MW00851912

Nehama Leibowitz

Teacher and Bible Scholar

Modern Jewish Lives
volume 3

Rabbi Shlomo Goren: Torah Sage and General (MJL, volume 1)
Rabbi Haim David Halevy: Gentle Scholar and Courageous Thinker
(MJL, volume 2)

NEHAMA LEIBOWITZ

TEACHER AND BIBLE SCHOLAR

BY YAEL UNTERMAN

URIM PUBLICATIONS
Jerusalem • New York

Nehama Leibowitz: Teacher and Bible Scholar
by Yael Unterman
Series: Modern Jewish Lives – Volume 3
Series Editor: Tzvi Mauer

Printed in Israel. First Edition.
ISBN–13: 978-965-524-019-1
Urim Publications
P.O. Box 52287, Jerusalem 91521 Israel

Lambda Publishers Inc.
527 Empire Blvd., Brooklyn, New York 11225 U.S.A.
Tel: 718–972–5449 Fax: 718–972–6307, mh@ejudaica.com

www.UrimPublications.com

For my parents, Rabbi Dr. Alan and Nechama Unterman,
with many thanks for their support.

CONTENTS

PART II: *EMUNOT VE-DE'OT* – BELIEFS AND OPINIONS

PART III: METHODOLOGY

PART IV: YESHAYAHU LEIBOWITZ

PART V: LOOKING TO THE FUTURE

NOTES FOR THE READER

A CERTAIN TENDENCY EXISTS today to call female scholars by their first names, as no rabbi or male scholar would be addressed. The use of Professor Leibowitz's first name throughout this book is not meant disrespectfully, but is in keeping with her own insistence that she be called "Nehama" by all. Her students still call her thus, and it seemed natural to follow their lead in this book. Moreover, as Dr. Gabriel Cohn points out, in the name of R. Sherirah Gaon, the greatest of the talmudic Sages were those addressed only by their first names, and not as "Rabbi." Hence, in calling her by her first name, we evoke Nehama's humility, warmth and greatness all at once.

The book is based on the reading of numerous primary and secondary sources, as well as close to two hundred interviews and conversations.[1] It is structured in two parts: Chapters 1 to 12 are largely biographical, with a detour into Nehama's pedagogical methods; while Chapters 13 to 24 develop analytically many of the themes mentioned briefly in the first part. Several issues and topics from Nehama's life relate to more than one chapter heading, and have therefore been repeated briefly and cross-referenced.

Quotes from Hebrew works are my translation unless otherwise noted. Although most quotes from the *Studies* series are from the English version, at times I have used the Hebrew *Studies* series (*Iyunim*) in part or in full, to preserve certain nuances lost in the English version.

The detailed footnotes will hopefully serve to open windows into many interesting issues surrounding Nehama's life. For brevity's sake, the names of several works have been abbreviated to acronyms, as shown in the key below. Other works, following their first citation, have been abbreviated in such a way that the reader may easily find the full reference in the bibliography. An index has been provided at the back of the book.

---

[1] Due to the large quantity of material, Nehama's worksheets and her book *Perush Rashi la-Torah: iyunim be-shitato* were not thoroughly combed and analyzed as her *Studies* were. However, analysis of these works by others has been quoted extensively.

KEY TO ABBREVIATIONS

WORKS BY NEHAMA LEIBOWITZ:

IBB: Iyunim be-SeferBereshit
IHBS: Iyunim hadashim be-Sefer Shemot
IHBV: Iyunim hadashim be-Sefer Va-yikra
IBBM: Iyunim be-Sefer Ba-midbar
IBD: Iyunim be-Sefer Devarim
KA: Keitzad anu lomdim tanach?
LP: Limmud parshanei ha-Torah u-derachim le-hora'atam: Sefer Bereshit
NSB: New Studies in Bereshit
NSS: New Studies in Shemot
NSV: New Studies in Vayikra
SBM: Studies in Bamidbar
SD: Studies in Devarim
TI: Torah Insights

OTHER ABBREVIATIONS

PN: Pirkei Nehama
VLN: Lecture at Van Leer Institute conference in honor of the hundredth anniversary of the birth of Nehama Leibowitz: *"Talmud Torah: limmud, parshanut u-mehkar,"* January 2–3, 2006 (video at http://www.vanleer.org.il/heb/videoShow.asp?id=231).[1]
VLY: Lecture at Van Leer Institute conference in honor of the hundredth anniversary of the birth of Yeshayahu Leibowitz: *"Yeshayahu Leibowitz: shamranut ve-radikaliyut,"* June 24–26, 2006 (video at http://www.vanleer.org.il/heb/videoShow.asp?id=1).

---

[1] Lectures from this conference are due to be published by the Van Leer Institute.

ACKNOWLEDGMENTS

M Y GRATITUDE GOES TO my publisher, Tzvi Mauer, for entrusting me with this project, and to my family and friends, for their support, kindness, and Shabbat invitations. I wish to express my appreciation of the National Library and its librarians. I would like to thank Dr. Gabriel Cohn for generously accompanying me through this process and for reading the manuscript. Sections of this book are based on my MA thesis in Jewish Intellectual History from Touro College Graduate School of Jewish Studies, and thanks go to my supervisor, Dr. Baruch Schwartz. Thank you also to my editor, Rahel Jaskow.

I also thank the following people, who read sections of my book and gave invaluable feedback: Helen Abelesz, R. Hayyim Angel, Shlomit Ben-Michael, Michael Berger, Dr. Stewart Brookes, Professor Florian Deloup, R. Yehoshua Engelman, Yaeer Ezekiel, Dr. Yoel Finkelman, Ruth Fogelman, Jared Goldfarb, Gila Green, R. Zvi Grumet, Tania Hershman, Nadia Jacobson, Jules Kaplan, Avi Katzman, R. Amy Klein, Gila Krygier, Judy Labensohn, Malka Landau, Dr. Leah Leeder, Morris Levin, Alex Margolin, Michal Meyer, Daniel Miller, Debbie Miller, Ursula McDermott, David Rapport, Gershon Rechtman, Professor Tamar Ross, Simi Peters, Zahavit Shalev, Avi Shmidman, Ester Silber-Schachter, Michelle Sint, Nizan Stein, Reena Barnett Tasgal, Chaya Kasse Valier, Dr. Naomi Wachtel, Rahel Reinfeld-Wachtfogel, Reuven Wachtfogel, Dr. Naomi Weiss, Dr. Deborah Weissman, Paul Widen, Dr. Tamra Wright.

Many other people had some part in this book in interviews, conversations and other help. I apologize if I omitted anyone from the list. I thank: Dr. Shmuel Adler, Yonatan Ahituv, Yosske Ahituv, Professor Moshe Ahrend, Aliza Alon, Chaya Amit, Mordechai Amit, Professor Yairah Amit, R. Nachum Amsel, R. Raymond Apple, Rut Azrieli, Joy Rochwarger Balsam, Yehudit Barashi, R. Avi Baumol, David Bedein, Dr. Ruth Ben-Meir, Professor Menahem Ben-Sasson, Yohanan Ben Yaakov, Else Bendheim, Dr. David Bernstein, R. Hershel Billet, R. Yoel Bin Nun, Rabbanit Malke Bina, Robert Bogen, Shoshana Brayer, R. Chaim Brovender, Rivka Burg, R. Emanuel Carlebach, Professor Tova Cohen, Dr. Howard Deitcher, R. David Derovan, Linda Derovan, R. Eitan Eckstein, Bruriah Eisner, Aryeh Felheimer, R. David Fink, Marsha Frank, R. Yitzhak Frank, Binyamin Ze'ev Frankel, Dr. Marla Frankel, Rabbanit Nurit Fried, R. Yohanan Fried, Professor Yehudah Friedlander, Sister Maureena Fritz, Zechariah Gamliel,

R. Yehudah Gilad, Rabbanit Blu Greenberg, R. Fred Klein, Toby Klein-Greenwald, R. Mordechai Goldberg, Yehudit Goldschmidt, Dr. Yonatan Grossman, Haim Hamiel, R. Nathaniel Helfgot, Rabbanit Chana Henkin, Professor Walter Herzberg, Azriel and Chana Hirsch, Michael Hochstein, Kibi Hofmann, R. Ben Hollander, Professor Carmi Horowitz, Frieda Horwitz, Professor Rivka Horwitz, Dina Hovav, Yehudit Ilan, Batya Jacobs, Professor Menachem Kadari, Professor Yaakov Kagan, Shimon Kalfa, R. Yosef Kapach, R. Tsvi Kilstein, Judy Klitsner, R. Shmuel Klitsner, R. Elyashiv Knohl, Professor Yisrael Knohl, Rahel Kossowsky, Professor Dov Landau, R. Pinchas Langer, Dr. Larry Laufman, Dr. Leah Leeder, Sol Lerner, Professor Ze'ev Lev, Dr. Yael Levine, Tzipora Levavi, Professor Barry Levy, Sharon Levy, Spencer Lewis, Professor Martin Lockshin, Hannah Malachi, R. Eliyahu Mali, Ruth Michaeli, Moshe Moskovitch, Sarah Leah Neventzal, Aryeh Newman, Meir Newman, Sarah Newman, Avraham Nissenbaum, Dr. Mira Ofran, Tzipora Ofri, R. Joseph Oratz, Moshe Oren, R. Stanley Peerless, Benjamin Pell, Professor Dov Rappel, R. Yitshak Reiner, R. Yaakov Koppel Reinitz, R. Shlomo Riskin, R. Peretz Rodman, Miriam Ron, R. Yerahmiel Roness, Leah Nehama Rosen, Dr. Rina Rosenberg, Professor Shalom Rosenberg, R. Yehudah Rosenberg, Aryeh Rotenberg, Ora Rotenberg, Professor Michael Rosenak, Professor Israel Rozenson, Eidel Rudman, Dr. Chana Safrai, R. Elhanan Samet, Yosef Shapira, Bat-Chen Schlesinger, R. Hanan Schlesinger, R. Larry Schwed, Dr. Don Seeman, Sissy Shelkovsky, Sharon Shenhav, Ruth Sherman, Walter Sherman, Werner Silberstein, R. David Sperling, Riva Sperling, Haviva Speter, Professor David Sykes, Nechama Tamler, Shmuel Teitelbaum, Aryeh Tepper, Anat Toledano, R. Daniel Tropper, Elyakim Una, Shlomo Wallach, R. Chaim Weiner, Gabi Weiss, Warren Wienburg, Dr. Joel Wolowelsky, Rami Yannai, Erella Yedgar, Professor Shaul Yedgar, Nissan Zisken, Dr. Avivah Zornberg.

INTRODUCTION

THIS BOOK will document the life and works of Professor Nehama Leibowitz (1905–1997) of blessed memory.

Nehama was a woman of contradictions. Fittingly, this biography too constitutes a contradiction, in publicizing the life of a woman who hated publicity, declaring: "I am not a museum!" Though she was happy to tell stories in praise of the "simple people" she met in her day-to-day life, Nehama would of herself say: "I'm not worth writing about – go learn Torah instead." Yet, since her death, much has been said and written about Nehama Leibowitz in books, articles, and conferences, by family, colleagues, students, friends and admirers. They hesitate, apologizing with a wry smile: "Had Nehama been alive, she would have forbidden us to do this." Nonetheless speak they do, under the motto: "*Aharei mot kedoshim emor*" (After saintly people pass away, speak), for they understand the need to try to encompass the meaning of the life that is gone, giving it continuance. Even those who kept silent during Nehama's lifetime are now speaking. When the newspaper *Kol ha-ir*, to Nehama's exasperation, prepared an article in honor of her ninetieth birthday, her student[1] Dr. Ruth Ben-Meir refused to cooperate with the journalist. But after Nehama's death she agreed to be interviewed in the *Jerusalem Post*, sensing the importance of exposure to the life of a great teacher, as in the verse "And your eyes shall see your teacher" (Isaiah 30:20).

There is a halachic discussion regarding what to do when someone requests not to be eulogized.[2] Some *poskim* rule that great persons may be eulogized against their express wishes, for such lives are public property.[3] Even Moses, the quintessential embodiment of humility, had no say after he passed away, and his life serves as an inspiration until this day.[4] Nehama

---

[1] When I refer to students in this work, I mean that the person began as Nehama's student. Many went on to become friends and colleagues.

[2] See *Shulhan Aruch, Yorah De'ah* 344:7, basing itself on the Talmud's question (Sanhedrin 46b) as to whether the eulogy is intended for the honor of the dead or that of the living.

[3] While the *Shulhan Aruch* makes no distinction between different kinds of people, some later *poskim* do. In *Meshiv Davar*, R. Berlin ruled to disregard the request by R. Bamberger of Wuerzburg not to be published after his death. The *Ruah ha-Hayyim* writes that what the *Gedolei ha-Dor* say and write is not their property. In a slightly different vein, the *Minhat Yitzhak* (9:135) suggests that praising a righteous person's deeds is always permitted so as to comfort us, even where a eulogy is precluded. (Thanks to Rabbis David Fink and David Sperling for this information).

[4] Thanks to Tzvi Mauer for pointing this out.

requested that there be no eulogy at her funeral and her request was honored. Nevertheless, Nehama's biography belongs not to her alone, but also to the Jewish people whom she loved so much, and to history, and it is under this premise that this book was written.[5] The only apology owed her is in writing this work in English, for she believed that the Hebrew language is the only proper medium for all Jewish life.[6]

In 1981, Nehama was awarded the Judith Lieberman prize for the Promotion of Torah Knowledge. The accompanying festive meal and praises of herself were anathema to her, and Professor Saul Lieberman felt compelled to explain in his speech why such public discomfort was necessary. He began by suggesting that even if the biblical character Job was not a real person, just a parable as the Talmud suggests, he was a true parable, one destined to be remembered forever. He added:

> And thus… there was once a woman in Israel, in the holy city of Jerusalem, and her name was Nehama; a virtuous and honest woman. And Nehama spent her days thoroughly scrutinizing the sacred Scriptures. She had the privilege of creating a revolution in Scriptural interpretation… not in the groves of academia or university halls, but within high-school walls… For those men and women for whom the *Mikra'ot Gedolot* are a part of their lives, the name Nehama Leibowitz has become synonymous with the weekly portion. (*PN*, 23)

Even before her passing, Nehama was larger than life. Now, only a decade after her death, she occupies a firm place in the pantheon of Jewish heroes and heroines whose lives have become a cultural legacy. For some, a hero is necessarily perfect; while for others, even a hero is first and foremost a human being, flawed and erring. This dispute is reflected in the different kinds of biographies written. Some of these, especially the kind chronicling the lives of saints, avoid criticism of their subject and mention only praises. R. Shimon Schwab explains:

> What ethical purpose is served by preserving a realistic historical picture?… What is gained by pointing out their inadequacies and their contradictions?… Every generation has to put a veil over the human

---

[5] Nehama was not against biographies; she encouraged her brother Yeshayahu to agree to have his biography written. Although he initially exhibited an attitude very similar to her own ("My opinions can be heard and read in my writings and lectures; my personality is of no interest!"), he subsequently relented. See his book *Al olam u-melo'o: sichot im Michael Shashar*, Jerusalem: Keter, 1987, 9.

[6] A Hebrew translation of this biography is planned.

failings of its elders and glorify all the rest which is great and beautiful…. We do not need realism; we need inspiration from our forefathers in order to pass it on to posterity.[7]

This position is one familiar to Jews, for the act of remembering in Judaism aims more often at a crafted collective memory than at objective, disinterested history.[8]

Although this biography is in a way an act of collective memory, being a composite portrait of many people's "Nehama," in contradistinction to the above position all voices will be allowed to speak, not only the complimentary ones. This was how Nehama taught her classes. She knew that suppressing critical opinions could only dull the experience of the Torah's truth, and that uniform and insipid portraits of the biblical heroes do not ultimately serve to inspire. Great people are to be loved, their failings notwithstanding, for to fail is human. Dr. Don Seeman writes:

> "Good people's contradictions," in R. Schwab's words, can serve an ethical purpose. In reminding us that the past was less tidy than we sometimes would like to imagine, it encourages us to be somewhat more forgiving of contradiction and complexity, of individuals who do not fit our easy typologies, right here in the present.[9]

Hopefully, the ultimate inspirational goal will be maintained: that as the readers encounter this great life, they will discover their own greatness within.

❧ ❧

This book is based on a significant amount of documented material – Nehama's own writings and a host of secondary sources. Letters referred to here are generally already in print, except for those kindly made available to me by Yonatan Ahituv and Professor Martin Lockshin. Much use has also been made of interviews and conversations. I am aware that human memory is an erratic and subjective instrument, and have myself come across fallacious memories or beliefs about Nehama, such as a report of the time she spoke in a synagogue in the United States (Nehama never visited America) or the notion that she put on *tefillin*. These have not been included, of course, but, with all the will in the world, not all reports could be verified.

---

[7] Shimon Schwab, *Selected Writings* (Lakewood, 1988), 233–234, cited in J. Schacter, "Haskalah, Secular Studies and the Close of the Yeshivah in Volozhin in 1892," *The Torah U-Madda Journal* 2 (1990): 111.

[8] See Yosef Hayyim Yerushalmi, *Zakhor: Jewish History and Jewish Memory.* New York: Schocken, 1989.

[9] Don Seeman, "The Silence of Rayna Batya," *The Torah U-Madda Journal,* 6 (1996): 105.

Therefore, this book reflects, more than how Nehama actually was, how she is remembered – a composite remembering based on each person's own Nehama.

Nehama explains in *Studies in Bamidbar*[10] that the spies sinned by inserting opinion into a factual report. But a biography is not the same as a factual report; it contains the subjective perception of the interviewees and also of the biographer, who over time creates a relationship with the subject. The reader is then invited to do likewise. Nehama's words seem appropriate here:

> Each student feels that one particular interpretation (depending on his personality and character) is compatible with his sentiments. He is drawn to that interpretation and makes a great effort to convince his friends that only "his" interpretation is correct... a personal connection is formed between the chapter and the student. (*TI*, 155)

I am writing as a biographer, and not as a student. While Nehama had many close students, I was not one of them. I learned her method from her students, my teachers; but my direct encounters with her were few. One of these took place on a Shabbat in the 1990s at a synagogue in Romema. There was a sudden disturbance in the rows behind me, and I noticed people moving aside, like traffic before an ambulance or – more appropriately for the setting – like the Red Sea parting before Moses. I witnessed a small, slightly hunched figure shuffling through. She took her seat at the front, while everyone waited respectfully; and when someone whispered to me: "That's Nehama Leibowitz," I knew that I was in the presence of a special person.

I was also lucky enough to hear Nehama teach on a few occasions. While researching this book I found an old note to myself: "I like Nehama Leibowitz. She's so straight." The young woman who wrote that note never dreamt that one day she would have the opportunity to become so familiar with her teacher and to learn so much from her. In 1999, Tzvi Mauer of Urim Publications invited me to begin the project and, never budging from his belief in my capabilities, waited patiently for almost ten years for its completion. This period, though longer than I had foreseen, provided me with the opportunity to attend conferences and to encounter – often unexpectedly – many people with memories of Nehama. It also allowed me to reflect more deeply and maturely upon Nehama's life through the prism of my own changing experiences.

---

[10] "Fact and Opinion in the Spies' Report," *SBM*, 135–142.

R. Nahman of Breslov writes that even if the student has only seen the teacher once, the act of looking in the teacher's face means that the teacher's wisdom has been transmitted.[11] I therefore hope that my encounters, though few, will enable me to transmit Nehama's "face" that I received in person, as well as the radiance and enthusiasm I witnessed on others' faces when speaking of her. It was gratifying to see my interviewees' pleasure in reminiscing about Nehama, a partial recompense perhaps for the generous gift of their time. Some have since passed away – Werner Silberstein, Professors Dov Rappel, Ze'ev Lev, Rivka Horwitz and Chana Safrai, Rabbis Yosef Kapach and Ben Hollander, and Joy Rochwarger Balsam, who left us while still a young woman.[12] May their memory be a blessing.

I have learned so much in writing this book, ceaselessly putting, in my mind, one all-consuming question to Nehama: "What does it mean to be a Jew?" Back came her manifold answers: It means to think, to probe, to discuss, to disagree. To take responsibility for self and society. To empathize with others, to act for the good. It means studying and teaching and studying again, maintaining the dialogue with Jewish traditions within current realities, while integrating world wisdom when useful. It means being simultaneously powerful and humble. All this is to be done with love, for God, Torah and fellow human beings.

Nehama's articulate and engaging voice has been constant in my ear, informing me, teaching me and making me smile. Once, while I sat in one of Nehama's favorite haunts, the National Library at Givat Ram, I was reading her discussion of Pharaoh's dream (Genesis 41:2):

> And, behold, there came up from the river seven cows sleek and fat; and they fed in the reed grass.

She mentioned Rashi's comments on these verses, where he suggests a symbolic meaning for these cows. Then, without warning, came Nehama's strident and almost sarcastic demand: "And who asked Rashi to interpret Pharaoh's dream?" and I had to stifle my laughter so as not to disturb the erudite hush.

One more personal moment before I step into the background and let other voices come to the fore: It is January 2006. I am sitting in a conference

---

[11] *Likkutei Moharan*, 230.

[12] Joy, an accomplished educator who touched many lives, passed away in 2004, aged thirty-seven. Her bond with Nehama was a special one, and her article in *Torah of the Mothers*, as well as the personal interview I had with her, have contributed greatly to this work. A memorial to her may be found at http://www.atid.org/joy/joy.asp.

at the Jerusalem Van Leer Institute marking the hundredth anniversary of Nehama's birth. I glance around me at the faces of many of those who knew her best. Suddenly I experience a fleeting vision that within this group remembrance, this tribute of affection, Nehama is actually present, as if her unique personality has been reassembled from its discrete parts lodged in the minds in the room, and she is sitting amongst us once again. Inspired, I write the following:

> Though you are gone
> a decade now,
> and I hardly knew you,
>
> Here in this room,
> inside these bodies; the
>   eyes that saw,
>   ears that heard,
>   hearts that loved you,
> Something of you
>   remains
>
> some orphaned shard,
>
> fluttering blindly around,
> hitting lights and walls,
> straining for life,
>   more, more life,
> as you did, always.
>
> I
> reach out my hand
> to capture it

Yael Unterman
Jerusalem, October 2008/5769

PART I

MEET NEHAMA LEIBOWITZ

Nehama's parents, Freyda and Mordechai Leibowitz. Courtesy of Mira Ofran.

Nehama's parents, 1931. Courtesy of Mira Ofran.

CHAPTER 1

EARLY YEARS:
"THIS YOUNG LADY WILL YET SPEAK A MOUTHFUL"

Riga

NEHAMA LEIBOWITZ was born on 3 Elul 5665 (September 3, 1905) in the Baltic port town of Riga, Latvia, two years after her brother Yeshayahu.[1] Witnessing their children's first steps, Mordechai and Freyda[2] Leibowitz probably nurtured typical parental ambitions for them. But even their fondest dreams must have been surpassed by reality, for Nehama and Yeshayahu Leibowitz went on to become arguably the most influential brother and sister of modern Jewish history, leading some to wonder aloud at the family's "extraordinary genes."[3]

Nehama's early development was slow. She liked to recount how when she was two or three her parents took her to "a professor" because she had yet to utter her first coherent syllable. The doctor answered – and here Nehama imitated him in an exaggeratedly serious voice – "'This young lady will yet speak a mouthful!' Thus," she concluded mischievously, "it's not my fault – this is the way God created me." The doctor's words proved prophetic, for once Nehama began talking she did not stop. In one of her books, Nehama describes the power of speech as

> this magnificent human instrument of expression and vehicle for transmitting values to future generations and for welding individuals into communities. (*NSV*, 201)

---

[1] The following information is based in part on the entry "Nehama Leibowitz" in the Hebrew Encyclopedia, Vol. 21, 1968, with additions by R. Yitshak Reiner, together with a chronology by Nehama from 1957, printed in *PN*, 13–15. More information on Nehama's intellectual background and influences may be found in Marla Frankel, *Toratah shel Nehama Leibowitz: darkah be-limmud ha-Tanach u-ve-hora'ato*. Yediot Ahronot: Sifrei Hemed, 2007. Frankel's book was published when this work was in its late stages, so its findings have not been included, except for some general pointers provided by the author (for which I thank her). More information based on interviews with people who knew Nehama in her youth may be found in Leah Abramowitz, *Tales of Nehama*. Gefen: 2003, 25–31.

[2] Her maiden name was Nimchevitch (phonetic pronunciation – the exact spelling is unknown). While Yeshayahu's family all knew their grandmother as Freyda, R. Yitshak Reiner reports that, desiring to pray for Nehama's health, he asked for her mother's Hebrew name and she wrote down "Sara Feigeh."

[3] Yair Sheleg, "*Kalat ha-Tanach*," *Kol ha-ir*, October 27, 1995, 70.

Nehama and Yeshayahu Leibowitz and their mother, circa 1908.
Courtesy of Mira Ofran.

It is the rare individual whose use of the faculty of speech matches this high standard. Nehama's often did.

Nehama recalled her childhood fondly as full of enjoyable activities and trips with friends. But the family environment also laid the foundation for the future trajectories of the children. Stereotypically, highly educated Jewish families were concentrated in Germany, while Eastern European Jews – labeled "*ostjuden*" by their more assimilated Western brethren – were considered relatively uncivilized. Riga, however, was no backwater. Jews had lived there for centuries, and several outstanding Jews were born there, including R. Abraham Isaac Kook and Sir Isaiah Berlin. The city boasted Jewish clubs and societies, schools and synagogues, as well as significant Zionist activity. Nehama's family integrated all of these elements. It was strongly religious, including some rabbis on the Leibowitz side; and also broadly educated. Yeshayahu described himself as having grown up in "a Jewish world in which Judaism and European culture were interwoven."[4] They were also Zionists, and the children spoke in Hebrew with their father (and German or Yiddish with their mother).[5] The Leibowitzes' social circles included the local intelligentsia and educated businessmen, many of them non-observant Jews. Nehama's was therefore not a sheltered upbringing, at least in that sense.[6] But they did not experience any overt anti-Semitism[7] or have to deal with painful realities such as financial deprivation. The heavy influx of Jews into Latvia in the latter half of the nineteenth century had created a thriving market economy, and Leibowitz senior was one of many Jewish businessmen who prospered by it. However, he chose to run his household simply, restricting luxuries and fripperies.

Of Nehama's mother little is known. She died relatively early on. Nehama once told Dr. Marla Frankel that her mother was a pianist, but many of Nehama's closest students and friends never heard any mention of her. Her father, on the other hand, was evidently an important influence. Nehama dedicated her book *Iyunim be-Sefer Devarim* to him as follows:

---

[4] Eliezer Goldman, introduction to Y. Leibowitz, *Judaism, Human Values, and the Jewish State*. Harvard, 1992, ix. This combination was not so common, for often the Jews of Eastern Europe lacked scientific and universal breadth, while Western European Jews, even those familiar with Judaism, adopted an academic approach to it rather than holding it as religious truth.

[5] Y. Leibowitz, *Al olam*, 172. Yeshayahu's reminisces of his youth may be found in *ibid.*, 172–176.

[6] Y. Leibowitz, *Al olam*, 69.

[7] Y. Leibowitz, *Al olam*, 70.

This book is dedicated to the memory of my father of blessed memory, who was my first childhood teacher of Rashi; and he – ever zealous for the Hebrew language – taught me above all to hear and to taste the fine flavor of Rashi's language and style.

Mr. Leibowitz was well versed in Jewish sources. Nehama quotes his Hebrew translations of Rabbi S.R. Hirsch in her writings (*IBBM*, 36, 56, 97). His philosophy on life and religion became instilled in his daughter, and many times she quoted his motto, "See how far the words reach!" This motto, which encouraged her to look beyond the surface of words, sums up to a large degree the essence of her life's work.[8] Although a somewhat introverted and severe person, Nehama's father smiled frequently and was fond of riddles and word games, as was the entire family.[9] He created weekly Tanach quizzes for his children, asking them for the location and context of random verses.[10] He was conversant with many other realms too, including politics, world affairs and general knowledge. On their walks together, he tested Nehama on quotes from Shakespeare and on general history. He teased his children for their ignorance of Western culture, granting them no respite long after they had both proved their brilliance and knowledge many times over. A family friend, Professor Dov Rappel, claims: "He was the only person in the world who could tell both Nehama and Yeshayahu to be quiet – and with just cause! Once in conversation he listed all the English kings who belonged to the Stuart dynasty. Not bad for a Latvian Jew."

The stories about her father that Nehama repeatedly told are also revealing. She often related how as a young girl she had once brought him his slippers, informing him: "I'm trying to be a good girl during the ten days of repentance between the New Year and the Day of Atonement." Her father replied wryly, "Nehama, that's not the hard part; I'd much rather you were good in the days between the Day of Atonement and the New Year!" Another story took place one snowy day when she was nine. Nehama was in a hurry to get to school, and, skipping her morning prayers, ran out, slipped on the snow and was struck by a passing tram. She later explained to her father, "This happened because I didn't pray this morning, but from now on I will." He retorted: "Do you think you are such a saint that God immediately reacts to your actions? I doubt there's any connection." This kind of outlook, shying away from superstitious thinking or an assumption

---

[8] See Moshe Ahrend, "*Mi-toch avodati im Nehama a"h*," in PN, 32.
[9] For an example of such a word game involving a Yiddish-Hebrew pun see *Haggadat Nehama*, edited by Yitshak Reiner and Shmuel Peerless, 119 (Jerusalem: Urim Publications, 2003).
[10] Sheleg, "*Kalat*," 70.

Nehama Leibowitz, circa 1920's. Courtesy of Mira Ofran.

Nehama studying, circa 1920's. Courtesy of Mira Ofran.

of direct knowledge of God's ways, would later characterize both Nehama's and Yeshayahu's thought.[11]

One exceptional aspect of Nehama's childhood was her schooling. She attended neither the traditional *heder* nor the Jewish school (which according to Yeshayahu was "not so good"),[12] nor the public elementary school, which held exams on Shabbat. Only after moving to Berlin did she join the tenth-grade class in the Berlin Gymnasium ("a terrible education," she recalled).[13] Before that, the siblings were taught by hired teachers and a private tutor who accompanied them on family vacations.[14] Nehama recalled how every time it snowed, they stood at the window, hoping and praying that he would not show up.

Berlin

In 1919, due to the upheavals of the Russian revolution and the creation of the independent Republic of Latvia, the family was forced to move from Riga to Berlin. As Yeshayahu later recalled, since they were not German, it took a while to acclimatize, and they were at times stigmatized as *ostjuden*.[15] However, overall it was a very positive experience.

Berlin of the 1920s contained the largest Jewish community in Germany at that time. A hotbed of Jewish and non-Jewish creativity, it was a stimulating place for an energetic young woman like Nehama to grow intellectually. This cultural bubble, so soon to be burst by the Nazis, nurtured several Jewish giants. On her way to study or teach, Nehama might well have passed on the street such figures as R. Menahem Mendel Schneersohn, the future Lubavitcher Rebbe; or R. Joseph Dov Soloveitchik, scion of a brilliant talmudic family and future leader of American modern Orthodox Jewry. R. Yehiel Yaakov Weinberg, R. Isaac Hutner, and R. Abraham Joshua Heschel all spent time there. Had all these Jewish luminaries gathered in one location, that would have been a sight to see; no doubt there would have been fierce debate, especially with the Leibowitz siblings present. Perhaps precisely because this notion is so appealing, rumors persist to this day that Nehama spoke with the Lubavitcher Rebbe

---

[11] Nehama, however, believed in some level of Divine Providence, while Yeshayahu rejected it out of hand. See pages 363, 545–546 below.

[12] Y. Leibowitz, *Al olam*, 173.

[13] From "Nehama Herself," *Kol Emunah* (Spring 1987): 18.

[14] Sheila Segal, *Women of Valor: Stories of Great Jewish Women Who Helped Shape the Twentieth Century*. Behrman House, Inc.: 1996, 103. Yeshayahu reports that his father learned Torah with him and also employed teachers for this purpose (Y. Leibowitz, *Al olam*, 173).

[15] Y. Leibowitz, *Al olam*, 73.

and R. Soloveitchik and studied with them at university. This is not true. Once, hearing that in an American apartment three large pictures were displayed on the wall – of the Rebbe, R. Soloveitchik and herself – Nehama laughed, and said: "Look what company I'm in!" But this was the only time the three "met." Habad Hasidim, desirous of knowing more about the Rebbe's early life in Berlin, would call Nehama every so often. One insisted, "Everyone knows that you sat drinking coffee with the Rebbe and R. Soloveitchik in the cafés in Berlin!" "It could be that we sat at the same table for lunch," Nehama replied, "but if we did, I didn't know it." Reportedly, the Rebbe later recognized Nehama's greatness and sent her groups of Hasidim, who were highly disgruntled at being ordered to study with a woman.

Nehama also never personally interacted with R. Soloveitchik. The story goes that Nehama was told of the brilliant young Jewish scholar who sat in the library "behind the tallest stack of books." With a description like that, she located him easily, but never introduced herself. (It is a tribute to her erudition that in another version, it was he who was told to look out for her, but could not locate her because *she* was hidden behind *her* tower of books!) In later years, Nehama evinced a great respect for R. Soloveitchik, employing adjectives such as "important" and "profound" about his thinking,[16] and enjoying tapes of his lectures in Yiddish. She was especially taken with his disclosure that what consoled him after his wife's passing was the study of Gemara. He said he felt God tapping him on the shoulder and demanding, "*Nu* – what's the answer?" Nehama was moved by his pain and that God was his address for consolation.

Though Nehama never got to meet R. Soloveitchik, her brother later did, conversing with him on visits to the States in 1974 and 1979. R. Soloveitchik was purported to have said that Yeshayahu was the only interesting religious thinker in Israel.[17]

---

[16] See *NSB*, 16, n. 4 ("profound and original"); *NSS*, 329; *NSV*, 224–225 ("highly recommended," "profound understanding"), and 233, 238; *SBM*, 52 (in its Hebrew parallel *IBBM*, 57 she expresses her sorrow that the book *On Repentance* is not his writing but rather translations of his oral discourses); and *IBBM*, 106, n. 11 ("important words"). She was also very taken with Soloveitchik's article "*Ra'ayonot al ha-tefilla*," (*Ha-Darom*, 47 [5739]: 84–106) and his essay "*U-vikashtem mi-sham*" (*Ha-Darom* 47 [5739], 1–83), which she describes as "spectacular" (letter to Yonatan Ahituv). However, Soloveitchik is not mentioned in Nehama's *gilyonot*, according to Sokolow's *Mafte'ah ha-gilyonot* (Index to the Worksheets), Department for Torah Education and Culture in the Diaspora, 1993.

[17] See Y. Leibowitz, *Ratziti li-shol otcha, Professor Leibowitz*, edited by Mira Ofran, Avi Katzman *et al.*, 482 (Jerusalem: Keter, 1999). See also his *Al olam*, where he notes that he never fully understood Soloveitchik and remarks, "Regrettably, he was not a fighter. What can you do?"

Nehama and Yeshayahu Leibowitz, 1920's. Courtesy of Mira Ofran.

Nehama in the late 1920's. Courtesy of Mira Ofran.

Nehama with a friend, 1929. Courtesy of Mira Ofran.

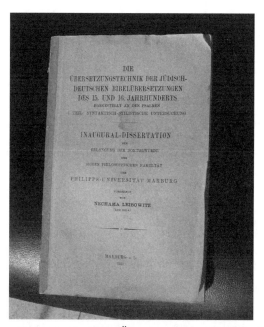

Nehama's doctorate. Cover reads: "Die Übersetzungstechnik der Jüdisch-Deutschen
Bibelübersetzungen des 15. und 16. Jahrhunderts. Dargestellt an den Psalmen.
(Translation Techiques of Judeo-German Bible Translations in the Fifteenth and
Sixteenth Centuries, as Exemplified by Translations of the Book of Psalms). By
Nechama Leibowitz from Riga, Philosophy Department, Marburg University,
1931." Courtesy of Mira Ofran.

෪ ෫

Nehama matriculated from the state high school at age twenty, the normal age. She spent the years 1925–1930 in the Universities of Berlin, Heidelberg and Marburg, studying English and German philology and literature, and Bible studies.[18] At the same time, she advanced her Jewish studies at the *Hochschule für die Wissenschaft des Judentums*, the Berlin college for the scientific study of Judaism. This resembled an academic department for Jewish studies but was not located within any university. Nehama was fortunate in her timing, for the Nazis later closed it down.[19]

The *Hochschule* was the only institution where Nehama did any formal learning of Jewish studies. The college's doors were open to all, including women and non-Jews, and it was the closest thing to a yeshivah that a woman could attend at the time. While the study was academic, it also had a *li-shmah* dimension, with the aim of studying Judaism for its own sake. Here, as nowhere else at the time, Nehama could interact on an equal footing with Jewish scholars, rabbis and rabbinical students. The faculty of the school included world-renowned Jewish scholars of both Orthodox and liberal outlooks, and Nehama studied with Professors Julius Guttmann,[20] Ismar Elbogen and R. Leo Baeck. One of her classmates in Julius Guttmann's seminar on Maimonides's *Guide for the Perplexed* was a young post-doctoral student by the name of Leo Strauss. Strauss subsequently became an important political philosopher, focusing on the ancient debate between philosophy ("Athens") and poetry/faith ("Jerusalem"). Nehama recalled that he would not let Guttmann finish an idea without attacking him; and indeed he later published a book critiquing Guttmann's approach, *Philosophie und*

---

(54). For more details of the connection between the two see Jeffrey Saks, "Letters on Religion without Theology" (review essay of *Ratziti li-shol otcha, Professor Leibowitz*), *Tradition* 34/3 [2000]: 93–94, n. 6. Avi Sagi has drawn up comparisons of their thought in "*Ha-Rav Soloveitchik u-Professor Leibowitz kete'oretikanim shel ha-halachah*," Daat 29 (5752): 131–148, and in "*Kitvei ha-kodesh u-mashma'utam be-hagutam shel Leibowitz ve-Soloveitchik*," *Be-khol derakhekha daehu*, 49–62.

[18] According to Nehama, the professors of Bible studies whom she heard included Sellin, Galling, Gressman, Bultmann, Meissner and Hölscher; and she attended an education seminar by Eduard Spranger. Although more a philosopher than a Bible scholar, Rudolph Otto also merits a mention in her list (*PN*, 13). Other scholars in Germany who impressed Nehama were Friedrich Gundolf, a leading historian and theoretician of literature, and Theodor Mommsen, a historian and professor in Berlin before she arrived there (d. 1903).

[19] See Richard Fuchs, "The *Hochschule für die Wissenschaft des Judentums* in the Period of Nazi Rule," *Leo Baeck Institute Year Book*, London: East and West Library, 1967, 3–31. Some of the historical information in the following paragraph is from this article, which was brought to my attention by Dr. Marla Frankel.

[20] She quotes Guttmann in *NSB* 2–3 and *NSS*, 506, n. 4.

Gesetz (1935). Although critical of religion in general, he formed an enriching intellectual partnership with Nehama, and together they pored over difficult texts. Strauss taught Nehama philosophy, reading Plato's *Gorgias* with her in the original Greek, while she taught him Hebrew, studying Saadya Gaon's *Emunot Ve-de'ot* and other Hebrew works with him.[21]

The University of Marburg was the opposite of Berlin in terms of Jewish social life, although several prominent Jews attended it, such as Hannah Arendt. Nehama studied there under Rudolf Otto, a Christian scholar who was a highly influential thinker on religion and knowledgeable about Judaism. At Marburg, Nehama completed her doctorate. At the time, it was very much the norm within German Jewry for Orthodox Jews, including rabbis, to obtain doctorates, without which advancement was difficult; and people liked to joke that "Dr." was a common Jewish first name.[22] Nehama's dissertation was on "Translation Techniques of Judeo-German Bible Translations in the Fifteenth and Sixteenth Centuries, as Exemplified by Translations of the Book of Psalms," a topic that lay, in her own words, on "the border between Germanics and Bible interpretation." It explored Yiddish translations of the Tanach, based on manuscripts in the Parma and Berlin libraries.[23] The period she had chosen allowed her to avoid biblical criticism, so predominant in the universities of the time. The Jewish translations of Bible were, to her mind, much more respectful and loyal to the original Hebrew language than the sloppy, condescending and often downright anti-Semitic Christian ones.[24]

In addition to her studies, Nehama also got her teaching career off to a good start. Although she qualified officially as a high school teacher only in 1930, she taught high school pupils before that. In her classes she used the *Ivrit be-Ivrit* method, speaking exclusively Hebrew during class so that it might be experienced as a living language. First used by Eliezer Ben-Yehudah in Jerusalem in 1883, this technique was still unheard of in German schools at that time. Nehama taught in such Berlin Jewish schools as that of the Adas Yisroel, R. Azriel Hildesheimer's breakaway Orthodox congregation, founded in reaction to the Reform movement in 1869. Their

---

[21] Professor Warren Zev Harvey, private communication; Alan Udoff (ed.), *Leo Strauss's Thought*, 27, n. 63, (Boulder: Lynne Rienner, 1991). In error it refers there to the teacher as Jacob Guttmann, Julius's father.

[22] Rivka Horwitz, "*Nehama Leibowitz ve-ha-parshanim ha-Yehudi'im be-Germania ba-me'ah ha-20 – Martin Buber, Franz Rosenzweig, u-Benno Jacob,*" in PN, 213.

[23] According to her own account (*PN*, 13) it was subsequently published in the journal *Paul u. Braune's Beiträge*.

[24] See Horwitz, "*Nehama,*" *passim*. See pages 416–418 below.

philosophy resembled that of R. Hirsch's followers. Hirsch's *Torah im derech eretz* philosophy appealed to Nehama since it combined Orthodox sensibilities with openness to Germanic culture and emphasized ethical behavior. However, she also felt distanced from the Hirschian camp, especially in her Zionism.[25]

By the time she left Germany at the end of 1930, Nehama had given her first lectures on didactics and published her first articles, on teaching Bible without translation and on the methodology of *Ivrit be-Ivrit*, written at age twenty-three. The stage was set for the next period in her life.

Marriage and Aliyah

Several misconceptions surround Nehama's marriage. Perhaps because she was so independent, or perhaps because her last name never changed, some are of the belief that she never married at all. Others suppose that she married, but kept her maiden name. Both are mistaken, as Joy Rochwarger, a close student of Nehama's in her later years, discovered to her surprise when asking Nehama's opinion on love. She began: "Nehama, how do you know when you love someone?"

"What do you mean, how do you know? You know!" replied Nehama.

"Well, what did your parents think of your husband?"

"What do you mean? They loved him."

"How do you know?"

"Well, he used to come to my house every day for lunch."

"Why did he come to your house every day for lunch?"

"Well, he was my uncle!"

Indeed, Nehama had married her father's brother, Yedidyah Lipman Leibowitz.[26] Her marital situation was puzzling to many. They wondered why she would marry a much older, ailing uncle. Not daring to discuss it

---

[25] See Mordechai Breuer, *"Professor Nehama Leibowitz a"h,"* in *PN*, 17. Hirsch himself is quoted abundantly and positively in her work, though he also comes in for some harsh criticism for his dubious grammar and philology. For example: "How far he is from the medieval giants!" (letter to Reinitz, *PN*, 678). See also Horwitz, *"Nehama,"* 212. For another example see *IHBS*, 166, where Hirsch's commentary is termed a "far more superficial view" than Ramban's. The English translation in *NSS*, 227 does not bring her criticism out as pointedly. Frankel argues that Hirsch had a great influence on Nehama and demonstrates how in their philosophy and outlook Nehama and Hirsch evince great similarities. However, she departed from him on two subjects: their hermeneutical orientations to the texts and the subject of Israel and the nations (see Frankel, *Toratah*, chapter 4).

[26] For some reason, while the *Vayikra* volumes of her *Studies* series are dedicated to her husband correctly as "Yedidyah Leibowitz," the *Bamidbar* volume bears a dedication to "my husband Yehudah Leibowitz."

Nehama's husband, Yedidyah Lipman Leibowitz.
Courtesy of Mira Ofran.

with her directly, some speculated that perhaps she had altruistic motives, for thus she could take care of Lipman without transgressing any Jewish laws. But the truth is that Nehama married for love. Professor Chana Safrai, a friend and colleague of Nehama's, on several occasions visited Lipman's gravesite with Nehama and heard the facts from her own lips. Apparently, the marriage was not without its obstacles – decades older than she,[27] he already suffered from a condition causing deteriorating eyesight; and her choice was resisted by some of those close to her. Nevertheless, she followed her heart and pushed ahead with it, waiting only, due to Lipman's insistence, to finish her Ph.D. first. With this accomplished, the couple were married in 1930 in Berlin, and Nehama declared to Safrai: "This was the wisest decision I ever made, and I have been extremely happy my entire life!"

Nehama viewed the job of looking after her husband as a lover's privilege rather than a duty. Simi Peters recalls long conversations with Nehama while collating worksheets together: "She talked about him not as one would speak about a revered uncle, but in the way any woman talks about her husband – with that mixture of affection and a certain knowingness." Nehama encouraged others to follow their hearts, too, even in the face of adversity. Her attitude towards love was similar to her attitude towards Torah – it should be completely intuitive, with no room for doubt, and things like age difference should not matter. The only thing she regretted was never having children.

Nehama and the Holocaust

At last, Nehama was able to move to the Holy Land, and to her joy, she did so the day after she married. She never left the country again except for one occasion soon after her immigration, when she went to meet her parents in Europe and accompany them back to Israel to settle. At that time, Nehama and Lipman took the opportunity to travel while he still had his sight. Fortunately, the couple departed Germany before the ascension of the Nazi party and the nightmares that were to follow. Perhaps they were sensitive to the unbridgeable gap between the German and Jewish identities, as per the Israeli novelist A.B. Yehoshua's words:

> Perceptive and self-critical German Jews such as the renowned scholar of Jewish mysticism, Gershom Scholem, and others, who could

---

[27] Abramowitz (Tales, 27) cites an interviewee who suggests that Lipman was ninety-six when he died. Since Lipman died in 1970 (see page 156 below), that would make him fifty-six at his marriage, thirty-one years older than Nehama.

perceive both the German and Jewish cultures' inner codes, acknowledged that timely "unilateral separation" from fateful integration with the Germans was a prerequisite. Consequently, they followed it up by immigrating to Eretz Yisrael as Zionists in the 1920s, so as to construct an independent, sovereign, autonomous Jewish reality.[28]

In any event, their timely choice meant that the Leibowitzes spent the Holocaust years safe in Palestine. Nehama later expressed her shock that many of her fellow students in Berlin, so polite and cultured, had become participants in the Third Reich.

In general, Nehama hardly ever mentioned the Holocaust. Even her close friends and students recall no significant discussions with her on this subject. Needless to say, she cared deeply about the fate of the Jews – R. Hanan Porat recalls seeing tears in her eyes when she told of Eastern European Jewish villages, so poor and yet so warm and hospitable, now lost to the Jewish people.[29] But she never suggested sophisticated theories or philosophies to account for the evil. Neither did she adopt the Holocaust as a core component of her Jewish identity, as many others did. Her Jewish identity was for the most part an affirmative one, stressing positive Jewish activity over persecution and anti-Semitism, and life over death. Her primary focus was on textual study and on ethical, Godly living, and not on persecutions past. History had its place, but the Tanach, an eternal, living work, held the Jewish future. For this reason she had mixed emotions concerning school heritage trips to Poland and Germany, including visits to concentration camps. Not only did the students thus spend money in the persecutors' homelands, but the ultimate effect on Jewish identity was unclear. Better that Jewish life be strengthened through Torah learning and other constructive experiences.

Nehama's life's work was, in part, a rebuilding after the destruction wreaked by the Holocaust. The publishers of her book "Chapters of Consolation and Redemption," written jointly with Professor Meir Weiss, suggested that such chapters of prophetic consolation ought to be distributed widely in the Diaspora, as a reminder of the consolation inherent

---

[28] "For a Jewish border," *Jerusalem Post*, July 19, 2002, B1. However, Yeshayahu Leibowitz said that the German Jews felt deeply German and no one could have predicted what had happened (Y. Leibowitz, *Al olam*, 73–74).

[29] *Me'at min ha-or* – weekly Torah sheet, *Va-yikra* 5767. See also her remarks quoted in Nili Ben-Ari, "*Makkot mitzrayim*," *Amudim* (*Nissan/Iyyar* 5767): 5–7.

in the new Israeli State, founded upon the ashes of the Holocaust.[30] Nehama too upheld the Holocaust-State connection. We see that concerning the events in Egypt, she asks:

> There has been no reference, direct or implied, to the name of God (except in connection with the midwives). Where had He disappeared to? Had he abandoned the world?... Where was He to be found in light of the bondage, persecution and suffering? (*NSS*, 17–18)

Rather than attempting a theological answer, she proposes that the absence of God's name is a psychological statement, reflecting the sentiments of the Israelites who felt abandoned. Subsequently a new chapter is opened, with God as redeemer, emerging from behind the barriers to "burst into the arena of history," hinting, perhaps, that in a similar way the horrors of the Holocaust were followed by the establishment of the State.[31] This discussion is the closest Nehama gets to asking "Where was God during the Holocaust?" Rather than engage in philosophical discussion, she read the text and commentaries and her comments sprang from this reading. Within these comments, Nehama had a lot to say about the persecution of the Jews. She viewed this as a significant theme in the Torah, serving as a model for future events. Thus she writes:

> there were transgressors in Israel who had Egyptian patrons and lived in affluence and honour and were loathe to leave. (*NSS*, 147)

She then adds that these words are "dreadful in their predictive power" for all of Jewish history and its tragic unfoldings (*IHBS*, 108). For Nehama the Holocaust was not unique; it was just one in a long line of incidents of cruelty towards Jews, as per the declaration at the Passover Seder: "In every generation, they have risen up against us to destroy us, but the Holy One, blessed be He, delivers us from their hand."[32] Nehama writes:

> The latest exponent of Jew hatred always promises never to make the mistake of his predecessor, but effecting a "final solution." The latest has been the worst. Realizing he cannot destroy the bodies, he destroys the Jewish soul, the body automatically falling his victim. (*NSB*, 283)

She viewed the Diaspora as one big breeding ground for this phenomenon. From the time of the patriarch Isaac until today, Jews have

---

[30] Introduction to N. Leibowitz, *Shiurim be-firkei nehama u-ge'ula* (with Meir Weiss), Jerusalem: WZO, Department for Torah and Culture in the Diaspora, 1957. A section of this book was printed in a volume dedicated to Israeli Independence Day themes (*Ma'ayanot* 7, "Yom ha-Atzma'ut," Department for Torah Education and Culture in the Diaspora, 1960, 46–62).

[31] Yedgar, *VLN*.

[32] Yedgar, *VLN*.

been accused of becoming rich and mighty on the backs of their gentile countrymen (*NSB*, 261–262). It is in this vein that she reads Pharaoh's strange statement regarding the Hebrews who had initially settled in his land with full permission:

> ... it may come to pass that in case of war, they will join our enemies, and fight against us and depart the land. (Exodus 1:10)

The phrase "and depart the land" is puzzling, for it is generally invaders who are feared, not emigrants. Nehama remarked that Pharaoh was attempting to solve his "Jewish problem" (*NSS*, 25), and wrote:

> It seems that this is the insanity of Jew-hating: Not to allow them to depart, but also not to allow them to live! Like in Soviet Russia. This question becomes clearer through the prism of recent history, when we see that they hate us, degrade us and despise our company, yet lock the gates against us, lest we depart the land. We have learned from our experience that no reasons are required for genocide and cold-blooded murder.[33]

Similarly, she wrote of the situation of the Jews

> in their wanderings from one exile to another. First they are welcomed and even invited but, subsequently, are not allowed to leave unmolested (as occurred in Germany, Poland and other places). (*NSS*, 58)

We also hear shades of modern Germany when she describes Pharaoh's initial, subtle measures against the Jews:

> Pharaoh, King of Egypt, the cradle of civilization, science and art, could not exterminate innocent people.[34]

Nehama occasionally made the connections to her own time explicit. She taught that in a tyranny, as in Pharaoh's domain or in Nazi Germany, people imagine that if only they can talk to the ruler and bypass the overseers, he will certainly understand them.[35] She wrote:

> And we have seen all this with our own eyes.[36]

> We know – and who better than our generation – that the progress of civilization does not necessarily imply or correspond with moral advancement.[37]

---

[33] Reiner and Peerless, *Haggadat*, 87, quoting the *Teacher's Guide* for *Shemot* 5718.
[34] *NSS*, 26. See a similar comment regarding Pharaoh's supposed lack of knowledge of his own overseers' activities in *IHBS*, 79.
[35] R. Nachum Amsel, interview.
[36] *IHBV*, 458; compare *NSV*, 592: "This holds true for modern history with added force."
[37] *IHBV*, 193; compare *NSV*, 245.

Regarding Pharaoh's appointment of Jewish overseers to brutalize their brothers, Nehama remarks, in a clear reference to the concentration camp Kapos:

> And this is well known to us, both then and also today.[38]

She mentions Eichmann (*LP* 138, n. 11) and illustrates the *Sefer ha-Hinuch*'s principle, "Actions shape character," with a contemporary example:

> For a moment recall all those concentration camp officials who had to carry out the orders of their masters and remember how ordinary folk who were neither angels nor devils became brutalized as a result of the brutal preoccupations to which they had been appointed. Though they might have, at the beginning, experienced revulsion, habit and custom soon got the better of them.[39]

Nehama notes that R. Meir Simha ha-Cohen of Dvinsk (a fellow Latvian, known as the *Meshech Hochmah* after the title of his book), prophesied decades before the Holocaust that without faith, humanity's intellect is liable to degenerate and conceive the most savage and diabolical plans.[40] She liked to contrast his farsighted assessment with the over-optimistic outlook of his older contemporary, Hirsch. On the question of whether Esau's kiss upon reuniting with his long lost brother Jacob (Genesis 33:4) was genuine or actually concealed some hateful motive, Hirsch wrote:

> Even Esau gradually relinquishes his sword and begins to feel the chords of love. It is Jacob who usually provides him with the opportunity for showing his innate humanity. (*NSB*, 375)

Nehama felt that this view reflected

> the overtones of the nineteenth century emancipation and liberalism.... We shall not quarrel with Hirsch, who did not know what we know today about the "sword" turning into holocaust and not love. (NSB, 375–376)

---

[38] See *IBBM*, 94, n. 1. Oddly, however, in the more obvious context – that of the slavery in Israel, where Nehama even discusses a statement of Rashi's that begs the comparison ("The foremen were themselves Israelites," *NSS*, 104) – she does not make the connection.

[39] *NSS*, 180. The principle "Actions shape character" is also quoted in *NSS*, 502; *NSV*, 10, 46, 346, 383, 449, 465 and 540; and *SD*, 245. Also, *SD*, 273 is similar.

[40] *NSV*, 448, and see also the supplement at the end of *NSV*, 618–623. Note too Nehama's letter to Reinitz (*PN*, 677) in which she writes that a certain *Baraita* had become "actualized in a dreadful manner in our days in the Holocaust."

Early years in the Yishuv

After their *aliyah*, the newlyweds moved to Eliezer ha-Levi Street in the Kiryat Moshe suburb in northwest Jerusalem. Not long afterwards, Yeshayahu Leibowitz also immigrated.

Nehama quickly became a well-known and beloved figure in the neighborhood, giving regular talks on the weekly Torah portion. She and Lipman lived in a small house. During the Israeli War of Independence, a bomb fell on part of the house, but they escaped unharmed. Their immediate neighbors were Yonah Ben-Sasson, a professor of Jewish thought, and his wife Junia, a former student of Nehama's. The Ben-Sassons welcomed the Leibowitzes as family. Nehama often sat and checked her worksheets in her neighbors' home, and they spent many Shabbat meals and Passover Seders together.[41] Their children, together with her nieces and nephews, were the nearest thing Nehama had to her own. Though the Ben-Sasson children grew up surrounded by numerous prominent Jewish figures, she was special to them. Professor Menahem Ben-Sasson states that Nehama was a part of his life from the day he was born. He learned to read from Nehama's father, whom he called "Grandpa." He recalls that Nehama demanded repeatedly to know what contribution he and his siblings were making to the State of Israel. "She was always very concerned with our development, giving us quizzes, discussing the weekly Torah portion, and telling us about various mistakes in Hebrew she had spotted." She built snowmen with them, and at night read them poems or declaimed stories from Agnon or the Tanach in melodramatic tones. They in turn helped her by delivering her worksheets to the post office.

Upon arrival in Palestine, Nehama gave herself over completely to teaching, primarily in teachers' seminaries. With her doctorate in hand and her talent for teaching, she easily found full-time employment in colleges for religious women run under the auspices of Mizrachi. This was the religious Zionist educational stream, established in 1926 as an official alternative to the public-school system, and its goals largely matched Nehama's.[42]

Nehama taught in three different programs, all located in a building in the city center, in a small alleyway near the Ethiopian Church and Hanevi'im St. The first program was the *Bet Midrash le-Morot Mizrahi Yerushalayim* (Mizrachi Teachers' Seminary of Jerusalem), where she taught for twenty-

---

[41] Sheleg, "*Kalat*," 70.
[42] Jacobus Schoneveld, *The Bible in Israeli Education: A Study of Approaches to the Hebrew Bible and Its Teaching in Israeli Education*, Amsterdam: Van Gorcum, 1976, 75, 76–83.

two years. Yeshayahu's wife, Grete, taught physics there, and he too came in occasionally to teach Maimonides. Nehama also gave lectures in the equivalent program in Tel Aviv from time to time. The students were Israeli girls aged fourteen to nineteen, from mixed backgrounds. They included daughters of well-known personalities such as Emunah Yaron, the daughter of author S.Y. Agnon, whose parents sent her there to benefit from the teacher training.[43] There were also girls from impoverished backgrounds who sought professional status. Some of the more well-off students who found it hard to live up to Nehama's unremitting demand for a simple lifestyle developed the habit of hiding their elegant coats before class for fear of her displeasure. In general, Nehama was very impressed with these students' knowledge of Torah, and saw it as a tribute to their education in the Jewish homeland. "*This* is our people!" she would exclaim with pride. Few went on to the university, but there were exceptions: Rivka Horwitz, for example, became a professor of Jewish philosophy at Ben Gurion University and maintained close contact with Nehama for many years.

Nehama also taught in a second Mizrachi framework, the *Bet Tze'irot Mizrahi* (Mizrachi Young Women's Institute), intended for immigrants. This was a time of great flux in the nascent Jewish society in Palestine. Many European Jews were transporting their children as far as possible from Nazi claws, either westward to England or America or eastward to Palestine, where the trickle of immigrant youth soon turned into a steady stream. In 1933 Henrietta Szold and Recha Freier set up the *Aliyat ha-No'ar* (Youth Aliyah) organization to send German-Jewish adolescents to complete their education in Palestine. Thousands were slotted into religious and non-religious educational frameworks around the country. These immigrants often possessed only a patchy Jewish identity and education, a situation reflected in Nehama's comments regarding the *tinok she-nishbah* (Jew brought up from childhood by non-Jews):

> In our times... many fall into this category and transgress the entire Torah unknowingly – be they children sent to Gentile households to save their lives, who have been influenced by their saviors' religion, or those who were brought up in homes that are Jewish but nonetheless far from Jewish tradition. (*IBBM*, 180)

Although the children lived mostly on kibbutzim, Youth Aliyah also subsidized a program within the *Bet Tze'irot Mizrahi* for immigrant girls to study Torah for a five-month semester. Nehama taught approximately ten

---

43 Emunah Yaron, *Perakim me-hayyai*, Jerusalem: 2005, 88 (thanks to Yael Levine for this reference).

girls, aged fifteen to seventeen, who had come to Israel, primarily from Germany and Austria, without their parents. There were many gaps to be filled. Unfortunately, not all of the teachers in the Mizrachi institutions knew how to teach Torah imaginatively, and Nehama found herself fielding complaints about others' dull classes. Remonstrate as she might that the other teachers were far more knowledgeable than she, the girls continued to favor her. This was the case in the other Mizrachi frameworks too – for instance, Emunah Yaron reports that she hated the majority of her studies, except for Nehama's lessons.[44]

In light of the refugees' weak Hebrew, Nehama surrendered her principle that students speak Hebrew at all times and spoke German with them, helping them to acclimatize gradually to their new surroundings. A powerful bond formed, and she frequently stayed after classes ended, chatting to the girls for hours over coffee about their lives and romances. She looked out for her students financially, employing them in her house or organizing a small stipend from Youth Aliyah in order to enable them to continue their studies after high school.[45]

In these frameworks, Nehama taught Tanach, literature, Jewish history and Hebrew expression, though later she would focus almost exclusively on the Tanach and its teaching. In her literature classes she analyzed the structure of books, demonstrating how novels are crafted such that when one thread of action ends, another begins, to keep the reader turning pages. She took the students to movies and plays, teaching them to employ a critical eye and differentiate between work of high and low quality.[46] She also offered a voluntary evening class in world literature.[47] She taught modern Jewish history, which Professor Rivka Horwitz enjoyed even more than her Tanach classes. "She brought documents to the lesson – for example, the French National Assembly's statement about the Jews' status, and we had to analyze them. She turned us into 'junior historians.'"[48] The Hebrew expression classes aimed at improving communication skills, especially important for the immigrants. The girls were treated to the sight of Nehama pantomiming scenes, and were asked to describe in Hebrew what she was doing. They enjoyed her acting, especially when she mimed herself dashing out of the seminar at the sound of the taxi horn. Additionally, Nehama

---

[44] Emunah Yaron, *Perakim me-hayyai,* Jerusalem: 2005, 89–90.
[45] Gedalyah Nigal, "*Morah degulah,*" *Ha-Tzofeh,* May 9, 1997, 6.
[46] Ahrend, "*Mi-toch,*" 47.
[47] Adam Baruch recollects his mother attending such a class (*Limmudim,* 115).
[48] Horwitz, interview. See also Nehama's article, "Active Learning in the Teaching of History," about how to make the study of history more interesting and fruitful.

taught her students didactics, and took them to see teachers in practice in other schools. By that time, she was already teaching Tanach with her famous question, "What's bothering Rashi?" The foundations of her life's work were already in place and did not undergo radical change in the years to come.

By 1941–1942, with the war fully underway, the teenage immigration ceased, more or less. It was therefore decided that those already in the country should be educated further. To this end Dov Rappel and Eliezer Goldman created, in conjunction with Batya Gottesfeld of the Mizrachi women's association, another program in the same building for graduates of the immigrants' course. Here they could "complete their education and promote cultural activity in their home locales." Two groups of approximately a dozen young women studied there in turn, each for half a year, focusing intensively on a few subjects in depth. Eventually these women who once could barely read Rashi became capable of learning Torah on their own.[49]

Nehama felt extremely comfortable in this environment, and it was this group that subsequently gave rise to her famous worksheets, discussed in the next chapter. Almost all the participants lived on religious kibbutzim, and they were older – three were aged thirty. This, together with the absence of tests and pressure to cover material, allowed her to depart from the text and let the class discussion take its natural course. She permitted forays into topical issues on which she had strong opinions such as religion, Zionism, pioneering and the kibbutz ideal. She sometimes held a lesson outside so as to enjoy the nice weather or read a story. Once, she displayed a booklet made by a student who had illustrated verses from Psalm 104 using photographs from *National Geographic* magazine.

Another institution in which Nehama taught in her earlier years, not affiliated with Mizrachi, was the *Seminarim le-Hachsharat Madrichei Aliyat ha-No'ar* (Seminars for Training Youth Aliyah Counselors). Set up by the Jewish Agency, these seminars aimed to prepare young Israelis to work with immigrant children in youth villages all over the country. They were overseen by R. Shimshon Rosenthal, a scholar of Talmud who taught at the Hebrew University, and took place in the Bayit Vegan neighborhood.[50]

Rosenthal hired the best teachers available for each subject, Nehama among them. When the graduates of this program went to work as

---

[49] N. Leibowitz, "*Keitzad lamadnu Torah im mefarshim*," in *PN*, 471; Dov Rappel, "*Horatam ve-ledatam*," *Amudim* 609 (5757): 233; Dov Rappel, "*Tehillim mizmor kaf-bet*," in *PN*, 441.
[50] Nehama mentions Rosenthal in *NSV*, 486.

counselors in youth villages, they often took Nehama's worksheets with them, to fill them out with their most promising pupils. Several graduates went on to become renowned academics, such as Yonah Frankel, an expert on Midrash, and Tamar Ross, a professor of Jewish philosophy. Ross studied for a year at the seminar, though she came not from war-torn Europe but from the USA at age sixteen. Nehama figured repeatedly and colorfully in Ross's letters to her parents. She sent lively descriptions of a chilly classroom in which Nehama bent over a kerosene oven to warm her hands, and once even sent home a sketch she had made of her teacher (see illustration). Ross reported that Nehama had "nearly exploded" when she caught her chewing gum in class, and spent the entire lesson lecturing the students on the lack of culture exhibited in this activity. Ross thought this rather ironic, since after the harangue, while still in class, Nehama "proceeded to have her famous cup of tea and sandwich," but this was ultimately justifiable as "there is no other time when she can do this. Indeed her life is very different and much more loaded than most people's." Alone in a foreign land, Ross was grateful for the personal attention Nehama extended to her.

Intellectual circles in the Yishuv

After Hitler's accession to power in 1933, cultural circles in Palestine were enriched by fleeing German Jews, who were forced to acclimatize rather abruptly:

> These people from Germany with their pink complexions and suits were now anxious individuals wearing rags. A group of Ph.D.s... worked together cleaning shop windows.[51]

These "*yekkes*," as they were called, stuck together, and in Jerusalem, many made their homes in the Rehavia neighborhood. A colony formed of artists, philosophers, politicians and scientists, who socialized and debated, whether in salons such as that of the famous Anna Ticho and her husband or in more casual encounters, such as on the bus.[52] Nehama mixed freely with these sophisticated Jerusalemites. She was personally acquainted with several of the scholars she quoted in her books and felt free to call upon them for advice:

> I asked several scholars in Jerusalem and they could not help me. (*PN*, 691)

---

[51] Gideon Ofrat, *One Hundred Years of Art in Israel*, translated by Peretz Kidron, Westview Press, 1998, 88.

[52] Thus, for example, in a letter to Gershom Scholem, Yeshayahu Leibowitz apologizes for their previous snatched conversation on the bus (Y. Leibowitz, *Ratziti*, 255).

Shimshon Rosenthal and Nehama at the Seminars for Youth Immigration,
Bayit Vegan, 1955. Photo: Tamar Ross

Sketch by Tamar Ross, 1955. "This is Nehama in real life. She appears serious
here, while in reality she often laughs; but I've managed to capture the eyes
especially. I drew for the duration of one lesson, but she disturbed me in the
middle and I had to complete it from memory. She said that if I study well she'll
agree to sit for me sometime, but I didn't accept, for it was only a fleeting urge on
my part. Her face is very interesting, it has a special expression. Her hat is a shade
of tan brown, and she always wears it (I'm sure for religious reasons)."
Courtesy of Tamar Ross.

Nehama liked and admired the German Jews and, despite her Latvian origins, did not feel an outsider among them, since she shared their strongly cultured background and rationalistic orientation. However, she did not possess the lingering love for German culture that some retained in spite of everything. Moreover, she was pained that German Jewry did not sufficiently look to the welfare of the entire Jewish people. R. Hirsch could afford to be optimistic because things were going well for his constituents, but what about his responsibility to his brethren in other Jewish communities?[53]

Nehama's close friends and colleagues tended to belong ideologically to the national-religious camps of the Kibbutz ha-Dati or Mizrachi. At the time there was a huge chasm between the national-religious camp and yeshivah society. Although she was strictly religious, Nehama clearly belonged to the former. She was outspokenly pro-army, disapproved of adults learning Torah at their parents' expense, and endorsed social contact between the sexes.

Her busy teaching schedule notwithstanding, Nehama found time to spend with her brother Yeshayahu. Although her brother's house was the larger, the Leibowitz family would periodically gather in Nehama's house for pleasurable discussions. She also socialized with her cousin, Dr. Yehoshua Leibowitz, a professor of medicine and the history of medicine at the Hebrew University, who specialized in Maimonides. Her close circle also included fellow teachers from the Youth Aliyah and Mizrachi programs, many of whom taught also at the Hebrew University in Jerusalem, such as Professors Meir Weiss, Ernst Simon, Isaac Heinemann, Aryeh Ludwig Strauss, Simha Assaf, Yehudah Elitzur, Haim Hillel Ben-Sasson and Yehezkel Kutscher.[54] Others with whom Nehama had a close connection included academics such as Professors E.E. Urbach, S.H. Bergman, Yaakov Katz, and Shlomo Goitein; and rabbis such as R. Yehudah Ansbacher of the Ihud Shivat Tziyon synagogue in Tel Aviv, R. Yissachar Jacobson and R. David Carlebach.[55] Nehama had cordial relations with author and Nobel laureate S.Y. Agnon, whom she brought to meet the students of Youth Aliyah, and to whom she wrote:

> Please send warmest regards to your wife. Whenever I visit you, I am accorded such a warm reception that I remain in good spirits for days after my visit. (*PN*, 667)

---

[53] Horwitz, "*Nehama*," 214.
[54] Haim Hamiel. "*Leibowitz, Nehama*," Ha-encyclopedia shel ha-tzionut ha-datit, Vol. 6, 573.
[55] Horwitz, "*Nehama*," 212.

Bottom row, from left: Nehama Leibowitz, Lipman Leibowitz.
Second row up, third and fourth from left: Shimshon Rosenthal, Meir Weiss.
Third row up, second and third from left: Junia Ben-Sasson, Yonah Ben-Sasson.
Courtesy of Mira Ofran.

She was also acquainted with Henrietta Szold, the American philanthropist and Zionist, having met her through her connection with the women's seminary, and with whom she shared a love of literature. The Israeli poet Zelda (Shneurson) studied with Nehama and reportedly was "extremely happy to meet someone like Nehama Leibowitz, who can sit and discuss poems." Nehama phoned her for explanations of modern poems. Nehama knew the Jewish philosopher and scholar Professor Martin Buber, and helped him with his monumental German translation of the Torah, which he undertook, together with Franz Rosenzweig, from 1924 onwards.[56] She held the Buber-Rosenzweig translation in high esteem because of its exacting loyalty to nuances of the original Hebrew.[57] She was involved in the project from its early days, when they solicited her aid in translating Psalms, the topic of her doctorate.[58] They also asked for her help with the book of Job, which contained particularly difficult Hebrew.[59] Nehama respected Buber's intellectual honesty in readily accepting her translation suggestions over his own. However, she had her criticisms of him too, and was unable to comprehend how a man who had read and translated the Bible could fail to know in which chapter the Ten Commandments appear. For Nehama, this exemplified his lack of the more intimate knowledge possessed by traditional Jews who hear the Torah read weekly in synagogue. She also told of visiting Buber's house and finding, to her great wonder, that the philosopher – famous for his model of the "I-Thou" relationship – neglected during the long hours to offer her so much as a glass of water. Since Nehama was never one for idle gossip, perhaps she mentioned this in order to illustrate that the "great people" of society sometimes lacked the basic decency of the ordinary people whom she loved.[60]

---

[56] Steven S. Schwarzschild, *Encyclopedia Judaica*, 14:301. See also Horwitz, "*Nehama*," 213.

[57] See pages 416–418 below.

[58] Sheleg, "*Kalat*," 70; Raphael Posen, "*Ha-targum bi-chetavehah shel Nehama*," in *PN*, 112–113. Nehama's comments in *NSS*, 312, n. 6 and *ibid.* 688, n. 5 demonstrate her extensive familiarity with the back-and-forth of the revisions, deriving perhaps from first-hand acquaintance. See also *ibid*, 333, n. 3.

[59] Horwitz, "*Nehama*," 215, n. 22.

[60] See also the story about Agnon, pages 446–447 below.

CHAPTER 2

THE *GILYONOT*:
HOW NEHAMA BECAME A FAVORITE
OF THE ISRAEL POSTAL SERVICE

Introduction

HAVING COVERED, in brief sketches, Nehama's work and social milieus in her younger years, we turn now to one of her key projects, which grew from humble beginnings into a landmark venture, affecting countless people all over the world.

During her lifetime, Nehama succeeded in teaching Torah via three different media. Two were familiar and time-tested – teaching and writing books and articles – but the third was unique to Nehama: her famous mimeographed pages of questions that she called "*Gilyonot* (Worksheets) on the Weekly Torah Portion." With these *gilyonot*, Nehama inverted a centuries-old Jewish practice. Since talmudic times, Jews have corresponded on matters of Jewish law with the greatest halachic decisors of their day, sending queries by mail across considerable distances, and receiving detailed replies. From the time of Geonim onwards these have been published in volumes, creating a body of literature known as the Responsa or *Shu"t* (*she'elot u-teshuvot*). But Nehama did the reverse: she sent out the questions, and the correspondents were the ones who wrote the responses! In doing so, she helped to restore the Holy Land to its rightful place as the central address for the Torah's dissemination across the world, helping fulfill the words of the prophet Isaiah:

> From Zion shall the Torah go forth, and the word of the Lord from Jerusalem.

How the *gilyonot* came into being

The story of this groundbreaking endeavor begins with the Mizrachi graduate program for young immigrant women mentioned in the previous chapter. Every week, Nehama assigned her students questions on the Torah portion, and the challenge of grappling with the commentators' approaches – Rashi, Ramban, Ibn Ezra *et al.* – became the highlight of their week. Every Shabbat afternoon, small groups of students might be seen sitting on the grass, discussing the current worksheet. After Shabbat they pooled their answers and handed in the group effort to Nehama. She felt free to rate their answers with words and phrases, such as "Good," "Not enough," and so on, rather than with formal grades. She encouraged them to fill out as many *gilyonot* as possible, believing that it was an excellent way to advance. In fact, it became known among the students that a surefire technique to restore Nehama's good humor was to mention having filled one out.

That summer of 1942, after the young women returned to their kibbutzim, a rare if not unique event in the history of education occurred: though the school year was over, the students asked for more homework! These young women, who had maintained a strong personal connection with Nehama, wrote to her asking to continue the questionnaires under her supervision. More than happy to oblige, she mailed the first sheet to the women at their respective kibbutzim.

The next thing that occurred, which was quite as surprising, was that the young women's kibbutz friends began to envy them their avid scribbling, and wrote to Nehama asking for worksheets too. She unhesitatingly agreed to the strangers' requests, despite the extra load it entailed – and that was how it all began.

Now, the above account is based on accounts by Professor Dov Rappel and others.[1] Nehama's version of the story of the birth of the *gilyonot* shows a little more premeditation:

> I noticed that all sorts of subjects are taught by correspondence, from architecture to accountancy, from advertising to stenography, and I said, "Shall not our perfect Torah [at the very least] resemble one of these?"[2]

Elsewhere, she explained:

> The problems of adult education began to occupy and trouble me. From my work in short courses ("seminars") for kibbutz members, and for immigrant youth and movement counselors, I realized that there was a need for these studies to continue. An idea came to me to carry on this brief seminar study via a guided correspondence course, leading to regular study over a prolonged period.

---

[1] See Dov Rappel, "*Horatam ve-ledatam*," *Amudim* 609 (5757): 233. Sheleg's suggestion that Nehama invented the worksheets to cope efficiently with the large numbers of people who wanted to study with her does not appear to be an accurate representation of their launch, although they may well have served that function subsequently ("*Keter shel Torah*," *Otiot* [Iyar 5757]: 9).

[2] N. Leibowitz, "*Sihah al limmud parashat ha-shavua be-michtavim*," in PN, 458.

And thus it was that in 5702 (1942) I began to teach Torah and
commentaries by means of "Worksheets for Studying the Weekly
Portion," whose chief aim was to bring the student (individuals or
groups) to independent study, to a deeper examination of the text
through comparison and analysis and a thorough exploration of the
commentaries (of all periods, from the Sages to Cassuto).... No exam
or certificate or even a set period was attached to this study. (*PN*, 14)

In any event, regardless of the exact causes and beginnings, an endeavor
unique in Jewish history had been born.[3]

⇛ ⇚

The *gilyonot* got off to a modest start as a single sheet, copied by stencil; only
in later years were they printed *en masse*. They initially arrived at the Mizrachi
building on Rashi Street, but from the following year onwards they went
straight to Nehama's home. The first sheets were sent at her expense, but as
the numbers grew the American Women's Mizrachi organization, under the
auspices of Dr. Joseph Burg, undertook to print and distribute the sheets as
part of its program of Torah and Education for Adults and Youth.
Subscribers were asked to send a small sum for postage, but the rest of the
costs were covered. Several years later the World Zionist Organization took
over the task.[4]

The numbers of subscribers quickly swelled, reaching five hundred by
the end of the third year, though only forty actually sent in their filled sheets
– and even this depended on the season, with farmers much freer in the
winter (*PN*, 460). Later on, Nehama was receiving upwards of a hundred
sheets, every one of which she checked and returned. By the tenth year of
the worksheets, the numbers stood at 560 in Israel and 30 abroad; though
Nehama surmised that the sheets were shared between families and groups
and therefore the actual number of students was over two thousand.

By 1957, Nehama could attest to three thousand recipients of her
sheets.[5] Word was spread both by enthusiastic correspondents and by
Nehama herself, who often suggested at the end of her courses: "If you want
to continue learning with me you can buy a set of *gilyonot*." She also often
built her lessons around one or more worksheets.

---

[3] Though Aryeh Newman reports that R. Chaim Klein, a British Rosh Yeshivah, similarly
sent out sheets to his students who had been drafted to the army in World War II,
containing quotes from the Talmud and questions, and they corresponded with him in return
(interview).
[4] Hamiel writes that this took place in 1951 ("*Morat ha-dor*," *Ha-Tzofeh*, April 18, 1997, 6). See
also Marla Frankel, "*Ha-te'oriyah ha-hora'atit shel Nehama*," in *PN*, 426, n. 4.
[5] Yehiel Zvi Moskowitz, *Parshanut ha-mikra le-doroteha*, Education Ministry: 1998, 201.

Nehama's *gilyonot* had expanded, by 1952, from one folio sheet to two. The mark of history is seen on the sheets. They skip several months in 1948, because, after her mimeograph machine took a direct hit during the War of Independence, she had difficulty locating another one in the city.[6] One year, two *gilyonot* were printed on one page because there was not enough paper.

From 1955 onwards, Nehama also began to include a study guide alongside the weekly sheet, printed through the Ministry of Education. This guide, called *Alon hadracha le-hora'at parashat ha-shavua* (Guidance Pamphlet for the Teaching of the Weekly Torah Portion), helped teachers and counselors to use the *gilyonot* properly, with recommendations of how to build lessons around them and which points to emphasize. Since the *gilyonot* were not easy, such guidance benefited non-teachers too (*PN* 14, 703). These teachers' pamphlets did not appear every week – possibly because Nehama was too busy to prepare them.

At the twenty-five year mark of the worksheets, Nehama's friend and colleague R. Yaakov Koppel Reinitz observed:

> Sometimes I wonder whether the students appreciate just how much effort and toil are invested into preparing the worksheets! What painstaking work goes into putting together a collection of the best of the best! And what reward does she seek? Only that we study – that we study meticulously and thoroughly. That we also invest effort – like her – in understanding the words of the living God, each according to his ability. (*PN*, 679)

By the time Nehama stopped producing her sheets, there were thirty years' worth in total, though the later ones contained some repetition.

The *gilyonot* were initially stored in Nehama's house according to years, separated by old pages of Lipman's Braille books. As they became more numerous, they were put into hundreds of bulky file jackets, according to weekly portions, and were also piled up in other locations in the small apartment – in closets, kitchen cupboards, on the balcony; and anywhere with room for shelves. Fully two and a half walls of her living room were taken up with these files – R. Hershel Billet describes the effect as "wallpaper filled with *divrei Torah*" – with each centimeter of the wall representing another weekly portion. When teaching at home, Nehama would often respond to a query by pointing to a file on the wall and saying, "I discussed that in that *gilayon*."

---

[6] Nissan Zisken, conversation. See *PN*, 711, where Nehama lists every week she had missed to that date.

Nehama with her worksheets in the background. Courtesy of Mira Ofran.

Nechama Leibowitz

Nehama's English signature.
Courtesy of Nachum Amsel

נחמה ליבוביץ

Nehama's Hebrew signature.
Courtesy of Nachum Amsel

No one spending any serious amount of time with Nehama could fail to be aware of the *gilyonot* and the buzz of activity surrounding them; and everyone was recruited to help, including her father. For the children close to Nehama – her brother's children, and the Ben-Sassons and their cousins, the Knohls – the *gilyonot* were an integral part of their growing up. It was exciting to watch them being sorted and sent, and even more so to be permitted to participate. The administrative aspects alone were staggering. People ordered the sheets by weekly portion or subject, and Nehama – together with friends, relatives, students and anyone else who was willing to help – prepared packages accordingly. One year's, five years' or all thirty years' worth of sheets were ordered. Each *gilayon* was painstakingly pulled from its folder and note taken of which folders were empty or running low. Then the sheets had to be folded and placed into the envelopes, which were sealed, addressed and dropped at the post office. The envelopes were used, and not necessarily the sender's original, granting her correspondents a small glimpse of Nehama's bustling postal life; sometimes they were even just folded-up newspapers.

Nehama continually asked for volunteers to help organize the *gilyonot*, offering in return a one-on-one study session or even payment. Over the years many friends and students gave up hours of their time, some on a regular basis, to this activity. The work of reaching up to the top rows and bending down to the bottom ones to withdraw the *gilyonot* could prove a severe strain on one's back; but this time with Nehama could also constitute a great treat, an opportunity to ask questions or discuss issues in confidence. While collating the *gilyonot*, Nehama sometimes felt more comfortable talking about personal matters – her own and her companion's.

Sending out the worksheets was, however, only half the story, for Nehama also had to check the numerous filled-in sheets returned to her daily. Nechama Tamler recalls: "She had a huge mailbox in the hallway of her apartment building. Everyone else's was lined up and was the same size; Nehama's was probably three to four times as big, since the mail carrier couldn't fit it all into the standard sized box." She used every spare moment to check sheets, whether at home, in cafés, traveling to lectures, and sometimes even by the light of a small flashlight.[7] Teachers especially, familiar with the drudgery of checking papers, understand what a Herculean effort it entailed. R. Shmuel Klitsner observes: "The bane of any teacher's

---

[7] Aryeh Strikovsky, "Nehama on Women and Womanhood," in *Traditions and Celebrations for the Bat Mitzvah*, edited by Ora Wiskind Elper, 187 (Jerusalem: Urim Publications/MaTaN, 2003).

existence is correcting homework. But for her this was a labor of love." In fact, nothing could have pleased her more than the sheets' success.

Here, then, was an example of someone who single-handedly, without office or aide, glossy brochures or lavish promotions, created a project of worldwide proportions, solely through dedication and hard work. At a gathering held in 1952 to mark ten years of the *gilyonot*, various professors and scholars in turn each praised a different aspect of the *gilyonot*.[8] Nehama's enterprise was termed a "one-woman Open University course,"[9] and R. Ben Hollander, Nehama's teaching assistant for many years puts it this way: "The *gilyonot* were the first, pre-computer website. That's what she won the Israel Prize for, and that's what connected her to all of the people of Israel."

Not everyone, however, approved of the *gilyonot*. One critic said he saw them as nothing more than a nice pastime. Nehama's retort was: "On the contrary – even our amusements should revolve around the Torah, along the lines of the verse in Psalms (119:16) – 'I will take delight in your statutes!'"[10]

Nature of the *gilyonot*

Such criticism notwithstanding, Nehama's work remained by far the most successful of its kind. This leads to the question: What was so special about these typed sheets that started off as homework for immigrant girls?

Part of their magic lay in moving beyond the local point under discussion to touch on broad issues, which made for thought-provoking reading. Another motivating factor was the detailed feedback that Nehama gave to each and every correspondent, creating an ongoing dialogue. Many were amazed and flattered that Nehama herself, rather than some secretary or assistant, wrote to them each time. In fact, she loved reading all the answers, and was only saddened that she had to return them to their owners: "Had I wanted to copy down every excellent thing I saw, I would not have found the time," she noted. For this reason, she was known to request that personal correspondence be sent on a separate sheet and not on the filled-in worksheet she had to return.

But the real secret lay in the questions. Her purpose was not to show off her erudition ("It is not my function to answer, rather to ask!" she declared).[11] Rather, Nehama provoked the student into intellectual investment. It was the act of sweating over her terse questions, and the

---

[8] Moshe Ahrend, "*Ha-katuv tzarich iyun*," *Bi-sdei hemed* 11 (1968): 30.
[9] Sheleg, "*Kalat*," 70.
[10] Breuer, "*Professor*," 17.
[11] N. Leibowitz, "*Sihah*," in *PN*, 459.

suspense of waiting to see if the answers were correct that created the enjoyable learning experience. The *gilyonot* were like puzzles, and people enjoyed trying to solve them. R. Chaim Weiner observes: "Nehama believed that answers are easier to find than questions. People are naturally curious, and when they see a problem they try to solve it. There are no limits to human imagination or to human ingenuity in solving problems. Study isn't a matter of memorizing answers." Professor Warren Zev Harvey adds:

> Not every crossword is challenging and not every dialogue is exciting – what makes the gilyonot special is Leibowitz's distinctive approach.[12]

Anyone filling out a worksheet learned a basic lesson about Torah text: that it should never be taken for granted. Shira Leibowitz Schmidt points out that the word for worksheet, *gilayon*, generally means a scroll. However, in Isaiah Chapter 3, the following is written:

> In that day the Lord will take away the bravery of their anklets, and their tiaras, and their necklaces… (v. 18).

> The gilyonim, and the fine linen, and the hoods, and the veils (v. 23).

The word "*gilyonim*" is interpreted by Rashi to refer to mirrors; he derives this from the root *g-l-h*, to reveal, because mirrors reveal the face of the viewer. Schmidt creatively applies this meaning to describe what Nehama's *gilyonot* did for the student. By the end of the process, readers had made the verse their own and had discovered the depths beyond seemingly trivial Hebrew words.

The contents of every worksheet were as follows:

Firstly, the student was required to examine the verse, section, or chapter of Scripture carefully; then read the commentaries under discussion; and finally try to answer the questions Nehama posed, which were of the type:

> What is the difficulty addressed by the commentator?

> What led the commentator to give additional explanations?

> What is the difference between one explanation and another?

> What do the other commentators add?

> What are the different problems addressed by each of several commentators on the same verses?

> What is the weakness of each commentary?[13]

---

[12] Warren Zev Harvey, "Professor Nehama Leibowitz, Israel's Teacher of Teachers," *Canadian Zionist*, 50/4 (April/May 1981): 11.
[13] Yitshak Reiner, "Introduction to *Gilyonot*" (www.moreshet.net/oldsite/nechama/ introgilyon.htm).

Some of the worksheets dealt with the specific approaches of particular commentators, especially Rashi. There were also general and linguistic questions, which became increasingly diverse as the years went on.[14] Nehama also sometimes added tips, such as articles for further reading for teachers.

Nehama wanted to train the students to search for the questions implied in the commentator's words. Her premise, repeated thousands of times over the course of her life, was that commentators did not write for their own pleasure, but were rather responding to difficulties in the text. Nehama reported that the task of pinpointing these difficulties was grueling for her worksheet students, but that

> the results demonstrate that [this task] educates towards accurate, "healthy" and necessary comprehension.[15]

Within her *gilyonot*, Nehama cited a range of materials: Tanach, talmudic and midrashic materials, commentators through the ages, ethical teachings from the Mussar movement, and contemporary religious philosophy. Her subscribers received a broad introduction to the corpus of Jewish thought, barring Kabbalistic and Hasidic works. Believing in the value of books over printed quotes, Nehama sent the reader to look up the more common sources (Rashi, Ramban, Ibn Ezra, Rashbam, Seforno) in the *Mikra'ot Gedolot* series. But from 1945 onwards she began to cite works unlikely to be found on the ordinary shelf, and these of necessity she quoted in full. In this way she introduced the fledgling Jewish society in Palestine to many little-known works, using the rich resources available even then, such as the National Library, to dig them up; for example, the commentary by the Italian scholar Isaac Reggio, which

> like many other heavy articles and commentaries printed in journals from the previous century, is difficult for the reader and student to access, since they are found only in large, scientific libraries.[16]

In a light-hearted tribute to Nehama after her passing, Nurit Fried suggested that upon ascending to heaven Nehama was met by hordes of

---

[14] Before 1945 her questions focused on the commentator's interpretation, for example: "What is bothering Rashi?" or "How does Rashi differ from Rashbam?" See Yehiel Zvi Moskowitz, "*Al ha-gilyonot ve-al ha-iyunim*," *Daf le-tarbut Yehudit* 228: *Nehama Leibowitz z"l*, edited by Aryeh Strikovsky, 11 (Torah Education Department of Education Ministry, Iyar 5757/1997).

[15] N. Leibowitz, "*Daf la-lomdim*," in *PN*, 456.

[16] N. Leibowitz, *Teacher's Guide* for *Yitro*, 5730.

commentaries, all thanking her profusely for rescuing them from obscurity.[17] Nehama's exhaustive surveys of often inaccessible sources and, perhaps even more importantly, her judicious selection of the most compelling ones, made her *gilyonot* – and later her books – a precious resource for teachers. An overworked teacher preparing lessons at ten o'clock at night was grateful to be able to locate speedily a variety of commentaries on any given weekly Torah portion. Even more significant was that Nehama made the commentaries accessible for the first time to the lay public who could now not only fulfill the mitzvah of reading the weekly portion with commentaries but also actually understand the latter.[18]

Nehama sometimes chose the subject matter for the worksheets based on what she was teaching in her regular classes. She once informed her class in Bar-Ilan, "This week the entire country is working on Ibn Ezra because of you!"

"*U-faratzta*": Spreading out in all directions

A broad spectrum of the Israeli Jewish population filled out the worksheets – from very religious to very secular. Nehama records that the members of the secular kibbutz Deganyah set up a study group, and this phenomenon spread from kibbutz to kibbutz in the Jezreel and Jordan Valleys and in the Galilee. It began with the older members, who wanted to recapture the religious flavor of their parents' homes, and then younger generations, who had never learned Rashi and Ramban, joined.[19]

Nehama naturally built pictures in her mind of her regular correspondents. When at times her curiosity propelled her to write and inquire who they were, this led to some surprises:

> And one correspondent from Tel Aviv who wrote intelligently for over a year, in reply to the curious inquiry of the worksheets' author as to his profession, wrote simply "Municipal street cleaner." And a young woman who writes with discernment and spelling mistakes, who stubbornly questions everything she does not understand and never skips a week, turns out to be a waitress in a café.[20]

Whilst several prominent figures regularly filled out her worksheets, Nehama was proudest of her less distinguished correspondents. The

---

[17] Nurit Fried, *VLN*. Fried wrote a poetic ode to Nehama based on this idea, which she reads in her lecture at *VLN*.

[18] Aryeh Newman, "The Joy of Tora Reading," *Jerusalem Post*, October 12, 1990, 11.

[19] N. Leibowitz, "*Sikkum beynaim al mifal ha-gilyonot*," in *PN*, 462.

[20] N. Leibowitz, "*Sikkum*," 462.

devotion of simple people to Torah touched her, and she mentioned this waitress far more frequently than she did the accomplished educators and rabbis on her mailing list.[21] She praised farmers who filled out the sheets after a long day in the fields or at a midday break sitting on the sweltering ground in the tractor's shade, and who wrote apologizing for getting manure on the answer sheet.[22] She admired the hospital midwife who begged forgiveness for her slipshod answers due to a tiring day involving two difficult births.[23] She also liked to tell of the time when a burly man approached her excitedly after a lecture and exclaimed: "I am Ezekiel who twenty years ago used to write to you every week from Morocco! Today I'm a stevedore in Ashdod!"[24]

The *gilyonot* went out as far as border settlements and Israeli army bunkers, uplifting the soldiers beyond the tedium and trepidation of army life. The IDF's Religious Services even requested specially prepared sheets for the soldiers; here, instead of "See Rashi on this verse" Nehama had to quote the commentary in full. During the War of Independence in 1948, the military rabbinate sent out over a thousand such sheets to soldiers. When R. Shlomo Goren, then chief rabbi of the IDF, saw the sheets, he immediately understood their exceptional quality. A brilliant Torah scholar, he admitted that even he wasn't able to answer all the questions.[25] Jewish soldiers abroad, such as the Jewish Brigade fighting in Italy in World War II, also filled out her *gilyonot*. One soldier offered a unique excuse for interrupting his studies – his *Humash* was currently at the bottom of the Mediterranean Sea![26] Nehama was always very warm towards soldiers, and a student once turned up to an exam in army uniform, hoping to take advantage of this soft spot.

Some of the soldiers even returned their answers to Nehama between battles, as she recounts:

> At the height of the siege, a soldier turned up in the bombed house of
> the author claiming he had been looking for her for two hours and had

---

[21] *Studies on the Haggadah from the Teachings of Nehama Leibowitz*, edited by Yitshak Reiner and Shmuel Peerless, 151 (Jerusalem: Urim Publications, 2002).

[22] N. Leibowitz, "*Ahavat Torah ve-limmudah*," in *PN*, 464; Harvey, "Professor," 11.

[23] Avigdor Bonchek, "Professor Nechama, Teacher of Israel," *Jewish Action* 54 (Fall 1993): 16.

[24] Harvey, "Professor," 11.

[25] For more on Rabbi Goren's life, see Shalom Freedman, *Rabbi Shlomo Goren: Torah Sage and General*, Jerusalem: Urim Publications, 2006.

[26] N. Leibowitz, "*Sikkum*," 463. See also the letter from Zvi Bass z"l, a volunteer soldier in World War II, in Elhanan Samet, "*Ha-morah le-Torah*," *Amudim* 581 (5757): 38.

come specially to get his sheet that he had sent a week ago and not yet received with all the usual corrections.[27]

[Soldiers] came on foot between bombings from the "Notre-Dame" front to bring me answers (since the mail was not functioning) during the War of Independence.[28]

Under the violent circumstances of war, correspondences were also abruptly terminated:

We shall not forget the memory of the holy members of Kibbutz Kfar Etzion who were amongst the first to participate in the study in 5702 and continued throughout the years until contact was lost between their settlement and Jerusalem and the enemies came upon them.[29]

And let us also remember here the kibbutznik from Deganyah B, who asked a question on Shabbat while he was studying the weekly Torah portion in his group; then on Sunday morning came into Jerusalem to bring vegetables, since Jerusalem was still only under partial siege, and was killed by the enemy in the alleyways, with his question that had been sent on to Jerusalem still unanswered. And the young man, an immigrant, from Kfar Darom, who wrote his answers regularly over a span of two years even when under battle-fire in the Negev, and I still have his answers, with nowhere to send them, for he has fallen.[30]

Professor Moshe Ahrend corresponded with Nehama while in the army, not knowing that he would later become her close colleague and friend. During these years (1949–1950) there was little Jewish study material available in the army, so his brother sent him a set of Nehama's worksheets. With time to kill, Ahrend began to fill them out at a prodigious rate: "Whether from stupidity or *hutzpah*, I filled out not one, but four or five sheets every week!" The indefatigable Nehama returned all of them faithfully, corrected with detailed comments.

As in the kibbutzim, "worksheet envy" hit in the army too. In 1970, a soldier named Yonatan Ahituv, having found his secular high school Tanach studies boring, was slowly becoming more interested in Judaism when the sight of his fellow soldiers scribbling away in their spare time piqued his interest. He wrote to ask to receive them too. At first, he noted his answers for his eyes only. Subsequently, however, he decided to take this "Nehama

---

[27] N. Leibowitz, "*Sikkum*," 463.

[28] N. Leibowitz, "*El kol lomdei parashat ha-shavua mi-toch iyun ba-gilyonot ba-asher hem sham*," in *PN*, 469.

[29] The reference is to May 13, 1948, when dozens of the defenders were killed.

[30] N. Leibowitz, "*Sikkum*," 463.

Leibowitz woman" up on her invitation to actively correspond. Before long, one of her recycled envelopes arrived with his corrected answers, together with a note that warmed his heart in the frosty terrain: "I have many envelopes sitting on my desk, but soldiers get served first without waiting in line. Please leave wide margins for my answers." She later asked him, "Are there other boys there who'd be interested in this kind of study? If so, please tell them about it."[31]

One of the first worksheets Ahituv filled out, for *Va-era* 5731, discussed the hardening of Pharaoh's heart and how free will can co-exist with Divine foreknowledge. This topic had kept Ahituv awake at nights; but Nehama, in quoting from Talmud and Maimonides, "made me realize I was not alone, and introduced me to a group of 'friends' who were also bothered by it. She exposed me to such treasures; I realized Tanach could be interesting!" After several *gilyonot* had gone back and forth, Nehama wrote: "If you're ever in Jerusalem, come visit me." He did; and they remained in touch long after he left the army, his wife eventually attending lessons too.

By 1977, when R. Chaim Weiner joined the IDF, more options existed for studying in the army. Yet he too chose Nehama's study sheets, resolving to fill out one a week, even though she had stopped producing the sheets six years earlier. Weiner decided to post his answers anyway and was delighted when he received a response. From then on, Weiner studied in every spare moment, forfeiting meals and sleep so that every Friday a completed sheet could be sent to Nehama. The case containing his study sheets and books went with him everywhere; it became caked in gun oil and tank grease, but the worksheets remained clean, and he even used special gloves to fill them out.

At one point Weiner was stationed with his unit in the Sinai desert, on the Egyptian border. One night, doing guard duty in the watchtower overlooking the border, he waited until first light of dawn and then took out the *gilyonot* to look at the questions. Suddenly a strong wind appeared and blew them out of the tower, scattering them across the surrounding desert. Without a second thought, Weiner climbed down from the tower and chased after the fluttering pages. With great effort he climbed over fences and crawled through bushes, hunting for all of the sheets in the dark. Making his way back fully two and a half hours later he discovered to his surprise a high fence intervening between himself and the watchtower, on the other side of which read the sign: CAUTION – MINEFIELD AHEAD. Weiner was

---

[31] Letter to Ahituv.

stunned: He had just spent several hours wandering around in a minefield! "But it was worth it!" he declares.

❧ ❦

In 1951, the World Zionist Organization began the work of distributing the sheets in the Diaspora too. They eventually made their way to destinations throughout the Jewish world, as Nehama attests:

> There is the doctor from Holland, who is an expert in grammar and traditional readings, and challenges our commentators based on the cantillation notes… and the highly educated social worker from Germany; and the university physicist who argues and debates so powerfully, who studied in an American yeshivah.[32]

Answers came in also from Switzerland, Morocco (addressed to "Our teacher in Zion"), Turkey, Tunisia and Libya:

> And how varied were these answers in outlook and style, from the lyric style of North African Jewry, with the bookish Midrashic style of their yeshivah students, to the linguistically poor yet analytically meticulous style of the academic from Western Europe.[33]

The sheets were translated into Russian by refuseniks in the 1970s and circulated secretly to anyone who knew even a little Torah.[34] *Gilyonot* could also be found in the offices of youth movements such as Bnei Akiva. Initially America, which was not a learning-oriented community at the time, was not among these destinations. Indeed, in 1954 Nehama remarked to her American student Tamar Ross that while she received *gilyonot* from correspondents all over the world she was yet to hear from the largest Jewish Diaspora. But eventually American Jews contacted her too, for example a study circle at Harvard University Hillel. Groups like this used the sheets as the basis for *havurah*-style learning.[35]

Nehama was pleased at this widespread dissemination, a rare expression of unity in a divided Jewish world. Here was one thing all Jews cared about – the study of the Torah. Not for prizes, not for tax reductions, but simply for love.[36]

With the backgrounds of the people filling out the *gilyonot* so varied, Nehama had to word the sheets in very general ways, without reference to particular realities, although certain references seem meant specifically for a

---

[32] N. Leibowitz , "*Sikkum*," 462.
[33] N. Leibowitz, "*Sikkum*," 463.
[34] Abramowitz, *Tales*, 37.
[35] Nathaniel Helfgot, "Recalling a Master Teacher," *New York Jewish Week*, April 1997.
[36] N. Leibowitz, "*Sikkum*," 464 and "*El kol*," 469.

Diaspora audience.[37] She also had to find ways to tailor the *gilyonot* to many different levels and capabilities.[38] Her solution was to make the questions range in difficulty, marked by Xs: No X indicated a relatively easy question; one X was more difficult; and the most challenging questions came with two Xs. But even the "easy" ones could never be answered mechanically or circumvented by waffling. R. Mordechai Spiegelman writes:

> Nehama's incisive questions in her study sheets never required long answers. If you didn't answer in less than three sentences, you knew that you should rethink the answer.[39]

She included encouraging instructions, such as:

> Each person should answer according to his level.

> You don't have to answer all of the questions.

> Answer to the extent that your time and ability allow.

The most difficult questions she preceded with warnings such as

> Only for those who look in the *Targum*,

> For the advanced student.

These warnings lured many, in a case of reverse psychology, into trying to answer the hard questions.[40] There were also occasional tips and pointers under the title: "A piece of good advice." Other instructions included on every sheet were "Write clearly and leave me room for corrections." Incidentally, her own handwriting was not so easy to decipher. One student claims that the first time he received a letter from her, it took him ten minutes to work out who it was from.

Rather than a grade, the student was rewarded with exclamation points and idiosyncratic remarks in red pen. Those who had already studied with her could hear her voice and intonation in her pungent responses. Besides her four types of "grades," all positive – N (*nachon* = correct), T.M. (*tov me'od* = very good), *be-vaday* (absolutely) and *metzuyan* (excellent) – she included complimentary comments using colorful language such as: "This is worth an orange."

---

[37] See Frankel, *Ha-te'oriyah*, 436, n. 50.

[38] Marla Frankel, *Iyun ve-hora'ah: hanharat shitatah shel Nehama Leibowitz* [A Clarification of Nechama Leibowitz's Approach to the Study and Teaching of Bible], Jerusalem: Hebrew University, 1997, 7.

[39] Mordechai Spiegelman, review of Shmuel Peerless, *To Study and to Teach: The Methodology of Nechama Leibowitz*, Jerusalem: Urim Publications, 2003, in Lookstein Center Internet archives, November 2003.

[40] Posen, "*Ha-targum*," 119.

But there was also criticism such "Where did you get that from?" "How can you write such nonsense?" and "Unintelligible waffle!" The letters L.N. did not bode well. "She told us that when we see the letters *lamed* and *nun*, it doesn't stand for '*Leibowitz Nehama*' but '*lo nachon*' (not correct)!" recalls Tamler. These forthright comments were not always easy to stomach. One correspondent whose scrupulously researched answers consistently failed to impress grumbles: "I might have got a '*tov*' just once!" He adds, "Nevertheless, I carried on, because it was Nehama."

Disgruntled correspondents could defend their answers a week later, on the next sheet, creating ongoing debates. Nehama sought this kind of dialogue, enabling the students to learn from their mistakes. She pleaded with her more passive subscribers to fill out the sheets, urging that they did not have to answer all the questions and could request guidance if it was too difficult.[41]

Impact

The *gilyonot* became somewhat of a sub-culture, though primarily amongst the national-religious sector in Israel. At social occasions, conversation between people with little in common turned to Nehama's Torah and became animated. Kibbutz members sat around after Shabbat lunch, puzzling together over the sheets, an enjoyable and frugal way for them to spend their free time. Neighbors compared answers, and couples did the *gilyonot* together, appreciating the opportunity to interact on a plane other than the mundane. "My husband and I would sit down on a *motza'ei Shabbat*, the first thing after *havdalah*, and write out the answers with a real sense of holiness," says Tzipora Levavi of Kibbutz Massuot Yitzhak. The *gilyonot* were even instrumental in the affairs of the heart. Azriel Hirsch and Hana Baruch, new immigrants who had settled on Kibbutz Be'erot Yitzhak, filled out *gilyonot* like many others. Knowing how communal kibbutz life is, Nehama sometimes permitted herself to save time by directing a kibbutznik to her comments on another member's sheet. Her instructions to Hana to "see what I wrote on Azriel's sheet" and vice versa got them talking, and eventually they got engaged. "We then decided to drop in on Nehama in Kiryat Moshe," they recall. "We came in and told her we were correspondents from Be'erot Yitzhak and she immediately said, 'Oh, you're Azriel Hirsch and Hana Baruch.' To this day we do not know how she knew it was us."

---

[41] N. Leibowitz, "*Daf*," in *PN*, 456.

The *gilyonot* were also given as bat-mitzvah presents, with Nehama personally climbing up her ladder to pick out sheets suitable for a twelve-year-old child. Sarah Leah Neventzal recalls that at the time she couldn't fathom why these "yellow crumbly typewritten things" were being given to her, and only later was able to appreciate their worth.

Nehama's efforts, while financially unremunerated, laid the foundation for much of her subsequent work, including her teaching, her training of other teachers, and her books. In 1957 she wrote:

> Putting together the worksheets every week and marking them consumed the majority of my time. But by doing so, I learned about exegesis on Tanach and began to explore the interpretative methodologies of Rashi, Ramban, Abravanel and others; and I [now] have an abundance of material on Rashi's method. (*PN*, 14)

End of the *gilyonot* era

In 1971, after completing thirty series of weekly *gilyonot*, Nehama at last ceased producing them, possibly due to the death in the previous year of her husband, her partner in Torah discussions. She did, however, continued to photocopy the existing worksheets, and to send and receive them. People not yet born when her sheets first saw the light came to acquire them now. Some bought all thirty volumes at once. Into her old age Nehama continued to correspond with around one hundred subscribers a month.[42] By 1986, she had responded to over forty thousand letters in total.[43]

Nehama's success brought others to imitate the format. Professor Joseph Heinemann did the same for the study of Mishnah. Nehama's student, Professor Dov Landau, inspired by the pedagogical efficacy of the sheets, used the format as a basis for his own worksheets on other topics; and when Moshe Moskowitz's wife, a regular *gilyonot* correspondent, passed away, her husband obtained Nehama's permission to put out a weekly sheet in a similar style in tribute. All these, however, kept to the basic format of Nehama's *gilyonot*, unlike the innumerable pamphlets on the weekly Torah portion of later years. Published by Jewish organizations of every religious and political stripe and distributed weekly to Jewish synagogues and homes, these broadsheets seem at first glance to be the offspring of the *gilyonot*. Nevertheless, Yosske Ahituv argues they are not an imitation but a "desecration" of her work. He notes that they are denominational while

---

[42] Harvey, "Professor," 10.
[43] Yairah Amit, "Hebrew Bible – Some Thoughts on the Work of Nehama Leibowitz," *Immanuel* 20 (Spring 1986): 9.

Nehama's work spanned the whole of society; and they are often dogmatic or political, with only a vague connection to the Torah text. Requiring no thought or interactivity, they are part of a culture of uncritical faith, the reader a passive consumer without responsibility towards the material. Therefore, in Ahituv's view, while loosely adopting the worksheet's form, they abandon its spirit and underlying purpose.

The *Studies* series: The Pamphlets

Nehama authored another important set of works besides the *gilyonot*, namely the pamphlets on the weekly portion which eventually transformed into her famous *Studies* series. The following is the story of how this process came about.

Some of history's eminent figures owe much of their fame to a friend or disciple with a stubborn vision of their potential. Haim Hamiel played this role for Nehama. While Nehama had achieved much even before she met Hamiel, he succeeded in propelling her work into a new league, "bringing forth her fountains of Torah" to reach an enormous number of people. Israeli society may well have been, as Dr. Yehiel Zvi Moskowitz suggests, ripe at this point for more output from Nehama;[44] but without Hamiel's push, the *Studies* might never have been born.

Hamiel had heard Nehama's lessons as a youth counselor and in the Jewish Agency's Youth Department. But only after he joined the Education Department did he suddenly perceive Nehama's possible impact. This epiphany came to him one day while attending a sample lesson for visiting Diaspora teachers. Hamiel suggested that rather than teaching what questions to ask, she give over a structured lesson with answers. He felt that this would suit these teachers better, and indeed the inclusion of answers changed the character of the lesson entirely. As it progressed, Hamiel became aware of his own emotional response, and a vision arose in his mind. "I knew already how powerful her teaching was, but now I suddenly recognized the novelty of what she was doing, drawing out hidden levels of the Torah, raising awareness of how much more there really was. This bore educational import of the first degree."

He decided to apply his idea to the *gilyonot*. In 1949, the Education Department of the WZO had undertaken to fund the sheets' dispatch to the Diaspora, with Hamiel heading the project. "For the Diaspora teachers the

---

[44] Yehiel Zvi Moskowitz, "*Al ha-gilyonot ve-al ha-iyunim,*" *Daf le-tarbut Yehudit* 228: *Nehama Leibowitz z"l*, edited by Aryeh Strikovsky, 12 (Torah Education Department of Education Ministry, Iyar 5757/1997).

gilyonot were not enough. Nehama's questions worked for Israeli students, more immersed in the world of Torah learning, but my Diaspora clientele wanted answers, and they wanted them packaged attractively – not as stencil copies from Degani's little printing shop in Jerusalem." Hamiel proposed that the *gilyonot* be printed up as booklets, with answers included, and he suggested that they be entitled *Iyunim (Studies)*. At first Nehama withheld her consent. She ignored a similar call by Professor E.E. Urbach in 1951:

> Nehama Leibowitz can and should provide us with the commentary we lack. It will be the fruit of her work in the *gilyonot* but it will contain not only the questions but also the answers.[45]

Nehama had no loyalty to her stenciled sheets, on the contrary preferring that people handle and hold books, a more tangible medium for learning. But she hated the idea of spoon-feeding students instead of training them to delve and analyze, and it was moreover difficult for her to change direction after years of success. In general, moreover, she did not approve of rushing to appear in print:

> The evil inclination that urges us to see ourselves in print is great, and it knows how to disguise itself as a positive impulse that tells us, "What you're doing is for the sake of heaven, these are important words."[46]

However, Nehama's strong personality had met its match in Hamiel, and he continued to coax her during many hours of conversation. At the time, he was cultivating a project called *Torah la-Am* (Torah for the people) aimed at circulating Torah far and wide; and he greatly desired to send quality material to the Diaspora. In the face of all her objections he insisted that in order to really reach "the people," answers must be included. In 1954, Nehama finally surrendered:

> Due to [Hamiel's] power of persuasion, I assented to his request and began the work – initially under the advice and guidance of my friend Professor Meir Weiss, and later on my own. Thus I sent out weekly *Studies* during the seven years 5715–5721, and they were translated into English and other languages. (IBD, intro)

Each of these *Studies* comprised an eight-page pamphlet on the week's portion, with an essay based around commentaries. There were also occasional teaching guides. Nehama thus became for the first time an author

---

[45] E. E. Urbach, *Ha-Tzofeh*, October 26, 1951, quoted in Uriel Simon, "*Ha-parshan nikkar lo rak be-shitato ela gam bi-she'elotav*," in *PN*, 241. Urbach repeated his call in "*Le-mikra ha-gilyonot le-parashat ha-shavua*," *Ma'ayanot* 4 (1954): 55–58.
[46] N. Leibowitz, "*Teshuvah le-mishal shel talmidim*," in *PN*, 623.

of Torah lessons rather than a facilitator who challenged with questions.[47] But her capitulation was not absolute; she insisted that the pamphlets be distributed outside Israel only, for the Hebrew-speaking population must continue to toil over her *gilyonot*.[48] She also appended "Questions for further study" at the end of each pamphlet for those interested in challenging their minds, and invited them to mail in answers.[49]

The *Studies* pamphlets proved very popular and were translated into English,[50] French, Spanish and Dutch. But Hamiel did not rest on his laurels. The enthusiastic response convinced him that the next step was to publish the pamphlets as books. Thus, each year's pamphlets were bound together and published as an annual, named *Studies in the Weekly Sidra*, seven in total. They proved very popular, and today are difficult to find.[51] In 1963, to mark the twentieth year of the *gilyonot*, Nehama republished the 1962 *gilyonot* and added a section of "explanations and answers."[52]

And still the indomitable Hamiel was not satisfied; something even more ambitious was in the offing. After the seven annuals had come out (1954–1961), he suggested to Nehama that they edit the material and redivide them, this time according to books of the Torah rather than years. She resisted this idea, too. Books were a far more serious undertaking than pamphlets or annuals, and she protested: "I'm not in the business of being an author! I'm a teacher and these pamphlets are teaching aids." However – perhaps motivated by her emergent academic career, with its requirement to "publish or perish," or simply realizing that Hamiel would never give up – Nehama eventually agreed to bring together in one volume all the material from seven years on the book of Genesis. Thus in 1966, the first book in her *Studies* series, "*Iyunim be-Sefer Bereshit*," came out. Finally the Hebrew-speaking population could access the essays too.

---

[47] See chapter 18 for more on these distinctions.

[48] Hamiel, from the introduction to "*Gilyonot le-iyun be-parashat ha-shavua: shnaton ha-esrim*," cited in *PN*, 704 n. 3.

[49] Hamiel, "*Morat*." The student was invited to send answers to "The Institute for Study through Correspondence," Department for Torah Education and Culture in the Diaspora (Simon, "*Ha-parshan*," 241).

[50] Nehama granted Aryeh Newman, her English translator, a fairly free rein; at some point she stopped looking over the translations, which are often an abbreviated and not literal form of the original.

[51] Samet, "*Ha-morah*," 38.

[52] Simon, "*Ha-parshan*," 242. The book is named Gilyonot le-iyun be-parashat ha-shavua: shnaton ha-esrim.

Avraham Burg, chairman of the Jewish Agency, and Eliezer Shefer, head of the Department for Torah Education in the Diaspora, bestow some of the department's publications upon Nehama in her home, on the occasion of the completion of her *Iyunim be-Sefer Ba-midbar*, December 1996.

Seated at far side of table, left to right: Yosef Burg, Rivka Burg, Nehama Leibowitz, Avraham Burg. Also pictured: Eliezer Shefer, his advisor Yitzhak Ben-Ari and Yehuda Ariel, director of the Elinor Library.

(Photo: Nitzan Shorer, courtesy of Eliezer Shefer).

The *Studies* series: The Books

Once she had agreed, Nehama threw herself heart and soul into the endeavor, producing the first two books of the series, in Hebrew. The material required a fair bit of editing to weed out duplications within the pamphlets. For *Iyunim be-Sefer Bereshit*, she reworked the material, added a pithy title to each essay and included footnotes, indices and brief biographies of the commentators quoted. This bestowed a more structured and academic form upon the material. Also included were some, though not all, of the sections from Prophets – the weekly *haftarah* – studied in her pamphlets.[53] The next Hebrew volume, on Exodus, was published in 1969 as *Iyunim hadashim be-Sefer Shemot*. Unlike the Genesis volume, this one included a lot of new material, including an important essay on Rashi, and therefore merited the word "new" ("*hadashim*") in its title.[54] As Nehama wrote:

> Not content to bring out the *Studies* for the other books in their original form, I expanded them and included additions, and I called the books of Shemot and Va-yikra "New Studies."[55]

Next, the English translation of the Genesis volume was published in 1971.[56] It was entitled *New Studies in Bereshit* because it, too, contained new material.

The above quote is a little misleading, as in actuality many years passed before the third Hebrew volume, the reworked material on Leviticus, came out in 1983 as *Iyunim hadashim be-Sefer Va-yikra*, followed by its translation, *New Studies in Vayikra*.[57] The *Bamidbar* and *Devarim* volumes also took a long

---

[53] The others can be found in *PN*, 531–576. The entire list of the portions from Prophets and Writings that Nehama covered may be found in *PN*, 712–713.

[54] Not on the cover, which for some reason says *Iyunim be-Sefer Shemot*, but inside.

[55] Introduction to *IBD*. See also translator's foreword to *NSS*.

[56] Aryeh Newman had already collected and edited much of the material from the pamphlets, which enabled him to put out this book relatively quickly after being given the go-ahead. This also explains the significant differences between the Hebrew and English versions – they were re-edited separately and based on slightly different sets of materials. Newman also wanted to spare the English-speaking audience the more complicated material and footnotes found in the Hebrew. In the other English books some material has also been moved around or simply does not exist when compared with the Hebrew (see e.g. *IBBM*, 237 or *IBD*, 158 and compare with the English versions); but, on the other hand, some ideas only appear in the English. Frankel even suggests that there was a deliberate element to all this, bearing in mind the different audiences (*Iyun*, 186, n. 160). In sum: To get the "full Nehama" one must read both the Hebrew and English books.

[57] A one-volume edition of studies in *Vayikra* in English, not written by Nehama but rather based on her work, was published before this, but the double-volume *New Studies in Vayikra*, the English translation of the Hebrew book, subsequently replaced it. See translator's note in the opening pages.

time to see the light, as Nehama preferred to spend her time teaching. They were published only at the end of her life, in reverse order, first *Devarim* in 1994 and then *Bamidbar* in 1996. Much of the work was not done by Nehama, and there was no new material, so they were not called "*New Studies.*" In her introduction to *Iyunim be-Sefer Devarim*, Nehama wrote:

> Many years have passed and I have, with God's help, attained old age and beyond. My learned friend, Rabbi Shmuel Bornstein... of the Department encouraged me to overhaul and expand the studies on the remaining books too, and I assented. He offered to do all of the editing, source checking, emendation of errors, proofreading, all of the technical work and much more than just the "technical" work, in order to make it easier for me. It is thanks to him and him alone that the studies in the book of *Devarim* which I put out over 40 years ago are now coming out.

While the material in these new books was methodical and analytical, guiding the student in reading the Torah text and commentaries, it was not too heavy, and could be read straight through by someone with a little background. Nehama presented sophisticated material in down-to-earth language, always trying to avoid the abstract by bringing concrete examples.[58] This was a didactic rule that she had espoused from a young age: "Learning occurs primarily from the individual specific case and not from generalizations."

Nehama had taught the art of essay-writing in her earlier years, so it is unsurprising that the essays in her books were crafted and polished, with a clear beginning, middle and end and everything laid out clearly for maximum comprehension by the unpracticed reader.[59] Although cross-references existed, each unit was basically self-sufficient. A title, containing the key concept or verse, was followed by brief background and context. Then came the biblical verses, always vowelled and often divided into phrases, with important words in bold. Parallel verses were presented side by side for comparison. After stating the difficulty, Nehama proposed various solutions, quoting, sometimes at length, from classic and modern interpretations. She added her own elucidations and comparisons and, occasionally, even her

---

[58] "Active Learning in the Teaching of History" (trans. Moshe Sokolow, introduction by Jon Bloomberg). NY: 1989, viii ("*Ha-amlanut be-hora'at ha-historiah be-vet ha-sefer ha-amami ve-ha-tichoni*," 633). "Active learning" is an English translation of "*Ha-amlanut*"; the latter was first printed in *Hed ha-Hinuch* 13 (various folios) and can now be found reprinted in *PN*, 631–650. The original article, by the same name, was in German.

[59] The descriptions in this and the following paragraphs are partly based on unpublished material by Yaakov Kagan.

own interpretations.[60] The piece built up to a climax or summary at its end, either a recap of a commentator's words, or her own words bearing some ethical or spiritual message. It might also be a quote from another Jewish source, demonstrating the breadth of her knowledge; or even a question, left open-ended for effect:

> Will Israel continue to cherish "the crown" of sound family life "for which they were praised" down the ages? (*SBM*, 339)

On rare occasions Nehama left the issue moot, letting the reader decide. For example:

> We have cited many different explanations of the problem of Moses's sin. We can do no better than conclude with Maimonides's own closing words on the subject: Set what we have said against what has already been said about it, and let the truth have its way. (*SBM*, 247)

The majority of the *Studies* also contained, following the essay, questions for further study, for those who liked a challenge. The reader was asked to look at new sources and to consider how they fit in with the preceding essay. Here, for the first time, Nehama did not extend an invitation to send answers to her.

In thus collating material and laying it out clearly in her books, Nehama was following in the footsteps of such Jewish giants as Maimonides and Rabbi Joseph Karo, who assembled halachic material in codices organized as a "set table." As Professor Yaakov Kagan comments, she was no mere seamstress, piecing the material together patchwork fashion, but was rather akin to a conductor working with hundreds of virtuoso soloists who play the same score but have rarely rehearsed together. Just as the conductor orchestrates the performance by spotlighting those soloists who perform any given piece best, Nehama selected the most significant commentaries on every passage. [61]

ॐ ॐ

The *Studies* series became a bestseller, reprinted many times; and Nehama followed the progress of the books with interest. Initially, the most enthusiastic audience was the relatively knowledgeable Jewish community in North Africa; but positive responses from other locales soon followed, from educators and laypeople alike. Although originally written with teachers in mind, the *Studies* were greeted eagerly on a mass scale. They opened up an

---

[60] This will be discussed later in chapter 21.
[61] Yaakov Kagan, "A Review of Nechama Leibowitz's *Eyunim – Studies on Torah*" at www.lookstein.org/articles/nechama.htm.

inaccessible world of Torah and commentary to people whose first language was not Hebrew. They were eventually translated into many languages: English, French, Spanish, Dutch, and more recently, Russian and German too. Selections from the *Studies* appeared in newspapers in the Diaspora.

The books ended up in out-of-the-way locations. Attending a synagogue service in a small community in Guatemala, Professor Chana Safrai was amazed to discover that despite their scanty knowledge of Hebrew and Torah, these Jews sat down faithfully every week after the services with Nehama's *Studies*. And it was not only Jews who admired Nehama's Torah. A Christian Zionist living in Dayton, Ohio studied the weekly Torah portion regularly with his group using Nehama's books, and was awestruck when he arrived in Israel and could finally meet the author. Sister Maureena Fritz, an octogenarian nun living in Jerusalem, first heard Nehama when attending her lessons at the Hebrew University. When she subsequently founded the Bat Kol Institute, bringing Christians from around the globe to study Bible from within the living traditions of Judaism, she used Nehama's *Studies* in her teaching. Upon returning to their home countries, each student received one of Nehama's books, and continued learning and teaching *parashat ha-shavua* to others, often using Nehama's works. This continues until today. "She was a great model of a teacher," says Sister Maureena, "She didn't teach academia, she taught in the trenches."

Rabbis and educators used the books for preparing their sermons and lessons, which pleased Nehama greatly.[62] But not all of them cited their source. "More than once I have heard a sermon taken almost word for word from Nehama's books, without her name!" complains Hamiel.[63] Dr Naftali Rothenberg elaborates: "I have visited many Orthodox synagogues in the States, and the rabbis' sermons fall into one of two categories: those who give over Nehama's questions and answers and cite her; and those whose entire sermon is copied from Nehama's books but with no mention of her!" (*VLN*). Kagan writes that to his knowledge,

> the only author to print a thankful acknowledgement of Nechama's great labor and labor savings for others... was Jacobson in the introduction to his popular *Binah ba-mikra*. As a well-known rabbi once remarked to the writer, "Practically everybody uses Nehama, but hardly anybody will admit it!"[64]

---

[62] Translator's introduction, *NSB*, xv.
[63] Sheleg, "*Kalat*," 71.
[64] Kagan, "Review." Yedgar also mentions the phenomenon in "*Parshanut nashim datiyot o parshanut nashit-datit la-mikra?*" *Lihyot Isha Yehudiya* 1 (2001): 114.

What is the reason behind this unseemly phenomenon? Some might hesitate to say things explicitly in the name of a woman. Others view themselves as quoting Rashi and Ramban, with Nehama simply the collector, and do not realize the extent of Nehama's own imprint on her work.[65]

The *Studies* spread Nehama's fame throughout the Diaspora, and eventually every group of teachers that came to Israel via the Jewish Agency demanded Nehama in their curriculum. She had become a star attraction. There were also repeated requests for Nehama to fly abroad and lecture, but she refused to leave Israel, even for the sake of Torah education. Precisely this result, bringing thousands to cherish Torah, was what Hamiel had intuited that day as he sat in Nehama's class. "All her protestations had no effect on me; I knew the Diaspora in a way she did not. Nehama came to realize I had been right all along, and would point to me and announce, 'It's due to this man that my books came out!'" Indeed, Hamiel is the first person she thanks in her introduction to *Iyunim be-Sefer Va-Yikra*.

Studies versus worksheets

The books and the sheets helped to boost each other's popularity, as students of one were curious to experience the other. But not all of the worksheet correspondents liked the transition to book format. The questions at the end of the essays appeared flat without the lively dialogue with Nehama. Even Hamiel, who had pushed so hard for the books, writes:

> There was a "written Nehama" and an "oral Nehama." These were two complementary worlds, and only those who had heard her teach could infuse into her writings her various tones of emphasis, her expressions and reactions, the joy with which she introduced every new idea.[66]

To those who had struggled with the worksheet questions, the books seemed like easy reading, picked up for a few minutes and then laid aside. Dr. Howard Deitcher periodically informs his students: "Nehama's questions are many times of more value than her answers." In her questions, he explains, she allows herself to identify the largest, most critical issues – moral, ethical and philosophical. The *gilyonot* forced the reader to see all the different possibilities, even if Nehama eventually suggested her own answers. Deitcher therefore prefers his students use the *gilyonot*, as do many teachers who take Nehama's didactic approach seriously. The *Bagrut* (Israeli

---

[65] Harvey, *VLN*. This topic will be discussed in chapter 21.
[66] Hamiel, "*Leibowitz*," 577.

matriculation exam) in Tanach is based on her worksheet-style questions such as "What's Rashi's difficulty?[67]

But Dr. Gabriel Cohn argues that the *Studies* also exposed the reader to various possible answers from among which the reader could ultimately choose. As for Nehama herself, to this day there is debate as to her true love and legacy – was it the *gilyonot* or the *Studies?* An analysis of her works by Dr Marla Frankel indicates that Nehama may indeed have respected the knowledgeable, industrious student of the *gilyonot* more than she did the casual, passive reader of the *Studies*.[68] R. Klitsner states: "The *gilyonot* were her life's work, and not the books. She claimed they twisted her arm to publish them." In truth, whenever Nehama tried to attract a visitor's interest to learning her material, it was to the worksheets. She was against giving answers to people on a silver platter. When teaching her course for the Open University in later life, she had to be convinced to include answers in her workbooks, objecting, "What's the point? They'll just go look at them!" Erella Yedgar points out that Nehama sometimes even addresses her *Studies* reader directly, as if he or she has asked a question – at these points we can perhaps intuit that, unhappy with writing a dogmatic essay, she wished she could be in dialogue with the reader.[69]

But Yedgar also claims that the lines between the two approaches are not as sharply drawn as one might think.[70] She notes that Nehama deliberates and questions within the body of the *Studies* essays when she could simply have delivered her conclusions. Furthermore, the books get the educational message across, a very important goal of Nehama's, while the *gilyonot* consist of a series of unrelated questions and lack a unifying thread.[71] Ultimately, suggests Yedgar, Nehama wished her lessons to contain both styles – the discussion-based learning characterizing the worksheets, as well as the educational messages found within the books.[72]

---

[67] Yedgar, "*Ha-iyunim shel Nehama Leibowitz ke-degem le-shiur Tanach,*" *Derech Efrata* 9–10 (2001): 14.

[68] See Frankel, "The Teacher in the Writings of Nechama Leibowitz," in *Abiding Challenges: Research Perspectives on Jewish Education.* London and Tel Aviv: Freund, 1999, 360; and also "*Ha-te'oriyah,*" 432; Samet, "*Ha-morah,*" 38; Yedgar, "*Ha-iyunim,*" 13–14. This will be discussed further in chapters 18 and 22.

[69] See for example *IBBM,* 199: "If you will ask…" (absent from the English version).

[70] Yedgar, "*Ha-iyunim,*" 14. She notes that the topics of the *Studies* are taken directly from the *gilyonot,* and that in the guidance pamphlets for teachers, Nehama recommends teaching the *gilyonot* using the topic order laid out in the *Studies.*

[71] Yedgar, "*Ha-iyunim,*" 34.

[72] Yedgar, "*Ha-iyunim,*" 34.

Other Writings

Nehama published five other books during her lifetime. Two were pedagogical works:

Limmud parshanei ha-Torah u-derachim le-hora'atam ("The Study of Torah Commentators, and Methods of Teaching Them") published in 1975. This dealt with Genesis. It was intended to be "an aid to the student, and especially to the teacher of high-school students," and contained questions and analysis on the text, and didactic tips. A companion volume for Exodus was published after her death.[73]

Lilmod u-le-lamed Tanach ("To Learn and to Teach Tanach"), published in 1995. This book appeared in English, arranged in a different order, under the title *Torah Insights*.

The other three books were:

Shiurim be-firkei nehama u-ge'ula ("Lessons in Chapters of Consolation and Redemption") published in 1957, written with Meir Weiss.

Gilyonot le-iyun be-Sefer Yirmiyahu ("Sheets for the Study of the Book of Jeremiah"), published in 1977, dealing with Jeremiah 1–9.

Perush Rashi la-Torah: iyunim be-shitato ("Rashi's Commentary to the Torah"), published in 1990. This was a two volume textbook written, together with Professor Moshe Ahrend, for her Open University course.[74]

She also published quite a few pamphlets and articles. See further details in the bibliography, and for a full list see *Pirkei Nehama*, 703–710.

---

[73] *Hora'at parshanei ha-Torah: Shemot*, printed by the Eliner Library of the World Zionist Organization. The same publishing house also reprinted the first book as *Hora'at parshanei ha-Torah: Bereshit*.

[74] In his work *To Study and to Teach: The Methodology of Nechama Leibowitz* (Jerusalem: Urim Publications, 2003) Shmuel Peerless has picked out many interesting ideas and examples from this volume (see his references on 163–170).

CHAPTER 3

NEHAMA'S PERSONALITY:
WHERE OPPOSITES MEET

> The test of a first-rate intelligence is the ability to hold two
> opposed ideas in the mind at the same time and still retain the
> ability to function (F. Scott Fitzgerald)

THE NEXT THREE CHAPTERS will be devoted to Nehama's character and
principles, after which we will return to the chronology of her life.

Introduction

Many will remember Nehama not so much for her scholarship but for her
special combination of traits: her vigorous, warm personality, which
expressed itself, as one student puts it, in her "fantastic mobile eyebrows"
and "warm and lovely eyes." Superlatives are commonplace in descriptions
of Nehama's character. R. Hershel Billet says: "Her personality was
outstanding – she had all the traits one could look for." Her combination of
forcefulness, honesty and humility, together with her broad Torah
knowledge and her principled value system, made her an exceptional figure.
She embodied a generation that has largely passed from this world, one that
preferred action and creation to introspection. R. Pinchas Langer remarks:
"They were content with just doing. People these days want to 'be' as well;
they want to make a name for themselves." Simi Peters adds: "They don't
make Jews like that anymore."

The following is an outline of various facets of Nehama's personality,
with references also to her thought, since the two are closely bound together.

Contradictory elements

The above quote from F. Scott Fitzgerald is anticipated by a similar idea in
the book of Ecclesiastes (7:18):

> It is good that you should take hold of this, but do not neglect that
> either; for he who fears God shall fulfill both.

And Isaiah Berlin writes:

Nehama's passport photograph. Courtesy of Mira Ofran.

Values may easily clash within the breast of a single individual; and it does not follow that, if they do so, some must be true and others false.[1]

Nehama's personality was such that she was able to contain opposing, even paradoxical, traits and values within herself. This important key to both her personality and her intellectual outlook will be emphasized throughout this book. While some adjectives, such as lazy or greedy, are not applicable to Nehama at all, in many cases she possessed both a trait and its opposite. She was sophisticated yet naïve, serious yet humorous, pious yet liberal, rationalistic yet emotional. Sensitive and subtle, she was also forceful and brusque. Firmly down-to-earth and logical, she might suddenly be swept away by the lyricism of a verse. Nehama was methodical and punctual, yet lived a hectic lifestyle, running out at the last minute to lecture and forgetting her pages. Her words regarding the patriarch Abraham's greatness in containing extremes could have been written, with little alteration, of herself:

> In other words, Abraham mustered all his inner resource, both his gentle and hard qualities, love and fear, mildness and boldness, ready to do combat on behalf of Sodom.[2]

Nehama was thus a complex person; and even her complexity was balanced by an equal portion of simplicity. This diversity was an expression of the quality of truth in Nehama, an appreciation of the multiplicity of this world. She liked well-roundedness in others, approving in a student such activities as tennis alongside more cerebral pursuits.

Intellectually, too, Nehama brought together several different systems and ideas. Her literary analyses intermingled with medieval commentaries, and she juxtaposed academic approaches with a religious outlook. She upheld seemingly contradictory philosophical positions such as Divine Providence together with human autonomy, or respect for civilization together with a rejection of its corrupting aspects.[3] Depending on the circumstances, she brought different elements to the fore. Between two extremes, she often maintained a dialectic motion, shifting sometimes in one direction and sometimes in the other; or synthesizing the two, finding a middle place.

It might be suggested that in doing this, she was taking her lead from Judaism, a religion with a composite and multi-faceted nature, reflecting life itself. Nehama did not hold one opinion in early years and later switch to

---

[1] "The Pursuit of the Ideal," in *The Crooked Timber of Humanity*, Princeton University Press: 1998, 12, and see further there.
[2] *NSB*, 182, and see also *NSB*, 164, quoted on page 112 below.
[3] For more on both of these, see chapter 16.

another. Rather, they co-existed from the start.[4] In another, such eclectic combinations may have led to accusations of wishy-washiness and fear of commitment to one path. But Nehama would have been appalled at any such claims. She explicitly criticized such opportunistic behavior:

> The Israelites were in the dangerous situation characteristic of many people to this day. They neither agreed with Korah nor actively opposed him, but stood aside to see how things would work out. (Our Sages condemned this attitude.) (*SBM*, 199)

In Nehama's case, she truly believed in all the contradictory approaches. If her heart told her something was true, she was willing to ignore certain intellectual inconsistencies. In her definition of truth, the highest truths are not scientific; they lie beyond empirical verification. Nehama quotes the Rashbam's declaration: "The truth speaks for itself." She adds:

> Such is the power of the truth that it bears its own telltale seal. This is its essence and strength, which requires no proofs. Often, the more important, the more profound the truth, the greater the impossibility of proving it – it bears witness to itself.[5]

and

> [The dreamer's] own heart is the witness of its truth. (*NSB*, 455)

It follows from this that any attempt to prove or disprove religious axioms using scientific tools is irrelevant – it is "artificial rationalization of things essentially non-rational.[6]

⇛ ⇚

In this biography, Nehama's facility in holding apparently opposed ideas in her mind at the same time will be called "complex thinking." This refers to two essential modes of being and thought. The first moves beyond the simplistic "Either this or that" to "*Both* this *and* that," as exemplified by the contradictory traits in Nehama's own self. The second, intrinsically connected to the first, rejects the simplistic judgment: "This is bad, that is good" in favor of "Good or bad depends on the context." As Ecclesiastes advises (3:1):

> For every thing there is a season, and a time for every purpose under heaven.

---

[4] Erella Yedgar, "*Bein megamah parshanit-didaktit le-megamah erkit-hinuchit*," *Limmudim* 1 (2001): 51.

[5] *NSB*, 427. With these words, Nehama explains how the baker could be so confident of the truth of Joseph's interpretation of his dream (Genesis 40:16).

[6] *NSB*, 366. See Frankel, *Iyun*, 52 and 82–83, n. 164.

We hear echoes of this in Nehama's writings. For example:

> Essentially, this – like many pedagogic questions – is not one that can be answered yes or no, but is one of quantity, of time and place. (*LP*, 138, n. 11)

The two modes are connected in that no trait is all good, but depends on the circumstances, and therefore its opposite trait should also be present for maximum flexibility. That no trait is all good may be seen in the following statements:

> The same instinct or impulse which can lead man to perversions, filth and destruction can also lead him to creativity, the building of a house and the continuity of the nation. (*NSS*, 694)

> This extreme quality of fierce hate and anger can be used for both destructive and constructive purposes. (*SD*, 391)

> The Torah was given to Israel on account of this polarity in their character, the "fierceness" or stubbornness for good or ill. (*SD*, 380)

It is not easy maintaining conflicting values and contradictory forces, and the correct balance is determined by the Torah, not by individual whim (*NSS*, 409). For instance, self-sacrifice, generally considered a positive value, may become distorted without the Torah's guidance. Jephthah, who sacrificed his daughter to God in fulfillment of a vow when he was victorious in battle (Judges 11),

> is not to be regarded as a national hero. His deed is not to be admired as one of self-sacrifice and greatness prompted by patriotic feeling. It was a cruel and unwarranted deed. We may rely on our Sages who saw him as an ignorant and unlettered person, a boor, empty and rash. Enthusiasm by itself is no guarantee of the desirability of a cause. Enthusiasm that is not backed by conscience and the self-discipline of Torah is liable to bring disaster.[7]

Since what is generally good may become evil in its extreme, Nehama at times recommends moderation. Zeal and hotheadedness were dangerous when

> concentrated in too great an intensity and only destructive. But in moderation, they were useful and indeed an essential ingredient of national life. (*NSB*, 545)

Fear should also be applied sensibly:

---

[7] *SBM*, 279. See also *NSB*, 545, where she cites a second opinion regarding zeal, that it is indeed dangerous in the homeland, but actually requisite in the exile – another example of the need for context.

> An attitude motivated by fear alone savours of idolatry which regards the godhead as a monster… [while] an attitude which is completely devoid of fear indicates that man fails to regard himself in the appropriately humble light as dust and ashes. (*NSB*, 85)

In fact, the very last paragraph of her *Studies* series advises against extremes:

> We are warned against two dangers in this explanation: racial hatred and prejudice on the one hand, and assimilation and aping of the ways of other nations on the other. (*SD*, 410)

In another example, while abstaining from hedonism is good, becoming an ascetic Nazirite, is, though permitted, ultimately not a positive step:

> Every extra effort, every further obligation that a person takes upon himself, is always at the expense of fulfilling other obligations (for a person's strength, time, energy and abilities are forever limited). And if a person took upon himself this prohibition by becoming a Nazirite – realizing perhaps that without this he would not be able to rectify his character – then inevitably he neglects his obligations in other areas. And for this he has to make atonement. (*IBBM*, 75–76)

In the above insight, Nehama is echoing in psychological terms Newton's third law of motion: "For every action, there is an equal and opposite reaction." In other words, there is a price for all choices, especially extreme choices, in terms of time and energy. A system of checks and balances needs to be in place.

In the biblical figures also, good and bad are not clear-cut. Some rabbinic sources turn Esau into an archetype of Jew-hatred, symbolizing the evil of the Roman Empire; but Nehama, like Rashi, insists that he be viewed also as an individual, with positive and negative characteristics.[8] Regarding the Joseph story, Nehama writes:

> The teacher should draw the students' attention to the manner in which the text maintains a balance in its opinion of Joseph on the one hand and his brothers on the other. Light and shadow appear on both sides. This chapter contains no categorically righteous people, nor any absolute villains – there is no black and white. (*LP*, 162)

---

[8] *NSB*, 283–284. But she does not emphasize this in every place – see for example *NSB*, 300, 372 or her reply to Professor Bergman's letter (pages 323–326 below). The subject of the imperfections of the biblical heroes will be discussed at greater length in chapter 15.

Indeed, she particularly liked this story for its blurring of such boundaries.[9]

🙦 🙧

Nehama managed all these diverse elements in herself with grace and flexibility. Not for her the agonizing over contradictions; instead, she brought the wolf to dwell harmoniously together with the lamb, so to speak. This differentiated her from many predecessors and contemporaries who suffered angst most particularly from the clash between two worlds, the Jewish and the modern. See, for example, this poignant description of young rabbis in Russia, by R. Yehiel Yaakov Weinberg:

> The most tragic figures are precisely the young rabbis who stand between two magnets. Their young hearts are pulled to where everything is exciting and alive, they hope and aspire, love and are loved. However, their feeling of Jewish responsibility tells them that it is forbidden to desert the sages and elderly righteous ones who carry the entire Jewish "spiritual wealth" on their weak backs.[10]

R. Weinberg, an older contemporary of Nehama's who authored the work *Seridei Esh*, was himself such a tragic figure, simultaneously attracted by two opposing forces.[11] But Nehama's personality and upbringing appear to have preserved her from such turmoil, and her various facets co-existed peacefully.[12] She had no time to spare for abstract problems, especially insoluble ones. Instead, she just got on with a productive life. Analytical, literary, comprehensive and incisive she was; but an existentialist philosopher she was not. In this she differed not only from R. Weinberg, but also from Rabbi J.B. Soloveitchik, whom she greatly respected.[13]

---

[9] Rosenak, "*Parashat Mi-ketz: ha-omnam tzaddik? Ha-Rambam, Yeshayahu Leibowitz ve-Nehama Leibowitz mesohahim al Yosef,*" in *Hogim ba-parashah*, edited by Naftali Rothenberg, 136–137, citing Frankel's work.

[10] Weinberg, *Li-frakim*. Bilgoraj: 1936, 419 (or Jerusalem: 1967, 333), cited in Marc B. Shapiro, *Between the Yeshiva World and Modern Orthodoxy: The Life and Works of Rabbi Jehiel Jacob Weinberg, 1884–1966*. Littman: 1999, 13.

[11] Shapiro, *Between*, 13.

[12] Julius Guttmann's words on Moses Mendelssohn resonate here, though they may not apply exactly to Nehama: "He is fully devoted to both of these worlds, and there is no conflict or tension between them. The idealism of his religion of reason, and the priority of his Jewish sentiment, are both genuine parts of his spiritual essence…. His personal integrity was unaffected by their joint occupancy of his soul…. He was thus saved from inner turmoil, because he separated the two sides of his existence, the two bases of his consciousness" (*Philosophies of Judaism*, Philadelphia: Jewish Publication Society of America, 1964, 300).

[13] Note that R. Soloveitchik was gripped not so much by theoretical problems as by the existential, practical dissonances in his own life. See *The Lonely Man of Faith*, Northvale, NJ: Jason Aronson, 1997, 1. "Whatever I am going to say here has been derived not from philosophical dialectics, abstract speculations or detached impersonal reflections, but from

Some believe that this harmony may have been procured at the expense of integrity. They argue that Nehama "overharmonized" and that a careful study of her work reveals some underlying tensions.[14] But others disagree.[15] Her repression of dissonance may have been unconscious or it may have been calculated, as she often steered clear of difficult questions to which she had no answer.[16] For example, while legitimizing the act of questioning Divine justice "in a cruel and unjust Divine world [which] our prophets and sages did not hesitate to do" (*NSV*, 394–395), in practice she did not ask questions such as "Where was God in the Holocaust?" Instead, as previously discussed, she chose to comment on God's absence in Egypt, and in general preferred to engage such issues within the parameters of Torah study and its educational messages.[17] She was a teacher of Torah rather than a philosopher. She disapproved of the countless articles that tried to "clarify issues" and "deal with contemporary challenges" in place of real Torah study.[18] Even in her off-duty moments, in more informal settings or private conversations, she did not challenge Jewish fundamentals; and any conflicts were kept close to her chest.[19]

Here, in fact, is another example of two opposite traits in Nehama. Despite her approachable manner, her many anecdotes about herself, and

---

actual situations and experiences with which I have been confronted." From page 7: "I have never been seriously troubled by [theories of evolution, mechanistic interpretations, historical empiricism, biblical criticism.] However, while theoretical oppositions and dichotomies have never tormented my thoughts, I could not shake off the disquieting feeling that the practical role of the man of faith within modern society is a very difficult, indeed paradoxical one."

[14] Rozenson points to hermeneutical tensions in the *Studies* between the use of classic commentaries and modern literary tools ("*Diber ha-Shem be-mahazeh: hashkafatah shel Nehama Leibowitz al ha-parshanut ha-alegorit*," in *PN*, 325, 334). See also Yedgar, "*Ha-iyunim*," 26, and "*Bein*," *passim* dealing with her conflicting approach to the text. See also the discussion of Nehama's selective readings of texts (page 327 below). Nehama also swept tensions within the commentaries under the carpet. Touitou critiques Nehama's claim that Rashbam felt no tension between *peshat* and Halachah ("*Bein 'peshuto shel mikra' le 'ruah ha-Torah': yahasah shel Nehama Leibowitz le-perush ha-Rashbam la-Torah*," in *PN*, 233).

[15] Ben-Sasson, for example, feels that Nehama took a critical approach, the very opposite of the harmonizing and unquestioning one ("*Ha-teshuva be-iyuneha shel Nehama Leibowitz – iyun be-megamatam ha-hinuchit shel ha-iyunim*," in *PN*, 357).

[16] R. Mordechai Breuer suggests that Nehama "consciously or unconsciously" avoided direct study of the text, fearing it might lead to biblical criticism ("*Yahasah shel Nehama Leibowitz el mada ha-mikra*," *Limmudim* 1 [2001]: 11).

[17] See page 38 above. For further discussion of Nehama's approach to difficult questions see chapter 15.

[18] N. Leibowitz, "*Teshuvah*," 623.

[19] Dr. Baruch Schwartz recalls: "Meir Weiss said more than once that he was not convinced that Nehama was always saying the whole truth, that she knew a lot more than she said" (interview).

her open home, Nehama Leibowitz was actually a very private person. She requested that her personal letters be burned after her death. Her doubts, challenges and low points were not on public display. She recounted her failures, but always in a joking manner that removed any sting. The insecurities she did express tended to relate to the quality of her teaching, in a bid to improve it. Only her closest female friends and a few students were privy to her innermost feelings. Others sensed that certain subjects were best sidestepped. Even some of her closest students never went beyond purely intellectual conversation or, if the conversation became personal, it was about them, not her, with Nehama shifting the spotlight from herself, or changing the topic.

All of the above is even more remarkable when we consider that Nehama spent her whole life exposing the struggles of biblical figures – for example:

> Only after overcoming his fears and faintheartedness does the real hero and believer in God emerge. For this reason, the Torah depicts Jacob in his hour of weakness. (NSB, 355)

> From this juncture, [Joseph's] sufferings begin and his character undergoes a corresponding refining process. (NSB, 433–434)

Dr. Howard Deitcher notes that Nehama's approach

> repeatedly emphasizes the contradictions, conflicts, controversies and tensions that confronted the biblical heroes in their various human interactions. In this sense Leibowitz affirms the Hegelian concept that the life of God, and thus also the internal life of the person, descends to a level of pointlessness and mere fulfillment of injunctions unless it involves seriousness, pain, suffering and the struggle with the innumerable forces of evil.[20]

Nehama did not come across as a person of "pain, suffering and the struggle with the innumerable forces of evil." She gave the appearance of a practical and positive personality. She underplayed her troubles, refusing sentimentality or self-pity. Only very infrequently was there a hint of difficulty, shared with a close friend, such as:

---

[20] See Howard Deitcher, "Between Angels and Mere Mortals: Nechama Leibowitz's Approach to the Study of Biblical Characters," *Journal of Jewish Education* 66:1 (Spring/Summer 2000): 21.

I have not written for a long time; perhaps you heard about the terrible blow that occurred in our family – that my brother's son died. We have all been in heavy mourning and I have not been able to do my work.[21]

Such an approach might elicit positive or negative reactions in students. Those who seek to learn from their teachers' existential issues as much as the information they teach would not have found their address in Nehama.[22] Some might also be disappointed that a courageous and non-stereotypical person like Nehama would go along with a prevalent sanitization of the more difficult aspects of religious life – that she would subscribe to a "don't tell" policy, dictating that public religious figures must appear pious and content at all times.[23] But others certainly welcomed her strong public face. For them, her discretion was appropriate to a prominent religious figure, in line with Maimonides's recommendation that the *talmid hacham* act in a restrained fashion, for example eating only at home so as not to degrade the Torah wisdom he is privileged to bear.[24] Her forbearance, sparing others from her troubles, may be seen an example of *mesirut nefesh* (self-sacrifice), deriving from her strong sense of responsibility to those who needed her to be their pillar of strength. It may also have derived from a particularly Stoic attitude characterizing her generation and an unsentimental upbringing as a rationalist.

In any event, Nehama exhibited great emotional and physical stamina. Outliving her husband and numerous friends and students, she forged on with her teaching and did not succumb to sadness. When unwell, she ignored her friends' pleas to cancel, reproaching: "How can you think of such a thing? People work all day in the heat, and look forward to hearing

---

[21] Letter to Ahituv.

[22] Sarah Malka Eisen's praise of her teacher, Chana Balanson, demonstrates this model: "I remember the image of the EKG that you used so often. You pointed out that the EKG graphically illustrates the movement of the heart – the life force of a person. It charts the heartbeat with a line that goes up and down, and up and down. If a long, horizontal line comes out on the screen, it indicates death – the absence of life. Struggle, symbolized by the up and down, is the sign of vitality. It is something that should be embraced and harnessed. Yet so many people spend their lives negating that reality, and yearn and strive for the smooth straight line. The peace of death" ("On the Sixth Anniversary of Your Parting from this World: A Letter to My Teacher Chana Balanson," in *Torah of the Mothers: Contemporary Jewish Women Read Classical Jewish Texts*, edited by Susan Handelman and Ora Wiskind Elper, 82–83 (Jerusalem: Urim Publications 2000/2006).

[23] As Don Seeman remarks, "Dissonance, pain and the stubborn intractability of personal experience are relentlessly rooted out of the text. They are just too disruptive to the seamless narrative of happy continuity which has become a central feature of popular *hashkafa*" ("The Silence," 96).

[24] Maimonides, *Yad Hazakah, Hilchot Deot*, 5:2.

some Torah in the evening. Should I deprive them just because my head hurts?"

This habit of putting her goals over her own grievances sustained her drive even when she was exhausted, ill and old. She emphasized the positive. After reading, in her eighties, Rav Soloveitchik's article *Ra'ayonot al ha-tefilla*,[25] she said:

> He is a great man. I am a simple woman. I cannot maintain the right intention during the entire prayer; so I try to say at least one blessing with the correct intention every morning – the blessing of "who has fulfilled all my needs.".... Thank God I can walk unaided on my two legs, and I can also get dressed independently. Is this not a kindness from God? There are so many old people for whom it is so difficult.[26]

Gratitude was very important to Nehama – she went so far as to classify ingratitude as a sin (*SBM*, 413). She hated the phrase "*magiya li*" (I deserve it), declaring, "*Lo magiya lachem klum!*" (You don't deserve anything!). Her approach was that one ought to thank God for what is received, but not to consider it deserved. When bad things happened, rather than lay blame or play the victim, she said: "This is all nonsense. Tomorrow is a new day; this will soon be forgotten." She liked to illustrate the lesson that the choice to be grateful or resentful is entirely up to the individual with a Midrash and a story. The Midrash says:

> "And they came to Mara [lit: bitter], and they could not drink the waters of Mara, for they were bitter; thus its name was called Mara" (Exodus, 15:23). Rabbi Levi expounded, What is the meaning of "for they were bitter"? For they were bitter – the generation was bitter in its deeds. Everything depends on the person – if he wishes, he will control himself; and if he wishes, he will become embittered.[27]

The story, told with great gusto, went like this:[28]

> Last spring, a week before Passover, I received notification of a package waiting for me, so I went along to the post office. There are still post offices in Jerusalem manned by only one clerk, and so there was a long

---

[25] *Ha-Darom* 47 (1979): 84–106, NY. It was a favorite of hers (see chapter 1, n. 16).

[26] Posen, "*Mehanechet idialit*," *Ha-Tzofeh*, May 9, 1997, 6.

[27] *Tanhuma yashan*, *Va-yakhel*, 9. Nehama quotes this Midrash in *NSS*, 283 n. 3: "As in many cases of this nature, both the homiletical and the literal sense complement each other. The waters were indeed bitter, but were it not for the fact that the people themselves were embittered, they would not have been disturbed or demoralized by the unpleasant taste of the water."

[28] See Ephraim Yair, "*Shabbat Nahamu*," *Amudim* 430 (5742): 24–25.

line of people waiting to be served. Indeed it is written of Passover time, "The sound of the *tor* is heard in our land!"[29]

She continued:

> I stood in line, waiting behind two old people who came to collect their National Insurance allowance. This is normally handed out at the beginning of the month, but due to the holiday, the State was handing out the money in the week before Passover, out of consideration for the pensioners.

> Well, the clerk requested that the old man in front of me show his I.D. card. The pensioner barked furiously, "Don't I have anything else to think about besides my identity card?! Typical of this country; it's all bureaucracy. You're never treated decently, they just make trouble for you everywhere you go! It's simply appalling!"

> The clerk apologized and asked the gentleman if at least he remembered his I.D. number. Even more enraged, his customer began yelling: "That's the last thing I need right now! What, do I have to remember my I.D. number off by heart? What on earth are you thinking? To hell with your State! Who wants all these headaches?! Everything becomes worthless in this country – money, apartments, people! The only option is to emigrate. No other country in the world has these kinds of hassles!" He banged on the counter and stormed out.

> Next in line was an old woman, also getting on in years. Quietly, she waited. Calmly, she passed over her I.D. for inspection. Serenely, she watched the clerk count and hand over her allowance. Then she thanked him warmly: "Thank you so very much! What a great country we have here! How wise of the ministers to allow the elderly an honorable livelihood – you no longer have to roam the streets or degradingly stick out your hand. Well done to all the clerks, and to the entire Jewish State – and a joyous and kosher Passover to all of Israel! May you all live long lives!"

> Suddenly she began to search for something on the table. The clerk asked, "Do you need anything else?"

> "The charity box, where is the charity box?" she asked. The clerk handed her the box and she counted her money and gave a tenth of it to charity, as we learn in the *Shulhan Aruch*. "You should put the box in the middle, otherwise someone might forget to give," she commented, and with a thousand blessings, left the post office.

---

[29] Song of Songs 2:12. This is a pun on the verse. "*Tor*," literally turtledove, can also mean line/queue.

Nehama concluded:

> They could not drink water at Mara for *they* were bitter. Everything depends on the temperament of the person!

This simple choice of Nehama's, made daily afresh, to appreciate the good and verbalize it, explains both her popularity and also her capacity to move forward despite burdens and obstacles. This attitude, some would claim, is the sign of a true Torah personality. Vanessa Ochs, a writer who spent time acutely observing the learned women of Jerusalem in the 1980s, including Nehama, writes:

> Unlike members of my women's circle, who, as adults, were preoccupied with licking the wounds of childhood (myself now included – I had readily gotten the hang of it), the learned women focused their energies on the present, honoring their parents and not blaming them, serving and praising God, striving to perfect themselves.[30]

If we learn nothing else from Nehama except to do this, we have learned much.

Curiosity and Innocence

Nehama possessed tremendous curiosity. This was one of those traits whose opposite – indifference – found little foothold in her. She never ceased to expand her intellectual horizons, to show interest in peoples' lives and in current events. This was true even into her old age, when she stayed after Shabbat services to hear R. Yohanan Fried's talk on Maimonides's *Mishneh Torah*, reviewing the lesson with him afterwards in the attempt to grasp it fully; or "pestered" Aryeh Newman to update her on the latest developments in linguistics and literary interpretation.

Nehama enjoyed talking upon any subject. Even the most casual sentence might kindle a thoughtful conversation. Professor Rivka Horwitz, who visited her on many a Shabbat afternoon, says: "Nehama was a superb conversationalist, and discussing things with her was a real pleasure. She listened well, developed the line of thought skillfully, and often pulled books off the shelf to shed light on the topic." Rather than holding forth in erudite monologues, as she might have done with ease, she liked to ask questions – either personal ones, or concerning subjects on which the other was well-informed and would enjoy discussing. Although some people never dared to

---

[30] Vanessa L. Ochs, *Words on Fire: One Woman's Journey into the Sacred*, San Diego: Harcourt, Brace, Jovanovich, 1990, 290.

speak to her about trivialities, she actually took pleasure in hearing the details of people's lives. R. Raphael Posen relished the "ordinary conversations" with Nehama, with her genuine and powerful words, even more than the learned ones.[31] She felt no obligation to speak Torah all the time, and could effortlessly sustain hours of talk with people of very little Jewish background.

In conversation, her attention was palpable. "You felt you had a unique connection to her, as she asked about the pressing issues in your life with great interest," says Judy Klitsner. She asked people about their jobs and lives; and those who returned from abroad were deluged with questions about life there. This interest was not false, not some role she felt constrained to play as a teacher. Driven home by a friend or student, she would tarry talking in the car, long after arrival at her doorstep. Indeed, offering to drive Nehama often led to a warm new friendship. Friends knew there was no such thing as a ten-minute conversation with Nehama, or a brief drop-in to say hello, for these inevitably stretched into hours; conversation drew her in completely, and she forgot the time. Aryeh Felheimer recalls: "Once, when I came to visit, Nehama asked me to wait a moment as she walked her previous guest to the door. Then the other person mentioned an involvement with Adlerian psychology, intriguing Nehama so much that she stood talking at the threshold, despite her eighty odd years, for another three quarters of an hour, inadvertently forgetting me completely."

With all her love for conversation, though, Nehama made efforts to avoid *lashon ha-ra* – slander and gossip. She hid the identities of the people she talked about, and intimate details told in confidence went with her to the grave. When the editors of the memorial volume *Pirkei Nehama* were looking over her letters, they found their plan to edit out any gossip to be superfluous, as there was so little to remove. When Nehama did talk critically about people, it was because she strongly disapproved of them in moral or spiritual terms.

Nehama's curiosity was such that, although she was generally content to glean information from others, occasionally the urge welled up to experience things first hand. She went to the beach "just to see what it was like," and felt compelled to visit the new Jerusalem mall just once (and of course ended up disliking it intensely, and failing to understand why anyone would go there!).

---

[31] Posen, "*Mehanechet*."

Nehama on the phone. Courtesy of Mira Ofran.

She particularly loved stories of the odd and extraordinary, and students went out of their way to remember unusual things to tell her. Their reward was an exclamation of almost child-like incredulousness: *"Be-emet?!"* (Really?!) She had a similar response when hearing of the evil in human nature, for her tendency was to think well of people. R. Hanan Schlesinger: "She had the moral innocence of a child. She was never able to understand how a person could cheat on taxes, or steal even the smallest sum of money." She found it hard to absorb that people lived in great distress and suffering, and stories of children abandoned or beaten to the point of hospitalization caused shocked disbelief every time. She also refused to let go of the belief that good schools, good homes and official titles were a guarantee that nothing bad could happen. She tried to judge people in the best possible light, searching for reasonable explanations for their behavior: "How can we know for sure – perhaps the truth is not what we think?" She let people take her books or pay later if they wanted. When a handicapped person knocked on her door and poured out a story about lack of funds for proper medical care, Nehama on the spot used her acquaintance with a wide circle of people to call two doctors and arrange an X-ray. When, after all her effort, the man did not return the next day, she wondered in amazement whether he could have been a con-man.

Nehama surprised people with her unworldliness about certain matters. Hearing that a friend's son was serving in the intelligence branch of the Israeli army, her response was: "Oh, he's a spy?" Even in the last decade of life she was still to be found posing ingenuous questions to an American visitor, such as: was it really true that an American's work clothes would serve in Israel as Shabbat finery?

Such naïveté might appear to some as unworthy of someone of Nehama's stature. But the very opposite is true. In the words of R. Soloveitchik:

> The great man, whose intellect has been raised to a superior level through the study of Torah, gifted with well-developed, overflowing powers – depth, scope, sharpness – should not be viewed as totally adult. The soul of a child still nestles within him... naïve curiosity, natural enthusiasm, eagerness and spiritual restlessness, have not abandoned him. If a man has aged and become completely adult, if the morning of life has passed him by and he stands, in spirit and soul, at

his high noon, bleached of the dew of childhood… he cannot approach God.[32]

In truth, when necessary Nehama could be very realistic. She was against giving students unsupervised tests, for she felt the temptation to cheat was too strong and would constitute "a stumbling block before the blind." Perhaps, therefore, the above quote helps us to understand that her innocence was a deliberate construction, a choice she repeatedly made to express the sweet and enthusiastic "soul of the child nestling within her" rather than a life-destroying cynicism that others adopt. For Nehama, in her heart of hearts, knew human nature. She knew that

> the heart of man is crooked and there is no light which man through his stupidity and shortsightedness cannot succeed in dimming and darkening. (*SBM*, 191)

and that

> Man – the Lord's flock – is petty, suspicious, views all greatness through the prism of his small-mindedness, slanders, blackens whatever shines. (*IHBS*, 479)

Indeed, she even criticizes Ramban for his belief in human goodness:

> How naïve is Ramban's assumption that a person is naturally moved to compassion at the plight of his fellow if he himself had shared the same experience![33]

Nehama was, in fact, quite interested in the evil inclination. She discussed its workings and the principle that "one sin leads to another" (*NSV*, 285), and it was no coincidence that a particularly beloved Shakespeare play, *Macbeth*, dealt with this topic. For her, the evil inclination was not an elusive and mysterious enemy that attacks suddenly, but a

---

[32] From a eulogy for R. Hayyim Heller in *Shiurei ha-Rav*, edited by Joseph Epstein, 16 (Hoboken, NJ: Ktav, 1994). Originally printed as "*Pletat sofrehem*" in *Be-sod ha-yahid ve-ha-yahad*, edited by Pinhas Peli, 289 (Orot: 5736), and in *Divrei hagut ve-ha'aracha*, Jerusalem: WZO, 1981, 159.
[33] *NSS*, 389, n. 6. Ironically, what she rejects here is precisely the assumption that, as she elsewhere notes, the Torah makes: "They themselves should experience the taste of slavery and humiliation" (*NSS*, 6–8). Although she goes on to imply that this empathy, rather than being a precondition, was to be simply a spur for what was ultimately "a religious duty" (*ibid.*, 8) there does nevertheless appear to be some contradiction between her position in the two essays, which she explicitly connects (*NSS*, 389 n. 5). Perhaps this duality, between an essay teaching a "naive" message and one teaching a "sophisticated" message, speaks of the combination of naivety and sophistication within Nehama's self. See further on these contradictory essays on pages 478–479 below.

psychological conglomerate of destructive impulses accruing over an entire lifetime:

> A person's desires and heart cravings are not disconnected from his personality, thought processes and lifestyle; they do not attack him out of the blue, against his will and in contradiction with his worldview and lifestyle. On the contrary, they are the product of his views, habits and way of life.... Covetousness does not materialize in the heart of someone who habituated and educated himself to regard what is forbidden to him as off limits – this is an incontestable truth. (*IHBS*, 254)

The best antidote is to focus on one's positive traits.

> Man cannot overcome his desires simply by consciousness of that which is prohibited.... He must also be conscious of and love that which is permitted him, that which is all important and deserving of his affections, the Lord his God and His Torah. If his heart is full to the brim with love of the good, where then will he have room for coveting the bad? (*NSS*, 350)

Sensitivity and caring

Nehama was greatly concerned for people's welfare, whether emotional or physical. Though she often misplaced her own glasses, she was mindful of details that were important to others, noticing a student's appearance and sensitive to people's dignity. In a class containing many Sephardic Jews, she praised R. Ovadia Yosef (a leading Sephardic rabbi) as an excellent halachic authority and Torah scholar. Nothing was made explicit, but the class appreciated her subtle compliment. If someone was late – be it friend, acquaintance or plumber – she phoned every few minutes to make sure there had been no car accident. Receiving a Rosh Hashanah gift of several apples, scarce in Israel of the mid-1950's, Nehama instantly cut them up into halves and quarters for her friends and family.

Though not one for demonstrative displays of affection, it was obvious how much she cared for people, and this was often expressed not in gushy words but in the most concrete terms, in many hours invested in favors for others, or money freely given. When tales of distress were brought to her Nehama immediately wrote out a check. But her charity did not stop there. For example, during a period when everything was bought with coupons, her housekeeper, Tzipora Ofri, saved up for a long time to buy some towels and sheets. Soon afterwards she could not find them, and when she inquired, Nehama apologetically explained that, lacking spare change, she had given away the new linens to a beggar at the door. Then there was the outfit Nehama bought for an upcoming festival. When her friend, Shoshana

Brayer, noticed that the suit was missing, Nehama said that she could not quite remember what had happened to it, but she supposed she had given it to someone who had knocked. Her shocked friend exclaimed: "But Nehama, that suit was new!" "Well?" Nehama demanded. "Should I give out old clothes?" Rut Azrieli similarly discovered to her amazement that the set of old silverware that Nehama had donated to Russian immigrants was in fact an expensive wedding gift to Nehama's parents, engraved with their names.

When petitioned for charity, Nehama would ask if there were hungry children. She had a particularly soft spot for children, making sure that her domestic help's children had the books and shoes they needed, and rallying friends' sons and daughters to tutor other children in need. She also went out of her way to think about poor people, asking friends to locate worthy causes, while doing her best to conceal its source, ordering: "Tell them the check came from somewhere out there. Don't mention Jerusalem" (*PN*, 686). A neighbor in Kiryat Moshe once saw Nehama carrying several books under her arms, and she informed him they were for sale. Surprised that Nehama had turned to book-selling, he was told that they belonged to an impoverished rabbi who had passed away, and she was selling the books to finance the funeral expenses. She also used her connections to help people, such as the immigrant who could not get an appointment with a high-ranking Jewish Agency executive. After exhausting the usual methods of bypassing bureaucracy, she realized she needed some "Vitamin P" – *protektzia*, inside influence. She creatively hit upon the famous author S.Y. Agnon as the solution and immediately went to inform him that he must arrange the appointment. When Agnon tried to claim that it was none of his business, Nehama ignored him. He then pointed out that he had no phone. "Then write a letter!" she insisted. The winner of the Nobel Prize for Literature protested, "I don't know how to write!" "You've written so many books. Can't you write just one letter?" urged Nehama. Grumbling to his wife, "Estherlein, what does Nehama want from me?" he finally capitulated, and Nehama forced him to go buy a stamp and post the letter forthwith.

Nehama looked out for her students, subtly trying to patch up a rift between husband and wife, or ordering people to look out for a match for unmarried students or to go talk to a student with low self-esteem. She firmly believed in the importance of hospitality, receiving visitors with a warm "*Shalom!*" Like the fabled Jewish mother, she plied her visitors and students with candies and wafers, not letting them leave until they ate something. Hospitality was not a simple affair, for she always had something else important to do. Since she valued her time and her goals, her compromise was to give a few minutes even to strangers, and then end the conversation with a pleasant but firm, "It was very nice to see you."

❧ ❧

Nehama's belief that a Jew must not have a heart of stone comes across in her teachings:

> The Torah cautions us regarding our behaviour towards a stranger no less than thirty-six times. No other mitzvah, not even the commandments to love God, keep the Sabbath, circumcision, refrain from forbidden foods or uttering falsehood or theft are so often referred to. (*NSS*, 380)

In discussing the case of the murder victim's body discovered outside a city (Deuteronomy 21:1–9), she writes:

> Nature is indifferent to the sight of those terrible evils screaming out to the heavens. It continues to blossom and grow on the graves of the slaughtered and murdered in every generation.[34]

She quotes Bialik's poem "City of Slaughter":

> The sun shone, the acacia blossomed and the slaughterer slaughtered.
>
> And you leapt up from there and went forth and behold the world as before.
>
> And the sun its brightness cast down, as of yore. (*SD*, 205)

She then adds:

> Man himself, also partly comprised of nature – the dust of the earth – similarly hears of the corpse lying in the field… and continues on his way home, preoccupied with his own needs. However, man is not like a tree in a field – only a part of nature; he has a soul and is created in the image of God, and his Creator does not wish to see him behave thus.[35]

For this reason, the Torah commands that a heifer be beheaded on the site, an act abnormal enough to prevent people from shrugging and returning to business as usual.

In discussing the command to give charity to "the poor man who is with you" (Exodus 22:24), Nehama employs the language of empathy rather than her more customary language of duty and responsibility:

> [The poor man] is "with you" together, a part of you. You share his problems. (*NSS*, 408)

---

[34] *IBD*, 196 (compare *SD*, 205).
[35] Combination of *SD*, 205 and *IBD*, 197.

She ends with a powerful quote from the Sages:

"With you" – regard yourself as if you were poor.[36]

Nehama practiced what she preached. One rainy winter's day, she phoned Leah Abramowitz, a friend and social worker. "I was looking at the rain and thinking that there must be people out there right now who are cold. Please give a sum of money to needy people in my name."

In another example, in her introductory essay to *New Studies in Shemot*, Nehama explores the reason for Jacob's descendants' exile and enslavement in Egypt. The only exile in Jewish history that is not obviously a punishment, its purpose remains obscure. She makes the following suggestion:

> The reason for the Egyptian exile, the persecution and suffering of bondage accompanying the birth of the Jewish people prior to the giving of the Torah and their entry into the Promised Land, was that they themselves should experience the taste of slavery and humiliation. They were to be made to realise just what it felt like to be subjected to the violence and domination of man by man…. [T]he redemption from Egypt serve[d] as a spur for a religious duty; that imposed on every Jew to redeem his fellow-being from the slavery he had been reduced to for lack of means. (*NSS*, 7–8)

In other words, this exile was to embed permanently the qualities of moral sensitivity and empathy within the Jewish collective psyche. From then on, a Jew ought never to be capable of hard-heartedness in the face of another's suffering.

Integrity and honesty

But together with her sensitivity, there was another, equally important aspect to Nehama's personality – her love of truth. These two elements do not always go together. They clashed two millennia ago, embodied in the arguments between the talmudic Sages Hillel and Shammai,[37] and in Nehama's case, they pulled in opposite directions inside one person. Truth was a watchword for Nehama, and she spoke explicitly of its value.[38] It sometimes took priority over her concern for people's feelings. When Nehama's student R. Yitzhak Frank brought his book, *The Practical Talmud Dictionary*, to her for appraisal, she received it enthusiastically. "Then," he adds, "my pride got the better of me, and I began to point out a couple of places which I believed were particularly well-chosen. She looked at them

---

[36] *Tanhuma, Mishpatim* – see *NSS*, 410.
[37] See for example in Ketubbot 16b–17a, and elsewhere.
[38] For example in the context of Joseph, *NSB*, 427 cited on page 81 above.

and shook her head. They were not good examples. Though she had no great knowledge of Aramaic, her good sense had guided her; and after she explained why to me, I agreed with her." Rather than smile and protect the author's ego, Nehama found it more valuable to tell the truth.[39]

Dr. Rina Rosenberg also had an encounter with Nehama's straightforwardness. She was attending a religious high school in Chicago where, though Nehama had not yet achieved widespread recognition, one of the rabbis happened to be an admirer. The students adored Nehama, finding her work revolutionary, and Rosenberg decided to liven up the school newspaper by including some of Nehama's Torah. Trembling, she wrote to her, and to her pleasure Nehama wrote back a little about herself. Rosenberg printed it in the newspaper and sent Nehama a copy. When Rosenberg visited Israel, she excitedly went to thank Nehama; but the latter rebuked her for putting out a newssheet full of "rubbish," leaving Rosenberg crushed. Years later, she met Nehama again and reminded her of what had happened. Nehama seemed very embarrassed. Rosenberg: "She had not realized she had upset me, and apologized profusely, saying 'But you see there were such childish questions in it about boys and girls!' I explained to her that in America, girls' interest in boys begins at a very young age. Nehama's eyes widened in surprise and she started asking me all sorts of questions about that." This same sense for truth made her zealous for Halachah, particularly with people to whom she was close. She found it difficult to keep silent in the face of actions contravening the Torah, believing them not to be in her students' best interests.

Nehama's intellectual honesty won out over other values besides sensitivity; such as her intense love for the State of Israel. Of *Megillat ha-Atzma'ut* (the Israeli Declaration of Independence) she said, "It's very nice, but doesn't compare with the American Declaration of Independence for power and depth." She was also often not willing to bend the truth even to protect the Torah. When secular students complained that parts of the Torah grated on their sensibilities, she did not resort to apologetics; whitewashing was not the way to get people to love the Torah.[40]

This basic trait of integrity explains many of Nehama's educational emphases, suggests Nurit Fried. These include: her emphasis on accuracy when reading; her principle of not teaching Midrashim to younger children

---

[39] See also the anecdote on page 434 below in which Nehama chose to speak her truth, risking the embarrassment of a young scholar.
[40] See pages 328–330, 400 below.

who might miss their true meaning; her dislike of people coming to meet her instead of to study; and her insistence on students bringing a Tanach to her lesson. All of these point to a determination that the work be taken seriously and understood accurately. To this list may be added Nehama's custom not to coddle her students – if she believed that their answers fell short, she would not say, "That's nice," but rather tell them to think over what they had said, or even move straight on to the next person. She also had no hesitation in arguing when she disagreed, and even with people she revered. She loved debate, and deliberately sparked heated discussions as a pedagogical technique.[41]

This approach was most likely learned growing up; her brother adopted the same direct and confrontational approach – if anything even more so. It was not a love of argument for argument's sake, but rather the no-holds-barred "argument for the sake of heaven," to be found on every page of the Talmud.[42] It was a tool in the service of truth, and the proof of this is the respect that remained between Nehama and her opponents. Intellectual disagreements did not become personal altercations, as R. Mordechai Breuer, whose ideas Nehama ruthlessly attacked, testifies.[43] Erella Yedgar, who spent many Shabbat meals with Nehama, recalls the atmosphere as one of passionate debate. Everyone looked forward to this and no one was ever insulted, she testifies.

But although Nehama's manner was often mitigated by her sensitivity, it could nonetheless be very brusque, and she was often unable to hear opinions that were different from her own, saying things like: "I've been teaching this for thirty-five years – why should I change now?" One educator who, in a public discussion, had his claims respectfully but firmly dismissed by Nehama, walked out mumbling, "Nehama is an autocratic woman. There's no point arguing with her!"[44] At these times, true dialogue became difficult, and many gave up after several hours of argument had created not the slightest dent in her outlook. "There were things you simply could not talk to her about," testifies one student. Even her admirers admit that she was too uncompromising at times. But those who loved her accepted this as part of the package that was Nehama Leibowitz, and in them it garnered even more respect. Her criticism, which she gave with love,

---

[41] See *KA*, entire article.
[42] See *Ethics of the Fathers*, 5:17: "Every controversy that is in the name of heaven is destined to result in something permanent," etc.
[43] Breuer, "*Yahasah*," 11. See also her exchange of letters with Reinitz, *PN*, 676–702, which also contain some blunt statements that did not damage the friendship in any way.
[44] Ahrend, "*Mi-toch*," 48.

served to shake people out of complacency into a re-assessment of their values.

☙ ❧

Nehama sensitized her students to the many occasions on which people bend the truth, using words that are not inherently false but are intended to deceive nevertheless. She taught that these constituted a lie, which is why Exodus 23:7 instructs "Keep far away from falsehood" instead of the more common format, "You shall not lie." She illustrated this with the story of the mother who calls out of her window: "Yossele! Go to the shop and buy some milk!" Her son, playing below, does not obey. Ten minutes later, she looks out again: "Yossele, *nu*, did you go?" "Mummy, the shop is closed!" shouts her son, adding in a whisper, "On Shabbat!"[45] Nehama explains:

> "Keep far" implies not only the negative avoidance of actual falsehood, but also meticulous care in refraining from anything which might conceivably savour of untruth, even though it was not obviously dishonest.[46]

She taught many lessons about honesty in the ethical realm, stating, for example:

> The rabbis regarded a man's attitude to robbery as a touchstone of his character and sterling worth. (*NSB*, 129)

She had this to say about bureaucracy:

> We live in a bureaucratic world. There is scarcely a field of human endeavour which is not regulated and governed by managers and administrators who have the power to determine matters both great and small for the community. It is well to be reminded in such a context of a truth that is often forgotten: office, as our Sages saw it, is not an opportunity to wield power but a matter of service, even slavery. (*NSS*, 148, n. 4)

She lambasts the corruption rife in government offices by first quoting the Talmud (Bava Metzia 111a):

---

[45] In a different version, the boy adds, "is a fib!" (Heb: *be-sheker*). See David Tamar, "*Pahim ketanim al isha gedolah*," *Ha-Tzofeh*, July 4, 1997, and Shoshanah Rabin, "*Mi-nitzotzot Nehama*," in Strikovsky, *Daf*, 7. See also the story quoted in *NSS*, 445, from *Va-yikra Rabbah* (and compare Nedarim 25a) about the man who hands his creditor a hollow staff containing money to hold, and then swears truthfully, yet still deceitfully, that he has handed over the money.

[46] *NSS*, 437; see essays in *ibid.*, 334–338, 437–447. See further the discussion of Jacob's deceit on pages 345–346 below.

What is meant by "oppression" and "robbery"? R. Hisda said: "'Go and come again, go and come again' – that is oppression"….

and then adding:

And how apt are these words for all times and particularly ours, which is a period of rule by administrators, bureaucrats and offices, where so frequently is heard the order to "Come back tomorrow, go to So-and-so, I have no time, this is not my jurisdiction, now is not office hours."… Taken altogether, how much exploitation is involved![47]

In the footnote, she writes:

Approximately 1800 years after [the Sages], in the late 1930s, the renowned labor leader Berl Katznelson, who was extremely wise, admonished the officials of the Labor Union and the Health Funds, and in general all government employees… for the malpractice of closing the door during office hours, hanging a sign "Back Soon," and then sitting and drinking tea while the public wait restlessly and go home, having accomplished nothing.[48]

Elsewhere she quotes Katznelson as follows:

There are so-called trivial sins that a person treats lightly, such as telling someone to come again, with the door locked during reception hours. Can you forget that cooling one's heels outside an office constitutes oppression? Ancient dicta need to be repeated. "An official who lords it over the public – the Almighty weeps on account of him daily." (NSS, 401, n.7)

Nehama remarked that the growth of bureaucracy and public organizations allowed people to shift responsibility onto anonymous abstract bodies (NSB, 327). She also joked: How did Joseph know after hearing Pharaoh's dream that seven bad years were coming? The answer: As soon as he advised Pharaoh to appoint *pekidim* (literally "officers," but in modern Hebrew, officials or clerks), it was inevitable that seven bad years would follow!

In her own life, Nehama was extremely scrupulous and protested the smallest infractions, such as eating an unpaid-for chocolate from the assortment shelf in the supermarket – whether child or adult, the person had committed a crime. She once discovered some money that an American had paid for worksheets that had not been sent. She immediately mailed them with an apology, saying that she didn't want him to consider Israelis crooks.

---

[47] *IHBV*, 237 (compare *NSV*, 289).
[48] Combination of *IHBV*, 237, n. 2, and *NSV*, 290, n. 1.

Her housekeepers attest that inside her home Nehama was exactly the same, insisting they declare every penny of their salary for tax purposes and that plumbers and other workers be paid with legal receipts, even at greater expense. One plumber who arrived directly from the *yahrzeit* for his brother, a soldier who had died in one of Israel's wars, asked Nehama to pay without a receipt. She sternly rebuked him: "Your brother died for the country! Can't you pay your taxes as you should?!" When a women's Torah learning institution, still in its early years, invited Nehama to give a talk, the staff, inexperienced in tax laws, sent her a gift certificate in lieu of payment. She sent it back, saying: "This is illegal. I didn't expect payment; but if you are going to pay me, you must pay tax on it." She could not stand plagiarism, and took care to cite by name those she quoted. Hypocrisy of any sort also earned Nehama's contempt, and especially amongst the religiously observant. She was once very upset when she heard about corruption within the *hevrah kadishah*, refusing to calm down for many minutes.

Professor Dov Rappel knew of Nehama's conscientiousness before he was even formally introduced to her. In 1936, he was standing in the bank of *Ha-Po'el ha-Mizrahi* (the religious labor movement) in Jerusalem, when a woman walked in and paid her monthly membership dues. After she left, the secretary divulged that this woman was the only member who paid up without being reminded. It was, of course, Nehama.

∂ ∞

Yet sometimes truth also lost in the clash of values, subordinated to even more important values. Nehama notes in her *Studies* that in exceptional cases – always outside of court – deviation from the truth is commendable, even essential, in the interests of peace.[49] Likewise, in an essay entitled "Truth Gives Way to Peace" she discusses a fabrication on the part of Joseph's brothers, concluding that truth is not an absolute value, for the Sages regarded the brothers' conduct as warranted under the circumstances. Nehama also notes that even God deviates from the literal truth for the sake of peace and of life itself.[50]

Principles

Another facet of her trait of integrity was Nehama's determination to do the right thing. She stood by controversial views that she held to be true, remaining in the minority position regarding the use of Midrash, for

---

[49] See discussion in *NSS*, 440–441.

[50] *NSB*, 568. Nehama also has no problem with the suggestion that Judah put words in his father's mouth (which may indeed have reflected what was in his heart); see *LP*, 200.

example, or, despite aspiring to acceptance within Orthodox circles, quoting non-Orthodox and non-Jewish scholars.[51] She refused to base her position on what was popular, for popularity is not a good guide for one's choices:

> Success often deceives the individual into imagining that it is synonymous with truth…. This argument from success has been echoed throughout the centuries by the revilers of Judaism…. The material success of Christianity in contrast to the persecuted and abject status of the Jewish people was adduced as evidence of its truth. (*SD*, 131–132)

Or, in brief:

> As a contemporary thinker once phrased it, among all the many names and attributes of God the title "success" cannot be found. (*NSB*, 385)

Nehama was ready to make great sacrifices for her convictions, as illustrated by the following incident. Since its earliest days in the mid-1950s, Bar-Ilan University, an institution aiming to encompass both Torah and academic study, employed Nehama in the Bible Department together with her close friend and colleague, Meir Weiss. After several years of teaching, both had become senior lecturers but not yet professors. Then Weiss suddenly left the department in stormy circumstances created by academic politics. Believing that her friend had been denied a deserved promotion, Nehama declared that if he left she would follow; and at the end of the academic year in 1961, she made good on her promise. Weiss went to the Hebrew University, establishing himself as a foremost Bible scholar and eventually receiving the Israel Prize; while Nehama focused her academic career at Tel Aviv University where she was already teaching. Her action left a profound impression on those she left behind. One editorial later described it as follows:

> It made waves, and set the tone for the discussion regarding the spiritual-religious nature of that university, as well as being an educational move. (*PN*, 621)

The students, for their part, were very upset. The departure of the two pillars of the department left a vacuum, in spite of the excellence of Nehama's replacement, Professor Uriel Simon. Professor Yehudah Friedlander never forgot the distress of those events: "I had only managed one year of study with her, but that was one of my best years as a student."[52] Professor Dov Landau, despite nearing the end of his degree, even

---

[51] See chapter 18 for further discussion.
[52] Sheleg, "*Kalat*," 70.

transferred out of the department, having lost the only teacher he trusted to supervise his thesis. Yehudit Ilan went even further, giving up her almost completed degree to follow Nehama to Tel Aviv University.

Bar-Ilan's loss was Tel Aviv's gain, and Nehama was able to open the eyes of the very secular population at the latter institution to the riches within traditional commentary. But she was deprived of the most natural environment for her – one that respected both religion and academia. Though she always maintained a discreet silence on the matter, it left an unpleasant aftertaste, and, according to Horwitz, in private she shared her negative feelings, and also suggested that at Bar-Ilan, women were not accorded their due status. Reportedly, in the years after the incident she refused to set foot on the campus even in order to teach. Evidently she later relented, lecturing in various forums at the university and eventually receiving an honorary doctorate from Bar Ilan.

৯ ৯

Nehama had several unalterable principles. She was a firm believer in self-discipline. This was the purpose of the Torah's precepts,

> to control man in his responses to his natural desires, in purifying and exalting him. (*SD*, 151)

> Every man, however perfect, is subject to weaknesses and frailties and his greatness lies rather in his measure of control over them. (*SBM*, 269)

She reserved a special wrath for unthinking obedience, even of the mitzvot, as well as for hypocrisy and for inferior interpersonal behavior. Witnessing a neighbor demanding that a stranger move from his garden bench, she rebuked him: "Our father Abraham would not have behaved this way." (The neighbor retorted, "Do you need this to prove to you that I am not our father Abraham?!") About to begin teaching a group of important Jewish educators in a too-crowded hall, she announced, "I will not begin until someone gives the lady standing at the back a chair."

Nehama was also principled about money, not only regarding honest transactions but also when it came to fair payment for services rendered. She believed in Torah teaching and taught for free on many occasions; people even had to persuade her to take money. Nonetheless, as the sole breadwinner of her family, she at times had to stand firm on being recompensed for her work. In doing so, she was thinking not only of herself but of all Torah teachers, who are too often expected to teach for free and cannot make ends meet.

Gifts, though, were a different matter. Mahatma Gandhi, in his autobiography, mentions that he refused to accept several expensive presents given in appreciation of his public service:

Meir Weiss, 1945. Courtesy of Gabi Weiss.

Nehama with students from Bar-Ilan, 1959. Inscription reads: "To Nehama, a momento from your students at Bat-Ilan University, first graduating class. *Sivan* 5719." Pictured behind Nehama: Leah Frankel. Courtesy of Mira Ofran.

I am definitely of the opinion that a public worker should accept no costly gifts.[53]

Nehama went further – she refused gifts of any sort, costly or not. This category extended to a plant when she was unwell, or a small gift at the end of the semester (she declared, "Teachers receive a salary!"). When a cake was brought for an end-of-year party in her house, Nehama only consented on condition that she pay for it, insisting, "This party is happening in my house, and it is *my* hospitality!" She was disturbed when guests brought flowers for Shabbat. "I wouldn't accept a bribe like that. If they bring red flowers, you start thinking, 'I'll invite them back next week – maybe they'll bring yellow flowers.' I won't let them steal my mitzvah like that!" In fact, Nehama's friends rushed to confiscate any flowers that were innocently brought before the blunder was discovered. Even flowers brought from a student's garden bothered her.

One summer in the mid-1980s, a group of American teachers, having just completed a three-week Tanach enrichment seminar at Machon Gold, presented Nehama, their primary teacher, with a silver salt and pepper shaker set at their final dinner. The next morning, she appeared at breakfast, just before their departure for the airport. The gift was lovely, she said, but she had not slept all night – she was paid to teach and also very much enjoyed it, especially in the case of teachers who wanted to learn, and this was payment enough. She had wished to respect their feelings, but it was an unethical act, and so return the gift she must. The surprised teachers decided instead to make a donation to the JNF in her name. A decade later, these same teachers came to study with her, this time in her home. Looking around in amazement, they suddenly understood the incident from years before. "As I sat in that apartment, surrounded by the treasures in the room," recalls R. Joel Wolowelsky, "I thought back to that salt and pepper set. What must she have thought of those American teachers who believed such a gift would enrich her home?"

Similarly, Nehama left her house every Purim so as to avoid accepting *mishloah manot* (Purim food parcels) and warned people not to bother coming. R. Yitshak Reiner and a group of close students who had studied with her weekly without payment over a long period wanted to express their gratitude. Instead of a gift, they brought her a large basket of *mishloah manot* before Purim, filled with useful items. But the plan backfired, as Nehama ordered: "You will not leave this here. You will take this with you when you

---

[53] M.K. Gandhi, *An Autobiography, or The Story of My Experiments with Truth,* Desai, Ahmedabad: 1997, 185.

go." When R. Reiner tried to leave without it, Nehama shouted at him down the stairs, "Yitshak! Come and take this away!"

Over the years, many determined efforts were made to find something that Nehama would accept. A scarf from overseas, specially chosen for its modest design and muted color, was met with "Thank you, but I don't need it." A coat, bought to replace the one she has used for thirty years, was rejected with, "Why do you claim that my old coat doesn't keep me warm? Have you ever worn it?" But some, with great aplomb, circumvented the blockade. Blu Greenberg thought long and hard and succeeded in getting Nehama to accept four folding chairs, slimmer and of a better quality than the ones she had, for the benefit of the students. R. Nachum Amsel bought her books that would pique her interest, such as a new book on Rashi, and inscribed them so that she could not return them. She also accepted candies for the students, or a ceramic bowl filled with raisins from her Youth Aliyah students, who told her that rather than teaching entire chapters, she picked out the "raisins," the exciting points in the verses.

Nehama herself, however, loved to buy gifts, keeping an eye out for special items that would bring happiness. She gave her housekeeper a gift on every festival, including *Yom ha-Atzma'ut*, rather than just twice a year. Since she gave away numerous books, some students ended up receiving an entire shelf's worth on topics close to their heart. Yet when they wished to reciprocate, she fended them off, saying, "I have all these books already" and "I'm older than you. It is the privilege of the elder to give to the younger."

The fervor with which Nehama cleaved to her principles derived from a combination of her passionate personality and her background, which emphasized excellence and precision. Joy Rochwarger reveals:

> One time, as I was helping her adjust her clothes before leaving the apartment, she went to the closet to look for a belt. I pointed out to her that there were no loops on her dress and hence there was no need for it. She picked up her head and gave me a look that made me wish I had never gotten out of bed that morning: "In my home no one ever left the house without a belt."[54]

Not quite a *yekke*, Nehama had some of the *yekke*'s stereotypical meticulousness. For example, when developing a course on Rashi for the Open University in the 1980s, she drafted Professor Moshe Ahrend to assist her. Together they wrote the important work *Perush Rashi la-Torah: iyunim be-*

---

[54] Joy Rochwarger, "Words on Fire: Then and Now – In Memory of Nechama Leibowitz," in *Torah of the Mothers: Contemporary Jewish Women Read Classical Jewish Texts*, edited by Susan Handelman and Ora Wiskind Elper, 78 (Jerusalem: Urim Publications, 2000/2006).

shitato, but Nehama was so exacting that it took an entire decade from idea to print, with every chapter Ahrend wrote returning loaded with comments on the smallest details.

Nehama's principles made her act forthrightly – some would say inflexibly – in certain situations. One time, she had hurried off immediately after Shabbat to give a lesson, but upon arrival discovered her prospective audience still singing at their third Shabbat meal. When they continued to sing, Nehama got up and left. This behavior was not due to a concern for her own honor but for the right way of doing things, which was one of punctuality and respect for both herself and others. Once, teaching in Michlelet Bruriah, a women's yeshivah, a rabbi erased the blackboard so that Nehama could use it. She announced: "It's not respectful for the teacher to clean the board – the students should do it!" and walked out. Similarly, on another occasion at the same institution, she needed some chalk. The rosh yeshivah, R. Chaim Brovender, volunteered to get her some, but Nehama objected that a student ought to run such an errand. Reassuring her that he did not mind, he went out. She was once again appalled and left the building, the rabbi's entreaties falling on deaf ears. Looking back at the incident, R. Brovender says: "I felt that she had a European value system of hierarchy and honor, something that Americans hold as less important. Nehama was a very conservative person." In his view, an educator should aim for reasonable goals for reasonable people.

Discovering a student doing a crossword puzzle before class, Nehama cried: "Crosswords! What a waste of time!" She could not tolerate mediocrity, remarking: "How could a person teach Tanach in a university without knowing the entire Tanach by heart? Would a person teach English literature without knowing Shakespeare by heart?"[55] Once, frequenting a university café with Eliezra Herzog, Nehama ordered a dish of lettuce with sardines, only to be informed that they were "all out" of that dish. "What do you mean, 'all out?'" Nehama demanded. "Go prepare!" And to Herzog's amazement, they did. Herzog adds that Nehama later self-mockingly recounted of the time she was asked to lecture on somewhat unfamiliar material. She objected: "But I'm unprepared." They replied, "What d'you mean unprepared? Go prepare!"[56]

Nehama was teaching a group of kibbutz schoolchildren the following verse (Leviticus 19:16):

> You shall not be a talebearer amongst your people.

---

[55] Strikovsky, "Nehama on Women," 187.
[56] Recounted at *VLN*, public session.

One child piped up: "Although this is written in the Torah, it's not something you can ever really do." In response, Nehama told the following story:

> My nephew told me one day that his class drives their teacher crazy. I said to him, "Tell me, are the kids in your class observant Jews?" He said they were. I then asked him: "Are there kids in your class who like soccer?" Of course there were. Then I asked him, "So what happens when there is a soccer game on Shabbat?" My nephew had no doubt that in such a case they wouldn't be able to go.

> "If they are so observant," I asked him, "why do they not keep the commandment of not embarrassing someone in public? Or honoring their teacher?" My nephew answered, "Well, that's different."

As Nehama finished, one of the kibbutz children interjected: "Well, it *is* different!" Nehama stood up, declaring: "I can't continue teaching you. I don't accept that the verse commanding Sabbath observance is more important than the others!" Without further ado, she left the classroom and refused to teach them until they came to apologize, and after her return, they sat and trembled.

However, Nehama acquiesced when she knew it meant a lot to someone. For example, she sometimes allowed herself to be photographed, though she detested it. Her empathy and humor prevented her from becoming a grouch or misanthrope. Her standards were channeled into educational ends, to spur herself and her students to higher achievements and more ethical living.

CHAPTER 4

NEHAMA'S HUMILITY:
"I'M NOT WORTH WRITING ABOUT!"

> Rabbi Yohanan ben Zakkai... used to say: if you have learnt
> much Torah, do not claim credit unto yourself, because for this
> [purpose] you were created. (*Ethics of the Fathers*, 2:8)

A model of powerful humility

NEHAMA LEIBOWITZ LIVED her life for the sake of something greater than
herself – in talmudic terminology, "for the sake of heaven." Her humility
and modesty were legendary. "I can honestly say that I have never known
anyone who possessed Nehama's humility," says Dr. Ruth Ben-Meir.

The word humility often brings to mind meekness and submission,
turning the other cheek. But in Jewish thought, humility takes on a different
meaning. While there does exist a Jewish value of self-effacement under the
heading of *mesirut nefesh* (self-sacrifice) or *bitul ha-yesh* (self-nullification),
humility appears to be comprised not only of these kinds of elements but
also of their opposite. Humility is "not just the absence of pride, but a
positive force that expresses itself in constructive action."[1] It is not low self-
esteem, but rather respect for one's strengths as Divine gifts and a
determination to act upon them. As the author of *Hovot ha-Levavot* writes:

> When a person is proud of his wisdom, or the righteous man of his
> deeds, and considers them a great favor of the Creator for which to be
> thankful and joyous... and is humble because of his inability to do as
> much as he would like.... This pride does no harm to humility... [but
> rather] assists humility and adds to it.[2]

Unlike the person who is meek or has low self-esteem, the truly humble
person who has a sense of responsibility to a mission will not allow others'
needs to override his or her own in every case.

---

[1] Zvi H. Szubin, *Encyclopaedia Judaica*, 8:1072.
[2] *Sha'ar ha-kenia* 9, quoted in Elyakim Krumbein, "On the Humility Dilemma and its
Solution," *Tradition* 39/1 (2005): 48. See this article for an in-depth discussion of the nature
of humility.

True humility requires something to be humble about. As Golda Meir said: "Don't be so humble – you're not that great!" Indeed, the figure described as "the most humble man on the face of the earth" (Numbers 12:3) is none other than Moses, the greatest Jewish prophet and leader. Though at times reluctant and self-questioning, he is also aware of the significance of his role and is willing to stand up boldly for his principles, even to the point of bloodshed (Exodus 2:12).

Such paradoxical humility is difficult to keep in balance without toppling to the side of either meekness or arrogance. A talmudic passage points to the existence of both extremes simultaneously in the Divine:

> In every passage where you find mention of the greatness of the Holy One blessed be He, there you find His gentleness.[3]

The liturgical hymn "*Ha-aderet ve-ha-emunah*" echoes this idea, placing the two extremes together in God:

> Power and humility – to whom are they attributed? To the Eternal.

Should we assume, then, that these two can meet only in the Eternal, the repository of all dualities? Nehama, for one, did not; she believed that humans could do so too. After quoting the above talmudic passage, she writes:

> We demand that the mortal king [and] the leaders of the people unite within themselves these two qualities. (*SD*, 82)

She describes Abraham, too, as holding on to both traits:

> Though the awareness that he is dust and ashes never leaves him, he nevertheless demands, argues and claims.[4]

However, Nehama herself provides living proof that this may be done not only in ancient times by kings, leaders and patriarchs, but also today. Like other contradictory elements, she somehow managed to uphold these two in equilibrium. Although she appreciated her own strengths and spoke with confidence, she did not permit her charisma and fame to make her arrogant, and all her success did not take away from her concern for others or her capability for self-critique. We are reminded of R. Simha Bunim of Przysucha's recommendation to keep two notes, one in each pocket. On one

---

[3] Megillah 31a; quoted in *SD*, 80.
[4] *NSB*, 164. However, in a different discussion she seems to suggest that the two traits contradict. In *NSB* (446) she strongly argues, against Ramban's opinion, that a man like Joseph, who attributed all his wisdom to God, could not possibly be pressing his own suit to work for Pharaoh. Nehama surprises us here with her assumption that shouldering responsibility contradicts Godliness.

is written: "For my sake the world was created," while the other reads, "I am but dust and ashes." These twin modes are exemplified in an exchange of letters between Nehama and Professor Shmuel Hugo Bergman. Bergman had written to her in great consternation after hearing her teach a lesson on the radio.[5] Nehama's reply began mildly:

> Had you informed me that my words were weak, pale and utterly inadequate I would have accepted your claim immediately, for I too am aware that I am an extremely cracked shofar from which to sound the words of the living God – the words of the Torah. (*PN*, 659)

Then she went on to disagree boldly with his claims; ending, however, once again with words of self-negation:

> Thank you so much for your aid and guidance, and how I wish I could teach Torah truly as it ought to be taught in this generation, but for this to occur would require a great amount of heavenly assistance. (*PN*, 661)

From our knowledge of Nehama we can safely assume that such words are not mere niceties, but sincerely felt.

℮ ℯ

Nehama was a human "doing" rather than a human "being." She took her deeds seriously, but not herself. Her goal of teaching Torah was her main focus, and her personal needs came second. She was also the one laughing loudest at her own failures.

Nehama somehow remained oblivious to her true worth. It seems as if she preserved an almost purposeful lack of self-awareness, as the poet Rainer Maria Rilke recommends:

> One of the most difficult tests for the creator [is that] he must always remain unconscious, unaware of his best virtues, if he doesn't want to rob them of candor and innocence.[6]

Often she paid no attention to compliments, as if her ears contained a mechanism to automatically filter out flattering words. She said that hearing positive things about her work gave her joy for the sole reason that it meant that she was achieving her goals, not because of her own honor (*PN*, 680). At times she even showed strong negative reaction to praise. Once she read out in class one of her favorite pieces, a midrashic description of Moses pleading to God to be allowed to enter the Holy Land before he died. Her profuse apology that the students must suffer her poor rendition instead of

---

[5] For the full text of the letters, see pages 345–346 below.
[6] *Letters to a Young Poet*, trans. Steven Mitchell, Vintage Books: 1986, 26.

hearing a recording of a radio personality was belied by the terrible pathos with which she, not far from death's door herself at the time, then proceeded to infuse the ancient text. She captivated her audience, declaring: "Really, God – what do you care if one more person crosses the Jordan? I will pass the leadership on to Joshua. Just let me go! Can you not overlook this one little thing?" Upon ending, she apologized once more. Her students rushed to tell her that no broadcaster could have conveyed the depths of this story as she had done; but Nehama reacted angrily: "What do you mean? I'm not a radio announcer, I'm not a professional! How can you say that?"

Similarly, she showed little desire to analyze or reflect upon her own work. When Marla Frankel, accompanied by Professor Michael Rosenak, broached to her the idea of writing a dissertation on her educational system, Nehama looked at them blankly and said, "What system?" Rosenak recounts: "She was in two minds whether she wished to be portrayed as having anything as 'highfalutin' as a theory of instruction."[7]

Being involved in the academic world was important to Nehama; titles were not. When Professor Moshe Ahrend called to congratulate her on becoming a professor she said: "I don't care about that." In her earlier years she hid from her Mizrachi seminar students the fact that she had a doctorate, and they only found out when a colleague let it slip.[8] She preferred to call herself "just a teacher"; though, in fact, for her this was an honorable title, demanding professional excellence. Indeed, she did allow herself to be aware that she was considered a first-rate educator. A powerful sense of certainty informed her teaching and writing, and she never shirked her duty to contribute pedagogical training and advice wherever she could. But she avoided letting her Torah study become a vehicle for self-aggrandizement or financial gain, as *Ethics of the Fathers* warns (4:5):

> Rabbi Zadok said: Do not make them [the words of the Torah] a crown with which to magnify yourself, nor a spade with which to dig.

Even after decades of successful teaching, Nehama did not coast on auto-pilot. What others experienced as an excellent lesson, she defined as "not so good." Linda Derovan remembers Nehama's nervousness before each annual Yeshiva University talk at the Israel Center in Jerusalem: "She would say, 'I'm so nervous – I hope people will come.' Then, walking in and seeing the place wall-to-wall with people, she was overwhelmed and said, 'All these people came to hear this old lady?' And on the way home she always

---

[7] Michael Rosenak, *Tree of Life, Tree of Knowledge: Conversations with the Torah,* Cambridge, Mass, 2001, ix–x.
[8] Nigal, "*Morah.*"

said, 'Was it good?'" Derovan believes that Nehama knew her own worth, but that she was concerned about being exact in her Torah message; the honor of the Torah, not her own, was at stake.

Humility inside and outside the classroom

One of the signs of genuine humility is that if another can do a job just as well, the person is content to let that happen. When, as her doctoral student, Ahrend found himself struggling with Nehama's demanding expectations – she wanted his work to be recognized as meeting the highest standards – Nehama suggested without rancor that she might not be so good at the job of "doctorating," and he might be better off with someone else. In another example, Nehama discovered at the end of her life that five hundred years previously, a Spanish Talmudist, R. Isaac Campanton, had developed a methodology similar to hers. Rather than feeling crushed or attempting to underline the differences, which doubtless existed, Nehama was delighted that her conclusions were well-founded, and even bought her students Campanton's book so that they too could experience the technique.[9] Additionally, when R. Shmuel Klitsner invited her to give a lesson at a women's yeshivah, she said: "What do they need me for? They've got you!" He explains: "It was partially a way of getting out of it, but it also represented her way of thinking: If you're a good teacher also, then what difference is there between us?" Similarly when offered teaching assignments around the country, she protested that there were so many worthy people; what did they need her for? But she often went nonetheless. Indeed, she made a special effort to go to distant places with greater need for a teacher. Traveling to an army base in the Jordan Valley on a hot day, she ignoring her own inconvenience, remarking to R. Ben Hollander: "Look at those soldiers! It's hot and they're exhausted, yet they turn up and pay so much attention."

Nehama's careful attribution of her sources was not only due to her honesty, but also so that no one should think it was her own wisdom.[10] In sharp contrast to the usual practice, she hid her own original ideas behind those of others.[11] She downplayed her scholarship, writing:

> [This] article is not intended to imply "this is the way to teach, in this manner, in this order, presenting these details." Not so. It is nothing

---

[9] Mira Ofran, *VLN*. See also page 373 below for more on this method.
[10] See for example in her letter to Reinitz, *PN*, 692, where she is careful to attribute her ideas to their source, the Malbim.
[11] See more on pages 476–481.

more than a letter to my friends, containing a few suggestions of what can be done, from which the teacher can choose. (*TI*, 21)

Nehama professed her ignorance repeatedly. She took pains to inform her class that her friend Baila Hinda, the wife of R. Isser Zalman Meltzer, knew more Tanach than she, being familiar also with the book of Chronicles. She wrote to R. Nathaniel Helfgot:

> Thank you for remembering me positively and for honoring me with an invitation to participate in this collection. I cannot accede to your invitation, both due to my inability to contribute anything of genuine importance to Tanach study, and also from lack of time.[12]

In this astounding claim of her inability to contribute, Nehama went further than her greatest critics. Although she frequently quoted from the Talmud, Nehama said repeatedly, "I never learned Talmud. I don't know how to learn it" and "I am unable to study the Ritva" (*PN*, 665). She wrote to her friend R. Yaakov Koppel Reinitz, who had asked her a Torah question:

> You have greatly honored me with your letter; and if I did not know that you wish me well, I would suspect that you are mocking me, for what do I know that you do not? But I will try with the little ability I have

and also

> I'm sure that Eisenstadt understands Ramban better than I do....

and

> In a disagreement between Goldschmidt and Nehama, we always hold like Goldschmidt.[13]

After she received the Bialik Prize, Nehama wrote to R. Reinitz:

> I studied the list of past recipients and I saw such names as Professors Epstein and Albeck, and Saul Lieberman and Abramson and more, all of them outstanding Torah scholars – and by what right am I placed amongst them? I suppose there has been inflation in prizes too. (*PN*, 689)

---

[12] *PN*, 662. This quote is cited more extensively on pages 482–483 below.

[13] These three quotes are from letters to Reinitz, *PN*, 686, 687 and 688 respectively. The Eisenstadt mentioned is most likely Menahem Zevi Eisenstadt (d. 1966), who published a critical edition of Ramban's commentary on Genesis. The other reference is to Nehama's friend Daniel Goldschmidt, an expert on liturgical texts.

True greatness is sometimes best gauged in the treatment of people whom one has no need to impress, such as bell-boys, waitresses or librarians. The latter in particular get to observe people closely undetected. The librarians at the National Library in Givat Ram, who for many years watched Nehama poring over books and preparing classes, have nothing but praise for her. They witnessed how she was available to answer people's questions and was constantly, with a smile, stepping outside with someone to talk. One of them, Aliza Alon, remarks: "You can tell a lot about a person from how they treat us. A lot of young doctoral students think we are there to serve them, and leave piles of books lying around for us to return to the shelves. Yet even in her old age, Nehama faithfully returned the books she used, or if she was too tired, apologized for troubling us." Nehama made friends with Alon, taking coffee with her in breaks from her studies. "She would ask if I could leave my position for a few minutes and thank me greatly, calling it an honor, when of course it was my privilege." In Alon's thirty years in the National Library, she cannot recall anyone else of similar stature using such respectful mannerisms with her.

In fact, it was not uncommon for Nehama to thank people when it should have been the other way around. She thanked her correspondents for filling out the worksheets, when it was she who was up until the wee hours checking them. Joy Rochwarger writes:

> Nehama always thanked me profusely for the time that I spent with her, although without a doubt it was I who was receiving far more from her than she from me. She always made me feel as if I were doing her a favor by simply sitting and engaging in a conversation, even though it was I who had asked for her time.[14]

People who believe themselves great, such as politicians, celebrities, academics, and so on, commonly erect barriers between themselves and others. But Nehama's manner was friendly and down to earth, and she asked about the other person in conversation, and made fun of herself. She made herself accessible, deliberately choosing to travel on the bus together with some high-school students on the way to a seminar that she was teaching instead of going by car. While she was, at her own request, universally addressed by her first name, answering the phone crisply with "*Nehama!*," she introduced others by their title, calling Martin Lockshin "The Professor" (though he is not convinced this was entirely complimentary!). Walter Ze'ev Herzberg was always, to his discomfort, introduced as "Dr. Herzberg." The

---

[14] Rochwarger, "Words," 71.

only occasion when she introduced him as "Ze'ev" was to her taxi driver – clearly in order not embarrass the driver, whom she had also introduced by first name. The sequel to this story took place over lunch in Nehama's kitchen. Herzberg mentioned that he had been thinking about Genesis 22:5, where Abraham, on his way to the *Akedah*, the binding of Isaac, tells his servants:

> Stay here… and I and the lad will go….

The root *n-'a-r* used to denote Isaac as "the lad" is the same one used for the servants, in place of the far more common *'a-v-d*. Herzberg mentioned an insight that Nehama's behavior had sparked in him: Perhaps Abraham, sensitive to his servants, deliberately used this word to indicate that his son was like them. Nehama simply said, "Hmmm." Herzberg adds: "It was a reaction of pleasant agreement. I had caught her – but in a nice way."

Nehama showed her students respect in other ways. She stood up for rabbis, even those freshly ordained, and when quoting a source, might preface it with "But you probably know this better than I do" even when they did not. She did not hesitate to appoint Joy Rochwarger, a quarter her age, as her sounding board in matters of education, and to benefit from the younger woman's experience of Diaspora teaching. She deferred to the expertise of her students in many realms. Once she asked her worksheet correspondents whether Pharaoh's new decree – that the Israelites must henceforth gather straw in addition to making bricks (Exodus 5:7) – was designed to extract better results from the slaves, or whether it had another purpose. She personally believed the former, but one correspondent troubled to respond in great detail in support of the latter. He wrote that giving the Hebrews, expert brick makers, the additional burden of gathering the straw would only backfire, as this was forcing menial work on professionals. It was tantamount to asking a skilled surgeon to mop the operating room floor. Therefore Pharaoh's sole purpose must have been to embitter their lives. Intrigued, Nehama asked how he could be so certain. He replied that he was an efficiency expert working for the Department of Labor.[15]

Nehama prized the doctors and lawyers in her class, appealing to their wisdom with, "Well, what do you say?" Studying the story of Jacob and the speckled sheep (Genesis 30:32), she asked someone in her class: "You do genetic research – do you think this is valid?" She wanted not only their

---

[15] Reiner and Peerless, *Studies*, 64.

knowledge, but also to make her students feel important; the exact opposite of building oneself up at the expense of others, which she describes here:

> The desire to make the great man small, to blacken the reputation of the famous, to belittle the character of the good man and minimise any symptom of human greatness is prevalent among the small-minded. (*SBM*, 132–133)

Although a master teacher herself, when Nehama heard of superb teachers, she sat in on their lessons so as to learn from them. She avoided complacency, constantly re-evaluating her goals and behavior as an educator. The spotlight of critique she shone upon others was directed no less frequently upon herself. Once, after she expressed some doubts regarding the effectiveness of her Hebrew University class, R. Hollander showed her the complimentary evaluation forms in order to change her mind. From then on Nehama looked forward to these forms, scanning them carefully and refusing to take any criticism lightly. Within a year of the first worksheets, she was already asking for feedback, with an eye to improvement: "Are the questions generally too difficult for you? What types of questions are the most difficult for you? Do you need explanations and aids for "difficult" words and unusual phrases…?" and so on.[16]

Professor Yehudah Friedlander, while still an MA student, was asked to look over Nehama's Open University course. Many senior lecturers would not have allowed a mere MA student to comment on their work, but Nehama said: "Of course I'll listen to every comment!"[17] When Nehama's friend Professor Meir Weiss read over the material for the same course and wrote "superfluous" next to a favored hypothesis of hers, she insisted that her idea be removed, even in the face of her own regret and Ahrend's objections. "Weiss is a great man, and we will have to take out what I wrote," she said, although in the end Ahrend convinced her to compromise and include it in an appendix.

As mentioned, Nehama held strong opinions, and most of her opinions remained unchanged over her lifetime. Nevertheless, some diehards never lost hope of one day persuading Nehama to modify her views, if only slightly. They were encouraged by her love for truth, by the fact that she generally listened carefully, and by her awareness that there were two sides to any argument, as she writes:

---

[16] See N. Leibowitz, "*Daf*," 456.
[17] Quoted in Sheleg, "*Kalat*," 73.

I try to explain that since both camps in the debate believe that their opinion is obviously correct, perhaps in fact it is not so clear and it would be better not to speak with such assurance; but no one listens to me. (*KA* 479)

Nehama knew the role that ego plays in opinions. Having argued the merits of a certain book for years, she one day turned round and commented: "Perhaps the reason I like this book is because I am quoted in it!" She sometimes surprised people with an unexpected retraction. About six months before her death, she turned to Erella Yedgar at the Shabbat table, during one of their regular debates, and amazed her by reversing a lifelong opposition to scientific research as an aid to understanding the Tanach.[18] As Nehama explained elsewhere:

You see, when a person reaches my ripe old age, fewer and fewer things appear absolute, and the uncertain element surpasses the certain in many questions. (*PN*, 694)

Ben-Meir argues that Nehama was in fact an intellectually flexible person. "She was always gaining new understandings of the Tanach and revising what she thought. Once, she asked us to answer a question on the book of Exodus. I answered it exactly as I had read in her *Studies*, but she responded, 'Wrong!' Clearly, in the intervening years she had changed her mind, and had come to a better understanding."

Another element contributing to Nehama's humility was her sense of humor. She put things into proportion by laughing at herself and at life. Professor Yaakov Kagan tells of the time he visited her, together with another former student of Nehama's. Nehama welcomed them and asked the latter what she was doing with herself. The young woman replied that she was writing a Master's thesis on Kabbalah, and spoke for a few minutes about forces, male/female aspects, and other esoteric topics. Kagan recounts that Nehama, for whom Kabbalah was not a favored topic, spent the entire time glaring silently, at last blurting out, "But this is heresy!" Taken aback, her student said defensively that this was Torah and great Jews throughout the generations had studied it. An argument ensued, until finally, wearying of the intellectual ping-pong, Kagan interjected: "It seems to me that neither one of you is going to convince the other – you're both pretty much set in your ways!" He then told them about William James's concept of "old-fogeyism," which sets in after the age of about twenty-five or thirty and

---

[18] See pages 463–466, 558 below.

causes great difficulty in accepting new ideas. Nehama looked up sheepishly and murmured: "Well, *I* have definitely reached the age of thirty!"

Nehama vigorously made fun of herself. Far from being ashamed, she repeatedly recounted her mistakes to others. For example, the reactions to her venture in writing an article on Rabbi A.I. Kook[19] became fodder with which to regale her students. She told them how her brother Yeshayahu had swiftly cut her down to size, scolding: "Nehama, stick to *parshanut* – you don't understand the first thing about Rav Kook!" Professor Bergman was slightly more tactful, but his comment, "Nehama you must have been referring to Plato here – why didn't you quote him?" still left her speechless. After this episode, she vowed never again to dabble in unknown fields; and to students from R. Kook's yeshivah, Mercaz ha-Rav, she would say: "You, the Mercazniks, know how to read Rav Kook. I don't dare to touch him!" She also told the following anecdote, in the context of a dispute between Rashi and Ramban as to whether animals possess free will. Once, walking in the street, she ran into a student, who mentioned apologetically that she must absent herself from the next lesson. Nehama chided: "What do you mean *must*? You've chosen between two options. What are you, an animal who goes by instinct alone?" Suddenly a passer-by stopped and scoffed: "I've never heard so much nonsense! Say whatever you want about humans, but what do you know about animals?" "Why, do you know about them?" asked Nehama, startled. "Yes!" cried the man, "It's my profession! So don't get involved with things beyond your comprehension!" Nehama would conclude her story with: "How right he was! Before talking and writing on unfamiliar matters, we should first go study them!" Similarly, she recounted how she heard a group of kindergarten children singing the hymn *Yigdal*, containing many philosophical statements about the Divine. She approached the teacher and said: "Do these children really understand the sentence 'He has no form of a body, nor is He a body?'" The teacher looked at her and replied: "Do you?"[20]

Nehama was not afraid to be lighthearted even with distinguished figures. In a letter of response to an Israeli High Court judge, Zvi Tal, whom she had never met, she wrote:

> Honored sir,

---

[19] The article, analyzing R. Kook's piece on the Song of Songs, was *"He'arot metodiyot le-keriyat ma'amar shel ha-Rav Kook (Le-metodika shel keriyat sifrut mahshavah be-kitot gevohot),"* Ma'ayanot 3 (5713): 144–146. Nehama's admiration for R. Kook was tremendous; see further on page 547 below.

[20] Quoted in Shoshanah Rabin, *"Mi-nitzotzot Nehama,"* in Strikovsky, *Daf*, 7.

When I received your letter and saw the envelope stamped clearly with "The High Court" I thought in dread: Of what crime am I suspected? Have I revealed any State secrets or smuggled State treasures abroad? And when I opened the envelope and read the contents, my eyes lit up. And I have never been this overjoyed, not even when I received the Israel Prize in 5717. Who am I that a High Court judge should not only study my words but find time to write to me and to praise me and show me supporting evidence for my words? (*PN*, 664)

Fleeing the limelight

For Nehama, fame was an undesirable by-product of being an excellent teacher. She ignored it as best she could, and frequently acted as if she had no idea that she was a celebrity. Ben-Meir mentioned to Nehama that when browsing in a bookstore in Arizona, she had come across a book about the century's great Jewish women, containing a brief biography of Nehama. She replied that she had no idea why she should appear in such a book. When Walter Sherman asked her to autograph her books for him, Nehama pleaded ignorance as to what an autograph was. If a stranger knew her, she reacted in surprise. After an admirer had asked her for her signature and a photograph, Nehama turned to her student, R. Shmuel (Stanley) Peerless, and commented: "Strange!" Peerless also recalls, "Nehama once got on the phone and said in all seriousness: 'Shmuel, do you remember me?' – as if I could ever forget her!"

Nehama would wonder whether anybody would show up to her lectures. When Rabbanit Chana Henkin invited her to lecture in the Bet She'an area, she gladly consented. Entering the hall, which was packed to standing-room only, she whispered: "Which important personage was here before me?"

Nehama wrote to R. Reinitz:

I am sending you [my new book, *Iyunim hadashim be-Sefer Va-yikra*] and it is an honor for me that it will sit in your bookshelf – although I am afraid that its neighbors on the shelf will say "What is this doing here amongst us?" (*PN*, 692)

She many times actively redirected attention from herself back to the Torah, where it belonged. Hearing the rumor that in Berlin she had lunched with Rav Soloveitchik and the Lubavitcher Rebbe, she said: "Don't people have anything better to do with their time than talk about with whom I used to lunch?" As a rule she did not permit herself to be taped or videoed, and contraband tapes made of her lessons met with her displeasure. There were several reasons for this. Firstly, the student would pay less attention in class. She said, "If you learned something from me and made it truly yours, then you have no need of tapes." Secondly, Nehama wished to be able to freely change her mind and not have a particular viewpoint recorded in perpetuity. But another reason was that she did not want attention drawn to herself, her voice, or her image. For years, R. Nachum Amsel urged her that videotaping lessons would enable more people to learn Torah, but she said that she did not want people to remember her, rather what she taught; and she rejected claims that teacher and teachings cannot be easily separated. One time, after Nehama had enjoyed listening to some tapes of R. Soloveitchik's lectures, R. Amsel struck while the iron was hot and raised the topic again, but she sidestepped him with her usual modesty: "How can you compare me to Rav Soloveitchik?"

Photographs too were only grudgingly allowed. Nehama liked to declaim the verse (Exodus 20:4): "You shall not make for you any engraved image, or any likeness of any thing!" Few dared to ask permission to take a photo, and even fewer met with assent. Chaviva Speter traveled in the early 1990s to the Former Soviet Union to teach Torah and fill the Jewish vacuum left by seventy years of Communism. Prior to her departure Speter paid a visit to Nehama. Nehama was overjoyed to hear of the mission, but when Speter, who planned to take Nehama's books with her, asked for permission to also bring a photograph for the students to see, Nehama flatly refused, exclaiming: "Who am I, Lenin?"

Nehama declined to be interviewed, declaring, "I've said everything I want to say in my books!" and "I'm not worth writing about in a newspaper!" [21] It did not matter which newspaper it was. A journalist from the religious paper *Erev Shabbat* tried to change her mind by drawing upon the paper's reputation, urging: "You won't be interviewed by *Erev Shabbat?*" (literally, "Friday night"). Nehama retorted: "I won't even be interviewed by *motza'ei Shabbat*" (Saturday night)! R. Hollander would implore that in interviewing her he merely wished to publicize how she transformed lives, as she had his; but she insisted: "Study Torah – *that* transforms lives!" Ben-Meir tried to persuade Nehama to allow people to come to meet her, but without success. "I argued for the value in actually seeing a teacher – as in 'And your eyes shall see your teacher' (Isaiah 30:20) – but in vain. She said she wasn't worthy, that there was nothing special about her, and everything she had to say was expressed in her *shiurim*." When a schoolteacher wanted to bring

---

[21] She agreed to be interviewed once only, by Avi Katzman. There is also an interview, by unknown authorship, entitled "Nehama Herself," (*Kol Emunah* [Spring 1987]: 18), but it seems Nehama did not define that conversation as an official interview, as the article begins: "Nehama Leibowitz flatly refuses to give 'interviews'… but she openly talks about many subjects, slowly leading the interviewer step by step, as she does in the classroom, to the information she wishes to impart."

pupils to meet Nehama in real life, or when she discovered people coming to hear her because she was famous, she would exclaim: "I am not a museum! This is not a parade of film stars! What is it they want – me, or a chapter of Tanach? You can't study the book of Jonah in one lesson. If they're serious, then we'll have to have several classes."[22] Indeed, especially in her later years, Nehama turned away requests to study with her in her apartment. She pleaded lack of space, but the real reason was that she did not want to be a "tourist attraction." Only serious students with recommendations were accepted.

There was certainly no shortage of people who wished to meet Nehama, for all sorts of reasons. A young convert from Czechoslovakia first heard of Nehama while attending a Jewish summer camp, as "a very special woman who gives *shiurim* on the weekly portion." Having chosen the name Leah, she was looking for a middle name, and found herself attracted to both the sound and the meaning of "Nehama" (consolation). She adopted the name, and subsequently always felt close to Nehama Leibowitz. Arriving in Israel, the young woman bought her books; but an attempt to meet Nehama was met with the response: "I'm not a person who people come to meet. I am a teacher – people come to learn with me." Though disappointed, Leah Nehama was impressed by Nehama's humility and felt even happier that she had chosen that name.

Vanessa Ochs, too, found that her writer's curiosity must remain unsatisfied:

> There was much I would have asked Nehama if not for her policy on privacy, which everyone respected. I didn't, I couldn't, ask…. What a mystery Nehama was to me. How frustrating not to know who or what had given her the confidence, the stamina to go on in Torah when the feat seemed so much more staggering for a woman.[23]

Nehama would defend her position by telling of the time when a school principal brought a class of students "to meet Nehama." Later, they were asked to write an essay on the topic of "Nehama's lesson." Nehama recalled: "He sent me the essays. Thirty-four essays, and every single one described how I wear my beret at an angle, and how the principal held my bag for me as he came into class. No one wrote anything about the lesson itself! If people meet me, what will they remember? An old woman? Let them read the books." She was particularly incensed at a writer who had mentioned the color of her shoes: "They come to learn Torah, but instead look at shoes!"

---

[22] Ben-Meir, interview; Fried, *VLN*.

[23] Ochs, *Words*, 281.

Nehama loathed being publicly feted. She insisted that an eightieth birthday party being planned in her honor be renamed from "birthday party" to "friendly gathering for no particular reason."[24] The many friends and acquaintances who came to the event to pay their respects did little to ameliorate her displeasure. Worst of all was the discovery, despite anxious efforts at concealment, that a student of hers was amongst the organizers. Nehama was furious: How could she be part of this conspiracy when she knew that Nehama hated these affairs?

Even appealing to Nehama's love of learning was to no avail in this matter. When R. Ben Hollander and Dr. Gabriel Cohn wished to bring out a book in Nehama's honor, a serious collection of articles by students using her methodology to analyze early Prophets, she rejected the idea. Only after her death could a work of tribute, *Pirkei Nehama*, be safely brought to press.

While receiving an honorary doctorate from Bar-Ilan University, she refused to wear the cap and gown: "It's not Purim. I'm not wearing a costume!" In her speech she remarked: "I did some research and I asked myself – what is an honorary doctorate? And I came to the conclusion that it has no significance whatsoever!"

Someone brave enough to take Nehama to task was the noted talmudist, Professor Saul Lieberman. In 1981, Nehama received the Judith Lieberman Award for her Torah teaching. After the ceremony, he wrote the following frank letter:

> I would like to say something regarding the issue of fleeing from honor. Of course, chasing honor is very reprehensible, and fleeing from it worthy, but the highest level of all is to scorn honor and ignore it completely. The very act of fleeing from it, hastily and furiously, inflates its importance. If people insist on paying you tribute, let them have their fun, especially if it will ultimately result in some benefit for an individual or the community. (*PN*, 22–23)

Lieberman also sent Nehama a copy of his speech from the ceremony, as he had promised her:

> We have tied an innocent woman to [a] mast to make her listen to a paean of praise. She protested loudly, saying, "I don't want to hear tributes and accolades!" I promised her that there was no danger in this paean, but she was adamant: "I don't want it!" Furthermore, she argued, what means this festive meal? For what is this celebration? And

---

we have coerced her, and here she sits tied to this mast under duress, against her will and not to her benefit.

The question arises – halachically, is this the correct course of action? After all, "What is hateful to you, do not do unto others." Well, I heard a story, and remembered the Halachah.

Once there was a Rebbe – I forget his name; perhaps Rebbe Nahum of Chernobyl, or one of the Lubavitcher Rebbes. Anyway, the story goes that the Rebbe noticed that his disciples were giving him too much honor, so he said to them: "Wait here. I am going into my room and will return shortly." He went into his room. The disciples were curious to know why the Rebbe wanted to be alone in his room and what he was doing there, so they put their ears to the door and heard him talking to himself: "Please sit down, our rabbi, Candle of Israel, Mighty Hammer, Right-hand Pillar, Anointed of God, Holy Light [and so on and so forth]." The Rebbe then opened the door and came out.

The disciples asked him: "Rebbe, we were eavesdropping on you and heard you talking to yourself – but what does it mean?" The Rebbe answered: I was going over a saying from *Ethics of the Fathers* [2:10]: Let your friend's honor be as dear to you as your own. Meaning, when honor is given to you, let it seem as if you are raining compliments and accolades upon yourself! Let it be exactly as important and significant!

This provides us with an opening to permit our actions... from now on, Professor Nehama Leibowitz, you may listen serenely and enjoy yourself. What do you care? You hear praise not of yourself, but of someone else whose name is synonymous with yours!

Nehama's response is, unfortunately, not available.

CHAPTER 5

SIMPLICITY:
"YOU CAN'T EAT BREAKFAST TWICE!"

> Outward distinction and grandeur bear no relation to inner greatness. Inward truth does not gain in authenticity from the glory and gaudiness of its outer casement (*New Studies in Shemot*, 58).

THOUGH SOPHISTICATED INTELLECTUALLY, Nehama embraced a large measure of simplicity in her life, both in her physical environment and in the world of her emotion and faith, and this is the topic of this chapter.

Physical simplicity

Nehama's material surroundings were an unforgettable sight. Even back in the Kiryat Moshe days, Nehama and her husband lived a relatively spartan lifestyle. Besides books, all the money went to the bare necessities, with the only extravagance being a housekeeper (and with Nehama out all day that too had become a necessity). But it was Nehama's next apartment, the tiny one behind the bus station in Romema, that is most remembered. The American Hebrew University students who came to her house for lessons would sit so silently at first that Nehama asked her teaching assistant, R. Ben Hollander, what was wrong with them. He explained that they were overwhelmed by her living environment. A great deal more sparse than their own homes, it certainly did not meet their expectations for a well-known personality. Through her, these young Americans got to experience first-hand the Israel of old, puritanical and non-materialistic. But Nehama refused to see her home as exceptional. She told the story of a young child who, upon entering her kitchen, blurted out: "Is Nehama really poor?" She would then laugh: "Am I poor? Don't I eat well?"

The apartment contained a small kitchen and two rooms – neither one a bedroom. One was her private study, and the other, a small living-room-cum-study where she gave classes. Baffled visitors would eventually detect her bed behind a curtain in an alcove in the hallway next to the front door. One student quipped in astonishment: "She slept on a shelf!"

The furniture in the apartment was well-used. The bed was brought from Germany in the 1930s. The candlesticks were old, and Nehama forbade her housekeeper to buy replacements. The kitchen, which was tiny, contained a small table and two chairs. The refrigerator was at least forty years old. In the living room were some twenty unmatched hard chairs and benches, for use during lessons, and an old couch. A very large desk sat piled high with open books, pens and papers – one good jolt would have brought them all tumbling down. Most of the time, Nehama's bed and floor were also piled with various reading materials. She never changed her old filing system, climbing up a ladder to get her books and sheets until her students begged her to let them do it instead. It was with great reluctance that she allowed her family to buy her a comfortable chair to use while she was working, and for long afterwards she felt uneasy about it.[1]

There were few ornamental items in the house. She had hung a framed needlepoint on the wall, bearing the legend in Hebrew: "How I love Your Torah; it is my conversation the whole day long" (Psalms 119:72). She also kept a photograph of Rabbi Aryeh Levin, the famous "Tzaddik of Jerusalem," on the desk. This was the only photograph on display. Nehama knew him personally and was a devotee, and it is not hard to see why – he, too, shied away from honors, neglecting his own needs and dedicating his energies to the Jewish people.

The only possession in which Nehama invested significantly was her books. Besides many books on Bible and commentaries, she also owned a considerable amount of literature. Her books lined the walls, announcing their titles in many languages, and were clearly well-thumbed. "As we sat in her library filled with torn and well-used books, I felt that in this home I was living Torah," recalls R. Avi Baumol.

Nehama's regular meals consisted of fish, crackers, bread, cheese, and unsweetened yogurt with jam. Her sole indulgence was a small stash of chocolate in the cupboard, and even this was primarily intended for students and visitors. There is speculation as to why Nehama abstained from meat. Some understood it to be health-related. Others, such as Dr. Shmuel Adler, clearly recall Nehama explaining that she simply did not want the bother of two sets of dishes in her kitchen. Yet we do find scattered throughout her *Studies* several references to the spiritual value in vegetarianism, including an essay entitled: "How permitted is meat?"(*SD*, 135–142) and lengthy excerpts

---

[1] Breuer, "*Professor,*" 18.

from an essay by R. Kook on the topic.[2] Here are some examples of her comments:[3]

> In Rabbi A.Y. Kook's opinion... the Torah implicitly disapproves of eating of meat. (*NSV*, 89)

> The late Rav Kook regarded these verses as providing a clear indication that the Torah did not look on the eating of meat and killing of animals for human consumption as an ideal state of affairs. (*SD*, 136)

Several times Nehama quotes R. Kook's evolutionary spiritual model regarding vegetarianism:

> By the end of time the knowledge of the Lord will extend to the animals also... whereupon this offering – the vegetarian *minhah* – "will be pleasant to the Lord."[4]

However, Nehama implies that she, like R. Kook himself, held vegetarianism to be a rarified ideal, not for the average person today:

> These are only for the wise ones.[5]

> In contradistinction to vegetarians, Rabbi Kook regarded the abstention from the slaughter of animals... as a sublime goal to be achieved after man had become completely accustomed to his duties to "those nearer to him." (*SD*, 140)

> The duty of relieving the suffering of animals must give way to the more important obligation of moral improvement.... We are not at liberty to make our own rules and regulations... like those who proclaim their solicitude for animals but ignore the suffering of humanity. (*NSS*, 434–435)

Nehama's clothing, too, was legendary in its plainness. On the first day of class, students were sometimes shocked to discover that the small woman

---

[2] R. Kook's article, from *Talelei Orot*, was reprinted as "*Hazon ha-tzimhonut*," in *Lehai Ro'i*, Jerusalem: 5761 (see *IHBV*, 77, n. 3).

[3] Other references to vegetarianism or to similar ideas appear in *NSB*, 77–78; *IBB*, 55–56; *NSV*, 388–397; *SD*, 137–140, and *IBD*, 184, footnote; and also in the teacher's guidance leaflets for *Re'eh*, 5705 and *Ki Tetze*, 5729 (thanks to R. Yitshak Reiner for these two references). An adapted version of the essay may be found in Chanan Morrison, *Gold from the Land of Israel*, Jerusalem: Urim Publications, 2006, 31–33.

[4] *NSV*, 43. Also "the progress of dynamic ideals will not be eternally blocked" (*SD*, 138). Her words in *SD*, 313 also point to R. Kook's philosophy, that human advance will bring the Messiah. See also *NSB*, 205, for another example of R. Kook's general belief in "the upward progress of the human soul," and *ibid.*, 391–392, for his evolutionary model regarding the use of the *matzevah*.

[5] *IHBV*, 42. R. Kook writes: "The time for this exercise of power of self-control has not yet arrived." See *SD*, 138, and *IHBS*, 301, n. 9.

in the modest outfit was actually the lecturer! One student remarks: "I never dreamed that this person with a beret and briefcase was destined to have such an impact on me." Some people are under the impression that she always wore the same brown suit and beret. This was not quite true, but all of her outfits were in a similar style, in brown or blue, with perhaps an occasional foray into black. She wore her clothes until they were no longer serviceable. Once, curious as always, Nehama asked Joy Rochwarger to describe current women's styles and fashions. Rochwarger told her about a dress that had been custom-made for a wedding and worn only once. "Nehama was dumbstruck by the wastefulness. She proudly informed me that not only was her own wedding dress inexpensive, but that she had continued to wear it for over fifty years!"

❧ ❦

Nehama's lifestyle choices did not stem from lack of finances or miserliness, or from an impaired sense of aesthetics. She noticed and complimented others on their looks, and cleanliness was important to her too. Rather, as she once explained to an inquiring friend, she preferred to invest minimal thought in clothing. "But," she added, "you're a young woman, and it's a good thing for you to be thinking about these things." Her frugality was motivated by her ideals. She opposed keeping up with trends and wasting useful possessions. She liked to quote R. Judah Halevi, the medieval philosopher and poet, on the Ten Commandments:

> The servants of time, slaves of slaves they be;
>
> The servant of God alone is truly free. (*IHBS*, 233; *NSV*, 565)

David Weinberg recalls:

> We students secretly would smile at each other. She never realized just how accurately Rabbi Halevi's words described her own self. She taught us that fashion – in dress, behavior and speech – meant slavery to time. What's "in" or "in style" is not important, she railed; only that which is timeless is of value.[6]

She placed many values above material gain. Invited to speak at a prestigious institution abroad, she turned the invitation down without a moment's thought, as no sum could tempt her to leave Israel. Indeed, upon reading their apology for offering "only" one thousand dollars plus expenses, she exclaimed in wonder. She could not even conceive what one could possibly do with this exorbitant sum of money.

---

[6] David Weinberg, "Remembering Nehama," *Jerusalem Post*, April 5, 1998, 8.

Nehama Leibowitz. Courtesy of Mira Ofran.

Nehama Leibowitz. Courtesy of Mira Ofran.

Her habits of restraint, imbibed early on in her parents' home, were reinforced by the Zionist ethos of hardiness and plain living, to which Nehama fully subscribed. Generations of *halutzim* (pioneers) had taken pride in an anti-bourgeois, austere way of life, valuing the land and the common people, alongside books and cultural and spiritual matters. They cultivated these habits deliberately in order to escape what they viewed as the hypocrisy of the civilized Jewish societies that they had fled. The emphasis was on community goals rather than on individual preferences.[7] This ideology fit in very well with Nehama's dislike of pretentiousness. Although she chose to live in the city, she sometimes outdid the kibbutzniks in her desire for plain living. When, on one of her regular visits to Kibbutz Lavi she found her room filled with new furniture, she entreated: "Do me a favor – bring back the old furniture so I can be comfortable!"

With the extensive changes sweeping Israeli society, Nehama's slight figure in her modest outfits and her small home became more and more remarkable to her students. Witnessing her lifestyle became a lesson in and of itself. "You walked into her apartment and saw her priorities immediately," recalls one friend. "Afterwards, I felt embarrassed entering my own home where I saw a completely different set of priorities – pictures and carpets and so on." Some found it excessive, though. One student remarks: "Her modesty went so far that I felt it to be almost immodest, with people sitting in her house, seeing into her kitchen and practically into her bedroom. For me, that would have been an invasion of privacy. But she would never have thought of it that way."

Functions of all kinds irritated Nehama. She almost never attended weddings and bar-mitzvahs. She pleaded that to accept all invitations would create a terrible burden on her time while to pick and choose would cause insult; but there was another reason – she abhorred the excess and waste. She felt that big weddings were unnecessary. "How many close friends does a person really have anyway?" Paying a photographer was ridiculous if a friend could do the job. "A bar-mitzvah?" she would say. "Invite as many guests as fit into your house! And people have food at home, so all you need is a little wine. My brother knows many more people than you, yet for his sons' bar-mitzvahs they simply had a bottle of juice and some cookies for *kiddush*. Give the money instead to poor people. That would be more educational." The point was not empty showiness but the spiritual import of the occasion.

---

[7] Anita Shapira, *Yehudim hadashim, Yehudim yeshanim*, Am Oved: 1998, 254.

Nehama at a wedding, 1971. The bride is Meir Weiss's daughter-in-law Tzili.
Courtesy of Gabi Weiss.

Nehama expected others to hold the same ideals regarding lifestyle, but to her consternation this became less and less prevalent over the years. Far from moving towards the utopian social standards set by her beloved prophets, Israeli society was instead becoming daily more materialistic. The simpler world that she knew and loved and preserved in her home gradually vanished, and she missed it terribly. Her stories of Israel of old, of the days in Tel Aviv when a front door key was unnecessary, contained a combination of joy and wistfulness. The extravagance of young people distressed her. She was amazed to hear about yeshivah students who had a refrigerator in each room. In the early 1980s she remarked disapprovingly to R. Shmuel Klitsner: "I've heard there's a new machine that takes wet clothing, turns it around and dries it. What do you need it for? What's wrong with the sun?" Discovering that were no optometrists in Kiryat Shemonah (a town located in the far North), Nehama complained to R. Klitsner that with so many Jewish optometrists in the world, why couldn't some of them move to Kiryat Shemonah? R. Klitsner suggested that the standard of living was not high enough there. Nehama replied sternly: "You can't eat breakfast twice!" This slogan left a deep impression on him.

Nehama worried about these developments in the Western world and Israel. She feared that too much free time and a life devoid of struggle would eventually lead to a decline of moral standards.[8] She taught that the Torah allows accumulation of wealth as long as it remains a means, not an end in itself (*NSS*, 320). She also writes in an essay on the festival of Sukkot:

> Rashbam... does not belittle the importance of material plenty, but on the contrary, values it as something to be thankful for. (*NSV*, 471–472)

However, she ends the same essay with the direction she favored more:

> Rabbi Y. Arama, on the other hand, sees in gold, silver and all worldly goods dangerous temptations likely to divert man from his real goal in life... [and] lays special emphasis on the fact that succa embodies a protest against and the negation of the commonly desired living standard, which he considers the principal form of idol worship in his time. (*NSV*, 471–472)

Despite an increasingly hi-tech Israeli society, Nehama never learned how to use new technology. It was not that she was of Amish tendencies or fiercely opposed to technology on principle; she was comfortable using the technology she already knew. For many years, for example, she used

---

[8] *TI*, 27. Nehama also refers to Herzl's play *Solon in Lydia* on the negative results of too much leisure (*IHBS*, 196, n. 4).

recordings as dramatic aids in her classes. For example, she played Psalm 22 read by two actors, Lawrence Olivier and Yehoshua Bertonov (from the Habimah Theater in Tel Aviv), demonstrating how their different inflections represented different interpretations of the Psalm. But she disliked new gadgets. It took a long time for her to admit that the computer might be of some value. Towards the end of her life, the idea was broached to transfer her *gilyonot* into computer format. It was predictable that Nehama, who had started out using carbon copy paper followed by mimeographed stencils and for years had resisted updating into printed form, would be strongly opposed. When R. Yitzhak Frank showed her the Bar Ilan Responsa, a compilation of hundreds of important Jewish works on one CD, and demonstrated its ability to search for any word, she was fascinated and declared: "It's like witchcraft!" She checked its results, and even disagreed with some. Yet when he encouraged her to buy it, she said, "I'm old-fashioned – this is not for me." R. Nachum Amsel also tried to convince her of the usefulness of this CD. It could reveal all the contexts in which a given word or expression was used. He discovered an interesting fact when he heard Nehama teach a lesson on the phrase "the king of Egypt died" (Exodus 2:23):

> And it came to pass in process of time that the king of Egypt died; and the people of Israel sighed because of the slavery, and they cried, and their cry came up to God because of the slavery.

Nehama noted that Rashi on this verse is surprising. Instead of staying with the plain meaning, that the king of Egypt had passed away, he quotes a Midrash to the effect that the king had become a leper. Nehama explained Rashi's odd choice by quoting the Vilna Gaon's insight that generally when a king's death is recorded in Tanach, he is referred to only by his first name, for he is now no longer a king. Thus, for example, I Samuel 31:6: "So Saul died." In this case, "the king of Egypt died" is an anomaly, and hence the Midrash's suggestion that he was not in fact dead but was a leper. However, a problem arose with this ingenious explanation when R. Amsel ran a computer search, for he unearthed two other instances of "and the king died."[9] Nehama looked at the screen for several moments and then said, "I guess the Vilna Gaon didn't have a computer!"

But this was not the end of the story. A year later, when Nehama taught this topic, she explained that in these two instances, since the king had never been named beforehand, the text had no choice but to write there "the king

---

[9] II Samuel 10:1 and I Kings, 22:37.

died"![10] She had demonstrated that the computer could never replace a good teacher.

∾ ∾

It goes without saying that Nehama was not part of the "leisure culture." She had little free time, and that was how she wanted it. Her work not only provided much-needed income but also was her pleasure and her love, and it spilled over into the small hours of the night. She did not like restaurants or newspapers, and the only thing she watched on her old TV was the news. Travel was done for a useful purpose, generally teaching, and even during vacations she often spent hours studying Torah. Her "down time" was generally spent in conversation with visitors. But she did have a few pastimes, for example, reading novels – which, she liked to point out, serve to satisfy our natural interest in people without transgressing the Halachah about gossiping, which does not extend to fictional characters. Nehama was *au fait* with Israeli literature, and also favored romances and mystery novels by early crime authors such as Dorothy Sayers, Josephine Tey and Agatha Christie. When returning these books to their owners, she loved to discuss the plot and finale. One student, seeing an Agatha Christie book in Nehama's hand, protested, "But Nehama – that's rubbish!" Unruffled, she replied, "Yes – but it's *good* rubbish!"

Nehama loved movies and theater and was familiar with many old films and actors. She often listened to the radio, savoring classical music in particular. She also had a penchant for buying lottery tickets, a hobby that R. Klitsner suggests derived from her trait of optimism. Although she took the trouble to explain that the money went to important causes, she clearly delighted in this activity. Indeed, before handing her shekels over the counter, she would announce to her companion, Rahel Kossowsky: "Now we are going to do something wicked!" Even here Nehama was generous to a fault, insisting that winnings would be split between them. Kossowsky replied that in that case she should also have to pay half the ticket price, but Nehama would not hear of it.

Inner simplicity

With all her erudition, when it came to her core religious life Nehama chose the path of simple faith, leaving her critical outlook at home. When she

---

[10] The first example, II Samuel 10:1, indeed deals with the anonymous "king of the Ammonites." The second, I Kings 22:37, is more problematic as it clearly refers to Ahab. However, we do see that in the chapters beforehand, the text consistently refers to Ahab only as "the king of Israel," and thus too at his death.

asked for halachic rulings, she avoided convoluted discussions, putting her questions "just as the simple people do" and asking only what was necessary to "be a good Jew." Her religious approach will be further discussed in a later chapter.[11]

Nehama also brought her fondness for simplicity to her emotional life. She loved children, and at the few social events she attended, sometimes elected to sit and study with them instead of the adults. Children were likewise drawn to Nehama, and one student recalls her younger brothers arguing about who would get to accompany her to Nehama's house for Hanukah. Nehama respected what children had to say and liked to quote unexpectedly wise or funny statements that came out of their mouths. She suggested that when stuck, teachers should ask a child, who might see things differently

Nehama also loved ordinary folk, favoring blue-collar workers over ivory-tower academics. While she genuinely enjoyed academic debates, she was ultimately anti-elitist, especially when it came to Torah:

> The Torah is not the property of a privileged caste of priests and initiates. It is not in heaven but in our midst. It is the duty of all to study, teach and practice its tenets. (*SD*, 325)

> The Torah addresses itself to the Israelites of all ages, classes and occupations; to the serving priest, practicing judge, children... youth... the farmer who is sowing, reaping the harvest and picking grapes, the shopkeeper. (*NSV*, 263)

> [Moses] did not... make Judaism into an esoteric cult for the initiated only, but imparted it to all Israel without discrimination, just as He received it at the hand of God. (*NSS*, 640)

More than churning out another seminar, another degree, another book, Nehama wanted to teach regular people Torah. The stories that she repeated with the most enthusiasm concerned taxi drivers, kindergarten teachers, factory workers and soldiers, and she reveled in passing on the folk wisdom that she gathered from them. In the words of Dr. Avigdor Bonchek:

> From cab driver to cardiologist, Nehama finds the "*pintele Yid.*"[12]

Nehama was once out walking with Dr. Ruth Ben-Meir when they were stopped by a street cleaner who wanted to share his Torah insights. Nehama listened attentively, head inclined. Though the man's grasp of the material

---

[11] See chapter 15, and in particular pages 336–338 below.
[12] Bonchek, "Professor Nehama," 18. This phrase refers to the "Jewish spark," the concentrated essence of Jewishness supposedly found inside every Jew.

was shaky, she commented encouragingly, and afterwards expressed to Ben-Meir her wonder at his stamina for learning, declaring, "And Your people are all saints" (Isaiah 60:21).

Nehama never denigrated any profession, maintaining that no type of work embarrasses its doer. Her housekeepers were treated as equals, and even walked over to visit with their children on Shabbat, their day off. Tzipora Ofri, Nehama's housekeeper from 1953 to 1975, became her student and close friend. "I switched roles very naturally," says Ofri. "She would come in at lunchtime, and I would be sorting out the *gilyonot* and I would ask her about some point in a worksheet, and we would discuss it and then turn to other topics." Ofri's successor, Yehudit Barashi, Nehama's neighbor on Ha-Tzvi Street, received the same treatment. "We didn't have an employee-employer relationship, but more like mother and daughter. Nehama helped me get my children into the right schools without my asking." When she noticed that Barashi was tired, Nehama released her from her chores, and if it was raining, would insist that Barashi take a taxi at her expense. Barashi's husband was once in danger of losing his job, and the couple asked Nehama to write a letter of recommendation for him. She instead phoned the head of the firm, and when unable to get hold of him, got into a taxi and went to speak to him in person. She used every plea she could honestly employ and eventually won him over. When Nehama passed away, Mr. Barashi still had his job.

ఈ ఆ

George Burns, the American comedian, once said: "Too bad all the people who know how to run the country are busy driving taxi cabs and cutting hair." Jesting aside, Nehama was able to glean great wisdom from such "common folk" about life and Torah subjects, which she would animatedly repeat in classes and conversation. Nehama's stories of ordinary people became famous amongst her students. This was especially true of her taxi driver stories, which merited a category of their own. Far from being patronizing – though perhaps a touch romantic – her interest stemmed from admiration for unpretentious and productive people. It also rested on her talent for discovering wisdom in nooks and crannies that others overlooked. R. Klitsner remarks that Nehama was an excellent example of the saying, "Who is wise? One who learns from every person."[13] Indeed, one of her taxi

---

[13] *Ethics of the Fathers*, 4:1.

driver stories was about this very subject.[14] It took place as Nehama sat grading papers in the back of the vehicle. The driver said to her:

"You're a *morah* [teacher], aren't you? Once upon a time, a teacher was called a *melamed*. What's the difference between the two?"

"Nothing. They're the same," she responded.

"No, there's a difference," insisted the driver. "Let me illustrate. Is whiskey good for you?"

"No."

"Do you drink whiskey?'

"No."

"If not, how do you know that it isn't good for you?" he challenged. "I'll tell you how. If you sit in a bar watching a respectable person, and observe his behavior after several drinks, you understand that whiskey is not good for you. That person becomes a *melamed*. That is why the verse "From all of my teachers I have gained wisdom" (Psalms 119:99) uses the word *melamed* for teacher, not *moreh*!" Nehama told this story to illustrate that children learn not only from formal instruction but also from personal example and life experiences.

Nehama used taxis from the early days, when there was only one taxi in Kiryat Moshe. When asked as a child what she wanted to do when she grew up, she had answered that she dreamed of being chauffeured around in a taxi. Her wish was granted, for her life was spent crisscrossing Israel in vehicles driven by others. She developed what Martin Buber would call an "I-Thou" relationship with the many taxi drivers she met; that is to say, she did not view them in terms of their function, as objects for her use, but as real, fascinating people. They reciprocated the interest, and sometimes upon arrival asked if they could come in and participate in her lesson. One such driver spent the entire journey home pointing out the errors in her teaching, as Nehama delightedly told her friends. Another time, she was teaching a group of visiting American rabbis, and one man was very involved, answering many of her questions, until the group coordinator asked him to be quiet. At the end Nehama asked why this man had been silenced. "To be honest," answered the coordinator, "it was a little embarrassing – he's the bus driver." Then there was the time she forgot one of her worksheets in her taxi. She returned at the end of her lesson to discover the waiting driver filling out the sheet. She checked his answers and they were correct. "Did you find it difficult?" Nehama asked. To her pleasure, he replied, "Not particularly!" She also marveled at the minibus driver who, in notifying the

---

[14] The following is based on Reiner and Peerless, *Studies*, 43, with a few embellishments.

girls in his bus that it was time to get off, employed the verse from Lamentations (4:1) "The hallowed stones shall spill out at the head of every street."

On another occasion, Nehama entered a classroom looking very uncomfortable. She told her students, American rabbis-in-training at the Gruss Institute in Jerusalem, that on the way her taxi driver had asked if she taught Americans. When she said yes, the man turned around in his seat and demanded: "Is it true that they talk during the Torah reading in synagogue?" He would not turn back to face the road until she admitted that they did.

The next story is told by Bonchek:

> A cabbie... noticing that his passenger was grading papers, and discovering that she was a professor of *Tanach*, took advantage of the Tel Aviv-Jerusalem ride to unburden himself of a question that had bothered him for some time:
>
> "What does Jeremiah mean when he says: 'Let not a wise man glory in his wisdom; and let not the strong man glory in his strength; let not a rich man glory in his wealth. But let him that glories, glory in this: that he understands and knows Me'? [9:22]."
>
> "Well," explained Nehama to her driver, "that means that human wisdom and human strength and riches are not really important values; the prophet is telling us that what really counts is knowing Hashem."
>
> "Yes, yes, I know," said the cabbie, with a trace of irritation, "but what does he mean when he says 'Let not a wise man glory in his wisdom, and let not the strong man glory in his strength, let not a rich man glory in his wealth...?'"
>
> Nehama tried again, in her patient pedagogical manner. "The prophet is teaching us a very important lesson in life. Those things that most men strive for – riches, wealth and strength – are...."
>
> "Of course, of course. Understood!" interrupted the cabbie with undisguised impatience. "But what does Jeremiah mean when he says '*A* rich man, *a* wise man,' but when he speaks of strength, he says '*the* strong man'?"
>
> At this point in her story, Nehama looks up with wide-eyed wonderment and a smile of admiration. "You know," she confides, "I never noticed that! That's a very interesting point!"[15]

Finally, here is one of Nehama's most oft-repeated taxi driver stories. She got into a taxi at a hotel on a Friday, and as they prepared to depart, the

---

[15] Bonchek, "Professor Nehama," 18.

concierge hurried out and rapped on the driver's window: "Guess what? A wealthy tourist wants to travel tomorrow to Caesarea. I told her it would cost a thousand liras and she agreed. You're in luck. It's your turn!"

The driver shook his head and said, "I don't travel on Shabbat."

"What's wrong with you? A thousand liras!" urged the other.

"Forget it. I don't travel on Shabbat!"

"But you'll get a free lunch in a fancy restaurant!"

"I said forget it! I don't travel on Shabbat!" The driver started the engine, and although the concierge continued to cajole him, drove away from the hotel. "I noticed," Nehama remarked, "that he was drumming his fingers on the window, and then I heard him muttering, 'One thousand liras… no, I don't travel on Shabbat! A free lunch… no, I don't travel on Shabbat.'" Suddenly the driver said in a determined voice: "Tomorrow I am going to shul with Tzemach and Zechariah and that's that!" (Alternative versions have the punchline as: "I'll go to synagogue and earn even more there!" or "On Shabbat I go to the synagogue to be with God!") Nehama told this story in the context of one of her favorite verses (Psalms 73:28):

> But as for me, God's closeness is my good; I have made the Lord God my refuge, that I may declare all Your works.[16]

From this driver, she explained, she learned what it means that God's closeness is our good – when we forgo greater profits, resisting temptation and preferring to go to synagogue. R. Raphael Posen, who retells this story, remarks: "The power in these words remains with me to this day."[17]

In a similar story, perhaps the same one, Nehama heard the taxi driver declaring to himself: "I won't drive on Shabbat! What would my wife do while I'm away? I'll come back and find her with someone else!" She saw this as a lesson in the psychology of temptation. In attempting to steel himself, he clutched onto every possible straw, using the power of the evil inclination to serve the good inclination.

Nehama traveled economically, many times using a shuttle taxi to save her employer money. She also used buses until the physical constraints of old age prevented her. Nehama had bus stories too, such as the time an older gentleman boarded a crowded bus and a boy offered him his seat. The man asked: "Because of which part of the verse did you stand up for me?" He was referring to the Leviticus 19:32, which instructs, "Rise before the elderly, and honor the aged." The commentators learn from the repetition in

---

[16] She quotes this verse also in *NSV*, 117 (describing it as the "*sumum bonum*") and in *SBM*, 73.

[17] Posen, "*Sofrim u-sefarim*," *Ha-Tzofeh*, March 30, 2007, 10.

the verse that it intends to include not only the elderly but also the wise. The boy responded, "Both!" and the man took his seat. Nehama always ended the story saying with a smile, "And nobody had to explain which verse they were referring to!"

Someone once asked Nehama whether she had any bad taxi driver stories. She replied, "Yes, but why should I tell them?"

Nehama with a taxi driver at the Seminars for Youth Immigration,
Bayit Vegan, 1955. Photo: Tamar Ross.

CHAPTER 6

THE MIDDLE YEARS:
IN WIND, RAIN OR SNOW

THOUGH SHE WORKED diligently throughout her life, the 1940s–1970s were Nehama's prime years.[1] The following chapter describes the developments that took place during that time.

Nehama's teaching career

Being the Renaissance woman that she was, in her early career Nehama taught several topics: essay writing, literature, history, Hebrew expression, Tanach and medieval commentaries. But gradually she gave up some of these subjects, despite her success; and while she continued to teach literature and essay writing, she began to focus on two key fronts: teaching Tanach and pedagogical training.

Already in 1932, at the age of twenty-seven, Nehama was training budding teachers at the Mizrachi seminaries. By 1938, she was well on her way to earning her title "Teacher of Teachers," providing professional development for teachers and counselors, including sample lessons. She also began teaching adult populations (*PN*, 14). As her career moved into full swing, she began to teach diverse populations – in schools, colleges, private classes, conferences and study days. The ministry of Education hired her to run courses for teachers (*PN*, 14). These were taught at the Givat Washington educational campus when it was still a one-room operation. Nehama traveled to IDF bases to do what she jokingly referring to as her *milu'im* (reserve duty). She also taught in what eventually became the longest-running informal Tanach class in Israel. Launched by Rahel Yanait Ben-Zvi, the wife of Israel's second president, it ended in 2003, over fifty years later.[2]

Her students included children and adults, men and women, separately and together. She taught sizeable numbers of non-Jews, including members of the Japanese Makoya sect and groups of priests. Believing that everyone should learn Torah, she taught all comers, secular, religious, learned and

---

[1] Frankel, *Iyun*, 10.
[2] Yaffa Goldstein, "*Shiur ha-Tanach ha-vatik magiya le-kitzo*," *Ha-Tzofeh*, July 13, 2003.

not.[3] With her blend of ancient and modern sources, Nehama catered simultaneously to liberal university-educated people and to much more traditional types. Her lesson spoke to both populations in their own language, and yet simultaneously revolutionized Torah study for both. She introduced secular Israelis to traditional commentaries, demonstrating to the university-educated that the Tanach could be an accessible and enlightened text; while those from very traditional homes, such as the members of the old *Yishuv* (Jews living in Palestine before the Zionist settlement) and the simple Zionist laborers, had their eyes opened to the riches of the Tanach and to analysis of the commentaries, as well as to modern ideas and scholars.

Professor Chana Safrai notes the urgent need for a teacher like Nehama in those turbulent times, when the Holocaust and mass immigrations had unraveled the traditional Jewish cultural fabric. Many had been deprived of Jewish education, and this threatened future generations. Safrai: "Nehama stepped into this society which had no books, no teachers, no study habits, no culture, with her little sheets and, a page a week, began sprinkling a little Rashi, a little Ramban, a few verses – but on a mass scale. Her work paved the way for the Bnei Akiva yeshivot, which in turn marked the gradual reestablishment of solid Jewish education. For this I think she deserves not the Israel Prize but the Nobel Prize."

Through her teaching, worksheets, and regular radio appearances, Nehama became a central figure for the entire *Yishuv* (Jewish residents of Palestine). A friend remarked: "Nehama, you encompass us from all sides – with your worksheets, on the radio, everywhere!" On one occasion her radio appearance was particularly dramatic.[4] The British Mandate permitted the Jews three hours of radio time daily, including half an hour for a chapter from Tanach with a brief explanation by various guests. Nehama took her turn one day in early February 1948, just after a shocking incident had occurred:

> There was already fighting in Jerusalem. They warned me the day before at Kol Yisrael to be careful of stray bullets. I came to Kol Yisrael thinking about the *Palestine Post* printing presses – today's *Jerusalem Post* – that had been bombed at dawn that morning.[5]

---

[3] Nehama taught that Torah learning must encompass all ages and levels of understanding. See Reiner and Peerless, *Haggadat*, 14; see also Reiner and Peerless, *Studies*, 39.
[4] The following is based on Rochwarger, "Words," 65–73, and on Nehama's own memory of the event recorded in the article "Nehama Herself" (see bibliography).
[5] "Nehama Herself."

At this point, when telling over this story, Nehama would lower her voice, adding that everyone knew that the British were the guilty party, though they denied it and nothing was ever proven.[6] The editors of the *Post* were determined to go to press, and mustered the resources to publish a special edition, in which they declared:

> The truth is louder than TNT and burns brighter than the flames of arson. It will win in the end. Last night's bomb smashed machinery.... It is surprising what some men will do to destroy truth. The tyrant... the fool... have tried to suppress the truth since history began; and tried vainly. They are still at their monstrous folly.[7]

Joy Rochwarger recalls that as Nehama told this part of the story, she

> sat back, folded her hands on her lap, and with a smile tugging at the corners of her mouth asked me if I could guess which chapter the radio station had asked her to read on the very same day. It was Jeremiah, Chapter 36.[8]

Nehama explained the background to the chapter she was teaching as follows:

> The section preceding describes how the King Jehoiakim grew rich off the people, built his own palace without concern for the nation, without justice. He exploited the workers. Instead of improving the society he involved himself in foreign wars. The prophet Jeremiah protests this corruption. And is thrown into prison.[9]

After these events, in Chapter 36, Jeremiah writes a scroll containing all of God's words of warning for the king. The king, however, scornfully burns it, so God commands the prophet:

> 28: Take again another scroll, and write in it all the former words that were in the first scroll, which Jehoiakim the king of Judah has burned.
>
> 29: Say to Jehoiakim the king of Judah: Thus says the Lord: You have burned this scroll, saying, Why have you written therein that the king of Babylon shall certainly come and destroy this land, and shall cause to cease from thence man and beast?

---

[6] Rochwarger, "Words," 73.
[7] From *Front Page Israel: The Jerusalem Post*, (Jerusalem, Israel, Fifth Edition, 1994), Monday, February 2, 1948. Quoted in Rochwarger, "Words," 72.
[8] Rochwarger, "Words," 73.
[9] "Nehama Herself."

Nehama explained to all the radio listeners that the words in the first scroll represented the truth, which in his ignorance, Jehoiakim thought he could expunge by the act of destroying the parchment. She added:

> In every period there are those who try to suppress the truth. If they don't want to hear something they burn it. But it doesn't help. The truth can't be suppressed. For God told Jeremiah to take a new scroll and write everything that had been on the first.

She continued quickly, before anyone could stop her:

> It won't help them to burn *megillot* [scrolls], and it won't help them to burn printing presses, or to bomb newspaper offices, for the truth will come to light. The Jewish right to Israel is a truth.[10]

Later Nehama received many congratulatory phone calls and letters and was stopped in the street by people proud that she had stood up to the British.

Teaching during Israel's War of Independence was challenging, especially during the six-month siege of Jerusalem, of which Nehama spoke frequently. With no petrol to be had, she arrived at her classes panting after the forty-minute walk from Kiryat Moshe to Bayit Vegan, having sometimes even dropped to the ground to avoid shells launched by the Arabs from Nebi Samuel. Nehama maintained strong ties with the kibbutz pioneers in the Gush Etzion bloc, harking back to the mid-1940s, when the pioneers had not yet moved to the Gush Etzion area and were still living in Kefar ha-Roeh and Petah Tikva. Some members of this group, called "the Masuot Group," had been her students in Jerusalem, and many filled out her worksheets. During the siege of 1948, a plane arrived regularly bearing bundles of Nehama's *gilyonot* amongst the regular mail. Nehama was one of the few lecturers who came to Gush Etzion whenever invited, despite the inconvenience of traveling by truck and sleeping overnight at the kibbutz. This close contact caused her to be terribly grieved when kibbutz Kfar Etzion fell to the Arabs, with great loss of life. She always retained a soft spot both for this group of kibbutzniks, who subsequently set up the Masuot Yitzhak kibbutz near Ashkelon, and for the area of Gush Etzion.

Indeed, Nehama held strong ties with the religious kibbutz movement as a whole.[11] Many of her most devoted correspondents lived on religious kibbutzim, including the students whose requests had initially created the

---

[10] "Nehama Herself."
[11] Nehama's brother, Yeshayahu, had great influence on the movement in its early years. See chapter 23 n. 22.

gilyonot project. She knew a lot of the kibbutz members well, read the kibbutz journals and was active in the *Ha-Po'el ha-Mizrahi* movement from which the religious kibbutz movement sprang, although not politically. Nehama and her husband spent many Passover holidays in Kibbutz Ein Tzurim in the company of prominent members of those circles. In turn, kibbutzniks often stopped by the Leibowitz home when they came to Jerusalem.

Nehama taught in all weathers and in all locations in Israel. She traveled to towns, kibbutzim, moshavim and army outposts, in buses, cars, taxis, and even planes to the farther North or South. She thereby fulfilled her own wordplay on the verse (Psalms 55:16):

> We took sweet counsel together, and walked to the house of God in company.

The Hebrew word for "company" is *ragesh,* and Nehama used to say: "We go to the house of God in *ragesh* – which stands for *ruah* (wind), *geshem* (rain) and *sheleg* (snow)." Neither concern for her safety or time nor physical discomfort were factors in these trips. She experienced it as a calling; this was her contribution to Israel. Someone once expressed astonishment that Nehama had traveled all the way to Kiryat Shemonah and back in one day simply in order to teach a lesson. She responded that this was her way of encouraging the people there after a terrorist incident had occurred. Even in her old age, she journeyed long distances – for instance to Safed once a month between 1977 and 1979 as part of a Gesher initiative to strengthen the local population. The truth was that she enjoyed traveling. For her, the time spent sitting in a vehicle was far from wasted, and often passed in stimulating conversation. Thus it is typical that R. Mordechai Breuer writes during a discussion of Nehama's approach to biblical criticism,

> Once Nehama encountered my son in a taxi.[12]

Some people even purposely offered to drive her to and from engagements, aiming for quality time with her, or wishing to witness the famous taxi driver stories in the making.

When Nehama taught in absorption centers for new immigrants, she encouraged them to tell their stories, prompting them to begin, "Where we come from in…." She rose to the challenge of teaching in Hebrew to newcomers by explaining in various languages such as German and French, or pronouncing English words in various ways until recognition dawned.

---

[12] Breuer, "*Yahasah*," 12.

Nehama at Machon Gold Seminary, circa 1950's. Courtesy of Ruth Ben Meir.

End-of-year photograph from Givat Washington, 1956.
Top row: Yonah Ben-Sasson (*second from left*), Meir Weiss (*fourth from left*),
Dov Rappel (*middle*), Nehama Leibowitz (*third from right*).
Fourth row, third from right: Shimon Kalfa. Courtesy of Gabi Weiss.

Nehama gradually became a well-known figure. People were attracted by the combination of diverse elements she presented: halachic commitment, depth of study, diversity of intellectual sources and expertise in Jewish sources. These qualities, combined with her magnetic personality and the novelty of her gender, made her a unique teacher on the Israeli scene, and people began streaming from near and far to hear her. For example, a kibbutznik from the Jordan Valley would arrive in Jerusalem at 4:00 AM for his fish business and then attend her class afterwards. Although many people came to hear Nehama out of curiosity – her suspicion that she was a "tourist attraction" was correct – she was not one of those charismatic speakers whose novelty wears thin after a while. On the contrary, friends and neighbors returned repeatedly, knowing they would always learn something valuable. Nehama taught in so many frameworks that some people ended up studying with her at several different points in their lives, separated by years or decades. One such student, Shimon Kalfa, says: "It was always the same Nehama each time. The same method, the same pathos." For her part, although she taught in so many places, Nehama was often able to recall the topic she had taught a given group in years past.

Her lectures generated their own publicity; little advertising was needed. Her reputation and personal connections – many of her former students worked in education – kept the teaching invitations rolling in. Unable to accede to all of the requests, she often sent her disciple, Leah Frankel, to teach in her stead. When Frankel passed away at a young age,[13] Nehama asked Professor Rivka Horwitz to substitute for her. Horwitz, however, soon discovered that people wanted Nehama and no one else would do.

Growing requests by individuals to study with her led Nehama to create new classes in her home. One such class on didactic methods, conducted twice a week to a closed group, gradually evolved into an intimate meeting with a family-like atmosphere, and if someone was absent Nehama phoned to inquire as to his or her welfare. The class, named *Amitei Tzion* ("Comrades of Zion"), ran for approximately two decades, from the mid-seventies until her death. Together they studied the books of Genesis, Exodus and Numbers, and also a course on the commentator Ibn Ezra. Nehama loved this class. She asked for no payment and could not resist inviting higher-level students to join, even after the class was full. This weekly lesson took on a great significance in the lives of the participants, and one of the reasons that R. Nachum Amsel made *aliyah* was in order to return to it. For R. Amsel, an added bonus was the expertise of the participants, an eclectic mix of

---

[13] Nehama dedicated her book *Iyunim hadashim be-Sefer Shemot* to her.

yeshivah students, educators, and – in Nehama's words – "two very interesting Russians."[14] All were highly educated and some knew the Tanach by heart – although, R. Amsel hastens to add, Nehama *knew* it better. The classes were lively, with much debate. The students, drawing upon long years studying with Nehama, challenged her using her own quotes, and she often allowed the participants to steer the discussion. Joy Rochwarger, who joined relatively late, describes her experience in this class:

> Nehama was then eighty-three years old. I was the youngest student there and definitely the least knowledgeable. Most of the other participants were either Israeli or had been living in Israel and studying with Nehama for many years, which put me at a distinct disadvantage. In addition, Nehama's style of teaching was different from any I had ever experienced.[15]

Nehama also particularly enjoyed teaching yeshivah students. They tended to have extensive knowledge yet few exegetical skills, which she was able to supplement for them. In the late 1960s, a group of Americans studying in the Mercaz ha-Rav Yeshivah in Kiryat Moshe expressed interest in learning with Nehama. Since she refused to "conduct a subversive movement in her home," they were forced to ask for special permission from their Rosh Yeshivah, R. Zvi Yehudah Kook. He responded: "On the contrary, it is not only permissible but praiseworthy!" Nehama was pleased with this approval and liked to quote it. In stark contrast, when she similarly ordered a student from an ultra-Orthodox yeshivah to inform his rosh yeshivah, he never returned.

Students from English-speaking countries especially were drawn to Nehama, and she developed many rich and enduring connections with this population. In the 1950s, there were few Diaspora students in Israeli yeshivot. Slowly more and more one-year programs and summer courses for educators and rabbis sprang up, and the Jewish Agency employed Nehama to teach on several of them. Word spread, and before long some teachers from abroad began conditioning their attendance of programs upon Nehama's presence.[16] This popularity derived, no doubt, from the fact that she was an excellent teacher, broadly educated, sophisticated and genuine. Despite never having left Israel since her mid-twenties, she was far from provincial in her thinking. Her interest in Tanach stretched beyond narrow

---

[14] Letter to Ahituv.
[15] Rochwarger, "Words," 57.
[16] Hamiel, "*Leibowitz*," 578, and Hamiel, "*Morat.*" The Jewish Agency also published many of her articles.

Nehama with students. Courtesy of Mira Ofran.

land-of-Israel aspects, to general ethical and spiritual messages that suited Diaspora Jewish identity.[17] She in turn liked the English-speaking population – perhaps for their more open and cosmopolitan approach; or perchance simply for their politeness. As Nehama liked to joke, Rebecca's gracious offer ("drink, my lord!") when encountering Abraham's thirsty servant proved that "she's not from Israel!"[18]

Academia

From the mid-1950s, Nehama's academic career flourished. It began at Bar-Ilan University, where she lectured in Tanach and in literature, and taught a class in the teaching of literature and of essay-writing. Her passion for the latter stemmed from her desire that students learn to express themselves coherently and use language well;[19] and only writing that stood up to strict logic and meticulous criticism was admissible. Her literature lessons, on the other hand, were much more flexible and intuitive, emphasizing emotional elements. Professor Dov Landau, her student and later himself a professor of literature at Bar-Ilan, says: "Nehama was one of the influences that helped me to understand literature in a deeper and more human way."

Starting in 1957, Nehama also lectured at Tel Aviv University, teaching "Approaches in Bible Exegesis" in the Bible department and "Methods of Bible Teaching in High Schools" in the Education department. In 1968 she was granted a professorship in Bible Education. Friends felt insulted on her behalf that she had not received her professorship in Bible proper, since education was taken less seriously. Professor Moshe Ahrend even made pointed remarks in a number of forums along the lines of "Cannot great intellectual and spiritual personalities become professors of humanities? Are professors to be only those who know something about one narrow field of research?" But Nehama was not doing the kind of research that the Tel Aviv

---

[17] David Ohana suggests that Nehama implements universal Jewish exegesis in contrast with the extreme localized approach of the Israeli "Canaanites" ("*Parashat Noah: Nimrod bein Nehama Leibowitz le-Yitzhak Danziger*," in *Hogim ba-parashah*, edited by Naftali Rothenberg, 31). See also Schoneveld: "In marked contrast to this religious-Zionist approach to the Abraham narrative stands Nehama Leibowitz's treatment of these stories.... It is significant that, when she comes to deal with the motif of the land, she sees fit to quote a Midrash that denounces an attitude of usurpation towards the land.... With regard to the story of the purchase of the Cave of Machpelah, Leibowitz rejects the favorite Zionist interpretation which Jacobson had also made" (*The Bible*, 158).

[18] From her column in the *Yediot* newspaper, weekly portion of *Hayyei Sarah*, November 8, 1990, reprinted in *PN*, 524.

[19] See further in her article "*Hadracha be-ketivat hibburim*," originally in *Hed ha-Hinuch* 10 (5696): Folio 11–13, 318–321, reprinted in *PN*, 625–630.

Bible department, heavily oriented towards biblical criticism and scientific data, would have required, so Bible Education remained her official field.

She also developed longstanding connections with the Hebrew University of Jerusalem. In 1956 she became a faculty member in its Department for Elementary Education. She also taught in the overseas program from 1955 until close to her death. She was assisted in this from 1973 onwards by R. Ben Hollander, who prepared small groups of her students in tutorials, so as to raise the quality of class participation. Though completely voluntary, these tutorials were well-attended as students felt the need for proper preparation. Nehama was the beneficiary of the Hebrew University's Katz Prize for the Study of Adult Education (1955), which allowed her the leeway to try out various methods on adult populations around the country, and to share her conclusions with others in the field (*PN*, 14). Several other prizes were awarded to Nehama, most notably the prestigious Israel Prize in Education in 1956, honoring "a scholar or writer whose overall life's work constitutes an exceptional contribution to progress in his/her field, or to the advancement of Israeli culture." The judges remarked that Nehama's "own character as a teacher – her dedication, modesty and integrity – may serve as a model to all."[20] In 1981 she also received the Judith Lieberman Award "for promotion of Torah knowledge and of biblical interpretation throughout the Diaspora, for unique dedication to studying and teaching, and for her contribution to Bible comprehension unrivalled in recent generations" (*PN*, 15). Professor Saul Lieberman wrote to her:

> There is none in our generation, man or woman, who has contributed to Jewish education as you have. You have merited having your Torah permeate into all sectors of the people, to an unsurpassed extent. (*PN*, 21)

Other prizes included in 1982, the Bialik Prize for Jewish Literature and Thought (Municipality of Tel-Aviv-Jaffa);[21] in 1986, the Samuel Rothberg Prize "for unprecedented success in the promotion of Torah study, for its advancement, and creating great interest in it amongst the Jewish people";

---

[20] Amit, "Hebrew Bible," 12. The full text of the judges' decision can be found in Nissenbaum, Booklet, 3.
[21] The explanation by the awarding panel is an excellent summary of Nehama's achievements. She is cited for her enlightening work with commentaries, her realization of the work of Jewish thinkers through her own original viewpoint, her aesthetic-literary analysis of the Tanach, her popularization of the commentaries and her sophisticated methodology (see Nissenbaum, Booklet, 4.)

and in 1988, the Prize of the Minister for Religious Affairs. Nehama also received an honorary doctorate from Bar Ilan University in 1983.

Starting in the early 1980s, Nehama taught for the Israeli correspondence college, the Open University.[22] She began as a guest teacher for the course *The Early Monarchy in Israel*. Avraham Nissenbaum explains: "Wanting to include some traditional interpretation in the course, I invited Nehama to come teach a lesson, which she based on her *gilyonot* for the books of Samuel." Nissenbaum subsequently asked her to design a full course on Bible interpretation, but Nehama said that she would rather cover one commentator in depth. Thus her course on Rashi's exegetical method was born. To help her with the academic writing required for the course textbook, she enlisted her friend Moshe Ahrend, then head of the Bar Ilan University School of Education, who espoused her method and mindset.[23] The resulting book, *Perush Rashi la-Torah: iyunim be-shitato*, represents Nehama's most systematic work. While her worksheets and *Studies* focused on specific topics and textual segments, in this book she analyzed Rashi's entire commentary and method. It was the first time anywhere in the world that an academic work on Rashi had been taught as a university course.

Although Nehama did not actually teach this course – it was, and still is, taught by Avraham Nissenbaum – she remained involved for many years. This contrasted with most course compilers for the Open University, who readily relinquished both ownership and interest as soon as they were done writing. With characteristic humility, she even thanked Nissenbaum warmly for the opportunity to stay involved. Periodically, she inquired how many had registered, from which parts of Israel they hailed, if they were kibbutzniks or city dwellers, soldiers or teachers, and how well they did in the final exam. She also requested to teach the first class of each course, which she devoted to the nature of interpretation, opening with: "What is the difference between a dictionary and a commentary?" This turned out to be such a riveting lecture that the students requested another session with her at the end of the course. Hundreds of students came to these lectures, not only those enrolled in her course but also others attending out of pure interest. Nehama was delighted with the challenge of teaching secular people and with the freshness and enthusiasm of these large audiences. She spoke

---

[22] Nissenbaum, Booklet, 21.

[23] The extent to which Ahrend's thinking was congruous with Nehama's may be seen in Aryeh Newman's review of Ahrend's book, "Fundamentals of Bible Teaching," in *Leela* 28 (September 1989): 47–48. Almost everything written there of Ahrend could be said of Nehama, such as his attitude to the biblical heroes and to *peshat* and *derash*.

each time for four hours straight, yet still leaving her audience eager for more.

Ordinary life

This middle section of Nehama's life also represents the bulk of her married life. It was not all easy sailing – Lipman's illness steadily worsened to the point where he became blind, and the couple were never blessed with children. Nevertheless, the years when Nehama lived in the house in Kiryat Moshe with her husband were filled with bustle and joy. Come Shabbat, the house filled with local intellectuals – Nehama's neighbor Professor Yonah Ben-Sasson, her brother Yeshayahu and others – who gathered for passionate discussions on many subjects.

Nehama's husband, whom she sometimes called affectionately "Yonteleh," was, like his brother, Nehama's father, a businessman by profession, yet also very educated in Jewish subjects. He was a man of both wisdom and humor and had a more easy-going and patient personality than either Nehama or Yeshayahu. But he was confident in his opinions, possessing the Leibowitz keenness of mind and interest in many topics, and sharing his family's love for Tanach quizzes. He invented rhyming quizzes with jellybean prizes for the children and set Tanach quizzes for the kibbutzniks when the couple stayed on kibbutzim over festivals. He even authored collections of rhyming riddles and poems on Tanach, under the pen-name *Lif-Lei* (for *Lip*man *Lei*bowitz).[24] Lipman loved Jewish texts. Once, after attending a mediocre concert of Bach cantatas based on Psalms, he turned to Nehama and remarked, "Well, the words were wonderful!" (Nehama told this story when about to teach some kibbutzniks who had heard her many times before, saying, "You know my tune and are tired of it – but read the text of the Torah! How beautiful it is!")

The couple's relationship was one of love, respect, and mutual appreciation. Despite her many obligations, Nehama remained devoted to her husband. Lipman was an invalid for many years, and since Nehama was out teaching most of the day, she paid yeshivah students, often from the nearby Mercaz ha-Rav yeshivah, to make him supper and learn some Talmud with him. Lipman loved Talmud, and it was unavailable in Braille script. His familiarity with segments of Talmud by heart, shared by many from a Lithuanian background, came in useful in these sessions. One of these yeshivah students, Moshe Oren, recalls his year of looking after Lipman in 1954 as a wonderful experience: "This was a man who lived the

---

[24] Hamiel, "*Leibowitz*," 572–573; Ahrend, interview.

155

Gemara, who lived the world of the Sages." Oren notes that he never heard Lipman complain once. "He did seem to have a certain sadness to him, but he never said anything about it. In fact, he was always expressing interest in me and my doings." Sometimes, Nehama would return early, and eat together with them. Lipman would inquire "Nehamaleh, what are you teaching this evening?" and offer his comments. Their conversations were generally about intellectual topics: art, music, literature, etc. She also enjoyed recounting her day for him, and valued his feedback and advice above all. He helped her improve her teaching by paying attention to the details, pointing to inaccuracies, and guiding her towards further sources of information. He was an influential force in Nehama's life, and encouraged her to write down her work.[25] When speaking of him to others, she frequently referred to his great learning. She said she owed much of her knowledge of Talmud and Midrash to him, though he was "a terrible teacher." She spoke little of their difficulties, sharing only with her close friends and students the hardship of her husband's deterioration. She once said that the day Lipman woke up and could not see anything was a cruel one.[26]

Lipman passed away in May 1970. The next week, Nehama wrote on her worksheet, "I did not send a sheet last week because I was in mourning."[27] His death was very hard on Nehama. She afterwards mentioned him constantly in conversation, recalling what he had said and gathering recollections of him from those who had spent time with him in the house such as her housekeeper, Tzipora Ofri. Although, with typical forbearance, Nehama stifled her sadness even at home, Ofri sensed that she never completely recovered; a kernel of pain had formed inside her. She now lacked someone with whom to share all the questions and knowledge that her day had brought, and had lost her *hevrutah* (study partner). She dedicated her Hebrew *Va-yikra* volume of the *Studies* series as follows:

> In memory of my husband, Yedidyah Lipman, may he rest in peace, from whom I gleaned most of my Torah, and especially all the halachic material. I did not merit to have him witness the completion of this book on *Va-yikra* that contains so many of his words. (*IHBV*, inside cover)

---

[25] See introduction to N. Leibowitz, *Lilmod u-le-lamed Tanach*, Eliner Library, WZO, Department for Torah and Culture in the Diaspora, 1995. This was published in English as *Torah Insights*, but in a different order and with slight differences.
[26] Reported by Simi Peters.
[27] Worksheet for *Be-hukkotai*, 5730.

Lipman Leibowitz, Jerusalem, circa 1930's. Courtesy of Mira Ofran.

Nehama and Lipman at home in Kiryat Moshe. Courtesy of Mira Ofran.

As R. Yaakov Koppel Reinitz points out, typically, rather than writing "*he* did not merit to see this book," Nehama expressed her own loss of his value. She also dedicated the *Bamidbar* volume to Lipman, writing that "much of his wisdom permeates this book."[28]

After Lipman's death Nehama moved to Romema, to Ha-Tzvi Street. Located behind the Central Bus Station, it was a convenient address for a frequent traveler like her. Never a stay-at-home type, it now became all the more important for her to get out as much as possible, "to flee loneliness, the empty house."[29] She began spending a lot of time in Kibbutz Lavi even before its hotel was built, including most of Passover and parts of the summer. Being with the kibbutz families was a balm to her after the loss of her husband, providing a domestic atmosphere, the company of children, and a comfortable *bet midrash* in which to spend hours reading and learning.

---

[28] *IBBM*, inside cover.
[29] Letter to Posen, *PN*, 670. For full quote, see pages 565–566 below.

CHAPTER 7

NEHAMA THE TEACHER: HEAVEN ON EARTH

Teaching as a calling

R. CHAIM WEINER SAYS, "Nehama taught me the true responsibility of being a teacher. Teaching is not a job, it's a calling. If you are able to do it, you have no right to turn from it."

Nehama took her profession very seriously. Without traveling abroad she managed to keep up to date with the world of education. When her student, Marsha Frank, mentioned a desire to teach English, Nehama was able to immediately inform her of a recently-launched English teaching program in America. She believed in obtaining degrees in education, but mostly for the teacher's own confidence. She did not use her own titles, insisting she was just a "teacher." She would say, "What do you want from me? I'm just a *melamed!*" Yet she also declared that of all honors and titles, none was more honorable than "*melamed.*"[1] She thus liberated this title from its frequent connotation of an underpaid drudge.[2] Nehama rejected the insulting maxim, "Those who can, do. Those who can't, teach." On the contrary, she wanted as many talented and capable individuals as possible to flock to the teaching profession. It distressed her to see good teachers being promoted into executive positions, out of daily contact with pupils. She herself never accepted a position as an educational supervisor or policy maker, but remained in the classroom.[3] Even as a professor at Tel Aviv University, she was first and foremost a teacher.[4] In her speech upon receiving her honorary doctorate from Bar-Ilan University, Nehama

---

[1] Hamiel, "*Morat.*"

[2] R. Soloveitchik similarly referred to himself as a *melamed*, yet also believed it an honorable title; for the Almighty Himself is referred to in the morning blessings as "the teacher of Torah to His people Israel." Teaching Torah is thus a fulfillment of the commandment of *imitatio Dei*, walking in God's ways (Jeffrey Saks, "Melamdim and Mehankhim – Who Are We?" *Leela* [51]: June 2001, 49.)

[3] However, she did serve in an advisory capacity to various departments connected with the matriculation examinations.

[4] Ahrend, "*Mi-toch,*" 31.

commented with deliberate ingenuity, "It's nice that for once this honor is being given to a teacher!" She went on to observe how hard it had become to get teachers, and to hope that this honor would encourage people to teach. She ended by quoting a Midrash that states that teachers go straight to heaven because they have more than their fair share of hell on earth. "But," she added roguishly, "this is one of the few times I disagree with the Sages, because I think that teachers have more than their fair share of heaven on earth!"

Nehama went far beyond the call of duty, working at all hours of the day and night. Besides her regular classes and lectures, she had many one-time engagements. Then, coming home after a long day, she still had her "homework" to do, namely checking the *gilyonot*, which she did until the small hours. After a few hours' sleep she got up again to another packed day. Sometimes it proved too much; and then her worksheet correspondents received their checked sheets after a delay of weeks or months with a note of apology from an overburdened Nehama.[5]

Her phone constantly rang with queries from around the world regarding the meaning of a passage or a difficult commentary. She always answered the phone, even during her own lessons, though then she might ask the caller to ring again, proceeding to pick up exactly where she had left off. Hurried, whispered calls came in from Moscow. People phoned at midnight or later – rumor has it that someone once telephoned at three AM. Nehama patiently answered these inquiries, though sometimes added, "May I ask why you are calling so late?" One person excused himself with: "Tomorrow I have my son's *brit* [circumcision] and I have to have something to say!" Another explained that he worked all day, only getting to the worksheets at these hours. She spoke enthusiastically of this caller: "Look how incredible *Am Yisrael* are, studying after an entire day's work! *Nu*, can you get angry at a Jew who gives up sleep to study Torah?" She had similar reactions when people fell asleep in her *shiurim*, praising them for coming despite their busy lives.

People also came to ask questions in person. Nehama told fondly of the carpenter who turned up at her house half an hour before Shabbat, breathlessly requesting an explanation for a difficult Ramban for a *shiur* based on her *gilyonot* that he planned to give the next day to a group of workers.[6] She was willing to go to great lengths to help someone with an answer. A man once approached her in her later years, while she was vacationing at a hotel during Sukkot, to ask her why the festival of Sukkot is

---

[5] Sheleg, "*Keter*," 9.
[6] N. Leibowitz, "*Ahavat*," 465.

mentioned in two separate sections in Leviticus 23. She promised to find out, and as soon as he left, turned to R. Yitshak Reiner and asked him to drive her to her home. There, after leafing through a book, she cried, "Here is the answer! Now we can return to the hotel!"[7]

On top of all this, Nehama volunteered hundreds of hours helping students prepare lesson plans, serving as mentor and first port of call for all sorts of difficulties. David Bedein recalls:

> Many years ago... I asked Nehama for advice about preparing the Tanach curriculum at a Jewish summer camp in the US. She asked me to meet her right away. I thought that a busy lecturer and author like this would not have the time for such things, but Nehama spent the better part of four hours helping me create a curriculum that transformed what might have been a bunch of boring lectures into an interactive Torah theatre for children, and the kids loved it.[8]

Even when a schoolchild wrote asking for help with a Tanach project, she made sure to pass this on to one of her students, and quoted the required sources impromptu.

Nehama demonstrated the importance of the trait of patience in a teacher. What appears to give immediate results is not necessarily the best method, since "education is a gradual process" (*SD*, 190). The Torah itself teaches this, she explained, by reforming people step by step, taking into account their human frailties.[9] Success can only be measured over time;[10] and in the meantime, there is the great satisfaction of the work. Nehama perceived special beauty in the classroom moments when all were focused and engaged. These could be times of intense debate over a verse, the students excited, eyes lit up and hands waving; or, in moments of silent concentration, bent over their books deep in thought, alone with the text; or even when the teacher

> pours out his soul to the class. No one argues or debates, they listen to the teacher, and there is a spiritual elevation.[11]

---

[7] Yitshak Reiner, *Mo'adei Nehama*, Eliner Library, WZO, Department for Torah and Culture in the Diaspora, 2005, 90.

[8] David Bedein, "Goodbye, Nehama," http://israelbehindthenews.com/Apr–14.htm #Nechama.

[9] *IBD*, 184, footnote there, and see likewise R. Kook's vision of gradual advancement (*IHBS*, 301, n. 9, and page 129 above).

[10] Ahrend, "*Mi-toch*," 48.

[11] *TI*, 147. Nehama qualifies this last mode – probably due to its risk of frontal lecturing – by writing that it "may not be allowed in excess."

Nehama and students. *Bottom row, from left*: Nehama Leibowitz, Naphtali Unterberg. *Second row, from left*: Yaakov Eliash, Baruch Tenebaum, Matityahu Olshin. Courtesy of Mira Ofran.

Nehama teaching Genesis 15:6. Courtesy of Mira Ofran.

Societal change through teaching

Nehama was of the old breed of German Mizrachi Zionists. One prominent example of this group was Dr. Joseph Burg, who tended towards a liberal perspective religiously and politically. But her affiliation with Mizrachi remained social, and she assiduously avoided the political side of things. Though she felt strongly about many issues, she was no crusader, and joined no causes or movements, at most expressing her approval. Although she at times discussed politics – and which Israeli citizen does not? – she mostly abstained from this topic, especially in her public life. Perhaps, as Yehudit Barashi suggests, this was because politics was the one question for which Nehama had no solution. She preferred the enduring values of the Torah over the ever-shifting agendas of parties and ideologies, which frequently constituted obstacles in the service of God:

> Not only are graven images and all physical objects of sight prohibited to us as deities, but our mortal desires, too, the "isms," slogans, ideologies, programmes and manifestos produced by the human mind. If we deify them, we take the Lord's name in vain.[12]

Nehama believed that a learning institution should not become involved with politics, even when these are connected to Zionism and Israel. She herself educated towards Zionist values in a non-political way. Her classroom was devoted to pure Torah learning, as Dr. Avivah Zornberg notes:

> There was nothing remotely political or vulgar about her teaching.... One did not think of her as a pioneer of any "ism;" you just learned from her.[13]

The few mentions of politics in her writings are negative ones. She identifies within the antics of Korah, the arch-demagogue of the Torah, elements recognizable in rabble-rousers until this day.[14] She cites R. Isaac Arama's intimate knowledge of

> the intrigues and tensions of court life and corruptions of office (*NSB*, 517),

---

[12] *NSS*, 331; see also *ibid*. 321, quoted on page 534.

[13] Dr. Avivah Zornberg, quoted in Uriel Heilman, "A Passion for Teaching," *Jerusalem Post*, April 18, 1997, 13.

[14] *SBM*, 189, *IBBM*, 209; and see there also for her in-depth analysis of these elements and of Korah's skewed arguments against Moses and Aaron. See further "*Kohah shel demagogia*," in *PN*, 597–601.

and also Don Isaac Abravanel's hatred of politics and public office (*NSB*, 21.) Hosea, she notes, rebukes Israel for the "political sins" of

> exaggerated militarism and respect for physical might alone.[15]

Nehama lacked faith in politicians, commenting in a letter to Professor S.H. Bergman:

> We can find callousness amongst political party leaders of all the parties, even the ones close to me; but not amongst our lofty rabbis whose sole intention was to teach the knowledge of God. (*PN*, 661)

In place of activism or politics, Nehama worked to shape fledgling Israeli society through the medium of teaching. She was not afraid to introduce social comment into her Torah lessons, not sparing even the institutions employing her. Once, teaching at a predominantly Ashkenazi school, she came to the verse recounting how the Egyptians "became weary of Israel" (Exodus 1:12), whose physical proximity made them a thorn in the Egyptians' side. Nehama gave a humoristic example: "Queen Nefertiti went to the theater, and discovered in the seat next to her – Mrs. Rabinowitz!"[16] She added that the modern version of this phenomenon would be when Ashkenazi and Sephardic Jews cannot tolerate each other's presence – a broad hint to her disapproval of the school's policy of segregation from Sephardic Jews.

Most of Nehama's influence was achieved not through explicit remarks, though, but rather subtly and over time. She was an excellent example of societal transformation through educational means alone. For her, Torah was in no way separate from life. Teaching Torah meant teaching correct living to a generation that needed it more than ever. In this, she followed a long line of Jewish commentators who, as interpreters of the Torah's message, were

> deeply conscious of the timeless quality of the Holy Writ, ever able to convey comfort, a warning or a summons particularly appropriate to their own generation. (*SD*, 51)

Nehama also saw herself as bearing this burden of moral and spiritual leadership for her peers.[17] This, she believed, is the duty of a public figure:

> The few can turn the scales and save the place if the righteous individuals concerned are "within the city," playing a prominent part in

---

[15] *SD*, 366 and see Menahem Ben-Sasson, "*Ha-teshuvah*," 367.

[16] Reiner and Peerless, *Haggadat*, 83.

[17] See Yedgar, "*Bein*," 72, "*Ha-iyunim*," 22. For more, see chapter 16. In "*Ha-iyunim*" 21, Yedgar quotes Nehama's view of Abravanel as just such a leader.

public life and exerting their influence in its many fields of activity. (*NSB*, 185–186)

However, unlike many of these commentators, and indeed most other outstanding Jewish teachers of her own time who were rabbis, heads of yeshivahs, professors or political leaders, Nehama influenced thousands without ever heading any institution or party. Thus her life is a lesson in the power of one individual to shape the world.

CHAPTER 8

NEHAMA'S PEDAGOGICAL METHODS:
"THE *GRANDE DAME* OF BIBLE TEACHING"

> Watching Nehama in the classroom was like seeing Yehudi
> Menuhin on the violin.
>
> – Yehudit Ilan

Introduction

NEHAMA WAS THE IDEAL educator in the eyes of many. Professor Michael
Rosenak, a leading philosopher of Jewish education, dubbed her "The
Grande Dame of Bible teaching."[1] She was so versatile that she could teach
complete beginners or university professors, kindergarten children or the
most sophisticated of adults. Everything about Nehama was educational,
down to her very gestures and body movements. "Everything about her
instructed and edified, as in the verse 'All my bones shall speak,'"[2] says Haim
Hamiel. "Those who only listened to her on the radio were missing out."
Her skill derived not from formal pedagogical training, of which she had had
very little,[3] but from fine intuitions. In the introduction to *Lilmod u-le-lelamed
Tanach*, she writes:

> This book, a collection of articles written over a span of several decades
> of teaching in the Holy Land, is not primarily the result of reading
> scholarly books about pedagogical methods and general didactic
> techniques. For this reason, it lacks a bibliography, and footnotes and
> references are few. It is entirely the product of actual teaching
> experience, findings drawn from the lessons I taught pupils, seminar

---

[1] Rosenak, *Tree*, ix. But Mira Ofran suggests that Nehama's methodology is applicable to
teaching of any subject ("*Le-ha'ahiv et ha-limmud: 'shitat Nehama' – be-chol ha-miktzo'ot*," in *PN*,
407 and *passim*).
[2] Psalms 35:10. This phrase is often used to represent the totality of an experience, done with
the entire body.
[3] Ahrend does note some principles that Nehama learned from educational theory ("*Mi-toch*,"
37). Frankel demonstrates the similarities between Nehama's methods and those of Johann
Pestalozzi, a Swiss educator whose work was popular in Germany (see Frankel, *Toratah*,
chapter 2).

students, teachers young and old, teachers from Israel and the Diaspora, university students and Kollel students.

She also writes:

> All these lessons were given once or several times in class during the past years and are, therefore, the fruits of experience and not of imagination.[4]

By her own account Nehama spent the first decades of her life creating her material and teaching it. Only later on did she begin to assemble it more methodically, prompted by Lipman:

> My husband of blessed memory, to whom I habitually recounted the events of my work in schools, encouraged me to write down my findings.[5]

This was fortunate for the world of teaching. Although Nehama denied having a coherent pedagogical theory, saying, "Well, I can teach you a few *trickim* (tricks)," in truth, she had invented a successful didactic approach from a combination of classical Jewish and modern academic materials.[6] She outlined parts of her approach in various writings. While in the worksheets and *Studies* Nehama rarely addressed the teacher directly and her pedagogy had to be teased out,[7] the *Alonei Hadracha*, the teachers' guides accompanying the worksheets, were explicitly pedagogical. She also published several articles and volumes aimed at Tanach teachers. While several were devoted to systematic outlines of methodology and pedagogical philosophy,[8] generally she preferred to focus on examples, interweaving her educational recommendations between them. An article by Nehama appeared in every volume of the first Israeli pedagogical collection, *Ma'ayanot*, produced by Haim Hamiel from 1952 onwards, alongside articles by the finest educational minds of the time such as Professors E.E. Urbach, Jacob Katz and Haim

---

[4] N. Leibowitz, "Active Learning," ix.
[5] Introduction to *Lilmod u-le-lamed Tanach*.
[6] Yedgar, "*Bein*," 79.
[7] Marla Frankel has probed these writings to reveal Nehama's instructional theory in them. See all of her articles.
[8] See, for example, "*Keitzad lamadnu Torah im mefarshim*," in *PN*, 471–473, and "*Keitzad anu lomdim Tanach?*"in *PN*, 475–484; "*He'arot metodiyot le-limmud Humash im mefarshim be-veit sefer tichoni*" (first printed in *Hed Hahinuch* 15 (1–3): 13–16 and (4–5): 58–60 (5741); reprinted in *PN*, 485–494); Nehama's brief introduction to LP; also "The Haftarah of the Second Day of New Year" (TI, 59–92) and "Tanakh for Advanced Students" (TI, 143–162).

Zvi Enoch;[9] and for an extended period she was the only woman writing there.

However, although it was possible to pick up many teaching skills from Nehama's written lesson plans and worksheets, those who saw her in practice were enriched tenfold. Dr. Ruth Ben-Meir: "It was a holistic experience, involving the mind, sentiment, and imagination." Nehama's enthusiasm did not come through on paper – it had to be seen. It was not a pedagogical method or act. Erella Yedgar recalls, for example, the day she was greeted by a delighted Nehama, who had discovered, at the National Library, a small pamphlet of commentary that solved a question she had puzzled over for forty years.

The following gives a further taste of what made Nehama's teaching unique.[10]

Preparation and condensation

Good preparation was a key factor in Nehama's teaching. "It was part of her respect for the students," observes Nurit Fried (VLN). She planned very thoroughly for her classes, sitting in the National Library for hours even if she had given the lesson many times already. It did not matter if it was for one student or one hundred. However, the material prepared need not all be crammed into the lesson. Refraining from trying to teach too much is just as important for good teaching:

> The teacher has to decide what to leave out and what topics should not be touched, because it is pointless to tackle a number of different topics and problems superficially or incidentally in a chapter. It is preferable to concentrate on just a few topics, but in depth. (TI, 22)

> We would not even want to introduce all these items in the study of just one portion, even if we had unlimited time... they would tend to swamp each other.... Choose just a few. (TI, 92)

---

[9] Enoch also taught at the Youth Aliyah seminars. He and Nehama were considered the educational luminaries of the time. He too espoused active learning (PN, 653), but focused on informal education and adopted more distance in teaching than Nehama did. Nehama praises him in her letters to R. Nathaniel Helfgot (PN, 662, 663). Hamiel notes that today Nehama is better known by far because Enoch taught technique, and to a narrow population of teachers; while Nehama taught Torah, and to all comers (interview).

[10] For further information see To Study and to Teach: The Methodology of Nechama Leibowitz, by Shmuel Peerless, especially his two model lessons – on teaching a legal section and a narrative section of the Torah (117–144 and 145–161 respectively). Nehama's teaching techniques are also summarized in Yitzhak Resler, "Hora'at ha-mikra al pi gishat Professor Nehama Leibowitz," Talelei Orot 5 (5754): 291–300.

Nehama warned also against overloading too many commentaries for comparison into one lesson (*LP*, 215). It was a higher priority for her that the students have enough time to work out the answers for themselves and discuss the issue than that more information be packed in.

It was also a mark of her confidence that she did not feel the need to show off her tremendous knowledge each time. In fact, students were often oblivious to how much she had left out. R. Nachum Amsel once mentioned to Nehama an obscure talmudic point relating to her lesson, and was surprised to discover that she knew the quote and had simply chosen not to bring it up in class. In general, she recommended only including material that there was time to explain properly, and especially if the language was difficult; otherwise the class would get bogged down and nothing would be learned (*LP*, 163, 203). Correct grammar, though of the utmost importance, must not be allowed to make a lesson dry and technical:

> In our *Studies*, we do not generally go overboard in explicating words. The study of the weekly portion – indeed all Torah study – must absolutely not become the study of language, grammar and philology… these are always meant to serve the subject matter. They are a means and never an end in themselves. (*IBD*, 336)

> There is no study more boring and self-defeating, liable to cause students to hate the Scriptures, than studying a whole row of "difficult words," dictionary style, without the pupil knowing what purpose they serve in the text. (*TI*, 67)

However, the teacher must beware of going to the other extreme, including exciting material at the expense of basic information.[11] As usual, a balance was necessary.

Thorough preparation also meant that Nehama was equipped to deal with students who tried to contradict her using extra sources. Furthermore, it provided backup material for adding new dimensions when teaching the same class again. Although she did not repeat lessons within the same year (for, especially in a school setting, teaching the same topic for too long or too many times makes pupils "fed up" [*TI*, 22]), any student hearing her over a span of years would notice some favorite classes cropping up again and again. Nehama allowed herself to linger on a favored topic for several weeks, even in a course which was supposed to advance with the weekly Torah portion. Some of the lessons she liked most included the story of the servant and Rebecca, Moses killing the Egyptian, Moses at the burning bush, "Do

---

[11] *LP*, 189. See also the second page of the introduction in *LP* and page 3, where she suggests excluding methodological examples that are not directly on the topic.

not take revenge and bear a grudge," the breaking of the two tablets with the *Meshech Hochmah*'s commentary,[12] the topic of Amalek, and the two and a half tribes.[13] She also particularly favored the book of Jeremiah.

Nehama's advice in preparing a Tanach lesson reflected the above two practices of preparation and condensation:[14] First, she recommended, study the material thoroughly, ignoring the fact that you are planning to teach it. Read it repeatedly, moving from a general impression to the particulars. Once this is done, decide what to select from all the available material, based on the age-group and time constraints. Search for the type of text that will best engage the students' attention, for not every text easily lends itself to analysis.[15] Finally, work out the best methods to engage the students and to activate them in the lesson:

> When you are preparing, the question is not "How can I transmit to them the substance and ideas that are now in my mind?" Ask yourself instead, "How can I prepare and lead them, so that they themselves should express that which needs to be said?" (*TI*, 65)

Nehama's classroom

The following is an attempt to reproduce at least some of the dynamic experience that was Nehama's lesson.

The lesson would commence with Nehama asking for quiet; only when there was complete silence would she begin. To a new group of students, she presented the following rules: "Bring a Tanach to every class, do not chew gum, ask lots of questions, and call me Nehama." Otherwise, the lesson began by introducing the text in hand, then following this up with a question on the text or commentaries, which led in to the rest of the class. Nehama's classes almost always revolved around at least one of her *gilyonot* (and

---

[12] *NSS*, 612–614. See pages 317–318, 536 below.

[13] R. Yitshak Reiner, having examined Nehama's worksheets and books, also notes the recurrence in her writings of the stories of Cain and Abel, the Tower of Babel and the *Akedah*; discussion of the phrase "*al tira*" and the revelation of the Divine presence; and themes such as civilizing the world, the centrality of Eretz Yisrael, vegetarianism and idolatry. He points out that she seems to use every opportunity to write on a favorite theme even if she has already dealt with it previously in her works, for example mentioning the theme of civilizing the world in her *Studies in Bereshit*, *Vayikra* and *Bamidbar*.

[14] The following is based on *TI*, 53–54 and Mira Ofran, "*Le-ha'ahiv*, 409.

[15] According to Peerless (*To Study*, 15–16), the types of text Nehama selected tended to be ones that (a) allow comparison with other texts; (b) contain textual difficulties, (c) exhibit unique biblical literary style; and (d) contain a significant educational message. She selected Midrashim and commentaries that aided in understanding the text. Nehama herself outlines her recommended selection criteria in her essay "*He'arot metodiyot le-limmud Humash im mefarshim be-veit sefer tichoni.*"

sometimes three or four). She would march in carrying two shopping bags, one containing work handed in the previous week, corrected with her famous red pen, and the other, new *gilyonot* for the lesson or for homework. Part of the time was spent going over last week's homework, and she took this very seriously – anyone who had forgotten to do it could not stay.

Nehama was a strict and meticulous teacher. Her attention to minutiae expressed itself both in the content of the lesson – in the detailed reading of text; and also in its form – in thorough preparation, a highly personal approach and strict management of the particulars of the classroom. This, combined with her strong personality, her humor and her remarkable knowledge, created the experience of Nehama's class.

The personal dimension was crucial to her educational approach, for the lesson must be geared towards the students and so the teacher must invest effort in getting to know them. Many decades after Nehama left Marburg University, she still spoke with disapproval of one of the Jewish professors, who insultingly invited the Jewish students to his house in rotation, with no recognition of the individual. While detailed attention to every student proved impossible in lectures for several hundred people, in other forums Nehama took the time to at least go over the students' names, and might even mention someone's birthday in class. She recalled many of her students well, and knew when they had last attended, interrupting herself in the middle of class to exclaim joyfully to a student trying to sidle in unnoticed: "How are you? It's been such a long time!" R. Shlomo Riskin was particularly taken aback when he walked into Nehama's class after a hiatus of fifteen years, only to have her look up and ask calmly, "Riskin, what took you so long to make *aliyah?*" She even remembered students from her Open University course whom she had met only once, asking Avraham Nissenbaum, "Whatever happened to that student from kibbutz So-and-so?"

This level of awareness helped Nehama intuit who understood the lesson and who did not, even when the student remained completely silent. She could choose whom to turn to first for answers, based on her familiarity with the students:

> Permission to speak should first be given to the more superficial students, those who see the external and obvious. Let them make their contribution first, followed by the better students, and, finally, the penetrating ones who spot what the others have missed.[16]

---

[16] N. Leibowitz, "Active Learning," 3.

She often tailored her questions in terms of their difficulty, to challenge each student within his or her range.[17]

Nehama was an accessible teacher, and her pupils felt more comfortable turning to her for advice than to other members of staff. Her personal touch also enhanced the connections between the participants. This approach was not a pedagogical device, but an expression of her caring personality. As one student says, "You could not separate between Nehama the teacher and Nehama the person." Teaching was not just a job. As soon as she was introduced to her students she was in relationship with them, and the end of class did not signal the end of the connection. Much of the satisfaction Nehama gained came from the bond with her students. Whether they had studied with her for years or only briefly, many remained in contact with her for long afterwards. Even people who came to buy a set of *gilyonot* were ensnared by her charms. R. Elhanan Samet and his wife Bruriah, both Tanach teachers, had read Nehama's books and discovered that in order to buy *gilyonot* they must go to her house. True to form, Nehama started an animated conversation, and a fast friendship based on Torah topics was soon formed. The couple subsequently made biannual visits to Nehama, each one beginning at 8:00 PM and ending at 2:00 AM.

Indeed, Nehama's students visited at all times. "She would be very happy to see us and would cry, '*Kinderlach*, come in, come in, I'm so glad you came!'" recalls R. Hanan Schlesinger. Her house was especially full on Shabbat afternoons, and it was hard to catch her alone. How Nehama felt about these visits comes across in a lesson she frequently taught. The weekly portion of *Va-yera* begins (Genesis 18:1):

> And the Lord appeared to him [Abraham] in the plains of Mamre; and he sat in the tent door in the heat of the day.

Here God appears to Abraham, yet does not say or do anything. For what purpose did the Divine manifest itself? Rashi suggests that since Abraham, according to rabbinic interpretations, was recovering at that point from his circumcision, God came to visit the sick. Nehama would add in explanation that God came simply "to be" with Abraham, as an expression of relationship with him. Judy Klitsner: "I always felt that Nehama related to this sentiment very strongly, and was pleased when her students came 'just to be' with her. I thought I needed a reason to call or to come to her apartment, until I realized how much she encouraged visits for their own

---

[17] Professor Martin Lockshin cautions that this technique runs a risk of embarrassment and must be used carefully.

sake. This message came from Rashi, but was delivered frequently and convincingly by Nehama."

Nehama's relationship with her students was closer than most professor-student relationships. She functioned as a surrogate mother and grandmother to many. When her student Shaul Yedgar became engaged, Nehama teased his fiancée Erella, "Do you really need two mothers-in-law?" Students frequently wanted to include her in the important moments of their lives, and she was deluged with invitations to festive occasions. At her own urging, students brought their future spouses to meet her. They also took advice with her about relationships and their future; her childlessness did not detract from Nehama's ability to relate to family problems. There were even students who requested Nehama's presence in their most difficult moments, such as dangerous operations or during terminal illness. At these times Nehama spoke words of Torah, comfort and encouragement.

Nehama had a tremendous knack for making people feel close to her, and these people were frequently unaware how many others felt the same. R. Yitshak Reiner reports his shock at hearing, at a memorial evening for Nehama, sentences beginning "For me, Nehama was…" on everyone's lips. "I thought she was *my* Nehama!" he says. "But it was only then that I understood her true greatness. When she was with someone, she was one hundred percent with them. She was able to be a 'mother' to all these people." R. Schlesinger's eyes were likewise opened one Shabbat when he witnessed a constant stream of visitors, all of whom considered themselves her best friends. He observes: "My relationship with Nehama meant so much to me; it was unique for me, although she had literally hundreds of such friends. At the basis of all of these relationships was her voracious appetite to know, to learn. She wanted to know who you were and what you did, and why, and where."

Her warm approach extended to her worksheet correspondents, most of them strangers, and she penned personal comments to them on the sheets. This led to amusing results in the case of Shimon bar Hama, who corresponded with her in the 1940s while serving in the army. Since his real address was classified, he chose the cover address: "Convalescent home, Ein ha-Shofet." The first time Nehama responded to this address, she wrote, "It's wonderful that people learn Torah even in convalescent homes." But as time passed and he continued to send his replies from this address, she became concerned and wrote: "Are you so ill, God forbid, that you need such an extended period of recovery?"[18]

---

[18] Cohn, "*Ma ahavti Toratecha,*" in *PN*, 25.

Nehama also wrote personal notes on exams. In this she prefigured the important experiment by Ellis Page (1958), who demonstrated that detailed, individualized feedback by teachers improves performance more than a numerical grade alone.

കം ൟ

At times Nehama's approach was perhaps even too attentive, as the latecomers who would fail miserably in their bid to creep in unseen discovered. She would stop the lesson, ask them if everything was all right, and even discuss their excuse in front of everyone before continuing. Bruriah Eisner comments that this strictness was not the result of any feeling of insult on Nehama's part, but was rather a pedagogical choice, punctuality being the basis for respect and fruitful study. Nehama even elevated punctuality to a moral imperative, stating: "Being late is a form of stealing."[19] Her unbending policy succeeded in its goal with a group of consistently late yeshivah students. Arriving one day to find the classroom entirely empty, she immediately called a taxi and went home. They never dared to be tardy again.[20]

It was once said in praise of Nehama that her only prerequisite was that the student want to learn.[21] But the student had to demonstrate this concretely by coming prepared to class, and Nehama refused to teach anyone who showed up without a Tanach.[22] She argued that sharing books prevents the student from looking at the text through his or her own eyes. She was astounded when people arrived empty-handed to a Tanach lesson, such as the kibbutzniks who proffered the feeble excuse, "Oh, we thought you were going to talk *about* the Tanach." Her reactions varied from silently waiting for the book to be procured, through commenting pointedly, "You know, this is a lesson in *Tanach*," to rebuking the miscreants at great length, or even demanding they leave the classroom. When two young yeshivah students admitted they had brought neither Tanachs nor notebooks, Nehama announced to the roomful of students, "It's the TV generation! They come to sit and watch!"

This strict policy also succeeded. People would run around frenziedly searching for Tanachs before class, terrified of Nehama's wrath (though at least one wily student got away with holding a prayer book instead). Once, a group of female students at Machon Gold played a trick on some visiting

---

19 Abramowitz, *Tales*, 57.
20 Aryeh Felheimer, "*Iyunei lashon ba-iyunim*," in *PN*, 308, n. 6.
21 Saul Lieberman, *PN*, 23.
22 Cohn, "*Ma ahavti*," 25.

male students from the Mercaz Ha-Rav yeshivah by deliberately omitting to warn them to bring Tanachs to Nehama's lesson. As a result, they spent the first fifteen minutes scrambling around while Nehama waited with folded arms.

Another principle in Nehama's class was that one was expected to have a basic understanding of the material. Dr. Rachel Salmon, a lecturer in English literature at Bar-Ilan University, recalls her first encounter with Nehama. She had arrived full of pleasant expectations for her first experience with classical Jewish studies:

> My anticipations proved short-lived. Nehama entered the classroom briskly – in the neat, dark, simple clothing she always wears, which makes a clear statement about her values – and got straight down to business. Each student was told to read a few verses aloud, and when my turn came – I don't think I pronounced one word correctly – I was told to leave the room. I soon had a companion. Nehama informed us that we could not rejoin the class until we had read the entire Torah, verse after verse, aloud to each other, and that we were not to attend any other lessons either until we completed the task. Permission was granted – if Nehama said so, it must be done. When we finally finished I returned to the class with trepidation. To my surprise, Nehama was warmly welcoming, encouraged me when I was near despair about ever being able to learn properly, and – in these long years – has never asked me to read aloud again.[23]

Other things that made Nehama impatient included students asking, "Which verse are we on?" or the presence of young children in her class, which she would not allow. The room's physical conditions were also important to her. She once said, "For my whole life I have prayed for two things – that I should see the State of Israel established, and that I should walk into a classroom and find a clean board, chalk and a board-eraser. The first one, thank God, has materialized, but I have yet to see the second fulfilled!"

Nehama's exacting control of her classroom, her self-assurance and her gestures all put her colleague R. Yaakov Koppel Reinitz in mind of Toscanini, the hot-tempered conductor who regularly threw his baton at musicians to make them play better. Nehama similarly always seemed to him on the verge of throwing her chalk at her students, although she never quite did. But, in contrast to Toscanini, Nehama's intimidating outbursts were

---

[23] Rachel Salmon, "Nehama Leibowitz, Scholar and Teacher," *Kol Emunah* (Spring 1987): 16.

most likely an educational device, designed to drum the message home. As she writes:

> Anger not prompted by selfish motives but by the desire to discipline one's household is not tantamount to idolatry. If a man wished merely to impress on the members of his household his shock and disappointment at their misconduct, in order to correct them, he is inspired by educational motives. (*NSS*, 610)

Also:

> Anger and bitter reproof should be deferred till the last possible moment, till there is no other alternative. (*NSB*, 341)

Professor Yaakov Kagan states: "It was feigned surprise and shock – all of it. She was in control, she wasn't the type to fly off the handle." Indeed, one incident illustrates this well. A group of tired Machon Gold students, returning from a field trip, were convinced by their teacher to go directly to Nehama's *shiur*. He assured them they were in for a treat, but when they walked in, Nehama discovered they had no Tanachs. She demanded loudly: "Did you come to look at my beautiful face?" and left the room. Outside, in her normal voice, she told the distressed teacher: "Don't worry. I'll wait here in the next room until they all bring their Tanachs, and then I'll come back."

Charade or not, it was not easy to digest. Some believe that Nehama was too blunt in the classroom and wasted time on trivial infractions. One person who was sent out of class for chewing gum was very annoyed and recalls: "It didn't teach me anything except not to sit at the front of the class!" Nehama's strictness even drove some people away. An older couple who turned up at Nehama's class at the Hebrew University without Tanachs, after Nehama's reprimand never returned. When the dean told her that that the couple had lodged a complaint, Nehama was upset and said she would have apologized that same day had she known. On another occasion, Nehama asked a student who she thought was chewing gum to leave. Informed that it was in fact medication and that the student was present against her doctor's advice, Nehama was pained by her mistake.

Joy Rochwarger once off-handedly remarked to Nehama that many people were frightened of her. Nehama was astonished – what was she doing to make students afraid? Her sole intention was to spark the will to learn and encourage incisive thinking. Nehama would say, "I'm one old woman and they are a hundred young people – and *they're* intimidated by *me*?!"

Her sensitivity brought Nehama to try to soften the effects of her forthright ways. After writing a frank letter to some young inquirers, she signed herself as follows, even underlining the last two words:

With blessings, writing to you with the best intentions.[24]

She would also sometimes say, "I don't understand" instead of the sterner "I don't approve." And once, she begged R. Reinitz not to pass her cutting remarks on to the authors of some articles she had been asked to read:

> I don't want any arguments or conflicts and, most of all, to cause pain to the authors who have invested so much effort – I'm sure [So-and-so] labored for several weeks and months on her article… and the questionable profit from my criticism will surely be eclipsed by the indisputable injury of the distress and disappointment I will cause. Perhaps even, God forbid, baseless hatred will ensue. (*PN*, 684)

Nonetheless, her basic approach was always to say what she thought and stick to it, and even in her old age she engaged in diatribes against people who came to class without a pen, lamenting the falling standards.

But some, far from being bothered by this, saw it as a lesson to all teachers of the importance of standards, both inside and outside the classroom. Dr. David Bernstein: "Her extreme stands were like a breath of fresh air. They made you think. She was a personal example of her views." Her seemingly pedantic behavior actually expressed caring for her students' welfare. Professor Yehudah Friedlander: "She kept us under tight rein. She didn't lecture from the podium, but rather walked about amongst the students, making remarks and drawing red lines on the answer sheets. A few years ago I met her and… told her that for every such red line I owed her profound thanks. Though she was very aggressive and made great demands, I am grateful, because her comments opened my eyes and got me thinking."[25] Simi Peters explains that Nehama came down hard only on students who opened their mouths without thinking: "Nehama could certainly get very testy and not suffer fools gladly, but it wasn't personal, promoting her ego at someone else's expense; it was a certain kind of integrity." R. Shmuel Klitsner agrees: "It was part of what a good pedagogue does. It wasn't a product of ego, so people didn't get insulted."

If Nehama did not coddle her students in the classroom, once outside it she often prodded people to grow, complimenting their strengths with reinforcing words such as "You're one of a kind." She also often accompanied her criticism with encouraging comments. R. Raphael Posen's

---

[24] N. Leibowitz, "*Teshuvah*," 623.
[25] Sheleg, "*Kalat*," 70 and Friedlander, interview.

first worksheet returned covered in corrections in red ink, and the remark: "Don't be put off by this *red stuff*!" She wrote to him again the next day: "Don't be alarmed by all the corrections!"[26] Nehama liked to foster independence and responsibility, and she took this attitude with everyone, not only her students. Once, when Nehama phoned Aryeh Felheimer at home, his little daughter answered and said that because she was only five she would not remember to tell her father that Nehama had called. "No," Nehama chided her gently, "you're a big girl and you *will* remember."

Nehama nurtured her students in other ways. For instance, she was willing to read their manuscripts, including books hundreds of pages in length – not skimming, but thoroughly reading and offering her critique. She guided inexperienced teachers through the tricks of the trade, still following their progress years later. She supported students and persuaded them to go on to study and teach. Friedlander always recalls how, after he had written a high school paper on Agnon, Nehama arranged for him to meet the famous writer; and her urging of R. Posen to study Onkelos influenced him greatly in that direction.[27] Rahel Sylvetsky writes:

> She happily gave me hours of advice while I was involved in various educational projects, and she encouraged me and even called me when I had some fateful decisions to make.[28]

This support could sometimes be quite forceful. R. Hershel Billet reports: "I have numerous books on Rashi and on the Targumim in my house because she made me buy them!" But she was also aware of the dangers of over-involvement in others' work.[29]

Methods

Some teachers are strong on methodology but weak on charisma, running orderly but dull classes. Others are highly charismatic but lack precision and structure in their teaching. Nehama was both exact and systematic, yet at the same time stimulating and dynamic. Despite her strictness and fixed basic format, her lesson was anything but dreary. The key was flexibility. She used varied aids to make the class interesting, appealing to different senses:

---

[26] Posen, *"Mehanechet."* The phrase she used was actually *"ha-adom ha-adom ha-zeh,"* a playful borrowing of the language of Esau's request to Jacob for some of that "red stuff," i.e., lentil pottage.

[27] Posen, *"Ha-targum,"* 110.

[28] Rahel Sylvetsky, *"Zichron la-holchim," Ha-Tzofeh,* May 14, 1997, 7.

[29] See her letter to Reinitz, *PN*, 676, where she writes, "And perhaps in the end it was best this way, that I did not intervene in your article; and it's good that that you wrote what you thought, without me specifying what I had intended."

> Remember that the success of the lesson depends on having plenty of class activities. (*TI*, 92)

> Classes in Tanakh should change their structure from time to time according to the material being studied, the needs of the class and the aim of the teacher. Not every chapter should be taught in the same way.... Do not stick to a single model. (*TI*, 22)

Nehama locates this approach in the Torah itself:

> The Torah was careful to utilize multiple means (optical, acoustic, practical, verbal) to make sure that we do not forget our past. (*PN*, 702)

When teaching difficult material such as later Prophets, which lacks plots, events and tales of heroism or failure, the teacher is especially in need of flexibility:

> The teacher needs to equip himself with a large number of instruction aids. The verse "When waging war, use good tactics" [Proverbs 20:18] applies equally to the battles of Torah, and particularly in the classroom! (*TI*, 40)

Hence, Nehama kept a veritable arsenal of methods up her sleeve to keep the classroom atmosphere lively. These included stories and anecdotes, humor, and drama.[30]

1. Stories

"The most important thing I learned from Nehama was the power of her stories to illustrate a point," recalls Nechama Tamler. "I'm sure she told those stories hundreds of times, but it never seemed like that."

As a child, Nehama had been a wonderful storyteller,[31] and as an adult she made the most of these talents, using both her own stories and those of others in her classroom. In every class she included some anecdote to elucidate a point in the text, often beginning, "Yesterday..." even when it had taken place years before, so that the students would experience it as fresh. As a skilled writer or artist does, she paid close attention to the ordinary events around her – on the bus, on the street and in the classroom – and to details that escape the notice of the majority. Perceiving deeper meanings in the most banal affairs, she saved them for her classes, where she linked them to the Torah subjects she taught. Newspaper articles, chance encounters, overheard conversations, her own adventures and mistakes – all were grist for the educational mill. Through her active imagination, this

---

[30] See *TI*, 92, for more detailed examples of various classroom techniques.
[31] Abramowitz, *Tales*, 27.

woman who had never traveled to wild corners of the world, spending much of her life in classrooms and libraries, was able to assemble a rich collection of personal anecdotes. To hear Nehama talk, one would think that every day of her life was full of adventure and drama – as indeed it was, for she made it so. Essentially, she applied her knack for finding the most interesting angles in the biblical text to people and events too.[32] The following passage says it all:

> Here there is no need to search for [God's] word in explicit texts or in heavenly voices, for the truly perceptive and understanding person catches the word of God in everyday occurrences, in current events and in the fate of individuals and peoples.[33]

Nehama's stories made complex issues simpler. A story could illustrate a difficult verse or commentary so that even beginners grasped the point. For example, when teaching the somewhat unclear directive (Leviticus 19:2) "You shall be holy," she told of the teacher who rebuked a teenage girl for behaving maliciously in the school yard. The girl exclaimed, "I didn't do anything wrong! What mitzvah did I violate?" The teacher replied, "The mitzvah of 'You shall be holy.'" Nehama then explained that the teacher was alluding to Ramban's interpretation that this is not a separate commandment, but rather a blanket injunction covering gray areas outside the letter of the law. Even in the absence of clear guidelines a person should behave according to a moral compass; this is holiness.

Nehama's stories, while not revealing much about her private life, did give the students a sense that they knew her better than they did many other teachers. Some of her stories concerned her own past students; participants in her classes little suspected that at the same time as they were learning from Nehama, she was learning from them, gathering raw material for future stories.

She drew her students in using language relevant to their reality. Her *Studies* contain Israeli slang and Yiddish idiom.[34] The American students from the Hebrew University were impressed by the metaphors from contemporary American society employed by this eighty-year-old Israeli woman, and were at times taken aback by elements of popular culture that

---

[32] It is interesting that Ben Zoma, who was perhaps the greatest interpreter of texts amongst the Sages (see Mishnah Sotah 9:16: "After Ben Zoma died, the expositors ceased") is also the one who said "Who is wise? He who learns from every person" (*Ethics of the Fathers* 4:1). Nehama, like Ben Zoma, possessed the talent of heightened intuition towards both texts and people.

[33] *IBB*, 174; compare *NSB*, 248.

[34] *IHBV*, 297, n. 3 and 429, n. 3; *NSV*, 551, n. 3.

Nehama teaching. Inscription reads: "In memory of the story 'Dust of the Land of Israel' [by S.Y. Agnon] from your student, David Prato, Grade 7a, Maaleh school, 10th February 1957." Courtesy of Mira Ofran.

Nehama sprang on them. She once quoted from the mafia blockbuster *The Godfather*, and when eyebrows were raised, said gleefully, "Yes, I've read some of that 'holy' book!"

At the same time, she was a living link to a bygone age. Through her these young Americans heard firsthand about the Beilis trial of 1911 and the siege at the founding of the State, with rations of five liters of water a day and yet no complaints while waiting on line. They heard of the terrible rainstorms of 1952, when immigrant children living in the *ma'abarah* transit dwellings were sent into the towns as their homes became mud – Nehama herself taught some of these Yemenite children. She also recalled the days when only two people in the city had telephones, and the sensational installation of the first traffic light in Jerusalem. For her students these were prehistoric times, but here was Nehama recounting them, clearly no dinosaur but rather a very much alive and fascinating first-hand reporter.

She also used others' stories when they were helpful, including novels, stories, poems. She mentioned John Steinbeck's *East of Eden*, in which the translation of the Hebrew word *"timshol"* plays a pivotal role. She recommended using a story by Shalom Aleichem, "The Penknife," about a little boy who steals a penknife and then, in his remorse, throws it down a well instead of returning it to its owner, to emphasize that the Torah demands the opposite behavior (*IBBM*, 60, n. 4). When Rochwarger wanted to study Jeremiah with her, Nehama did not turn to any of the classical biblical exegetes, nor to any of the Midrashim. Instead,

> after searching a back bookcase for a solid five minutes, she pulled out a small, well-worn book. She told me to sit down and listen carefully because she had a "story" to tell me. As Nehama began reading from the book, the characters were brought to life and I felt as if I was witnessing the events first-hand. The chapter from which she was reading was a modern literary rendering of Jeremiah 36, entitled *Va'ani kotev al ha-sefer be-diyo, o ha-pahad mi-penei ha-nisgav*, by D. Kimhi. Nehama's choice of reference was guided by her continual insistence that one must read and understand the text as if it were happening at that very moment.[35]

2. Humor

With all her erudition, Nehama had a lighter side, and her stories often had a humorous angle to them. This aspect was primarily expressed in person rather than in her writings. True, the careful reader of her *Studies* will

---

[35] Rochwarger, "Words," 64–65.

find a few lighthearted examples, for instance when she comically describes people entering a shop who "sniff around," (*NSV*, 549) or tells us that in German, the word "affe" means monkey (a play on the Hebrew for "nose"; *NSV*, 617) or remarks that when the Israelites were called to desist from their contributions to the Tabernacle, "this was perhaps the only fundraising campaign in our history which it was necessary to cut short" (*NSV*, 93). But for the most part her writings are very serious. As R. Amsel recalls, "Before I met Nehama I thought her style very dry and textual, but when I sat in her class she made it come to life. This eighty-year-old woman had the whole place cracking up. I learned more about teaching from that than from anything else."

Nehama felt that educators ought to overstate, exaggerate or put things across in a funny way in order to get the message across, like the Sage R. Judah ha-Nasi, who resorted to preposterous statements such as "One Israelite woman in Egypt gave birth to six hundred thousand children at once" to rouse his sleeping audience.[36] David Bedein writes:

> Who will ever forget Nehama's unique way of introducing the Joseph story: "Now what was that Jew-boy doing in the palace of a king, and how did he get there?"[37]

Nurit Fried still remembers her teacher's voice and smile as she acted out the Israelites' complaints after the miraculous crossing of the Red Sea: "*Mud over there – mud over here!*" (i.e., what have we gained?).

Nehama always had a quick comeback, thinking on her feet and moving the class along at a brisk pace. This, together with her entertaining stories, invigorated the lesson immensely. Walking into her classroom for the first time, one might imagine that a wrong turn had been taken – for this appeared to be a stand-up comedy show, where a diminutive woman in a beret, with an innocent, playful voice, kept an entire audience in fits of giggles, waves of laughter following her every sentence. Nehama's style proved a shock to those hailing from the far more serious yeshivah atmosphere, until they became used to the new approach and then grew to love it, realizing that the frivolous form held lofty content. She tossed in puns, one-liners, imitations and sidesplitting examples in the middle of important ethical messages or methodological points.

The following are some examples, although they lose much in Nehama's absence. The first is yet another of Nehama's famous taxi driver stories, one which she told repeatedly, about the book of Jonah, read on Yom Kippur

---

[36] *Shir ha-Shirim Rabbah* 1:64, 4:2; quoted in *TI*, 144.
[37] Bedein, "Goodbye Nechama."

afternoon in synagogue. Nehama loved the book of Jonah for its treatment of the psychology of repentance and its suggestion that every individual has a mission. She liked to describe it as a "mystery story."[38] Here is how Nehama told it:[39]

> You know, Eretz Yisrael is a wonderful country – you can travel around in a taxi and learn important things! I've learned a lot from taxi drivers. Two years ago, the day after Yom Kippur, I was in a taxi and the driver told me:
>
> "I'm so upset – I didn't sleep the whole of last night."
>
> "What's the matter? You ate too much?" I said.
>
> "No, that's not it," he said.
>
> "So why are you upset?"
>
> "I've been upset since *Minhah* time."
>
> I said, "Why, what happened?"
>
> He said, "Tell me, did He forgive them?"
>
> "Who?" I said.
>
> "What do you mean who? Nineveh? Who else?"
>
> "Yes, He forgave them."
>
> "Completely?"
>
> "Yes," I said.
>
> "Is that written? Is that written?" he demanded.
>
> "Yes!" I said.
>
> "Then why," said the driver, "does it say at the end of the book of Jonah, 'While I will not spare Nineveh, that great city'?"
>
> See that? Thousands of people sit through the reading of Jonah and what do they care? Nothing! They're busy looking at their watches and wondering when it's all going to be over, and hoping the cantor won't take too long over *Ne'ila*. But *he* listened to the *haftarah* and it pained him. He was right. The verse was not written with a question mark. So I said to him, "That's a good question."

---

[38] Quoted in Simi Peters, *Learning to Read Midrash*, Jerusalem: Urim Publications, 2004, 54. Peters explains there: "The story is characterized by so many critical gaps that it is nearly impossible to make sense of the narrative flow." For some of Nehama's teachings on the book of Jonah, see Reiner, *Mo'adei*, 362–379, based on two of her lessons.
[39] For a slightly longer version see Raphael Posen, "*Sofrim u-sefarim*," *Ha-Tzofeh*, March 30, 2007, 10.

And he thought and thought and then said, "Should I be reading it as a question?"

"Yes," I said.

"*Ohhhhh*," he said. "So it's a *good* thing!"

I was so impressed! Here was a person reading the Torah and actually caring what he was reading instead of sitting and thinking about who got called up to read the *haftarah* of Jonah![40]

The point of this story is that since punctuation is lacking in the Torah, the way in which we punctuate it is a form of interpretation.[41]

Nehama taught Rashi's comment on Exodus 5:1 "and the elders slipped away one by one," in the following fashion:

> Moses arrives in Egypt and sends a message to the seventy elders: "Come!" But only sixty-five of them show up – one is ill, one is abroad, one's wife is about to give birth, etc., etc. Next, when they hear the mission – to go to Pharaoh – ten more refuse. So they set out fifty-five. By the time they arrive at the palace there are only forty, and the imposing sight of Pharaoh's guards sends even more scurrying away. In short: When Moses and Aaron finally walk into the king's chamber, there is not a single elder left!

Here Nehama would remark that during the Mandate period, demonstrations took place against the British, with cries of "Free immigration! A Hebrew State!" "Then," she added, "we would walk towards the King David Hotel, the Mandate's headquarters; and if five hundred people had set out, by the time we got there, only a hundred remained."[42]

Nehama explained the concept of *genevat da'at* (acting under false pretenses) as follows: "It's like a woman in a shoe store. She's trying on shoes, making the salesman run around and bring her shoe after shoe – only to walk out empty-handed, never having planned to buy anything in the first

---

[40] Nehama spoke often of the problem that familiar material seems dull, with nothing new to offer, and especially that read in synagogue. In fact, she made it her business to teach this material in particular. See the introduction to *Shiurim be-firkei nehama u-ge'ula*.

[41] In another example of this, Cain, having been cursed by God, cries out (Genesis 4:13), "My sin is too great to bear!" It sounds as if he is repentant, but Rashi reads it as a question – a rhetorical one, closer to a petulant demand – "Is my sin then too great to bear?!" Nehama paraphrases Cain's plea in a mocking tone: "So what if I killed someone? Is that so bad?" She adds that of course verses cannot be turned into questions wholesale. Otherwise every verse in the Torah could be read as a question, and we would end up asking, "Love your neighbor as yourself??" (*LP*, 9).

[42] Yedgar, interview. Compare *NSS*, 88.

place. This is *genevat da'at*."[43] This in itself was a good illustration of the point; but Nehama's gift lay in adding humor, as she continued: "The other people in the store ask the salesman why he puts up with such a customer. The salesman explains, 'No one in this woman's home listens to her – her husband won't take out the garbage when she asks, the children ignore her. Here's the one place where she gets to tell someone what to do!'"

In the following excerpt from a letter to R. Reinitz, Nehama uses some amusing examples to drive home her critique of a scholarly article that used inconsistent categories:

> I've already told you on the phone – I was so perturbed that I couldn't restrain myself and so I attacked you from afar – that this [supposedly scholarly article] is a scandal and a disgrace! [What the author did] is comparable to sorting shirts in a textile factory as follows:
>
> 1. Cotton shirts
>
> 2. Woolen shirts
>
> 3. Newspaper advertisements for the factory's products
>
> 4. Nylon shirts
>
> All my life I have battled against this phenomenon in grades 9 and 10, until they grasp that you cannot describe three brothers by saying one is a redhead, the second studies in a yeshivah and the third is mentally unstable. And that if the first is a redhead, the second has no choice but to be blond or dark-haired. (*PN*, 683)

However, though she used it so frequently, Nehama rarely wrote about the uses of humor as a pedagogic tool or helped teachers to notice humorous dimensions. One exception was:

> It is worth pointing out to students the humor of the situation, according to this Midrash, where giants look down from a great height on tiny men walking among the vines looking like grasshoppers. (*TI*, 10)

3. Dramatics

Another use of story was to dramatize the narrative so that it would be truly experienced as a story. "Nehama was ahead of her time in dramatization of the Bible," remarks Yedgar. Rochwarger writes:

> Her unique pedagogic style consisted of bringing the text to life by placing the person within the context of the story, the time period, and

---

[43] See also *NSV*, 549–550 where she illustrates the concept of *ona'at devarim* with a similar example.

the historical circumstances.... When Nehama taught Torah, she was always telling a story. She was the "narrator" par excellence, knowing how to create a dialogue between the text and the student.... Nehama was able to transport me back to a distant time and place – sixth century B.C.E., Palestine... by infusing the text with the spirit of her voice and soul.[44]

A born actress, Nehama used her voice and her gestures to add color and depth to her teaching. Her observation about the Sages, who "clothe [a biblical story] in dramatic and pictorial form" (*SBM*, 273) could equally have been applied to herself. She advises:

> You might begin the lesson by reading [the text] to them, the changing tone of your voice conveying emotion (such as pain or joy, excitement or calm, fortitude or despair) indicated in the text, so as to impress them deeply with its contents and captivate their hearts even before it has entered their minds. (*TI*, 65)

> This great speech of Judah's should be read to the students at the beginning of the lesson, non-stop from start to finish without explanations. The dramatic and rhetorical power it contains will be experienced if the students hear it read proficiently and with emotion. (*LP*, 193)

One story Nehama liked to read in class was Bialik's "*Aleph-bet ben ha-shittin*," about his childhood in the *heder*. Employing great pathos, she enraptured the students with the story of the wayward child who, in order to break away from the teacher's discipline, created an imaginary society of his own. She also recommended getting the students to read the text dramatically themselves:

> Ask three pupils to read a line each [of Jeremiah 31:3–4]... and the whole class to read the fourth line together in chorus. This way they will not only understand the poetical repetition, but also see it with their eyes, sound it with their voices and hear it with their ears. Once their senses are gratified, they might also express the meaning of this repetition in conceptual terms. (*TI*, 73)

Well into her old age, Nehama not only stood for the duration of her lesson but walked around, using the classroom space as her theater. She marched up and down the length of the classroom several times to demonstrate the effort Rebecca made in drawing water for many camels. She got children to act too. Teaching a class of elementary-school children about Dathan and Abiram's defiance (Numbers 16:12), she asked a student who

---

44 Rochwarger, "Words," 61–65.

had lethargically read the verse to come to the front of the room and demonstrate it instead. This time he put his full effort into it, stamping his foot on the floor and shouting: "*Lo na'aleh!* (We will not come up!)"[45] She used dramatic techniques in order to create emotional identification with the text in ways that would be developed as progressive educational techniques decades later. For example, there is a scene in Genesis when Jacob's sons return from Egypt without their brother Simeon and then inform their father that they must take Benjamin back to Egypt. Jacob responds (Genesis 42:36):

> You have bereaved me of my children. Joseph is gone and Simeon is gone, and you will take Benjamin away. All these things are against me.

Here Nehama asked her students, "At whom do you think Jacob was looking when he said this sentence?" Suggestions were offered, each one a form of interpretation. Nehama's own view, which she mentioned at the end, was that he was looking at the floor. She employed similarly creative methods in teaching younger grades, drawing them into the subject matter.[46] Teaching the confession of Joseph's brothers (Genesis 42:21),

> But we are guilty concerning our brother, whose distress we saw when he pleaded with us and we did not listen.

she asked the children to write down what Joseph might have said as he was pleading. Stepping into Joseph's shoes, they came up with "Help, help!" "What will you tell Father?" and "See you in Egypt!"[47]

Another talent that Nehama shared with the best actors was the ability to take lines already declaimed a hundred times and make them seem fresh. Once, R. Amsel, convinced by Nehama's spirited manner that she was giving a particular lesson for the first time, happened to attend another of her courses in the same week. To his surprise, she taught the same material, word for word, with identical passion. Suspicious now, he opened her books and discovered the lesson printed there from years before. "From this I learned that a good teacher is excited every time. I was not taught this; I learned it by watching."

---

[45] Spiegelman, review of Peerless.
[46] Professor Moshe Sokolow notes that Nehama believed that children were capable of taking in more complex ideas than teachers gave them credit for. She liked to tell of the second-graders who, when asked, "Why did Joseph leave his garment in Potiphar's wife's hand and flee?" responded: "She wasn't his wife and that's yucky" and "He didn't want to be a male prostitute" ("*zon,*" creating a neologism). See Sokolow, "Re: Ethics and Parashat Shavua," Lookjed archives, November 29, 1999.
[47] This example, together with the previous two, seems to me to be an early foretaste of an interesting educational technique called Bibliodrama. For more, see pages 570–572 below.

Goals

Nehama had three goals in teaching: imparting knowledge, activating the students and transmitting love for the Torah.

First goal: Imparting knowledge

We have already mentioned Nehama's emphasis on teaching digestible chunks. In general, she believed in quality over quantity. She was against *bekiut*, the speedy accumulation of knowledge through superficial study. She was provoked by the mere mention of the Barkai method, in which children study the entire Tanach before reading any commentary or Midrash, asking rhetorically, "How can you teach the book of Job to sixth-graders?" R. Schlesinger: "She always said it didn't matter how much you knew, but rather to understand profoundly what you do know. When I poured out my sorrows to her, complaining about my late start in learning and the little Tanach I knew, she always comforted me, saying, 'It's not important, because you know how to learn, and what you do know you really know.'"

Hearing of a particular Tanach teacher who liked to test his students on tables packed with details, Nehama said: "I really can't feel enthusiastic about this – in any event they're going to forget everything!"[48] Indeed, one of her educational mantras was "Students never remember anything!" Students, she felt, care little for the fact that a lifetime's worth of concentrated knowledge and information is handed to them on a silver platter. If it does not interest them, it will not stick in their minds. Learning things by heart was useless; it would only lead to distaste for the material, as happened to Nehama as a girl:

> I remember long ago when I had to learn by heart an ode "Upon the ascension to the throne of the Empress Catherine," and subsequently lots of other odes, and how we repeated them and went over their stanzas and rhymes *ad nauseam* until they had lost all vitality and were utterly flat. (*KA*, 482)

The only recourse, therefore, is to devise strategies for students to discover the knowledge for themselves. Rather than teaching the Tanach as a mass of details, give the students exercises to carry out on the text. Let them internalize it, even at the price of learning fewer verses.[49] This brings us to her next goal:

---

[48] Ahrend, "*Mi-toch*," 40.
[49] N. Leibowitz, *Darkei ha-hora'ah shel Humash im mefarshim le-aliyat ha-no'ar ha-dati*, Jerusalem: Organization Committee for Youth Aliyah Counselors, 5701, 7.

Second goal: Activating the students[50]

In order to make sure that information is retained, the educator must nurture the skills for independent research and analysis.

> Most of all, [the student must] learn how to study when there is no teacher in front of him and there will no longer be any teachers either.[51]

For Nehama, Torah learning was about thinking and not learning by rote. She guided the student, through an interactive process, to explore a small quantity of material in depth. This method, now accepted in many educational theories, was already in ascendance in early twentieth-century Germany.[52] She writes:

> All the leading educators have reiterated time and again that a person does not learn by merely listening, by being spoon-fed. (TI, 65)

She held by the maxim: "In the nineteenth century, they said that the student speaks too much. In the twentieth century, they said that the teacher speaks too much." But she also claimed that, far from a twentieth-century invention, active learning appears in classic Jewish sources – for example, the sixth chapter of *Ethics of the Fathers*. This chapter is known as *Baraita Kinyan Torah*, as it discusses the elements necessary to attain Torah. Frontal teaching, Nehama noted, is only one of the numerous methods suggested:

> *Baraita Kinyan Torah* lists forty-eight means by which Torah is acquired, one of which is "listening." Only one out of forty-eight, yet in practice we tend to push all our Torah studies into that category, in the belief that Torah is acquired through listening exclusively.... But it's not that simple.... In the past few decades educationalists in various countries have carried out research and discovered that it is difficult for a student of any age to learn by listening alone. (TI, 143)

She then pointed out another of the forty-eight means to attain Torah, namely *pilpul talmidim*, analytical discussion by students. This one, claimed Nehama, represents active learning (TI, 144).

Elsewhere the Sages also urge that "the only learning that endures is that acquired through effort."[53] Passive learning, says Nehama, weakens the

---

[50] This topic appears throughout her pedagogic writings (see for example TI, 64). For some delightfully melodramatic descriptions of her classes in the Mizrachi seminar see KA *passim*. See also N. Leibowitz, "Active Learning" concerning how to make the study of history more interesting and fruitful.

[51] Letter to Aaronson, PN, 653.

[52] Nehama notes the similarity between modern methods and those of 1920s Germany and 1930s Palestine. See letter to Aaronson, PN, 653 and TI, 144, 145.

[53] *Kohelet Rabbah*, 2:12 and see further discussion in Ahrend, "*Mi-toch*," 36, n. 9.

muscles, saps the students' spiritual energy, and leads to drowsiness and sleep (*TI*, 143); and if the student is asleep, it is almost always the teacher's fault (*KA*, 475).

> In lectures people fall asleep. I studied at the Gymnasia. It was a terrible education. The teachers were boring. But I had two good teachers. One was a teacher in German Literature who could draw things from the students. That had a great influence on me. Here, in Israel, there was an outstanding Mishnah teacher – I would go to his lessons, and saw how he involved people, connected the Mishnah to the students' lives. He even brought items from the newspaper and applied it to the Mishnah.[54]

Active learning forces students to pay close attention to the texts, to experience familiar words from a fresh angle. Nehama warned against the all-too-common habit of skimming through the text and assuming that it has been understood. This leads to the dismissal of the Torah narratives as children's stories:

> Young people do not tend to see the greatness and depth in simplicity, in a text that avoids pathos... we need to teach them to read between the lines.... For this reason *Humash* should be taught with Rashi or the other commentaries, for this opening of eyes, decoding the hidden layers is the essence of their work.[55]

> Our young people who are used to great literature and to reading it hurriedly, interested only in the plot, who love to speed along... Rashi will stop them and force them to examine the language meticulously. [56]

The book of Genesis must be taught again in secondary school so that children will not remember it as a book of lovely stories about good and bad people;[57] for this is only the first layer of a multilayered text:

> The study of Tanakh is partly the study of a simple narrative in simple language, which does not call for extensive interpretation; and partly the study of complex texts in difficult language, requiring explanations and commentaries. (*TI*, 144)

Nehama's goal was to teach those who saw the first to see the second too.

---

[54] "Nehama herself." She may here have been referring to R. Yaakov Koppel Reinitz, her long-time correspondent and colleague, who created a methodology to teach Mishnah (see *Shma'atin* 15 [52]: 30–33). Nehama attended a lesson of his and was very impressed, urging him to invite her to every lesson he taught.
[55] N. Leibowitz, "*He'arot metodiyot le-limmud*," 485.
[56] N. Leibowitz, "*He'arot metodiyot le-limmud*," 486.
[57] *TI*, 21; see also *Darkei*, 1.

৵ ৶

Nehama listed five common practices from which teachers should refrain if they wish to avoid classroom passivity.[58]

1. Thou shalt not lecture.

Nehama refused invitations to lecture. When asked to speak at a girls' high school, she rejected all the topics suggested by the principal, explaining: "I cannot speak *about* this and I cannot speak *about* that, but if you want me to come and teach a simple Rashi I'd be happy to." Whenever she found herself compelled to give a lecture, she complained to her husband. He would try to reassure her that she was doing a good deed by preventing her audience from speaking *lashon ha-ra* (gossip) for over an hour![59]

Nehama believed that when the teacher talks too much it limits the interaction essential to learning. Even a highly charismatic lecturer will find, within a few weeks, the effect waning due to repetition, replaced by a "gentle sweet sleep" on the part of the students.[60] Accordingly she herself did not rely on her personal magnetism, but rather encouraged discussion, even with two hundred people in the room. With such a large group, she might first ask students to get into pairs, like the *hevrutah* of the traditional yeshivah world. This way they got to discuss the sources together before they were dealt with in the larger forum. Then she tried to encourage as many people to speak as possible. Ben-Meir, while listening to about twenty tapes of Nehama's lessons at the Ichud Shivat Zion synagogue in Tel Aviv, noticed something that she had generally overlooked as a participant – that Nehama never spoke for more than a couple of minutes consecutively. Instead, the group discussed the topic, while Nehama interspersed her comments. Ben-Meir: "I imagine this is how the talmudic Sages studied – with give and take, grappling together over questions."

In Nehama's classroom, students forgot that they were being educated, as the discussion flowed naturally from one person to another, like a conversation. There was no need to raise hands, firstly because everyone spoke freely, and secondly because Nehama fired questions at whoever she

---

[58] The following is based on Peerless, *To Study*, 13–14, but with some changes and expansions based on additional material as cited.

[59] Letter to Reinitz, *PN*, 682, and Reinitz, interview. Reinitz adds that the audience make up for it afterwards with all their comments about the lecturer!

[60] N. Leibowitz, "Active Learning," 5, n. 3. Jon Bloomberg, in his introduction to the translation of this article, writes: "It is my view that Professor Leibowitz's strong condemnation of the frontal lecture method is too extreme" (iv).

chose – and especially at those who had been sitting silent for too long. She explained this practice as follows:

> Such silence presses heavily upon the heart of the teacher! Why are they silent, these ones? Because are still undecided?... [or] bored? Who knows? Best to turn to them and pull them in by force: "And what's your opinion?" (*KA*, 477)

Nehama loved the give-and-take of her class discussions, and was frustrated when her students were inhibited by their awe of her. This tended to be truer of Diaspora students than their more audacious Israeli counterparts, and she would urge their teachers, "You have to tell them not to be afraid of me!"

In encouraging discussions, Nehama was exploiting the innate human tendency towards conflict:

> If students love a good argument, let us encourage them to argue about Torah. They will learn how to debate using sound arguments... and – by means of the arguing they love – they will develop a love of learning. (*TI*, 145)

Against those who would criticize this position, she wrote:

> Some may complain that this will encourage disputes and factionalism, from an excess of which we are already suffering. On the contrary, this proves the point! Since this loathsome tendency already bedevils the world at large and has certainly infected our students, and since we are unable to remove it, let us drag it into the *beit ha-midrash* and purify it. The Talmud advocates utilising the world's evils to do good: "Someone who has been born under the sign of Mars should become a bloodletter, a butcher or a mohel." (*TI*, 145)

This technique allowed those with little Jewish background to study Tanach on an equal footing, since they could argue based solely on what they learned in class (*TI*, 148).

2) Thou shalt not allow students to write while the teacher is speaking.

In Nehama's class, students could note something down occasionally, but the common practice of automatically writing everything the teacher says was not acceptable. Nehama would scold: "What are you writing notes for? You're not going to look at them anyway. It's all written already in my books, and better than you could ever phrase it. If you're writing, you're not thinking!" She felt that a person could always, having effectively absorbed the information, transcribe it afterwards if necessary.

Nehama lecturing on the topic of Moses at Beit Pevsner, Haifa, 1983.
Courtesy of Mira Ofran.

3) Thou shalt not ask factual and rhetorical questions.

Nehama deliberately challenged students to overcome obstacles in studying and understanding the material (*PN*, 654). Her basic pedagogic tool was the question – both student questions ("It is more important to train a student to ask his own questions than to give him your answers" [*TI*, 75 n. 15]) and teacher questions.

Students' questions must be treated with the utmost seriousness. She explained that the main difference between the Wise Child and the Wicked Child in the Passover Haggadah was that the Wise Child asks a question, as it is written, "And when your son *asks* you…" (Deuteronomy 6:20), whereas the Wicked Child declares his position – "And it shall come to pass, when your children *say* to you…" (Exodus 12:26). No matter how brazen the question, as long as the student is asking and looking for an answer, he or she is not a Wicked Child.[61] Elsewhere she laments:

> How rare [genuine questions are] in the adult world! Most of the inquirers are entirely uninterested in the answer![62]

Student questions can provide an excellent springboard for class discussion. Nehama explained, with a twinkle in her eye, that she had a great strategy for dealing with difficult questions – to turn to the class and say, "Well, class, what do *you* think?" Joking aside, she repeatedly used this technique to start a good discussion, and it worked well.

However, if questions are not forthcoming from the students, then the teacher needs to ask some in order to stir up thought processes and bring the students to see the difficulties for themselves. Even history lessons should begin with a question.[63] The teacher must at all costs avoid launching into a lecture before having made the students care about the material. "People should not be offered solutions before they are aware of the problem!" she declared (*TI*, 23), and "We teachers appear, all too often, as someone trying mightily to solve a great problem for a friend while the friend doesn't feel it is problematic at all."[64] R. Hollander: "Rabbis are fond of announcing, 'We have a very rich heritage!' but Nehama didn't do that; she would ask questions and let you discover it for yourself."

---

[61] See *NSS*, 208; Reiner and Peerless, *Studies*, 38 and *Haggadat*, 48; and also *IHBV*, 119 ("It is not the Wicked Child who asks here 'What is [the meaning of] this work to you?'").
[62] Letter to Posen, *PN*, 669.
[63] N. Leibowitz, "Active Learning," 1. History is a subject particularly prone to passive learning (*ibid.*, vii).
[64] N. Leibowitz, "Active Learning," 1.

The teacher should not rush to reply after asking a question. Instead, it should be left hanging until the text has been thoroughly studied (*TI*, 3). A well-chosen question serves to focus the lesson, to dictate the choice of commentaries brought, and to give a framework for looking at the answers and deciding their validity.[65] Nehama built entire lessons around her famous question, "What's bothering Rashi?"[66] Already back in the 1930s, Nehama was criticizing teachers who only wanted to hear the "correct" answer, their questions merely a manipulative device. Rather than extracting answers from the students, such a teacher is using questions to deposit the desirable answers into their mouths; and the only thing the students learn is how to expertly guess what the teacher wants to hear, "like a mechanical echo of the teacher."[67] In contrast, the use of compelling questions gradually moves students away from looking for the "right" answer and towards generating their own. Hence, Nehama avoided questions whose answer was obvious from the context. The teacher's questions had to be real questions, containing genuine ambiguities and several possible valid answers; thought-provoking questions that made for a lively lesson, not rhetorical-factual ones sounding its death-knell (*TI*, 145).

Nehama noted that students need to be trained to do the work to answer these questions, and to be encouraged to look beyond the spitback answers they are used to. R. Hollander recounts that when Nehama asked, "What did Joseph say while he was down in the pit?" her pupils would reply, "We don't know; the verse doesn't tell us!" She then retorted: "If it did, I wouldn't be asking you!"

If possible, though, questions should not be spoon-fed to a class. Students must learn to ask on their own. Nehama writes:

> It is not the teacher who asks and provokes, but rather the text. (*PN*, 654)

She illustrated this point by telling of the time when she began a class by reading out several problematic – even outrageous – verses. She sat back, but instead of the expected storm of protestations she was greeted with stony silence. Perplexed, she demanded: "Don't you have anything to say?" Came the reply, "You haven't asked us anything yet!" "I think this is very common," she later remarked (*PN*, 654). She writes:

---

[65] Yedgar, "*Ha-iyunim*," 28.

[66] Avigdor Bonchek, "*Darko shel Rashi bi-ferush milim mukarot ba-Torah, le-fi gishatah shel Nehama*," in *PN*, 143.

[67] N. Leibowitz, "Active Learning," viii–ix.

> It is not a good sign if the students do not ask this question and the teacher instead has to prod them into it. (*LP*, 65)

> If the students do not ask this question, this indicates that they have not got used to the idea of raising problems on their own, but simply try to answer those raised by others. (*TI*, 15)

4) Thou shalt limit the types of activities and questions used.

The teacher must vary the methodologies or the lesson will become routine. For this reason, Nehama was against workbooks, which required the same methodology lesson after lesson. Students should even be invited to choose the particular technique themselves every now and then. The teacher can ask, "What would be the best way to understand the text at this point?" and hopefully receive answers such as "Let's go back to chapter so-and-so" or "Let's look in the commentaries," and so on (*PN*, 655).

5) Thou shalt not give introductions.

Introductory lessons are seen as *de rigueur* in many educational frameworks. Nehama agreed that one cannot simply jump into the material cold, but she rejected the usual type of introduction as rather tedious. Hence, in her book on Rashi, the historical background appears at the end instead of as the more standard first chapter.[68] She recommended that, rather than reeling off introductory information, the teacher set an assignment obliging students to read the chapter carefully and think about it. This assignment might be to designate a title to the piece, to find a key verse, or to imagine the text as a play, answering questions such as:

> How many set changes are there in this play?

> Who is the main character?

> In what tone of voice does a certain character speak?

> Where do the speakers' words begin and end?[69]

She also recommended asking them to rewrite a reported conversation in direct speech (*TI*, 28). One of her favorite exercises was dividing the text into a specified number of categories or subsections, giving each one a definition. She discovered that students' attempts to divide the Ten Commandments into first two categories and then three invariably produced several different answers.[70] For the portion of *Ki Tetze*, students had to allocate its numerous commandments according to headings such as "In the

---

[68] This also stemmed from her dislike of historical material. See pages 461–469 below.
[69] Peerless, *To Study*, 17–22 and *TI*, 66.
[70] Peerless, *To Study*, 21–22. See also *NSS*, 343.

shop," "In the bedroom," "On the road." This helped them to organize the material in their heads.[71]

The answers to these exercises were almost irrelevant. It was the act of looking that was key (*TI*, 66–67). Nehama would give out an exercise: Read the chapter and give it a title. After a few minutes she would say, "Actually, your title is not important – the main thing is that you've read the chapter!'" Her aim was to make students examine the text closely, but in an enjoyable and challenging way that would help them to remember it better. To do this, the tasks must have a conceptual component. Setting a mechanical task, such as "Locate each verse containing fourteen words," would be pointless.

Nehama found this technique particularly useful when studying difficult texts that required several readings to be understood, as it avoided the boredom of repetitive re-readings. It could also work as a more focused homework assignment, since the traditional instructions "Write an essay on the topic of…" are too vague and invite meaningless waffle (*PN*, 683).

Much of Nehama's pedagogical approach tied in to this goal of active learning, and this was what made her courses so demanding. Students who took her class at the Hebrew University as an "easy option" soon discovered their error. One admits: "I came out of the first class with a migraine. It was very taxing. But she stunned us with her whole demeanor." Nehama did everything she could to conquer the "in-one-ear-and-out-the-other" syndrome. And she succeeded; through her, complete beginners in Tanach came to understand and own the chapters and verses they learned with her, such that even years later it was still familiar territory for them.

No one was allowed to audit Nehama's class. All participants were required to work and might be picked upon at random with a demand such as, "You! Please explain to me – what's bothering Rashi?" Professor Carmi Horowitz, dean of Touro College, discovered this when he dropped in on the first day of Nehama's Touro class to see how it was going, when she suddenly gestured at him and demanded to know what he had to say on the topic. However, picking on students in this fashion requires great confidence on the part of the teacher, and there is a risk of student resentment. Rochwarger: "I was always anxious that Nehama might call on me. Having witnessed the discomfiture of others who had not conformed to Nehama's concept of the correct answer, I strategically established my seat out of her range of vision!" Even this strategy did not always work. Nehama informed

---

[71] For another example see *TI*, 3.

R. Ben Hollander: "It won't help anyone to sit in the back. They are the first ones I pick on!"

Professor Dov Rappel observes that what Socrates achieved in the field of philosophy, Nehama did for Jewish texts. She "midwifed" ideas, enabling students to refine their own thinking processes. This role requires great patience – the teacher must wait, giving hints if necessary and only providing the answer if all else fails.[72] One example of this is seen in the story of the taxi driver and the book of Jonah mentioned above. Rather than immediately giving the answer, Nehama remarked, "That's a good question," and waited for him to arrive at the solution himself.

෯ ෯

One famous pedagogical invention connected to active learning for which Nehama will always be remembered was her writing technique. Here it is described in her own words in a letter to R. Nathaniel Helfgot:

> I am happy to hear you are now a high-school Bible teacher.... Be careful not to deliver sermons; rather allow the students to work, search, discover, compare and analyze. And the most important thing is to get them to answer questions in writing and to check them – and I don't mean that they should write an essay on a Tanach topic. That is very undesirable. Instead they should answer specific questions briefly and precisely; questions such as "What is the difference between these two commentaries? What is the key word in this passage? Why did Rashi find the simple reading dissatisfactory, quoting the midrashic passage? What is the nature of Ramban's attack on Rashi?", and so on. This teaches students to engage in careful reading, and brings them to love and respect the text.[73]

The essence of the technique was to ask a question and, instead of eliciting the usual verbal responses, to require students to write down their best guess. Then she would pick someone to read it out loud. She walked up and down the aisles as they wrote, looking over shoulders and loudly whispering comments; or, in her less mobile years, asked for the notebooks to be handed up to the front. Seeing a correct answer, Nehama whispered a new question in the student's ear, or pointed to other sources for further

---

[72] A model for how the teacher must withdraw to create space for the student, based on the Hasidic idea of *tzimtzum*, has been put forward by Asher Friedman, in "As Gardeners in the Garden of God: Hasidic Thought and its Implications for Teacher-Student Relationships," in *Wisdom from All My Teachers: Challenges and Initiatives in Contemporary Torah Education*, edited by Jeffrey Saks and Susan Handelman, 112–136 (Jerusalem: Urim Publications, 2003).
[73] I have slightly revised Helfgot's own translation from his article "Recalling," based on the original, printed in *PN*, 663.

comparisons and analyses. But if it was wrong, the unfortunate students would be berated with "What is this?!", "Where did you get that from?", "No, no, no!", "You didn't read what it said!" and made to try again.[74]

R. Klitsner recalls those exercises fondly: "There would be this wonderful quiet, with everybody searching in the text, and thinking. Nehama liked to say that these periods are the most precious moments for a teacher." Nehama writes:

> This silent work takes up time. It takes the students ten minutes or more to study, think and write that which the teacher could explain in three minutes. But the reward of independent effort certainly outweighs the loss of time. (TI, 5–6)

However, she never took up the entire lesson with it, for that would be monotonous.

Nehama outlined several advantages to this method: First, a discussion, however lively and interesting, never involves all of the pupils and cannot be sustained for long periods without minds wandering; giving them a limited problem to tackle in writing will return their minds to the subject under discussion (TI, 74, n. 12). Secondly, in a verbal discussion, the brightest students jump in immediately with answers. This leaves slower students with no time even to understand the question properly, never mind offer their own answer; yet the teacher is deluded into believing that all have understood, and moves on. The writing method is therefore especially useful in a weak class (TI, 23). Thirdly, when students claim, "I know the answer but I can't put it into words," the material has not been fully understood. Writing compels students to think more precisely, and to articulate and commit to an answer.

To encourage maximum precision of thought, Nehama stipulated that the answer must contain only two or three words, or one sentence only (LP, 60, 164; TI, 5). This pushed students beyond the lazy habit of paraphrasing words, without any real understanding. For instance, she asked the students to read the verse (Isaiah 1:3):

> The ox knows his owner, and the ass his master's crib; but Israel does not know, my people does not consider.

They were to encapsulate in one word the difference between Israel and the animals mentioned. Most students wrote something like "The ox and the ass know their owners whereas Israel do not know God" but Nehama repeated that she was looking for one word only. Some then came up with

---

[74] See also TI, 23.

"Knowing owners versus not knowing God" but this was still not good enough. Only after great exertion and thought did the students eventually come up with the answer: "Loyalty."[75]

The method was particularly useful in teaching commentaries, where paraphrasing is especially insidious. Nehama would demand: "Don't tell me in your poor Hebrew what Rashi says in good Hebrew! I already know what Rashi says!"

> A paraphrase of the text is merely a translation from good style to bad style, and does not indicate that the text has been understood. (Remember this; do not forget it!) (TI, 26)

At other times she would ask the students to punctuate a verse. This would also force them to commit to one avenue of interpretation.[76]

Through the writing method, Nehama trained the students to approach text analytically, as she herself did, and to think about the philosophical dimensions behind the words. It brought to light new aspects of verses read countless times before, and even for teachers who had taught them.[77] It also helped her get to know her students and their level of understanding, maximizing the personal attention in the classroom, as she walked around giving each participant a mini-tutorial. Most of all, it transferred the responsibility for education from the teacher to the pupil, which was her chief aspiration.

Over the years, Nehama encountered resistance to this technique. In her old age, she was able to cajole people into writing by pleading poor hearing. But even as a younger woman she refused to allow slackers; everyone had to be activated. In Nehama's class, which included accomplished rabbis, Jewish educators, scholars and businessmen, all were stripped of professional status, all worked diligently and wrote their answers. The anxiety concerning her response was palpable, and any children participating in the class were amused to witness these adults trembling in fear. When Nehama said, "Very good!" these distinguished professionals looked as if it was the high point of their career. "After the class she would chuckle about it and be surprised that they actually did the work," says R. Klitsner.

---

[75] Ofran, "Le-ha'ahiv," 412. For further examples of the writing method, see TI, 30 and 89. Moshe Sokolow brings some of his own examples of brief encapsulation ("succinctness") in Hatzi Nehama: Studies in the Weekly Parashah, Based on the Lessons of Nehama Leibowitz, Jerusalem: Urim Publications, 2007, 26–27, 37 and 48.
[76] See LP, 16–17, 56, 170, 208.
[77] See for example in Ofran, "Le-ha'ahiv," 422.

Not everyone liked this method or the feelings it evoked. One fellow teacher from the Mizrachi seminar termed it "Spiritual athletics" because those who had not learned to think the way Nehama did would not get the right answer. Learning to think like Nehama was very valuable, but it could be exasperating to have to work within a word quota and to have to hit upon the exact phraseology that she wanted. Some people felt reduced by the method to the helpless feelings of childhood. Rochwarger says: "The method did have its faults. Depending on your ego, it could be extremely frustrating or it could just be fun to try and work out exactly how she wanted it phrased. It might shatter an insecure person. It was intimidating and did not allow you to think freely, teaching you to analyze in one very specific way; and only talented students were able to take that and apply it in other ways. Having said this, Nehama did modify her remarks based on the student. To an old-timer, she might suggest that he should know better than to submit such an answer, while newcomers were encouraged and given hints. She held fast to the dictum, 'Train a child according to his own path' [Proverbs 22:6]." Rochwarger also points out, as evidence for the value of Nehama's methods, that thousands of students still talk about how much they learned from her. Michael Hochstein recalls, "There was an enormous thrill to getting it right. It did not bother us to be made to feel like children." Dr. David Bernstein adds that this leveling experience is an important and positive one that teachers ought to note.

Nehama designed her exams so as to promote active learning. In the Mizrachi seminar she introduced the "open book" test, in which the students learned something new even during the exam.[78] Although she approved of the act of revising, crucial for the comprehension and retention of material, to force the students to read the chapter yet again in the test itself and to give mechanical answers was wearisome. Instead, she included unseen material, testing the internalization of already-taught principles; or she set a fresh assignment which would require combing the chapter thoroughly to find the answer, for example: "Which verse expresses the following ideas?" "Which verses in your opinion are the most encouraging?" This gave students renewed motivation to search the material for answers. Even more successful were questions such as "Which verses in your opinion are the most pertinent to current events?" Nehama recounts that her students took

---

[78] She tried to encourage others to do likewise, for example R. Reinitz (*PN*, 681).

such assignments straight to heart, and after the test papers were collected a lively discussion ensued, with students feeling that

> it was very difficult to pick only two or three verses since it suddenly appeared that nearly all of the verses were pertinent to modern realities, as if they had been spoken today. (*KA*, 484)

Third goal: Love for Torah[79]

For Nehama, the most essential level of education was about more than just knowledge and skills. She once asked a group of teachers and principals: "What's the purpose of teaching Tanach?" One answered, "To learn about the history of our people." Another said, "To learn about the mitzvot." A third cited ethical behavior. "No! No! No!" she responded each time. Finally, she said: "The purpose of teaching Tanach is – so that our students should not hate the Tanach!" There was a stunned silence, but everyone understood the truth of what she had said.

This then was her third, and most important, educational principle: That above and beyond the transmission of information or skills, the teacher must engender an abiding love for the subject matter. Though applicable to any area, this was especially true for Torah:

> All of our work must be aimed at bringing our students to an affinity for the Torah; to ensure that when they leave school they will have both the inner need for it, and the possibility to continue studying it. (*He'arot*, 485)

> May you succeed in impressing on your students the love of Torah which is more important than knowing and being expert on a few more chapters. (*TI*, 37)

Similarly:

> Our main aim in school is not to disseminate large quantities of information; and it is beyond our capacity to produce scholars proficient in all areas of the Torah. Our aim is rather to propagate love for the Torah, so that the words of the Torah will be cherished by the student, who will behold the great light that radiates forth from our commentaries and illuminates the verses, and his heart will be warmed by their light. (*LP*, intro, 3)

She brought up this topic repeatedly. Professor Menahem Ben-Sasson recalls: "As children, we would hear Nehama say over and over again that she wanted to promote Torah and that was her sole interest." Nothing riled

---

[79] Peerless adds a fourth goal – to encourage the observance of mitzvot (see *To Study*, 12). But this is a more complex issue, as will be discussed on pages 397–399 below.

her more than an inferior lesson that made the pupils hate the Torah instead of loving it.

Nehama understood the nature of the student population, for whom being in school was not an ideal occupation. School did not encourage an atmosphere of enjoyment or even learning. Reportedly, when her students once informed her that sex education was now being taught in schools, she exclaimed: "*Oy vey*, now they won't like *that* either!" She also joked, "When the bell rings, the students have left – even if they are still there!" R. Yoel bin-Nun recalls arguing with Nehama in a car on the way to Gush Etzion about a Midrash that describes how the Israelites fled from Mount Sinai "like a child running home from school." The Midrash suggests that just as a child wants to avoid being given more homework, the Israelites did not want to be given any more laws.[80] He said that it must be referring to the end of the year, when the children long for the summer holiday; but Nehama argued that it was true of any ordinary school day:

> Every teacher, whether Jewish or not, witnesses this sight daily – the child running away from his school. (*IBBM*, 117)

Similarly, in her acceptance speech for the Bialik prize in 1982, she said that she had had various pupils, from the very young to the old, but one thing she knew they had in common: All were happy when the teacher did not show up. "No lesson can ever be as good as a free lesson."

Once, the fourteen-year-old Nehama was sitting in Berlin at the back of her schoolroom. When the teacher rolled out a map of Hungary, Nehama's friend leaned over to her and whispered "Just what I needed right now!" This sarcastic sentence stuck with Nehama, and her educational philosophy developed from there. She resolved that no student of hers would ever say such a thing. This story affected Nehama's student Blu Greenberg more than any class in teaching methodology, and until this day every time she prepares a lecture, she hears in her mind Nehama's voice saying: "Just what I needed right now!"

Students have to be persuaded to enjoy the material. A lesson needs careful preparation and must be suited to the students' capabilities. For this reason, Nehama did her best to avoid sections of the Tanach that would be too complicated for young minds – for example, the sacrifices. Rami Yannai explains: "She preferred that students say, 'The teacher said we don't have to study the sacrifices' rather than that they hate the Torah after being forced to

---

[80] *Midrash Yelamdenu* on *Be-ha'alotcha*, 3:17. See *IBBM*, 116.

learn it. When she heard that I was about to give a sample lesson on the topic of sacrifices, her face plainly said that I was wasting my time."

Nehama's passion for Torah was conspicuous, and it reproduced itself in her students' hearts. Dr. Gabriel Cohn declares unequivocally: "I don't think there was anyone who brought about such a love of Torah as Nehama Leibowitz did. She wanted to make the Torah beloved, and the students wanted to love the Torah, so it was a perfect match!" Another student, long parted from his teenage years, reported to his friends with shining eyes, "I've been to a class with Nehama, and I'm in love!"

CHAPTER 9

NEHAMA'S IMPACT:
"SHE'S THE REAL THING"

To her thousands of weekly listeners on Kol Yisrael in the 1950s she is Professor Nehama Leibowitz. To the tens of thousands of readers of her books in Hebrew, English, French, Spanish and other languages, she is Nehama Leibowitz. To the dozens of graduating classes of her students throughout Israel from the 1930s onwards, she is simply "Nehama." More than a scholar, more than a teacher, Nehama Leibowitz is an institution in the field of Tanach study and its teaching. (Professor Yair Hoffman[1])

General Impact

THE KABBALISTIC WORK *Sefer Yetzirah* (6:1) speaks of three dimensions in which holiness may be created: time, space and being (soul). Nehama's life's work covered all three, spanning almost an entire century, thousands of kilometers, and countless people over several generations. Lesson by lesson, page by page, she built up the inner life of Judaism in high schools and universities, seminaries and yeshivahs, through worksheets, teacher-training manuals, lectures, books, radio shows and conversations – in person or on the phone – in Israel or with her Diaspora correspondents, in the city and in the country, for religious and secular, men and women, Jews and non-Jews. She brought Jews with disparate backgrounds together to study their common sacred text, a scene which today, with the polarization in Israeli society, must often be artificially engineered in religious-secular encounters. The existence of common texts strengthens societies. Nehama, in teaching the Text of Texts, nurtured Israel's culture, its national pride and stamina. Yet she did all this in an atmosphere of critical inquiry, not mindless propaganda. Thus she succeeded in appealing to these extremely different populations.

---

[1] Yair Hoffman, "*Yoter me-hokeret, yoter mi-martzah,*" *Yediot Ahronot*, Culture Supplement, December 24, 1982.

Nehama skillfully clarified the often dense text, creating order out of a jumble of commentaries. It was as if she had walked into a chaotic room and rolled up her sleeves, forgoing rest until everything was in place. Professor Saul Lieberman states:

> She redeemed biblical interpretation from eclectics and reduced it to a scientific discipline. (*PN*, 23)

R. Aryeh Strikowsky parallels her work with the greatest of Jewish intellectual methodologies:

> Just as R. Hayyim Soleveichik of Brisk established a conceptual method for learning Talmud that transformed the *yeshivah* world, just as Professor Gershom Scholem created a scientific approach to learning Jewish mysticism, so Nehama paved an innovative pathway toward understanding Torah through *midrash*, commentaries, and translations into the vernaculars as well.[2]

R. Soloveitchik, Professor Scholem, R. Meir Shapira of Lublin who initiated the *daf yomi*, R. Pinhas Kehati on Mishnah, R. Adin Steinsaltz on Talmud – many are convinced that Nehama's name rightfully belongs amongst this handful who systemized Jewish study with immeasurable impact.[3] For, as Professor Walter Herzberg notes, Nehama went beyond simply decoding or translating difficult texts, a task accomplished by others before her, such as Bialik in his *Book of the Aggadah*. Her achievement was to make them interesting and up to date.

Note, too, that with the exception of Professor Scholem, all of the names in the above list relate to work on talmudic materials. Dr. Gabriel Cohn points out that Nehama – though probably unintentionally – also revolutionized the Jewish world by presenting another book besides the Talmud through which to build oneself as a Jewish person. Women, who were barred from the world of the Talmud at the time, benefited especially, and many religious high schools for girls and advanced learning institutes for women were founded upon this basis. Cohn notes that this change was assisted by the way Nehama taught, creating lively and spiritually satisfying exegetical discussions.

In fact, Nehama's teaching was so superb that some found it difficult to enjoy any other Tanach course afterward, even a high-level one; and many former students automatically processed all subsequent courses through the prism of Nehama's methodology.

---

[2] Strikovsky, "Nehama on Women," 186. See also see Breuer, "*Professor*," 18, regarding Nehama's Lithuanian dialectic approach.
[3] See Yuval Cherlow, introduction to *Pirkei ha-avot* by Yoel Bin-Nun, 11.

By dint of solid teaching for more than seventy years, Nehama influenced generations of teachers and students. The widespread interest she generated in Tanach and commentaries and her new approach to them was tantamount to a movement.[4] For the first time, Tanach became a subject in the regular curriculum in many Zionist yeshivahs, the direct result of work by some outstanding scholars, among them Nehama.[5] She receives much credit for the fact that today, Tanach and commentaries are widely studied in schools and private homes, and discussed in periodicals and other publications. Gedalyah Nigal goes so far as to write:

> I do not think I exaggerate in saying that we may divide the study of *Humash* throughout Jewish history into two periods: Pre- and post-Leibowitz.[6]

Nurit Fried uses similar phrasing regarding her pedagogical development. "I divide my life into before Nehama and after Nehama. After I met her I saw just how many mistakes I had been making as a teacher, though I was already training other teachers at the time!" (*VLN*). Superlatives abound concerning Nehama's teaching. Vanessa Ochs writes:

> She is the source, the real thing. To have studied with Nehama is to have been in analysis with Freud, to have been educated in nursery school by Maria Montessori, to have been inoculated against polio by Dr. Salk.[7]

Ochs describes the first time she sat in Nehama's class as follows:

> I was catching around seventy percent of Nehama's Hebrew. It was exhilarating to understand; frustrating to miss words here and there. I would learn Hebrew better immediately, I vowed.... I wanted to be one of the thousands of students who knew Nehama's love, interest, approval. I would learn Hebrew for her! I would learn Bible for her!

---

[4] I say "tantamount" because it lacked a cohesive force. While some of Nehama's students developed a special bond of friendship through their common study with her, ultimately her students were too numerous and far-flung to qualify as a community *per se*. Though we certainly may speak of "Nehama's school of thought" and "Nehama's disciples," there is no structured movement or court of the kind surrounding hasidic Rebbes, something that might have happened had Nehama been a less democratic and more cultish personality. More of this will be discussed in chapter 24.

[5] From R. Haim Sabato's article in *Ha-Tzofeh*, May 23, 2002, discussing the publication of R. Elhanan Samet's book on the weekly portion.

[6] Nigal, "*Morah*."

[7] Ochs, *Words*, 268.

Was this a crush, was it idolatry? I felt as if I were nine years old and in the fourth grade.[8]

Some only realized after several decades the extent of the debt they owed Nehama. Professor Michael Rosenak, a leading theorist on the philosophy of education, writes:

> As this book developed... I came to realize the enormous influence the revered Bible teacher of the generation now passed, Nehama Leibowitz... had on my reading of Torah.... [Her] methodology changed my view of what Bible study is.[9]

Nehama was seen as scholarship incarnate, and as the paradigm of the *maskil dati* – the Orthodox enlightened Jew, the best that the national-religious framework had to offer.[10] She became an icon on the Israeli scene, part and parcel of its religious and Zionist history. Thus, in the book *My Grandfather Was a Rabbi: A Religious-Secular Lexicon* by Israeli satirist Uri Orbach, he writes regarding the "Cultural Heroes" of Zionist-religious Israeli society:

> The mere mention of these names is enough to get the nostalgia glands working.... Rabbi Neriah, Rabbi Zvi Yehudah [Kook], Zevulun Hammer, Dr. Burg, Nehama Leibowitz, Rabbi Goren.[11]

Yair Sheleg writes:

> Until recently, you could see an elderly, petite woman with old-fashioned glasses walking slowly through the streets of Jerusalem. She was recognizable by the brown beret that she had worn for decades. Many people knew her and greeted her, "Shalom, Nehama. How are you, Nehama?" When you saw Nehama with her beret, you knew that with all the changes Jerusalem had been through over the years, one thing remained constant: Nehama Leibowitz.[12]

Nehama even makes a cameo appearance in an Israeli mystery novel, *Death in the Literature Department*, by well-known Israeli author Batya Gur:

> When he raised his glance he beheld Professor Nehama Leibowitz, whom he considered one of the last giants of the old world; and when he saw her approaching the librarian's counter, her head inclined to one side and her perennial brown beret immobile, and despite her attempted whisper heard her saying to the librarian: "But this cannot be

---

[8] Ochs, *Words*, 276.
[9] Rosenak, *Tree*, ix.
[10] Schoneveld, *The Bible*, 81, 242.
[11] Uri Orbach, *Saba sheli haya rav: lexicon dati-hiloni*, Keter, 2002, 29.
[12] Sheleg, *"Keter,"* 9.

referring to me, it's not my book; it must be my brother's," and saw the amicable smile that lit up her face when she returned to her seat, he breathed a sigh of relief.[13]

Even the Israeli tourism office knew that when it came to Tanach, Nehama was the address. A visiting priest who expressed interest in Tanach was sent directly to Nehama's house, where she obligingly helped him plan his trip![14]

ৡৈ ৵ঌ

It is impossible to guess how many people were touched by Nehama. She received dozens of letters from people around the world thanking her for increasing their Torah knowledge and for her personal approach (*PN*, 21). If we include not only those who learned from her lessons and writings, but also those who learned from her students, the number certainly runs into the tens of thousands. She influenced more lives than she could ever know, and only a fraction of the stories filtered back to her. One of these was brought to her by a man who one day knocked at her door and walked in, dressed in the long black garb of an ultra-Orthodox Jew. As Nehama sat there open-mouthed, he informed her that, growing up as a highly assimilated American Jew, he had served in the Korean War and had been injured. In the hospital, the chaplain brought him Nehama's worksheets, and, lacking other diversions, he began to fill them out. Thus began his process of return to Judaism, which led to who he was today. After he left, Nehama exclaimed repeatedly to Dr. Ruth Ben-Meir, "Can you believe it?" Then there was the boy who received her *Studies* as a bar-mitzvah present. His non-Jewish father began to read them and was affected to the point of converting to Judaism.

However, Nehama disliked blatant outreach in religious education. She compared it to Elijah's showdown with the prophets of Baal, which, with its all its drama, had little lasting effect. She preferred a steady process; though she also, witnessing a prominent Israeli rabbi teaching secular kibbutz youth in the 1970s, poured out her frustrations into her friend's ear: "I hear him talk and talk and – *nothing!* He's not saying *anything!* And yet he's succeeding in bringing them to religion! I'd sell all my wisdom to know his secret!"

While her primary audience was Modern Orthodox or national-religious, Nehama frequently went beyond those bounds, teaching Reform, secular,

---

[13] Batya Gur, *Mavet ba-hug le-sifrut*, Keter, 1989, 154 (referenced in Aviad HaCohen, *Shema ha-emet mi-mi she-omra: zeh kelal gadol be-Torat Nehama Leibowitz*," *Alon Shvut* 13 [5759]: 71). Nehama is the only truly recognizable real-life figure in the book (see the review, "Literary Remains," by Vivian Eden, *Jerusalem Post*, June 16, 1989, 14).
[14] Ephraim Yair, "*Shabbat Nahamu*," *Amudim* 430 (5742), 25.

ultra-Orthodox and non-Jewish students. Her non-political approach allowed her to transcend denominations, to shun the sectarian categories that plague much of Israeli society. She would say, "*They?* Who is *they?* Let's not talk of us and them. I see only individuals." She instructed teachers not to weigh up whom to teach, which nationalities or affiliations. "The answer is *kol dichfin* ('all who are hungry')," she said, borrowing the phrase from the Passover Seder. "Anyone who comes to hear you. You can't know what the power of the Torah is, and what effect it will have on the students." She writes:

> It is impossible… for one human being to judge the character of another and appraise his moral worth. This only the Almighty can do. (*SBM*, 270)

This respect was based on a genuine appreciation of human qualities. In fact, she divulged to one secular friend that she had a better rapport with him than with some who prayed three times daily but had no understanding of their prayers. "You aren't religious, but at least you know how to think!" she complimented him.[15] She admired secular public figures, such as Chief Justice Hayyim Cohen, who was fair in all his dealings, while at the same time she strongly disapproved of radically secular Israeli politicians who hated the religious.

Nehama courageously rebuked those who would discriminate against certain Jews. R. Lee Buckman, a Conservative rabbi, attended Nehama's class. When some yeshivah principals objected to his presence, claiming, "All they do is violate Halachah," Nehama responded:

"All Conservative rabbis? Even the respected Conservative talmudist, Rabbi Saul Lieberman? And by the way, there is no shortage of Orthodox rabbis who would say that you're violating Halachah by studying Torah from a woman teacher."

"But they are trying to destroy our State!"

"Conservative rabbis are responsible for destroying our State? Was it a Conservative rabbi that killed Rabin?"

"They are heretics! They don't accept Maimonides's thirteen principles of faith."

"Many Orthodox Jews burned Maimonides's books," she parried. To each argument Nehama had a response, lucid and convincing, never raising her voice. Finally, her disputants gave up. R. Buckman was very moved:

---

[15] Abramowitz, *Tales*, 20.

That Thursday evening session in her tiny one-room schoolhouse, I was treated to Nehama's finest hour. This time it wasn't the words of Rashi or Ramban or Buber or Rosenzweig. This time Nehama Leibowitz was the text. It was her words and temperament that we were privileged to study. To her, the verse *Torah tziva lanu Moshe morasha kehillat Ya'acov*[16] meant that the Torah was the inheritance not just of the Orthodox but of the entire community of Israel. There is one Torah and all of us find our way through it as best we can.[17]

Nehama succeeded in highly secular environments. Supposedly, she might have seemed alien or threatening, a member of the "other" camp; or simply downright archaic, walking through the corridors of Tel Aviv University in her plain outfit and old briefcase. Yet she was highly esteemed there. Her educational background in Berlin University helped, as did her warm personality. Professor Yairah Amit, who succeeded Nehama in the department, recalls, "She wanted to expose us to traditions from our culture. What we did at home did not interest her. She was tolerant – had a live-and-let-live approach." In the early days of the State, when the average Israeli was more familiar with Tanach, Nehama had many secular students. Her worksheets were studied in ultra-secular kibbutzim, such as Kibbutz Yotvata, to which she flew once a week. At the School for Senior Educators, teachers from the non-religious stream specially requested to attend her lessons. R. Daniel Tropper, director of the dialogue organization, Gesher, found Nehama to be the only religious person who could speak to secular Tanach teachers. "They worshipped her. She was the one academician that spoke to them on their level – and she really cared about them."

The many non-observant students with whom Nehama developed close relationships included a philosophical man who spent hours talking with her; a brilliant female American law student, who got more answers correct than many of the religious educators in the same class; and a female school principal from Ramat Gan. Nehama became part of their spiritual lives, and when one woman fell terminally ill, she asked Nehama, sitting by her hospital bed, questions about the immortality of the soul. Many of these students remained secular, but they left Nehama's class with new perspectives. A group from Argentina told her at their festive parting meal: "Our main goal in studying Torah was, in truth, to improve our Hebrew; but you taught us that through studying *parshanut* we can be wiser and better

---

[16] "Moses commanded us Torah, the inheritance of the congregation of Jacob" (Deuteronomy 33:4).
[17] Lee Buckman, Internet (website has since been removed).

people." The worksheets also served over many years to fill in gaps in Judaic knowledge for some correspondents.

Dr. Marla Frankel was once sitting at the Jerusalem Academy of Dance and Music, studying Nehama's *Studies*. A young woman next to her struck up a conversation, telling Frankel that she used to be ultra-Orthodox, and that the only books remaining on her shelves from those days were Nehama Leibowitz's *Studies*. This story illustrates two points: that Nehama's work was able to sustain its appeal even after rejection of everything religious; and also that Nehama's books could be found on ultra-Orthodox shelves. Indeed, significant numbers of Jews from this sector studied her books and attended her lessons, and she also trained teachers from this community. R. Ben Hollander observes: "I'll be sitting at a wedding with a Haredi person, wondering what we have in common. Then he mentions Nehama's name – he's seen her work, he was in a class. It's remarkable." While there were certainly ultra-Orthodox institutions where Nehama's books were not welcome,[18] her writings showed up in surprising places. A lecturer at a college affiliated with Shas, the Sephardic-Haredi political-social movement, once took out one of Nehama's books and quoted from it. The students gasped, but the lecturer reassured them that he had received approval from the Council of Sages. R. Yohanan Fried explains this phenomenon: "Diaspora Haredim, including rabbis, used her books, and some of their children attended her lectures and seminars in Israel. This attitude then permeated the world of Israeli Haredim."

Despite her gender and the non-Orthodox sources she cited, Nehama's books were even sold in ultra-Orthodox bookshops. Nehama loved to tell of the occasion when she noticed her book in a shop window in Meah She'arim, a stringently ultra-Orthodox neighborhood. Entering to inquire, she was asked by the owner if she was surprised. Nehama replied, "Yes, pleasantly surprised!" He leaned over and, gesturing, said in a low voice, "If you want, I'll take you to the back of the store – I have even worse there!"

For many Diaspora Jews, meeting Nehama was part of the romance of discovering Israel and the Jewish renaissance taking place there. "It was very inspiring to learn with her," says Rosenak, who studied with her in 1954 as part of a Jewish Agency program. "She belonged to a circle of people who focused on Jewish traditional learning and on being Jewish in a rooted way. It seemed almost as though this enterprise had been interrupted in Jerusalem

---

[18] For example, Gateshead Seminary, according to Aryeh Newman (interview).

for seventeen centuries and was just now getting back on track. It was natural, and yet somehow supernatural. Sitting in Jerusalem with Nehama and Klausner and Scholem was a rarified experience, like a sort of 'heavenly Jerusalem.'"

Mordechai Kramer recounts his encounter with Nehama:

> Spring 1968 and the Hebrew University campus at Givat Ram was filled with English speakers. The Six Day War aroused young Jews around the world, and there was a surge of pride and curiosity in being Jewish. The enthusiasm made itself felt after the war when thousands came as volunteers. Some of them volunteered to serve in the Israeli army. Many took advantage of the opportunity to study one year at the Hebrew University at the expense of the Jewish Agency.
>
> I personally did both, serving a year in the army and then in September of 1968, starting my first year at the Hebrew University. Part of our first year of study was composed of what was called *mechinah* or preparatory classes. These were studies provided to give some Jewish background to the majority of us who knew very little or nothing about Judaism and Israel. Nehama Leibowitz gave the Bible class. Everyone had to learn the stories of Joseph with her.
>
> At first I wondered why we had to learn Bible. I had never found it interesting. I once tried to read it and after a few *begats*, I gave up.
>
> Whatever knowledge I had was common knowledge, which I had picked up from movies, casual reading and television – more from the popular Christian culture of the media than from Jewish sources.
>
> However, while I can't speak for the other few hundred students who attended the class, I personally needed some spiritual justification for being in Israel. I didn't like the kibbutz I was on before the army, I did not enjoy the army, I did not appreciate the people, but I loved Israel. And I knew that being a Jew and Judaism had something to do with it. Hence, I approached Nehama Leibowitz's Bible class with both a suspicion that I would be bored with the *begats* and a hopeful curiosity.
>
> We were seated in a large lecture hall when a short elderly woman with a beret and a long skirt hurriedly descended to the front of the hall. "How many of you have ever learned Bible before?" asked Nehama. A few dozen hands went up.
>
> Then she asked us to open our Bibles to the appropriate pages dealing with Joseph. I don't remember how she started the lesson, it has been more than thirty years, but I do remember the enthusiasm she generated in myself and the class. She wanted to know how we understood every line and she asked us to explain. She read the commentators with us and wanted us to explain what bothered the commentator and why he answered as he did. We found it intellectually

stimulating and even fun. She interlaced the study of text and commentators with stories from her life. I found myself entertained and enthralled every moment of the class. She gave us so much homework that we gasped in unison. Reading Hebrew was no easy task for us. At the end I remember her standing in front of us with a broad warm smile on her face which I assumed meant that she had succeeded in what she had set out to do.

Next to me sat a student with long hair dressed in the hippie style of the sixties. He stood up to leave and said to someone, "Hey, this Torah stuff is cool." This caused laughter among those who heard it.

The classes continued every week with the same enthusiasm. I found myself looking forward to them. After a few months I took a *kippa* with me to the class and put it on when we started learning. I noticed a few of the other students doing the same.

All I can say is that she was the first person to show me some of the beauty of the Torah. After that I started learning privately and eventually went to yeshivah and after I married joined a Kollel.

About twenty-five years later I saw Nehama walking in front of my house. She was more stooped than before and walked with a stick, in stark contrast to the brisk gait of former years. She seemed to be looking for an address. I approached her, calling her by name and asked if I could be of help to her. She said she was looking for Rabbi Aharon Lichtenstein, who was my neighbor. I said I would show her to his door. As we walked I told her that she had been the first person ever to teach me Torah and make me love it. I told her that I would be forever in debt to her for opening the door to Judaism for me. I wanted her to know that her endeavors in life had been justified. She smiled but said nothing. I think she knew. I think many people had said similar things to her. But I was glad I said it. It was the least I could do for her.

Occasionally, I see the student who had remarked after the first lesson, "Hey, this Torah stuff is cool," in Jerusalem. He is now the head of a yeshivah.

Classes are rarely the subject of a poet's fancy, but Nehama's teaching even inspired some to poetry.[19] One particular lesson galvanized Hamiel to put pen to paper in an ode to Torah study.[20] He recreated the experience of

---

[19] For example, Nurit Fried wrote a poem about Nehama (can be heard in *VLN*).
[20] See Haim Hamiel, *Be-odi*, Jerusalem: Carmel Press, 1990, and Nissenbaum, Booklet, 23–28.

learning with her, the sights and sounds in her modest Jerusalem home one summer's day in 1985 in the company of

> many students in a room who have come from far away and overseas; but none of them complain that there is no space.

Hamiel: "After I came home, her words and her voice continued to bubble in my brain. The experience of her riveting teaching simply would not leave me alone." He recorded the dialogical atmosphere, and the dramatic effect of Nehama's reading of a Midrash describing how at the hour of Moses's death he pleads to be spared the fate of all mortals.[21] This Midrash struck an almost mystical note in the listeners. The class went into overtime and no one noticed. In Hamiel's poem, one old man stands up and declares:

> How momentous is this place – it is Torah study as it was at Mount Sinai!

Impact on teachers

Nehama's example inspired a number of people who studied with her to become Tanach teachers, including some for whom that was initially the farthest thing from their mind. Deena Nataf's background in Torah was so limited that she failed her first course with Nehama. Today, she teaches it to others. "When I teach, I want my students to learn to love Torah, to be thirsty for it. I try to engender excitement." Nataf learned from Nehama not only to highlight the beauty of the language, conceptual relationships, and parallels in Tanach, but also to give the teaching the respect it deserves by dressing with care and starting punctually.

Ben-Meir, who initially filled out Nehama's worksheets, went on to study with her in Machon Gold in 1968. From the first lesson, Dr. Ruth Ben-Meir knew that she had found herself a "teacher with a capital T," one who would be worthy of the recommendation from *Ethics of the Fathers* [1:6]: "*Aseh lecha rav*" – make for yourself a teacher/master"; that is to say, have someone to follow and learn from at every opportunity. Ben-Meir was impressed by Nehama's precision and openness, and her goal of teaching people to think: "I had studied with a wide range of lecturers, but instead of saying 'I'll teach you' she was saying 'Let's study together.'" After meeting her, Ben-Meir concluded that academic research is sterile, influencing few people in contrast with the many lives Nehama changed. Consequently, she chose a

---

[21] *Yalkut Shimoni, Devarim*, 3:821.

career in Tanach teaching and teacher-training, a field that, according to Ben-Meir, carries little prestige in today's academic climate.

R. Chaim Weiner tells of the rabbi who rebuked his student for failing to attribute something to him properly. The student replied, "Everyone knows that I have learned all I know from you; therefore, I do not need to quote in your name." He explains: "When it comes to Bible study, everything I know I have learned from Nehama. Every *shiur*, every explanation of a verse, I either learned from her lectures or books, or deduced indirectly using the training she gave me. Nothing is my own, and I give her full credit for it all." Weiner also notes that ever since Nehama made time for him, a stranger whose only qualification was his desire to study, he feels obliged, no matter how busy he may be, to find time for anyone wishing to learn from him.

Professor Martin Lockshin similarly announces at the start of his courses that he is unable to footnote Nehama Leibowitz every time he mentions something learned from her: "Just assume that anything good I learned from her, and anything lousy I made up myself!" Few are the classes in which Professor Walter Herzberg does not mention Nehama. For R. Ben Hollander, the greatest compliment is to be told that there is some Nehama Leibowitz in what he teaches. "That is her greatest living memorial – the thousands who were influenced by her." Linda Derovan, too, was highly complimented by someone who said after her lesson, "I thought we were back in Nehama's class!" Indeed, Nehama's style and thinking are instantly recognizable to those in the know. To one Diaspora educator, for example, it was obvious that most of the local *shlihim* were using Nehama's methods. R. Hollander even spotted Nehama's influence in an exam given by a student's student.

Some have also developed their own methods based on Nehama's. R. David Derovan developed a step-by-step Torah study method, influenced by the Midrash and Nehama's work. Nissan Zisken developed interactive software for Tanach text study, inspired by her. Haim Hamiel created a method for studying biblical text that followed Nehama's lead in its sensitivity to motifs and context. R. Hanan Schlesinger spent years perfecting a system of Talmud study only to realize after Nehama's death that its main principles were based on her worksheets and pedagogic method: "Unbeknownst to her, she actually aided me in teaching material which she herself barely touched!" he says. And countless academics and Bible teachers, including some of the top lecturers and writers in the field today, have gone on to use and expand upon Nehama's methods in their own approach to Tanach.[22]

❧ ❧

Nehama's pedagogical goals and suggestions often left a profound impression. Throughout his entire teaching career, R. Joseph Oratz kept Nehama's third goal in mind: "Those words 'Students never remember anything' still echo in my ears, as twenty years later I continue to teach with the goal of not just knowledge but love of Torah. They might forget the information, but the love will remain in their hearts forever."

When trainee teachers who gave imperfect lessons are exposed to Nehama's "tricks" – for example, writing what was said on the board and involving the students in discussion – the second time, the lesson is much improved. To this day Nehama's writing method is still used and is being passed on to a new generation of teachers, for example by Rami Yannai, who tries to include it in every teacher-training lesson. R. Hollander agrees that it proves its worth almost every time, as the more inattentive students suddenly sit up and inquire, "Excuse me, what was the question?" Nurit Fried learned from Nehama that the exact phrasing of questions is very important. "I learned to ask students first what does Rashi say, and then what does Ibn Ezra say, and only then what is the difference between them, so that they won't just say, 'Rashi says this and Ibn Ezra says that'"(*VLN*).

There were those who even ended up talking like Nehama, using her inflections, gestures and the element of dramatic presentation without realizing it. But not all of her techniques translated well when others tried them. Ben-Meir admits wryly that when she attempts to ask questions like Nehama did, people sometimes inform her that they came to hear a lecture, not to be asked questions. "I don't recall this ever happening in Nehama's class!" she protests. Linda Derovan's pupils were outraged when she included unseen material on her tests; they were not prepared to do that much thinking. Due to such occurrences, many realize that Nehama's approach is beyond exact replication and do not even make the attempt. R. Hollander permits students without Tanachs to attend his class. When Nehama once advised him indignantly, "Ask them to leave! I would!" he replied with a smile: "Yes, but *you're* Nehama Leibowitz!" In the words of Professor Yair Hoffman:

> To follow her path is possible; to imitate her, impossible.[23]

---

[22] For more on this see chapter 24.
[23] Hoffman, "*Yoter.*"

Professor Carmi Horowitz observes that more than a Nehama Leibowitz pedagogy, there was a Nehama Leibowitz personality. She knew how to sustain attention and concretize it, to break down ideas and translate them for every level.

Dr. Marla Frankel, whose career is in education, feels that Nehama influences everything she does. She says: "My mother gave me life and taught me how to live. My teacher, Nehama, showed me a path of learning and taught me how to study basic Jewish texts. She made it intellectually challenging." Frankel observed Nehama teaching, first while a student at the Hebrew University and subsequently when training teachers at the Melton Center. Intrigued by Nehama's teaching of ancient texts in modern times, she chose to write a doctorate analyzing Nehama's writings for her overall instructional theory. She wanted to delve beyond Nehama's charisma to her educational principles – not just her methodology, but the system behind it. "I was not interested in what kind of questions she asked, but why is the question important in the context of studying a religious text." Through her research, Frankel has drawn up a picture of Nehama's ideal Tanach teacher. This person knows much of the Tanach in depth; can speak several languages; is comfortable with modern scholarly research useful in understanding the *peshat*; and uses Jewish and universal works to unearth meanings and translate them into modern terms.[24]

Such an ideal not easy to live up to. Many of Nehama's students are not as nearly as well-read as she was, and are unable to include Shakespeare, Steinbeck and Dostoevsky to illustrate biblical topics as she did. Israeli Orthodox educators are often uneasy with Western culture; but even Nehama's citations of the Hebrew poets Alterman and Tchernichowsky, on the Ten Commandments and the witch of Endor, may be beyond today's Israeli teachers. Indeed, Nehama constantly complained of the ignorance she encountered. She challenged secular people who claimed, "I'm not religiously observant, but I believe in the Ten Commandments" to name them – often they could only remember two or three. Yeshivah high school graduates suffered from low levels of both Tanach and general knowledge. When Nehama's Tanach questions met with blank looks from them, she would mutter pointedly: "What are they teaching there? I don't know what they're teaching them there!" And when a question from Shakespeare was also met with mute silence, she cried, "No Tanach! No Shakespeare! What *are* they teaching in these schools?" She was dismayed that yeshivahs, instead

---

[24] Frankel, "*Ha-te'oriyah*," 434–435; *Iyun* 134, n. 64.

of centers of learning and excellent scholarship, had instead become centers for inculcation of religious social norms.[25]

Nehama was aware of the difficulties in imitating her, and therefore recommended that students take her pedagogical method and reshape it in their own image, according to Herzberg: "Some teach too much Nehama and not enough themselves. The idea is to be yourself as she was herself," he explains. Ultimately, good teachers used Nehama's tools well, and poor teachers misused them. Like anything else, Nehama's method could become trivialized, routinized or applied inappropriately; but when applied properly, it made the lesson soar. This will be discussed further in chapter 24.

Impact of values

Nehama's strong values also left their mark. For instance, her disapproval of lavish functions influenced R. Yerachmiel Roness to hold his son's bar-mitzvah celebration at home instead of in a hall. Her ethical views affected Shlomo Wallach, who says: "She told us that if you go into a *garinim* (sunflower seed) shop and taste even one *garin*, that's stealing unless the shop owner gave you permission. I'll never forget that." In a lesson that Vanessa Ochs attended, Nehama criticized the new *asimon* (telephone token) machines, for now the poor old men who sold the tokens, sitting on the ground for ten hours a day at the Central Bus Station, would lose their source of income. When the students left Nehama's house and walked through the Bus Station, as if by reflex they bought a handful of tokens from the first peddler they saw. Ochs observes:

> To learn with Nehama was to learn to be more human.[26]

When Nehama taught Genesis 24:19, the portrayal of Rebecca's selfless offer to draw water not just for Abraham's servant but also for his camels, she urged that when people, especially older people, ask for directions, one should make the extra effort to accompany them a little way to make sure they don't get lost. Herzberg internalized this, and when a lost elderly woman stopped to ask him the way, he got into her car to show her. When she thanked him, he replied, "It's to Nehama Leibowitz's credit." Shimon Kalfa still recalls, fifty years later, almost word for word how Nehama

---

[25] In *Off the Derech* (Jerusalem/New York: Devora Publishing, 2005) a book discussing why young people leave Orthodoxy, Faranak Margolese describes an incident in which three young men from a world-renowned yeshivah could only remember nine of the ten commandments between them. The author notes that this omission of teaching of the fundamentals may be one reason why students cease to be connected to Torah (217–219).
[26] Ochs, *Words*, 280.

compared Rebecca to the girls of that time: "Imagine a stranger, even one who seems well dressed, asking a girl today to water his camels, and her running to refill his bucket over and over! Where could you find a girl like that? Nowadays, even if you want just an address, would you ever be treated with this kind of patience? And this is Rebecca before she even came to the house of our father Abraham!"

R. Michael Melchior was struck by Nehama's observations regarding the modern Hebrew word *"freier,"* meaning pushover, someone who gives too much. To her vexation, this had become the worst possible insult in Israeli society, and she objected: "Generations of Jews aimed for precisely that, to be a *freier*!" She writes:

> Today, we call this a *freier*. The Torah's opinion is that this is a *tzaddik*.[27]

> Those realists and practical folk who might be drawn to pity the simplicity of the maiden, who went to all this trouble to quench the thirst of a total stranger and his camels, would do well to remember Akavia ben Mahallalel's maxim in the Mishnah: "Better that I be dubbed a fool for the rest of my days than become a wicked man for one hour before the Omnipotent." Similarly Rebecca entered into no calculations of profit and loss when she gave man and beast to drink. It is just such "fools" who have always succeeded in becoming benefactors of mankind. (*NSB*, 227)

Rahel Kossowsky was influenced by Nehama such that, upon being told by someone, *"Magiya lach* – you deserve it" she found herself retorting exactly as Nehama would have, *"Lo magiya li klum!* I do not deserve anything!"

There is also the ultra-Orthodox student who was deeply affected by Nehama's suggestion that in exempting themselves from the IDF, yeshivah students missed a valuable opportunity to propagate Torah values in society. He says he returns to this conversation many times in his thoughts.

›‹

One of Nehama's more famous stories was told in the context of Judah's promise to Jacob to bring Benjamin safely back from Egypt. Judah promises his father that if he fails in this, "I will have sinned to you all my days" (Genesis 43:9). This appears at first glance a rather flimsy guarantee, and one could ask, "So what?" Yet behind it lies the notion that a misdeed is its own punishment, for the burden of guilt will continue for the rest of one's life.

---

[27] From her column in the *Yediot Ahronot* newspaper, weekly portion of *Hayyei Sarah*, November 8, 1990, reprinted in *PN*, 525.

The story that Nehama told took place at the Youth Aliyah seminar where she taught. A spate of thefts began, poisoning the atmosphere and horrifying the teachers. Here is how she recounted it:[28]

> First of all, a sum of money disappeared. A week later, someone missed his fountain pen, and after a few more days a pupil's expensive watch was stolen. Now it was plain to all – a thief was in our midst! How dreadful! No one knew who it was; and we had no choice but to call in the police. On Friday afternoon, the principal and a policeman walked into the classroom. A hush fell upon the class, and the principal read out the names of the pupils – fifty all told – ascertaining that all were present.
>
> Then the policeman said: "I've been a policeman for many years, and seen scores of cases like this one. It's clear this was an inside job. I am one hundred percent convinced that the thief is sitting right here in this classroom. So now I wish to speak personally to the thief:
>
> "Besides God, you alone know who the thief is. You have stolen three times already, getting away with it each time. Maybe this isn't even your first time – maybe you tried before and failed. In any event, know that this won't be your last time. Stopping is tough. After you've seen that you can do it, you'll steal a fourth time, and so on indefinitely. A long chain of thefts stretches ahead of you! You'll own all sorts of beautiful things: Money, jewelry, watches; possessions that other people, hard workers, can never afford. And you won't be caught – our experience in the police force is that most thieves aren't – so you'll be a rich, respected person. But you'll always be a thief! For your entire life, you'll be a thief! And you'll never be able to free yourself from sin, ever.
>
> "So I'd like to give you a little advice. It's now 12:30. We'll all go home, Shabbat is fast approaching. Between 1 and 2 PM, put the stolen items in a public place where they can be found easily. No one has to see. Then you'll no longer be a thief." The policeman put on his coat and his hat, wished us all Shabbat Shalom, and left.
>
> Silence in the classroom. No one said a word as we exited. At the bus stop I met the policeman, patiently waiting for his bus. I said, "Sir, how do you know your advice will work?"
>
> The policeman replied sternly, "Madam! How many years have *you* served on the police force?"

---

[28] This is a paraphrased version of this story as it appears by Ephraim Yair entitled "*Ha-ḥet u-teshuvato: ma'aseh she-siprah Nehama,*" *Amudim* 347 (Tishrei 5735): 32–34 (also reprinted in Strikovsky, *Daf,* 8; Nissenbaum, Booklet, 39–40).

An hour later, I received a phone call from the principal, who excitedly informed me that the articles had been found in the school corridor – out where everyone could see them.

At this point Nehama would break off, and inform her listeners that this was the end of Act I. Act II took place a few years later.

A series of ten-minute conversations were being broadcast on the radio, on the topic of "The most important person I ever met." These included such figures as Menahem Ussishkin, Rav Kook, Winston Churchill and others. They asked me to participate, so I decided to tell the story of the policeman who saved someone from being a thief forever.

A week later, a teacher in a girls' school phoned me and told me the following story. Her class was about to set off on a trip up north, and she had just collected five liras from each pupil. The teacher turned her back for a second to pick up her bag, and then, just to be certain, counted the money once again. Ten liras were missing! Frantically she searched the classroom, not knowing what to do. Then she suddenly remembered hearing me on the radio a few days earlier. So the next day, she assembled the pupils and informed them of the theft. "There is a thief amongst us, right here in this classroom! And she won't be able to resist, she'll do it again and again! And she might never get caught because even the most alert of police forces can't catch everyone. But she'll always be a thief, for the rest of her life…."

Then the teacher handed out thirty empty envelopes and thirty blank pieces of paper, so that the thief could return the money anonymously, folded in the paper. When the teacher later opened the envelopes, the money was there!

Thus ended Act II. But there was to be an Act III.

Five years later, I received an urgent letter from the principal of an educational institution near Be'er Sheva, asking to meet. I immediately sent him a postcard and set up a time. We met, and he informed me agitatedly that in all his years as a principal he had never experienced such a thing. Within a few weeks, several valuable pens had mysteriously disappeared from the classrooms, one after the other, but the culprit's identity remained unknown.

Then he remembered what he had heard on the radio a few years before. He called everyone together and explained the situation to them at length – how the thief might remain at large, but he would never be able to wean himself off his deeds, moving from light misdemeanors to serious ones, since sin brings further sin. And when he died, although no one would know the truth behind his prosperity, since no police force catches everyone, God would know, and this person would be a thief forever, in this world and the next!

The principal then announced that from now on the staff door would be kept open, and any child might enter freely. Thus, the guilty child could deposit the stolen items without anyone seeing. Three weeks passed, and the principal was close to despair; but then in the fourth week, a pupil came in and with lowered gaze, placed the valuables on the table. The principal asked him: "Please tell me – why did you wait until three weeks went by?"

The boy answered: "The other children were watching the door to see who would return the pens, and only now, with the whole thing forgotten, did I get a chance to come in without anyone seeing."

The principal was speechless. But still the boy did not move. It was obvious that his conscience was bothering him; and why had he returned the pens deliberately when the principal was in the staff room? Finally, the pupil said hesitantly: "Perhaps you could place some kind of penance on me?"

The principal replied, "Look, by the very act of returning the pens you've proved that you've repented. You are no longer a thief; you're an honest man now. So go in peace and God be with you."

But the boy insisted: "No, I need to do some act. Maybe I could go every week to the Institute for the Blind, and read them stories? I've done something wrong, and good should atone for bad, right?"

"You're right. Do this and be blessed, because you are doing a good deed. You shall do only good and lovingkindness all the days of your life."

Many people heard this story from Nehama, and the ruse was used on further occasions to return a budding thief to the honest path. She recommended this strategy, observing: "Other methods simply teach students to polish their lies." The above insight of Nehama's also serves as a response to the conundrum of why the righteous suffer while the wicked prosper. The answer: The good person enjoys guiltless sleep, while the evil person, though flourishing materially, bears inside a worm of self-loathing that destroys all peace of mind. One of Nehama's students, Sharon Shenhav, an attorney working with Israeli women trapped in unwanted marriages, remarks that this idea comforts her in her regular encounters with extortionate husbands who go unpunished; she reminds herself that their own consciences will punish them for long after.

The next generation

Nehama's Torah was studied at many a Shabbat table. She became a legend in many homes, especially in "dual-Nehama" homes, where either the parents had been connected to Nehama independently while still single, or the spouse had been "converted to Nehama" after marriage. There, Nehama was a household word, the children aware of her from the day they were born. Returning from her lesson, parents would be entreated, "Let's hear something from Nehama!" For example, Avraham Burg, the son of Dr. Joseph and Rivka Burg, calls himself a "grandson to Nehama's Torah." These second and third generation Nehama fans learned her Torah from their parents, and some wrote projects on her, interviewing their parents for material. Bat-Chen Schlesinger introduced her assignment as follows:

> I chose to write about this distinguished person because she was my father's teacher, was very famous and contributed greatly to Torah learning. From the start I looked forward to knowing more about her, and I was very sorry that I had had several opportunities to go see her with my father and did not go! And now I can't turn back the clock, but I can still know about her and give her respect after her passing.

One son, ordinarily very bashful, came up to Nehama and said, "My mother will never forgive me if I don't introduce myself to you." Other children seized eagerly upon the first chance they had to see the myth with their own eyes. Sarah Leah Neventzal says: "When I saw the apartment, I finally understood what my mother had been describing all these years!"

Nehama was often able to recall, if not their names, then what her students' children did. She particularly loved to teach these students. Professor Moshe Sokolow writes of a visit to her:

> I introduced her to my then three-year-old son, Shalom. While plying him with chocolates, she said: "When you are older, you will come to learn Torah with me."[29]

She took great satisfaction in telling people: "I taught your parents and I taught your grandparents!" and reproached a rabbinical student in class with, "Your mother would have done better!" Another young offender was ordered: "You should be ashamed of yourself! Your mother misses you! Call your parents!" On the application form for her Hebrew University class appeared the question: "Why do you want to study with Nehama Leibowitz?" When a student wrote, "My father studied with her, as did my

---

[29] Moshe Sokolow, "Nehama Leibowitz z"l," *Jewish Action* (Summer 1997): 46.

mother, brother and sister," Nehama accepted the candidate on the spot. At times, several members of a family studied with her simultaneously, the mother and daughter in a class, while the soldier son filled out worksheets. However, deeming it inappropriate for children to see their parents' suggestions rejected in the take-no-prisoners atmosphere of her class, she generally did not permit them to study together.

Some students named their daughters in honor of their beloved teacher even during her lifetime: Shira Nehama, Tehillah Nehama, Hannah Nehama, or just plain Nehama. David Bedein:

> I had long ago made a quiet prayer that if I were ever to have a daughter, that she would be able to understand and teach the Torah with the love and the vigor of Nehama.[30]

His prayer was answered, and he named his daughter Rivka Nehama. These little namesakes gave Nehama great pleasure. She called them "Nehamaleh," and perhaps felt that these babies were in some sense hers. The girls often felt a special connection to her too. When Ora Nehama Ahituv reached bat-mitzvah age, her parents took her to meet their teacher, who gave her a signed copy of *Studies in Devarim*, while little Nehama Yaffa Derovan, after her visit, commented: "That was a nice Nehama!"

---

[30] Bedein, "Goodbye Nechama."

Nehama with students. Courtesy of Mira Ofran.

Nehama in her home with a group from the Senior Educators' Program, 1990.
Courtesy of Mira Ofran.

CHAPTER 10

LATER YEARS:
"THE TANACH-TEACHING GRANNY"

MANY PEOPLE WHO REACH their golden years find themselves alone precisely at the time when they have the most wisdom to share. Family members and a few friends may visit, but it is the rare octogenarian who has people lining up at the door. Often it is the individual who has already given much who is rewarded with continued opportunities to give in old age. Nehama was one of these sought-after senior citizens, with constant visitors and classes into her nineties. Though increasingly tired, she was very glad to continue teaching, writing in a letter to Rafi Aaronson:

> I want to thank you very much for including me in your work; for a person my age it is a great gift to be allowed to continue contributing my accumulated knowledge, experience and highly focused lifelong work, and not to throw it all away – if not into the garbage, then at best onto the bookshelf. (*PN*, 653)

∂~ ~∂

In 1972 Nehama retired from her academic position at Tel Aviv University (*PN*, 15); but she continued to teach as much as ever. Shoshana Brayer recalls: "During the Yom Kippur War the universities were closed, but Nehama did not sit idle, instead opening classes in her house, three times a week. She was very serious about these classes and even gave homework." In 1976, already seventy-one years old, Nehama wrote to R. Yaakov Koppel Reinitz to apologize for her overdue response to his letter:

> I have taken upon myself far too much. I have taught and taught and then taught yet again, without one day of vacation. I was asked to give enrichment sessions for teachers, both elementary and primary school, with teacher's certificate and without, and also groups and courses of teachers from Europe and the United States – in brief, I am so exhausted that "no spirit remains in me any more." (*PN*, 682)

Nonetheless, she did not cruise on autopilot, relying on past learning, but continued to prepare thoroughly for her classes. R. Peretz Rodman witnessed his teacher, in her late seventies, trudging home from the National Library, bulging bags in hand, and complaining about recent cutbacks:

"They've started closing at seven instead of ten – how do they expect anyone to get any work done?"

Nehama remained extremely young at heart. In her late eighties, vacationing at the Reich hotel for Passover, she complained that she was not enjoying herself.

"What's the matter?" asked a friend. "Is it the food?"

"The food is fine."

"What then, your room?"

"No, the room is fine."

"So then what's wrong?"

"Well... everyone here is old!"

At the age of eighty-five, Nehama remarked in all seriousness to her friend Miriam Ron: "I'm very envious of you – you are always doing different things, while I always do the same thing. When I retire I'll also do different things!" But she never really intended to retire. On the contrary, she began in her old age to teach in new frameworks. In the 1980s she wrote a course for the Open University, and also began teaching in several men's and women's yeshivahs and in programs for yeshivah graduates. R. Elyashiv Knohl, who had known her since childhood, attended her class at the Herzog teaching seminary of the Har Etzion yeshivah. He recalls that "the excitement in the room and her concern that everyone understand was exactly the same as always, as was indeed the very soul of her Torah."

Nehama desired to continue teaching Torah as long as she had clear thought and breath in her lungs. And others concurred with her desire. Every year, R. Ben Hollander and the administration of the Hebrew University Overseas Students Program adopted a variety of tactics to persuade Nehama to stay on for "just one more year." In this way they kept her with them for twenty years. In 1990, R. Hollander suggested moving the university class to her house for her convenience. Nehama exclaimed, "If every teacher gives lessons at home we might as well close down the university!" But she eventually agreed, and a record forty-eight people were crammed into her small apartment. She also moved her Open University course to her home, and students made the pilgrimage to Jerusalem from as far away as Ma'alot in the north and Dimona in the south. Nehama's modest house on Ha-Tzvi Street became a temple of learning. Once, when she gave her home address to a taxi driver, he asked her, "Are you going to hear the Tanach-teaching granny?" Astonished, she said, "How do you know about this person?" "Well, I once took an American student, and he said to me, 'Hurry up, I'll be late for my lesson with the *savta melamedet Tanach.*'" Nehama smiled. "Yes, that is where I'm going."

Nehama in her home with students from the Gruss Kollel, 1992.
From left: Bruriah Eisner, Elie Tuchman, Adam Berner, Boaz Mori, Adam Klein,
Bruce (Yochanan) Klein. Courtesy of Mira Ofran.

Nehama in her home with students from the Gruss Kollel, 1995. Inscription reads:
"Spring 5755, Gruss Kollel. A small gift to thank you for the privilege you granted
me to study from the source of living waters, and to read Megillat Esther to you.
With much affection and thanks, Mordechai Sicklick."
Top row, from left: Moshe Sendowski, Dov Schreier. *Second row, from left*: Bini Krauss,
Chaim Hagler, Shaul Erlbaum, Andrew (Mordechai) Sicklick, Nehama Leibowitz,
Jonathan Kroll, Menachem Linzer. Courtesy of Mira Ofran.

During these years, she also wrote a column on the weekly Torah portion for the daily newspaper, *Yediot Ahronot*.[1] Although she phrased herself succinctly and simply to suit their readership, she still managed to incorporate her usual favorites: Verses, commentaries and Midrashim, and themes of responsibility, honesty, and Zionism; and garnished, as always, with humor and references to contemporary events. Here she succeeded where many intellectuals fail, writing on weighty subjects without being heavy.

In 1991 Nehama started teaching in Touro College; and she also taught a course at Machon Pardes in the same year. She was still capable of tremendous impact on her students. It was during this period that a group from Canada noticed that their Tanach teacher, recently returned from studying with Nehama in Israel, had noticeably improved her skills.

Nehama reached such advanced years that many of her students were elderly themselves. She was known to ask after "the young people" when referring to seventy-year-olds. But her old age also did not prevent youngsters, who had grown up in drastically different realities, from attaching themselves to her. R. Hanan Schlesinger recounts: "I was a twenty-year-old, recently arrived in Israel, with only rudimentary Hebrew and Torah knowledge, meeting a seventy-year-old with an encyclopedic knowledge of Bible and its commentaries. Fifty years of life separated us, but you'd never know it – she bridged what should have been a yawning chasm with incredible ease." Even teenagers found Nehama appealing. R. Hollander's son brought his yeshivah high school friends to study with her on Saturday nights. She loved this fact, commenting that today's youth were certainly not worthless druggies if high school students who studied Torah all week – in her opinion, too much – wanted more on a Saturday night. As an eleventh-grader, Chaviva Speter heard Nehama's lessons in the Tikvateinu center in Romema. Inspired, she decided to spend the month of Elul attending daily lessons in Nehama's house. After two weeks, Nehama said to her: "What are you doing here? Doesn't anyone from your school know that you're here every day between eight and ten o'clock?" When Speter confessed that they did not, Nehama was shocked; and Speter's excuses citing parental permission fell on deaf ears. Quite affected by this incident, Nehama quoted it many times, to persuade teachers they must pay more attention to what their students are doing.

Bruriah Eisner was only thirteen when she decided to attend Nehama's lecture at the Gruss Kollel. Nehama told her she would be wasting her time;

---

[1] Reproduced in *PN*, 503–530.

but after the first lesson, let her continue. "She was very grandmotherly and wise," recalls Eisner, but adds that she also always felt a fear and trembling, never knowing what would come next with Nehama.

಄ ⚬⚬

Already back in 1954, the young Tamar Ross had described Nehama in an essay for Hebrew class as follows:

> Her energetic soul urges her body, slow and cumbersome as it is, onwards.

This only became more true as the years passed, with Nehama's agile mind increasingly hampered by her physical limits. She drafted all the energy she could muster to get through her intense days in one piece. Dr. Shmuel Adler was enlisted in 1993, four years before her death, to attend to Nehama's medical needs. In their first conversation, she complained of constant fatigue and asked for a prescription to keep her awake. Smiling, Adler commented that most people came to him with the opposite problem, needing sleeping pills. She was taken aback, and kept returning to this topic: "Really, doctor? There really are people who want pills to make them sleep?" Adler recalls: "She was a very old woman – but I've never seen anyone younger. Her desire to know, to learn, was like that of a two-year-old." He was surprised at the ability of this ninety-year-old woman to develop deep personal connections with new people. "Her systems were barely functioning – muscles, ears, etc. – but her brain and her heart were still going strong," he says.

Nehama was eighty-seven years old when she entered the hospital for the first time in her life, in 1992. Though she was unwell, her high standards were still intact, and she was dismayed to discover that even in a Jewish hospital in the State of Israel, the doctors could talk about the patients as if they were not present. Nonetheless, she put her trust in the doctors as Divine agents of healing, and, as was typical of her, she created spiritual connections with some of them, who came to her *shiurim* or talked Torah with her. Her conversation with a young cardiologist, as she anxiously awaited the results of some heart tests, is recorded by Dr. Avigdor Bonchek:

> The doctor looked at his graphs and then up at his silent, apprehensive patient; again a look at his papers and again an inquisitive glance at his increasingly nervous patient. Then, hesitantly and in a barely audible voice, he asked, "Do you also explain the Abarbanel? Because I have a question…." Nehama breaks out in a laugh as she retells the story. "Nu!" she summarizes, as if to say: Would you expect any less of a Jew?

232

> They are meditating on the Torah all the time and in the strangest places.[2]

True to form, she also brought back from the hospital new stories to tell in class. There was the doctor who, before he gave her an injection, asked her to tell him what Rashi says on a certain verse. "How did you know I'm familiar with Rashi?" she inquired. The doctor responded, "Nu, Nehama, *be-emet* (really)!" Ever fascinated by language, she explained to her students that here the word *be-emet* is not to be translated literally as "in truth," but rather as, "You must be joking!"

Nehama clung to her independence and only reluctantly permitted people to help her. Not wanting to relocate to an old-age home, she employed someone to take care of her needs. Students and friends volunteered to escort her for walks recommended by her doctors or join her weekly shopping expeditions on Friday mornings; and they recall these experiences fondly. Joy Rochwarger: "My Friday mornings before had felt like a waste of time. But now, with Nehama, they were a spiritual experience, the beginning of my preparation for Shabbat. Whenever I couldn't come I arranged for a replacement, but was always nervous that I was going to lose it to someone else." Rochwarger used this time to share her dilemmas with Nehama, whose reactions always helped her resolve any doubts. "Her sense of right and wrong always threw me back on track. It was not that I didn't already know what she was saying, but the way she said it, the power and weight behind her words, expressed her entire being."

Despite her increasing tiredness Nehama determinedly continued to teach. In fact, it invigorated her, and her doctor said to her: "Whatever it is that you're doing – carry on!" Her dynamism and vitality while teaching lay in stark contrast to the person she became at the lesson's end, picking up her cane and shuffling away like the elderly lady she actually was. One evening, R. Hollander arrived for the regular lesson, and found her lying on the bed, too weary to teach. She rejected his idea of canceling the class, insisting that she must teach something since people had come specially. He suggested that twenty minutes on the weekly Torah portion would satisfy them, and she agreed. Two hours later, Nehama was still going strong, while students fell asleep over their papers. Rochwarger recalls:

> Sometimes she would begin a *shiur* at 8:30 at night and visibly grow stronger and more determined as the hour grew late. At 10:30 she

---

[2] Bonchek, "Professor Nehama," 18.

would abruptly stop and announce that it was time for everyone to go home since they were surely worn out.[3]

Nehama said, "Walking up the stairs is difficult, but teaching is easy. If I teach, I'm well; if I don't teach, I'm ill." She wrote in a letter:

> Thank God, in my old age I am still a sought-after teacher in kibbutzim, cities and Kollels, in Nahal army outposts and in seminars, and this tremendous amount of work is not a burden; on the contrary it gladdens me and gives me strength and health. Great are His mercies. (PN, 690)

Indeed vacation time, at Passover and Succot, was when Nehama felt most unwell.

In these years, she tried to limit her visitors, but her students missed her sorely and got her to agree to short visits, for if she agreed to five or ten minutes, it would likely turn into a conversation of two hours. Even now, Nehama did not turn the talk onto herself or sink into nostalgia, but was the same intelligent and interested conversationalist she had always been.

ॐ ॐ

As illness took its toll, for the first time in her life Nehama found herself unable to travel, and this greatly upset her. "I used to listen to the conversations on the bus and learn so much, and now I can't travel anywhere," she confided sadly to a friend. It distressed her that she had to sit down frequently during the Yom Kippur service. But she was able to laugh even about these distressing developments. When, outside the National Library, Professor Shaul Yedgar encountered Nehama feeling dizzy and headed for home, she still managed to quip: "I thought to myself: It would be typical of me to die in the library!"

Nehama's lessons were not what they used to be. They got shorter as her strength failed, and her short-term memory became limited. Rochwarger:

> The last year... the spark also began to wane from Nehama's eyes and her spirit began to falter. Our walks became shorter and shorter, until finally we would only be able to walk once up and down the block. I felt as if I was watching the light of a dimming flame.[4]

But her classes were still full of wisdom, and people still came to hear her. She continued to look over students' doctorates on request, to read new material and expand her horizons. Mere weeks before her death, students

---

[3] Rochwarger, "Words," 60.
[4] Rochwarger, "Words," 77.

heard new ideas from her.[5] She also continued to have meaningful encounters and conversations, for instance with Dr. Avivah Zornberg.

Zornberg was familiar with Nehama's books and had also attended a few of Nehama's classes in the Hebrew University, principally to learn from her didactic methods. Impressed by how Nehama engaged "every single brain in the class" with the text, she later adopted some of these methods.[6] But, like Nehama, she went on to forge her own path in Torah. Indeed, many would argue that she was Nehama's successor, at least in the English-speaking world, as the foremost original and erudite (female) voice of Torah scholarship.[7] The two shared several students, through whom Nehama had heard about Zornberg's creative interpretations. Over the years, her typically pithy messages got back to Zornberg: "It sounds very interesting – but why do you teach in English?!" Zornberg was also aware of Nehama's influence on her students, and about a year before Nehama's death, called to arrange a meeting. She had no intention of debating the merits of teaching in English: "I knew there would be no chance of persuading her of my views; actually we didn't touch on that until the end of the conversation." Instead, they spent several hours talking about life and literature. "I was grateful for the opportunity," says Zornberg. "I thought I would be tiring her, and kept indicating that we could finish if she liked, but she stayed for hours. Although unwell, her mind was completely there." She experienced Nehama as very warm, supportive of her work, and cosmopolitan in her approach to world literature. She presented Nehama with her book *Genesis: The Beginning of Desire*, and Nehama said she felt honored. This was not lip service, for, to Zornberg's surprise, she read and complimented the work.

---

[5] See Ruth Ben-Meir, "*Le-darkei parshanuto shel Ramban*," in *PN*, 138, 57.

[6] See Heilman, "A Passion." Zornberg's style is however very different from Nehama's; there is far less discussion. See also Calev Ben-David, "One Woman's Exodus," *Jerusalem Post*, March 23, 2001, B12.

[7] For more, see pages 568–569 below.

CHAPTER 11

LEAVETAKING:
"DO NOT LEAVE US"

> The children of Israel pleaded: "Do not leave us.".... Then Moshe said to God: "Until now I asked for my life, but now my soul is given over to You" (*Midrash Tanhuma, Va-et'hanan* 6).

EVEN WITH DEATH LOOMING, Nehama's forceful personality made itself known. She wanted to have a clear mind, and to be fully prepared, and asked R. Yohanan Fried to teach her the laws pertaining to a person on her deathbed. Despite her repeated urgings, R. Fried felt compelled to refuse.[1]

Nehama continued teaching at home through the first few months of 1997, until a few weeks before her death. David Weinberg recalls:

> Her very last lectures in life, in which I had the privilege of participating, were devoted to the studying of morality in thought and action, based on chapters 21–23 in Exodus. Despite the fact that the *parashat ha-shavua* advanced weekly, Nehama couldn't get away from *Parashat Mishpatim*, as if she knew this was her last time around to expound upon the biblical prohibitions against duplicity, prevarication and the telling of lies, the causing of mental or verbal anguish, and the mistreatment or abuse of neighbors and strangers.[2]

In her last *shiur*, given the night before entering the hospital, she quoted her favorite *Meshech Hochmah*, explaining why Moses dashed the two tablets to the ground.[3] She was coughing, but the lesson took place.

Finally, Nehama went into hospital for the last time. Many students visited her, trying to keep her spirits up. R. Ben Hollander came in to her room declaring heartily, "Oh, I'm just in time for the *shiur*," and she laughed. Another visitor, a former student from the Mizrachi seminar, reminisced with Nehama, who still remembered all her students from more than sixty

---

[1] He followed the *Hatam Sofer*'s position that it is not customary to learn these Halachot until they are about to be used (interview).
[2] Weinberg, "Remembering Nehama."
[3] Weinberg, "Remembering Nehama."

years before. But now, at last, Nehama lost her grip on optimism and love of life, and she became depressed, quoting to Bruriah Eisner from Jonah (4:8):

> … And he fainted and wished to die, and said, It is better for me to die than to live.

Eisner: "This was the only time I can remember that she spoke bitterly. Even when she talked about not being a mother, she had never been bitter." Even in hard times, Nehama spoke her feelings through Torah. Even when she was practically unconscious, when a student asked her a question on Rashi, she roused herself and whispered an answer.

֍ ֎

It was an unhappy day when the world was deprived of Professor Nehama Leibowitz. The date was April 12, 1997 (5 Nisan 5757). Here is Joy Rochwarger's account of that day:

> It was a Shabbat afternoon and… I chose to take a walk and visit Nehama, who had been in the hospital for almost a month. I had been visiting her almost every day and had witnessed the distressing progression of her illness. Most of the time, I would sit at the side of her bed hoping she would awaken for just a few moments so that I could share some words with her. Many times I would hear her mumbling to herself, barely conscious. Even in her weakened state, I could make out words that always had something to do with Torah. Sometimes she would be reciting verses; other times she would be clarifying a point that had possibly been raised by a previous visitor, or maybe a student from long ago. Whenever I would try to engage her in conversation, the topic I introduced always had something to do with *Tanakh*, and in this vein she responded. On that same afternoon, I expected to walk in and find her resting, possibly with one or two students sitting nearby.
>
> As I approached the doorway to the Intensive Care Unit, I realized something was wrong. The person lying in Nehama's bed was bareheaded. For all the years I had known Nehama, not once had I seen her without a hat…. I braced myself for news that her situation had worsened and she had been transferred to a different ward. When I entered the Unit and asked the nurse where I could find Nehama, the response was clipped, "Who are you?" Instinctively, I answered that I was someone who was very close to Nehama. I can only assume that I was misunderstood, as the Hebrew word for "close," *karov*, is the same as that for "relative." I was then informed that Nehama had passed away early that morning, and I was curtly dismissed. I walked out of the hospital in a daze, not sure how to absorb the news. With my stomach churning, I began to make my way back to my apartment….

Rochwarger happened to meet one of Nehama's great-nephews. He said that the family were still unsure about the time of the funeral and would have to consult a rabbi after Shabbat, for the Jerusalem custom to bury as soon as possible would prevent many of Nehama's out-of-town students from attending. Rochwarger went home, where she spent some time mulling over an important halachic question:

> The news that Nehama had died was a devastating blow. I had lost my teacher and friend. But Nehama was not only *my* teacher. In my eyes she had grown to the level of a *talmidat hakhamim*, a revered teacher of Torah who imparts her lessons to the masses. One should tear *keriyah* as a sign of intense mourning. Although my grief was overwhelming, I was not an immediate relative and therefore not necessarily obligated in this commandment. Nehama, however, did not have any children, and her husband had died many years before. It didn't seem right that there would be no one performing the *keriyah* ritual. Would I be permitted to do so?

After Shabbat the phone rang, and she was told that the funeral had been delayed until Sunday to enable the students, who in the case of a *talmid hakham* are considered as relatives, to arrive. However, the decision of tearing *keriyah* would be hers to make.

> At this point I was left to my own devices, and instinctively reverted to a well-rehearsed habit that I had developed to help me resolve difficult questions: I turned to Nehama. But for the first time in more than ten years my question was met with a bleak silence. What would she have said? Would Nehama have viewed herself as a *talmidat hakhamim*? Or would she have considered this title to be too pretentious and undeserved?[4]

Nehama would undoubtedly have picked the latter. Nevertheless, several students did end up ritually tearing their clothing.[5]

ಸ ೕ

Unsurprisingly, Nehama tried to orchestrate that even her passing draw as little fuss as possible. She requested that no customary death notices with information about the funeral and *shivah* be plastered on Jerusalem's walls. Yet her funeral, in the Har Tamir cemetery, was attended by thousands, and many had to stand outside the site. The assembled included all ages and all religious affiliations, men with black hats and long sidelocks next to bare-

---

[4] Rochwarger, "Words," 77–80.
[5] Abramowitz, *Tales*, 19.

headed men; young Americans next to elderly Israelis; students, colleagues, friends, family, and those who had simply come to pay their last respects to a great Jewish person.

Nehama had specifically instructed that no eulogies were to be said. In the end, she passed away in Nisan, when eulogies are traditionally forbidden anyway.[6] Professor Meir Weiss had already prepared a eulogy before he heard this, the opening line of which was: "From this day on, if you want to know what's troubling Rashi, you won't have anyone to ask."[7] The absence of a forum to express all the grief and love was saddening, but Hamiel observes:

> What the mourners, from the oldest to the youngest, said to each other at the funeral said more than any eulogy could have.[8]

When the time came for the *kaddish* prayer, Nehama's nephew, Yossi Yovel, announced: "It says in *Ethics of the Fathers* [6:3] that anyone who has learned even one letter from his friend must give him respect as a parent. So all those who feel as I do, like Nehama's son, may join in the *kaddish* prayer with me...." He had barely finished his sentence when an extraordinary thing occurred. From all quarters, a host of voices declaimed tearfully and in unison: "*Yitgadal ve-yitkadash shmeh rabbah.*" As R. Hollander later noted, Nehama's passing on the Shabbat of weekly portion *Tazria*, which begins with subject of birth (Leviticus 12:2) was fitting, for she truly had many children. Whether students, or students of students, all felt that level of connection. The mourners thronging outside thought that they were hearing a heavenly choir. "The only time I have ever heard anything like it was at Yad Vashem on Holocaust Memorial Day," says Yehudit Ilan.

When it was over, nobody wanted to leave. Many lingered, reciting Psalms and speaking with long-lost acquaintances, a living connection with Nehama. Those on the outskirts now made their way into the burial site, already covered in a huge mound of stones. In accordance with Nehama's wishes, no tribute was engraved on her tombstone. Besides her name and dates of birth and death, she permitted only one other word. It was the title she had preferred above all others as the greatest possible honor, the one encapsulating best her passions, her wisdom and her contribution to the world: *Morah* (teacher).

---

[6] See *Shulhan Aruch, Orah Hayyim*, 429:2.
[7] Baruch Schwartz, interview.
[8] Hamiel, "*Morat.*"

Nehama's grave at the Har Tamir cemetery, Jerusalem.

Nehama's gravestone reads: "Nehama Leibowitz. Teacher.
3rd *Elul*, 5665 – 5th *Nisan*, 5757"

The loss began to sink in gradually. For R. Hollander, it was only when he walked into the university after Passover and realized that he could not phone Nehama that he was overcome by emptiness. The work of making meaning of Nehama's life began almost immediately. Sarah Leah Neventzal: "Her death fell within the Passover school break, and my first thought was one of regret, that I would not be able to speak to my students about her. Then I reflected that with her modesty, Nehama might not have wanted it anyway." Rochwarger:

> Nehama's loss for me was like a *hurban* (destruction of the Temple)....
> However, given the overriding principle she had taught me concerning the main lesson of *Tisha b'Av* – to find the kernel of hope amidst the decimation, I felt the imperative to find a similar way to understand her loss. Nehama's life provided me with a pattern after which I could model my own.... Nehama's ultimate success is in creating the next link in the chain of transmission that connects us back to Sinai, adding her voice to the collective experience of the oral tradition, and enabling us to participate as well.... In all her actions and teachings Nehama was the embodiment of a Torah scroll. Her essence was eternal truth which nothing can diminish or divert – "She [the Torah] is a tree of life to those who lay hold on her: and happy are those who hold her fast."[9]

A week after Nehama's death, a night of learning in her memory took place at Ohel Nehama Synagogue in Jerusalem.[10] In the New York area, members of Congregation Ohab Zedek and others undertook to learn the whole Tanach together in memory of Nehama. A few weeks later, a memorial evening was held at the house of Danny and Rivka Bash, a Swiss couple who had joined the *Amitei Tzion* relatively late. Many of the *Amitei Tzion* crowd were there, as well as other students, neighbors, relatives and doctors. Some were silent, still in shock. Others found words: "I never realized that I could love a person so much. It's like losing a parent." "It's astounding that this woman was as close to us as our own relatives. We are all orphaned children." Indeed, this gathering seemed to fill an emotional vacuum left by the lack of halachic obligation upon those present to sit the traditional *shivah*. The evening was dedicated to learning Nehama's Torah, but an event in memory of Nehama could not remain all solemnity and mourning. A family atmosphere reigned, with much laughter. As a worksheet was handed out to be studied, one participant called out, like a

---

[9] Rochwarger, "Words," 80–81. The reference is to Proverbs 3:18.
[10] Uriel Heilman, "Teacher of the People of Israel Mourned," *Jerusalem Post*, Monday, April 14, 1997, 12.

delighted wine connoisseur, "Which worksheet is this? Ah – a good year!" Inspiring personal stories poured forth, reflecting who Nehama was and her bond with those present. During the course of the evening, students asked each other to recall where particular teachings of Nehama's were located; their memories had become a living index to her works.

As they quoted her, people consciously or unconsciously imitated Nehama's voice and gestures – her voice, her strong facial expressions and hand motions. It was almost like a meeting of the regular *Amitei Tzion* class – a place was even kept for the chronically late student – but without the beloved teacher. The stories told seemed to bring her back to life, and every so often, someone noted what Nehama would have said. Private jokes abounded – only this Nehama coterie understood the full significance when someone called out in a rousing voice: "Did everyone get a sheet?"

For many, Nehama was irreplaceable. Students and friends note: "When she died there was the feeling of the last of a certain generation," "Until today when I pass by her house I feel completely orphaned," and "I have all these questions that I wish I could have asked Nehama, but it's too late." Those seeking answers and advice must now fend for themselves or refer to worksheets, letters or information held in the memories of those who knew her.

However, Nehama's death did not signal the end of her work or its impact, as we will see in the next chapter.

CHAPTER 12

NEHAMA'S LEGACY:
"*ZOT NEHAMATI:* THIS IS MY COMFORT"

> This is my comfort in my affliction; for Your word has revived me. (Psalms 119: 50–51).

Introduction

NEHAMA'S THOUGHT AND WORK had its continuance via the writings she left behind and the people she taught, who passed it on to those who never got the chance. At a conference at the Van Leer Institute, marking the hundredth anniversary of Nehama's birth, Dr. Bryna Levy suggested that the event be named "From the Fruit of Her Hands" because the fruits of Nehama's Torah endure to this day.

Ongoing publication

Nehama's estate turned up a few surprises – an unpublished article; some writings on Psalms; chapter headings; and discussions and talks for the radio. There was also a manuscript for a book on teaching Exodus, paralleling somewhat her book on teaching Genesis, *Limmud parshanei ha-Torah u-derachim le-hora'atam.* This was subsequently published, unedited, in late 2003 as *Hora'at parshanei ha-Torah: Shemot* by the Eliner Library of the World Zionist Organization, who also reprinted the earlier book on Genesis under the title *Hora'at parshanei ha-Torah: Bereshit.* In the meantime, the *Studies* series continues to be translated, most recently into Russian and German. Some of the questions at the end of the *Studies* have been published, with suggested answers and insights by R. Mordechai Spiegelman.[1]

Another active front has been that of the *gilyonot.* The JNF's Department for Activities in Religious Organizations published four glossy pamphlets entitled *Darchei noam,* containing one worksheet and one teachers' guide for each portion in Genesis and Exodus, alongside pictures of Israel's flora.

---

[1] See http://www.jewishagency.org/JewishAgency/English/Jewish+Education/Compelling+Content/Jewish+Time/Jewish+Sources/Insights/.

Edited by R. Yitshak Reiner, they included answers that he provided, based on students' answers that Nehama had validated during her lifetime.

Since the worksheets are unavailable for purchase today, they are being transferred to the Internet so that they may continue to be a resource for future generations. Two groups of people have undertaken this mammoth task. The first group is directed by R. Reiner. Selections of *gilyonot* and teacher's guides, edited by R. Reiner and with suggested answers, have been posted on two Internet sites, including translations into English.[2] Because many of the questions are too difficult for today's student, it was decided that these Internet *gilyonot* should include answers based on information heard directly from Nehama or feedback to her worksheet correspondents, or simply an educated guess.

The second group is the Leibowitz family, who have undertaken to transfer all of the worksheets and most of the teachers' guides to the Internet.[3] These are not accompanied by answers, but with an invitation for people to post their suggested answers on the site, and guided forums for learning and discussion.

Since Nehama never provided answers in her worksheets, an argument may indeed be made that they should be left open. On the other hand, as Nehama once told R. Nachum Amsel, though she disapproved of the translation of her worksheets into English at the time, calling it "watered down," she felt that "after 120 years you can do as you like."[4] Only time will tell which formats will bring the most benefit.

Books about Nehama continue to be published. In 2001, a 750-page tribute to Nehama appeared. Entitled *Pirkei Nehama*,[5] it contained articles written by students, colleagues, friends and family on a variety of topics connected to Nehama's work. Here, for the first time, many aspects of her work that she had left unsystematized, preferring to invest her time in teaching, were laid out clearly. Examples include her approach to Midrash,

---

[2] The World Council for Torah Education site contains English versions of the *gilyonot* and also teacher's guides (http://www.moreshet.net/oldsite/nechama/gilayonarchives. htm), and the Jewish Agency site has Hebrew ones (http://www.jafi.org.il/education/torani/nehama /index.html). Those interested are also referred to some new studies, based on Nehama's worksheets, by R. Shmuel Peerless and R. Aryeh Strikovsky, on the Lookstein site (http://www.lookstein.org/nechama_parasha.htm).

[3] This project opened to the public in April 2008 at www.nechama.org.il.

[4] Abramowitz, *Tales*, 81.

[5] Literally "Chapters of Consolation," often referring to chapters from Isaiah read on the seven Sabbaths between Tisha be-Av and Rosh HaShanah. This volume was printed by the Eliner Library, who published her *Studies* series – see the bibliography for further details.

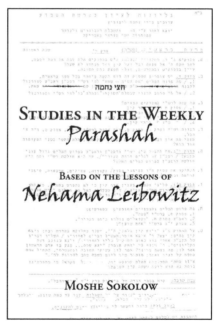

A selection of books about Nehama Leibowitz's work.

Hebrew language, or Targum. The volume also included a variety of writings and letters by Nehama, published and unpublished.

The story of the compilation of *Pirkei Nehama* says something about its subject. Normally, editors of a memorial volume have to toil to assemble a group of people willing to write articles, especially new ones. But in this case, those who were approached agreed at once. In fact, many more articles could have been included, and some people were even upset at not being approached. This fact testifies to the devotion inspired by Nehama and her work, as do the personal tributes inside. The editors were also amazed and amused to discover that many authors – writing on topics varying from the Bible's cantillation through various commentators and educational issues – were convinced that their field was *the* area of Nehama's specialization, the one that she loved most. Such was the breadth of Nehama's expertise and her passion for everything to do with Torah.

However, this 770-page book was not the last word in studies on Nehama – far from it. In 2002, *Studies on the Haggadah from the Teachings of Nehama Leibowitz*, edited by R. Yitshak Reiner and R. Shmuel Peerless, was published by Urim Publications in English; followed by an expanded *Haggadah* in Hebrew in 2003. Adhering to the question-and-answer format of Seder night, these books contain questions culled from Nehama's works, together with answers, and with the more difficult question indicated by wine goblets in place of Nehama's usual Xs. In 2003, R. Shmuel Peerless published *To Study and to Teach: The Methodology of Nechama Leibowitz* (Lookstein Center and Urim Publications), containing pedagogical material and lesson plans, useful to teachers worldwide. Also in 2003, Leah Abramowitz's *Tales of Nehama* was published. In 2005, R. Yitshak Reiner assembled Nehama's writings on the festivals as *Mo'adei Nehama*, and in 2007, Dr. Marla Frankel published *Toratah shel Nehama Leibowitz: darkah be-limmud ha-Tanach u've-hora'ato*, dealing with Nehama's intellectual background and her philosophy of education. Also in 2007, Professor Moshe Sokolow published *Hatzi Nehama: Studies in the Weekly Parashah Based on the Lessons of Nehama Leibowitz* (Urim Publications). A Hebrew account of Nehama's life story was published in 2008.[6] From all the above it becomes apparent how varied and interesting were Nehama's life and work, providing material for many volumes of analysis, and surely there will be more to come.

Nehama was pleased at the documentation of her intellectual work, for thus it would endure. She enjoyed hearing Frankel read selections from her

---

[6] Hayuta Deutsch, *Nehama: sippur hayyehah shel Nehama Leibowitz*, Yediot Ahronot, 2008. It was published as this work was at printing stage, so its findings have not been taken into account.

doctorate on Nehama's pedagogical theory. Frankel deliberately chose her least contentious paragraphs, but even in her later life Nehama's powers of observation were keen, and she demanded, "Next time read me something that has more substance!"

Teachings

Nehama's Torah also lives on.[7] It influences much of the Tanach curriculum in Israeli schools of the religious-national stream. The religious Tanach *bagrut* (Israeli matriculation exam) is largely based on her approach. In fact, between 1975 and 1996, Nehama helped to write the exam questions.[8] Jewish adults continue to study her Torah in various ways. The novelist Naomi Ragen wrote, in her newspaper column of June 2001, following a traumatic week for Israel:

> Sunday evening ushered in the holiday of Shavuot, in which we Jews rejoice at having received the Torah from God at Sinai. Our women's study group stayed up late Sunday night poring over the last study sheet of the late professor Nehama Leibowitz on Genesis, completing five years of intensive study. To celebrate, we gathered with our families for much the next day. Recalling the pleasure of our collective learning experiences, we forgot for a few hours the tragedies all around us, remembering our striving to be near God by understanding His words a little better week by week.[9]

A group meets every month in the Ohel Nehama synagogue, led by R. Yitshak Reiner, to swap answers on the worksheet for the week's portion. There, people who never met Nehama are treated to a flavor of her Torah. A group in the Tel Aviv area also set up a monthly lecture in Nehama's memory.

In the 1940s Nehama began giving a *shiur* on the weekly Torah portion every Shabbat for the women of Kiryat Moshe and any husbands who wished to tag along. After five years, she withdrew in order to spend more time with her husband, but not wishing the group to disband, she invited different lecturers, primarily her own students, to come every week. When she left the neighborhood, the participants continued bringing in diverse lecturers, using her reputation to convince them. Miriam Ron, the organizer, attests: "Some of Nehama's students never refused, because it was her *shiur*." Nehama was amazed at the longevity of this lecture series, and was delighted

---

[7] For a more in-depth analysis of the future of Nehama's legacy, see chapter 24.
[8] Abramowitz, *Tales*, 94.
[9] Naomi Ragen, "Save Us from Ourselves," *Jerusalem Post*, June 1, 2001, B9.

to discover that "her" *shiur* was the longest-lived in Israel. The group of over sixty women continues to study together to this day.

Several conferences and study days on Nehama's work have been held, including joint study days on Nehama and Yeshayahu. Her legacy continues also in the world of academia. Her student at Tel Aviv University, Professor Yairah Amit, adopted Nehama's method of comparing and contrasting commentaries. Amit trains her students to brainstorm what each commentator's difficulty with the text might be, what the argument between them is, and how each one makes his case. However, in Amit's classroom there is no attempt at deciding who was right; rather, the aim is to understand each one's logic based on his historical background.

To this day Nehama is frequently mentioned in classes all across the globe. R. Nachum Amsel feels that anyone who asks the question "What's troubling Rashi?" is drawing upon Nehama's approach. Even those who do not agree with her method still sometimes quote it, for she represents an entire school of thought that cannot be ignored.[10]

Nehama's Open University course on Rashi continues to be taught; and although her method is now well-known, a surprisingly large number of participants in this course still find her close reading method fresh and eye-opening. Teachers also continue to use her books as a resource for preparing their lessons. Chaviva Speter: "I frequently find myself wondering why I am trying to reinvent the wheel, and return instead to Nehama's collection of sources and analysis." Nehama's name also crops up in various writings, from the predictable, such as books on Jewish commentary and Bible scholarship, to works further afield, for example in *Exodus and Revolution* by Michael Walzer[11] or in a survey of halachic literature about surrogate motherhood.[12]

A prize named for Nehama and her brother Yeshayahu was inaugurated, and just after her death in 1997, the Nehama Leibowitz library for Jewish Studies was opened in an Israeli religious girls' school, Neve Ruchama. A

---

[10] See further in chapter 24.

[11] New York, Basic Books, 1985, x and 54 (and see also in footnotes).

[12] J. David Bleich, "Survey of Recent Halakhic Periodical Literature: Surrogate Motherhood," *Tradition* 32/2 (1998): 162. He cites *IBB*, 111–112 (*NSB*, 156–157), applying Nehama's lesson regarding Sarah's overidealistic behavior (see page 346 below) as follows: "Sarah is described as having desired to displace Hagar and to raise Hagar's child as her own. But in practice the arrangement does not succeed. The child is not Sarah's; it is Hagar's. People may believe that they are capable of transcending biological realia, but in practice, they find that they cannot. Despite the best intentions of all concerned, biological facts give rise to psychological consequences and human beings frequently find it impossible to rise above, or to suppress natural instincts and emotions."

street was also named for Nehama in Jerusalem's Har Homa neighborhood in April 2002.

Here we conclude the biographical section of our book.

Nehama Leibowitz. Courtesy of Mira Ofran.

PART II

EMUNOT VE-DE'OT
BELIEFS AND OPINIONS

We begin the second part of this book, the analytical section, with some topics upon which Nehama held strong views: Zionism and the Hebrew language, feminism and femininity, religious identity, humanism and the approach to biblical heroes, and themes of autonomy and responsibility.

CHAPTER 13

ZIONISM:
"DIGGING WELLS ONCE AGAIN"

SOME OF NEHAMA'S most cherished values related to the Jewish people, its land and its language. In Germany, Nehama had pioneered the teaching of *Ivrit be-Ivrit*, teaching in Hebrew, and her emigration to Palestine at the first possible moment indicated where her heart lay. She wrote to the Israeli High Court judge, Zvi Tal:

> If someone had informed me during my childhood in the Diaspora at the beginning of this century (I am now ninety years old) that I should merit that we should have a High Court in Jerusalem and that a High Court Judge would write to me with talmudic sources, we would have thought – I and my brother, of blessed memory – that these were fairy tales, like the Leviathan that the righteous shall eat in the World to Come, and that Father was telling us this to bolster our Jewish and Zionist education. And yet this is no fairy tale from the *Ein Yaakov*. The envelope is actually in my hand, with "High Court" written on it. And now that we have merited this, it reinforces our faith that you, Honorable High Justice, will yet be seated in the Sanhedrin of seventy-one, and Jews from the four corners of the earth shall dwell with us here, awaiting your every word. (*PN*, 665)

Israel never lost its magic for Nehama. She especially loved Jerusalem. The very first time she traveled to Jerusalem, Nehama noticed a traffic sign that said, "*Slow Down – Drive in Low Gear.*" Turning to her husband, she remarked in a voice filled with reverence: "This is what you have to do when you come to Jerusalem!" Only later did she discover that it was a regular traffic sign, seen all over Israel. She told this story repeatedly, laughing at her own unworldliness.

Religious Zionism

Nehama firmly belonged to the religious-Zionist camp. She loved Israel and Hebrew not only for their own sake, but also because they represented the Torah's natural environment. She exhorted Diaspora teachers:

> May you also succeed in inducing your students to come up to Zion so that they may study our holy Torah in the holy language in which it was given, on holy soil. (*TI*, 37)

Though not part of the politically messianist Zionist camp, Nehama took much pleasure in going on tours of ever-expanding Jerusalem, crying: "This is the redemption!" Unlike for her brother, for Nehama the State held spiritual import.[1] In a letter to Professor Bergman, she writes of herself as

> educating towards loyalty and love of Israel as our State and country, the beginning of our redemption. (*PN*, 660)

She supported R. Kasher's suggestion to mark the State's founding and the ingathering of the exiles by drinking a fifth cup of wine at the Seder; and she held the many Jews who did not immigrate to Israel in 1948 responsible for the fact that this custom did not take hold.[2] She did not view the establishment of the State as a unique event, isolated from the rest of Jewish history, but rather as a fulfillment of all the prophecies from the "covenant between the pieces" to those of the final prophets.[3] Rejecting the secular Zionist belief that the existence of the State meant safety from all enemies, she wrote:

> Our position [is] as a lamb amongst seventy wolves (and I fail to see what difference the existence of the State makes). (*PN*, 659)

She was not particularly interested in political Zionism, although she mentions Herzl's *Der Judenstaat* in her writings.[4] But she did espouse the movement's socialist ideals and values, its emphasis on self-sacrifice, and its back-breaking pioneer work, draining swamps and building settlements. Nehama approved of hard work. She quotes the Midrash (*Bereshit Rabbah* 39:8) describing how Abraham, having passed through several lands inhabited by idle loafers, enters Canaan, where he sees the natives weed at weeding time and hoe at hoeing time. Abraham declares: "I wish that I could live in this land!" and Nehama points out that in this "he preempted A.D. Gordon."[5] The pioneering spirit also makes a cameo appearance in Nehama's essay on the weekly portion *Toldot*, entitled "*Yishuvo shel olam* (Settling the World)"[6] discussing Genesis 26:12–19, and specifically verse 15:

---

[1] See discussion on pages 536, 540, 545 below.

[2] Reiner and Peerless, *Haggadat*, 72.

[3] Yedgar, *VLN*.

[4] *NSB*, 526 and worksheet for *Va-yigash* 5708/1947. Herzl's play *Solon in Lydia* is mentioned in *IHBS*, 196, n. 4.

[5] From her *Yediot Ahronot* column, *Lech Lecha*, October 25, 1990, reprinted in *PN*, 524. Gordon believed in personal and national redemption through physical toil on the land. Pioneer work held a semi-religious significance for him.

[6] *IBB*, 180–184. The English title, "A Reclamation Controversy," is less evocative.

For all the wells which his father's servants had dug in the days of Abraham his father, the Philistines had blocked them up, and filled them with earth.

Nehama writes:

However, in our generation, privileged to see the descendants following in their forefathers' footsteps and once again digging wells – real wells, with living water – in the Negev and in the entire promised land, we can finally appreciate the patriarchs' greatness, in combining their dissemination of the true faith with physical digging of wells and land irrigation.[7]

She adds that this idea is found in the Midrash:

Great are the righteous, since they occupy themselves with the habitation of the world.[8]

In this way Nehama discovered, so to speak, the religious Zionist ideal of "Torah and Labor" in the patriarchs' lifestyles. Elsewhere she praises the pioneer

who deliberately forsakes all considerations of career for the mission of building with his own hands the future of his people in Eretz Yisrael. (*SBM*, 379)

In discussing God's command to Adam to "control the earth," Nehama writes:

The phrase therefore refers to man's conquest of the desert and his constructive and civilizing endeavors to build and inhabit the world, harness the forces of nature for his own good and exploit the mineral wealth around him. (*NSB*, 5)

Although it pertains to the entire world, this statement has strong echoes of the pioneer work in Israel that was being done at the time. While Nehama never actually lived on a kibbutz or tilled the land, she was intimately connected with those who did, visiting and teaching often on kibbutzim. Kibbutzniks filled out her worksheets as spiritual and intellectual nourishment after a long day in the fields. She felt concern for the future of the kibbutzim and was upset when people left them to live in other settlements, even idealistic ones.[9]

Nehama believed that the Torah was more comprehensible to people living in Israel just by virtue of their connection to the land:

---

[7] Combination of *NSB*, 260 and *IBB*, 182. See also Nehama's column in the *Yediot Ahronot* newspaper, weekly portion of *Toldot*, November 15, 1990, reprinted in *PN*, 525.
[8] *Midrash Hefetz*, quoted in *NSB*, 260.
[9] Letter to Ahituv.

> The frequency of the stealing exemplified in "pasturing their animals in other people's fields" is particularly familiar to our students in our land, where flocks are often grazed on land that does not belong to the owner. (*LP*, 94)

However, she was against making all of Jewish life revolve around land-based elements, for example the secular Zionist practice of turning the Jewish festivals into harvest festivals:

> Modern pioneers of Eretz Israel sought to "revive" the biblical precept of reaping the *omer* and turn it into an exclusively agricultural ceremony… transform[ing] the original biblical precept into a purely materialistic affair, fanning man's pride in his toil and glorifying his prowess and wealth. (*NSV*, 417, n. 1)

> There have been attempts to present Succot mainly for the children as a pagan nature feast, as an agricultural festival like that of other nations, and denude it of its religious character.[10]

Nehama rarely made political statements, but for her, the ability to settle the land signified its true ownership:

> The forerunners of the *Hovevei Zion* [the Lovers of Zion movement], when the land was still devastated, its hills bare, its valleys infested with swamps, and the Negev a wilderness… saw that none of the gentile would-be settlers had succeeded in extricating it from its barrenness, and they too saw in this a potent promise and proof… that since we left it, no nation nor tongue has been accepted by it, and that all have tried to settle it, but have never succeeded. (*NSV*, 589–590)

Elsewhere she notes that if Esau were to claim that he had been promised the Holy Land alongside his brother, this was not accurate, for

> it was the suffering of the bondage, the refining effect of the iron furnace of serfdom in Egypt, which alone gave title to the land. (*SBM*, 252)

Nehama wholeheartedly subscribed to the Zionist focus on the State's responsibility to the individual. She was proud of the State's concern for every Jew both inside and outside its borders. When Operation Solomon brought fourteen thousand Ethiopian Jews to Israel in one weekend, Nehama marveled at the fact that "each had a place to sleep." But individuals must do their part for the State, too. Upon hearing from Rabbanit Malke Bina that her husband was teaching in a yeshivah and learning Torah at that time, Nehama responded that although this was highly

---

[10] *SV*, 467. See also *NSV*, 442, and *SD*, 151.

commendable, it could not compare to the contribution of his father, R. Aryeh Bina, who, in addition to being a great Torah scholar, was extremely active during the pre-State era and the early years of the State in farming, smuggling munitions, and fighting in the Jewish Brigade. Learning and teaching were not enough; one must also observe and do, bringing Torah to all areas of life:

> The student needs to emerge from the lesson with the sense that '[The Torah's] ways are ways of pleasantness and all her paths are peace', and with a desire to redeem the Torah from her exile, her desolation and constriction into paltry corners of our lives; to spread her light once more throughout all of our deeds, at home and outside, in the family circle, in business dealings, in government and economics.[11]

This included serving in the Israeli army. Nehama took the religious kibbutz movement's line, rejecting any exemptions on religious grounds. Even the *hesder* program of Torah study with shortened army service was not ideal; she preferred that everyone serve the full term.[12] Nehama was zealous on this point. She once challenged Yeshivat HaKotel's policy of allowing outstanding students a three-year deferment of army service. When the director argued that universities also postpone service for exceptionally gifted students, Nehama replied that there was a fundamental difference. "The university wants to develop the student's intellect, but the yeshivah wants to build a fully integrated Jewish personality, a model to society. Yeshivah students should be the first ones ready to do army service."[13]

Although she had been too old to serve when she arrived, Nehama also advocated women's military service. She argued this point for hours with rabbis and educators and was unhappy with those religious girls' high schools that discouraged it. She even initially opposed Sherut Leumi (National Service) as a substitute, though she reportedly came round to the idea eventually.[14]

Hebrew language

The Zionist movement aspired to resurrect the Hebrew language. Nehama too was a very strong proponent of Hebrew both for religious-nationalistic

---

[11] *Teacher's Guide* for *Be-har*, 5731.

[12] Aryeh Felheimer, interview.

[13] Cohn, "Nehama Leibowitz – Teacher of Torah," *Be-khol derakhekha daehu: Journal of Torah and Scholarship* 6 (Winter 1998): 14 (slightly paraphrased).

[14] Some allege that one reason Nehama refused to teach at the Michlalah College for women in Bayit Vegan was because they accepted girls who had done neither army nor national service; but others, who spoke to Nehama about this explicitly, claim this is false.

reasons (this was the language of the Tanach and of the Jews in their land) and pedagogical ones (good Hebrew was a prerequisite to learning Torah properly). She thus encouraged familiarity with both biblical and modern Hebrew.

Nehama herself had learned her excellent Hebrew early on, from her father and from tutors (*PN*, 13). Though her bookshelf groaned with German, English, French and Spanish books, she almost always spoke Hebrew on principle unless the person really could not get by in Hebrew, such as a visiting non-Jew. She was even known to claim an inability to speak English – hardly likely for someone who had studied English language and literature at university.

By the time Nehama arrived in Palestine, the strict language regime adopted by the *Yishuv* to boost Hebrew speaking in a multilingual population had in the main succeeded. As the language became widely spoken, the social pressure and patriotism associated with Hebrew speaking gradually dwindled, but Nehama never let go of that early zealotry. Once, asked for directions in English, Nehama turned to R. Nachum Amsel and said, in (feigned?) shock: "He asked us in English! We're in Jerusalem, the Holy City! We can't speak English here!" She informed him that once upon a time, people would whisper in German on buses, for all public talk had to be in Hebrew. On another occasion, during class, Nehama got up to answer her door. In her absence, the students, including many English speakers serving in the army, began to discuss the material. Returning, Nehama protested: "Gentlemen, you're in Jerusalem now. How can you speak English?" They were thunderstruck. Then one student piped up: "But Nehama, your books are translated into English!" In a scandalized voice, she retorted: "That's for people who don't know Hebrew, but you do!" She even opposed speaking to young children in English, advising, "They need to speak to their parents in the Holy Tongue. A teacher can be hired to speak English with them."

Nehama was sensitive to errors in Hebrew, and when marking the papers for the *bagrut* (Israeli matriculation exams) she deducted points for poor Hebrew. She also hated "Heblish," the mongrel mixture of Hebrew and English often affected by Anglophone immigrants to Israel.[15]

Nehama also opposed translating the Torah. She firmly believed that given a basic 250-word vocabulary, the Torah may be taught in its original language. Her somewhat radical advice to senior educators was that instead of studying *Humash*, Diaspora first-graders would do better learning the

---

[15] Nonetheless, even Nehama occasionally slipped from purist Hebrew, using the English words instead of the Hebrew equivalent, for example "provisory" (letter to Aaronson, *PN*, 655) or "projection" (*IBB*, 138) and more (see Kagan "Review" for more examples).

most common biblical words so that by second grade they could enjoy the book in its original language. Similarly, if the language of the classroom is *Ivrit* the children will pick it up easily and be able to study the book of Genesis in the original. Better to get this out of the way earlier on, she said, for too much class time spent on translation rather than content makes for a negative experience,[16] while reading only in English is even worse. She joked that learning Tanach without Hebrew is like *inuy* (torture) instead of *iyun* (in-depth study). She insisted that some Japanese Christian Bible scholars study in Ulpan for six months before joining her class. Asked in what language a Torah class should be taught to a beginners' Ulpan group, she responded: "What a question! How could you teach Torah in an Ulpan in any language besides Hebrew?" Requested, if so, to come and show how it could be done, she happily complied, giving a successful Torah lesson in Hebrew to immigrants of just three months.

She was particularly exasperated that adult Jewish studies were being taught in Jerusalem in English. R. Chaim Brovender, whose women's yeshivah, Michlelet Bruriah, catered for women with little Hebrew and Jewish knowledge, argued the point with Nehama. "I thought at the time that it was more important to learn. But she was very opposed," he says. Nehama wanted all the yeshivah programs to be *Ivrit be-Ivrit*. She even refused to teach for the Touro College Jerusalem branch in its early years because some of its classes (not hers!) were in English. Invited to speak at an international conference about Bible teaching, Nehama was likewise appalled that some talks would be given in English. "But Nehama," reasoned the organizers, "the people from abroad need to understand!" "That's their problem!" she replied, and only with great reluctance agreed to stay. She was also greatly perturbed by the poor Hebrew of the future Diaspora educators and rabbis whom she taught. To R. Larry Schwed, who had a degree in Hebrew, Nehama said: "You? A Hebrew teacher? You still write with mistakes!" To R. Nathaniel Helfgot, she wrote:

> I must caution you to write in correct Hebrew. I think the problem with [you] teachers in the Diaspora, even those who teach in Hebrew, is that you don't read books in Hebrew. (*PN*, 663)

When a group of Makoya, a Japanese Judeophilic sect, came to study with her for the first of many annual sessions, Nehama inquired as to their language preference. They indignantly replied: "In what language did Moses give over the Torah? That's the language we want!" Nehama loved this and later teased her Kollel students at Gruss: "The Makoya speak better than

---

[16] Reported by Steve Bailey, "Re: Teaching primary sources in Hebrew," Lookjed archives, November 11, 2002.

you! They have a beautiful Hebrew!" The aspiring rabbis in Gruss were "excellent young men" (*PN*, 690), but their Hebrew, to her mind, was appalling, and she would ask them sardonically if they thought God said in English, "Let there be light!"

With all this emphasis on Hebrew, Nehama underestimated the role that fluency in languages played in her own scholarship. It allowed her to read many books that did not exist in Hebrew translation, and to teach populations with weak Hebrew. She also gained a tremendous amount from studying translations (mostly English and German), frequently referring to them as a form of commentary:

> And if the students know other languages (besides Hebrew) they should search in the translations. (*LP*, 199)

> For the benefit of those who know foreign languages, we will bring some translations. (*IHBV*, 65)

Attitude towards the Diaspora

Another Zionist value that Nehama wholeheartedly adopted was that of *shelilat ha-golah* (negation of the Diaspora). She insisted that no one could be fully Jewish outside Israel:

> The Torah cannot be observed in its entirety except in a society wholly governed by its precepts and not in an alien framework ruled by other ideals. Admittedly there are personal religious obligations that can be observed anywhere, even by a Jewish Robinson Crusoe on his desert isle, but the Torah, as a whole, implies a complete social order, a judiciary, national, economic and political life. That can only be achieved in the Holy Land and not outside it.[17]

Nehama scolds assimilationists of recent generations who deliberately distorted the Sages' statements so as to claim that the exile and dispersion of the Jewish people were blessings from God:

> They deliberately ignore the tens, perhaps hundreds of sources in Torah, Prophets Writings, Midrashim and Aggadot that testify and underscore the fact that the most severe and terrible of punishments is exile.[18]

David Weinberg writes:

---

[17] *SBM*, 399–400. In *SD* (115–118) she cites the radical *Sifri* that suggests that observance outside Israel is merely a practice or a preparation for the real thing, like a queen who adorns herself in readiness for her husband when they reunite. Nehama hurries, however, to dispel the impression that in the Diaspora precepts can therefore be taken lightly.

[18] *IBD*, 339; compare *SD*, 349.

There were no half-truths in Nehama's life, nor could she countenance less than full devotion to the cause. For this reason, she was completely impatient with Jewish life in the Diaspora, which she viewed as Jewishly false, dangerous and "thank God, no longer necessary."[19]

In his opinion, even Nehama's correspondence with hundreds of students from abroad was primarily motivated by pity and concern. Indeed, Nehama bemoans:

> And why, why do they still live there?[20]

> In our day, whole Jewish communities have forgotten their traditions as a result of divorcement from Jewish learning and their remoteness from centers of scholarship. (*SBM*, 153)

She was very worried about the future of such Jews:

> What of those who have only caught second or third-hand glimpses of their ancient traditions and shadows of the ancestral image during moments of Torah study in their childhood? Do they similarly stand a chance of being saved amidst alien cultures and climes? (*NSB*, 415)

The world beyond Israel's borders, a non-Jewish cultural and political domain in which Jews were subject to gentile rule, could be of no interest to a committed Jew. Nehama associated Eastern Europe especially with negative events; only the "handful" of Jews remaining there were of importance. When R. Shmuel Klitsner returned from a trip to Riga he was surprised by Nehama's indifference to news about her birthplace.

On the other hand, countries where Jews had not been murdered by the millions but instead allowed to prosper had their own attendant dangers. She writes that the patriarch Jacob

> was not afraid of the persecution... but rather of the wealth and prosperity that might turn their heads and cause them to repudiate their historic national destiny to leave Egypt for the Promised Land. (*NSB*, 536)

Nehama did not believe that serious Torah learning could take place there. Upon being informed that her books were selling well in England, South Africa and America, she retorted: "Are you crazy? Nobody would sit on Shabbat and read my books – they'd read a novel instead!" As she met more and more Jews from the *"Goldeneh Medina,"* Nehama became increasingly concerned about this comfortable Diaspora. Meeting a fourth-generation American, she exclaimed, "And you're still Jewish?" She declared it "sad and tragic" that such a high percentage of American Jews never

---

[19] Weinberg, "Remembering Nehama."
[20] N. Leibowitz, "*El kol*," 469.

visited Israel. Every time Blu Greenberg came to visit her, Nehama badmouthed America with gusto, telling the same stories again and again to prove Israel's superiority and America's unsuitability for Jews. "If you gave her a bad statistic about America, she would play on it for five years," Greenberg recalls. When explaining to her Hebrew University students, mostly Americans, why God destroyed the world at the time of Noah, she liked to parallel his contemporaries to America's materialistic "me generation" and call New York "a hotbed of sin."

Alongside this, though, Nehama was also very curious about America, interrogating people particularly about the Orthodox Jewish lifestyle. She asked whether men wore *kippot* to work, and was astounded to hear about numerous afternoon *minyanim* at firms in New York City, or the *daf yomi* learning in the early morning hours. But her curiosity to see Williamsburg and Boro Park, where only Jews walked the streets, was destined to remain unquenched, for leaving Israel, even temporarily, was for Nehama an offense of the highest order. Although willing to travel anywhere within Israel to teach, she never left Israel's borders. She refused scores of offers to lecture abroad, even just for a weekend, announcing: "Anyone who wishes to hear me will please do me the courtesy of coming to Israel," (*PN,* 673) and "I do not want to die outside Israel." The only enticement she might have taken at all seriously was the opportunity to hear *shiurim* from Rav Soloveitchik. From the list of those Nehama admired most,[21] R. Soloveitchik was the only American. Yet she never went. Hence, Dr. Gabriel Cohn was dumbfounded when in a New York City synagogue he saw a large poster announcing "Shabbat with Nehama Leibowitz." Had Nehama capitulated after all these years? It turned out that three of her students had organized a Shabbat of Torah study according to her method.[22]

It dismayed Nehama when others left Israel, even for short periods. She berated a young Israeli wishing to study for a year at Yeshiva University in New York, despite her being at that very moment in the employ of the Yeshiva University recruitment office. In self-defense, the young man cited the quality of the rabbis and the learning. This was a colossal blunder, and Nehama's scolding grew even more vocal. To go abroad to study Torah? Not sciences or humanities, which she could understand, but Torah? An outrage! There was no Torah like that of Eretz Yisrael! Other students, friends and colleagues were treated to similar tongue-lashings, and no excuse was acceptable. Professor Chana Safrai, while abroad, actually wanted to

---

[21] This list included Rabbis Aryeh Levin and Yeshayahu Shapira (known as the *Admor he-Halutz*) and Professors Aryeh L. Strauss, Meir Weiss, Eliezer Shimshon Rosenthal, Isaac Heinemann, Shmuel Hugo Bergman and Nathan Rotenstreich (Ahrend, "*Mi-toch,*" 33).
[22] Cohn, "*Ma ahavti,*" 30.

hear these tirades; they were like booster shots of Zionism, to push her into returning. "I owe to Nehama the fact that I came back," she says. It made no difference if the student in question was not Israeli. Weinberg:

> When I informed her… that I was returning to Canada to study (after having studied here in Israel, and with her, for several years), Nehama became apoplectic.[23]

She expected her Diaspora students to stay, and was upset when year after year they consistently returned to the Diaspora. Ever hopeful of convincing the next defector, Nehama persevered, and her typical tactics included firing a salvo such as: "You'll never come home! You have nothing to gain from *hutz la-aretz*! It's just a waste of time! You can achieve the same in Israel!" To one student, promised a position at a Bible department abroad, she declared, "Well, of course! They can't find anyone! It's hard to find good people in Jewish Academia in the Diaspora, since good people don't leave Israel!" In a letter in 1974, she wrote to Professor Martin Lockshin:

> I hope that all the Jewish warmth over there and the *Yiddishkeit* that apparently (for I have not been there myself) exists, and is felt more strongly than in Rehavia in the Holy City of Jerusalem, will not weaken your resolve and bring you to make the *tragic and dreadful* mistake that many tens of thousands (literally) of Kotsker, Belzer and Gerer Hasidim made, believing Kotsk, Belz and Ger etc. to be a genuine substitute for Jerusalem; or like the Torah scholars of the city of Vilna who named it the "Jerusalem of Lithuania" and thus felt as if they were citizens of Jerusalem; and we know what price was paid for this mistake.

Lockshin: "I made the terrible mistake of asking her to write me a letter of recommendation for graduate school abroad, adding, 'I hope that you don't consider this as the transgression of aiding sinners.' She wrote back 'Meir, I never considered you the kind of person who would use halachic terminology flippantly! How can you ask me to write a letter so that you can go be a monk in your academia?'" On another occasion Nehama said to Lockshin: "Are these intellectual things so important? Why don't you come back here and pick tomatoes?" When David Sykes left Israel due to what he experienced as "a virulently anti-Torah atmosphere," Nehama sent him a letter written, on her own testimony, in tears. She pleaded that he not "abandon the battlefront," for only his evil inclination could tempt him, under the pretext of learning better Torah, to return to a place with a sixty-percent intermarriage rate.

Even the altruistic excuse of going abroad as a *shaliah* (emissary) was less than satisfactory. R. Raphael Posen describes how, after he left an

---

[23] Weinberg, "Remembering Nehama."

Letter to Martin Lockshin 1974/75. Courtesy of Martin Lockshin.

Letter to Martin Lockshin 1974/75.

educational post in Israel to teach for a limited time in Canada, he called
Nehama a few days before his flight to bid her farewell:[24]

> A deafening silence followed. After several interminable seconds, she
> responded in a severe tone: "You should not be going abroad! Your
> place is in Israel – how can you take your wife and seven children into
> the 'exile'"?

After this harangue, Nehama offered a grudging farewell that left Posen
shocked and shaken. He was, after all, leaving for important educational
purposes, and for the short term only. Upon arrival in Canada, with
Nehama's words still burdening him, Posen sat down and wrote her a
description of his work with teachers who were *yordim* (emigrants from
Israel). By arguing that these Jews too should be taught how to learn and
pray, Posen hoped to calm the troubled waters; but it had the reverse effect.
Soon he received the following letter of (in his words) "explicit rebuke
together with veiled affection":

> My dear friend,
>
> What can I say? I read your letter and the article you sent; it told me
> nothing new. It's a known fact that the *yordim*, who want to live
> amongst the gentiles and breathe the air of the "foreign world," are
> prepared to pay any price – even that of "praying"... for what will a
> person not do for material gain, especially if it will allow him to live in
> the Diaspora? As long as he does not have to live in his country
> amongst Yids like us.
>
> I have often heard from these teachers when they return for a
> vacation... a little surprised at themselves, at the fact that there they
> "had" to pray and did, and made sure the students prayed, and learned
> to sit down and stand up in the right places: "And now I am, thank
> God, free of all that." And some add, "Overall, it was quite nice."
>
> And I heard from one highly intelligent mother... whose son studied in
> an Orthodox high school – according to her, a very good school with
> progressive methods – who said: "It's not so bad that he learned how
> to pray, it's actually a good thing. He even took it seriously, since he's
> not a cynic. But now of course he has forgotten it all; we weren't
> worried, we knew it would quickly pass."
>
> You may save some girls from the clutches of intermarriage and
> assimilation. It is possible, for I really do esteem your ability as a
> teacher, educator, a good Jew, honestly! But to take such a wonderful
> family (and I will always remember the evening I spent in your home

[24] *PN*, 671. The following description and letter appear in Posen, *"Te'uv ha-golah," Ha-Tzofeh*, March 27, 1998, reprinted in *PN*, 671–673.

with your children, and how blessed I felt to be in such a Jewish home), to take your children away from our land at this difficult time – in my opinion, nothing you do there can make up for it. It burns in my heart like a flame.

I am distressed about this, if not daily, then very frequently. Your children, who right now should be Bnei Akiva counselors, traveling the length and breadth of Israel, volunteering as all good high-school students do, working with the Sephardic Jews, doing outreach, fortifying the religious movement – so feeble and divided – in its connection to the land… will instead get to know the Diaspora in all its hypocrisy. Thirty-five years after our independence they do not dream that it's not proper, simply not proper for a Jew to continue freely (not out of coercion) to dwell amongst the gentiles!…

As someone from Toronto Mizrachi said to me: "Toronto is our Jerusalem." And I recalled how at the end of the eighteenth century the maskilim of Berlin said, "Berlin is our Jerusalem…"[25] And I was aghast when I read that *you* have to repeatedly promise that there is no chance they will stay there! What has befallen us – that *you* have to emphasize such a thing! Oh, the benefit you could bring our country, simply by being here – that alone would be much!

My only hope is that your children feel miserable there, experience the inauthentic life of those who pray for the return to Zion, who declaim unthinkingly at the Seder and on Yom Kippur after all the confessions, "Next year in [Jerusalem]" and dare to pronounce this utter falsehood before God!

And how can you teach, "And return us to Zion in joy" – for if this is taken seriously, the person who says it should get up and return! No one would pray "And feed us in Your mercy with kosher food every day," and then go buy meat at a non-kosher butcher!

I read carefully over and over what you wrote me about the role of the *shaliah*. My heart still hesitates over the question of whether *shelihut* does not simply help the Jews, the best ones, continue to live their counterfeit lives in the Diaspora, to get along there "Jewishly." They will live there and, in the best scenario, not marry non-Jews (the percentages are still on the rise) and will leave to the small handful of Jews who live here the task of suffering, being killed – literally – almost

---

[25] Similarly, Vilna was referred to as "the Jerusalem of Lithuania," Gateshead as "the Jerusalem of England" and Djerba as "the Jerusalem of North Africa." Nehama writes in her studies, regarding Dathan and Abiram's descriptions of Egypt as a land flowing with milk and honey: "The land of uncleanness is given the title applied exclusively to the Holy Land. It is a symbol for all time to those who in the lands of their dispersion proclaim: Here is our Jerusalem" (*SBM*, 210).

every day, and if not being killed then doing reserve duty, lying in the mud in wintertime, etc. etc. Must someone like you, who dealt with the slain during the Yom Kippur War (of which I am totally in awe), make Diaspora life comfortable (in the most elevated sense of the word)? I write this with an aching heart and from my deep friendship with you and your family. Answer quickly! If only you would leave in the middle, out of sheer disgust! (PN, 671–673)

Nehama did not even sign her name, leaving her words to reverberate in Posen's heart for the rest of his time abroad. So perturbed was he that he even read it to local school principals and asked for their response. Predictably, they were absolutely livid, and when a recording of this discussion fell into Nehama's hands, she told Posen that she had enjoyed it tremendously and for this alone it had been worth writing to him. For years afterwards, she sent anyone seeking her opinion on *shelihut* to read this letter, which said it all. Her words to R. Yaakov Koppel Reinitz were no less cutting:

I still haven't digested the fact that you are going to teach Torah in the accursed atmosphere of Vienna, and that Jews, who for pure material gain live shamelessly amongst their parents' murderers, will merit to hear your Torah in their community. Do they really deserve this honor?

Perhaps, just perhaps, when the children born there (and these lambs, what sin did they commit?) hear your Torah, their hearts will be opened to a different world, as you anoint the air with the fragrance of your Torah, driving away the stench of the noble city Vienna. Perhaps? And if thus a few young people turn their back on this accursed world – well then…. (PN, 693)

Nehama once met a priest who told her that he had witnessed Diaspora Jews mourning on Tisha be-Av for the destruction of the Temple and Jerusalem, and then, on arriving in Israel, had exclaimed in wonder: "What a beautiful country the Jews have! So luscious, ample and fertile!" But all Nehama could think was:

But why do not the Jews from every country return home? In their exile they remembered Jerusalem for two thousand years. They cry, mourn and lament – but why do they not return home?[26]

ð ó

To her credit, despite her strong feelings Nehama mostly refrained from making her classes a platform for preaching at her Diaspora students. The agenda was Torah learning. Her words, written about the Ramban, are instructive:

---

26 Ephraim Yair, "*Shabbat Nahamu,*" *Amudim* 430 (5742): 25.

Note that is specifically Ramban – who loved Israel, who went to live there, to cherish its dust, lamented its destruction and rejoiced when he laid a foundation stone to set up a synagogue in Jerusalem – who does not take advantage of this opportunity to exploit the verse to "recount the virtues of Eretz Yisrael," but on the contrary takes Ibn Ezra to task for doing so, since his is not an interpretation that fits the verse. This teaches us that opinions and beliefs, likes and dislikes, are not to dictate the interpretation, but only the text – its language, style, grammar and context.[27]

Nehama's overall messages were universal ones, or general Jewish ones.[28] At times, however, when the Torah lent itself to it, she plied her Zionist educational messages. This, after all, was a religious injunction too:

And the teacher should not worry that the students will groan reluctantly, "*Zionism*...." In the framework of Torah learning as the word of the living God that obligates its students, we must explain and remind them that settling the land of Israel is a mitzvah and not some random human program.[29]

She blamed much of the reluctance to make *aliyah* on a false sense of belonging and on materialism. In her writings she suggests that this phenomenon predates the Israelites' even becoming a nation:

[Joseph] was enamored of the new life of luxury that he was living in Egypt, the country of wealth and culture.... He forgot his slavery and that he was a stranger among them, he forgot the spiritual chasm separating him as a son of Abraham....[30]

"Slavery? It's not so bad. I'm a manager." "Exile? Who says? This is a civilized country and they treat me nicely."[31]

Jacob, who was reassured (Genesis 46:3), "I am God, the God of your father; fear not to go down to Egypt,"

was haunted by [the] fear [that] perhaps, once the famine or even the bondage was over, they would no longer be eager to leave this country of plenty to return to claim the land of Canaan, which alone had been promised them from the days of the Patriarchs. (*NSB*, 507)

---

[27] *LP*, 83–84. See also *NSB*, 208 for a similar point.
[28] See chapter 6 n. 17.
[29] *Teacher's Guide* for *Matot-Masei* 5716.
[30] *NSB*, 414. Nehama mentions Egypt as the cradle of civilization several times – see page 39 above, and see also *NSS*, 310: "... center of ancient culture, the home of the wise men, famed for its pyramids and art."
[31] From her column in the *Yediot Ahronot* newspaper, weekly portion of *Va-yeshev*, December 6, 1990, reprinted in *PN*, 527.

This fear was justified, Nehama notes, for, living separately from the Egyptians in Goshen – the "ghetto of choice" – Jacob's family forgot the temporary nature of their sojourn and the country promised them by the God of their forefathers.[32] Such were the dangers of assimilation, then and now.

Nehama also quoted a Midrash that describes the Israelites loitering on the shores of the Red Sea, harvesting the jewels floating up from the drowned Egyptians' chariots. She commented, "If people don't come to the land flowing with milk and honey, it's because of the jewels!" She liked to point out that the patriarchs did not have to be tempted to come to Israel, unlike their descendants who needed the promise of milk and honey – or, in today's terms, tax exemptions and electric appliances.[33] One of her favorite lessons revolved around the Israelite tribes who settled in trans-Jordan instead of mainland Israel (Numbers 32). She loved to explain that the words "and your servants have cattle" (32:4) demonstrate that their reasons were purely materialistic; their animals came first.

Whenever this issue reared itself in the classroom emotions ran high, for Nehama genuinely felt that her students' welfare was badly served outside Israel and that her job was to convince them to stay. In the next chapter, we will explore another subject that caused many a fierce argument: feminism.

---

[32] *NSB*, 517–518. Note Nehama's comments regarding the Netziv's Zionism and its influence on his commentary (similarly *NSB*, 510). Here she deviates from her claims regarding commentators such as Rashi, who in her view was never influenced by his background (see page 467 below). We can only speculate as to whether Nehama, possesing a Zionist agenda similar to the Netziv, ever asked herself if her own ideologies affected her teachings or interpretations as his did.

[33] Reiner and Peerless, *Haggadat*, 141.

CHAPTER 14

FEMINISM AND FEMININITY:
"A WOMAN IN THE INNER COURTYARD?"[1]

Introduction: What's in a street name?

IT WAS THE LATE 1990s, and Anat Hoffman, staunch feminist and councilwoman in the Jerusalem Municipality, was concerned about Jerusalem street names. Hoffman had discovered that only three percent of Jerusalem's streets were named for women. The classic biblical figures and Zionist heroines – Deborah, Esther, Hannah Szenes – were represented, but they appeared in other Israeli towns too. Then there were anonymous titles such as "Women's Brigade Street," "The Nurse Street," etc. Where were the honorable women of the city? Hoffman went sleuthing and discovered many of their names on plaques in tiny plazas, while, in her words, "treasurers of local football teams and second-rate building contractors were given real streets." Dismayed at the implied message to young women that their impact on the city's life could only be minimal at best, Hoffman went around trying to collect names of additional prominent women. To her frustration, there was only one name on everyone's lips: Nehama Leibowitz.

The novelty of a prominent female Torah scholar

S.Y. Agnon opens his story "The Wisdom of Women" as follows:

> There lived in the city a great woman of good lineage; and she knew Scripture and Mishnah, Midrash, Halachot and Aggadot, and she had discussions with the Torah scholars in the *bet midrash*.[2]

As the story proceeds, the denizens of this *bet midrash*, perturbed by the woman's presence in their midst, place an attractively bound volume on the shelves entitled *The Wisdom of Women*. Elated, the woman leafs through it only to see that every page is blank. The men laugh loudly at her. Although furious, she is forced to admit that the blame begins with her female predecessors for leaving no written legacy of Jewish wisdom.

---

[1] My thanks to Professor Tamar Ross and Dr. Deborah Weissman for taking time to look over this chapter.

[2] Mentioned in Elhanan Samet, *"Ha-morah,"* 37.

R. Elhanan Samet points out that in Agnon's story, the wise woman ends up writing stories to fill the book. Agnon's imagination could not stretch to encompass a female Torah scholar; and yet right there in front of his eyes was the woman who would prove him wrong.[3] In 1943, when this story was printed, Nehama had already launched the worksheets that would eventually lead to the first volumes of Torah scholarship written by a woman. After this, *The Wisdom of Women* could never again be considered a blank book.

As a female Orthodox Tanach scholar, Nehama was a rarity. She was, in effect, the woman in the *bet midrash*. But she would certainly have been less captivated by a book entitled *The Wisdom of Women* than by a book entitled *The Close Study of Tanach and Approaches of Its Commentators throughout the Ages*. This was another book that was blank, and whose pages she filled with great industriousness.

Although she herself denied her gender any importance in her scholarship, it may have played a significant role. Tanach scholars existed when Nehama began her teaching – all male, of course. However, by and large, traditional Jewish men gravitated to the Talmud, which was considered the superior field, while the women had not yet achieved a significant level of erudition in Tanach, which was then the only accepted area of study for them. This left the field wide open for Nehama, and she went on to rectify this sorry state of Tanach study by introducing to its study the kind of analytical thinking previously reserved for the world of the Talmud.

Many intelligent women – and men too – eagerly embraced this approach, both in the traditional world and in academic circles, gaining great proficiency in Tanach along the way. The yeshivah world, however, remained resistant to change. Nehama often spoke disapprovingly of the "ignorance of the yeshivah boys" in Tanach, and wrote:

> It sometimes breaks my heart to hear what they're doing there [in yeshivah high school Torah education].[4]

She wondered how they could analyze Ramban's comments on the Talmud but not on the Torah. Yet even after her reputation was established, there proved no shortage of yeshivah students who believed they knew Tanach better than any woman, Leibowitz or no Leibowitz. This was the case for R. Hershel Billet. He arrived in Israel in 1972 as a newlywed to study in Yeshiva University's Kollel faculty, the Gruss Institute. When his Rosh Yeshivah, R. Dovid Miller, suggested that he study with Nehama Leibowitz, he did not take it seriously: "I had already spent five or six years in Rav

---

[3] Samet, "*Ha-morah*," 39.
[4] Letter to Reinitz, *PN*, 680. See his description of his own Tanach knowledge before encountering Nehama's work, *PN*, 678.

Soloveitchik's shiur – what could a woman teach me about Torah? So she wrote a few books, quotes a few commentators – simplistic stuff!" But after continued urging, he eventually phoned her. They found no mutually convenient time for study except Friday, so she consented that he come then, for a personal session. R. Billet recalls: "I walked up a couple of flights of stairs, knocked on the door, and a feisty lady opened it, saying, 'Come in, you're two minutes late.' Then she sat me down and gave me a worksheet to fill out. I thought it would be piece of cake. The first question was a breeze, but the second wasn't – it had an X, and the third had two X's, and I couldn't believe this was happening." Nehama looked at what he had done, and sat with him at length, after which he walked out chastened. "That's how our relationship began – my arrogance and her humility." When he asked to learn with her regularly, Nehama replied: "I'm a busy lady too!" but agreed to give him an hour and a half a week. These visits, often together with his wife, considerably broadened his horizons, he says.

R. Yaakov Koppel Reinitz recalls: "A yeshivah student, I happened to walk one Friday afternoon into my friends' room at Yeshivat Hebron [a prestigious ultra-Orthodox yeshivah]. These friends subsequently became respectively a yeshivah head and a rabbinical judge. I noticed books piled around them. They were filling out some sheets, and they invited me to join them." The result:

> Out of curiosity I took a peek, and was – burnt! Burnt, because the questions made me feel mortified. But the shame was sevenfold when I read 'Arranged by Nehama Leibowitz.' A woman in the Inner Courtyard?![5]

After recovering from his shock, he began to fill out the sheets, and a rewarding relationship of many years ensued; and Nehama was very pleased that finally some Tanach was being studied in yeshivahs.

For decades, Nehama was the only woman able to dissolve this wall of prejudice.[6] Her very existence overturned the usual order of things. People hailing from both traditional societies, such as Algiers, and progressive societies such as Germany where educated women were common, were stunned at the sight of a female Torah lecturer. At least one man, in a reversal of the "Yentl" scenario, sneaked into the back of an all-female lesson in order to hear her. On another occasion, a distinguished looking

---

[5] "Twenty-Five Years of the *Gilyonot*." Reprinted in *PN*, 678. The reference is to the *azarah*, the inner sacred courtyard of the Temple, into which women were not allowed.

[6] Reportedly, Dr. Avivah Zornberg says of her own encounters with certain male students, who walk away still convinced of their superior knowledge: "I'm sure that I'm partly to blame.... Nehama Leibowitz doesn't get that kind of reaction I'm sure. She terrifies them out of their seats" (Ochs, *Words*, 124).

Ultra-Orthodox man walked in to her class at the Efrata College (formerly the Mizrachi teaching seminar), requesting to sit in. Nehama agreed. At its conclusion he introduced himself as a student's father. He had felt the need to substantiate with his own eyes that the teacher behind his daughter's impressive class notes and worksheets was a woman.

৵ ৵

Women have frequently been intellectual pioneers in Jewish history, observes Professor Israel Rozenson. He suggests that Nehama's gender played a crucial role in her ability to bring together diverse elements because, in his words, "no one expected her to have a beard!" No man could have taken on her role – he would have had to belong either to the academic or to the yeshivah world. But less was expected of Nehama. She was not considered an enemy of the yeshivah world. Erella Yedgar adds that another result of Nehama's not having studied in yeshivah was that she was less bound by regular study methods and was freer to introduce elements such as literature and drama.

But the novelty of her gender was a minor consideration for most students, compared to her stimulating and original teaching. Indeed, some female students attended despite, rather than because of, her gender, and actively reject her as female role model, as one explains: "There was nothing feminine about her, to my eyes; her uniqueness lay in other areas. I never wanted to be like her in everything, I was too much of a woman."

Nehama claimed ignorance of the reactions she caused in people:

> I did not realize at all that my being a woman would be factor in the acceptance or rejection of my worksheets. (*PN*, 680)

She was not, however, entirely gender-blind. For instance, although she purportedly did not believe that one sex learned differently from the other, these words, written at the first anniversary of the worksheets, imply otherwise:

> Frequently, our students (and especially female ones), instead of the commentator's difficulty, suggested as their answer the content of his explanation; until they learned that where there is an explanation, there must of necessity be some difficulty – for which one must search first and foremost....

> There were male students (not female ones) who feared we would thereby forego our own independent notion of the verse, becoming instead habituated to seeing it through the eyes of others, whose time and viewpoint differs from ours.[7]

---

[7] N. Leibowitz, "*Mi-bereshit ad le-einey kol Yisrael: bi-melot shana la-gilyonot,*" in *PN*, 453.

Here then is an appraisal of the strengths and weaknesses of the genders. Nehama also breaks down her tally of the number of worksheet correspondents for the first year by gender – from a handful of all-female students, the correspondents had grown to forty-six men and twenty-nine women.[8]

Gender in Nehama's scholarship

Over the course of the twentieth century, as female scholars became increasingly common in every field, female Bible scholars also made their mark. Gradually they introduced new ways of reading through feminine and feminist eyes, pinpointing issues that had been previously overlooked. This eventually had its effect within Jewish religious circles, where women also began to focus more on issues such as laws affecting women, the concept of Jewish femininity, biblical and talmudic heroines, and renewed Torah interpretation through female eyes.

In general, feminist readings may take one of two broad focuses: *absence* of women's voices in the text and negative attitudes towards women; or the positive emphasis, amplifying and celebrating women's *presence* as much as possible. Jewish observant women have become involved in both these approaches; but most cannot join wholeheartedly, if at all, with the secular feminists' explicit critique of sacred text, the so-called "hermeneutics of suspicion." Such readings, often unsympathetic, may appear to devout people to distort the Scripture's meaning. Therefore, the second activity is often preferred, accepting the status quo and studying female topics primarily for their inspiring and devotional value.[9]

Nehama however, seeing herself not as a "female scholar" but rather as a scholar who happened to be female, did neither. She was never critical of the Torah's approach to women, and was unconcerned with female power or legal approaches to women. In general she preferred to let the text speak without imposed social agendas. As a reviewer of a book of Jewish exegesis by female rabbis writes:

> Nehama Leibowitz's commentaries would be out of place in this volume, not because she was not a rabbi but because she explicated the text, not her society.[10]

---

[8] N. Leibowitz, "*Mi-bereshit*," 454.

[9] See Yedgar, "*Ha-iyunim*," 111, 119–120.

[10] Grace B. McMillan, "Fifty Feminist Rabbis on Torah," *Jerusalem Post*, January 5, 2001; B12, reviewing *The Women's Torah Commentary: New Insights from Women Rabbis on the Fifty-Four Weekly Torah Portions*, edited by Elyse Goldstein. Her remark is not strictly true, since Nehama granted some role in interpretation to the needs of each generation.

For similar reasons she disliked reading texts by topic, preferring to read a specific text in its own context, without an imposed category:

> I neither recommend nor approve of studying "topics" or "themes" instead of studying books. Here is not the place to discuss my reasons. But since such study has become fashionable, I am obliged to mention it. (*TI*, 61)

Hence, she did not search for feminine voices or motifs in Tanach. Upon hearing from Dr. Gabriel Cohn that he was teaching a course on women in Tanach, Nehama remarked: "Well then, next time you should give a course on *men* in Tanach!"

In light of the above, it is surprising to discover that Nehama gave a series of talks on the radio on female figures in Tanach: Rebecca, Rachel, Eve, Michal, the woman of Tekoa, Abigail, Tamar and the witch of En-Dor.[11] But besides this, any feminist or feminine-themed motifs in Nehama's writings are discovered only by careful examination, and are largely speculative. R. Aryeh Strikovsky lists certain topics absent from Nehama's teachings, arguing that they illustrate her notion of Jewish womanhood in that they made her uncomfortable.[12] These include the laws of the *sotah* (suspected adulteress – Numbers 5:11–31); the punishment described as "chop off her hand and do not have mercy on her" (Deuteronomy 25:12); or the book of Ruth – Nehama was uncomfortable with Naomi's advice to Ruth to lie with Boaz (Ruth 3:4). R. Strikovsky also notes her omission of the book of Proverbs, which, opening with an incestuous woman and closing with the ideal woman, omitted the most essential roles for women, of mother and guide to children.

It is, however, difficult to prove anything conclusively from absence. And when we search for topics from which we can, in contrast, learn positively about Nehama's view of Jewish womanhood, they prove difficult to find. She deals little, if at all, with female identity, whether within Halachah – issues such as women's Torah learning, the laws of *niddah*, marital laws, the law of the chained wife, etc. – or in the psychological realm, such as a woman's independent existence, the search for partnership,

---

However, Nehama would no doubt have defined these needs very differently. See chapter 22.

[11] Strikovsky, Aryeh. "*Nehama Leibowitz al nashim ve-nashiyut*," in *Bat Mitzvah*, edited by Sara Friedland ben Arza, 310 (Jerusalem: MaTaN and Urim Publications, 2002), citing Dr. Mira Ofran, Nehama's niece, as his source. Ofran recalls that the program was called "For the housewife," and the talks were only a few minutes' duration each (interview).

[12] Strikovsky, "Nehama on Women," 188–189. Professor Ahrend has told this author that he does not in fact support this view as suggested there (interview).

motherhood, infertility or being a female in a male-dominated world. Yedgar is particularly struck by the fact that Nehama was able to read the parable of the harlot from Ezekiel 16, which some find shocking in its attitude towards women, and remain unmoved.

It has been said that Nehama was against the abusive treatment of women.[13] We cannot doubt that this is true, but it is more accurate to say that Nehama opposed all abuse and injustice. She writes:

> The Torah was not concerned with favouring one side or according privileges to the other. It does not underwrite the privileges of a particular class but is concerned with human welfare.[14]

Much can be learned about her real attitude from the story of the rape of Dinah. In her study of this story, she chooses to focus on Jacob and the brothers rather than on Dinah; and, most significantly, criticizes the brothers, Dinah's defenders, for their violence.[15]

In fact, besides the radio course mentioned above, Nehama almost never paid attention to the gender of the personalities in the Tanach as an issue in itself.[16] In Nehama's discussion of Eve's sin, the latter's gender is not a factor in any way. Rebecca is deemed interesting not as a woman but as an exemplar of *hesed*. In fact, at times Nehama seems to be actively avoiding granting the biblical women any sort of three-dimensional existence. An interesting example is Potiphar's wife. As Dr. Marla Frankel notes,[17] both the Midrash and Thomas Mann, whose book *Joseph and His Brothers* Nehama greatly esteemed, wrote about the human face of Potiphar's wife. Nehama, however, ignores the social and emotional aspects, not even bothering to demonize this character as the eternal female seductress. She is instead entirely focused on Joseph's restraint and righteousness in the face of temptation. Potiphar's wife is no more than the embodiment of his test and of the foreign cultures that will forever threaten the Abrahamic faith. Indeed,

---

[13] Strikovsky, "Nehama on Women," 191.

[14] *SD*, 233. Strikovsky cites Nehama's discussion of Genesis 6:1–4 describing "the sons of God – i.e., the sons of the judges" who "took for themselves wives whomsoever they chose," as demonstrating Nehama's concern for women ("Nehama on Women," 191). Yet Nehama says there explicitly, "The stronger enslave the weaker, the classic example of exploitation being the subjugation of the daughters of man." Clearly her primary interest was in general societal morality.

[15] See Erella Yedgar, *"Parashat va-yishlach: ha-shiput ha-musari be-iyunehah shel Nehama Leibowitz: ma'aseh ha-ahim bi-Shechem ke-mikreh mivhan,"* in *Hogim ba-parashah*, edited by Naftali Rothenberg, 102–116 (Tel Aviv: Van Leer Institute: Maskel, 2005).

[16] Strikovsky's suggestion that Nehama utilized every available opportunity to discuss female Tanach personalities ("Nehama on Women," 188–189) does not stand up to the test of a reading of her *Studies*.

[17] Frankel, *Iyun*, 53.

Frankel argues, so engrossed is Nehama in bolstering the Sages' view of "Joseph the righteous" that she ignores a primary layer of the text.[18] Even more startling is her sidelining of the daughters of Zelophehad, whose story is replete with drama and educational messages. They have only the most fleeting of cameo roles in her *Studies*;[19] and Nehama instead devotes no less than three of her six essays for that week's portion to the *haftarah*! In the few cases where Nehama places some focus on women, none of them constitute convincing proof that she was interested in the feminine experience. Of Samson's mother she writes:

> The tidings regarding the birth of the son… were first given to the mother… because the primary bond both before birth and in infancy is with the mother. (*SBM*, 80)

In another example, at the end of a long essay ignoring the gender of the two midwives in Egypt in favor of general lessons about civil disobedience, Nehama at last adds a note which possibly – though not necessarily – reflects gender awareness:

> Moab and Ammon produced a Ruth and Naamah respectively, Egypt two righteous midwives. (*NSS*, 36)

A further example is cited by R. Strikovsky. In a radio lesson regarding Tamar, Nehama remarked:

> As opposed to the Book of Ruth, which divides its action between Naomi who plans and Ruth who acts, Tamar both plans her actions and carries them out.[20]

All that these latter two demonstrate is an occasional impulse to compare some of the female figures in the Tanach with each other. The overall picture is one of an essential indifference to female identity in the Tanach, and it would certainly prove difficult to build "Nehama's view of womanhood" upon this rickety structure.

ॐ ॐ

Moving now from content to method, we can ask whether Nehama's gender influenced her approach and techniques in any way. Deena Nataf believes so. She remarks that Nehama always remained a "lady" in her Torah teaching: "One of the occupational hazards of women learning and teaching Torah is that some of them fail to put the 'feminine touch' into Torah; one

---

[18] Frankel, *Iyun*, 54.
[19] "Since the daughters of Zelophehad inherited their father, Moses said: now is the time to make my claims" (*SBM*, 342). Moreover, this sentence appears in a Midrash; Nehama does not mention them at all.
[20] Strikovsky, "Nehama on Women," 192.

senses a certain coldness or 'toughness' in the classroom." Nehama's attachment to her students and her personal approach may be seen as expressing a nurturing side. Some also argue that men would not study the weekly Torah portion with such sensitivity to the text's emotional tone.

Yedgar prefers to suggest that Nehama combined a rigorous "male" analysis with "female" elements, such as imagination and visualization of the scene, ethical dilemmas, and emotional and psychological aspects. All these are subtle elements, and not intentionally feminine.[21] We must note that those who influenced Nehama tremendously in the development of her biblical sensibilities (Buber, Rosenzweig, Weiss, Cassuto, Jacob, Strauss), as well as all of the traditional commentators and indeed every one of her intellectual influences were, without exception, male. Her *Studies* lack even a single reference to a statement or commentary by a woman, and similarly, of the approximately 250 sources mentioned in Professor Moshe Sokolow's index to the worksheets, not one has any connection to female authorship. The only female figures present in her work are those from the Tanach and Midrash.

In all fairness, as suggested by Agnon's blank book in his story, very little female scholarship existed for Nehama to quote.[22] As Avraham Grossman notes:

> Throughout the Middle Ages, which continued for about a thousand years, we do not find so much as a single Jewish woman of importance among the sages of Israel… not a single Jewish woman wrote a halakhic, literary, theoretical, mystical, ethical, or poetic work, with the exception of a handful of poems written by Jewish women in Spain.[23]

Even in the earlier part of the twentieth century, very few women were involved in Nehama's field, and those who later entered it were largely her own students. Frankel argues, however, that had Nehama lived today, she would surely be citing some women scholars, for example Mary Douglas.

Whatever the cause of Nehama's avoidance of specific women's issues, the great paradox is that it ultimately resulted in allowing her to contribute more than would otherwise have been the case – not just to Bible study and the

---

[21] Yedgar, "*Parshanut*," 115–116; interview.

[22] In *Jewish Women: A Comprehensive Historical Encyclopedia*, Shalvi Publishing, Jerusalem: 2007, Nehama Leibowitz is not only the sole female Bible scholar mentioned; she is the only post-biblical woman appearing in the entire "Bible" category!

[23] Grossman, *Pious and Rebellious: Jewish Women in Medieval Europe*, University Press of New England, 2004, 278. He notes there that this stands in contrast to Christian and Moslem societies, where creative writing by women did take place.

Jewish world, but even to the cause of women's scholarship. Had Nehama restricted herself to overtly female angles, her scholarship would probably have been relegated, particularly by the Orthodox, into the marginalized category of "women's issues." But by innovatively teaching a wide range of topics central to Jewish thought, she placed herself squarely within the mainstream and gained the respect of Orthodox society, thus opening the door for other women to follow suit. Yedgar: "Nehama is the model for a woman who writes, interprets, has social opinions and is a leader. Had she been more feminine in her approach, she might not have had the courage to do what she did."

Enabling factors

So how did Nehama manage to achieve what no Jewish woman had before her?

Undoubtedly, one important factor was her upbringing. Reportedly, her mother never allowed her into the kitchen. She was treated as the intellectual equal of her brother, subject to the same demands as Yeshayahu, with no doors closed to her as a woman.[24] Nehama, by her own account, was greatly influenced and educated by her father, brother and husband. She hardly ever mentioned her mother or any female role models, except for a grandmother, whom she once described in a letter:

> I've always been told that my grandmother – whom I never knew – was able to competently study a page of Talmud; and the rabbis of Lithuania, the greatest of the generation (and we are talking about eighty to one hundred years ago) would playfully engage with her in words of Torah and even accept her ideas – if she was correct.[25]

Changes were also taking place in the wider community. Nineteenth-century Eastern European Jewish women had learned their Torah in Yiddish from the *Tse'ena U-re'ena*, whilst the men learned it in Hebrew in the *bet midrash*; but by the beginning of the twentieth century, significant numbers of women were exploring new educational frameworks.[26] Even so, Nehama was exceptional. With the advantage of an excellent education in Hebrew

---

[24] See comments by Bambi Sheleg, "*Morat ha-morot*" in Strikovsky, *Daf*, 4. In general, being treated as intellectual equals by their father was a formative experience for several unusual women. Sometimes it occurred by default due to absence of teachable male siblings, as in the case of Henrietta Szold, who was an only child, or perhaps even of Bruriah, the Talmud's foremost female scholar, whose brother was a reprobate (see *Masechet Evel*, 12). But this was obviously not true of the Leibowitz household.

[25] Letter to Reinitz, *PN*, 680.

[26] Shaul Stampfer, "Gender Differentiation and Education of the Jewish Women in Nineteenth-Century Eastern Europe," *Polin, A Journal of Polish Jewish Studies* 7: 70–72, 81.

and constant conversation with the brilliant men in her family, she went on to study at university and in the *Hochschule*, interacting with many learned men there. This gave her unusually unmediated access to the world of Jewish knowledge, which brought with it a sense of confidence and authority unavailable to most women of the time, and even many men.[27]

Lipman's infirmity may have had some effect too, in forcing Nehama to be the breadwinner. Under the best of circumstances she might have invested little time in domestic activities, preferring to spend it in other ways. The need to make a living made this all the more acute, with Nehama out all day, teaching and studying, and leaving her affairs to her housekeeper. Thus she was free to do things such as teach on Friday afternoons when most are overwhelmed by pre-Shabbat mayhem. But she never disparaged practical pursuits. On the contrary, she always marveled at people who cooked or could hammer in nails. When she complimented Joy Rochwarger on her prowess in hosting Shabbat meals, Rochwarger was astonished to discover Nehama's lack of culinary expertise. She asked:

"But what did your husband eat for all those years?"

"Whatever the hired person cooked for him," replied Nehama.

"Was your husband upset that you didn't cook?"

"He didn't care who made the food."

"But why did you never learn to cook?"

"He preferred me to spend my time studying and teaching!"

Nehama was known to say that she wished her parents had taught her to cook and bake, but she was not necessarily believed. "These things were simply not within her frame of reference," says a close friend.

Nehama's background and personality gave her the confidence not to be disturbed by her radical departure from the traditional Jewish female role. True, alongside her encouragement of her female students to learn and teach Torah, she never downplayed the importance of family life. But she also never viewed herself as less of a good Jewish woman for this departure.

It is instructive to compare for a moment Nehama's situation with that of Rayna Batya Berlin, granddaughter of R. Hayyim of Volozhin and wife of R. Naphtali Zvi Yehudah Berlin, the Rosh Yeshivah of the prestigious Volozhin yeshivah. Like Nehama, Rayna Batya was very uninvolved in the running of her household, as reported by her nephew, R. Baruch ha-Levi Epstein, in his memoir, *Mekor Baruch*.[28] In fact, her husband sometimes even went without meals while she spent her days learning Torah. Dr. Don

---

[27] Stampfer notes that lack of education, for both men and women, was part of a system conditioning people to accept the authority of the more knowledgeable (*ibid*. 74).

[28] See Vilna edition, 1928, volume 3, 1949–1950.

Seeman describes poignantly in his article "The Silence of Rayna Batya"[29] the bitterness with which she poured out her feelings to her nephew of being deprived, as a woman, of important mitzvot and of real opportunities for Torah study. In this, her position was the opposite to that of Nehama, who never felt deprived (except possibly in her lack of full talmudic expertise[30]). For Nehama, the gates of Torah were wide open, both to study and to teach. The Torah was a source of pleasure and not pain.

Rayna Batya knew she was atypical. The young Epstein once made what was by his own admission a thoughtless joke to a friend, to the effect that Ben Azzai – the sage who actually encouraged teaching women Torah – himself consistently refused to marry, because "he must have known that a woman who studied could never keep a proper home."[31] When this came to his aunt's ears, she was deeply offended; it clearly touched a raw nerve in her. Nehama, in contrast, always laughed at her own ineptitude in the kitchen and seemed unfazed by societal expectations.

Personality factors may have played a role here. Nehama always made of her life what she could, choosing optimistic paths, while Rayna Batya, in contrast, gradually descended into a negative and frustrated (though challenging and uncompromising) silence.[32] However, we must not ignore their different historical contexts, and the limited choices facing the latter.[33] Fulfilled in the intellectual and spiritual realm, Nehama could afford to laugh at her cooking. Rayna Batya died a disappointed woman, whilst Nehama had the satisfaction of leaving behind a tremendous legacy. Had Rayna Batya lived later,[34] or under slightly different circumstances – for example, in a

---

[29] Don Seeman, "The Silence of Rayna Batya," *The Torah U-Madda Journal* 6 (1996): 91–128. Note, though, that other scholars have called into question the veracity of the *Mekor Baruch*'s portrayal. Some anecdotes and conversations may have been fabricated. See Dan Rabinowitz, "Rayna Batya and Other Learned Women: A Reevaluation of Rabbi Barukh Halevi Epstein's Sources," *Tradition* 35 (2001): 55–69, and also Internet discussions by Marc B. Shapiro, Yehoshua Mondshine and the author of the blog *Ishim ve-shitot* (ishimshitos.blogspot.com). (I thank Professor Shaul Stampfer for drawing my attention to recent developments.)

[30] See page 293 below.

[31] *Mekor Baruch*, 1965, cited in Seeman, "The Silence," 103.

[32] Seeman, "The Silence," 108, and private communication.

[33] Seeman remarks that an individual's suffering will be an outcome of both socio-cultural factors, and the individual's personality, which will dictate how to approach those factors ("The Silence," 121–122). His reading is kind to Rayna Batya, emphasizing her "opportunities for transcendence and meaningful choice-making" within her painful circumstances (*ibid.*, 127, n. 62).

[34] Exact dates of birth and death are unavailable, though they were approximately 1817 to 1876 (Seeman, "The Silence," 113 and 116, n. 7). Although she lived contemporaneously with Hirsch, several important changes occurred after her death,

Hirsch-influenced Western European household, encouraging of women's education – she might have become a Nehama, fulfilled in her Torah instead of thwarted to the point of paralysis. This scenario of "what might have been" makes Rayna Batya's life seem all the more unnecessarily tragic. At the same time it shows how fortunate Nehama was in the timing and circumstances of her life, enabling her talents to be fully expressed.

The fact that Nehama never had children was probably also significant, for it gave her the time to teach and travel freely, a truism of which the Midrash is aware:

> When a woman has no children, she is free to come and go at all times to her mother's house or her relatives' house. When she gives birth to children, she will not have as much freedom to go out, and will stay at home.[35]

Indeed, several prominent Jewish women of the modern period have been either single or childless, such as Henrietta Szold and Sara Schenirer.[36] Undoubtedly even with children Nehama would have achieved tremendous things, with her intellectual drive and passionate goals for changing society. In fact, she made famous a Torah piece that touches on this very question of women's roles. In Genesis 30:1, the matriarch Rachel implores her husband Jacob:

> Give me children or else I die!

Jacob's response is one of anger, but why this is so is not readily apparent. R. Isaac Arama (known as the *Akedat Yitzhak*), writing in the fifteenth century with very modern-sounding sentiments, suggests the following reason:

> The two names, "woman" and "Eve," indicate two purposes. The first [name, in Hebrew *isha*, similar to the word for "man," *ish*] teaches that woman was taken from man, stressing that like him you may understand and advance in the intellectual and moral field just as did the matriarchs and many righteous women and prophetesses and as the

---

such as the establishing of the Bais Yaakov schools. See Seeman, *ibid.*, 113 and 127, n. 65; also Stampfer "Gender Differentiation and Education of the Jewish Women in Nineteenth-Century Eastern Europe," *Polin, A Journal of Polish Jewish Studies* 7: 81, regarding changes in the twentieth century.

[35] *Bereshit Zuta* 29:35, quoted in Uri Cohen, "Childless or Childfree?" *Leela* 52 (December 2001): 43–50, referencing Yael Levine, "*Ha-akrut ba-aggadah*," *Teudah* 13 (1997): 107.

[36] Other single or childless women include Bertha Pappenheim, Nettie Adler and Rebecca Graetz. See Sally Berkovic, *Under my Hat*, Joseph's Bookstore, London, 1997, 88–114.

literal meaning of Proverbs 31 about "the woman of worth [valor]" (*eshet hayil*) indicates. The second alludes to the power of childbearing and rearing children, as is indicated by the name Eve – the mother of all living. A woman deprived of the power of childbearing will be deprived of the secondary purpose and be left with the ability to do evil or good like the man who is barren. Of both the barren man and woman Isaiah (56:5) states: "I have given them in My house and in My walls a name that is better than sons and daughters," since the offspring of the righteous is certainly good deeds (see Rashi on Genesis 6:9). Jacob was therefore angry with Rachel when she said, "Give me children or else I die," in order to reprimand her and make her understand this all-important principle that she was not dead as far as their joint purpose in life because she was childless, just the same as it would be, in his case, if he would have been childless. (*NSB*, 334)

Nehama taught this piece frequently. When invited to lecture on women's issues, she would refuse and instead teach this text. It left a deep impression on her students, some of whom resolved to educate their daughters accordingly. Many also heard echoes of Nehama's own experience in these words and assumed that she agreed with its message. But she confided in friends that she in fact disagreed, for a woman's primary role is to be a mother. Perhaps this is why she does not choose to end her essay in her *Studies* with Arama's explanation, instead bringing a midrashic opinion far more sympathetic to Rachel:

> Our Sages accused Jacob of giving an unworthy answer to an appeal from an embittered and troubled soul.[37]

Nehama showed great interest in motherhood, and always made sure to ask pregnant women how they were feeling. She waxes poetic at the end of an *Iyun* dealing with the offering brought subsequent to childbirth:

> The woman was privileged to experience in her self, in her flesh, the greatness of the Creator. In seeing, sensing and living the developing embryo inside her, she felt her own insignificance and unimportance, her status as "dust and ashes," her impurity. Hence she must bring a sin-offering.[38]

But she also knew in her humility that she could never entirely understand a mother's experience. Once she taught a group of women the story of the banishment of Hagar and Ishmael from Abraham's house, reading the following verse in a dramatic voice (Genesis 21:16):

---

[37] *NSB*, 335. My thanks to Joanna Bruce for drawing my attention to this ending.

[38] *IHBV*, 148; compare *NSV*, 181. Strikovsky notes that Nehama chooses this out of all possible explanations for the mother's sin-offering – an explanation that relieves the mother of any taint of genuine sin. See his comments in "*Nashim ve-nashiyut*," 313.

Nehama with some young visitors and their mother. Courtesy of Mira Ofran.

And she went, and sat down opposite him a good way off, approximately a bowshot; for she said, Let me not see the death of the child. And she sat opposite him, and lifted up her voice, and wept.

Nehama paused and asked: "What do you think of this verse?" No response was forthcoming, so she continued: "I always suppose that the Torah is teaching us the difference between a non-Jewish and a Jewish mother. Hagar, an Egyptian, sits far away from Ishmael because she cannot bear to see the death of her child. But a Jewish mother would never do that; she would stay with her child till the bitter end! Do you agree?" After a moment's pause, a chorus of voices was raised in opposition: "Nehama, you're wrong! We would also do the same thing! What mother could watch her child dying?!" Nehama backed down gracefully. But the story did not end there. At the end of the lesson, a man approached her and said: "You were right. These women didn't go through the Holocaust, they're talking hypothetically. But I was in the camps and I tell you you're right!" He then told her of his five-year-old sister being cradled in his mother's arms right up to the moment of death.[39]

The Talmud (Sanhedrin 19b) states:

He who teaches his friend's son Torah, it is as if he had given birth to him.

According to this, Nehama had numerous spiritual children. Tzipora Levavi: "Nehama was surrounded with love, and she needed it. We were like the children she didn't have." Indeed, she channeled her motherly instincts into her students. Dr. Leah Leeder recalls that while she was at the Hebrew University studying with Nehama, Nehama noticed and fixed her incorrectly buttoned shirt. She did it in such a nurturing way that Leeder felt a pang, knowing of her childlessness.

Lipman tried to console his wife, pointing out that with children of their own she would never have created such close connections with students. But students could never adequately substitute. Friends sensed her pain when around children, and she reportedly once even tried to adopt one of her students.[40] Nehama said explicitly she would have given it all up for a child.[41] In response to a disparaging comment regarding women who choose children over career, she retorted, "Do you think I'd be writing these *gilyonot*

---

[39] From Raphael Posen, "*Al ereh be-mot ha-yeled*," *Ha-Tzofeh*, September 25, 2003.
[40] Abramowitz, *Tales*, 99.
[41] Szold expressed similar sentiments (see Sally Berkovic, *Under My Hat*, Joseph's Bookstore, London, 1997, 112).

if I had children?!"[42] And the delegation of Jewish women from the Women's Liberation Movement who asked for permission to use Nehama's name to spearhead their movement were startled by her reply: "Writing books? That's nothing! Raising six children, now that's an achievement!"

A friend even speculates that certain surprising lapses of confidence in her, such as asking others anxiously if her lesson went well, may have derived from – lying underneath all the poise and light-heartedness – a self-image as a failure in the most traditional Jewish role for women.

Feminist or not?

Now we come to the question of Nehama as feminist.

The word "feminist" is not simple to define, covering the range from self-image and personal opinion to political affiliation and social action. But whatever the definition, one thing was very clear – in Nehama's own eyes she was not a feminist of any stripe, and she adamantly refused to be classified as one. She saw herself as a teacher, and any other title or agenda was extraneous. The topic of feminism produced in Nehama reactions ranging from distaste to wrath. To her, it was just another faddish "ism," and it too would eventually pass. Yet Nehama will, by all accounts, go down in Jewish history as having tremendously empowered Jewish women and served feminist goals extremely well. So what deserves the most credence – a fiercely defended self-definition or a label bestowed by others based on actual deeds and impact? This question, so pertinent in today's age where individuals battle for the freedom to define their own race, religion and even gender, lies at the heart of the issue.

Opinion A: "Nehama was a feminist"

To this day feminists find it difficult to understand how Nehama could have been so hostile to their cause, and they refuse to cooperate with her attempts to divert attention from her gender. "We feminists see Nehama as an important figure in our context," remarks Professor Chana Safrai. Nehama furthered feminist goals by creating a different model of Jewish womanhood than was customary until that time. By taking previously off-limits activities for granted, she beat out a path for other Jewish women to follow.

It is easy to see why many of Nehama's achievements are labeled feminist ones. Professor Tamar Ross, a former student of Nehama's, is today involved in exploring the philosophical implications of radical feminist

---

[42] Heard from several people in interviews. See also Strikovsky, "*Nashim ve-nashiyut*," 311.

critique.[43] She notes that Nehama did away with the myth that women are incapable of becoming *talmidot hachamim* (Torah scholars). For Nehama, women were unqualifiedly capable of scholarship, and Torah study was a natural activity for them. She acted as if no obstacles even existed. When two female students approached her saying, "We'd like to come to Israel but what can we do here for a living as women?" she replied, "Well, I'm a woman – I teach Torah!" As with all her firmly-held beliefs, Nehama stalwartly defended this view. On one occasion, a well-known rabbi came to address a group of Nehama's students, all male except for one woman who had special permission to attend. The rabbi declared, "I won't begin until *she* goes out." "Very well," said Nehama and immediately stood up. "No, no, until *she* leaves," said the rabbi. "I understood you perfectly," she said, "but if she goes, I go!"

Nehama allowed women to sit in on classes given to men. She had no problem with mixed seating, but she conciliated conservative audiences by having the women at the back. There were limits, though. Arriving one day at the Meretz yeshivah in Mevasseret Zion to discover the women sitting behind the *mehitzah*, Nehama announced: "If all the women are over there behind a curtain then I must join them!" The women hurriedly moved into the men's section so that the lesson could begin.

In one remark she also seems to actively defend women from rabbis' low opinion of them, writing with regret:

> Sometimes women come to ask [halachic questions] and they are scolded – why have they come with their bothersome nonsense? (*PN*, 681)

Nehama took equality for granted, upholding equal pay and rights for women. This expressed itself even when it came to dating norms. "When we were young, there was no such thing as the man paying for the woman," she said, adding with distaste: "You know what that's called!"

ॐ ॐ

Another arena where Nehama might arguably be seen as behaving in line with feminist sentiments was that of modesty. The concept of female modesty, when interpreted as requiring concealment inside clothing and homes, is viewed by feminism as a patriarchal suppression of women's rights to their own bodies.

---

[43] Although, like Nehama, Ross developed within a largely male-dominated intellectual arena, she gradually found herself identifying more and more with the feminist issues she had once rejected. Conceivably there is a generational factor involved in their different trajectories – Nehama, born forty years later, might have viewed feminism differently. This is, of course, only speculation.

On the one hand, Nehama always dressed very modestly and did not question the need for a modest dress code. On the other hand, she lived her life as an extremely public figure, and her personality was the very opposite of reserved. She did not let any false societal notions of modesty stand between her and her dearest goals of Torah teaching. In her classroom, she was in charge, speaking her mind no matter who the students were. She taught in front of men, with a manner far from meek – on the contrary, it was outgoing and even theatrical. Professor Rivka Horwitz states that Nehama enjoyed teaching men; it was important to her and she had no specific desire to teach all-female classes. Only on rare occasion did Nehama express discomfort, as when teaching a class of very religious rabbinical students, to whom she presented herself almost apologetically: "They asked me to teach you."

It is marvelous to see that no matter how much time Nehama spent outside her home, traveling the country and teaching in front of hundreds of men, and no matter how little time she spent in her kitchen, she was still praised repeatedly with the verse representing the ideal of Jewish female modesty: "The honor of the king's daughter is within" (Palms 45:14).[44] The muted colors and conservative style of her clothing had something to do with this, for, being the very opposite of provocative or alluring, they broadcasted a message of piety. She was sufficiently covered up for a society that often measures the devoutness of its women in terms of extra centimeters on their sleeves and skirts. But beyond such judgments of fabric length and color, her clothes also reinforced the clear impression that Nehama's purpose in all these travels and teaching was not one of self-aggrandizement, and that she did not want the focus to be on her. Her humility and altruistic nature made even the most public lecture seem somehow less exposing; as if she retained that elusive "innerness" no matter where she went.[45] Such a paradoxical balance of modesty with a highly

---

[44] See Breuer, *"Professor,"* 18, and also Peerless, *To Study*, 178, though his emphasis there is more on humility than on female modesty.

[45] Another reason that Nehama might be praised in this way is because this is the traditional Jewish language used to praise women. Traditional language lacks praises for women such as "confident, bold, groundbreaking," all words belonging to the modern lexicon of compliments for women (thanks to Kibi Hofmann for drawing my attention to this). Nehama did also receive some of the traditional compliments reserved for men who are brilliant Torah scholars and disseminate Torah widely, but there may have been more emphasis placed on her humility and modesty than would have been in the case of a man of her stature. This topic, however, requires further research, including analysis of the traditional language of praise and how it is customarily employed towards men and women.

public lifestyle is another example of Nehama's harmonization of elements at opposite extremes.

It should be noted, too, that while she strictly conformed to standards of modesty in her personal life, as an educator she was lukewarm about the issue. In some Orthodox circles the value of modesty is considered top priority for women, and in some girls' schools is measured daily in slits, sleeves and necklines, at the expense of intellectual, ethical and spiritual issues. But Nehama did not number it amongst the many topics she passionately wished to discuss, and never labored to convince others to dress modestly, as she did with other principles. A female student reports wearing culottes (a skirt split in the middle) in Nehama's presence: "Why are you walking funny?" Nehama demanded. "Are you embarrassed because of me? If you don't think it's right, don't do it! But if you really want to know, I think it's halachically fine; perhaps even preferable to a skirt!"

The subject of modesty does not appear in Nehama's *Studies*.[46] In general she avoided the topic of the body and sexuality in Tanach, argues R. Strikovsky.[47] He notes the absence of the topics of *sotah*, Naomi's advice to Ruth, and the books of Esther and Song of Songs. Esther in particular cries out for Nehama's analytical-didactic method, he says.[48] But, he suggests,

> she was uncomfortable with the book's emphasis on Esther's physical beauty. The Shulamite woman in the Song of Songs, even if the book is taken entirely on a metaphorical level, is still described sensually and erotically, and Nehama was careful to refrain from discussing such matters in her lectures and conversations.[49]

One exception was her discussion of the Israelite women's copper vanity mirrors, used to make the laver in the Tabernacle (*NSS*, 691–695). Here

---

[46] In one instance she discusses clothing-based modesty, quoting Benno Jacob to the effect that clothing is the mark of human dignity and that nakedness symbolizes immorality. But the context of the discussion is the priestly garments, and – the priests being male – not pertinent to questions of female modesty (see *NSS*, 528, and 534, n. 1).
[47] Strikovsky, "*Nashim ve-nashiyut*," 305. This reticence informs her approach to Joseph. For Nehama the appellation "Joseph the Righteous One" (*Yosef ha-tzaddik*) refers to much more than mere sexual restraint. Although she does deal with the incident with Potiphar's wife in an essay ("Joseph's Good Looks," *NSB*, 410–416), the essay actually entitled "Joseph the Righteous One" deals with his arrogance and humility in his general relationships (see *NSB*, 430–438). See further Michael Rosenak, "*Parashat Mi-ketz*," 139. Nehama mentions sexuality in her worksheet to *Bereshit* 5713, citing Arama: "God's wisdom saw fit that the union of man and woman should not be based exclusively on sexual relations, like all other animals. Rather, they should have a special personal relationship that will strengthen their love and companionship," etc.
[48] Strikovsky, "*Nashim ve-nashiyut*," 305.
[49] Strikovsky, "Nehama on Women," 189.

Nehama prefers to close with Rashi's praise of the women for using the mirrors to attract their weary husbands over Ibn Ezra's suggestion that in donating the mirrors they were renouncing such vanities and desires. In doing so she affirms the role of sexual desires when channeled into positive ends.

∞ ∞

When some young people today are asked "Who was Nehama Leibowitz?" they reply, "She was like a rabbi, but a woman." This attitude is not limited to children. Pinchas Peli, an Israeli scholar, wrote in 1965:

> Nehama Leibowitz is the most astounding living Israeli rabbi.[50]

People have also been known, either in affectionate respect, or simply in an understandable slip of the tongue, to refer to her as "Rabbi Nehama." But the aptness of this comparison of Nehama to a rabbi depends on which aspect of the rabbinical role is in focus. Many rabbis are primarily teachers; and in fact, in certain circles it is becoming the norm to call even those teachers lacking ordination "Rabbi," reverting to the original meaning of the word *Rav*, "master."[51] This goes some way to explain why slips of tongue occur so naturally, and why Nehama might be viewed as a *Rav* even without the official title. Indeed, R. Aharon Lichtenstein, Rosh Yeshivah of Yeshivat Har Etzion, ruled that students were to stand up when Nehama walked in as they would for a rabbi.

Furthermore, though she was far from the Hasidic outlook, Nehama functioned for her disciples in ways similar to the Hasidic Rebbe – the sage/guru figure. She guided and inspired, offered advice to those who sought it, and passed on her Torah to the younger generation. She created a spiritual community of sorts through her worksheet correspondents and students, though they did not all know each other. It is important to note, however, that Nehama shunned personality cults, and therefore the element of blind devotion or submission found in many Rebbe-disciple relationships was absent.

One of her disciples was Blu Greenberg. Today a leading Orthodox feminist, she considers Nehama one of her two greatest teachers. Greenberg studied with Nehama in 1955 in a framework called the *Seminar le-morim mi-ḥul* (Seminary for Diaspora Teachers). Located in the Palatin Hotel in Jerusalem, it numbered around thirty students, some destined to become prominent educators. Greenberg was profoundly impressed with Nehama's

---

[50] Quoted in Sheila Segal, *Women of Valor: Stories of Great Jewish Women Who Helped Shape the Twentieth Century*, Behrman House, Inc.: 1996, 102.

[51] See the thread "The Value of Origami Semikha" in Lookjed archives, June 2007.

familiarity with commentaries, her teaching methods, and especially her talmudic knowledge. Never having experienced any of these in a woman, Greenberg was, in her words, "blown away." At the program's end, Greenberg very much wanted to continue studying with Nehama and traveling with her as she lectured, just as a young male yeshivah student might accompany the *talmid hacham* in his daily rounds, acting as his *shamash* (attendant), doing errands for him and learning from his example. This was a radical idea, but Greenberg reasoned that if a female *shamash* was unheard of, so was a female Torah scholar until Nehama came along.[52]

Greenberg's idea was not so far-fetched; later, many students, both women and men, played this role at one time or another, organizing worksheets, driving Nehama, and giving her physical help. But at the time it was socially unacceptable for a young Orthodox female to travel around on her own, and Greenberg's family torpedoed the plan, though a young man with a similar desire would have been given every encouragement, she believes.[53] Reluctantly she returned to America, maintaining contact with Nehama from afar.

Batya Jacobs's attempt met with more success. She was only eight years old when her father, R. Shlomo Riskin, announced: "We're going to Israel to meet my Rebbe." She exclaimed: "But I thought Rav Soloveitchik was your Rebbe?!" Her father explained that Rabbi Soloveitchik was his Rebbe in Talmud, but this was his Rebbe in Tanach. His plan to surprise his daughter, who expected a venerable old man with a beard, was successful – the encounter led to a "lifelong reaction." When Jacobs subsequently came to Israel in 1982 and discovered discussions of the evacuation of Sinai dominating in her women's yeshivah to the detriment of her Torah learning, it was Nehama she called for advice. Nehama arranged for her to transfer to a religious kibbutz movement framework and also offered to study privately with her. Nehama supported her army service, and for many years Jacobs studied under her personal guidance. "She added a lucid and stately jewel to the crown of Torah," says Jacobs. "Her vivid and earnest voice still echoes

---

[52] In general, women seem to be at a disadvantage when it comes to this type of mentoring relationship. Within academic circles, male professors might hesitate to take on female protégées, and potential female mentors are few in the upper academic echelons (see Gary Olson and Evelyn Ashton-Jones, "Doing Gender: [En]gendering Academic Mentoring," *Journal of Education* 174/3 [1992], 114–127). This seems to hold even more true for potential mentor-protégé relationships within the Torah world. (My thanks to Rachel Furst for this information. See her article "En-gendered Identities: Accounting for Gender in Religious Educational Role Modeling" at www.atid.org.)
[53] Blu Greenberg, *On Women and Judaism*, Jewish Publication Society of America, 1981, 26.

behind every verse and Rashi that I read to myself or with my children. For me she is not a memory, she is a living reality."

Another person who considers Nehama his Rebbe is R. Avi Weiss, American Modern Orthodox rabbi and activist. He calls Nehama *morateinu* (our teacher).[54] Weiss had studied Nehama's *gilyonot* for years, but was afraid to send his answers to her. "I felt she was too holy," he says. They finally met when she was very old, and talked for four hours. Weiss presented Nehama with his book on women and prayer;[55] and Nehama, true to form, subsequently sent him a letter strongly critical of women's prayer groups. Walter Sherman also calls Nehama his rabbi, and her books are an indispensable part of his Shabbat reading of the weekly Torah portion. "It's the best section of my prayer; every year I get a new idea." One further rabbi-like element was activated when R. Nachum Amsel asked Nehama for a *haskamah* (endorsement) for his new women's seminary. She agreed, though this was the only one she ever gave.

But Nehama differed from rabbis in one vital respect – she was not a *posek*. Every Orthodox rabbi has learned the basic halachic codices, and is expected to be able to rule in questions of Jewish law. While Nehama made brief excursions into halachic works,[56] it was always as part of her Torah teaching, and she never pretended to be a dispenser of rulings. The late R. Yosef Kapach was once discussing women's capabilities for Torah learning with his students. When one of them attempted to cite Nehama as proof that that women could become highly Torah-learned, R. Kapach said, "Yes, Nehama knew a lot of Torah, but when she needed to know a Halachah, she came to me." Nonetheless, Nehama's immense Torah knowledge led students at times to turn to her for halachic advice. In one of the more unusual telephone conversations Nehama ever received, an American student anxiously asked: "Nehama, you know how we learned about the commandment to take the eggs and shoo away the mother bird?[57] Well, I'm standing next to the bird... *what do I do now?*" Nehama obligingly explained the issue to her as she understood it. Another time, a former student came to Nehama for advice. She had been married for nearly ten years, but the

---

[54] This term is one of the suggestions for how to address Orthodox women serving in community religious positions, "Rabbi" being considered inapplicable by most. See Debra Nussbaum Cohen, "Search is on for Names for Orthodox Women Leaders," *The Jewish News Weekly of Northern California*, February 20, 1998.

[55] Avi Weiss, *Women at Prayer: A Halakhic Analysis of Women's Prayer Groups*, Ktav, NJ, 1990.

[56] See for example in letter to Reinitz, *PN*, 694, where Nehama mentions *Teshuvot ha-Rosh*.

[57] Deuteronomy 22:6.

couple was childless. Should they divorce, as some halachic decisors rule in such a case, and try again with a new spouse?[58] Nehama replied that she was not qualified to answer, and they should go to someone else. But the woman persisted, stating that she respected her opinion and wanted to hear it, so eventually Nehama said:

"Tell me, do you love your husband?"

"Very much."

"Does he love you?"

"Yes, he does, very much."

"Well," said Nehama, "if you love him and he loves you, then I think you are meant for each other and you should continue with your marriage. And may God grant you your wish."[59]

❧ ❧

Nehama supported some initiatives that created an entrée for women into the world of Talmud and Halachah. Nurit Fried, director of an Ohr Torah Stone program training Orthodox women to be rabbinic pleaders in the Israeli rabbinical court of law, reports that Nehama supported this ground-breaking program, which allowed women to be official players in the Jewish legal realm for the first time. "Nehama saw it as an important move in preventing discrimination against female litigants," says Fried.

Nehama was also in favor of women studying Talmud, deemed largely unacceptable until the late twentieth century. She herself studied it from early times. When people visiting the Berlin library were surprised to see a woman taking down a volume of Talmud, it was inevitably Nehama. Much of the Talmud she knew she learned from her husband, and she included it in her teaching often. For her, it was a rich interpretative resource and she never felt it was off-limits. Once, an ultra-Orthodox rabbinical student asked Nehama a question from the Talmud. She shot back: "You know, it says in the Talmud, 'Anyone who teaches his daughter Talmud has taught her frivolity.'"[60] There was an awkward moment, but Nehama immediately

---

[58] See Mishnah *Yevamot* 6:6 and Maimonides, *Yad Hazakah, Hilchot Ishut* 15:7.
[59] Bonchek, "Professor Nehama," 20 and 27. This is, of course, what Nehama chose to do in her own life in similar circumstances. Incidentally, the childless couple visited the Lubavitcher Rebbe in New York, who echoed Nehama's words almost exactly (*ibid.*, 27).
[60] This sentence serves as a key text for the position forbidding women's Talmud study. The original statement, from Mishnah Sotah 3:4, actually reads: "Anyone who teaches his daughter *Torah* has taught her frivolity," but the word "Torah" is not traditionally understood to be referring to Tanach, but rather Oral Law.

continued: "You should look in *Tosafot* in such-and-such tractate," and the entire group of Orthodox men burst out laughing.[61]

Professor Chana Safrai had known Nehama from early childhood. Her mother was Nehama's student in the Mizrachi seminary, and her father Nehama's substitute in giving *shiurim* in the neighborhood on Shabbat. So when in the early 1980s she opened the Judith Lieberman institute for advanced Jewish women's studies, with Talmud on the curriculum for the first time ever in a such an institution, she immediately invited Nehama to join the faculty. Nehama offered her unreserved support, and commented in prophetic fashion: "You'll see, some day there'll be tens of thousands of young women who know how to learn, and this whole issue will become a non-issue." By Nehama's passing in 1997 this prediction was well on its way to coming true, and today, it is unremarkable to see women, young and old, engrossed in Talmud study, in women's yeshivahs and other forums. This sight would no doubt have pleased Nehama, though she disapproved when the women imitated the *Kollel* model, being subsidized to sit and learn instead of earning a living.[62]

However, this movement of change came too late for Nehama, who learned Talmud only piecemeal. There is something sad about this fact, for the Talmud was the seminal Jewish work upon which all her beloved commentators had been brought up. When students brought proofs from the Talmud, she sometimes said with a shrug: "This is your field," "I'm not a Talmud scholar" or "I'm an ignoramus when it comes to Talmud." Or she would ask someone with her childlike wonder: "How does it feel to learn Talmud in yeshivah?" R. Samet once clinched an argument with a talmudic quote, and when Nehama said, "I didn't study in the yeshivah like you, I don't have your background," he sensed her sadness. But the fact remains that she never attempted to study Talmud systematically, and even turned down opportunities to do so. When Professor Rivka Horwitz would propose on a Shabbat afternoon that they learn Talmud together, Nehama always suggested instead the *Ein Yaakov* – a collection of Aggadic material culled from the Talmud and considered much lighter fare. And when yeshivah

---

[61] *Tosafot* is a medieval collection of commentaries on the Talmud, and by mentioning it, Nehama was demonstrating that she had no problem with women learning or discussing Talmud.

[62] Nehama writes in her *Studies:* "The patron of Torah scholars is thus investing his money, the return on which is half the Divine reward bestowed on the Torah scholar for his devotions. This approach is of course fraught with danger…. Maimonides roundly condemns [it]" (*SD*, 396–397). In the Hebrew her language is even stronger – she says the approach contains an aspect of *"hillul Hashem,"* desecrating the name of Heaven (*IBD*, 381).

students came to study Talmud with Lipman, Nehama did not join in the conversation – though this may have been so as not to steal from her husband's precious studying time.

So where does all of the above leave us regarding the question of Nehama as feminist? It gives quite a mixed message. On the one hand, she came as close to being a rabbinical figure as an Orthodox woman can. She not only endorsed women's access to previously fenced-off realms but also led the way. Yet on the other hand, she remained firmly on the conservative side of certain red lines, which brings us to the other side of the discussion:

Opinion B: "Nehama was not a feminist"

"I wish the women's lib organizations would learn from Nehama," complains one Orthodox woman. "She was just herself and did not try to copy anyone else."

Nehama must have known she was exceptional. But while she frequently quoted her brother's statement –"The greatest revolution of the twentieth century is the entrance of women into the world of learning"[63] – she herself shrugged off the label "revolutionary" with all her might. Perhaps she understood that it would alienate part of her audience, placing her outside the bounds of the traditional camp where she felt most comfortable. Or perhaps she genuinely did not believe herself to be a revolutionary. Professor Alice Shalvi, a well-known feminist, suggests: "Nehama was an innovator, not a revolutionary."[64] Examining what Nehama did in practice, the phrase "evolution, not revolution," appears apt. Nehama built upon preexisting materials, gradually and subtly, making as few waves as possible. Professor Barry Levy remarks, "I think she liked to be controversial, but within the parameters of what she (and some other important figures) thought to be acceptable Orthodoxy. I have many examples that support this evaluation." It is unlikely that this was a thought-out strategy. It probably stemmed from an intuitive sense of how to balance her various goals and beliefs.

Even the label "innovator" would not have sat well with Nehama. She classified herself as a teacher, a role filled by religious women for centuries, familiar and safe territory. She also claimed that women's Torah learning was not new:

> In several rabbinic families even fifty years ago, the women knew Torah – even Oral Torah – and they never saw this as being a bad thing. But it seems that in this generation, this too has changed in a certain direction. (PN, 680)

---

[63] Strikovsky, "Nehama on Women," 187. Yeshayahu was the more radical of the two in pushing for halachic change regarding women. See page 293 below.
[64] Quoted in Heilman, "A Passion."

Similarly she commented in the mid-1980s, when women's Torah learning was just beginning to flourish:

> Women's Jewish education, has it improved? Well, there are certainly more institutions for women to study Tanach and Jewish subjects. And women from Kibbutz Hadati come from all over the country to my *shiurim* at Beit Meir. But there have always been women participating actively in my *shiurim*.[65]

Safrai, for one, feels that Nehama was fooling herself: "Nehama is one of these women who enjoy the fruits of the suffragettes' efforts but won't entertain the social and theoretical implications of the movement for change." In any event, Nehama's low-key approach succeeded in convincing opponents of feminism that she was one of them. They were delighted that she went about her work without turmoil, propaganda or politics. They felt no threat in her achievements, only pride. Thus, though Nehama's books contain no *haskamot*, they were widely accepted, except in far-right religious circles. Her broad Torah knowledge, respect for rabbinic authority, strict halachic observance and modest dress, her referring to herself as "a simple teacher" and her avowed anti-feminism – all of these were the passports Nehama held while unobtrusively smuggling female Torah scholarship into Orthodoxy. What, after all, could be objectionable about lovingly learning and teaching Torah, the tree of life?

Once again, the irony is that ultimately this nonchalant approach achieved much more than aggressive, overtly feminist tactics would have.

Nehama and the Jewish feminists parted ways on another major issue: Rituals and commandments. Jewish women have traditionally been exempt from certain mitzvot, loosely defined as "positive time-bound" precepts. Over time they accepted some of these upon themselves in a rabbinically ratified manner. In recent decades, however, there has been a push towards the adoption of further commandments, including reading from the Torah in synagogue, wearing *tzitzit* (ritual fringes) and *tallit* (prayer shawl), laying *tefillin* (phylacteries) and, in general, taking communal leadership roles. This trend has met with much resistance in the Orthodox community, and Nehama opposed it too. In her own life she rejected all actions that were not customary, refusing for instance to speak from the synagogue dais, which she felt to be an inappropriate place for a woman. R. Yaakov Ariel writes that Nehama

---

[65] From "Nehama herself."

refrained from giving discourses in shul. She told me this herself on a number of occasions. I attended her *shiurim* and I learned a lot from her, but not in *shul*.[66]

In keeping only those mitzvot customary for women, Nehama did not feel deprived in any way. She viewed the desire to take on more mitzvot as a modern innovation resulting not from authentic religious emotion but from the influence of secular feminism. She was very outspoken on this issue. Had women fulfilled all their present obligations that they needed to go pursue some more? Had they run the gamut of charitable deeds? If God did not want women to lay *tefillin* then they should not – what need had they for a black box on their heads? Whoever wanted more devotion every morning should get up early and visit the sick. Far easier to wrap leather straps around one's arm than to go comfort irritable invalids!

Nehama rejected the argument that women's spiritual needs must be met more fully than convention currently allows. Shira Leibowitz Schmidt recalls that Nehama

> unsympathetically labeled as "sport" the untraditional, demonstrative prayer by Women of the Wall,

and documents how one woman, for whom Nehama was a role model, felt initially hurt by this attitude:

> At first the rebuke stung. But I gradually realized it was Nehama's pithy shorthand for the halachic concept that "greater is one who does a mitzvah because he is obligated to, than one who does an optional mitzvah...." I was chagrined at the time but it helped me reevaluate my premises. [67]

The question might be asked why the same should not be said of Torah learning. Women might be motivated to study Torah not only to strengthen their religious identities, but also to be equal to men in a crucial Jewish realm that represents Jewish power and authority.[68] But Nehama separated between the two in her mind. She explained to Safrai, in one of their many discussions: "To deprive someone of the gratification and intellectual enjoyment of Torah study is unjust; but when it comes to keeping mitzvot, you just have to do what God told you." In this, she strongly echoed her

---

[66] Yaakov Ariel, "How Should Bat Mitzvah Be Celebrated?" in *Traditions and Celebrations for the Bat Mitzvah*, edited by Ora Wiskind Elper, 123 (Jerusalem: Urim Publications, 2003). Ariel's position is also mentioned in Moshe Stern, "*Rav tarbuti*," *Maariv*, 20 December, 2002, and Oriah Shavit, "*Zara be-tocham*," *Haaretz*, December 28, 2001.

[67] Shira (Leibowitz) Schmidt. "In Need of a Fifth T," *Jerusalem Post*, May 30, 2000, 8. The Women of the Wall are a group of women of varied affiliations who pray together every new moon at the Western Wall. They have been the subject of much opposition.

[68] Yedgar, "*Parshanut*," 111.

brother Yeshayahu's philosophy. He believed that taking on extra mitzvot is pointless, as their entire significance derives from their being commanded, but that Torah learning is a "basic Jewish right" and not to be withheld from women.[69]

By and large Nehama was not interested in confronting aspects of Judaism that might be considered problematic for women. Yaakov Fogelman says: "I once told Nehama that the Abravanel does not believe that woman was created in the image of God. At first she said, 'No!' and I said, 'Yes.' Then she said, 'Show me.' When I did, she whispered, 'Don't tell anyone!'"[70] Dr. Deborah Weissman, an active feminist, once sent out letters to many prominent Jewish figures asking for their views on women's issues and feminism. Her letter to Nehama met with a reply recommending that she stop wasting time on these ridiculous topics.

For Nehama, the Halachah was the ultimate arbiter, and she was willing to surrender even her democratic rights to its authority. When Rabbi A.I. Kook ruled to prohibit women from voting, she obeyed without a murmur. At *Minhah* time, Nehama would smile and tell her yeshivah students, "Now I have to leave." She had no problem with being one moment the revered Torah teacher, with every student under her thumb, and the next vacating the room, not counted in the quorum.

Nehama's feminist friends tried for years to persuade her to their way of thinking. Safrai ran various materials by her, though she knew that she did not tend to think along sociological and historical-critical lines as the feminists did. Dutifully Nehama read the feminist writings, but was never convinced of their worth. "I didn't expect her at her age to change her opinions," says Safrai. "I appreciated her willingness to read it, and wanted to share my world with her, a respected colleague." But Safrai admits that it was also a small provocation on her part. Blu Greenberg also tried. She maintained a close connection with Nehama, visiting whenever she came to Israel, often accompanied by her husband, R. Irving (Yitz) Greenberg. Over the years, the conversation turned increasingly to feminism, with Greenberg trying to persuade Nehama that traditional Jewish roles excluded Torah study also from women's lives. Greenberg even informed Nehama that she was her model for her feminism. But every visit she would be treated anew to Nehama's frank disagreement; and the latter's response to Greenberg's book, *On Women in Judaism*, was: "What do you need this stuff for?"

It is a tribute to the affection Nehama inspired that both Safrai and Greenberg continued their close friendship with her. Even Nehama's

---

[69] See page 549 below.
[70] Yaakov Fogelman, public session, *VLN*. The reference is to Abravanel's commentary to Genesis 1:27 (page 69 in the Bnei Arbal edition).

unbending opposition to Greenberg's life's work did not change her opinion that Nehama could do no wrong: "She was unique, extremely powerful as a model. I took the whole package, the whole picture and personality of Nehama."

The yeshivah world

With her reputation established, Nehama was, uniquely for a woman, permitted to teach at several men's yeshivahs. This included not only the more liberal institutions, such as the religious kibbutz movement's yeshivah, whose heads knew Nehama well from many kibbutz visits, but also more conservative establishments such as the Meretz yeshivah. The latter first consulted an ultra-Orthodox rabbi. He ruled that they should take a female teacher only if they could find no male teacher of equivalent capabilities. Without further ado, Nehama was hired.[71]

She also taught in teacher-training programs for religious men, such as the Herzog Teacher's College at Yeshivat Har Etzion and Machon Lifschitz. She taught at the Gruss Kollel of Yeshiva University, probably the only woman teaching Torah in a kollel anywhere in the world. Rabbis and teachers attending seminars in Israel – and even ultra-Orthodox ones such as the Lakewood-connected Torah UMesorah – wanted to hear Nehama. Only the small minority refused to be taught by a woman.

Of course there were many yeshivahs that would not employ Nehama. She was not offended; it was only to be expected. Students from these yeshivahs who wanted to study with Nehama had to come clandestinely. Today, there are ultra-Orthodox rabbis who in the past enjoyed Nehama's classes, but could never admit this publicly. One yeshivah student, desiring to quote her Torah to his friends but afraid that he would get into trouble for studying with a woman, arrived at a creative solution – and unbeknownst to her, Nehama was summarily transformed into "Reb Nahman"!

Nehama was such a mistress of understatement that she managed to pull off Torah teaching within these sanctums of male learning without making headlines – that is, until one day late in her life, when it all snowballed out of her control. The year was 1984. R. Shlomo Riskin had become the director of a program to train rabbis for Diaspora work, its participants hailing from institutions ranging from the Zionist *Hesder* yeshivahs to the ultra-Orthodox Ponevezh yeshivah. R. Riskin felt that talmudic knowledge was not enough for a Diaspora rabbi, especially with sermons such a central element to the role: "So I looked for the best Tanach teacher Israel has to offer – Nehama

---

[71] Abramowitz, *Tales*, 44.

Leibowitz, of course. She did a wonderful job, in terms of both substance and pedagogical material."

The rabbis-in-training enjoyed Nehama's teaching tremendously. R. Mordechai Goldberg recalls Nehama laughing at their ignorance of Tanach. Once, after they could not locate a certain verse from Prophets, she said merrily: "You should be ashamed of yourselves – it was in last week's *haftarah*!" According to Goldberg, some students changed their approach to Tanach entirely after meeting Nehama; and all came to respect her intelligence and look forward to the lively discussions. R. Riskin and some of the high-powered board members liked to sit in on the classes too.

A sizable component of the student body was ultra-Orthodox, and some were still attending their yeshivahs at this time. Shmuel Teitelbaum was studying at R. Shlomo Zalman Auerbach's yeshivah, Kol Torah. Teitelbaum insists that despite the novelty ("Who can forget the impressive sight of Nehama sitting at the head of a table, with thirty rabbis and *talmidei hachamim* learning from her?"), they never gave Nehama's gender a second thought. "She was so modest, and her teaching style made it appear the most natural thing in the world," he explains. If anything bothered them, it was her views on secular culture.

But there was a cloud on the horizon. Things began to heat up when one of the teachers complained about the program to R. Eliezer Schach, the doyen of the Lithuanian yeshivah world, and it ended with R. Schach ruling against the institute. The impression given out was that the ruling was based on the fact that a woman was teaching there.

R. Riskin states that the original complaint was motivated by personal rancor, since the teacher had been asked to leave. R. Eitan Eckstein, a participant in the program and student at the ultra-Orthodox Itry yeshivah, presents a different version of events: "A group of us who wore black *kippot* had approached R. Schach early on about studying with Nehama. He replied that it was inappropriate for a woman to teach, but since it was to be only for nine sessions, and she would be hurt if the students pulled out, it was allowed. I think he respected her integrity and learnedness, and I remember he explicitly said that she was 'not like her brother.'" But when the schedule was altered to include many more secular subjects, the students returned to R. Schach, and now he unequivocally disapproved, saying: "It has turned into a 'rabbinical seminary' like those in Berlin. Rabbis are not meant to be doctors or professors." Yet even according to this version, the controversy was never actually about Nehama. At most, there was an objection to too much Tanach teaching. "I think that Rav Schach's words were not properly understood. People took Nehama's gender as the excuse, because it was easier to comprehend than his real objections," suggests R. Eckstein.

In any event, when R. Riskin heard the ruling, he was dumbfounded. The students were in their twenties and Nehama in her eighties – what was the problem? He approached R. Avraham Shapira, then Ashkenazi Chief Rabbi of Israel, who, he says, pronounced it acceptable for Nehama to teach.[72] But the defamation continued nonetheless. R. Riskin found himself forced to turn to R. Shlomo Zalman Auerbach, the greatest living halachic authority, who, he says, clearly stated his view in favor of Nehama teaching. However, a few weeks later on May 1, 1987, *Yated Neeman*, the ultra-Orthodox daily, headlined its front page: "Studying in the Rabbinical Training Seminary for the Diaspora is strictly prohibited!" The article included an announcement signed by both R. Elyashiv and R. Auerbach, stating:

> Since we have been informed of the truth regarding the schedule and lecturers in the Rabbinical Training Seminary for the Diaspora, we hereby announce a strict ban on studying there.

The article continued:

> The most illustrious rabbis of our time this week signed an absolute ban on studying at the Rabbinical Training Seminary for the Diaspora, funded by the Rothschild Foundation, which recently became a *bet midrash* for rabbis, with all the negative ramifications of this [type of institution], strictly prohibited by all the great rabbis over the generations. Secular lecturers, including women, teach the students.... The institution has [expanded from one day a week to the entire week, taking the men away from their kollel studies]; and worst of all, the lecturers include very few rabbis, but rather secular lecturers from various universities. The views of these lecturers, and of Professor Nehama Leibowitz, who teaches Tanach in front of yeshivah students, are unacceptable, being the complete antithesis to the views of our respected teachers and rabbis, the great rabbis of the Torah....

> Our reporter has been informed that Riskin told the yeshivah students that the Chief Rabbi, Rabbi Avraham Shapira, endorses Professor Leibowitz's lecturing... but upon investigation, our reporter discovered that Rabbi Shapira too completely opposes Leibowitz's lecturing in front of yeshivah students; so Riskin's claims are entirely fabricated.

> A number of students have already announced that they are leaving.

---

[72] Nehama also noted that she had received the consent of the Chief Rabbi, and it troubled her that she nevertheless was still criticized for teaching male yeshivah students. See B. Barry Levy, "On the Periphery: North American Orthodox Judaism and Contemporary Biblical scholarship," in *Students of the Covenant: History of Jewish Biblical Scholarship in North America*, edited by S. David Sperling, 204, n. 79 (Atlanta: Scholars Press, 1992).

Appended to this article was a letter received from R. Schach:

> I heard and was appalled.... I have seen the schedule of classes and lecturers who hold foreign views of heresy and apostasy that contradict our holy Torah, and moreover a woman teaches there.... Woe to us that we have come to this. Worst of all, one of the heretics is titled "Rabbi," to blind the eyes and tempt Torah-true students.

There was also an editorial inside the same edition of *Yated Neeman*, entitled: "A factory for rabbis." The authors railed at the transformation of the program from a yeshivah into a university framework with semesters, exams and professors. They lambasted Riskin for deciding that the students must study Tanach –

> and not just ordinary Tanach, but in depth, under the microscope, and on a high academic level. And he has a wonderful lecturer – Professor Nehama Leibowitz. Well, what can we say, that's a refreshing novelty – a woman lecturing Kollel students! And the classes are mandatory. But there's more, much more. Mrs. Leibowitz is a big name in Tanach study, a giant in her field. Which is precisely the problem – this giant grew within a field that is nebulous, disorganized, and distorted. She takes a verse, and brings all kinds of comments, from the appropriate to the objectionable and deplorable. She judges what is good and what fit to dismiss; she gives out grades. She even carves her own path, steering downhill all the way. Moshe Rabbenu went out to his brothers, and saw their burdens? He was a seeker of justice, a universal revolutionary. He killed an Egyptian? Therein lies a moral problem....

> The students resisted, rebelled. They were naïve; little did they know that this was just the tip of the iceberg, the first experimental foothold.[73]

Another Ultra-Orthodox paper, *Hamodia*, also published the ban on May 1. R. Riskin was shocked to see R. Auerbach's signature, but was not able to get the ban reversed.[74] Religious sanctions were declared against R. Riskin's institutions, while R. Schach continued to refuse to grant him an audience. Half of the student body left. "All those who wore black *kippot* had no choice," recalls Teitelbaum. "It was an unavoidable decree from a higher power." Although he obeyed the ruling, Teitelbaum felt it was politically

---

[73] "*Beit haroshet le-rabbanim*," *Yated Neeman*, May 1, 1987, *Musaf* supplement, 6.

[74] According to R. Riskin, R. Auerbach explained to him with great sorrow that he could not come out openly against R Schach. R. Riskin then phoned R. Elyashiv, who said he did not recognize his name. "I said 'Rav Elyashiv, you just placed all my institutions under sanctions! If someone asked me a question about a chicken, before I would pronounce it non-kosher I would want to see the chicken; wasn't I also worth a ten minute discussion?!'"

motivated, with little connection to authentic religious matters: "We had already finished the entire semester, and nothing had happened to us," he points out.

Half of the faculty also resigned. R. Riskin remembers two of the remaining teachers receiving threats of having their legs broken; and R. Riskin and other teachers, such as Dr. Howard Deitcher, were put into *herem* (excommunication). Public emotion ran high, and the incident had the status of a scandal for a while, providing centrist Orthodoxy with more fodder for anger at what they saw as ultra-Orthodox excess. Then R. Ovadia Yosef, a leading halachic decisor, came out with his own ruling: Nehama could teach, but from behind a curtain.[75] There were historical precedents for this. In the twelfth century, the daughter of R. Samuel ben Ali of Baghdad taught through the window of a building, invisible to the male students below,[76] while in the sixteenth century, Miriam Shapira taught Halachah to the brightest yeshivah students from behind a curtain.[77] But this ruling only served to further inflame liberal sensibilities. If Deborah the Prophetess did not have to stand behind a curtain, why should Nehama? One *Jerusalem Post* reader recommended indignantly:

> Let Professor Leibowitz be treated with respect and consideration and lecture from a podium like all the other lecturers in the programme. Rabbi Schach and all his ilk can attend wearing burlap bags over their heads so they will not be distressed or distracted by the sight of an educated woman.[78]

Afterwards rumors circulated that Nehama capitulated and taught from behind a curtain;[79] but in truth she never did so. She lay low for a while, making no public statement and refusing the newspapers – religious or non-religious – her side of the story, saying: "I'm just carrying on." It was hard for her that the quality of her teaching had been slighted, though that was

---

[75] "Yeshivah Head Rejects Attack on Woman Teacher," *Jerusalem Post*, May 7, 1987, 4.

[76] *Sibuv ha-rav Petahya mi-Regensburg*, edited by Greenhut, 9-10 (Jerusalem: 1905), and Benisch, A., *Travels of Rabbi Petachia of Ratisbon*, London: 1856, 19. R. Eleazar ben Yaakov, the greatest Babylonian poet of the period, wrote an elegy for this woman, describing her as an outstanding scholar (Avraham Grossman, *Pious and Rebellious: Jewish Women in Medieval Europe*, University Press of New England, 2004, 163).

[77] This is mentioned in the Responsa of R. Solomon Luria (Maharshal), 29, quoted in Breuer, *"Professor,"* 19. See also Rashi, II Chronicles 34:22, regarding the prophetess Hulda who taught Torah from between two walls (thanks to Batya Wachtfogel for this reference).

[78] E.M. Solowey, letters, May 26, 1987.

[79] For instance, "At one point she taught in an Orthodox yeshivah, albeit from behind a screen in order to modestly shield her from the male students" (Calev Ben-David, "No More Yentls," *Jerusalem Post*, April 2, 1999, B3).

never made explicit. But above all she was pained at being dragged, after decades of successful avoidance, into a political controversy. For the first time in a lifetime of tiptoeing between the raindrops, Nehama had got wet.

Despite everything, Nehama managed to weather this incident with humor, laughing at the idea that after many decades of teaching men it was suddenly improper at eighty years old to be doing so. She was not angry with the ultra-Orthodox rabbis involved; on the contrary, she was upset at their negative portrayal in the press. Deitcher notes that it was important to Nehama to be accepted by them. Rather, what distressed her deeply was the pain caused to others. That R. Riskin was now in *herem* simply because she was doing what she always did seemed inconceivable. Nehama offered her resignation, but he adamantly refused. The program continued, and R. Riskin, ignoring requests by students and faculty to be allowed to return, reconstituted his program from *Hesder* graduates. The following year, he notes, enrollment was higher than ever.

Nehama and the women of today

If we drew up a pyramid representing female Torah scholarship, Nehama would be at its apex. Below her would be a handful of learned women, the prominent female Torah scholars of today – many of them Nehama's students; some not.[80] Moving down the pyramid, there would be increasing numbers of female scholars, many of whom studied with Nehama or with her students (male and female). At the pyramid's base are their students, the thousands of young Jewish women who have attended high schools, seminaries and women's yeshivahs, for whom Torah learning is almost second nature. Interestingly, Nehama lived and taught for so long that a relatively young female Torah scholar of today, near the pyramid's base, might have learned directly from Nehama herself, or might just as easily have studied with her student's student's student.

This diagram concretizes the changes in women's Torah learning. As mentioned above, Nehama's non-feminist approach advanced feminist goals, propelling the next generation of female Torah teachers forward, in a gradual yet drastic transformation. Today, women who teach Torah, even Talmud, are regularly viewed as assets instead of aberrations. If, as Seeman argues, after Rayna Batya Berlin no one could in all conscience claim: "What need is there for these changes? Our grandmothers were all happy!"[81] then after Nehama Leibowitz, learned Jewish women could no longer be treated as (again in his words) "exceptional and perhaps eccentric personalities, not

---

[80] See for example those mentioned in Yedgar, "*Parshanut*," 114.
[81] Seeman, "The Silence," 105, 123, n. 39.

subject to the usual norms."[82] Rather, they take their rightful place as passionately religious people, worthy of respect, just as learned men are. Educated, intelligent women have moved from the margins to the center. Although few have gained the access that Nehama did to the bastions of men's learning, they teach Torah in impressive numbers of yeshivahs, seminaries, universities, colleges and schools. They publish in journals, are quoted by men, and teach male students; and have introduced valuable new perspectives to the world of Torah study. Much credit for this is due to Nehama. As one female Torah teacher declares: "Rabbis sit in my lesson. Had Nehama not done the pioneering work, I would have had to do it myself."

And this credit is indeed given. Institutes for women's learning boast Nehama's picture on the wall, just as pictures of rabbis traditionally adorn yeshivah walls. Bat-mitzvah programs, for instance that of MaTaN, encourage mothers and daughters to learn about Nehama amongst other great Jewish women. And even amongst the increasing numbers of accomplished female scholars, Nehama's image remains unique. As late as 1989 the novelist Naomi Ragen could still remark:

> There aren't a whole lot of role models for Orthodox women apart from Nehama Leibowitz who teaches Torah at the Hebrew University. She's very revolutionary in her own way.[83]

However, this uniqueness has, in a way, made things more difficult for women, as complaints about obstacles to women's Torah learning are countered with: "Nehama succeeded when women's learning was even less common, so why can't you?" This brush-off refuses to address the fact that Nehama was Nehama. Letty Cottin Pogrebin calls this "the Golda Meir syndrome," in which a great woman's achievements are used as proof of the non-existence of biases against women. The syndrome constitutes

> a widespread belief that any woman can get to the top if she wants to ("Look at Golda!") and that the only reason Israeli women haven't achieved more success in politics or business is that they don't want it,

though in reality the woman in question is unique, for the good and the bad:

> A woman in the back of the room called: "Yeah, but if you want to be a Golda, you'll have to divorce your husband and abandon your children like she did."[84]

---

[82] Seeman, "The Silence," 98.

[83] Vivian Eden, "Ragen to Riches," *Jerusalem Post*, September 15, 1989, 11.

[84] Letty Cottin Pogrebin, *Deborah, Golda and Me: Being Female and Jewish in America*, NY: Crown Publishers, 1991, 171 and 174.

Few women can be a Golda; and just as few possess the brilliance, drive and personality of a Nehama that enabled her to glide elegantly through solid walls of prejudice.

ҩ҂ ҩ҂

Today, after her passing, Nehama's name continues to appear regularly in discussions of Jewish feminism and Jewish leadership roles for women.[85] Any history of Jewish women's scholarship would be seriously remiss without a mention of Nehama Leibowitz.[86] In an exhibition at Bar-Ilan University entitled, "She Opens Her Mouth in Wisdom: Women, Religion and Scholarship in Jewish Society,"[87] the brochure announced that the exhibition paid tribute to

> the pioneers of women's learning, including the second-century Bruriah; the nineteenth-century poet Rachel Morpurgo; Sarah Schenirer, founder of Beit Yaakov; philanthropist and scholar Flora Sassoon; and of course, the twentieth-century Torah giant, Nehama Leibowitz.

On display were Nehama's photograph, books and worksheets. The organizers, however, took care to note that Nehama did not see herself as a feminist.[88]

Both pro- and anti-feminist elements have adopted Nehama for their polemics. Anti-feminists find her statements useful. R. Yaakov Ariel often quotes Nehama's contention: "Have I already done all the mitzvot I am bound to do? Have I done enough kind deeds?" – for example, in the

---

[85] Thus, for example, she is cited in the *Jerusalem Post*, in various articles – about feminist exegesis of the Torah, (see McMillan, "Fifty Feminist Rabbis," page 273, n. 10 above); about pseudo-rabbinical roles for women (Marilyn Henry, "I Don't Want to Be a Rabbi, But…" Jan 19, 1998, 17); or about female Orthodox rabbis (Sue Fishkoff, "Just Call Her Rabbi," Aug 23, 1991, 12; see also Reuven Hammer, "The Changing Role of Women," June 1, 2006, 34: "When women like the late Nehama Leibowitz are viewed as authorities on Torah who can teach men and women alike… there is a natural tendency for women to want a more active – if not equal and identical – place within synagogue life.")

[86] Nehama appears in Emily Taitz and Sondra Henry, *Remarkable Jewish Women: Rebels, Rabbis and Other Women from Biblical Times to the Present*, Philadelphia: JPS, 1996, 180–181 (with errors – they refer to her brother as Yehoshua). She also appears in Carolyn Starman Hessel, *Blessed Is the Daughter*, Shengold, Rockville, 1999, 82–83, where we are told: "Many Orthodox Jews, especially women, believe she deserves the title 'Rabbi'" (83).

[87] Sponsored by Bar Ilan University's Fanya Gottesfeld Heller Center for the Study of Women in Judaism.

[88] This was a condition stipulated by Professor Dov Landau when he contributed notes to the exhibit. See Calev Ben-David, "No More Yentls," *Jerusalem Post*, April 2, 1999, B3.

documentary film *Who Created Me a Woman* by Yaakov Friedland, exploring the parameters of female Orthodox identity.[89] And Hagai Segal, complaining that this same documentary is liable to be pounced upon by the anti-religious, writes:

> A similar film has never been made about Professor Nehama Leibowitz, of sainted memory, who taught Torah to many without creating one provocative ripple around her. In contrast to the heroines of *Who Created Me a Woman* and to her famous brother, she never drew secular interest and showed no desire whatsoever to wrangle with the rabbis. Instead of starring in documentaries or organizing well-publicized rallies, she simply studied and taught. The impressive numbers of her books on the shelves of religious-Zionist *batei midrash* points to Orthodox men's openness in principle to female Torah scholarship. They are willing to hear Torah novellae from women, and many are open to more than that. What alarms them for the most part is the feminist griping that characterizes the learned women's uprising; they sometimes suspect that the struggle's prime movers aim to imitate Shulamit Aloni more than they do Leibowitz.[90]

Feminists, for their part, cannot afford to ignore the brightest star of female Torah scholarship, and they focus on her achievements. Nehama makes an appearance in the Jewish Orthodox Feminist Alliance's calendar, and also in a new feminist ritual dedicating the four cups of Passover Seder wine to the honoring of Jewish women, keeping company with Dona Gracia Nasi, Asenath bat Samuel Barazani, Gluckel of Hameln, Emma Lazarus, Bella Abzug and Judith Kaplan Eisenstein.[91] She even played a role in a cutting-edge issue – that of Orthodox ordination for women. R. Aryeh Strikovsky, an Orthodox rabbi trained in prominent ultra-Orthodox yeshivahs, agreed in the late 1990s to Haviva Ner-David's request to study for ordination with him. It was Strikovsky's experience of being taught by women such as Nehama, as well as his own experience of teaching women, that led him to conclude that the time was ripe for women's ordination.[92] Thus, intentionally or not, Nehama helped to set a ball in motion – or, some might say, to open a Pandora's box; the chosen metaphor is a matter of perspective.

To summarize: Many of Nehama's achievements will go down in history without reference to her gender, but her impact will also continue to

---

[89] See Hagai Segal, *"Rabbaniyyot horgot le-Elohim,"* *Maariv*, May 23, 2002.
[90] Hagai Segal, *"Rabbaniyyot horgot le-Elohim,"* *Maariv*, May 23, 2002.
[91] See http://www.ritualwell.org (taken from *The Journey Continues: The Ma'yan Haggadah*).
[92] Haviva Ner-David, *Life on the Fringes*, JFL books, 2000, 215. See also Strikovsky, *Daf*, 5–6, for his thoughts on Nehama and on women's study in general.

reverberate in gender-related issues. This chapter, having made a start in addressing the issues, should certainly be seen as an invitation for further research on the topic.[93]

---

[93] In *Pirkei Nehama*, the most comprehensive work on Nehama to date, there was little or nothing related to Nehama's gender. In the *Daf le-tarbut Yehudit* dedicated to her memory, two articles out of nine focus on her gender; but I have not yet seen even one in-depth analysis of Nehama and feminism.

CHAPTER 15

RELIGIOUS IDENTITY AND VALUES:
HALACHAH, HUMANISM AND HEROES

Religious identity

IT WILL HAVE BECOME CLEAR to the reader that Nehama was a deeply religious person. Now we will delve further into the specific elements within her religious make-up.

The first point to note is Nehama's distance from all things ecstatic and mystical. Her religious energies were primarily focused on this world and on her society, as she writes of Jacob:

> Jacob's communion with his Creator, his beholding of the Divine Presence at Bethel did not turn him into a recluse, contemplating the Heavenly mysteries. Rather his experience spurred him to practical action, to promoting welfare and justice in society. (*NSB*, 315)

Nehama was also no religious existentialist, grappling with the tragic situation of humankind. Her focus was intellectual, ethical and practical, nurtured by strong currents of Jewish rationalism. She was a "Lithuanian *par excellence*,"[1] educated within a critical Germanic-type mindset which distrusted abstruse or occultic religion. Nonetheless, she was not an absolute rationalist by any means, and in fact, explicitly warned against overdoing the rationalistic approach; against the "artificial rationalization of things essentially non-rational."[2] She critiqued Ibn Caspi's approach, writing:

> Let us not be among those who seek for rational explanation for those things to which the laws of reason do not apply.[3]

The rational approach is not the best key to unlocking the text:

---

[1] Breuer, "*Professor*," 17.

[2] *NSB*, 366. See also *IHBS*, 54, and *NSV*, 185–187 where she comes out strongly against over-rationalistic explanations of *tzara'at* as a physical disease. See further on page 81 above, and n. 6 thre.

[3] *SBM*, 235. Ibn Caspi comes in for some criticism for his demagogic style and hyperbolic language (see *IBBM*, 161–164). Nehama argues that he was influenced in this by his intellectual environment (*ibid.* 163, n. 16). She refers to him as "one of our strangest and most interesting commentators" (*LP*, 90).

> Here we have a convincing example of how the so called rationalist, the adherer to the strict literalness of the text… may be forced into deviating from the plain sense. (*NSS*, 68)

Her natural passion and imagination would not let her fall into the kind of error exemplified by certain of Maimonides's followers who

> in their attempts to eradicate all traces of anthropomorphism from the biblical text tended to dull the sense of Divine immanence and transform the Jewish religion into a remote mechanical monotheism. (*NSS*, 357)

Instead, her rationalistic bent expressed itself in her avoidance of speculating on the unknown and supernatural. She authored few essays on metaphysical topics such as the world to come, prophecy and revelation,[4] focusing instead on what is knowable – what is demanded by the Torah in this world.[5] She was interested in human nature and holiness; and not as philosophical concepts, but as ethical and symbolic ones, relating to mitzvot and upright behavior. Angels were for her a symbol of Divine protection or of a psychological state, and therefore she interprets Rashi's remark (Genesis 28:12) that Jacob saw in his vision two sets of angels, one to accompany him in the Holy Land and another outside it, as follows:

> In other words, man's experiences in his own country are not to be compared with his situation in a strange land. To make his way on foreign soil he needed different guardians.[6]

She recoiled, as Maimonides did, from anything that smacked of superstition:

> It is common knowledge that the Torah vigorously rejects all forms of magic. (*NSV*, 35)

> A number of rabbinic dicta [are] designed to counter the belief in magic and its supernatural powers, and to discredit the role of chance and fate in the conducting of human affairs.[7]

---

[4] Horwitz, "*Nehama*," 207. Her one essay on the afterlife is "The Blessings," *NSV*, 569–579.

[5] Frankel (*Iyun*, 94) quotes the *Teacher's Guide* for *Yitro*, 5730 as an instance where she emphasizes the demand on human behavior rather than the nature of God.

[6] *NSB*, 301. Another example of Nehama's demystifying tendencies is her explanation that the ten righteous men needed to save Sodom would protect the city not through some mystical mechanism, but through direct proactive work (*NSB*, 186).

[7] *SBM*, 217. See further in *SBM*, pp. 299, 303, 306. See also discussions of *nihush* (divination) in *NSB*, 224 and, 241.

When thefts in dormitories or other misfortunes occur, people's morals must be checked, not their *mezuzahs*, no matter what marvelous stories were brought as evidence for superstitions. She writes:

> A miracle constitutes no proof of the truth. The magicians of Egypt too succeeded in their sorceries; even the false prophet is sometimes capable of producing signs and wonders.[8]

She did her best to reframe strange Jewish practices in a down-to-earth way. For example, of the concept known as "not opening one's mouth to Satan," i.e., not mentioning negative topics, she writes:

> And if we want to state [this] position in rational terms we could say that a person must not be pessimistic and cynical but must rather always hope for the best from God, and so he should not state [a negative prognosis] because it may still [turn out false].[9]

Hearing a student describe certain bizarre steps taken to ward off the evil eye, such as boiling pieces of iron in water, Nehama insisted that the evil eye mentioned in the Talmud is something we cannot comprehend today. For her, such activities bordered on idol-worship:

> The context calls on us to eradicate magical practices and keep away from sorcery and enchantments. There is evidently then some direct connection between this and the admonition to be wholehearted in our service of God. (*SD*, 183)

She writes with deep conviction:

> Herein surely lay the difference between superstition, idolatrous media of intercession and the pure undefiled prayer of man to his Maker! The former imagine they can bend the will of God (whether through the medium of sacrifices, charms, incantations and other sorts of mumbo jumbo – so long as man's purpose is to subject the Divine by the potency of his own man-made media to his own will, he is purely a sorcerer and worshipper of idols) to theirs. (*NSB*, 333)

Yet with all her strong views on sorcery, Nehama made some surprising exceptions. In discussing whether curses carry any power, she disregarded several prominent commentators who deny this premise, choosing instead to conclude with a quote from *Sefer ha-Hinuch*, who "does not reject the objective power of the curse" and who believed that the soul had "the power to affect things beyond its confines" (*NSV* 303). In another discussion, she criticized the ancient Egyptians for attributing magical power to a dream's interpretation, yet alongside this cited the talmudic statement: "Dreams

---

[8] *NSB*, 385. See also *NSS*, 166–167; *SD*, 132.
[9] *IHBV*, 172; compare *NSV*, 218.

follow the interpretation (lit: 'the mouth')," which might imply something similar.[10]

ﭏ ﭏ

Nehama also kept away from mysticism. This was partly because she was not a dabbler. Her integrity demanded that she master a field before commenting on it – a lesson learned early on, after she wrote an article on R. Kook.[11] Following that incident, Nehama said: "At least I can be credited with knowing I do not know." She admitted the same of mysticism, writing:

> The true reason can only be explained solely according to mystical teachings, and therefore we too cannot continue to accompany [Ramban] due to our lack of understanding of this lore.[12]

This is no disgrace. Few can follow Ramban into the thickets of his Kabbalistic interpretations, and Nehama took seriously his warning that the esoteric layers of the Torah are reserved for a select few.[13] But she was not as ignorant as she made out to be. She demonstrated a working familiarity with the Zohar, the principal Kabbalistic work, though the passages she quoted were of a midrashic-exegetical flavor.[14] In truth, she had considerable reservations about this entire discipline, due to her rationalistic orientation. Professor Rivka Horwitz, who studied Kabbalah under Scholem, found Nehama very resistant to talking about this topic. "We had many arguments. Nehama would say, 'Do you really understand Kabbalah? I don't!'" When Nehama discovered that R. Shlomo Riskin was taking a course in the Zohar at the Hebrew University, she exclaimed, "Riskin! Have you filled your stomach with Talmud and Responsa, and with the five books of the Torah, that you now feel the need to study the Torah's secrets?" She viewed the fascination with the arcane as perilous, warning, in Abravanel's footsteps, of the danger involved

> when man strives to grasp that which is beyond him, to soar higher and higher to that which is hidden and concealed. "The heavens are the heavens of the Lord but the earth He has given to the sons of man," said the Psalmist (Psalm 115:16). It is sufficient for man to rest content

---

[10] *NSB*, 423. The statement is from Berachot 55b. Nehama does not deal with this contradiction in the body of her essay, but challenges the reader in a question at the end: "Can it be explained in any other than magical terms?" (*NSB*, 428 question 1).

[11] Mentioned inpage 121 above.

[12] *IHBV*, 14; compare *NSV*, 9. See also *NSV*, 613.

[13] Ben-Meir, "*Le-darkei*," 126, and see also Nehama's letter to Reinitz, *PN*, 689. Nehama even mentions Ramban's Kabbalistic interpretations in places where their absence would have gone unremarked (e.g. *NSS*, 528).

[14] See the citations in *NSB*, 61, 181; *NSS*, 279; *NSV*, 486–487; *SBM*, 264; and *LP*, 19 ("highly recommended to show the students") and 115.

with that which has been granted him to understand, with that which has been entrusted to him in his tasks, both sacred and profane. He should not strive to "break through" to realms beyond his ken, "lest he die." (*SBM*, 27–28)

She also largely avoided Hasidic thought. No matter how many times Professor Bergman phoned up on a Saturday night to complain about the dearth of Hasidic sources in her worksheets,[15] Nehama continued to exclude Hasidic material from her writings, with very few exceptions.[16] She did not repudiate Hasidism – one could be "a good Jew following the approaches of *Sefat Emet* or *Habad*" (*PN*, 652) – but she was far from its way of thinking, with its basis in Kabbalah and its radical textual interpretations. She claimed not to understand Hasidic commentary, saying: "It's an entire separate Torah."[17] Hasidic stories, a staple in contemporary Jewish inspirational education, also rarely appeared in Nehama's pedagogic arsenal.[18] Additionally, she objected to certain prevailing Hasidic assumptions – for example, that God is too distant, necessitating an intermediary, the Rebbe, to connect on one's behalf. She suggested that when the Israelites worshipped the Golden Calf, "they too needed an intermediary."[19] In some streams of Hasidic thought, the Rebbe is seen to have supernatural powers. The following words by Nehama, though referring to the priestly blessing, would seem applicable here too:

---

[15] Warren Zev Harvey, *VLN*.

[16] The exceptions include a non-mystical citation of the Ba'al Shem Tov (*IHBS*, 362, n. 1, involving a Hasidic version of Buridan's donkey) and two incidents involving R. Shneur Zalman of Liady, containing clear moral lessons (*NSV*, 364; *LP*, 217 – both are from secondary sources). She was familiar with the halachic works by the Hasidic Rebbe, R. Abraham of Sochaczew (*Eglei Tal* and *Avnei Nezer*).

[17] The Hasidim shared with Nehama a preference for spiritual-psychological meanings over historical-geographical ones, creating a direct encounter between modern reader and ancient text. But they treated the text as an extremely loose starting point for interpretative pyrotechnics, far removed from *peshat*. According to Horwitz (interview), Nehama claimed that the Hasidic reading was basing itself on things said elsewhere in the Torah. For example, on "When you shall go out to war upon your enemy" (Deuteronomy 21:10), the Hasidic masters remove from the physical battlefield to comment: "Your enemy – this refers to the evil inclination" (see e.g. *Noam Elimelech* on *Ki Tetze*). Rather than acknowledge the daring innovation in the interpretation, Nehama suggested that the evil inclination was a concept transplanted from elsewhere in the Torah. Yedgar notes that Nehama avoids the atomistic exegesis typical of Hasidic and Kabbalistic exegesis, reducing the text to letters or words and lacking the broader context ("*Bein*," 57, n. 29).

[18] One exception appears in her column in the *Yediot Ahronot* newspaper; see *PN*, 511. She also analyzes different versions of the famous story of the small boy and the flute in "Active Learning" (17–18), but here she is teaching a critical historical lesson on the essence of Hasidism and on the tendentious revision of folklore, not a spiritual lesson.

[19] Abramowitz, *Tales*, 90.

Anyone who sees the priests as having their own independent power to do good or evil, views their blessings as magical, and thus has no part in the Torah of Israel. For he has already been seared by the fire of idol-worship, of belief in charms and spells, in people with special supernatural powers who can by their actions force God to their will, heaven forbid.[20]

It is important to note that Nehama was no stranger to religious passion, as the poetry and fervor in the following quotations indicate:

Accordingly it is the dancing soul (the Meshekh Hokhma uses this metaphor for religious ecstasy in Ki Tisa) that the shaking of the lulav represents, the human being whose every fiber trembles before the Lord. (*NSV*, 464)

Having understood the form and structure, we do not abandon the verse, but linger a while to ponder over the phrase that overflows with holy feeling: "and I have loved you with eternal love" – an attachment that is boundless and everlasting. (*TI*, 71)

This Psalm… is so dear to me, and to it I owe a great deal of the happiness and joy and poetry in my life.[21]

But she disliked the emphasis on ecstatic experience in Hasidic life.[22] She did not believe in spiritual "highs," declaring, "To get a high you can take drugs! My brother goes to *shul* every day at five o'clock. Why? Because you have to pray, not to get a high." She was apprehensive of where the ecstatic approach might lead – one might try to preempt God's will, acting without commandment.[23] R. Joseph Albo asserts that a prophet may indeed do this, but Nehama brings a sharp refutation based on Arama:

It is highly significant for us to observe how the approach of humility and discipline reflected in the *Akedat Yitzhak* triumphs over the ecstatic

---

[20] *IBBM*, 81. This segment has no equivalent in the English version.

[21] N. Leibowitz, "*Iyun be-mizmorei Tehillim: Tehillim perek yud-gimmel*," in *PN*, 590.

[22] She seems to have made an exception for her beloved R. Kook, allowing ecstatic dimensions as a legitimate part of the discussion. For example, she analyzes whether true religious ecstasy and devotion might exist in "the clear, rarified atmosphere of a higher religion" or only in savage paganism (*NSB*, 204–205).

[23] In addition to the following examples, see also Nehama's discussion of the Nazirite who goes beyond the commanded, and especially Epstein's comments and the Netziv's opposition (*IBBM*, 72, n. 2 and 73, n. 3). See further her discussion of Nadav and Avihu (*SBM*, 30, question 3) and of the rebels who stood with Korah (*ibid.*, 221–222). Of the 250 men who joined with Korah Nehama writes: "The Torah here teaches us that all self-torment designed to elevate the spirit beyond one's capacity denotes 'sinning against the soul.' So, too, these men sought to intensify their adoration of the Lord, and pay the penalty of contravening Moses, whom they knew to be right. Hence their designation as 'sinners against their souls'" (*NSV*, 106, n. 3).

miracle working approach of Albo. We have to obey the commands and precepts of God and must certainly avoid any resort to miracles, to a revolution in nature. Even the greatest prophet has but to carry out the commands of his creator. (*SBM*, 245)

She feared that superficially understood, the revolutionary nature of Hasidism would appear to devalue Torah study and mitzvah observance, making it almost indistinguishable from the Reform movement.[24] She herself knew the difference of course; but perhaps she had this in mind when writing of

"the fit though few" who may be tempted to disparage some details of the Torah from an overabundance of religious ecstasy, looking down from their pedestal of mystic elevation and considering themselves released from the prosaic discipline of Jewish precept. (*SD*, 46)

This type of approach could not lead to an enduring religious life, she felt. David Weinberg observes:

Nehama did not put stock in transformatic spiritual experiences nor appreciate emotional highs in religion. The thunder and lightning of revelation at Mt. Sinai, or the fleeting thrill of a rapturous Hasidic dance, ultimately were ineffective, Nehama felt. After all, it didn't take long before the Jews who experienced Sinai debased themselves in worship of the Golden Calf.[25]

Nehama indeed writes:

We should not believe or expect a one-time experience – even the most intense and exalted one – to transform a person from a midget into a giant overnight…. The immense jolt that shocks a person (or a community) "to the depths of his heart" after great and marvelous events may indeed transform him for a short time, but after that brief period of elevation chances are that he (and even more likely in the case of the community) will return to the trivialities of mundane life.[26]

And she notes:

the inconsistency in our lives… in observing (sometimes very strictly) certain mitzvot that appeal to us, mainly those which occur on specific festive occasions when the spirit is elated, while neglecting (sometimes completely) the more mundane daily observances in the dull moments

---

[24] N. Leibowitz, "Active Learning," 17.
[25] Weinberg, "Remembering Nehama."
[26] *Teacher's Guide* to *Pekudei*, 5722. Also *NSS*, 556: "One single religious experience, however profound, was not capable of changing the people from idol worshippers into monotheists" and Reiner and Peerless, *Haggadat*, 159: "It is… a lot more challenging to carry out daily chores, to keep going even after the initial excitement has waned, when the shimmering splendor of the vision has dimmed."

when there is not a flash of beauty or festivity. This is what Amos is complaining about. (*TI*, 51)

Enthusiasm by itself is no guarantee of the desirability of a cause. Enthusiasm that is not backed by conscience and the self-discipline of Torah is liable to bring disaster. (*SBM*, 279)

And she quotes Ramban's warning to people who

are over-generous in their pious declarations and noble protestations, who readily announce decisions which are not followed up by practical steps to fulfill them and who experience sudden surges of enthusiasm which are soon extinguished. (*NSB*, 157)

When it comes to mitzvot, obedience and action are paramount. Nehama quotes the Netziv, who

frequently expressed his disapproval of uncontrolled, ecstatic, undisciplined acts of worship not covered by the normative rules of Judaism and its codes. The highest form of Divine worship combined sincerity and individual expression with absolute loyalty to those norms. (*NSS*, 705)

She quotes his opinion that even if meticulous compliance with the mitzvot interferes with *devekut* (piety), this is

the great merit of those who adhere to the Torah, that they forgo the infinite delight of union with God for the sake of fulfilling faithfully and scrupulously their religious routine.[27]

While Nehama did not rule out individual expression, loyalty to norms came first:

Obligatory performance is more valuable than voluntary performance. (*SD*, 280)

The offering up of a sacrifice must not be an impetuous act spawned by a momentary elation and liable to degeneration into idol worship. (*NSV*, 4)

She, like many Jewish thinkers before her, conceived of the Halachah as the practical manifestation of the Jewish spiritual essence. God does not "dwell in the hearts of the people" unless "first of all they carry out their obligations"; good intention alone is not enough (*NSS*, 670). The Halachah is pre-set, not determined by whims:

It is neither through momentary passion nor even through self-sacrifice that the religious goal is attained but rather through the discipline

---

[27] *NSV*, 107. R. Yitshak Reiner notes that Nehama frequently cited comments by the Netziv, asking, "And who was he arguing with?", hinting at his polemic with the Hasidim (see also pages 531–532 below).

spelled out in the precepts of the Torah. Many consider such submissions to the commandments, as against spontaneous worship stimulated by personal and subjective sentiments, as mechanical and objectionable. Yet... it was precisely the unrestrained desire to ascend to forbidden heights that constituted an unpardonable sin. (*NSV*, 124)

Nehama was charmed by the picture of Abraham, rushing to greet his three guests and paying no heed to the Divine presence visiting him at that very moment. She likened this situation to someone who had waited all day to hear a favorite symphony on the radio, and at the very moment when it finally begins, the neighbors come knocking, wanting sugar. Yet Abraham did not perceive it as such, for

> practical good deeds take precedence over any abstract spiritual enjoyment.... He did not linger for a moment in the toils of mystic communion with his Creator, but ran to attend to the practical tasks of making welcome some tired and weary wanderers.... (*NSB*, 162)

> It is not the ascendance to the highest heights, intellectual refinement or perception of the Divine which is the climax in the service of God; but rather something that is utterly mundane: the day-to-day concern for others.[28]

In another place she teaches the same lesson from Abraham, though this time from an absence of action. His declaration to the King of Sodom is a noble one (Genesis 14:22–23):

> I have lifted up my hand to the Lord, the most high God, the possessor of heaven and earth, that I will not take from a thread to a sandal strap, and that I will not take any thing that is yours lest you should say, I have made Abram rich.

Yet Nehama writes, in the footsteps of the Talmud (Nedarim 32b):

> True, this was a great moment; but had [Abraham] passed up the wonderful, fleeting moment of sanctification of God's name in the eyes of the world, and instead accepted upon himself the thankless, unassuming mundane effort of setting right the souls of the Sodomites, his deed would – according to Rabbi Yohanan – have been infinitely greater.[29]

---

[28] *IBB*, 116–117. Her repeated emphasis of this line of reasoning (she subsequently states that Abraham is concerned with preparing the food and not "immersion and isolation and communion with his Creator and attaining of Divine perceptions") might indicate a polemic with the Hasidic position, especially since the words she uses for isolation and communion – "*hitbodedut*" and "*hityachadut*" – are central Hasidic concepts. Her words here also remind us of the maxim by R. Yisrael Salanter, founder of the Mussar movement: "My neighbor's material needs are my spiritual needs."

[29] N. Leibowitz, "*Kiddush shem shamayim o asiyat nefashot le-giyur – ma adif?*" in *PN*, 592.

Such a practical approach might seem antithetical to the soul of religion. But Weinberg writes:

> In place of passion and sentimentality, Nehama preferred self-discipline and repetition. Character, she was wont to say, is formed through constant learning and tenacious devotion to good deeds. Religious belief is a function of intellectual sophistication and discovery, and clear thinking. She demanded that of herself, and of her students. And we loved her for it.[30]

Thus, Nehama made the separation between spirituality and emotion. With all her poetics, her spirituality was not ensconced in pretty words or fleeting feelings but in the practical (the Halachah), the intellectual (the text) and the ethical (lessons from the Torah) – in every moment of her life, as Rochwarger notes:

> The countless hours that we spent together, in sickness and in health, revealed to me that Nehama's greatest concern was the synchronization of God's will with every thought and action... integrated into the very depths of her normal thought processes... in every task she undertook, and every word she spoke.[31]

The reader will have noticed that, in some of the quotes above, Nehama liked to compare superstition, magical thinking and even a religious act done with the wrong intention, to idolatry. In fact, the term "idolatry" was a watchword for both Nehama and her brother, to describe many types of behaviors and thoughts that they believed unacceptable to the Jewish creed.[32] "Polytheism is alive and well in modern society," Nehama would say. She believed that there were many types of idols, such as sports, money, glamor and technology.[33] Symbols are dangerous too, for they are also liable to be granted semi-Divine status:

> It is not only religious symbols or rite that are exploited as an escape route – this avoidance exists in the secular world too: Every ceremony, memorial day, commemorative service, flag, may transform from a spur into an object for personal satisfaction.[34]

One of her favorite pieces of Torah revolved around this topic.[35] After the sin of the Golden Calf, Moses dashes the first set of the Ten

---

[30] Weinberg, "Remembering Nehama."
[31] Rochwarger, unpublished paper.
[32] See more on page 534 below.
[33] Weinberg, "Remembering Nehama."
[34] *IHBV*, 24; compare *NSV*, 21.
[35] See *NSS*, 612–614.

Commandments to the ground, and it is unclear why. Nehama was fond of the explanation by R. Meir Simha of Dvinsk (the *Meshech Hochmah*), that after witnessing the Israelites invest holiness in the Golden Calf, Moses feared a similar deification of the tablets. He broke them to teach the key lesson that investing holiness in objects is idolatry. Holiness comes about only through response to the Divine:

> There is only one source of holiness. No intrinsic holiness resides in places, houses or vessels, not even in the greatest of men. (*NSS*, 612)

Along these lines, Nehama liked to tell of the time she saw a little boy running to kiss the Torah, only to have his father wag his finger at him: "Rather than kissing it you'd be better off doing what's in it!"[36] The worship of departed saints was likewise anathema to her. Once, visiting Rachel's Tomb, she witnessed a woman crying out, "Rachel, Rachel, please help me!" Highly distressed, Nehama exited, and complained to her waiting husband that this was no less than idolatry. Overhearing Nehama's scandalized comments, an elderly man approached and said: "Look, this woman is saying to herself, 'Rachel lived down here. She dealt with earthly problems of barrenness and marital issues. Up in heaven, what does God understand about it?'" This explanation, however, failed to make a dent in Nehama's opposition.

Religious Humanism

Nehama grew up in an atmosphere that may perhaps be characterized as "Orthodox neo-Maskilic."[37] Although the period was already post-Haskalah, the family's ethos resembled that of Orthodox maskilim of the nineteenth century. She quoted some maskilim in her works,[38] and, like them, she was interested in scientific thinking and in importing universal material into her Torah teaching.

Her writings also contained many lessons consistent with certain humanistic emphases, such as ethical integrity, personal responsibility and free will, all lynchpins of Nehama's thought. She makes statements such as

---

[36] Reiner, *Mo'adei*, 198.

[37] This term is not a commonly used one, but it appears apt here. The Haskalah as a movement had disappeared by around 1810, but the Leibowitzes adhered to its general spirit. They more closely resembled the Berlin maskilim who emphasized love for the Hebrew language, Tanach and openness to secular sources, than the maskilim who wrote in German. Professor Martin Lockshin remarks of Nehama, "It's almost as if one of the Orthodox Maskilim of the nineteenth century was transported to the twentieth century."

[38] e.g. Yehudah Leib Shapira (known as *"Ha-rechasim la-bik'a"*). She also quotes the authors of the Biur freely, including Mendelssohn.

Since all men are brothers, then the murderer has shed his brother's blood.[39]

She notes that the conquering of other nations is not seen as a positive act[40] and that the command to do so is accompanied by exhortations to pursue peace (*SD*, 31), another core humanistic value. She taught that ritualistic aspects of religion should not come at the expense of moral dimensions:

> The Talmud comments, in an outraged tone, on the fact that ritual defilement was apparently more important to them than human life. (*SBM*, 29)

Another example is Nehama's attitude towards non-Jews. She interpreted the Torah's statement that the Jews are the chosen people to refer solely to their sacred mission to bring understanding and peace to the world.[41] When speaking of Abraham's chosenness, she uses language indicating her awareness of the problematics entailed in such selection:

> The Divine act of singling out one human being has the taint of discrimination and unfair privilege. (*NSB*, 116)

Nehama did not believe that Jews were inherently different from non-Jews, and cautioned against feelings of superiority and concern only for Jews.[42] She writes:

> Our Sages thus learned a lesson in love of humanity and respect to all created in the image of God.[43]

The epistle from Maimonides to Obadiah the proselyte

> utterly repudiates any racial theory that would evaluate human character in terms of ethnic origins. Maimonides well and truly bases man's merit in the eyes of his Creator on his conduct and deeds alone. (*SD*, 267)

Likewise, she writes:

> Let it not be imagined that Abraham's preference for his own kin sprang from concern for "ethnic purity." No idea is more foreign to our Torah and Judaism. (*NSB*, 216)

---

[39] *NSB*, 44. Here she is quoting Cassuto.
[40] See *Teacher's Guide* to *Matot-Masei* 5716: "How important is the Ramban's emphasis here against imperialistic ambitions to conquer lands that are not ours."
[41] See more on pages 363–364 below.
[42] Erella Yedgar, "*Ahrayut ishit u-beinishit bi-chtaveha shel Nehama Leibowitz – iyun be-megamatah ha-erkit-hinuchit*," in *PN*, 403.
[43] *SD*, 356. See also *LP*, 6, n. 7 regarding the maxim, "Anyone who destroys one life…" i.e., any life, not just a Jewish one, emphasizes Nehama.

It was the purity of Jewish family life then which thwarted Balaam's malicious designs. It was not a racial purity but a moral one, which only persisted so long as the Israelites preserved their moral integrity. (*SBM*, 337)

Furthermore, non-Jews are just as capable of moral behavior as Jews:

Neither moral courage nor sheer wickedness is an ethnically or nationally determined quality. Moab and Ammon produced a Ruth and a Naamah respectively, Egypt two righteous midwives. (*NSS*, 36)

She also believed it important to show kindness and give charity to non-Jews as fellow humans. Regarding the commandment to "Love your neighbor as yourself" (Leviticus 19:18), she asserts:

The text... employs the neutral, comprehensive term – fellow. The identification of this term with an "Israelite" is conclusively refuted by its use in "Let every man ask of his neighbor and every woman of her neighbor, jewels of silver and jewels of gold..." (Exodus 11:2), where it evidently refers to the Egyptians. (*NSV*, 367)

She taught that Sarah should not have been cruel to Hagar, her own humiliation notwithstanding (*NSB*, 156), and that even nefarious characters such as Esau must be given credit where credit is due (*NSB*, 283).[44] Moral standards must be maintained even towards enemies, and thus Abraham's flock was not to eat of the land promised to him, for at the time it still belonged to the Canaanites.[45]

Nehama held that God wishes to educate all peoples, not just Israel, towards correct thinking. Instead of ending one of her essays with a lesson for the Israelites about disobedience, she chose to end with:

The Almighty turned Balaam's curses into blessings not to save Israel from their hurt but all the peoples from being led further into superstitious beliefs. (*SBM*, 306)

However, for Nehama, universal and humanistic messages are not detached from the particular history of the Jewish people, but on the contrary emerge from it:

Our portion [*lech lecha*] begins with extreme particularism: Bidding farewell to all – land, birthplace, father's house, leaving him [Abraham] alone, cut off from all humanity... but the end of our portion is

---

[44] "The Almighty, who takes note of our tears, also takes note of those shed by the wicked Esau. They also are noted and cry out for retribution" (*NSB*, 272.)
[45] *NSB*, 126 and see page 152 n. 17 above.

characterized by Messianic universalism. The former is merely a stage in the historical ladder leading up to the latter.[46]

The first Jew serves in his commitment to God, and to his duty to improve the world, as a sign for all mankind.[47] Another example concerns the laws of charity, in which the injunction of "The poor people of your city come first," seemingly advocates priority giving to Jews. Nehama, however, read the word "first" as implying "first, but not exclusively." Needy Jews have precedence, but must not be the sole object of assistance. Both national solidarity and humane action are Torah values, and when they clash, it is the Torah which lays down the correct priorities. The Torah exhibits complex thinking in rejecting "only universalism" or "only particularism" in favor of "universalism emerging from particularism":

> For the Torah does not desire our love of humanity or of nation by skipping over our obligations to those closer to us; this love will not be implanted by uprooting natural bonds of love, but rather the opposite is true. The way the Torah selects to achieve loving another and loving humanity is via the continual widening of one's group, whereby parent's love for their own children expands to loving others' children, not only of relatives but also eventually of random neighbors... and from there to the nation and all humankind.[48]

Nehama expressed these beliefs in her actions. She protested that too few trees had been planted at Yad Vashem to commemorate righteous gentiles.[49] She frequently taught non-Jews Torah, rebuffing her detractors with: "We don't know where the redemption will come from, and the truth needs to be told."

తారా తారా

All of the above does not mean, however, that we can state unequivocally: "Nehama was a humanist." Her belief in divinely revealed texts, her commitment to obey a system of laws resting upon elements beyond the natural, contradict this premise. Her strong loyalty to the Jewish people also caused her to take up non-humanistic positions. Nehama mentioned in a letter that she considered so-called cosmopolitan ideas such as "Only a tree has roots, the greatness of humanity is in its rootlessness" to be pretentious rubbish.[50] Rather, her humanistic emphases came through unevenly. She

---

[46] *LP*, 29. See also *NSB*, 112.
[47] Frankel, *Iyun*, 40.
[48] *IHBS*, 301–302; compare *NSS*, 409–410. Much of the above discussion is taken from Yedgar, "*Ahrayut*," 394–395. See also *NSB*, 216.
[49] Strikovsky, "Nehama on Women," 193.
[50] Letter to Ahituv.

passed up obvious opportunities to teach humanist lessons, for example, Rashi's statement (Genesis 32:8):

> Jacob was greatly afraid and distressed. He was afraid lest he be killed; he was distressed that he might kill others.

She was evidently very familiar with this tribute to Jacob's sensitivity regarding human life, yet it does not merit a prominent place in her *Studies*, relegated instead to a question at the end of an essay.[51] Nehama suspected the seeming altruism of humanism – it might be tainted by baser motives, for

> [the] sudden recognition of the brotherhood of man under the pressure of outside circumstances and dictated wholly by self-interest is a common phenomenon.[52]

Her brand of humanism, whatever it was, was not the utopian one of the emancipation, but the more skeptical one of a generation that had witnessed the Holocaust. In Genesis 33:4, we read:

> Esau ran to meet him [Jacob], and embraced him, and fell on his neck, and kissed him; and they wept.

Hirsch claimed that this brotherly kiss from this same Esau who previously had vowed to murder Jacob (Genesis27:41) was a sincere one:

> Esau gradually relinquishes his sword and begins to feel the chords of human love. (*NSB*, 375)

But Nehama shot down this romantic interpretation:

> We can hear the echo of the blind optimism of the nineteenth century in his words.[53]

She prefers the words of the Netziv, who is more impressed by Jacob and his forgiveness, writing:

> Whenever the seed of Esau is prompted by sincere motives to acknowledge and respect the seed of Israel, then we too, are moved to acknowledge Esau: for he is our brother. (*NSB*, 375)

She similarly concludes the essay with Benno Jacob's opinion that the kiss was not sincere (*NSB*, 377).

This particular study prompted an exchange of letters in December 1957 between Nehama and Professor Shmuel Hugo Bergman. Bergman, a philosophy professor and the Hebrew University's first rector, phoned

---

[51] *NSB*, 356. It is however mentioned in her column in the *Yediot Ahronot* newspaper, weekly portion of *Va-yishlach*, November 29, 1990, reprinted in *PN*, 526–527.
[52] *NSB*, 419. This is perpetrated by Egyptians and Jews alike (*ibid.*).
[53] *IBB*, 261; compare *NSB*, 375.

Nehama every Saturday night to discuss his answers to her questionnaires, and clearly respected her work.[54] But as an avowed humanist and founding member of Martin Buber's peace movement Brit Shalom, when he read Nehama's worksheet and also heard her express similar sentiments on the radio, he felt compelled to write to her:[55]

> My very dear Nehama Leibowitz,
>
> I must inform you of the great distress you caused me with your interpretation of Jacob and Esau's encounter. I was shocked to read that "everything that occurred to our forefather with Esau shall occur to us eternally with Esau's children"; and I was even more shocked to hear your words on the radio, and how you rejected Hirsch's opinion and concluded your broadcast (as if with an exclamation mark) with Benno Jacob. Do you not grasp that you are sowing hatred in the hearts of students and listeners?
>
> Even if we might understand the commentators' intolerant approach from a historical perspective, should we perpetuate this appallingly anti-humanistic tradition now that we have a State? Is it thus that we will transform the seeds of redemption into a full redemption?
>
> Yours sincerely,
>
> S.H. Bergman

Nehama was moved to respond within ten days with a passionate, articulate defense:

> B"H, first night of Hanukka
>
> Esteemed Professor Bergman,
>
> I was amazed at your words. Had you informed me that my words were weak, pale and utterly inadequate I would have accepted your claim immediately, for I too am aware that I am an extremely cracked *shofar* for sounding the words of the living God – the Torah's words. However, I never, ever could have imagined that my words might sow hatred for human beings created in the image of God (which for me is most certainly not some flowery phrase). On the one hand I had assumed that I had presented both opinions of our Rabbis: that [Esau] kissed him sincerely; and that he did not kiss him but rather intended to bite him.

[54] Harvey, "Professor," 11. Bergman is also quoted in Nehama's work; see *NSV*, 401, n. 2; and see also the worksheets for 5710 (*Naso*) and 5711 (*Emor*).

[55] This exchange, taken from Bergman's archive at the National Library, was first printed in Aviad HaCohen, "*Ha-im Esav soneh le-Yaakov?*" *Meimad* 12 (5758): 17–19, and reprinted in *PN*, 659–661.

On the other hand I do not see how describing our position as a lamb amongst seventy wolves (and I fail to see what difference the existence of the State makes) could lead to hatred. As a teacher and educator, I don't intend to let our pupils forget our history – neither the Crusader massacres of 1096, nor Spain, nor the Chmielnicki pogroms of 1648, and certainly not the recent Holocaust; nor the words of R. Judah Halevi: "O dove, borne upon eagles' wings…"[56] and those of the contemporary poet: "You have the axe-arm, even a spade, and all the earth is to me a hanging-block."[57] Nonetheless, I don't believe that this creates prejudice against the masses of mankind. (I likewise see it as my obligation to stress all the corruption and vice, narrow-mindedness and intolerance, superficiality and imitation of the basest gentile behavior within our own State – and yet am certain that I am educating towards loyalty and love of Israel as our State and country, the beginning of our redemption.)[58]

Surely you yourself agree that we shouldn't teach love for our fellow humans, in anticipation of the end of days, whilst simultaneously concealing and suppressing everything done to us – just as you certainly agree that we must teach the fear of heaven and love of God without covering up all the failings, flaws and wrongdoings of generations of Jews who selectively applied their fear of God, using it as it suited them, to conceal their debasements.

So I don't understand why we cannot note Esau's attitude towards Jacob throughout the generations without necessarily creating hatred and vengefulness, but instead the anticipation for the end of days and a genuine prayer that "All the inhabitants of the world shall recognize and know that to You shall every knee bow."[59]

Perhaps I misunderstood your words and my entire response is irrelevant. But I simply cannot fathom what difference the establishment of the State has made. Is our prayer "Notice, we beseech you, our affliction, and fight our battles, and speedily redeem us for the sake of Your name"[60] any less applicable today?

I also fail to understand why you claim that I set up Benno Jacob in opposition to Hirsch, when as a counterweight to Hirsch I explicitly cited Naphtali Zvi Yehudah Berlin, head of the Volozhin Yeshivah, whose words indubitably breathe love of mankind. I wanted to

---

[56] Hymn for the Shabbat before Shavuot – see *PN*, 659–660 for her full quote and references.

[57] Hayyim Nahman Bialik, excerpt from "On the Slaughter."

[58] This paragraph constitutes another example of Nehama's ability to hold two contradictory thoughts in her mind at once.

[59] Quote from the *Aleinu* prayer.

[60] Quote from the *Amidah* (silent prayer).

demonstrate that Hirsch, educated within German humanism, arrived at his love of humanity by closing his eyes and refusing to see, or being incapable of seeing, what transpired around him (during this very period when he saw Esau relinquishing his sword, Jewish children were being kidnapped in Russia, handed over to the army and tortured horribly into renouncing their religion). Whereas the wise old talmudist from Volozhin wrote words of authentic humanism – drawn solely from the words of our Sages – and without forgetting everything done to us.

Above all, one thing in your letter caused me sorrow – your reference to the "the intolerant approach of the commentators." You yourself taught me, after I claimed that the gentile commentators' anti-Semitism overrides their wisdom, to be careful with such generalizations – after all, do I know every single one of them?[61] So how can you call intolerant the approach of such saintly giants as Ramban and his companions, who delve into Divine secrets, viewing the soul as a fragment of the living God (which for them is not an expression of hubris and technological accomplishment, but rather of a feeling of immense responsibility not to destroy that image, for "The soul You gave me is pure,"[62] etc.)?? Intolerance is to be found in political party leaders – of all the parties, even the ones close to my position; but not in our lofty rabbis whose sole intention was to teach the knowledge of God.

In any event, a radio talk is not measured by the speaker's intentions, but by what actually comes across, and if my words sounded like a call to hatred then I admit that this is not good and caution should be employed, including perhaps a shift of emphasis or exploration of a further angle. My thanks and blessings to you for letting me know how it sounded to you. I include my draft for the lesson; perhaps you will be convinced that it represents no call to hatred. Conceivably I should have left out (Benno) Jacob, whose words – as I see them now – are no more than *eine gestreiche Bemerkung* (an interesting aside), perhaps somewhat glib. I didn't notice when I wrote it. In general, I am influenced by Franz Rosenzweig (of sainted memory) who remarked of Benno Jacob that he was *der beste Bibelkenner der Jetztzeit* (the best Bible expert in our generation). Hence, perhaps, I followed him blindly.

---

[61] Nehama learned this lesson well, and was very careful not to generalize. To others she would say, "What do you mean, 'everybody'? Do you know? Whom did you speak to? You only heard? If you have not seen it with your own two eyes, you cannot say. That's forbidden; it's *motzi shem ra* (slander)" (Rochwarger, interview).

[62] Quote from *Shaharit* (morning prayer).

And once more, thank you so much for your aid and guidance. How I wish I could truly teach Torah as it ought to be taught in this generation – but this would require a great deal of heavenly assistance.

with great respect and thanks,

Nehama[63]

As can be seen, Nehama listened respectfully to the claims, but also defended her position. She held no grudge against Bergman, and several years after this exchange, attended his lessons at the Hebrew University and thanked him for the opportunity to do so.[64]

This letter sharpens our understanding of Nehama's humanism. Of especial interest is her belief that the Netziv spoke "words of authentic humanism – drawn solely from the words of our Sages."[65] The word "authentic" here is key. Nehama emphasized that the Sages were not modern humanists, or indiscriminate pacifists:

> Some of our Sages voiced their disapproval of Jacob's behavior as savoring of unnecessary debasement and appeasement. (NSB, 345)

For her, the Torah's moral guidelines were supreme. The value of saving human life is for the purpose of

> maintain[ing] our association with the Divine – the ultimate goal of life. (NSV, 173)

In fact, Nehama suspected Hirsch's philosophy of being influenced by a non-Jewish outlook.

Professor Moshe Ahrend suggests that she may have been influenced by her brother's view that humanism is atheistic and does not coincide with the Jewish viewpoint. Yeshayahu notes:

> "You shall love your neighbor as yourself" does not, as such, occur in the Torah. The reading is: "You shall love your neighbor as yourself; I am God."[66]

---

[63] Bergman's reply, missing from PN, appears in Hebrew in HaCohen, "Ha-im," 19, and in English in Abramowitz, Tales, 278–279. He remained unconvinced, arguing that even a difference of tone was an important distinction. We also hear of his distress at the dawning realization that Jews, though no more moral than others, indulge in sentimental self-vindication as if murder by their hands is somehow different. "When I sense, on occasion, such sentimentality residing in you too, it pains me doubly, for I so admire your work," he writes.

[64] HaCohen, "Ha-im," 16–17.

[65] The Netziv's introduction to his commentary on Genesis sounds very humanistic to the modern ear – see there.

[66] Y. Leibowitz, Judaism, 19.

Nehama also rejected the attitude that historicizes the Torah's morals, suggesting that the Torah, while advanced for its time, is cruel in today's terms, with the rabbis' interpretations

> a later toning down of ancient barbarity, humanization of the severity of the Torah by subsequent generations. (*NSV*, 494)

᪥ ᪥

Nehama does not stop at Hirsch; she implies that Moses Mendelssohn was likewise influenced by humanism (*NSS*, 678). Yet some scholars similarly claim an influence of early twentieth-century German humanism on Nehama's own outlook. She believed firmly that Torah and the highest morals coincide. But her notion of those morals was shaped by her environment, they argue, bringing her to see the Torah and commentaries in a romantic light, reading and even quoting them selectively,[67] and at times highlighting minority opinions that were more in line with her sentiments.[68]

For Ahrend, selective quotation is part of an educator's job, and it was a sign of Nehama's excellence at it that

> she had a sure sense of… what to omit from the excerpts she quoted from the commentators.[69]

And Erella Yedgar adds: "It is every educator's dilemma how much of the integrity of the texts to preserve when the students may not be mature enough to hear the truth." For while Nehama was dedicated to truth and integrity, it was not at the expense of all other values, as her words at the end of her essay "Truth Gives Way to Peace" indicate:

> Our Sages regarded [Joseph's brothers'] conduct as warranted on the principle that truth has sometimes to be subordinated to more important values. (*NSB*, 568)

---

[67] Elazar Touitou demonstrates how Nehama quotes both the Torah text and the Rashbam selectively so as to avoid an appearance of discrimination against non-Jews ("*Bein Peshuto*," 236). Also, when expressing radical ideas, Nehama leaned upon heavyweight commentators, while sometimes expanding them beyond their intended meaning (see Yedgar, "*Bein*," 75; "*Ha-iyunim*," 30 for examples, and see Deitcher, "Between," 19.) Yedgar also notes that the very selection of what words to quote constitutes an interpretation, for Nehama skipped passages she deemed unnecessary or confusing, such as Ramban's esoteric comments, even though they might impact his meaning (Yedgar, interview).

[68] Such as her suggestion that the Egyptian midwives were not Jewish (see *NSS*, 31–35) or the questionable morality of Moses's slaying of the Egyptian (*NSS*, 41–46) – see discussion on page 345 below.

[69] Ahrend, "*Mi-toch*," 35.

One such crucial value may have been to highlight the Torah's morality according to modern, humanistic sentiments. For Nehama was aware of the tension between the two, and, while against historicizing the Torah *per se*, was willing to admit that certain commandments or religious practices are no longer applicable for historical reasons. She warned that today, reckless application of the Torah's injunctions could actually lead to immoral results:

> We should also oppose all sorts of unfounded and invalid analogies (as appear in current actualizations), for the Sages already declared "Sennacherib came and confused the nations," meaning that the actual Amalek no longer exists.[70]

Similarly, Professor Moshe Sokolow reports that Nehama liked to say: "Suppose you saw a neighbor in the company of his young son starting off on a journey equipped with fire, kindling and a butcher's knife. When asked what he was doing, he replies: 'God appeared to me last night and told me to take my son up the mountain and sacrifice him.' What would you do? The obvious – and correct – answer is to restrain him while the men in white coats come to take him... because it is well known that God has long since stopped talking to people, and so his dreams must have been delusional."[71] In other words, no contemporary actions can be justified on grounds of Divine imperative, because it is no longer operative.[72]

Nehama taught that the commentators were likewise sensitive to these issues. She observed that the general assumption that – with the exception of the *Akedah* – throughout the Tanach morality and religion are in perfect harmony, was not the viewpoint of the classic commentators and the Sages. They asked critical questions concerning the stories of Saul and Amalek, the sons of Aaron, Uzzah, David and the Gibeonites, the hardening of Pharaoh's heart, and many more.[73] This brings us to the next subject within Nehama's religious identity:

Confronting challenging issues

Nehama's concept of a religious person was one who searches for solutions and admits lack of knowledge, rather than producing preset answers to every subject.[74] Her religious line was not one of dogmatic faith. She saw herself as following a great Jewish tradition of critical inquiry, not shying away from

---

[70] *Teacher's Guide* to *Va-yikra*, 5722.
[71] Moshe Sokolow, "Re: Dealing with the Sins of the Avot," Lookjed archives, December 6, 2001.
[72] Sokolow, private communication.
[73] N. Leibowitz, "*Al nituaḥ safruti ve-al parshanut*," in *PN*, 618. This essay was published after her death.
[74] Yedgar, "*Ha-iyunim*," 28.

sections of Tanach that seem morally problematic to modern eyes. On the command to wipe out the Amalekite nation she writes:

> All of our great commentators, from the Sages to the moderns, grappled with the question of how the Torah, whose "ways are pleasant and all her paths peaceful" (Proverbs 3:17) could, in certain circumstances, mandate terrible and dreadful commandments.
>
> Any teacher attempting to silence a student who asks difficult questions, who struggles and who is angry, by claiming that "generations upon generations for two thousand years" have studied and taught these chapters without difficulty, and "only you seem to have trouble with it" is slandering our ancestors and our outstanding commentators. [Such a teacher] is creating the totally erroneous impression that there is an unbridgeable abyss between all the generations of Bible students who supposedly sensed nothing, felt no emotion, and did not ask or object, and our generation who do raise these difficult questions. Familiarity with the great commentaries down the ages will preserve us from such a mistaken view, proving that our questions, soul-searching, and problems were their questions, soul-searching and problems.[75]

But Nehama adds that though the struggles of our predecessors legitimize the modern struggler, they do not allow us to rest idle, and their questions do not substitute for our own. We still need to ask, for

> while the one-time nature of this commandment eases the severity of the question, it still does not answer it.[76]

This is not the only time that Nehama rails against the suppressive teacher. In another example, she writes:

> There is nothing less educational than barking at a questioning student: "Why are you raising problems?" Nor is anything more detached from the Jewish tradition and alien to the spirit of Torah study than the groan often heard from elderly teachers regarding "that arrogant youngster who keeps on asking questions and raising problems, when our ancestors used to study Torah and accept it all without a murmur." (*TI*, 157)

A silent class, notes Nehama, signals that the students, sensing the teacher's awkwardness in facing difficult questions, have despaired of any satisfactory reply:

> From many years' experience I can say the following. When a teacher enters a class expressing the hope that he will not be asked a certain

[75] *Teacher's Guide to Va-yikra*, 5722.
[76] *Teacher's Guide* to *Va-yikra*, 5722.

specific question, or with a prayer that a particular problem or argument will not be raised, acceptance of his prayer is guaranteed: he will receive assistance from Heaven to ensure that his class will sleep the sleep of the just without questions, difficulties or problems. When a teacher hopes 'Let at least one person stand up and demand satisfaction concerning A, raise difficulty B, complain bitterly against C, raise arguments against what I said concerning D,' then in the course of time his class will gradually include more and more who raise questions and problems and demand better explanations from the teacher… and the lessons are guaranteed to be illuminating, interesting and enjoyable. (*TI*, 84–85, n. 20)

A good teacher ought to ignore personal insecurity and must encourage questions, preparing a number of commentators' answers with which to respond. Nehama encouraged teachers to study difficult sections, which harbor

> eternal questions that have been raised ever since the Tanakh began to be studied[77]

and to offer the students the range of opinions to choose from.

Practicing what she preached, Nehama herself grappled with many challenging texts. Rahel Kossowsky recalls: "She said you must teach it the way it is, even to a child, and even difficult stories like the *Akedah*." There was the Israelites' "borrowing" of the Egyptians' gold and silver, never to return it;[78] or Moses's request to "go and serve God for three days" while – ostensibly – planning a permanent exit,[79] and more.[80] Abba Oren, a veteran kibbutz educator, writes that he was

> curious to see how Nehama Leibowitz would handle the "sacrilegious" possibility that Balaam was as great as Moses. I was predisposed to believe that the Orthodox, and whatever else you may say of her, Nehama Leibowitz is surely that, have serious problems in the nexus of universalism and Jewish chosenness.[81]

While not entirely happy with Nehama's conclusions, Oren calls it a "noble attempt" and writes:

---

[77] *TI*, 156; and seepage 400 below.

[78] See "The Valuables that the Israelites Took," *NSS*, 183–192; worksheets for *Bo*, 5709, 5715 and 5719; Reiner and Peerless, *Haggadat*, 67–69, and in shortened version, Reiner and Peerless, *Studies*, 48–49.

[79] See Reiner and Peerless, *Haggadat*, 205–207, and "Moshe v. Pharaoh: Round One," *NSS*, 89–102, where Nehama rejects several apologetic and weak explanations.

[80] See *TI*, 156 for more examples.

[81] Abba Oren, "That Thy Word Hath Quickened Me: Review of *Studies in Bamidbar*," *Forum* (Jerusalem: World Zionist Organization) 38 (Summer 1980): 158.

It is not to damn Leibowitz with faint praise to say that on this issue, as on many others, she does not equivocate but faces it squarely.[82]

Nevertheless, Nehama believed that certain issues were too delicate for the classroom. In one case at least, she recommended actively avoiding a topic in class, unless brought up by the students:

> If you are unlucky, one of the class may ask you a question that has often troubled the rabbis (and which has served the Church leaders as a means for attacking us): "Is the ultimate good that we can look forward to from God in that glorious future simply material?" (*TI*, 78–79)

Here she adds a warning:

> Do not raise this particular question yourself or enter into the subject unless one of the class raises it. Do not give medicine to someone who is not ill. (*TI*, 78 n. 17)

There were also subjects and verses with which Nehama would either only engage in conversation and not in writing,[83] or not at all.[84] R. Aryeh Strikovsky suggests:

> Nehama did not always state her opinion explicitly. However, it is possible to learn of her views by considering the topics she chose to treat extensively as well as the topics she refrained from teaching.[85]

> Her great desire to have her students identify with her subject matter led her at times to choose to not teach certain topics, and even books of *Tanakh*.[86]

Some of the sections that she skipped may have been due to sexual themes, as previously mentioned. But there were others. For instance, Yedgar notes that Nehama did not teach the laws of the condemned city (Deuteronomy 13:13–18) or the commandment to kill witches (Exodus 22:7), or the incidents in which Abraham and Isaac pass off their wives as

---

[82] Oren, "That," 159.

[83] See *PN*, 682 where Nehama points out that an article is different from a lecture, and carries greater responsibility. Nehama was reportedly against the publication of some transcripts from tapes of R. Soloveitchik's lessons; material given over verbally is not always meant to be published.

[84] See chapter 3 n. 19.

[85] Strikovsky, "Nehama on Women," 189.

[86] Strikovsky, "Nehama on Women," 188. In this too she was like the traditional commentators, who, as Mondschein notes, are known as much by subjects omitted as the ones mentioned ("*Akedat Yitzhak – bein emunah le-tehiyah,*" *Bet Mikra* 44/2 [5759]: 108).

their sisters.[87] Another case, noted by Dr. Howard Deitcher, is Genesis 35:22:

> And it came to pass that Reuben went and lay with Bilhah, his father's concubine.

Nehama, who elsewhere explicitly defended an ambiguous action by this same Reuben,[88] never discussed this verse, and when asked directly about the incident, responded, "It's very problematic" but would say no more. This omission becomes even more conspicuous when we realize that the Talmud's statement (Shabbat 55b),

> R. Samuel b. Nahmani said in R. Jonathan's name: Whoever maintains that Reuben sinned is mistaken

is one of a set of teachings that also contains the statement (Shabbat 56a):

> R. Samuel b. Nahmani said in R. Jonathan's name: Whoever says that David sinned is mistaken.

This statement, as will be discussed shortly, was one Nehama openly opposed. Perhaps the difference is that, unlike in King David's case, in Reuben's case there was no admission of guilt in the text or clear moral lesson to be learned. In this case, Nehama valued silence, and she quoted Ibn Ezra's comment on this very verse, where he repeats the words from Proverbs (12:16): "A prudent man conceals disgrace."[89]

৵ ৶

In sum, Nehama's attitude towards humanism, and her treatment of Torah passages challenging to humanistic and other sentiments were not cut of one cloth. Hence, for some students Nehama did not offer satisfactory answers to the gap between modern mores and biblical morality, whilst others found her interpretations inspiring from a humanistic viewpoint. Oren, an educator at a secular Kibbutz seminary, falls into the latter category:

> Such are the vagaries of Jewish spiritual creativity as it unfolds in Israel that it took a Bible teacher with a Marxist orientation at Oranim to call our attention to Nehama Leibowitz's approach, warning us that not

[87] Genesis 13:12, 20:2 and 26:7. Neither Abraham's excuse (Genesis 20:2) "Yet indeed she is my sister, the daughter of my father," nor the absence of overt criticism of the two patriarchs, nor even God's protection of them, are sufficient reason to prevent Nehama from condemning their deceit, as she does in other cases such as that of Simeon and Levi. Yet she maintained silence on these chapters in both her writings and her lessons (Yedgar, interview).
[88] Nehama proposes that the Rashbam's interpretation, that Reuben intended to save Joseph (Genesis 37:22) is the closest to the *peshat* – see *LP*, 175.
[89] Note, though, that Ibn Ezra actually said it in praise of the rabbinic explanation that clears Reuben!

only the Jewishness of our pupils would be impaired, but their humanism as well, if we did not include Nehama Leibowitz in our teaching of the Bible.[90]

Modern- and Ultra-Orthodoxy

Having explored some of Nehama's inner religious life, we turn to look at it through a more sociological lens. Although she herself disapproved of generalizations about various streams of Judaism, if we can permit ourselves to generalize somewhat then it appears that, though sociologically and philosophically Nehama affiliated with the Religious-Zionist and Modern-Orthodox camps, she had also had something in common with Jews further to the right.

True, the most extreme ultra-Orthodox groups were experienced by her as quite alien in their divergence from her broad, rationalist, Zionist upbringing. She was, for instance, taken aback at the concept of *shidduchim* (arranged matches) and felt that she would never have agreed to meet a stranger for dating purposes. She also opposed the line that a Jewish educator's main goal is to teach *yirat shamayim* (fear of heaven). While Nehama supported this value in general – it was one of the founding values of the religious-Zionist Mizrachi educational stream[91] – she feared its distortion into an unexamined piety or a cover for indoctrination. "If you want to teach *yirat shamayim*, teach it outside the classroom," she recommended.[92]

However, she also shared several important elements with ultra-Orthodoxy, such as a deep love for Torah and traditional Judaism, piety, modesty and a simple lifestyle.[93] She had some contact with the most prominent rabbis and yeshivah heads in the Haredi world. She was gratified to hear that a particular *rosh yeshivah* had said of her: "She knows what she's talking about." She conducted several conversations with R. Yosef Kahaneman, head of the Ponevezh yeshivah in Bnei Brak. In one of these, she inquired as the number of students in the yeshivah. When he replied that

---

[90] Oren, "That," 157.

[91] Schoneveld, *The Bible*, 77.

[92] Compare *NSS*, 34–36 for Nehama's understanding of the phrase "*yareh elokim*" (God-fearing) which she sees as indicating a high moral standard; in *SD* she explicitly interchanges this notion with "*yirat shamayim*" (252–253). See also page 357 below. It is also interesting to compare Yeshayahu's notion of this phrase, important to him too (see *Deot* 20 [5722] 67–69). For further reading on this subject in general, see Rosenak's lengthy discussion in *Roads*, 92–144.

[93] Some might insist that "true" (as opposed to "liberal") Modern Orthodoxy also encompasses these elements; but I would argue that sociologically they are less prevalent in this community overall, while for Haredi Jews they are generally an overriding norm.

there were several hundred, Nehama asked if all were studying well. "No, only about twenty are learning properly," he said. Surprised, Nehama inquired: "So what are the others doing?" "They're creating the right atmosphere for the twenty excellent students to emerge." Nehama suggested that the less proficient ones might, instead of learning Talmud, be taught Tanach using her methods. The rabbi's answer was not terribly enthusiastic or flattering, to put it mildly.[94]

o o

Another element more common to ultra-Orthodox than Modern Orthodox circles was the simple faith by which Nehama held. Nothing delighted her more than to overhear two religious girls talking in a university cafeteria, one agitatedly demanding: "What is life all about? Why are we here?" and the other replying, "To serve God, of course." She deliberately kept her analytical side separate from her beliefs, for there was a time to be critical, and a time to be reverent:

> [The purpose is] when we recite Psalms – not to scrutinise and dissect them, not even to explain them, but [to] say them as prayers and personal supplications. (*SD*, 360)

She intuitively knew that sophisticated theories may destroy the wonder that underlies faith, as illustrated by some anecdotes she liked to tell, all located on buses. The first incident took place during the 1936–1939 insurgencies, when the Jerusalem–Tel Aviv highway was at risk from Arab snipers. A passenger on Nehama's bus remarked that the British police were introducing sniffer dogs onto the buses, so that if the vehicle was shot at, the dog would instantly be set on the scent. The narrator recounted enthusiastically that one such dog steered unfalteringly for several kilometers straight to an Arab village and into a house where the sniper stood, gun still in hand. The speaker then exclaimed: "How wondrous are your creations, O Lord!" (Psalms 104:24). But his friend interjected: "What do you mean? That's just an *instinct!*" With that one word, Nehama explained, he quashed all of his companion's enthusiasm.

Some ten or so years later, Nehama overheard two elderly female passengers speaking of a wonderful new invention:

"My daughter just got a Frigidaire from the USA – it works without ice!"

"Impossible! If there's no ice, how does it cool?"

---

[94] Marc B. Shapiro notes that the mission of the great yeshivot in Europe was to create outstanding Torah scholars, even at the expense of less talented students, some of whom left Orthodoxy altogether as a result. He mentions Maimonides's position, from his introduction to the *Guide for the Perplexed*, that the instruction of a tiny elite is more important than educating a mass audience (*Between*, 28, n. 61).

"It works on electricity."

"Well, of course, electricity! That explains it!" Once more, marvels are reduced to mechanisms, and all wonder disappears. As Nehama notes, in ancient times miracles were summarily dismissed as "magic," while today they are written off as "science" (*IBBM*, 242).

The third incident took place after the Six Day War. A passenger on Nehama's bus said to his friend, "I know you are no great believer, but you can't deny that this war was a miracle." The other replied: "I'm afraid to disappoint you, but it's perfectly logical. We were well coordinated, everything went like clockwork, we struck the first blow, and the victory ensued." A third person then chimed in indignantly, "Well coordinated?! Everything like clockwork?! By us, that's not a miracle?"

These stories also illustrated the human tendency to belittle the extraordinary. Nehama quipped: "Split the sea for someone, and he'll demand that you also put down a carpet!"[95] and writes:

> Man… in his blindness tends to detect the guiding hand of Providence only when vouchsafed visible miracles… he fails to see the hidden miracles performed for him, continually.[96]

Even so-called "visible miracles" are not foolproof:

> Miracles do not, necessarily, change human nature and cannot by themselves make man fear and love God. (*NSS*, 260–261)

> The sign or wonder can only impress the one who is psychologically prepared to be convinced. (*NSS*, 166)

> Miracles cannot change men's minds and hearts. They can always be explained away. (*SBM*, 231)

Israel's arch-enemy Amalek, for example, chose to ignore the wonders of the Exodus, declaring:

> But had not other peoples gone forth from the midst of other nations? Who could prove that they had been brought out by God? (*SD*, 256)

The Israelites, too, remained hard-hearted:

> The signs and wonders did not lead the Israelites to the proper acknowledgment of their Creator. Only the experience of forty years wandering in the wilderness [and] the trials they had been subjected to by the Almighty… accomplished that. (*SD*, 290)

---

[95] Reiner and Peerless, *Haggadat*, 137.
[96] *SD*, 93, and see also *NSB*, 243. For more on hidden miracles, see *IHBS*, 166, n. 2.

Nehama's attitude to rabbinic authority bore some similarities to the ultra-Orthodox approach. She maintained an unquestioning attitude towards the religious establishment and its representatives. She exhibited great deference towards rabbis, talmudic scholars and anyone involved in learning, even if many decades younger than she. She believed that rabbinic authority was sacrosanct, and devoted an entire essay to the topic of obeying the Sages, remarking:

> We have a very serious obligation in accepting the discipline of the central religious authority, even if its decision seems mistaken.[97]

Nehama abided by the halachic rulings of her day, refraining from voting, in compliance with R. Kook's prohibition of women from doing so. She took her halachic questions to rabbis she admired – to her local rabbi, R. Yohanan Fried, or R. Shlomo Zalman Auerbach and R. Shlomo Min Hahar. She also asked halachic questions of R. Isaac Herzog, the second Ashkenazi chief rabbi of Israel. Of him she said that he could truly be called a rabbi, for besides knowing the answer to every question she asked, he was also erudite in the "fifth book of the *Shulhan Aruch*: Experience and common sense."[98] In the final decades of her life she regularly phoned the late R. Yosef Kapah with her questions. He recalled that she knew Halachah very well, and frequently already knew the answer. Nehama was turning to him, not for information, but because it was important to her to rely on a recognized authority in her religious practice. Thus she was careful to ask about seemingly minor issues such as making tea on Shabbat, even calling again to double-check. These were not necessarily habits picked up from home. R. Yitshak Reiner recalls her saying to him: "My father taught me Torah. I don't know why he did not teach me Halachot."[99]

Nehama believed that legal verses in the Torah were only to be read accompanied by rabbinic interpretation:

> The light hidden in the halachic verses of the written Torah will only be revealed to the student, young and old alike… when studying the Oral

---

[97] *SD*, 172. In the body of the essay, "Obeying the Sages" (*SD*, 168–174), she quotes the Talmud and Mecklenburg to the effect that if one is absolutely certain that the Sages are mistaken, one does not have to listen to them (*ibid.* 170–171); but her summing up words return to the inviolability of rabbinical authority.

[98] Abramowitz, *Tales*, 57.

[99] R. Yehiel Michel Epstein wrote, before Nehama was born: "It was never the custom to teach women [Jewish law] from books… our women are energetic in every case of doubt and ask and do not rely on their [book] knowledge in even the slightest matter" (*Aruch ha-Shulchan, Yoreh De'ah* 246:19, quoted in Stampfer, "Gender," 65). Yeshayahu Leibowitz's great respect for Halachah might have been nurtured by their joint home environment; or alternatively, Nehama was influenced by Yeshayahu directly.

Torah's interpretations. Only upon observing how the Oral Torah defines terms, expands or amplifies stipulations, and sets limits of applicability will the student realize that these are not simply "recommendations," verses containing wisdom, ethics and sermonizing; but rather law, decree – Halachah.[100]

Yet her simple faith stopped short of promoting Torah scholars and leaders to a different league altogether, as is often done in ultra-Orthodox circles. She did not subscribe to the practice of viewing them as infallible, omniscient, even prophetic; as possessing a facility called *"da'as Torah"* (lit: knowledge of the Torah) which enables them to access God's will in all matters, whether halachic or not. She was against any attribution of mystical powers to human beings:

> There is no intention of basing the commandment [to accept the decision of current halachic authorities] on any superior Divine Spirit [Hebrew: *ruah ha-kodesh*] resting on the Sages.[101]

Nehama was dismayed to hear that the "correct" answer to the examination question given within the ultra-Orthodox Bais Yaakov school system, "How does Rashi know this?" was "Through *ruah ha-kodesh*." This was completely unacceptable. For her, this term referred to the kind of inspiration any great writer might have, from Rashi to Shakespeare. She suggested *siyata di-shmaya* (heavenly aid) as a more appropriate term, for if all of the commentators received Divine guidance to the absolute truth, how was it that they disagreed with each other? Indeed, students from religiously right-wing backgrounds sometimes became agitated when Nehama compared the strengths and weaknesses of Rashi's argument with Ramban's. They feared to look at a text critically, informing her: "We were taught that we are not capable of understanding." On principle Nehama resisted such trends even for younger students who found it difficult to absorb conflicting ideas.[102]

Nehama's moral philosophy did not sit well with blind obedience, which entails handing responsibility for decision-making to another:

> Deeply rooted is man's instinct to shirk responsibility for himself... he would much rather saddle his superior with the burden of providing for him, let him do all his thinking for him, give him orders, lead him. (*NSB*, 524)

---

[100] *Teacher's Guide* for *Kedoshim* 5718.

[101] *SD*, 173; *IBD*, 167. She observes that Maimonides emphasizes time and again that no prophet is authorized to legislate Jewish law. So "if the decision is traced exclusively to the inspiration of the Holy Spirit we do not heed it" (*SD*, 173). See also *IBD*, 308–309.

[102] See Ahrend, "*Mi-toch*," 48.

Leaders should not automatically be assumed honorable; the onus is upon them to prove it so. In her *Studies* she quotes a vivid midrashic description of the Israelites gossiping about Moses, accusing him of nepotism and of appropriating money from public coffers; while Moses insists that he has appointed his relatives to office by God's command alone, and offers to render the full accounts of the Tabernacle's construction to the people (*NSS*, 683–685). Nehama, of course, condemns the Israelites' behavior, but she is more interested in Moses's response. Rather than ignore the complaints as beneath him, Moses strives to clear the air and demonstrate his innocence. From this Nehama derives the lesson that a leader – even the greatest prophet – cannot overlook even the basest of gossip, but must take pains to keep up a spotless reputation. She also wrote in a letter to R. Reinitz, responding to an article she had read:

> I found the sentence "Everything that the rabbis say, expound and do must be accepted unreservedly and unconditionally" jarring. This is absolutely dreadful, completely opposed to the spirit of traditional Judaism. Clearly anyone whose role includes castigating the many, and teaching them, must go over his own deeds with a fine-toothed comb, and must recognize that all his words and deeds are subject to his community's scrutiny. And I still remember from my childhood how the householders criticized their rabbi if they thought he had acted inappropriately, although some defended him by saying it could not be helped, "*Er iz nit keyn groyser hochom*" ["he's no great intellect"]. Since the establishment of Jewish rabbinical leaders, criticism of them has been plentiful, and hence, perhaps, they were so careful with their words and deeds, knowing they had to serve as an example. And here comes this author and turns the rabbis into – Stalin! God forbid. And if this person (I do not know him) wished to pay tribute to the great Torah scholars, a commendable desire certainly, it should not be in giving them carte blanche, free of any responsibility or caution, dispensing with the verse "and you shall be guiltless before the Lord and before Israel" [Numbers 32:22].[103]

Nehama herself, albeit on very rare occasions, expressed criticism of rabbis where she felt it warranted:

> In Jerusalem… where a rabbi [supposedly] sits before Passover in a particular place, ready to be asked questions – when you actually come to ask him he is not there! This happened to me personally.[104]

---

[103] *PN*, 681, referring to *Shma'atin* 7, 84. See also *Teacher's Guide* for *Pekudei* 5722.
[104] *PN*, 681. Note that her intention in the context in which this is brought was not to criticize rabbis but to explain why people do not ask halachic questions, "sometimes for the strangest reasons."

જ઼ ઼જ

Nehama's religious approach diverged from the ultra-Orthodox line in several other important ways. She did not believe in isolating oneself from the world, to achieve holiness, but on the contrary in involvement in society in all its aspects. She did not go on crusades in the name of religion, and was wary of religious zealotry, praising the Netziv for his approach to the biblical Pinhas's actions, his

> acute sensitivity to the dangers of zeal, to the witch-hunting that accompanied verdicts reached without due process of trial and calm, cool objective investigation,

and adding:

> It was difficult for religious zeal to be unmotivated entirely by personal interest…. Only one who really knew himself, who had attained the love of God over and above that granted in the normal way to mortal man, might win Divine approval for such an action. But no general directive could ever be given to authorize it…. Such an act must be exclusively inspired by hatred of sin, not of the sinner…. Righteous indignation can so easily turn into obnoxious fanaticism.[105]

In her dress, she did not take upon herself stricter positions than those accepted in her circles. For instance, she covered her hair with a beret, not a headscarf or wig; and, as per the mainstream German Orthodox custom, she shook hands with men in a social gesture of greeting. The price paid for religious stringency may sometimes be too high, she felt. Regarding a certain rabbi's answer on the radio as to whether the laws of modesty require that a woman cover her legs, Nehama wrote to R. Raphael Posen:

> I was unhappy with his answer regarding socks. He himself said that the *Mishnah Berurah* explicitly permits [wearing no socks], but immediately added that R. Ovadia Yosef did not accept the *Mishnah Berurah's* opinion, and since it is commendable to be strict they should follow his ruling. What's this "commendable to be strict" business? Doesn't he realize that something like this might cause a young girl, unable to withstand peer pressure, to leave our [religious] camp entirely?! And things like this have actually happened: "I can't avoid wearing pants, and I can't always wear socks, they'll laugh at me; and so I've decided that I won't be religious at all." Just so! Even though for both these things there are rulings that permit them (for the pants, from R. Ovadia Yosef,[106] and for the socks from the *Mishnah Berurah*). Surely it is

---

[105] *NSS*, 625–626 and see also 627, n. 6, expressing similar sentiments.

[106] In *Yabia Omer*, 6, *Yoreh De'ah* 14, R. Yosef rules that pants, while not considered "men's clothing," are immodest and not to be worn unless the girls will otherwise wear mini-skirts.

preferable to spell out what the halachic consensus requires, which laws must never be flouted and which [in contrast] depend on one's particular community? (*PN*, 669–670)

Recalling her own upbringing of mixed socializing, Nehama opposed gender separation in schools and *shiurim*. She strongly encouraged membership in youth movements, even if mixed. Wagging her finger, she told a student who taught in a single-sex institution, "I'm an old woman who, believe me, is well-acquainted with the *yetzer ha-ra* (evil inclination), and I'm telling you, in the mixed classes that I teach, they learn Torah!"

Nehama not only supported men serving in the army, which many ultra-Orthodox oppose, she also supported women serving, which was rejected by many within her own circles. She also believed that exposure to new ways of thinking was not to be feared but embraced. Nehama taught at Gesher seminars, that brought secular and religious youth into encounter with one another. She approved of these dialogues, and did not fear, as some educators did, that the religious youth would become corrupted. She opposed isolationism and encouraged involvement in the broader world,[107] even at the expense of Torah study. When a student sought Nehama's advice regarding studying for the Rabbinate, she recommended that he instead become a scientist, for a religious scientist might have more influence than a rabbi who is expected to automatically advocate traditional Judaism. Dr. Rachel Salmon similarly reports:

> I once asked Nehama's advice about the possibility of changing professions in order to concentrate my efforts on Jewish studies. Nehama was not encouraging – in fact, she disapproved. In her opinion, it is of the utmost importance that religious women teach "secular" studies in the university.[108]

Salmon subsequently became a lecturer in English literature.

Nehama Leibowitz *teaching Genesis, chapter 45. Courtesy of Yitshak Reiner.*

---

[107] See page 365 below.
[108] Salmon, "Scholar," 19.

The humanity of the biblical heroes[109]

Now we come to another point on which Nehama deviated from more conservative religious lines. Recently there has been much discussion amongst Jewish educators as to how the Tanach should be taught: emphasizing its distance, or in a down-to-earth fashion? As a Divine work beyond human understanding or highlighting its human dimensions in order to speak to contemporary readers?[110] One central axis in this discussion concerns the biblical heroes (patriarchs, matriarchs, kings, prophets, and so on.). Should they, to borrow Dr. Howard Deitcher's language, be approached as "angels" or as "mere mortals"? Placed on a pedestal, a veil of holiness separates them from us, leaving little room to identify with them. But if their humanity is emphasized, we risk a lack of reverence, with the Bible stories little more than soap operas, its heroes mere schemers and shrews.

Those who would call them "angels" often quote the famous talmudic statements mentioned above, attributed to R. Samuel b. Nahmani (Shabbat 55a–56b) that the belief that Reuben, King David, King Solomon and others sinned is mistaken. But this statement is far from definitive in Jewish thought. Abravanel, for example, writes:

> The verse explicitly testifies to his evil deed... therefore I cannot be persuaded to disregard David's sin. I am pleased that it says that David sinned and confessed much, and did true repentance.[111]

---

[109] Some of the material in this discussion is based on a talk given by Dr. Gabriel Cohn ("Moral problems in the Tanach through the prism of Nehama's interpretation") at a seminar in Kibbutz Lavi, February 27, 2003, and see also his article "*Shiput musari li-demuyot mikra'iyot?: le-ha'arachat demutah shel Sara Imenu*," in *Derachim ba-mikra u-ve-hora'ato*, edited by Moshe Ahrend and Shmuel Feuerstein, 199–213 (Bar Ilan University Press, 1997), referencing a number of useful sources. Erella Yedgar is also currently writing a doctorate on the approach of several Jewish thinkers to moral problems in the Tanach, amongst them Nehama. See also the articles by Deitcher and Berger (details in bibliography).

[110] This debate is a central part of what has become known as the "*Tanach be-govah einayim*" (Tanach at Eye-Level) argument, whereby certain new, *peshat*-orientated readings encourage in-depth examination of the complexities of the biblical characters. R. Uri C. Cohen has assembled a list of the pertinent articles as they developed – see http://www.atid.org/resources/tanakhdebates.asp# where links to the articles are provided. Some of Nehama's students are themselves engaging in this kind of interpretation – see for example Shmuel Klitsner's *Wrestling Jacob*, Jerusalem: Urim Publications, 2006; and see also Cherlow, 19, for his discussion of Bin-Nun's work in the context of this debate.

[111] From his comments to II Samuel, chapter 11, near the end.

Nehama's view followed Abravanel's, and – she would argue – the Torah's own. In cases where there is clear wrongdoing and punishment, as with King David, she certainly believed that the *peshat* ought to be followed. These, she noted, are the rarer instances, for the Torah generally does not make explicit judgments of behaviors:

> As a rule, Holy Writ allows the events it describes and the action of its characters to speak for themselves.[112]

The Torah's opinion of certain behaviors comes across subtly, and needs to be drawn out of the text by those willing to look for them.[113]

In line with this argument, Nehama brought a dual approach to the text, reading respectfully but honestly. The quality of the biblical heroes was never in doubt, and her works are filled with their praise;[114] yet this did not mean that they had to be flawless. She saw herself as simply following the Torah's lead:

> The Torah does not confine itself to recording the good in man. It paints with equal objectivity the bad, giving the whole human picture with its light and shade. (*SBM*, 77)

> The Torah is at pains to present both sides of the biblical heroes, not concealing their but human faults. Even Moses is not described as the perfect man, but we see him also in his moments of impatience and weakness. Though he displayed these in reaction to the provocation of the generation of the wilderness, their grumblings and lack of faith, the Torah does not excuse them or gloss over them. (*SBM*, 121)

We are to learn from their failures, not to cover them up. Their imperfections in no way detract from their heroic status. Excuses such as "the moral code of their time was different" are neither necessary nor acceptable, for these people are to serve as eternal guides in their behavior.[115]

৵ ৶

Nehama did not invent this approach. It had its antecedents in talmudic materials and other commentaries, as she notes:[116]

---

[112] *NSB*, 264. Yedgar makes this point at greater length in "*Parashat Va-yishlach*," 116.

[113] Nehama did this, for example, with Jacob (*NSB*, 266 – quote cited below, page 346.

[114] At one point, Nehama writes: "All our ancestors' deeds, even the material ones, are a dwelling place [Tabernacle] for the blessed Lord" (*PN*, 472). This appears to be a quote, but it is unclear where Nehama derived this idea from – the human heart is often referred to as God's dwelling place, following Exodus 25:8, but not human deeds.

[115] Deitcher, "Between," 16 –17.

[116] Cohn notes that we can get a sense of the talmudic and midrashic materials by looking through Yishai Hasida's *Ishei ha-Tanach* (Encyclopedia of Biblical Personalities), under the sub-sections describing the sins of many important biblical characters (Cohn, lecture). For some instances where Nehama cites commentators who critique the

It is accepted – generally by those unfamiliar with our early commentators, or knowing of them only second hand – that they favored the patriarchs and national heroes, defending all their deeds and justifying them "at any price." This is a gross error. From the Midrash – and especially there – and until the Middle Ages, we find great latitude in the treatment of biblical figures. Even the greatest and most admired are treated to the critical yardstick. (*LP*, 33)

Our Sages feel at liberty to censure even the founding fathers of our people, the prophets, and even Moses, the greatest of all the prophets. He was by nature quick-tempered…. Our Sages, rather than ignoring such shortcomings, exhorted us to draw the proper lessons. (*NSV*, 138)

Our Sages were very exacting in their standards where the patriarchs are concerned. If they found their conduct wanting, they had no qualms about drawing attention to it…. Not all our later commentators have shared this approach.[117]

This last sentence is important. The medievals often would not criticize the forefathers, and the post-medievals were divided. For example, Hirsch was in principle willing to examine the biblical heroes critically, whereas Mecklenburg was not.[118] The later commentators might have been influenced in part by a modern devaluation of religious authority. Berger, however, believes that it was also affected by a shift in non-Jewish biblical scholarship. Where once unfavorable comparisons were drawn between the flawed biblical characters and the unblemished Christian saints, in the modern period the attack on traditional Judaism shifted from the morality of the Tanach's characters to that of its authors. Some traditionalists preferred to sacrifice the characters' saintliness if it meant that the Bible's morality was preserved, in that the Bible criticized the improper behavior of its characters. Berger locates Nehama amongst these defenders.[119] The important insight

---

biblical characters, see worksheets for *Devarim*, 5704, *Lech Lecha*, 5705 and 5710, *Va-era* 5706 and 5711, *Shemini* 5711, *Be-ha'alotecha* 5712 *and* 5718, *Va-yishlah* 5714, and *Shemot* 5715 (thanks to R. Yitshak Reiner for this list).

[117] *NSB*, 331. See also discussion in Deitcher "Between," 15 onwards.

[118] See Amos Frisch, *"Shitato shel RSh"R Hirsch be-sugiyat hetei ha-avot,"* in *Derachim ba-mikra u-ve-hora'ato*, edited by Moshe Ahrend and Shmuel Feuerstein, 181–198 (discussion of Hirsch) and 191–192 (discussion of Mecklenburg) (Bar Ilan University Press, 1997).

[119] See David Berger. "On the Morality of the Patriarchs in Jewish Polemic and Exegesis," in *Modern Scholarship in the Study of Torah*, edited by Shalom Carmy, 140, n. 21 (Northvale, NJ: Jason Aaronson, 1996). He also includes Yissachar Jacobson and Nehama's student Leah Frankel in this category. Furthermore, he states (*ibid.*, 138–139) that Buber, Jacob and Cassuto all noticed patterns of retribution running through entire books of the Torah (particularly Genesis); and these three scholars influenced Nehama greatly (see chapter 20).

here is that, rather than damaging the Torah's spiritual authority as her critics might suppose, Nehama was actually strengthening it.

But there was probably another reason too – her own integrity. When comparing Hirsch with Mecklenburg, Dr. Amos Frisch writes:

> While the author of the *Ketav ve-ha-kabbalah* gives priority to the educational value of the patriarchs' honor, Hirsch, according to his own statement of principles, prefers the truth as a religious value.[120]

Nehama held on to both of the values mentioned in this paragraph. Though an educator through and through, she also wished to go beyond defensive readings of the Tanach and engage truthfully with what is written. This too was educational, for otherwise she would act as do the suppressive teachers whom she condemned:

> The teacher... must avoid overdoing various attempts at "justification" – including explanations that distort the texts.... Such efforts do not further investigation of the stories' true meaning, and are also likely to irritate the students who sense that the teacher's motivation is not the quest for truth but rather the inclination to conceal from them the flaws of our ancestors – which the Torah (itself) does not intend to conceal.[121]

❧ ❧

Thus, Nehama was to be found, on occasion, boldly querying the behavior of biblical characters from Moses down:

> Moses, the greatest of prophets but nevertheless human.... (*SBM*, 341)

> There is here no excusing of Moses's conduct.[122]

She opposed commentators and colleagues who went overboard in their praise or apologetics. At a conference at Bar Ilan University, a certain professor mentioned the Aggadic approach to the story of King David's relations with Bathsheba, which portrays the king in a more positive light than does the Tanach itself in the second book of Samuel.[123] The moderator had not yet even managed to thank the scholar when Nehama rose from her

---

[120] Amos Frisch, "*Shitato shel RSh"R Hirsch be-sugiyat hetei ha-avot*," in *Derachim ba-mikra u-ve-hora'ato*, edited by Moshe Ahrend and Shmuel Feuerstein, 192 (Bar Ilan University Press, 1997).

[121] *Teacher's Guide* for Toldot 5727.

[122] *NSS*, 109. However, at the conclusion of this essay, after bringing the criticisms of Moses, Nehama brings the opinions that defend him, and ends on that note (*ibid.*, 110). See also her comments in *SBM*, 267–268 regarding Moses's fears.

[123] In this version, Bathsheba is hidden from view behind a screen. Satan appears as a bird and the king shoots an arrow at it, inadvertently breaking the screen and revealing the woman (Sanhedrin 107a).

seat in the audience and proclaimed: "You must never teach this chapter without teaching chapter twelve too!" In chapter twelve, the prophet Nathan rebukes David, who instantly admits his guilt – and for Nehama, as for the Abravanel, it was this repentance, not some unblemished perfection, that was the chief lesson of the story.

We must note, though, that Nehama tended to advance her more controversial statements in the name of accepted commentators such as the Midrash, Ramban or Radak. For example, after spending most of one essay defending Moses's slaying of the Egyptian taskmaster, in the end she brings *Midrash Petirat Moshe* (Midrash of Moses's Passing) which contains the following exchange:

> Said the Holy One: "Did I in any wise tell thee to slay the Egyptian?" Said Moses to Him: "But Thou didst slay all the firstborn of Egypt, and shall I die for the sake of one Egyptian?" Said the Holy One blessed be He to him: "Canst thou liken thyself to Me who causeth to die and bringeth to life? Canst thou, in any wise, bring to life like Me?[124]

She then feels more confident in criticizing the great Jewish leader at the conclusion of her essay:

> Taking the law into one's own hands [is] a serious crime. No man can take a leaf out of his Creator's book. (*NSS*, 46)

This reliance on her predecessors was not simply a tactical move in order to protect herself from rebuke. Rather, she genuinely viewed herself as following in illustrious footsteps:

> Our Sages were no respecters of persons, however great. They were ready to see the faults of both patriarch and prophet. Rashi echoes their approach. (*NSS*, 81)

Rashi, however, does not always adhere to this line, sometimes preferring to defend the biblical heroes, and Nehama certainly knew this too. When Jacob disguises himself as Esau in order to receive the firstborn's blessings, he informs his father (Genesis 27:19):

> I am Esau your firstborn.

Rashi deals with this apparent falsehood by splitting the verse into two sentences:

> I am [he that brings you (food)]; Esau [is] your firstborn.

Nehama omits this explanation from her *Studies*, an omission that might be construed as a rejection. Not only does it clearly run against the *peshat*,

---

124 Quoted in *NSS*, 46.

reason enough for Nehama to reject it;[125] but she would surely have denied its validity for moral reasons too. Even under duress, Jacob was not permitted to deceive his father. Even words that are seemingly true are still lies if they are said in order to mislead, for the Torah adjures: "Keep far away from falsehood."[126] Her own essay on this portion is, in contrast, devoted to proofs of the Tanach's critical attitude towards the patriarch:

> The vicissitudes of Jacob's life teach us at every step how he was repaid, measure for measure, for taking advantage of his father's blindness.[127]

Later, Nehama reads the text closely to demonstrate how Jacob was punished by Divine retribution with a lifetime of misery for causing Esau's "exceeding bitter cry":

> The moral lesson remains clear – sin and deceit, however justified, bring in their train ultimate punishment. (*NSB*, 324)

Nehama also discusses Sarah's problematic treatment of Hagar (*NSB*, 153–157). She initially praises Sarah for selflessness and excuses her envy of her taunting rival as "natural." But then she goes on to cite unusually disapproving comments by Radak and Ramban. Many disputed with her about this ("it was the only time I had a real argument with her," remembers one close student). After all, even a careful reading of the text seems to hold a positive view of Sarah's actions.[128] Sarah is not rebuked or punished, and the angel of God in fact urges Hagar to return to her mistress for more of the same. Furthermore, if we look at the historical context, the laws of Hammurabi allowed the mistress of the house to re-enslave a former handmaiden.[129] But Nehama writes:

---

[125] In his essay, *"Pulmus dati u-megamah hinuchit be-ferush Rashi la-Torah,"* (in *PN*, 192), Avraham Grossman quotes R. Menahem ben Shlomo (the *Sechel Tov*), who rejects such a reading, for we could similarly posit the existence of two deities by reading the Ten Commandments as *Anochi* = "I am speaking," YHWH *Elohecha* = "YHWH is your God." Grossman suggests that Rashi's interpretation was a defensive move against Christian accusations that Jews were deceitful in business like their ancestor Jacob. This theory is not something Nehama would wish to entertain. See also Israel Rozenson, *"Ha-parshanit, ha-perush ve-ha-historiah: he'arot al tefisat ha-parshanut shel Nehama Leibowitz,"* in *Al derech ha-avot*, 2001, 443, and Hayyim J. Angel, "The paradox of *Parshanut*: Are our Eyes on the Text, or on the Commentators? Review of *Pirkei Nehama*," *Tradition* 38/4 (Winter 2004): 115–117, 123.

[126] Exodus 23:7. See page 101 above.

[127] *NSB*, 266; see further, *ibid.*, 266–268.

[128] Cohn, *"Shiput,"* 203–204.

[129] Cohn suggests that indeed the word in Genesis 16:6, *Va-te'aneha*, generally assumed to refer to mistreatment or persecution, may actually mean that she curtailed her independence and brought her under her jurisdiction (*"Shiput,"* 205).

Even had Ramban known that according the laws of the ancient Near East Sarah was permitted to re-enslave her ex-handmaiden, he would certainly not have changed his negative evaluation; for not everything allowed and accepted at that time was the kind of behavior fitting for Sarah or Abraham, who were launching a new period of history. (*LP*, 52)

Thus it was precisely her esteem for Sarah that led to Nehama's high expectations from her (and the same might be suggested of her attitude towards the other biblical heroes). But rather than leaving the matriarch's misdeed to fester in the student's mind, Nehama, ever the educator, drew a lesson from it, by analyzing how Sarah could have fallen quite so low:

> Perhaps the Torah wished to teach us that before man undertakes a mission that will tax all his moral and spiritual powers he should ask himself first whether he can maintain those same high standards to the bitter end. (*NSB*, 156)

In other words, Sarah had bitten off more than she could chew in believing herself capable of standing by humbly while another woman gave birth to her husband's son. In Nehama's view, this was not humility but hubris; and she ends with the following extraordinary suggestion:

> Had Sarah not… dared to scale these unusual heights of selflessness… there may not have been born that individual whose descendants have proved a source of trouble to Israel to this very day. Who knows? (*NSB*, 157)

A further example of Nehama's audacity is seen in her condemnation of Simeon and Levi's slaughter of Shechem's male inhabitants in revenge for the rape of their sister Dinah.[130] Nehama opens the essay with emotional language:

> We have here in chapter 34 an account of a massacre of men, women and children, the inhabitants of a whole town? Was such a deed justified? (*NSB*, 380)

Yedgar notes that by adding the words "women and children" here, Nehama amplifies the heinous deed, for the narrative reports differently:

> They slew all the males…. All their little ones and their wives they took captive.[131]

---

[130] Genesis, chapter 34. See "The Story of Dinah," *NSB*, 380–387, and "Simeon and Levi," 542–547. See also comments by Breuer ("*Yahasah*," 15–16); Yedgar ("*Parashat Va-yishlach*," *passim*); and discussion on pages 505–551 below.

[131] Genesis 34:25 and 34:29. See Yedgar, "*Parashat Va-yishlach*," 104.

Nehama does discuss why the brothers might have believed they were justified, but she makes her own opposition clear throughout the essay.[132] Desiring an unequivocal message to be presented in this particular study, she deliberately omits the many commentaries that defend the brothers.[133] Even though, as Nehama herself notes, God Himself apparently stood behind their action (Genesis 35:5):

> … And the terror of God fell upon the cities that were around them,

she ends the essay with the following comment:

> As a contemporary thinker once phrased it, among all the many names and attributes of God the title "success" cannot be found. (*NSB*, 385)

Nehama realized that this essay was controversial. But despite all the phone calls she received, informing her that such punitive measures are the only way to ensure women's freedom to walk around safely, she stuck to her view.

Some further examples of Nehama's willingness to see flaws in the biblical heroes appear in her discussion regarding Rachel's cry (Genesis 30:1),

> Give me children or else I die,

and Jacob's angry response in the next verse. Both come under fire from commentators, whom Nehama unhesitatingly quotes (*NSB*, 331–336). Additionally we have her description of Joseph's "overweening pride and self-importance" before he became mature (*NSB*, 433) and of Pinhas's zealous act of murder, which Nehama critiques as a terrible deed. God's seemingly favorable reaction to Pinhas's action (Numbers 25:12),

> Therefore say, Behold, I give to him my covenant of peace

is reinterpreted by her as a necessary protection, representing

> a guarantee of protection against the inner enemy… against the inner demoralization that such an act as the killing of a human being without

---

[132] Yedgar points out that everything about Nehama's essay indicates her aim to denounce the violent act, including the structure, the questions and the commentaries she selects; and that she reviled both the killing and the deception involved ("*Parashat Va-yishlach*," 104).

[133] For a summary of the defending positions see Yedgar, "*Parashat Va-yishlach*," 103–104. In Nehama's worksheet on this story she is more balanced, bringing counterarguments supporting the brothers' actions, such as Maimonides's position (see *ibid.*, 106, 110); perhaps because the worksheet student is seen by Nehama as more reflective, industrious and committed.

due process of law is liable to cause.[134]

In closing, it is important to reiterate that Nehama venerated and loved the biblical heroes. Her close reading of the Torah was used to expose not only their flaws, but also their virtues. Her careful words about the Sages in the following quote apply also to herself:

> However, just as they bring to the fore Moses's rare failings, so our Sages no less diligently probe into the folds of the Torah to uncover his outstanding qualities.[135]

---

[134] *SBM*, 331. The explanation she brings is the Netziv's. In the Hebrew version, the word translated here as "demoralization" is *pegam*, which literally means "stain."
[135] Combination of *IHBV*, 114 and *NSV*, 138.

CHAPTER 16

AUTONOMY AND RESPONSIBILITY:
IN THE IMAGE OF GOD

AFTER LAYING OUT Nehama's opinion on a variety of issues, we will now undertake to answer the more encompassing question of Nehama's central philosophy.

First we must ask if she had an overall philosophy at all., Nehama never clearly explicated her philosophy or value system anywhere in her writings, unlike her didactic and methodological approach, which is laid out in various places.[1] Only those who knew her well or read her work carefully noticed the recurring themes.[2] By means of isolating these from their contexts, Nehama's *weltanschauung* may be delineated. This must be done cautiously, for, as such artificial separation contradicts Nehama's entire approach, running the risk of making her words sound more preachy than they should.[3] Yet, as will be demonstrated here, the stirring educational impact when aspects of her Torah are drawn from their half-shadow justifies this risk. When this is done, a pragmatic philosophy of ethics, study and action comes through strongly in her work.[4] Therefore, instead of a "philosophy," it might be better to speak of a "value system of human behavior in relationship with the Divine."

Nehama was not a philosopher in the accepted sense; she was a reader of text and an educator. In her works she did occasionally deal with philosophical questions, such as the purpose of the soul (*SD*, 100–101) or of the sacrifices (*NSV*, 1–22); or how God can be contained within physical space, in the Temple (*IBBM*, 106). She was also conversant with works by many Jewish philosophers, including Maimonides and Rabbis Kook and Soloveitchik, as well as non-Jewish philosophers – in her youth, she studied Plato, and she quotes Socrates (*TI*, 143) and Kierkegaard.[5] But she tended to steer clear of abstract theological questions such as how distant God is from

---

[1] Yedgar, "*Ahrayut*," 377.

[2] For a list of recurring themes see chapter 8 n. 13.

[3] See Yedgar "*Ahrayut*," 405–406 where she outlines the limitations of this approach and of her findings.

[4] See Yedgar, "*Ahrayut*," 377, n. 1.

[5] Worksheet for *Va-yera*, 5707.

mankind or how exactly God metes out reward and punishment. She believed it impossible to answer such questions.[6] She preferred to focus on what is knowable – what is demanded by the Torah of humans, in this world.[7] Even a philosophical essay dealing with the nature of prophecy, she ultimately channels out of the abstract and into more immediate questions of human behavior, psychology and religious faith.[8] She always turned to the applied and concrete, citing examples before fleshing out more conceptual material.

The beginning of Nehama's *New Studies in Bereshit* illustrates this well, setting the tone for the rest of the *Studies*. There, she skips all the questions of cosmology and Creation dealt with at length by many of her favorite commentators, instead launching directly into a discussion of "man in the image of God" and mankind's role in the world,

> charged with a special task over and above those applying to the rest of creation…. The pinnacle of it all. (*NSB*, 4–5)

Two scholars who have, in different ways, thoroughly combed Nehama's works for her philosophy and value system are Dr. Marla Frankel and Erella Yedgar. Frankel, who knew Nehama first as her teacher and then as her colleague and friend, searched Nehama's writings for her instructional theory. She discovered a marked preference for dichotomous themes such as authority and freedom, tradition and modernity, the metaphysical and physical, individual and community, and Israel and the Diaspora.[9] Yedgar, who attended the special *Amitei Tzion* lesson for twenty years and had a close personal relationship with Nehama, also discovered several recurring elements, amongst them a central theme of responsibility.[10] When this element is isolated, the result is a profoundly inspiring Jewish worldview, fostering positive, concerned action. Much of the following chapter is based

---

[6] See Frankel, *Iyun*, 132, n. 39 and 121.

[7] Frankel quotes the *Teacher's Guide* for *Yitro*, 5730 as an instance where Nehama emphasizes the demand on human behavior rather than the nature of God (*Iyun*, 94).

[8] See "The Prompting of the Holy Spirit," *SBM*, 225–232. In *LP*, 121, n. 2 Nehama also deals with the nature of prophecy, and whether it is conditional or not.

[9] Frankel, "*Ha-te'oriyah*," 438, and private communication.

[10] See Yedgar, "*Ahrayut*," 378, for her five criteria in drawing this conclusion. Some view Yedgar's premise as a little too sweeping, for at times Nehama passes over conspicuous lessons of responsibility. For example, in her essay "Moses Seeks Out his Brethren" (*NSS*, 39–48) she gives little space to Moses's courageous act of concern towards a suffering Israelite, preferring instead to focus on the value of human life. Note also for example *NSV*, 310, where she demands responsibility from one who misleads someone else to transgress, but without requiring it likewise from the transgressor ("But this is not so, the victim being blinded by his passions").

on Yedgar's work, as well as that of Professor Menahem Ben-Sasson and others.[11]

Autonomy

Underlying Nehama's notion of responsibility was her belief in human autonomy. Without the freedom to choose, there can be no responsibility for one's actions.

The question of human autonomy is a crucial one within life in general, and religious life in particular. Are we free to shape our own lives, or rather beholden to external factors, God included? The religious answer may go in two opposite directions. Many believe feelings of dependence on a higher power to be a prerequisite in religion. But some suggest that self-empowerment and confident action are not antithetical to religion, and may indeed be central components in religious life.[12] Nehama did not have a monolithic opinion on this question. She fully believed in accepting the yoke of heaven and of Jewish law, but her teachings also imply that the religious ideal is not attained through erasing one's individuality.[13] Human beings are at liberty to create their inner and outer environments. They do not function automatically, but have the power to choose; and, having chosen, to carry it out.[14] God demands active, independent choice: "Choose life!"[15] Self-governance, security, finances, and the general facility to shape our life and fate – all lie in our own hands, according to Nehama.[16]

Nehama made the important point, often overlooked in Jewish thought, that autonomy is not merely a gift but also an obligation. As such it is not to be diminished unnecessarily. We see this when she contrasts the Torah's and Mahatma Gandhi's approach to vows. Gandhi writes:

> The importance of vows grew upon me more clearly than ever before. I realized that a vow, far from closing the door to real freedom, opened

---

[11] For more see Ben-Sasson, "*Ha-teshuvah*," and Yedgar, "*Ahrayut*." Note her discussion of how the topic of responsibility connects to five main axes in Nehama's worldview (402).

[12] Erich Fromm, for example, writes: "Freud states that the feeling of powerlessness is the opposite of religious feeling. In view of the fact that many theologians – and... Jung too, to a certain extent – consider the feeling of dependence and powerlessness the core of religious experience, Freud's statement is very important" (*Psychoanalysis and Religion*, London: Victor Gollancz, 1951, 22.)

[13] Horwitz, "*Nehama*," 208.

[14] Yedgar, "*Ahrayut*," 379.

[15] Deuteronomy 30:19. See *NSB*, 50; Yedgar, "*Ahrayut*," 380.

[16] Yedgar, "*Ahrayut*," 380.

it…. To be bound by a vow was like a passage from libertinism to a real monogamous marriage.[17]

In contrast, Nehama notes:

> Our Torah wished man to remain free in those matters not covered by its commands and prohibitions. Man should act in accordance with the dictates of his own mind at the moment of decision and not be bound by any previously determined resolve or vow. (*SD*, 227)

Nehama also writes:

> A servant has to do the behest of others…. A free agent, however, is only bound by his conscience…. Man should conduct himself as a free agent rather than be bound by external artificial bonds. (*NSB*, 533)

Since she would not apply such sentiments to matters under the Torah's authority, but only when taking on extra restrictions,[18] Nehama is here once again exhibiting her complex thinking. Instead of absolute dependence, or absolute freedom, she advocates full heteronomy and obedience up to the perimeters of the Torah's laws, and beyond that, full autonomy.

The theme of free choice expresses itself strongly in Nehama's teachings, stories and writings.[19] She taught that when Adam is created, the phrase "And God saw that it was good" is noticeably absent because in humans the good is not assured but depends on free choice.[20] She demonstrated that the prophet Balaam freely made his decision to go with the Moabite messengers (Numbers 22). God not only allowed this choice but even facilitated its implementation, and it was only then that Balaam's free will became curtailed. For the more one follows an evil path, the harder it becomes to forsake it (*SBM*, 314), and God will remove the obstacles to it.[21] This was not just a theological statement for Nehama, but a psychological one – having chosen either good or evil, one is more likely to keep moving in that direction.[22]

As an educator, Nehama put her philosophy into practice. She tried to bring her students to a freely chosen love of Torah, not through

---

[17] Quoted in *SD*, 227. The exact reference is M. Gandhi, *The Story of My Experiment with Truth*, Desai, Ahmedabad: 1997, 173.

[18] However, acts beyond the letter of the law, striving for a higher religious level, are allowed even if restrictive. They are included in the Torah's directive "And you shall do that which is good and right" (Deuteronomy 6:18). This point came across clearly in several of Nehama's teachings (See e.g. *SD*, 57–63 "Doing the Right and Decent Thing"; see also *NSV*, 266–267).

[19] See for example her lesson on the waters of Mara on pages 88–90 above.

[20] *NSB*, 14; see Yedgar, "*Ahrayut*," 379.

[21] See *NSS*, 158, regarding the hardening of Pharaoh's heart.

[22] Ben-Sasson, "*Ha-teshuvah*," 343.

indoctrination or fear. She not only bestowed but actually thrust autonomy upon her students, demanding that they choose critically and independent-mindedly between several commentaries.[23]

Autonomy leads to responsibility

Freedom to choose places the burden of accountability on the individual:

> A person is no speck of dust or cog in a machine, but is created in the image of God, responsible for his every action – towards himself, society, the world. Every act, however minute, is fraught with consequences for future generations, for his immediate environment and even for the entire world.[24]

This theme is a recurring one in Nehama's work. It follows trends within the teachings of the Sages, mandating responsibility for one's actions even when working on behalf of an organization or community, for "there is no proxy for criminal acts" (*NSB*, 328).

Nehama condemned unethical behaviors with an intensity largely absent in her discussions of other prominent religious areas such as faith in God or the Sabbath.[25] This was because she viewed personal responsibility as fundamental, a prerequisite for correct functioning of individual, society and world.[26] We mentioned above that Nehama launched her *Studies* series with the creation of humankind as an autonomous and responsible being, and this was not by chance. In the first chapter of the creation story, humans are singled out and distinguished from the animals as the appointed ruler of the world and crown of creation. Nehama notes that in Genesis 1:27:

> The style of the verse is poetic and elevated, the fact of man's creation being referred to three times. The chasm separating man from the rest of creation is stressed twice in the statement that he was created in the image of God. Both the duties, responsibilities and glory of man derive from this (*NSB*, 2).

She then quotes Professor Julius Guttmann's understanding of the "image of God" as representing the trait of independence. This is what allows relationship to occur:

---

[23] Ben-Sasson, "*Ha-teshuvah*," 368. See further in chapter 18.

[24] Combination of *IBB*, 125, and *NSB*, 175.

[25] Yedgar, "*Ahrayut*," 403.

[26] Yedgar notes that Nehama brings a statement by Maimonides (*Yad Hazakah, Hil. Teshuvah* 3:4) to buttress this position, but that she stretches it beyond its actual meaning; and she similarly expands the meaning of the statement from Mishnah Sanhedrin (4:5) "For me the world was created" (*Bein*, 73–74). In other words, she reads the call to responsibility towards the world into sources that do not necessarily intend that message.

> *Zelem* (image) refers to the personal relationship that can only be found between "persons." The personality of man is placed vis-à-vis the personality of God. For there is a religious approach (not Jewish) that sees the religious ideal in the effacement of man's personality... but this is not the case with an ethical religion. Only as long as man is a person can he preserve his relationship with God. Man is a world of his own and he is not required to merge himself in nature. (*NSB*, 2–3)

But no sooner is human autonomy created than it is brought under certain constraining guidelines. God charges Adam and Eve to be fruitful and multiply, populate the earth and control it (Genesis 1:28), but this is not only a privilege and a blessing, it is also an obligation and a responsibility.[27] Wary of the belligerent-sounding phrase "control it" – much unlike the "peaceful ideals which our Sages considered to be the goal of mankind" (*NSB*, 4) – Nehama is careful to clarify what kind of control is referred to:

> Man, [Ramban] says, was thereby given dominion over the earth to do as his will with the rest of the animal creation, to build uproot, plant, mine metal from the earth and the like. The phrase ["control it"] therefore refers to man's conquest of the desert and his constructive and civilizing endeavors to build and inhabit the world, harness the forces of nature for his own good and exploit the mineral wealth around him.... It was man's privilege accorded him by his Creator to have dominion over the creation and to rule over the fish of the sea and the fowl of the air and over every living thing that moved. (*NSB*, 5)

Conquering the world thus means civilizing it.[28] And even this may be done incorrectly, as Nehama points out elsewhere, sounding uncannily like a modern environmentalist:

> The Torah is well aware that with all the blessing contained in this civilizatory work, improving upon the raw materials given to mankind at creation, there is also a danger of indulgence, decadence and egotism, which are always accompanied by enslavement and exploitation of others. (*IHBS*, 460)

---

[27] The administering of justice is also "a Divine charge... both a duty and a privilege" (*SD*, 14).

[28] As Nehama writes in a later essay: "Our Sages have said, 'The works of Creation must be complemented (by man),' i.e. must be cultivated, perfected, and adapted to human needs. This includes the unceasing war against all kinds of natural risks and dangers, from the manufacture of clothing to the building of houses, improving and increasing food supplies, and medical research.... But the Torah does not state the ways of developing farming, of digging tunnels or building bridges, or how to transform arid land into fertile soil, for all this is the task of man... [who] has been endowed with the ability to think and to invent, to investigate..." (*NSV*, 186).

We are not precluded from making use of God's creations. Indeed we are bidden "subdue it," exploit to the full the natural resources he has placed at our disposal, conquering the desert and uprooting vegetation where it causes damage. But it is willful destruction of the gifts of nature that have been bestowed on us that we are warned against. (*SD*, 198)

These warnings notwithstanding, Nehama certainly believed that Judaism is pro-civilization, and takes Abravanel to task for his anti-civilization approach.[29]

Individual, society and evasion

Nehama believed that the individual and society are responsible to each other. No one is an island. We come to this world not in order to implement our rights but to make some return for its benefits[30] and to work for future generations. We must look out for others, especially for weaker members of society, such as the poor person:

He is your responsibility. He is not simply at your side, in a physical, locational sense – you in your compartment and he in his. He is "with you" together, a part of you. You share his problems.[31]

Society must not be used to escape one's responsibilities. It is a sign of weakness to hide behind community norms, as Laban did when tricking Jacob (Genesis 29:26), declaring:

It is not done so in our country, to give the younger before the firstborn.

Nehama writes:

In this way man splits himself in two, into his personal "I" who does good and is acceptable and pleasant in the eyes of his friends, and the "I" which is but a cog in the anonymous public machine, be it the state of which he is but a functionary and servant, the army of which he is but one of its nameless soldiers, the party of which he is but one of the rank and file, the enterprise which he does not direct but merely serves. What blame can therefore be attached to him?[32]

One shining example of those who did not hide behind "superior orders" is that of the two midwives, who defied Pharaoh's decree to kill the

---

[29] Nehama views Abravanel's "violent antipathy" to civilization as a very non-Jewish approach. See *NSB*, 18–21, 92, 95 and *NSS*, 485, n. 4; also Yedgar "*Ahrayut*," 388, and discussion of Abravanel's subjectivity on pages 397, 469, 471, 491 below.

[30] See Ahrend, "*Mi-toch*," 35.

[31] *NSS*, 408. See also Yedgar, "*Ahrayut*," 382, n. 12.

[32] *NSB*, 327. See also Yedgar, "*Ahrayut*," 383.

Israelite male babies (Exodus 1:15–22). The overwhelming majority of commentators understand them to be Jewish, but Nehama inclines towards the opinion that they were Egyptians. She thus paints a beautiful picture of civil disobedience, and demonstrates that moral courage is not an ethnically or nationally determined quality.[33] In fact, she goes so far as to argue that the biblical term "Godfearing," used of the midwives, signifies primarily a concern for the defenseless outsider. For it is precisely this attitude that reveals whether one fears God or not;[34] and without fear of God, ethical approaches are liable to dissipate, as "man's intellect may degenerate and conceive of the most savage and diabolical plans."[35]

Members of society are to shoulder their part in supporting it, and not act as parasites. In quite a radical piece of interpretation, Nehama taught that the "idolatrous sinner" mentioned in Deuteronomy 29:18 is a person who

> wishes to follow the stubbornness of his heart, and shake off all responsibility for his deeds by casting his burden on the community. Judaism, on the other hand, demands that the individual take upon himself the responsibility for the community as a whole.[36]

Here, she has interpreted shirking responsibility as "idolatry" – it was clearly anathema to her, the very opposite of her ideal.[37] Yedgar notes that the contemporary incarnation of this "idolatrous sinner" is therefore no other than the citizen who commits the most banal of crimes – tax evasion!

It appears from here that Nehama raised responsibility to the level of a cardinal Jewish principle. She viewed even its passive avoidance as an evil in itself:

> One of the characteristics of the wicked man, standing in the way of reformations, is the flight from personal responsibility. (NSB, 327)

> Evil is evil and we are to avoid it. The struggle is between the good and evil impulse, between altruism and egoism, between the acceptance of responsibility and the shirking of it. (NSS, 409)

Simply being a law-abiding citizen is not enough. One may not sit passively, simply doing no harm, but must actively go out to do good and combat evil:

---

[33] NSS, 36. Another person who disobeys an unjust social norm is Pelotit, daughter of Lot, a midrashic character whose death was the catalyst for the destruction of the city. See NSB, 173–175.

[34] NSS, 36 and see also SD, 252–253.

[35] NSV, 448. Intellect is not a guarantee of morality; on the contrary, it can lead to ever more devilish and refined means of extermination (see NSB, 283).

[36] SD, 309. See Yedgar, "Ahrayut," 398, 402–403.

[37] "Ahrayut," 399.

For by the very act of not protesting, not raising your voice in dissent, not marking out dangerous spots, the responsibility for the evil devolves now upon you, and you have transgressed the prohibition of "You shall not put a stumbling block before the blind" (Leviticus 19:14).[38]

Nehama approvingly quoted Alshech to the effect that a Jew is "physically unable" to ignore lost property that needs returning (SD, 214); and of course one cannot stand by a widow's or orphan's cry of distress.[39] The lesson also comes through in the laws of the "beheaded heifer." When the corpse of a murder victim is discovered outside a city, the Torah instructs that the respected elders of the community must make the following declaration (Deuteronomy 21:7):

Our hands have not shed this blood, neither have our eyes seen it.

This is astonishing. Who accuses these pillars of society of murder? The equivalent today would be to gather the mayor, the police chief, the university deans and the chief rabbis to collectively deny that they are murderers. Many commentators explain the declaration to mean that all proper precautions of hospitality were taken by the guardians of the city towards those within its gates, and they were not accessories at any level to the crime. Nehama follows these lines, but expands them to include all citizens:

The concept of "bloodshed" is interpreted here in a very broad manner to include even indirect responsibility for the death of a human being through neglect.... The public as a whole... are all responsible. (SD, 207)

Responsibility for wrongdoing does not only lie with the perpetrator himself and even with the accessory. Lack of proper care and attention are also criminal. Whoever keeps to his own quiet corner and refuses to have anything to do with the "evil world," protecting his own self as much as possible; who observes oppression and violence but does not stir a finger in protest, cannot proclaim with a clear conscience that "our hands have not shed this blood.[40]

Nehama emphasized that God was willing to save the corrupt city of Sodom only if there were fifty righteous people *"within* the city," i.e.

occupied, involved and exerting their influence on the public life of the city – its business transactions, etc.,... but if these individuals hide themselves away and live their lives of righteousness in seclusion, they

---

[38] *IHBV*, 257; compare *NSV*, 311.
[39] See her essay "I Will Surely Hear His Cry," *NSS*, 390–401.
[40] Combination of *IBD*, 198, and *SD*, 208.

will – perhaps – save themselves, but their merit will certainly not protect the entire city.[41]

There is no mystical mechanism causing God's protection; it comes through the cumulative effect of individuals' proactive work for the good. For this reason, one person's effort should not be underestimated – when joined to the collective, it contributes exponentially.[42] Another lesson here is that a city that prevents its righteous people from being active is worthy of condemnation. Implied in this lesson, as Yedgar notes, is criticism of those religious people who are concerned only for their own religiosity, disregarding the collective – the "saint in a fur coat," who forgets that others are cold.[43] Even God Himself is not immune to claims of "idly standing by" while injustice prospers![44]

℞ ℥

Yet human nature is wired to avoid accepting responsibility whenever possible, by rationalizing and making excuses, be they theological or practical.[45] Nehama detested such behavior. Once, when student after student made an excuse for not having done her homework, Nehama said sharply that they reminded her of a secretary she had once encountered who said, "I'm not going to do this today; *lo ba li* (I just don't feel like it)." Nehama hated the "*lo ba li*" mentality; feelings are not an excuse to shrug off one's duty:

> The fulfillment of Jewish precepts, even the performing of good works, is not a purely personal hobby, determined by individual whim and fancy. The Torah has laid down clear rules defining our duties and a scale of priority in their performance. (*NSS*, 409)

Nehama's *Studies* often deal with the attempt to shirk responsibility and the Torah's disapproval of it.[46] As soon as there were humans, there were excuses. Adam blames Eve; Eve accuses the snake. Adam then tries to escape his reckoning with God. Nehama quotes Buber's words:

> Adam hides so that he will not have to give an accounting, so as to avoid taking responsibility for his life. Thus does every person hide, for every person is Adam, is caught up in Adam's situation… and as he repeatedly hides "from God" he gets more and more caught up in deceit. (*LP*, 218)

---

[41] Combination of *IBB*, 132 and *NSB*, 186.
[42] See also *NSV*, 583–584.
[43] Yedgar, "*Ahrayut*," 393.
[44] *NSS*, 391. Nehama quotes the Netziv's understanding of Isaiah.
[45] See *NSB*, 524, already quoted in full on page 337 above.
[46] *IBB*, 37; see Yedgar, "*Ahrayut*," 379.

Along comes Cain; and like father, like son. Nehama paraphrased the midrashic list of Cain's assorted excuses for Abel's murder as follows:

> Was I to blame? Does the responsibility devolve on me? *You* were to blame for creating me thus, with such base instincts – for not saving me, for giving me cause to envy him, for not saving him from my clutches. Where were Your providence, Your miracles and wonders? You are to blame for steering my fate, for it was due to all the troubles and traumas I have experienced that I did what I did.[47]

Nevertheless, Cain was fully responsible for his actions. Nehama taught this lesson through the verse in Genesis 4:1:

> And Adam knew Eve his wife; and she conceived, and bore Cain, and said, I have acquired a man from the Lord.

There Rashi comments:

> *And Adam knew.* Already before the events related above [took place] – before he sinned and was driven out of the Garden of Eden; thus too the conception and birth [of Cain, had also already taken place before the expulsion]. Had the verse said *va-yeda ha-Adam*, the implication would have been that he had children [only] after he was expelled.

Rashi seems to be making a simple grammatical point, but Nehama's *forte* was in revealing the crucial lessons in small details. Had Cain been conceived after the banishment from Eden, he would have been born into a world where sin was a given – and then small wonder if he too sinned. But if he was conceived beforehand, then he had no excuse, and this was Rashi's message, Nehama explained.[48]

Cain should have taken ownership of his misdeed,[49] and he should have repented. God tries to empower him to do this:

---

[47] Combination of *IBB*, 36 and *NSB*, 50.

[48] See Nehama Leibowitz and Moshe Ahrend, *Perush Rashi la-Torah: iyunim be-shitato*, Open University, 1990, 1, 129. Incidentally, for Nehama this Rashi also proves that sexuality existed in Eden, before the sin. She contrasted this view with Christian notions of "original sin" (*ibid.* 128–129). Once, a priest studying with Nehama informed her of the Christian view that Adam and Eve had sexual relations only after the exile from Eden. When asked, he did, however, admit that Rashi's grammatical point made sense. Nehama queried why he then championed the other interpretation, and he replied with one word: Dogma. Catholics believe implicitly in the innate sinfulness of sex. (Some indeed argue that Rashi's interpretation was driven by the polemic with Christianity, but Nehama never accepted these types of claims. See for example *LP*, 2, and also pages 467–468 below.)

[49] Though Nehama does not directly connect it to Cain, she writes that the prohibition against murder "was not explicitly transmitted to Adam, since the image of God in which he was created provided in itself sufficient warrant for such a prohibition," but was given explicitly to Noah after the deluge (*NSB*, 79).

> Thus the Torah from its outset emphasizes for us a person's ability to conquer his evil inclinations before the deed, and to rectify wrongs afterwards, to repent and to get up again after a fall. God tells Cain a truly great thing – He has given him the strength and power to be a true ruler. (*IBB*, 31)

In fact, repentance is another theme appearing in many *Studies*. Nehama believed that repentance is entirely attainable, providing one's will is bent to the task.[50] In general, she was not terribly interested in punishments; the sin, the deviation from God's will, is the source of the real pain.[51]

ֿ࿏ ⊛

Escape from responsibility comes in many guises. A person can easily cite any number of excuses, such as "technical reasons," "necessity" or "reasons beyond my control" (*SD*, 226). Psychological explanations are proffered, as if good intentions atone for everything, but they are unacceptable. Moses, when pleading for the Israelites before God, tries to find any justification he can for their poor behavior. Yet when he turns to rebuking the people directly, he

> does not seek psychological factors in extenuation of their sins and in understanding the motives that give rise to them. (*SD*, 23)

Similarly, no matter how humiliated and envious Sarah felt of Hagar, she was not vindicated in dealing with her so harshly:

> Our commentators find no excuses to condone Sarah's behavior, look for no psychological explanations in extenuation of her deeds. (*NSB*, 156)

Escape from responsibility is a very powerful mechanism. It even made the Israelites nostalgic for their time in bondage:

> In Egypt they had admittedly been slaves, borne down by suffering and misfortune, but they had, at least, been free, like all slaves, from one thing: from responsibility for their own destiny. (*NSS*, 265)

The sin of the spies had similar causes. In their slave mentality, and fearful of governing themselves, the spies preferred to relinquish their decisions and fate to someone else (*SBM*, 146). For their part, the Israelites tried to blame the spies; but Nehama taught that a people cannot pass the buck to its leaders, for it is their choice to follow them.[52] As she notes elsewhere:

---

[50] See Ben-Sasson, "*Ha-teshuvah*," 360 and *passim*.
[51] See *NSB*, 24, and Ben-Sasson, "*Ha-teshuvah*," 359.
[52] *SD*, 20–21. See Yedgar's discussion, "*Ahrayut*," 382–384.

Each individual has ultimately to be his own leader, responsible for his every action and not just a cog in the vast machine called society. (*SD*, 24)

No one else can be held at fault for one's sins, not even a manipulative enemy:

Though it was Balaam who instigated the daughters of Midian to strike a blow at the purity of Jewish family life, though he was the evil genius who thought out the plan, the moral responsibility ultimately rested on the Israelites themselves. They were guilty. (*SBM*, 377)

Also:

But the Almighty metes out punishment to every human being for his actions…. The existence of a provocateur does not absolve the subject of the provocation from responsibility. (*SD*, 22)

Technology and tools are sometimes blamed for the evil in this world, but this is a fallacy, argues Nehama, for it is the humans who wield them who are responsible. Objects have no independently good or bad uses. Humans have been endowed with wisdom and craftsmanship to produce these implements; whether they will be used as a blessing or a curse is entirely up to them (*SD*, 157). Technological advance may cause moral degeneration and hubris;[53] yet doing away with them is not an option, for God explicitly commanded progress. Nehama here once again rejects an "either-this-or-that" viewpoint – neither an Amish, deliberately old-fashioned perspective, nor today's techno-craziness involving blind acquisition of every new gadget; but rather a balanced use of technology, informed by the religious outlook.[54]

Even religion is no guarantee of right living, for faith in God itself may be used to avoid responsibility:

We shall misunderstand… if we imagine that wholehearted devotion to God rules out human effort and initiative…. "If a man has worked he is blessed; if not, he is not blessed." (*SD*, 185–186)

We cannot leave it to God to put our society in order; we must do that for ourselves. The fact that God is the only true judge does not imply that all justice may be left to Him. On the contrary, the point is to emulate Him (*SD*, 165). Divine Providence does not cancel out autonomy:

---

[53] See her remarks in the context of the Tower of Babel (*NSB*, 102); and, from her letter to Bergman: "viewing the soul as a fragment of the living God (which for them is not an expression of hubris and technological accomplishment, but rather of a feeling of immense responsibility not to destroy that image)" (*PN*, 660).

[54] See Yedgar, "*Ahrayut*," 388.

Divine instruction… [guides] man to the right path, lest he stumble and fall. However, the choice remains with man, and whoever wishes to stray, will do so.[55]

Nehama teaches this message in discussing the Joseph story:

On the surface, the actors in the story make their own way in life, set in motion their own plans… in fact, however, it transpires that it is Divine Providence which is carrying out, through mankind, its own predestined plan…. The Torah points out that Joseph's own diligence availed him not. Only the predestined decree of God working behind the scenes led him to his brothers.[56]

Therefore, Nehama emphasized, Joseph's brothers remained guilty of their crimes against him even if their actions ultimately led to Divinely ordained emigration to Egypt.[57]

Responsibility and Holiness

All this brings us to Nehama's unusual conceptions of holiness. For her, the roots of holiness lie in autonomy and responsibility, via chosenness. True, responsibility for the world was delegated not to the first Jew but to the first human, created in God's image. But it is particularly required of the Jews, and hence they were chosen. For Nehama, being chosen means being entrusted with extra obligations.[58] It does not, as many think, automatically confer a higher spiritual level. Rather, this depends on one's deeds:

Man's natural qualities do not determine his spiritual status, nor do the talents bestowed upon him from the Above. Even the supreme gift of

---

[55] *NSV*, 96. Also: "The righteous man who has been guaranteed Divine protection does not make the mistake of regarding his favorable destiny assured" (*NSB*, 353). And of Nathan the Prophet and King David: "They did not regard prophecy as freeing them from action, absolving them of responsibility for their destiny. On the contrary, they accepted the promise of God as obligating them to work and strive to the best of their ability and understanding" (*NSB*, 255). See also "Gifts, Prayer and Battle" (*NSB*, 359–365) and *NSB*, 459.

[56] *NSB*, 394 and 397. The entire essay is devoted to this theme ("Providence's Mystery Man," *ibid.*, 394–399). Similarly *NSB*, 498.

[57] For more discussion see Yedgar, "*Ahrayut*," 402; Rosenak, "*Parashat Mi-ketz*," 138–139.

[58] See Seforno on Exodus 19:5–6, mentioned by Nehama in worksheet for *Yitro*, 5710. See discussion in Frankel *Iyun*, 100; worksheet for *Yitro*, 5715 (cited in Reiner and Peerless, *Haggadat*, 61) and *NSV*, 131.

prophecy cannot turn him into a saint against his will or without his own endeavors.[59]

Nehama agreed with Rashi's opinion, that in buying the birthright from his brother, Jacob acquired not perks but responsibilities (*LP*, 112–114). Furthermore, when the Israelites were taken out of Egypt,

> not a privilege but a responsibility awaited them. Not so much as a reward for past good behavior but as a prelude to their future destiny. (*NSS*, 71)

Even the land of Israel is not a free gift:

> Israel is aware that this land was granted to it by the Almighty. This is not just a matter of history but involves for Israel a moral obligation, the responsibility to observe a particular way of life in that land. (*SBM*, 401)

In all of the above, chosenness is identified with responsibility. Moving to holiness, we find that the Torah itself makes the connection between chosenness and holiness (Exodus 19:5–6). Nehama took the next logical step, connecting holiness with responsibility. Thus, Korah's faction erred in that

> they interpreted the mission of holiness, the role of the "chosen people" with which they had been charged by God, in the sense of conferring upon them superiority and privilege rather than as constituting a call to shoulder extra duties and responsibilities. (*SBM*, 183)

In other words, as Yedgar demonstrates,[60] Nehama is reading the command of "You shall be holy" (Leviticus 19:2) as "You shall be responsible" – to actualize the image of God, to govern the world, civilize it and improve its moral (and not religious or ritualistic!) state,

> to be just, kind to the weak, to respect one's parents and the aged, be compassionate, not bear a grudge, not to oppress and rob. (*NSV*, 260)

Nehama later writes:

> Thus each person's responsibility extends to the whole world. The phrase "Nor shalt thou put a stumbling block before the blind" reflects the essence of our Portion which requires us to be holy. (*NSV*, 308)

This teaching was radical in two ways. Firstly, though Nehama never says this explicitly, one logical extrapolation would be that a righteous, proactive

---

[59] *SBM*, 326. For more of Nehama's views on chosenness see "The Kindness of Thy Youth," *SBM*, 347–356, particularly "Israel was passive. They were not chosen for their own goodness or merit" (354).
[60] Yedgar, "*Ahrayut*," 389.

non-Jew is more holy than a passive, self-absorbed Jew. And secondly, this definition of holiness, as involvement in, and improving of, the world, stands in direct contrast to the prevalent Jewish conception of holiness. This, as promoted by the Sages and Rashi and many others, is defined as separation from the world, isolation from sinful society, sexual depravity and vanity of all types.[61] Nehama does feature a version of this definition, in her essay "You shall be holy," following Ramban's interpretation of this command as referring to "a general exhortation of restraint also in things permitted."[62] But she was also willing to entertain several other definitions of holiness;[63] and amongst them the "holiness equals responsibility" lesson comes through strongly in several statements indicating that she did not believe in separation from society, only from sin:

> Our Torah demands service of God not by distancing ourselves from the noise and turbulence of life, in escaping from the earthy and material, but rather through the sanctification of the earthy, the tangible, the mundane, through the meticulous commandments and measures.... Our Torah does not demand... fleeing from world, society and family, but on the contrary obliges us to apply its principles throughout the breadth of life in its most expanded form, to instill holiness into daily life at home, in the field, family life, work and rest. (*IBBM*, 105)

Religion pulls us into the world, not away from it,[64] and negation of the world is not desirable. In discussing the case of the Nazirite, who abstains from earthly pleasures to achieve purification, Nehama is chiefly interested in the sin-offering he must bring at the end of his period of abstinence. Taking on ascetic vows means neglecting other important obligations, hence the need for a sin-offering.[65] As Yedgar remarks, this viewpoint puts Nehama in a polemical position vis-à-vis those Jews who detach from the world, desiring to improving the world through religion while leaving the

---

[61] See, for example, the *Sifra, Kedoshim* 1: "You shall be holy – [this means] you shall be separate."

[62] Here she includes Eibeschütz's opinion on "You shall be holy" – that this commandment implies involvement within society – only in her questions at the end of her essay, instead of in the body, where Ramban's definition is central (*NSV*, 268–269).

[63] For example in terms of agricultural work and socialist values (*IHBV*, 217–220) or relating to idol worship, which, by contradicting the Divine mandate of "Be holy as I the Lord am holy," prevents the Israelites from feeling the Divine image in their hearts (*NSS*, 634).

[64] See the quote beginning, "Jacob's communion with his Creator..." on page 308 above.

[65] "Every extra effort, every further obligation that a person takes upon himself, is always at the expense of fulfilling other obligations (for a person's strength, time, energy and abilities are forever limited)" (*IBBM*, 75).

civilizing role to non-Jews.[66] Disagreement on this point is a pivotal axis defining different Jewish camps to this day.[67]

Conclusion

This chapter has illustrated how powerful Nehama's value system appears when it is drawn out of her writings and put into concentrated form, even if she herself never did so, preferring to stay close to the text. The effect becomes even stronger when we note the motif of responsibility ever-present in her own life: From her demand that all serve in the army and fulfill their obligations to the State, to her principle never to leave Israel so as not to legitimize the Diaspora; to her charitable deeds and tremendous dedication to teaching Torah. Her educational philosophy was also one that charged her students to take responsibility for their own intellects and choices.

Perhaps it would not be an exaggeration to suggest that if Rabbi J.D. Soloveitchik speaks of Jewish religious typologies such as "Halachic Man," "Majestic Man" and "Religious Man," we can term the archetype emerging from Nehama's work and her life "Responsible Man."[68]

---

[66] Yedgar, "*Ahrayut*," 405.

[67] In "Point-Counterpoint," *Jerusalem Post*, June 28, 2002, Itamar Marcus argues that Judaism desires the rectification of the world, while Jonathan Rosenblum writes: "All mankind is commanded to subjugate the world; the Jewish people alone were given the unique task of studying the Torah. Though we recite a blessing over a great gentile scientist, we would not do so over even the greatest Jewish scientist, such as Einstein, for his principle purpose in life is the attainment of Torah, not secular, knowledge."

[68] R. Soloveitchik himself had a "profound understanding" of "man's tendency to escape from himself," as Nehama notes (*NSV*, 225). Rabbi Jonathan Sacks also describes the Jewish responsible religious personality in *To Heal a Fractured World: The Ethics of Responsibility*, Schocken, 2005.

PART III

METHODOLOGY

In the next six chapters, we will examine the methodological underpinnings to Nehama's work, asking: "With what materials did she work? How did she organize them? What was her methodology? What beliefs underpin all these issues?"

There were three foundations to Nehama's approach:

1) Use of Jewish commentators from a wide variety of periods and outlooks – though primarily traditional ones – while employing innovative and analytical methodology to extract the most benefit from their insights.

2) An exacting and literary reading of the Tanach text, generally in pre-selected units rather than whole books.

3) Deriving educational messages from the Torah and its commentaries. Tensions exist between these three foundations, creating differences of opinion in observers of her work regarding questions such as whether Nehama was pluralistic or not, a Bible scholar or not; and these will be dealt with too.

Since a large part of Nehama's work involved quoting, analyzing and comparing commentaries, this seems a good place to start.

CHAPTER 17

COMMENTARIES:
"LIGHTING UP THE TORAH"

NEHAMA USED TO SAY, "All of life is *parshanut*." Certainly, all of *her* life was *parshanut* and *parshanim*. This was the arena in which her work made the most impact. Her work was groundbreaking in two opposite directions at once, overturning dismissive attitudes at both ends of the religious spectrum. At one extreme lay the yeshivah world. There, the very same Talmud commentators who were most beloved and revered had their writings on Tanach treated with indifference – or, at best, studied for their emotional, rather than intellectual, significance. An apocryphal story tells of a man learning Rashi with his son. Arriving at a somewhat technical comment, he skipped over it. "But what does it say?" insisted the child. His father declared: "It says you have to be a good Jew! That's what Rashi is always saying!" Nehama combated this attitude her entire life. Once she was discussing Rashi on the Torah with a *rosh yeshivah*, when he remarked: 'Well, Rashi on *Humash* is *stam geredt*!" (casual/imprecise speech, not worth examining closely). Nehama wondered how someone who taught entire lessons on just one of Rashi's talmudic comments could gloss so cursorily over Rashi's Torah interpretation.

At the other end of the spectrum, equally uninterested in *parshanut* though for different reasons, lay the secular Israeli camp. For many decades even before the State, both Tanach and Hebrew language had been strongly emphasized in certain Jewish circles.[1] But at the time Nehama began teaching, the secular Zionists had taken this trend to an extreme, deeming these two subjects the sole valuable elements from Jewish tradition and granting them an honorable place in early gymnasia school curriculum. The Tanach was read as a guidebook to human nature and also to the flora, fauna and topography of Israel. It was used to imbue young immigrants with love of their homeland and a sense of entitlement to it, and also served as a manifesto for the spread of Socialist values.[2]

---

[1] Pinchas Sandler, *Ha-be'ur la-Torah shel Moshe Mendelssohn ve-siyato*, Jerusalem: Reuven Mass, 5754, 5–6. This was true for Sephardic Jews, the Maharal, and those who studied Bible in Mendelssohn's generation.

[2] From Anita Shapira, *Yehudim hadashim, Yehudim yeshanim*, 262.

Nehama shared this passion for Tanach and Hebrew, though as secular Israeli society gradually moved towards critical, universal and demythologizing approaches to Tanach, she had less and less in common with it.[3] But she was not willing to skip almost two thousand years of rabbinic literature along the way. No amount of scientifically up-to date interpretations could replace the classic Jewish commentaries.[4] She fiercely defended the commentators from accusations of narrow horizons, demanding of Professor Bergman:

> How can you call intolerant the approach of such saintly giants as Ramban and his companions, who delve into Divine secrets, viewing the soul as a fragment of the living God…? (PN, 660)

Nehama worked to counter David Ben-Gurion's statement that "the Bible shines with its own light."[5] Nothing, she contended, shines without being lit by some source – in this case, the commentaries.[6] The commentaries were not intended to be studied on their own, but alongside the Tanach, so as illuminate it, she believed.

ॐ ॐ

But if the commentaries were the spotlight, Nehama was the electrical power source. She brought them to life for those who found them obscure. Through her, their interpretations lit up the Tanach and also the eyes of those who studied it. This, in a nutshell, was Nehama's life's work. She understood that familiarity and identification with Jewish intellectual giants might go a long way to inculcate faith.[7] So she took an age-old Jewish idea, expressed by R. Yose ben Yoezer's recommendation,[8]

> Let your house be a meeting-place for the wise, sit in the dust at their feet and drink up their words thirstily,

and expanded it to include sages who had passed from the world, leaving a legacy of writings. Students found themselves spending an otherworldly hour "around the table" with rabbis and sages of centuries past, listening to their debates with each other – whether existing debates, or those set up by Nehama – and joining in themselves. Dr. Gabriel Cohn notes that in this, Nehama replicated in the realm of Bible what R. Soloveitchik describes as occurring in his Talmud study, namely the vital and personal experience of

---

[3] Yedgar, "*Parshanut*," 107.

[4] Ahrend "*Mi-toch*," 38.

[5] In his book "*Iyunim be-Tanach*," Tel Aviv: Am Oved:, 1969, 49. See the entire letter, entitled "*Ha-Tanach zore'ah be-or atzmo*," Ibid., 41–49.

[6] Ahrend, "*Mi-toch*," 35.

[7] Ahrend, "*Mi-toch*," 37.

[8] *Ethics of the Fathers*, 1:4.

generations of talmudic commentators coming together simultaneously to debate around his table.[9] "This experience is part of what has always drawn Jews to Talmud," says Cohn. "You sense how the room is filled with these great personalities; and every student becomes a partner in discussion with these renowned exegetes." As Nehama writes:

> What have we moderns to contribute to this debate between the commentators and expositors of a bygone era? (*NSB*, 349)

She hoped that time spent in such company would go a long way to prevent the watering down of Jewish spiritual life, and combat the powerful bombardment of negative stimuli that is part of modern life.

Methodology

Nehama's most famous question was "*Ma kasheh le-Rashi?* – What's troubling Rashi?" She asked it consistently from her early years,[10] finding it much more useful than "What does Rashi say?" – a question that often elicits a spitback response with no true comprehension. The question "What's paining Rashi?" had long featured within the *Heder* system;[11] but in Nehama's hands it became a real tool, an overture for a nuanced examination of the verse. Her opening salvo at the beginning of every course was: "We're not going to study *what* Rashi said, but *why* he said it." To apply this to every verse was something that even Rashi's numerous super-commentaries had never attempted. Dr. Avigdor Bonchek, who authored a series entitled *What's Bothering Rashi?*[12] writes:

> Were it not for Nehama's method to read every word of Rashi's meticulously, we would not ask the questions we ask or discover what we have. Her approach to understanding Rashi is a new one.[13]

"*Ma kasheh le-Rashi?*" can also be translated as "What's Rashi's difficulty?" and over the years people nicknamed Nehama "Mrs. Difficulty" because she asked this question so frequently. Some also quipped: "Nehama makes a living with difficulty!"[14] The reason why Nehama asked this question so often, and not just about Rashi, was due to her basic premise that the commentators did not write to give over information, to educate, or simply because they liked the sound of their own voices. They were actually

---

[9] Cohn, "*Ma ahavti*," 26, n. 2, referencing Soloveitchik, *Ish ha-halachah*, Jerusalem: 5749, 232.

[10] See for example in her article *Darkei*, 6.

[11] Hamiel, "*Morat*."

[12] Jerusalem: Feldheim, 2000–2001, 2004.

[13] Bonchek, "*Darko*," 147.

[14] Ben-Sasson, "*Ha-teshuvah*," 357.

responding to irregularities within the text. Nehama's goal was to discover those irregularities:

> Where there is an explanation, there has to be a difficulty! And it is this that I need to discover, first and foremost![15]

She taught the difference between a question, whose answer is mere information, and a difficulty, which requires an explanation. A difficulty is a contradiction between our expectations of the text (for example that it be grammatically, theologically or philosophically consistent) and what is actually written. Judy Klitsner: "She loved to quote some non-Jewish scholar whom I never heard her mention by name, who said, 'To find and elaborate on the question, that is the question.'"[16] Nehama trained students to differentiate between questions that inhere in the text, and those that inhere in the reader and might be irrelevant. She illustrated this point with a quote from *Macbeth* (Act I, scene VII) where Lady Macbeth says,

> I have given suck, and know
>
> How tender 'tis to love the babe that milks me.

Here it is valid to ask why Shakespeare used this particular expression or wording, but not how many children Lady Macbeth had.[17] True difficulties derive from the world of the text, and it was these to which the commentators were responding:

> The commentaries are not extraneous or decorative, but they reflect their appellation: they help us to understand in depth the chapter, the verse, the issue and the idea. They aid us in resolving difficulties arising when we study Torah, and most of all in opening our eyes to notice the difficulties, irregularities, deviations and contradictions which the casual reader would not notice.[18]

Nehama spent much time training students to pinpoint the difficulty behind the explanations. She particularly liked to lay out two or more commentaries side by side so that students could easily compare them, evaluating each interpretation for its strengths and weaknesses in dealing with the difficulty and choosing the one closest to the *peshat*, in their

---

[15] *PN*, 679. However, this did not apply though when she did literary analysis, which does not require a difficulty in the verse, deriving meaning from its very structure. See Yedgar, "*Bein*," 68, n. 51.

[16] This may be Gadamer; see his article "Religious and Poetical Speaking," in *Myth, Symbol and Reality*, edited by Alan M. Olson, 87 (Notre Dame and London: 1980).

[17] Based on an essay by L.C. Knights named "How Many Children Had Lady Macbeth?" in *Explorations*, London: 1946, 15–54. Quoted in Weiss, *The Bible from Within*, 50.

[18] *LP*, introduction, first page (first half translated by Peerless, *To Study*, 33).

opinion.[19] In doing so, they were to be as specific as possible, avoiding general statements such as "This is very nice" or "This one does not speak to me." This process helped the students make sense of the profusion of commentaries on the same verse. Breaking the method down, it allowed the student to learn the following:[20]

That a difficulty existed.

That there were several possible answers.

That each interpreter's answer derived from a different reading of the text, to be understood within the larger system of his philosophy.

That each answer had its strong and weak points and could therefore be evaluated.

That one answer might be more convincing, and a case could be made for its superiority.

Nevertheless, a decision between the answers did not have to be made; all answers were legitimate, and often completed each other.

(Explanation was required when deciding between the final two positions.)

This kind of comparison was one of Nehama's main tools. She warned against implementing it mechanically; it must lead to understanding:

> Never allow the student to get away with knowing (and repeating on the exam) that "this commentator says this and that commentator says that." Rather, the different views must be studied within the comparison between the opinions, with discrimination between the similar and the different. (*LP*, 115)

A good question to avoid mechanical answering and get students thinking was: "Why does Rashi *not* explain like Ramban?" Or she would ask students to write down the difference in one word, or arrange the commentaries in groups.[21]

るる *ら*

Nehama's method has been compared to the rabbinical dialectics used to study the Talmud, and particularly the Brisk method, for which she was

---

[19] See *TI*, 146 onwards for some examples, and *ibid.*, 160 for her suggestions as to how to implement this technique. See also Sokolow, "*Samchut ve-atzma'ut: ha-hashva'a ve-ha-mahloket be-mishnatah shel Nehama,*" in *PN*, 302.

[20] For a good example of several of these principles see *NSS*, 248–255, and notably: "The difference in interpretation between the two commentators reflects a radical difference in approach, and is not mere accident or idle preference" (249), and "A closer study of the problem should convince us of the essential soundness of Rashi and the Midrash's approach and the inadequateness of Ibn Ezra's" (251).

[21] Sokolow, "*Samchut,*" 304, n. 29.

known to have an affinity.[22] The similarity lies in the sensitivity to nuance, in pointing out underlying assumptions hidden from the casual reader, and in comparing different commentaries, for a larger understanding of the debate.[23] Dr. Mira Ofran, Nehama's niece, has also noted the similarity to the "Sephardi speculation" methodology of the fifteenth century Spanish Talmudist, R. Isaac Campanton. In his book *Darchei ha-Talmud*, he emphasized, amongst other elements, active learning, in-depth study and finding the commentator's difficulty.[24] But Ofran is convinced that Nehama did not take her methodology from Campanton, for she only heard about his method three years before her death. Instead, both must have developed their somewhat similar techniques through intense study and knowledge of Torah.[25]

Such antecedents meant that Nehama's methodological mindset was not entirely foreign to her traditional audience. The Brisk school had introduced the notion that talmudic commentators possessed specific and consistent approaches to Halachah. One anecdote tells how R. Hayyim Soloveitchik of Brisk reportedly disputed the accuracy of a quoted Tosafot. When his amazed students asked whether he knew the entire Tosafot by heart, he answered: "No, but I know that the Tosafists could never have said that!" Nehama could often have done the same with the Bible interpreters. Through her extensive study, she gained an understanding of each

---

[22] See also page 207 above. Several people have made this point: Schoneveld, *The Bible*, 81; Strikovsky *Daf*, 5; Kagan "Review" quoting R. Mordechai Spiegelman. Kagan adds a qualification: "However, in Nechama's analyses, there is constant evaluation of each interpretation's faithfulness and congruence with the Holy written text. In Oral Law, by definition, there is no sacred inviolate text written by the same Divine Author."

[23] Shmuel Wygoda suggests that Nehama's idea to study commentators in tandem was derived from the "polyphony" (many voices) of the Talmud, whereby all opinions and ideas are presented, though not necessarily accepted (*VLN*). As Emmanuel Levinas says of the talmudic structure: "A valid thesis is never effaced, but remains as one of the poles of a thought that circulates between it and the opposite pole" (E. Levinas, *Difficile Liberté*, 112. See ghansel.free.fr/wygoda.html for Wygoda's article on this topic). Warren Zev Harvey compares Nehama's approach with the Platonic dialogues, where each figure represents a different standpoint and value, and has different difficulties. Nehama takes on Plato's role, in defining the difference between each thinker quoted, and Harvey even suggests that the close reader of Plato will ask "What is Socrates's difficulty?" (*VLN*). Although no direct influence is imputed, Nehama did in fact study Plato with Leo Strauss in Berlin (see page 32 above).

[24] *VLN*. Campanton (alternative spelling: Canpanton), like Nehama, evinced a precise approach to Rashi (Grossman "*Pulmus*," 188).

[25] Unlike Nehama, Campanton concentrated all his rules within one book. His method was largely neglected until a recent renewal of interest, notably Daniel Boyarin's book *Ha-iyun ha-sepharadi: le-parshanut ha-talmud shel megurashei sepharad (Sephardi Speculation: A Study in Methods of Talmudic Interpretation)*, Ben-Zvi Institute: 1989.

commentator's principles and outlook, and was able to explain what brought him to differ from, or even actively argue with, another's interpretation. She demonstrated how their differences of opinion were often not local, but rather conceptual disagreements, emerging from an overall philosophy:

> The clash between two opinions over the narrow ground of one verse may indicate a difference in outlook on fundamental concepts. (*TI*, 150)

Generally Nehama analyzed the commentaries while she was in the process of discussing a text. Only at university, with its demands for systematization, did she agree to leave the texts and isolate a commentator for a more across-the-board look at his approach. This did not come naturally to her. Her comprehensive book on Rashi's method, her only written work of its kind, was prepared for the Open University, and would likely never have been written on her own initiative.[26] Nehama also focused on Ibn Ezra during an entire year with her *Amitei Tzion* class of 5747 (1986–1987). This, however, was quite exceptional.

Nehama's favorite classic commentaries

The following, in chronological order, are some of the main pre-modern commentaries figuring in Nehama's work (her later influences will be discussed in coming chapters):

1. Translations

Nehama's doctorate was on translations, and she made extensive use of them: the classic Aramaic translations, the Septuagint, the Vulgate, five different English translations, and many German ones, including the Buber-Rosenzweig, which she respected, and had contributed to herself.[27] She liked to compare translations with each other, demonstrating that they were really interpretations; and she liked to point out the untranslatable nature of slang and idioms.

2. The talmudic sages

Nehama revered the Sages. Her study and teaching methods bear their mark – for example, in her preference for concrete examples over abstract

---

[26] Though not her own initiative, it was her own idea. Avraham Nissenbaum of the Open University recounts that Nehama was initially approached to teach a course on *parshanut*, but did not want to teach isolated segments, preferring something more encompassing and suitable to an academic framework, so she suggested a course on Rashi.

[27] See chapter 1 n. 58 and chapter 20 n. 50.

concepts.[28] Nehama used some of their rules in interpretation, and also extracted from their words other rules, not explicitly laid out by them.[29]

3. Rashi

There was no doubt about it: Nehama loved Rashi. Professor Martin Lockshin testifies: "She would read other commentaries, and then when she came to Rashi, her voice would change, she would read with pathos." In fact, it was once remarked that had Rashi been appointed to a professorship at university, he would have taken Nehama as his assistant. Nehama quoted Rashi hundreds of times in her work – according to Dr. Ruth Ben-Meir, he is mentioned 523 times in the worksheets alone. Her book on Rashi's approach ran to 618 pages. Nothing like it had been previously undertaken, and it established Rashi as a subject for general scholarly research.[30] Methodological comments about Rashi appear in her other works too, for example:

> We may take this opportunity to peep into Rashi's laboratory and follow his method of exegesis. (*NSB*, 281)

> As a rule Rashi never explains the same word twice in his commentary.[31]

Nehama possessed over one hundred books of supercommentaries on Rashi.[32] She observed that the more commentaries exist on a particular work, the more proof of its brilliance and complexity – as in Shakespeare's case. In particular she utilized the commentaries of R. Elijah Mizrahi (*Re'em*), R. Isaac Horowitz (*Be'er Yitzhak*), and the commentary by R. Judah Loew of Prague (the *Maharal*), called "*Gur Aryeh*."

Nehama raised the level of study of Rashi's commentary, while simultaneously making it accessible and beloved to the community of learners. Few, if any, read Rashi so closely, or exposed so many dimensions in his words. She underscored how Rashi could read one way for a five year old and a different way for a ninety-five year old, one way for a simple reader and another for an expert in Torah; writing earnestly of the need to

> eradicate the viewpoint that is so stupid and so prevalent – even amongst Torah scholars, to my astonishment – that Rashi is some light,

---

[28] See her words in *IHBV*, 254; *NSV*, 548–549.

[29] David Zafrany, "*Darkah shel Nehama Leibowitz z"l be-hava'at ma'amarei Hazal*," in *PN*, 77 and see his entire article for more on this topic.

[30] Cohn, "Nehama Leibowitz," 11.

[31] *NSB*, 434. See also the essay "Just Wait for Father's Death," *NSB*, 280–285, which in the Hebrew is subtitled "*Le-derech perusho shel Rashi*" (*IBB*, 197).

[32] In *TI*, 142, Nehama notes that two scholars collected a list of 143 and 133 supercommentaries to Rashi respectively.

popular commentary, a congenial grandmother figure who tells educational fables that elevate the soul. (*PN*, 676)

In particular Rashi's Torah commentary – which is not merely an aid to understand Scripture, but is in itself a part of the world of Torah, integrating the written and oral traditions – necessitates a special method of teaching. (*TI*, 39)

For Nehama, Rashi was the prince of commentators, in his depth, style and precision, balancing an interest in grammar and language with a love for Midrash:

This is what Rashi's supercommentaries meant by their statement "the entire Torah was laid out before him like a set table" i.e. just as an experienced housewife looks from above at the table laid out before her and grasps in a glance that in one place a plate is missing and in another there is an extra glass, so too Rashi viewed each verse in interaction with all the parallel and similar verses in the Torah, and noticed every discrepancy. (*LP*, 78)

But rather than heaping praises on Rashi, she recommended that teachers bring an example, in order to show the students his tremendous sensitivity to the text, and his brevity and precision of language (*LP*, 61–62). Rashi's words, like those of the Torah, were carefully chosen, Nehama believed. Rashi read the Torah text closely, and Nehama read Rashi closely, pulling out her magnifying glass where others passed blithely on. Her guiding principle, that some textual difficulty must exist behind a commentator's words, and that he is relating directly to the verse, was most pronounced in his case:

We may observe how Rashi is thoroughly consistent in his explanations to the text in different places, and does not interpret based on any preconceived ideas, but rather reflects the plain sense of the verses.[33]

Hard work was involved here, for Rashi does not usually spell out the difficulty.[34] But even when one of Rashi's comments appeared

singularly uninformative, merely paraphrasing the text (*SBM*, 251),

Nehama did not let it rest, but searched for its deeper meaning. She insisted:

Rashi would not have interposed such a comment without having a warrant in the text.[35]

Rashi generally explains difficult words, phrases or passages rather offering moral homilies.[36]

---

[33] Combination of *NSS*, 82 and *IHBS*, 64.
[34] See however *LP*, 69 for one example where he does do this.
[35] *SBM*, 311. See also *NSB*, 283 and 320; *LP*, 133.

Nehama applied these rules not only to Rashi's first explanation, but also to his additional explanations, under the assumption, shared by many of Rashi's supercommentaries, that he held his first explanation to be insufficient in some way.[37] She also argued that Rashi's citation of Aggadot and Midrashim, even fanciful ones ostensibly far from the plain meaning, were also spurred by difficulties.[38] Similarly, there is significance to when exactly Rashi chooses to explain the meaning of a word, for he does not always do this on its first appearance in the Torah.[39]

Nehama did not demand unquestioning agreement with Rashi:

> It is not the teacher's job to try and justify Rashi's position; but it is important to show the students why Rashi nonetheless adopted it. (*LP*, 206)

Yet she almost never rejected Rashi's interpretations as implausible.[40] Such were her expectations of him that she expressed surprise when he did not notice something she herself had detected (*NSB*, 248). This was modest of Nehama, as in practice she was able to carry out types of interpretation that Rashi did not know of.

Nehama's persistent refrain "What's troubling Rashi?" was followed by the magical extraction before the eyes of her mystified students, like a rabbit from a hat, of some small detail lurking within the folds of the text that provided an answer. For example, in Genesis 18:9, Abraham's three visitors question him:

> And they said to him, "Where is Sarah your wife?" And he said, "Behold, in the tent."

Rashi comments there:

> "Behold, in the tent": She was modest.

---

[36] *NSV*, 284–285.

[37] See *LP*, 107 (in the name of "many of Rashi's supercommentaries" – she explains that Rashi is dissatisfied with *both* explanations when he brings two); and Amnon Shapira, "*Ha-im 'Davar Aher' be-Rashi meyatzeg shnei perushim alternativi'im o simultani'im,*" in *PN*, 277–279. He disagrees with Nehama on this issue.

[38] See *NSB*, 35, question 1, and also *NSV*, 473 question 2; *NSS*, 48, n. 2. *NSS*, 609.

[39] Bonchek "*Darko,*" 143. See for example *NSB*, 320, *NSS*, 680, *IBBM*, 30, question 3, and *LP*, 178. Nehama limited this principle to the Torah only, unwilling to commit to it absolutely in Rashi on Prophets and Writings (see *TI*, 136, n. 5). For further discussion of this topic see "Rashi's Criteria for Citing Midrashim," *TI*, 101–142 (this article first appeared in *IHBS*, 497–524).

[40] For some exceptions, see *IBB*, 103, n. 2, where Rashi's claim is in her words, "far from the subject and context of the verses"; *IBBM*, 89 – "Rashi's explanation is strange" and, more subtly, *SD*, 86.

Many perceived Rashi's statement as educational – an ode to female modesty. But Nehama, who denied that Rashi ever wrote purely educationally, asked as usual what was troubling him in this verse. Her answer: The language used. The word for "where" in this verse is "*ayeh*," as opposed to "*eyfoh*." "*Eyfoh*" is a request for information, while "*ayeh*" refers to "where" in the existential sense.[41] Hence, when God asks Adam "Where are you?" (*ayeka*) after he sinned, He is not inquiring as to Adam's whereabouts but rather as to his state of being.[42] "*Ayeh*" is also used to indicate surprise that the person is not present.[43] By using "*ayeh*," the visitors therefore are expressing surprise as to why Sarah is not outside with her husband, and asking where she is in an existential sense. Abraham's answer "She is in the tent" is therefore not simply a prosaic piece of information, but is interpreted by Rashi as an existential answer: She not outside with her husband where we might expect her to be, because she is modest.[44]

Many disagreed with Nehama on this point, that Rashi only brings something when relating to a difficulty.[45] Professor Moshe Ahrend, working with her on *Perush Rashi la-Torah: iyunim be-shitato* over the span of a decade, had a number of opportunities to try and persuade her that Rashi was both an interpreter *and* an educator, and that many so-called "difficulties" might be better termed "springboards for educational remarks." But in vain; Nehama would simply retort: "Call it what you like!"[46] Yet in one place she does write:

> When Rashi brings a Midrash… the "difficulty" in the verse is not a real one, more a hook upon which Rashi hangs the *derash*.[47]

---

[41] See *NSB*, 51, question 2.

[42] See *LP*, 217–218, quoting an essay by Buber.

[43] *LP*, 6. Thus, "Where (*Ayeh*) is the Lord?" (Jeremiah 2:8) expresses surprise at His withdrawal (*SBM*, 409–410).

[44] See Bonchek ("Professor Nehama," 19–20, n. 4). This also answers Nehama's question in *NSB*, 51 (question 2) regarding "Where is Abel your brother?"

[45] See Gottlieb, Isaac, "*Lama nismecha' be-ferush Rashi*," in *PN*, 149; and see his conclusions in *ibid.*, 174. Grossman argues that some educational and polemical agendas also informed Rashi's interpretations ("*Pulmus*," 187), as did Yonah Frankel (thanks to Dr. Gabriel Cohn for this information). See further Shmuel Pinchas Gelbard's citations of the opposition, such as Grossman, Touitou and others ("*Aggadah meyashevet mikra*" in *PN*, 178). Gelbard claims in his article to validate Nehama's position for the most part, but Hayyim Angel remarks: "It is specifically through the defense of Nehama's outlook by [Gelbard] that one can readily identify its shortcomings" ("Paradox," 115).

[46] Ahrend, interview. He also argued with her over Genesis 21:7 – she claimed that the unusual use of the word *milel* is a true difficulty, yet when he published an article with a different opinion ("*Perush Rashi la-Torah*," *Mahanayim* 3 [1992]: 92–109), she approved of it, he reports.

[47] N. Leibowitz, "*He'arot metodiyot le-limmud*," 492.

Lockshin: "I don't think that Nehama entirely believed that Rashi was always relating to a difficulty. I know that she taught and wrote this, but I also learned from Nehama that Rashi's first comment on each book of the Torah speaks in praise of Israel (i.e., is educational)." Moreover, on rare occasion, Nehama found herself unable to locate Rashi's difficulty. On one such occasion, noting that "Rashi's words are perplexing," she suggested omitting them from the lesson (*LP*, 27).

Nehama in no small measure resembled Rashi in her own approach and educational philosophy. Like Rashi, she proclaimed herself interested in the plain meaning of the verse, yet also brought Midrashim that were clearly not *peshat* but – many would argue – had some educational agenda.[48] Like Rashi too, she instigated a revolution inside a traditional package. Yedgar: "Why did Rashi, the great revolutionary, rely on the Sages so much? Rather than quoting their words selectively, as he does – changing words, suiting them to the context, citing certain Midrashim – he could have said it better in his own words. I think that Rashi intuited that his audience would reject the plain meaning if brought in his own words. Instead, he remained a link in the chain of tradition. Nehama, a university-educated woman in an Orthodox world, went through a similar process to Rashi. If you want your community to listen to you, you must speak in their language." This does not mean to imply anything artificial or manipulative about their approach; this language came naturally to both Rashi and Nehama, who were undoubtedly members of the communities that they wished to address. Many of the educational values that Rashi held dear were of major importance to Nehama too, including humility, responsibility for fellow Jews, the land of Israel, and avoiding gossip.[49] Additionally, both were uninterested in abstract philosophy, as can be seen by their (albeit very different) first comments on Genesis.

Nehama's partiality to Rashi was contagious. During one of Nehama's classes, Deena Nataf wrote her friend a note saying, "I hate Rashi." Yet she persevered, and today is a Torah teacher, "perhaps in no small measure because for Nehama he was the quintessential way to understand Torah.

---

[48] Erella Yedgar wrote an article entitled *"Ha-yesodot ha-ra'ayoni'im shel perush Rashi be-firkei ha-beriya"* (*Derech Efrata* 4 [5754]: 89–105), in which she demonstrated Rashi's educational agendas. Knowing of Nehama's strong feelings, she initially did not dare to show her article to her. But Nehama got wind of it and phoned Yedgar, demanding, "I heard you wrote an article! I want to read it!" Yedgar reports that Nehama afterwards said: "You convinced me."

[49] These values are brought in Grossman *"Pulmus,"* 200–204 as characterizing Rashi; the connection to Nehama is my own suggestion.

Now Rashi's my best friend." Rashi became a constant in some of Nehama's students' thoughts. One night, R. Yitshak Reiner even dreamt that he met Rashi. The next day, he told Nehama about his dream.

"What did he look like?" she asked.

He replied that he did not resemble his portrait.

"So how did you know that it was Rashi? What did he say?"

"He said, 'I'm Rashi.'"

Nehama then announced: "*Lo ra'ita* (You didn't see him)!" She was of course correct, because the real Rashi would have introduced himself not by his acronym Ra*SHI* (Rabbi *Sh*lomo Yitzhaki) but by his first name, Shlomo. R. Reiner later reflected that her questions probing his dream derived perhaps from a yearning for a certain kind of religious experience – she wanted to know if he had "really met Rashi," for she regretted not having such dreams herself. Similarly, he suggests that when Nehama read R. Soloveitchik's words describing God peering over his shoulder while he was learning, she was disappointed for not feeling the same way. R. Reiner points us to Nehama's words:

> This revelation... is not a means to an end... but simply a revelation or experience of Divine communion for its own sake, as a mark of grace and honour... an opportunity for the person so fortunate to be 'satisfied, when I awake with Thy likeness.' (*NSB*, 163)

Cohn, however, questions such an interpretation, for many students did feel a palpable sense of holiness in Nehama's classes. "Her personality and her method of study created for them a unique atmosphere of God's nearness, like the one described by R. Soloveitchik," he says.

4. Other commentators

We end with a brief survey of some of the other commentators Nehama utilized widely; the reader is referred to the footnoted articles for further study.

To begin with, Nehama highly admired Ramban (Nahmanides).[50] Second only to Rashi amongst the classical commentators, she pointed out his complexity and the principles of his method. He too was an expert at reading closely:

> We have seen from Ramban how a decision in a small grammatical point can have such all-important moral implications. The grammatical question cannot be divorced from that of content and idea. They are all

---

[50] See Ben-Meir, "*Le-darkei*," for an in-depth treatment of Nehama's approach to Ramban.

part and parcel of the teaching of Judaism called Torah, and require study. (*NSB*, 328)

While valuing Rashi's sparse language, she also esteemed Ramban's wordier and more complex commentary, spanning realms as diverse as theology, philosophy, psychology, and social comment.[51] She was partial to his disciplined thinking and his intensely rational belief in God.[52] She also liked the fact that

> unlike Rashi who gives a "localized" explanation – one confined to the point arising out of the actual text he is commenting on, Ramban often appends a "comprehensive" one which solves a number of difficulties that extend over a chapter or more. (*NSS*, 28)

Additionally, Ramban explains the Midrash in a way that Rashi does not.[53] Nehama also respected Ramban's integrity in defending Rashi even when he disagrees with him.

Another important commentator in Nehama's work was Rashbam.[54] However, she admired him less than she did his grandfather, Rashi. In fact, Lockshin discovered that her language indicates more objection to Rashbam's interpretations than to those of other commentators. For example:

> Apparently Rashbam, a literalist par excellence, veers far from the plain sense here. (*NSS*, 606)

This sentence is particularly damning for one who defines himself as devoted to the *peshat*. Rashbam's problem, according to Nehama, was that he associated the *peshat* with the literal meaning instead of the intended meaning. Lockshin also believes that she objected to Rashbam's mocking of his grandfather's explanations.

Nehama liked many other commentators. She was fond of Ibn Ezra for his word games and emphasis on language and poetry, and she knew some of his poems by heart. He too comes in for criticism, though, when he takes the text too literally, missing its point. She also loved to quote Maimonides, though he never wrote a systematic commentary on the Torah. She never tired of telling R. Yohanan Fried how she venerated Maimonides's brilliance and precision and even the literary side of his monumental halachic writings.

---

[51] Ben-Meir, "*Le-darkei*," 132. For some examples of Ramban's psychological analysis see *NSS*, 48, n. 4, and *NSS*, 79: "How appropriate do Ramban's words fit the picture psychologically!"

[52] Ahrend, "*Mi-toch*," 39.

[53] *IBB*, 115 – more clear than the English version (*NSB*, 160).

[54] See Elazar Touitou's article "*Bein peshuto*" for an in-depth treatment of Nehama's approach to Rashbam.

Additionally, she quoted extensively from traditional commentators such as Abravanel, the Netziv, Radak, Rabbenu Bachya, the *Akedat Yitzhak*, the *Or ha-Hayyim* and many others, as well as less traditional ones such as Martin Buber and Benno Jacob.[55]

This survey of Nehama's work with biblical commentaries has been rather brief. It should be supplemented by the many demonstrations of her use of them in the rest of this book.

---

[55] See Sokolow's *Mafte'ah* and Cohn, "*Ma ahavti*," 29, for more complete lists.

CHAPTER 18

PLURALISM WITHIN LIMITS:
THE FRUIT AND THE PEEL

IN THE CHAPTER on Nehama's pedagogy, we saw that many of her techniques fit well into the spirit of contemporary education, with its emphasis on individualism and pluralism. Today's students are encouraged to express their opinions and to create personal connections to the subject matter, while the teacher's role is to validate the students, not to critique them or guide them too strongly. In fact, a conversational style is adopted, with the text "sneaked" into the discourse.

Nehama's lesson partly conformed to this model, in its encouraging of maximum participation and lively discussion. Yet she also diverged from it sharply, in teaching with didactic rigor and unhesitatingly using a formula of positive and negative reinforcements. "Her grading system was very funny," remembers one student. "There was *yafeh* (nice) and *tov* (good). *Lo nachon* (not correct) meant you hadn't been paying attention; and if you got something wrong in class, she would get this tone of voice and say '*BICHLAL LO!* (totally incorrect!)' and you knew she wouldn't talk to you for the rest of class. It was really mortifying." Few educators in tune with today's trends would read a student's answers out in front of everyone and then declare, "That's completely wrong!" and some might well label Nehama's style authoritarian. Yet she herself would be repulsed by this term, detesting anything that smacked of indoctrination.[1]

In her multifaceted personality, Nehama encompassed simultaneously the openness of pluralism and the strictness of rigorous methods. This was true both of the *form* of her class – her pedagogical technique, and the *content* of her class – her approach to text. In both these realms, Dr. Marla Frankel's terminology helps us to examine the different ways in which Nehama approached her work. Frankel suggests that Nehama wore at least two teaching "hats," and that this granted her a large measure of flexibility, crucial to good education.[2] The first "hat," or role, is that of the *facilitator*.

---

[1] See Ahrend, "*Mi-toch*," 48.

[2] Frankel uses Michael Rosenak's educational theory as her organizing structure, including his terminology of the "deliberative-inductive" and "normative-ideational"

This kind of teacher steps back from the students, enables discussion, challenges them intellectually, and trains them in problem-solving. It is the process, not the solutions, that is important. The facilitator's religious focus is on existential, emotional dimensions rather than on enforcing norms and laws. The second "hat" belongs to the *pedagogue*. This teacher gives over a discourse or lecture, using rhetorical and analytical skills to answer his or her own questions instead of letting the students answer them.

In the first model, the individual student is important; in the second, it is the community and the content that matter as vehicles for belief and practice. These two broad roles (though obviously other models are possible)[3] will help us to organize what otherwise appears a confusing patchwork of contradictory elements. Through the opposite poles they represent, we will be able to shed light on the measure of pluralism in Nehama's work.

Sources

1. Nehama as facilitator vis-à-vis sources

Nehama embraced the facilitator role in being more student-focused than the majority of her Orthodox teaching peers. Moreover, one of the facilitator's aims is to help the student explore all the options, by creating a broad range of possible answers to choose from, and Nehama indeed believed in offering a diversity of interpretations. The method she invented, of presenting different commentaries side-by-side, was a true facilitator's technique. It activated the students, and also taught them that many options existed, and that their questions were not heretical. Nehama writes explicitly about these issues:

> It is important to include this opinion too so that the students will not assume that Rashi's explanation is the only one possible, and anyone who is bothered by it… is, so to speak, an utter heretic who has no part in the Torah of Moses. (*LP*, 188)

She makes an even stronger statement here:

> It is not our way (mine and yours) to say that only what is propounded in the Hebron Yeshivah, or by Rav Schach, or in the Malbim's commentary, is true and may be presented to the students. I believe it

---

approaches. For more on this, see Frankel, *Iyun*; Frankel "Teacher"; Frankel "*Ha-te'oriyah*," 438–439; and Deitcher, "Between," 8–9.

[3] Yedgar posits three models: the "Facilitator" who brings the student to a personal interpretation; the academically-oriented "Scholar" who puts across rules and a methodological approach; and the religious "Interpreter" who passes on the personal meaning of the text, thus including elements of preaching ("*Bein*," 65–67).

very important for the student to know that any doubts in his heart regarding the snake talking, or the ass, etc., do not constitute heresy – he is in very good company, and he can be a good Jew according to Maimonides's and Saadia's approaches, just as he may of course be a good Jew following the approaches of *Sefat Emet* or Habad.[4]

Nehama also legitimized the act of not choosing between commentators:

We do not ask the students, in their discussion, to decide between these two opinions and make a choice, but to understand each viewpoint and find supporting evidence for each in the Torah and in rabbinic sources, to appreciate the basis of each opinion and its implications. Studying conflicting interpretations therefore not only stimulates students by motivating them to argument and discussion; it can broaden their intellectual horizons…. (*TI*, 152)

Although this last aspect makes Nehama's approach appear highly pluralistic, in practice she often did not let the students get away without choosing. She was afraid that they might end up becoming lazy or hide behind relativism instead of using their critical faculties to determine the superior and inferior. In a parody of the statement, "These and those are the words of the living God," often cited as a basis for Jewish pluralistic approaches, Nehama was known to remark: "These and those means no learning!" She also observed, "When Ramban says of Rashi's explanation 'This is incorrect!' his intention is not 'You are also right'!"[5] She often encouraged her students to reduce the options and actively select the explanation closest to the *peshat*. Especially when the teacher is unsure which viewpoint is most valid, this is the time to get the students to argue the pros and cons and make a choice, she suggested (*TI*, 145).

Furthermore, she recommended that even the comparison method be used judiciously – that is to say, only on occasion, with more advanced classes,[6] and

where both opinions, both interpretations, have something to rely on and both are reasonable. (*TI*, 145)

On rare occasion she even skipped the evaluation stage entirely, bringing one source only, the one that sounded "most plausible" to her.[7] She explains:

---

[4] Letter to Aaronson, *PN*, 652. See also see *TI*, 2.

[5] Sokolow, "*Samchut*," 297.

[6] See, for example, N. Leibowitz, *Gilyonot le-iyun be-Sefer Yirmiyahu*, Department for Torah and Culture in the Diaspora: 5737, 81.

[7] See, for example, *SD*, 374, where she, unusually, gives us only the Gersonide's view.

The teacher can decide on his own which opinion he finds more acceptable and offer it to the class, without showing them the other possible explanations. The purpose of [this] approach is to study the verse as such. This saves time, and shortens the approach to topics that may be of greater importance than lengthy involvement with the verse under consideration. It all depends on the subject, the class and the needs at the time in question. (*TI*, 70)

Overall Nehama's method was pluralistic relative to her contemporaries and to the traditional approaches that preceded her. The Tosafists, for example, aimed to reconcile discrepancies, while Nehama loudly broadcasted them:

How wide indeed is the chasm that separates Maimonides's approach from Ramban's! (*SBM*, 56)

Nehama was criticized for teaching that many opinions may be equally legitimate. She was told that this was confusing, for students need to know that there is one truth only.[8] Such reservations were voiced for both educational and religious reasons. The educational concern was that students, especially children, could not easily grasp that multiple opinions could co-exist. Nehama once mentioned to a group of American Torah teachers that, since more than one correct answer exists, their role was simply to help their pupils understand each commentator's opinion. One teacher exclaimed: "Nehama, you don't know our students! They will *insist* we tell them who is correct!" She retorted: "We are not Catholics! We have no Pope to decide who is right!"[9] She liked to justify her position with an anecdote. She was once standing at the bus station, when suddenly there was a thunderclap. A child next to her exclaimed, "God's angry!" Dismissively, his friend explained that their kindergarten teacher had told them that it was all to do with the water in the finjans that the old women placed outside, which, when it evaporated, made rain. Nehama then turned to her class and asked who was right. She explained that actually, both could be right. The first child was answering the question of "Who?" and the second one "How?" Since these are two different questions, the two answers don't necessarily contradict.[10]

Professor Shalom Rosenberg, who was familiar with Nehama's work back from the days when he filled out her worksheets in Argentina, also argued with her, but for different educational reasons. Basing himself on the famous saying that "The Torah has seventy facets" (*Bamidbar Rabbah* 13:16),

---

[8] Ahrend, "*Ha-katuv*," 36, and "*Mi-toch*," 35, 48. See also page 337 above.
[9] Sokolow, "*Samchut*," 297.
[10] Moshe Yismach, conversation.

he claimed that each facet should be taught separately, even dogmatically, by a specific teacher. Only thus will students be able to truly appreciate that point and evaluate it suitably, whereas if all the opinions are cited by the same teacher, each will be only a partial representation.

There were also religious objections. It is true that in the yeshivah world, multi-source and indeed multi-generational discourse upon the Talmud constantly takes place; and perhaps, as mentioned, Nehama's innovatory work was even inspired by this model.[11] But yeshivah thinking draws sharp generational separations, between *Tannaim* and *Amoraim*, *Rishonim* and *Aharonim*, while Nehama granted equal status to early and later commentators.[12]

Even worse, she felt free to reject a commentator's words outright. The ultra-Orthodox daily, *Yated Neeman*, decried how "she judges what is good and what fit to dismiss."[13] Indeed, Nehama's language in rejecting rabbinical opinions could be quite brusque. Sometimes she praised the explanation before its dismissal:

> Alshech's explanation, ingenious though it is, is unacceptable. (*NSS*, 105)

> But with all its pointedness, the forgoing answer [of the *Or ha-Hayyim*] does not carry conviction.[14]

At other times she got straight to the point:

> In other words Abravanel misunderstood the text as did all the other commentators. (*NSB*, 567)

> Hizkuni's proposal is similarly unacceptable. (*NSS*, 94)

> This seems a far-fetched theory [of Malbim's]. (*NSV*, 332, n. 1).

> This is rather astounding [of R. Yaakov ben Asher, the *Rosh*]. (*NSV*, 427)

> A baffling answer is proffered by Abravanel.[15]

---

[11] See chapter 17 n. 22.

[12] R. Reinitz writes: "Her comparison of the *Rishonim* with the *Ahronim*, whether favorable or not, jars somewhat. But she sticks to her position: 'What is important is the *peshat* meaning of the text.' And we 'forgive' her for this too, for we know the integrity and love of truth that guide her" (*PN*, 679).

[13] "*Beit haroshet le-rabbanim*," *Yated Neeman*, May 1, 1987, *Musaf* section, 6. See pae 301 above.

[14] *NSS*, 125; in the Hebrew, "It does not seem convincing to us" (*IHBS*, 93).

[15] *NSV*, 437. See also "this explanation seems odd" (of Bekhor Shor, in *NSV*, 445). See her astonishment at the explanations by Ramban (*IHBV*, 379 and *NSV*, 477) and Abravanel (*IHBV*, 413 and *NSV*, 530), in each case rendered more tamely in the English. See also for examples of her rejection of Rashi's position, chapter 17 n. 40.

This confidence was due to Nehama's view of herself as taking her cue directly from the traditional commentators, who freely contradicted not only each other but also the Sages.[16] Oftentimes, far from attempting to reconcile their views with those of their predecessors, they set out to prove themselves right and the others wrong. Abravanel, for example,

> cavalierly rejects Rambam's explication as "very feeble" and Gersonides's as "tedious and far-fetched."(NSS, 473)

Arama is so astonished at one explanation of Ralbag's that he wonders if the latter had another version of Scriptures in front of him (NSS, 639). Ramban constantly rejected Rashi's interpretations. Hence, Nehama too allowed herself to fearlessly reject the interpretations of her predecessors.[17] Professor Yaakov Kagan writes in her defense:

> Nechama was one of the most competent scholars in this generation in her areas of expertise, Bible with commentaries, and is therefore entitled to voice her opinions. Let objection come from those who have taught as many students in as many varied contexts, over as many years and who have submitted their views to the learning public for scrutiny!... Infallible? Certainly not! But power of judgment and a sense of "connoisseurship"? These she possessed, and the reader is much enriched by their expression and through study of the analytic processes involved in selecting "the best."[18]

Her critics might respond to this that it was one thing for Nehama, with her level of expertise, to choose between answers, and quite another to permit and encourage teenagers to "crown winners" amongst the Jewish interpretative giants. Nehama did not accept such a view:

> Finally, a reply to the critics who complain that encouraging students to argue over and select commentaries does not educate them to maintain a correct attitude towards our teachers and masters who wrote such commentaries – Rashi, Nachmanides, etc.; and that further, it is

---

[16] See examples in Zafrany, "Darkah," 89.

[17] Although she does not quote the following words by the sixteenth-century commentator, R. Eliezer Ashkenazi, they seem particularly apt, and prove that her approach is not a new one: "We should learn from our predecessors. Just as they rejected some of the opinions of those who came before them, so we should do the same to them. Certainly not one author intended by writing his book to command those who followed, 'Accept my opinion!' but rather simply to state his own view, so that they might note it and choose for themselves. For through the gathering of many separate opinions, the truth will become manifest... and even if we make a mistake, this will not be a sin, for our intention is for the sake of heaven. On the contrary, we are guilty only if we abstain from searching out the depths of the Torah" (Ma'asei Hashem, Balak, chapter 31 at the end).

[18] Kagan, "A Review."

disrespectful for fifteen to sixteen-year-olds to judge them, accepting one and rejecting the other.

It seems to me, however, that if all this is done in the appropriate spirit, the spirit of serious in-depth analysis of the commentaries – and the purpose of this method is to train the student to analyze, and to prevent haste and superficiality – there is no disrespect. On the contrary, proper regard for scholars consists of studying in depth what they have written. Rashi, who was modest enough to say "I don't know," would certainly have approved if through studying and analysing his words students might, at times, come to prefer the explanation of his grandson (Rashbam), or even to agree with his critic, Ramban. If granting students "the right to vote" *vis-à-vis* the commentators strengthens their degree of attachment to Tanakh, which I am certain it will, the scholars can receive no greater respect than to have the Torah brought closer to its students as a direct result of what they wrote. The essential is that they should study Torah from all angles, search it out, choose interpretations and reject interpretations – provided that they engage in Torah out of love. (*TI*, 161)

She also says:

I emphasize this aim because students will come to realize that there is great – albeit not unlimited – leeway for any Jew to approach the Torah according to his own individual taste and outlook, without his being heretical.[19]

Nehama's approach was an empowering one. Cohn observes: "The student gained a place around the table together with the great Jewish minds, and a voice in the debate, and the atmosphere was one of seriousness." Nurit Fried experienced this empowerment directly. As a twelve-year-old, she had written on a test: "Here, Rashi gives a nice explanation." Her ultra-Orthodox teacher rebuked her: "Who are you to give grades to Rashi?" Only years later, when Fried met Nehama, was she able to lay this unpleasant memory to rest.

જી ન્જ

Besides her use of multiple sources, a further pluralistic aspect in Nehama's work lay in the type of sources she put at her students' disposal. In general she brought anything that she thought would be useful for interpretation,[20] and this included ideas from non-Orthodox Jews and the occasional non-Jew. Nehama adhered to Maimonides's dictum: "Accept the truth from

---

[19] N. Leibowitz, *Darkei*, 2. See also *TI*, 156–157.

[20] In her worksheets 5724–5727 she included *ta'amei ha-mikra*, the cantillation notes, as an interpretative tool (see Leah Himmelfarb, *Ha-zika she-bein parshanutah shel Nehama le-vein ta'amei ha-mikra*, in *PN*, 53; see also *ibid.*, 60).

whomever speaks it."[21] She welcomed universal sources of wisdom for their contribution to understanding. Her upbringing and her university years all reinforced her broad Orthodoxy. All of the well-known rabbis who studied in Berlin in contemporaneously with her – Rabbis Heschel, Hutner, Schneersohn and Soloveitchik – were more open to Western culture than were their communities of origin.[22] The Sages' motto, "Let the beauty of Japhet dwell in the tent of Shem,"[23] was embraced by many German Jews; and R. David Zevi Hoffmann, whom Nehama respected greatly, believed the Sages' intention here was to permit entry of all culture and learning – insofar as it ennobled humanity – into the houses of study.[24] Nehama indeed chose only sources that she believed ennobled humanity and advanced the love of the Torah.

Nehama enlisted non-Orthodox sources in two primary capacities: first, to generate a language and atmosphere more accessible to the modern, educated reader, whom she was anxious to convince of the Torah's profundity.[25] When Moshe Yismach, a religious student, asked Nehama why she must quote such sources in her lesson, she replied: "Look, the very mention of Ramban makes a person like you stand to attention, but not others. A Spanish commentator from seven hundred years ago? They dismiss him with a wave of their hand. But if I tell these students that Thomas Mann said something, and add that Ramban said it too, then they're convinced and say, 'You're right, you're right.'"

For example, in order to illustrate Maimonides's interpretation of Pharaoh's hardened heart – that it represented Pharaoh's descent into sin, to the point where free will was no longer available – Nehama quoted a passage from a favorite Shakespeare play, *Macbeth* (Act 3, Scene 11, line 55):

Things bad begun make strong themselves by ill.[26]

This was followed by the observations of a certain Shakespeare commentator:

---

[21] Maimonides, introduction to *Shemonah Perakim*. Maimonides quoted Aristotle liberally in his works, as did other commentators – Nehama quotes a passage from Arama where Aristotle is cited (*NSB*, 545).

[22] Dr. Shmuel Wygoda, *VLN*.

[23] Megillah 9b, based on Genesis 9:27.

[24] Hoffman, "Thora und Wissenschaft," *Jeschurun* 7 (1920): 498, quoted in Shapiro, *Between*, 29.

[25] Frankel, *Iyun*, 40.

[26] *NSS*, 160, n. 3; and *LP*, 170, n. 9. Nehama also writes: "The race of desire toward its objective, and precisely after the confident announcement of its attainment (even without man's diligent efforts) – is described with all its machinations by Shakespeare in *Macbeth*" (*TI*, 147).

Gradually he so hardens himself in the custom of evil that he becomes eventually incapable of altering the pattern in which his very being is fixed.[27]

Here, the external wisdom source is used to support a point already made by the traditional commentator (Maimonides). It serves a somewhat cosmetic function – what Professor Yaakov Kagan refers to as "a dash of color."[28]

This usage was relatively palatable even to conservative elements, who approved of the agenda to bring those distant from Judaism closer. However, Nehama's second agenda in bringing non-Orthodox sources was that of unearthing new layers of the Torah – and this was far more radical. It implied that people outside Orthodoxy can reveal dimensions in the Torah overlooked by traditional commentators, including such non-Jewish sources as *Fear and Trembling* by the Danish philosopher Søren Kierkegaard, who highlighted previously unplumbed aspects of Abraham's character;[29] and Thomas Mann's *Joseph and His Brothers*, which, in Nehama's opinion, succeeded in "illuminating the text with a great light."[30]

She also quoted widely from the work of such heterodox figures as Martin Buber,[31] Benno Jacob, Franz Rosenzweig and Umberto Cassuto – respectively, a non-Orthodox Jew, a Reform rabbi, a formerly secular returnee to Judaism, and an Orthodox rabbi who viewed the Torah as an amalgam of different sources. She bestowed compliments on these scholars, such as "Buber expresses the difference in his felicitous fashion,"[32] and quoted them abundantly. This was not done simply to show off her erudition or to impress her readers, as Frankel explains: "Nehama quotes Kaufmann not because of his popularity but because he wrote something significant. To be a Bible scholar and not have read Kaufmann was to narrow one's perspective."[33] At times, Nehama gave these scholars' words great prominence by featuring them as the take-away message of an essay. At other times she used them in order to make crucial arguments. Frankel notes that while Nehama certainly quoted them less than traditional

---

[27] D. Cummingham, quoted in *NSS*, 160, n. 3.

[28] Kagan, "A Review."

[29] Worksheet for *Va-yera*, 5707.

[30] Worksheet for *Va-yeshev* 5708. See Frankel, "*Ha-te'oriyah*," 428–429; also *TI*, 174; worksheet for *Va-yeshev* 5708 and *NSB*, 458.

[31] Buber says in his introduction to *Moses* that he wrote it "on a presupposed basis of critical inquiry without bias, research that does not depend upon the religious tradition, but also not upon the accepted assumptions of the scientific schools."

[32] *NSB*, 64. Also "For a penetrating and satisfying explanation of this Midrash see Buber" (*NSB*, 304, n. 2); "Buber aptly comments" (*NSV*, 537).

[33] Frankel, interview. See further in Frankel, *Iyun*, 219.

commentators, she often brought them at critical moments: "When she has to argue against the documentary hypothesis, she turns to Benno Jacob. It's a question of quality, not quantity." Nehama cited non-traditional sources for support in major Jewish philosophical issues, for example, the value of the Sabbath, where instead of rabbinic commentators she turns to Moshe Glickson, the writer and editor of the left-leaning newspaper, *Haaretz* (*NSS*, 539). She even occasionally quoted them on topics with halachic ramifications – for example, Buber on the prohibition of taking the Lord's name in vain.[34]

The non-traditional sources she used fall into four main categories: translations; Bible interpreters; political world figures; and authors.[35] They include such figures as Krochmal, Segal, Gutmann, Herzl, Yadin and Heschel; poetry and prose from Meltzer, Hazaz and Agnon; and non-Jewish figures such as Gandhi, the American economist Henry George and the English poet, William Blake.[36] She quoted from the Apocrypha, for instance the book of Ben-Sira (*IBBM*, 38). She read the New Testament and quoted it in her book on Rashi;[37] and when R. Yaakov Koppel Reinitz suggested to her that citing it was unnecessary, she disagreed.[38] R. Tsvi Kilstein, an anti-missionary activist, reports a conversation in which Nehama expressed astonishment when he showed her the biblical errors in the book of Acts, explaining that in her reading she had never caught these mistakes, because she read it as literature and never paid much attention to it.

For Frankel, the fact that Nehama quotes Mann, Buber and *Haaretz* signifies that for her the Oral Law "has a contemporary shelf" and that it can expand in every generation. Therefore, Frankel feels that to teach in Nehama Leibowitz's footsteps today would require incorporating contemporary scholars, literary personalities and thinkers.[39]

---

[34] *NSS*, 330. More often, however, she quotes these scholars in connection with non-halachic issues, concerning human existence or the human response to the Divine, Rosenak notes – he terms these the "implicit" aspects. See *Commandments and Concerns*, Philadelphia/Jerusalem: Jewish Publication Society, 1987.

[35] Wygoda, *VLN*.

[36] For a fuller list see HaCohen, "*Shma*," 75; the indices of the *Studies*; and Sokolow's *Mafte'ah ha-gilyonot*.

[37] One quote was cited in order to demonstrate how Ramban aimed to refute the New Testament (*Perush Rashi la-Torah*, 1, 159, citing Romans Chaps. 4 and 10, regarding the superiority of faith over works).

[38] *PN*, 700– 701. R. Reinitz recalls that, noting the strength of his feelings on the matter, she said she understood since he had been through the Holocaust, but stood her ground nonetheless (interview).

[39] See page 578 below.

Nehama had to defend herself for this practice too. In reply to a concerned letter from R. Yehudah Ansbacher, the rabbi of the Ichud Shivat Tzion synagogue in Tel Aviv where she taught many times, she wrote:[40]

> It is true that I quote people who are not observant, if I like what they have to say, and their words can illuminate the Torah's holiness and greatness for the student; as per the tenet: "Accept the truth from whosoever speaks it." What can I say? From Benno Jacob, who was an extreme Reformer and served in the *Sonntags Gemeinde*,[41] and certainly transgressed numerous commandments of our holy Torah (besides being a radical anti-Zionist, etc., etc), I learned, from his books...[42] more than I did from many, many books by God-fearing people. His claims against biblical criticism, his proofs of their recklessness and inaccuracy, are unparalleled even by R. David Zevi Hoffmann of sainted memory (difficult as it is for me to mention the name of this luminary in the same breath as B. Jacob).... [And also] many of my friends... learned much from his books, and he opened our eyes to see things that we had not previously noticed – to the truth of the Torah.

> Whereas Professor Cassuto *z"l*, who was a God-fearing and scrupulously observant Jew, said several things that are very far from my belief in Torah from Sinai, which I will have no part in publicizing. Therefore I heed not the speaker but the spoken.

> There is no need to state that Buber was not a good Jew – in the usual meaning of the term. I knew him – and he was not at all of my way of thinking! Absolutely not!...[43] But the fact remains that I, and many observant teachers, learned several correct things in the Bible from him, and especially the topic of the *Leitwört* and the deep significance hinted at in the Torah by its means; though our Midrash too knew of this principle....[44] It is however to Buber's, and even more so to Rosenzweig's, credit that they elaborated upon this topic, discovering several places that I did not find in any earlier source. And I shall not withhold benefit from students by keeping this hidden....

---

[40] *PN*, 657–658. I have made some use of Avidan Friedman's English translation in Yeshivat Chovevei Torah's journal, *Milin havivin*.

[41] A Reform congregation that held prayers on Sunday instead of Saturday.

[42] Here Nehama adds in parenthesis: "For example, [his book] *Aum an Auge, Zahn um Zann. Talion im Judentum*, Berlin: 1929, has excellent proofs that "an eye for an eye" according to the simple meaning means monetary compensation; [and] *Quellenkritik und Exegese, Genesis, Exodus* is a forceful work against the documentary hypothesis."

[43] Here Nehama discusses an incident reported of Buber that shed a negative light upon him.

[44] Nehama brings examples of this Midrashic sensitivity: "It says here... and also says there" and "measure for measure." See page 441 below.

Even non-Jews sometimes (although in my opinion seldom) offer a good and apt interpretation, and even Abravanel occasionally quotes the words of a Catholic cardinal, preferring his opinion over Radak's and Gersonides's....

Shall I hide the source [of my teachings]? I cannot. "Whose are the waters that we drink yet whose names we fail to mention?"[45]

She defends this position in her *Studies* too:

We should not imagine that all the knowledge of the nations of the world, and their wisdom and science, are prohibited under the commandment "You shall not do as they do." (*IHBV*, 194)

Abravanel claimed that gentile wisdom either agrees with the Torah or is included in it. But the Netziv goes further – in his opinion it is crucial to understanding the Torah and to piercing its depths; and the Torah in turn enriches the gentile disciplines. (*IBBM*, 108)

In the Talmud, we are told that the great sage, Rabbi Meir, continued to learn from his former teacher, the apostate Elisha ben Abuya. The following metaphor is used (Hagigah 15b):

Rabbi Meir found a pomegranate; he ate [the fruit] within it, and the peel he threw away.

Nehama wished likewise to eat the good "fruit" of these thinkers while discarding their "peel," of which she was well aware. She was thus able to give credence to two contradictory thoughts at once: Rejecting the author's lifestyle while accepting his work selectively.

Nevertheless she was criticized, both publicly and privately, for citing sources that many in the Orthodox world did not endorse. If, for example, we compare her work with Rabbi Yehudah Nachshoni's compendium of commentaries on the weekly Torah portion, we find a huge difference. He takes care to write:

As a matter of principle, I have not used any commentator not rooted in our tradition; not only because of my negative attitude toward any commentary not written with a sincere desire to study Torah for its own sake, but because I have not found anything of value in their works that does not appear in the classic commentators that preceded them.[46]

---

[45] Paraphrase of Horayot 14a.

[46] Yehudah Nachshoni, *Studies in the Weekly Parashah: The classical interpretations of major topics and themes in the Torah* (trans. Shmuel Himelstein). Artscroll Judaica Classics: 1988–1989, author's preface, viii. Nachshoni also differs from Nehama in his inclusion of non-*peshat* material, such as Hasidic and Kabbalistic writings, side by side with *peshat*. He

It was all very well to quote selectively, said her critics, but some heresy might still creep in and students might be tempted to read beyond the quoted segments, studying the heterodox work in its entirety.[47] And often, Nehama's more traditional students, having just recovered from the shock of a female Torah teacher, were once again floored when they heard her quote non-Jewish commentators: Could a person's lifestyle really be separated from his work?[48]

For these reasons, some students tried to downplay the non-traditional elements in her work, as Professor Rivka Horwitz reports:

> When I told friends I wished to write about Nehama and the German Jewish Bible interpreters, several of her students remarked that in that case I was surely going to be discussing Hirsch and perhaps Hoffmann; for despite their having read her worksheets and books and encountering in them the names Martin Buber and Benno Jacob, they did not dream that Nehama was genuinely interested in them… [whereas]… anyone who has studied her writings will actually conclude that [Buber and Jacob] interested her more than Hirsch did.[49]

Comments came from even the closest quarters. Nehama's husband once pointed to the existence in the Talmud of an idea she had quoted from a modern source, exclaiming, "Nehama, why do you quote external sources when you could bring the same idea from our own sources?" She conceded the need to cite from Jewish works before others, but not instead of them, as her husband suggested.[50] Nehama not only defended her stance but was prepared to make sacrifices for it.[51] She knew that Jewish life had always included elements of censorship. Once she showed R. Hershel Billet a blank page in his new volume of *Mehokekei Yehudah*, a recent reprint from Bnei Brak. In the volume in her possession, printed in Odessa in 1898, the page appeared, and it contained a quote from a maskil.

---

explicitly notes that the two are "treated with equal regard, until one cannot detect a distinction between them" (*ibid*).

[47] For example, she refers to several essays by Buber and Kaufmann. Mentioning the latter's comments on Isaiah 40:3 exposes the student to a work that promotes the notion of Deutero-Isaiah (Frankel, *Iyun*, 200–201, 220).

[48] See Ahrend, "*Ha-katuv*," 36, for discussion of this question and citation of some articles that present this problem; and see also HaCohen, "*Shma*," *passim*.

[49] Horwitz, "*Nehama*," 212.

[50] Moshe Oren, interview.

[51] Supposedly Nehama did not teach at Michlalah, an Orthodox college for women, because the principal, R. Yehudah Copperman, felt it proper to expose students only to commentaries by observant Jews. But Chana Rabinowitz recalls that it was Nehama who refused R. Copperman's repeated invitations, and it may therefore have been for other reasons.

Nehama had her champions in this matter too. Professor Moshe Ahrend was one, and he argued that this kind of censorship would disqualify great commentators including Ibn Ezra, Maimonides, Radak, Saadya Gaon and others, all of whom wrote views that might classify them as heretics.[52]

Nehama's example inspired others. One student from an ultra-Orthodox background was so impressed with Nehama's teachings that, upon returning to her hometown, she introduced Cassuto's books. Thus it came to pass that students in an ultra-Orthodox school began studying Prophets using some unfamiliar big brown books, never knowing that they had been written by a "heretic."

2. Nehama as pedagogue vis-à-vis sources

So far, Nehama has seemed to play the role of a facilitator, in granting students the right to compare sources and in providing a relatively wide spectrum of opinions to choose from. But she also took on the pedagogue role, placing constraints on the use of universal sources in her commitment to Orthodox Judaism. Firstly, worldly wisdom was not to be equated with Torah. Although Abravanel was

> particularly distinguished for his familiarity with classical and patristic literature, contemporary Christian Bible scholarship, the various schools of Arab philosophy, not to speak of his own Judaic heritage.... Nevertheless it was he who stressed time and again in his works the limitations of the secular sciences... they could not compete with [Torah]. (*NSS*, 503)

Secondly, the non-Orthodox sources to which Nehama referred always remained a precisely selected minority. She chose to quote with frequency only those scholars who treated the text with reverence, regarding it as a unified literary document and a focal point of faith. Although she considered them "insiders,"[53] she still objected to certain aspects of their thought and therefore approached them with more caution than she did the rabbinical commentators.[54] She used their insights only in topics that would not

---

[52] "*Ha-katuv*," 37. Ahrend also warns any would-be censors that they in turn will find themselves disqualified by those whose beliefs are even more extreme.

[53] Frankel, "Teacher," 364. This included Buber, who was strongly connected to traditional Jewish roots (Cohn, "*Ma ahavti*," 28, n. 9); Agnon and Bialik, whose writings were solidly based on Torah sources (Frankel, *Iyun*, 136); and even Thomas Mann, who assumed the Torah to be the result of Divine inspiration (Frankel, *Iyun*, 62).

[54] For example, she cites some classic commentators alongside Mann's words in order to give his opinion more legitimacy (Frankel, *Iyun*, 61–62) and quotes Buber, Jacob *et al.* primarily in philological and literary contexts, from narrative, historical and prophetic sections – i.e. the non-halachic material, not those which would undermine the assumption of the Torah as a given ("*Ha-te'oriyah*," 427, n. 11, and 429). Deitcher

undermine the authority of the Torah. When criticizing the biblical heroes, for example, a sensitive topic, she cited only accepted commentators such as Ramban, Radak or Midrash.[55] In dealing with difficult narratives, such as the *Akedah* story, she similarly kept her sources very selective.[56]

In quoting from "non-insiders," she was doubly cautious. "Nehama's goal was to teach the Jewish Bible," explains Dr. Gabriel Cohn. "For this reason she used almost exclusively Jewish sources of interpretation. Not including translators, the non-Jewish Bible scholars that she cites can be counted on the fingers of one hand."

The reasoning behind all of this was that while Nehama believed that such sources helped to illuminate the Torah, it was the Torah itself that defined what topics were to be illuminated.[57] One of the objectives of learning Torah is

> to demonstrate the "seventy facets of the Torah," so that the student realizes that that within the limits of traditional Judaism there are many options for understanding the verses and topics of the Torah.[58]

"The limits of traditional Judaism" was as far as Nehama's pluralism went. She had an intuitive sense of what these ought to be, and on rare occasion she delineated them explicitly; for example:

> The teaching that Abravanel outlines here is astonishing. Is this the approach of Judaism, of our prophets and sages to manual labour and human toil? (*NSB*, 21)

Thus, Nehama was happy to import ideas from many different thinkers, but within limits, promoting pluralism within traditional parameters.

Norms of Torah and Mitzvot

In the area of religious norms, we find that Nehama's approach was again a mixture of the facilitator and pedagogue. This time, we begin with the pedagogue.

1. Nehama as pedagogue vis-à-vis norms

From early on, Nehama taught the halachic parts of the Torah in a way that was involving and fascinating, not dry and legalistic.[59] But here she was

---

remarks that in this she followed the lead of the Midrash, which also has much more freedom of movement in non-halachic sections (interview).

[55] See Deitcher "Between," 18–19, and see further discussion on page 345 above.

[56] Frankel, *Iyun*, 64. See "God Tried Abraham" in *NSB*, 188–193, and "The Near-Sacrifice of Isaac" in *TI*, 21–38, which is a shorter version of Nehama's essay "*Parashat ha-Akedah*" in *Derachim ba-mikra u-ve-hora'ato* (5757), 11–34.

[57] Frankel, *Iyun*, 62.

[58] N. Leibowitz, *Darkei*, 2.

significantly less pluralistic, citing almost exclusively traditional sources such as Talmud and Maimonides. There are entire sections and essays devoted to halachic discussion, leaving the realm of *peshat* behind;[60] although she always remained a Tanach teacher, avoiding halachic minutiae. Halachic beliefs and practice permeated her work. Frankel discovered an underlying, subtle assumption within Nehama's works that the ideal Tanach teacher is committed to Halachah;[61] and a more explicit assumption that the student was Jewishly knowledgeable and observant too.[62] For example, Nehama quotes Abravanel as saying: "This section… is a familiar part of our daily devotions" (*NSB*, 188). This wording presumes that the reader belongs to the community that prays daily. She refers often to prayers and customs as part of her discussion in a way that assumes familiarity and that "every Jew" observes them.[63] As she herself points out, such references are only meaningful if they are known:

> For example, if I wish to illustrate a certain atmosphere, and I say: "It was like on Rosh Hashanah, after Psalm 47 is recited for the final time, just before the blowing of the Shofar," who will understand me and who will not? Those who have been in synagogue on Rosh Hashanah will understand me, as I evoke those feelings of dread and anticipation… but imagine what those who have never been to synagogue think. Even knowing that there is shofar blowing and that Psalm 47 is said still tells them nothing about the emotional tone.[64]

Nehama wanted to educate not only towards learning Torah but to the practice of mitzvot, the expression of God's will.[65] The idea of study without practice troubled her. "What is the point of all this study and the efforts to attract people to it? How many people will start observing Shabbat, laying *tefillin* or keeping the laws of family purity, even if they do fill out my *gilyonot* and attend my lessons for years?" she demanded.[66] Since Torah study does not *ipso facto* lead to observance, she strove to win over the reader by

---

[59] See "*Keitzad lamadnu*," 472; and see *LP*, 109, n. 4 for an unusually halachic discussion.
[60] See pages 499–500 below. Nehama outlines a methodology for teaching these topics in "*He'arot metodiyot le-limmud*," 487.
[61] Frankel, "*Ha-te'oriyah*," 435; "Teacher," 366–367.
[62] See Frankel "*Ha-te'oriyah*," 433, and *Iyun*, 103, 158–159.
[63] *NSB*, 134 and *SBM*, 171. Other examples include: *NSB*, 70, 87; *NSV*, 43, 76, 340; *SBM*, 43 question 5, and 60; *IBBM*, 91; and *SD*, 24 where she even grants the liturgy status as an authoritative opinion ("'Because of our sins we were exiled from our land' our festival liturgy states, and not because of the sin of Titus.") See also *TI*, 76 where Nehama sets homework requiring a search through the *Musaf* service, and *ibid.*, 91.
[64] Lecture, 1941, quoted in Ofran, "*Le-ha'ahiv*," 418.
[65] See Frankel, "Teacher," 368; "*Ha-te'oriyah*," 425, n. 1; *SD*, 221.
[66] Ahrend, "*Mi-toch*," 34.

outlining the advantages of the Jewish value system and bringing favorable comparisons with other Near Eastern laws (e.g. Hammurabi's[67]) and with world wisdom.[68]

2. Nehama as facilitator vis-à-vis norms

Nevertheless, Nehama drew the line at preaching, believing that missionizing forms of education would not have the desired impact. She knew that she could only make demands in moral and personal realms, not in personal practice.[69] She addressed her readers using *we* or *he* rather than *you*, avoiding a sermonizing tone.[70] Her conclusions were generally phrased, without reference to specific communities or ethnic groups. All of these factors prevented people from feeling threatened when studying her work, a factor especially important in the Israeli context, where sensitivity to religious coercion runs high.

To sum up this section: In the realm of norms, Nehama's pluralism, such as it was, was not ideological but pragmatic. Ideally, her students would practice mitzvot and keep Halachah, but pressuring them to do so would have an adverse affect. Beyond this, she genuinely welcomed all comers to her classroom, no matter what their level of commitment.

In the classroom

Within the classroom itself, the picture of Nehama's pluralism becomes even more complex. Her students experienced her teaching style in very disparate ways. Much depended on their own personalities as well as on which of her classes they attended, for she pitched them differently to different audiences.

1. Nehama as facilitator in the classroom

For many students, Nehama's teaching techniques were their first experience of the teacher as facilitator. The fact that her class was founded upon dialogue, between commentators of different periods and between participants, in the form of spirited discussions, was a breath of fresh air. Unlike old-school lecturers, she was open to diverse viewpoints in her lessons, and students were even allowed to contradict her, though not the text. She was interested in the individual student and in nurturing original thought, emphasizing process – discussion and analysis – above answers (*LP*, 37). Her aim was active learning. She drew out responses by asking a question and, after taking suggestions from everyone, using one student's

---

[67] *NSB*, 154; *NSS*, 361.
[68] See Frankel, *Iyun*, 155–156 for examples.
[69] Yedgar, "*Ha-iyunim*," 31.
[70] Frankel, "*Ha-te'oriyah*," 437; "Teacher," 367.

answer as a springboard for discussion by asking if anyone disagreed. She asked students which commentary they preferred. This not only increased their personal connection, but also required them to look back at the text repeatedly in order to refine their position and to articulate their opinion to each other and themselves.[71] Students were actively engaged in the exegetical process and in certain circumstances even contributed to it.[72] All the above are classic gambits of the facilitator, who remains chiefly in the background of the lesson. Nehama writes:

> Obviously the teacher's aid, trigger, or question needs to become less and less prominent as the grades get higher. The route is from the highly active teacher, to cutting back to the point where the teacher is simply a chairperson giving permission to speak, making sure to stay on topic, recommending references and aids, and transmitting information when required and otherwise inaccessible by the student from any resource close to hand. (*PN*, 654)

Nehama confronted difficult questions in her class.[73] She wanted students to speak freely and not to feel that what they said would be held against them. Her satisfaction in engaging with a bluntly-spoken secular Russian immigrant student was evident. She insisted on the right to ask the thorniest theological questions, part and parcel of the study of Torah. By asking, the student

> has not placed himself outside the camp of faithful Torah learners, but on the contrary he is engaged in their very activity: Torah study! (*TI*, 157-158)

2. Nehama as pedagogue in the classroom

However, Nehama functioned also as a pedagogue in her classroom, and certain types of interaction were out of bounds. While she believed that challenges by students must be met even if they sidetrack the lesson (*LP*, 112 n. 6), she also firmly steered her class, rigorously training her students to approach the text correctly as she saw it. There were also limits to her tolerance of critique of faith-based principles in her lesson. Those who studied with her remember occasions when students disagreed with her and it was obvious to all present that it was out of place. "We never felt that we were Nehama's equals, and we never expected her to talk to us as equals," says Professor Martin Lockshin. "She was running the class, and for someone to introduce some new agenda was completely inappropriate." Students were there to learn from Nehama, not to advance their own

---

[71] Sokolow, "*Samchut*," 300.
[72] Frankel, "Teacher," 369.
[73] See page 328 above.

theories. She countered opposition with responses such as: "You didn't understand," "You need to learn more about this issue," or "This is off the topic." She did not allow substantial deviation from the topic unless people were clearly anxious to discuss something, for she did not want her lesson to become too diffuse:

> It is pointless to tackle a number of different topics superficially or incidentally in a chapter. It is preferable to concentrate on just a few topics, but in depth.[74]

This policy frustrated those who wished to broaden the field of inquiry, or who thought along different lines to hers.

Text and commentary[75]

This discussion of Nehama's classroom dynamics is related to another question – that of the correct approach to the Tanach text. This subject warrants a brief introduction.

As noted above, Nehama liked to say, "All of life is *parshanut.*" This is certainly true of traditional Jewish life. The Jewish corpus contains multiple generations of interpreters, and for most of post-biblical history, Jews did not engage the Tanach directly but rather through its expositors. The Sages' interpretations became authoritative primary texts in themselves, to be interpreted by the next generations, whose comments in turn became fodder for the generations after, and so on and so forth to this day. Thus for many centuries every Jew has been born into a reality of explanations, and explanations of explanations; and the phrase "Torah learning" has long referred not to the study of biblical text, but rather to almost anything but.

The crucial question of who may be a legitimate biblical interpreter has historically been the source of much Jewish tension. Entire sects and movements, such as the Sadducees and the Karaites, were founded upon opposition of the prevailing rabbinic interpretative hegemony. Attempts to put aside – whether temporarily or permanently – the Talmud and commentaries and approach the Bible directly were also part of the intra-Jewish polemic in the nineteenth century. This issue is also important in our context, for a pivotal question of modern Jewish education is – should students be permitted to study the text unmediated by commentaries? May students freely suggest their own interpretations and ideas?

---

[74] *TI,* 22. See however *"He'arot metodiyot le-keriyat,"* 145–146, where she advises the teacher not to fear tangential discussions, even if they lead to general topics unconnected to the subject material of the lesson, as long as the teacher ensures that by the end of the lesson the material under discussion has been read, otherwise the students will come away with a partial experience.

[75] For further discussion of this topic see Angel "Paradox," *passim.*

In answer, the facilitator-teacher says that yes, the student should be encouraged to discover meanings independently. But the pedagogue-teacher says no, this must be left to experts and authorities, for the student's interpretation will necessarily be inferior and perhaps heretical. Once again, Nehama is found to have adopted elements of both.

1. Nehama as facilitator vis-à-vis texts

Nehama encouraged her students to read the text closely and directly, and she set creative assignments to make this happen. She wished the commentators' answers to be presented only after the students attempt to solve textual problems themselves, whether successfully or not (*TI*, 2). She emphasized that her goal was to teach Tanach and that nothing, not even the greatest of commentaries, should overshadow the students' own understanding of the text:

> Certainly school, even high school, is not the place to examine in depth the different approaches of the major classical commentaries, such as Rashi, Nachmanides and Ibn Ezra, because we are not studying commentaries, we are studying Torah, Neviim and Ketuvim with the aid of the opinions of the commentaries. (*TI*, 39)

> In elementary and high schools, we do not study *parshanut* or exegetical methodology for their own sake; rather, we study Torah with the assistance of its interpreters. And if, God forbid, the Torah should be pushed to the side – its stories and laws, its teachings and ideas, its guidance and beauty – because of overemphasis on *parshanim*, then any small gain my book achieves will be overshadowed by the damage done.[76]

Likewise:

> Rashi is not the central focus of our study, rather it is the Torah itself, so [the teacher] should be sparing [in spending large amounts of time reading one Rashi]. (*LP*, 61)

Nehama never equated the interpretation with the text, writing, for instance, that the Tanach should be known extremely well, while commentaries can always be looked up.[77]

2. Nehama as pedagogue vis-à-vis texts

But Nehama also did not believe that it was possible to correctly read a text unaided:

---

[76] *LP*, introduction, first page. I have used Angel's translation ("Paradox," 112) except for last few words.

[77] N. Leibowitz, "*He'arot metodiyot le-limmud*," 493.

At the center of the lesson stands the chapter, the verse, the story, the law, the issue, the idea. But, on the other hand, the commentaries are not extraneous or decorative, but they reflect their appellation: they help us to understand in depth the chapter, the verse, the issue and the idea.[78]

She pointed out that all reading automatically involves interpretation, and therefore if the Torah is read without the correct explanations as a guide, it risks being distorted. For example, if we choose to punctuate the Torah by ourselves, we can end up reading every commandment as a question – e.g. "Love your neighbor as yourself?!" Nehama illustrated this point with an example taken from the Japanese linguist Hayakawa (*LP*, 5). A motorist breaks down by the side of the road, puts his hazard lights on and stands waving to passing cars. One car stops and its occupant hails the motorist with, "Flat tire?" If the motorist then replies impatiently: "Hello?! Can't you *see* I have a flat tire, you dumb ox?" it means he has not understood the intent of the question, which is "Can I help you?" and is intended to open a line of communication. God's question to Cain, "Where is Abel your brother?" (Genesis 4:9), can be understood like this, for, if taken literally, it conflicts with the perception of God as omniscient. Rashi indeed explains that God is initiating a conversation using pleasant words, so that Cain will confess to the murder. She also liked to demonstrate the inherent ambiguity of text by quoting (in a gruff, melodramatic voice) the line from *Macbeth* (Act 4, scene 3),

He has no children.

Here the "he" could refer either to Malcolm or to Macbeth. For this reason, commentaries are necessary and vital.

Some stories were too sensitive to ever be read unaccompanied by commentaries, such as the *Akedah*.[79] But Nehama taught even less problematic stories primarily through the lens of commentary, one step removed – and not even all the commentaries, but only pre-selected ones. Yedgar: "Selecting commentaries was the secret to Nehama's success, but it was also problematic. She read all of the commentaries, and the student did not. Also, using a worksheet meant that the student had no need to open the *Mikra'ot Gedolot*. Sometimes, in order to really understand a commentator you have to read him in context – to read his comments on five verses and not just one."

The commentators' lead was to be followed when studying text critically, with the student's own ideas in second place. The questions Nehama wished

---

[78] *LP*, first page of introduction (translation Peerless, *To Study*, 33).
[79] Frankel, "Ha-te'oriyah," 435, n. 44. See also Frankel's comments in *Iyun*, 211–212.

to nurture were those that the commentators had asked, or very similar ones, for the commentators were, for her, role models of sensitive reading, examining every facet of the text and its nuances. No more valuable way of looking at the Torah existed, and it would be a crime to overlook such a rich resource. *They* read intelligently; *they* asked the right questions; and she was surprised when they overlooked something that she caught:

> What is puzzling is the fact that this deviation has not been noticed by many of our medieval commentators, not even those who are otherwise sensitive to the slightest anomaly. (*NSS*, 91)

Nehama instructed that, depending on the text, the teacher can start with the commentary and work back to the text, or alternatively bring the text first with its difficulties, and only later the "solution." In the latter case, the students do get to grapple with the Tanach text directly; but they must still be given the "correct" answer and there is no option to omit the commentaries entirely.[80]

જ ৬

Nehama also played the pedagogue role in keeping the students' attention far away from biblical criticism and sacrilegious ideas.[81] Additionally, while she dealt with genuinely difficult issues, such as the effect that God's command to sacrifice his son had on Abraham's faith, ultimately she does not leave such questions open, concluding in her essay that Abraham and Isaac went obediently and of one mind to fulfill God's instructions.[82] At the end of the day, Nehama upholds the expected religious answers. In fact, Professor Michael Rosenak suggests that even Nehama's questions, which appear to encourage freethinking, are in fact paradoxically instrumental in

> maintaining the invulnerability of the sacred texts. The question is not: is the text itself worthy of support? The question whether the text itself is perhaps unacceptable rather than just "difficult" is never raised.[83]

Dr. Howard Deitcher elaborates on this point, noting that while questions such as "What's Rashi's difficulty?" or "Who was more correct in his interpretation?" may seem pluralistic, they actually serve to deflect more

---

[80] Thus, for example, "And when they have stated their views, read to them the comment of Kimchi to confirm that they have hit upon the solution expressed by one of the classical authorities" (*TI*, 78).

[81] R. Mordechai Breuer connects these two approaches to text, suggesting that Nehama was afraid – consciously or unconsciously – to read the text independently, without the commentators' help, as it would lead her to biblical criticism ("*Yahasah*," 11).

[82] *NSB*, 200. See Frankel, "*Ha-te'oriyah*," 432, n. 35, *Iyun*, 22–23, and *Iyun*, 72, n. 63.

[83] Rosenak, *Roads*, 14. See Frankel, "*Ha-te'oriyah*," 432. Yet, Frankel adds, it might also open up the possibility of further, more probing deliberation (*Iyun*, 73, n. 66).

troubling questions on the nature of the biblical text itself. Attention is diverted from other problems that might challenge fundamentals of faith. Moreover, Deitcher says, Nehama's use of commentators for whom the text was invulnerable also kept the discussion within specific boundaries.[84]

It was while sitting in Nehama's class one day that Rosenak first realized that her use of commentaries served to defend the text itself. She was teaching Exodus 32:27, in which, following the sin of the Golden Calf, Moses commands the Levites:

> …Thus said the Lord God of Israel: Put every man his sword by his side, and go in and out from gate to gate throughout the camp, and slay every man his brother, and every man his companion, and every man his neighbor.

Here Moses implies that the command comes from God. But of all the interpretations on offer, the majority of the class preferred to believe that it was Moses's own initiative.[85] Nehama became agitated and said, "This is a terrible interpretation! It's PR for God at the expense of poor Moshe Rabbenu!" Rosenak says: "At that moment I realized that she got people to deliberate about things that are normative by taking one step back. In other words, the commentaries were the subject of deliberation, and this protects the text. She would say 'What do you think of Ibn Ezra?' not 'What do you think of the text?'" The text was perfect; it was to be treated with awe and reverence."[86]

રેંગ જ

Nehama was critiqued for obstructing the "authentic" reading of the text, pushing the verse aside to focus on the commentaries.[87] Reportedly, when her brother Yeshayahu first saw the worksheets, full of quotes from Rashi, Ibn Ezra, Ramban *et al.*, he remarked: "She wants to know everything: What Rashi says, what they all say. Only one thing does not interest her: what the Tanach itself says!"[88] The prominence of her work prevented others from

---

[84] Deitcher, "Between," 18–19.

[85] This follows *Yalkut Shimoni* (32: 391): "I bring as my witnesses the heavens and the earth that the Lord did not tell Moses, 'Stand at the gate of the camp and say, "Who is on the Lord's side?"'"

[86] In his later work Rosenak developed these ideas further, noting that in the *Mikra'ot Gedolot*, the physical layout of the page has the text in the middle, "shielded" by a surrounding ring of commentaries (see *Roads*, 16).

[87] Mondschein, "*Akedat*," 118; Reinitz, *PN*, 678.

[88] Breuer, "*Yahasah*," 11.

going directly to the Tanach, says R. Yuval Cherlow.[89] Her name even became synonymous, in certain circles, with the principle that now that we have the commentaries, the Tanach can never again simply be studied on its own.

Indeed, some of Nehama's students felt the need to modify her methods in line with contemporary educational trends by systematically introducing the students into the equation a stage earlier – allowing them to first grapple critically with the text and locate its difficulties and only then to study the commentaries. This will be discussed further in the final chapter.

3. Mixture of approaches vis-à-vis text

What we see, therefore, is that Nehama's method adopted a combination of approaches to text. She trained students to look for the "correct" answers and be self-effacing before the commentators, yet at the same time to think critically and to take responsibility for their learning.[90] Even the title of her *Studies* can theoretically support both directions. The first English volume was entitled *New Studies in Bereshit* with the subtitle *In the Context of Ancient and Modern Jewish Bible Commentary*. This creates ambiguity as to whether the commentary is primary or secondary to the text. Some scholars, such as R. Elhanan Samet and Professor Israel Rozenson, are convinced by the subtitle that the commentaries were the foundation stones of her work, her field of research and the area in which she invested her effort.[91] But Dr. Gabriel Cohn argues that her aim was to study the Torah itself and the commentaries were but a tool to this end, training the reader to read closely and think analytically in order to arrive at independent interpretations. It was not that she was afraid of biblical criticism if the text was studied unmediated, he asserts.[92] Rather, she wished to teach the Jewish Bible and therefore drew upon the sources of interpretation necessary for the Jewish understanding. R. Raphael Posen agrees that Nehama's primary interest lay in the text itself, but adds that her appealing presentations and vast knowledge of the commentaries may have subverted her own aims, leading her to be remembered as a superb teacher of commentaries.[93]

---

[89] Cherlow, 8, 12. He complains that this does not reflect genuine Jewish practice, as seen in the custom to study the weekly Torah portion twice over before reading any translations or interpretations (12).

[90] Yedgar, "*Ha-iyunim*," 34.

[91] Rozenson, "*Ha-parshanit*," 435.

[92] Here he opposes R. Breuer's claim – see n. 81 above.

[93] Posen, "*Ha-targum*," 109–110.

The larger picture

Although the picture that emerges from Nehama's approach to sources, texts and her classroom is one of combined approaches, there is some rhyme and reason to this mix. We find that the particular ratio of pedagogue to facilitator in her work depended on several factors: the subject being studied, the type of text being studied, the medium through which she was teaching it, and the audience.

First, the subject. Problematic subjects, as mentioned above, needed to be learned with commentaries, whereas other stories might be approached directly. Concerning the second factor, the type of text, the following answer by Nehama to a challenge put to her in the early years of the worksheets is enlightening:

> This is also an appropriate place to answer a question that I was asked in writing and in conversation: Would it not have been better had the questionnaires been oriented directly towards comprehension of the Torah rather than of its commentators? And there were male students (not female ones) who feared we would thereby forego our own independent notion of the verse, becoming instead habituated to seeing it through the eyes of others, whose time and viewpoint differs from ours.

> The answer to this is that the best way to arrive at one's own understanding of the Torah is to learn how the Torah greats understood it! Whoever, in order to preserve a child's originality, prevents him from reading books and hearing conversations of wise and insightful people will not end up creating an original thinker, just an inarticulate and unintelligent person.

> Notwithstanding, there were some questions in the worksheets that related directly to the Torah text, which the student had to answer without the aid of supercommentaries These dealt especially with the literary aspect of the Torah, the architectural structure of the chapter, analysis of the literary elements, etc.[94]

Also note in the above-cited text Nehama's persuasive explanation as to why it is so important to read using commentaries.

With regards to the third factor, the medium, we find that her focus on text was greater in her classroom and *Studies*, whereas in the pedagogical works and in the worksheets, which were more demanding,[95] she was more interested in commentaries. She explains this explicitly, noting that her *Studies* were primarily devoted to helping the student

---

[94] N. Leibowitz, "*Mi-bereshit*," 453.
[95] *IBD*, introduction.

understand various sections of the Torah, through selected verses; to comprehend the actions, narratives and events, characters and their modes; and to view all these in light of past and recent commentators

while her pedagogical work, Limmud Parshanei ha-Torah u-derachim le-hora'atam aimed

> to be an aid to students, and especially to high school teachers in understanding the words of the commentators, their language and style, the difficulties they spotted in the text… and what "large questions" they tackled within the religious philosophy of the Tanach, and how they resolved all these…. [Therefore] this book is only an aid in understanding commentaries, and not a guide for teaching Torah. (*LP*, intro)

The medium is closely linked to the fourth factor, the audience. In general, Nehama felt that changing one's style and agenda for different populations was a prerequisite for good teaching. Thus, as we saw earlier, she recommends allowing the comparison method only with advanced classes. Frankel, who has extensively analyzed how Nehama's instructional approach varied in her writings, discovered that the picture of the teacher and audience emerging from Nehama's teachings differs from medium to medium. In the worksheets, the teacher seems to be one who does not teach dogmatically and encourages independent thinking by the students, who, for their part, are skilled, actively committed "insiders." Such students may be given tricky theological or moral issues to chew over and even presented with problems to solve entirely on their own,[96] though within certain limits.[97] In contrast, the *Studies* readers are, though educated, not proficient or committed. They need guidance in the methods and norms of Torah learning. Therefore the *Studies* do not contain the same abundance of questions, but focus on just one or two of them, and on a more limited range of topics.[98] Also (barring a few exceptions,[99]) Nehama made sure to

---

[96] Frankel, *Iyun*, 28–29, 60, 121. For example, Yedgar notes that, in examining the story of the rape of Dinah, Nehama allows the worksheet reader more latitude than the *Studies* reader ("*Parashat Va-yishlach*," 110).

[97] In "master stories" shaping religious faith, such as the revelation at Sinai, and also in discussions of ritual mitzvot, Nehama allowed comparison of sources and some deliberation, but not independent opinions or questions of the type: "What do *you* think is the reason?", "What is *your* answer to this question?" See Frankel, *Iyun*, 100 and 170, 211–212.

[98] Yedgar "*Ha-iyunim*," 27. Frankel notes that the *Studies* are mostly concerned with the interpersonal realm – it is only the *gilyonot* that contain topics between man and God (*Iyun*, 156–157). Another difference is that the *Studies* contain more external (non-Jewish) sources.

create closure at the end of each essay, providing the reader with correct guidance in basic Torah values instead of abandoning him or her to "distorted perceptions."[100]

However, Yedgar emphasizes that even in the *Studies* Nehama was not a "preacher" *per se*. True, the essay resembled in many ways the rabbinic sermon in which questions are asked, sources examined and a message derived. But all of Nehama's questions were genuine, stemming from the text itself; and the transparency of her thinking process, together with her explanation of her choice of texts, also allowed the reader the possibility of critiquing her position.[101] In addition, her answers were not intended to be the bottom line; in the questions for further study at the end of every section, she relinquishes her power as interpreter to the student, who is thereby encouraged to continue solving the issues independently.[102] Yedgar argues that in doing so, Nehama implies that the preceding essay, educational message and all, is only one of the many routes to be taken and that, despite her strong desire to inculcate values, she is aware of her own limits.[103] Furthermore, in her footnotes Nehama opens windows to critical viewpoints by alluding to essays that challenge normative Orthodox understandings. The more capable and advanced students may then look up these essays and confront difficult questions.[104]

Turning to the *gilyonot*, Yedgar again emphasizes that the picture is a mixed one, with Nehama not as much of a facilitator as one might think. Her questions on the commentaries are still more numerous and difficult than those on verses.[105] And, as Rosenak suggests, all these questions and discussion left the focus strongly on commentary while protecting the sacred text – passing on tradition and initiating the students into the community of learners.

A slightly different resolution of the dichotomy within Nehama's work between pedagogue and facilitator is offered by Frankel. She suggests that

---

[99] These include *NSB*, 150 ("we do not want to force any particular interpretation on the student"), *NSB*, 545, *NSV*, 579; *SBM*, 247 (see quote on page 73 above) and 410–411. See Frankel, *Iyun*, 95, 96, 98–100 and Yedgar, "*Ha-iyunim*," 29. See also chapter 21 n. 123.

[100] Frankel, *Iyun*, 29.

[101] Yedgar, "*Ha-iyunim*," 27-29.

[102] Yedgar, "*Ha-iyunim*," 32. Note, though, that the vast majority of questions revolve around the classic commentators.

[103] Yedgar, "*Ha-iyunim*," 32.

[104] See Frankel, "*Ha-te'oriyah*," 429, n. 21; Frankel, "Teacher," 365, and also Frankel, *Iyun*, 26.

[105] Yedgar, "*Ha-iyunim*," 34.

Nehama's belief system and choice of texts tended towards the pedagogue, but her method of study and teaching leaned toward the facilitator.[106]

Students' reactions

In the classroom, Nehama's students reacted to this mix of facilitator and pedagogue in different ways. Many liked the balance between the two. They enjoyed the discussion while also appreciating her firm control of the class which, by preventing too much digression, allowed mastery of a specific topic. Joy Rochwarger states: "She allowed arguments to continue for just so long, knowing exactly when to interrupt and return to the original point that she had made." For these students, what Nehama lost in openness of discussion she gained in sharpening the student's mind. With a firm hand, she invited them into a new way of looking at a text, beyond their existing opinions, and she restrained overimaginative students with unsupported interpretations. In her class, even highly opinionated and voluble people learned to defer to her in order to gain what she could give. One charismatic educational figure, today the director of several institutions, recalls, "She would tell me what she thought, and I learned to keep quiet."

Simi Peters asserts: "Nothing in her method stifled creativity; it created common ground for argument. A creative person might have experienced her methodology as restrictive in some ways, but would also be missing an opportunity to learn intellectual rigor." The method forced Peters to "stretch certain muscles" and provided her with a new language. Lockshin says: "We learned some fantastic answers to questions we would not necessarily ask. Those only interested in answers to the questions they normally asked would lose out. For the most part, these commentators were not bringing to the text the same questions as the twenty-first century person would. Exposure to these questions could open one's mind to all sorts of avenues." Sharon Shenhav adds: "I personally could never answer her questions the way she wanted. She once turned to me and said, 'What is it that you do?' 'I'm a lawyer!' I replied. 'Well, then, you ought to be able to answer my questions!' she exclaimed. But I loved her. To have someone I admired and respected tell me consistently that my answers were wrong was a wonderful, constructive experience. It gave me a sense of humility."

Yet the atmosphere was too strict for some. In the words of Professor Chana Safrai: "A free spirit, though learning a lot, might feel uncomfortable in her class." Individualistic or critical students might experience Nehama's classes as rigid, her constant demand to justify oneself using strict and rational tools cramping a looser, more associative relationship with the text.

---

[106] Frankel, *Iyun*, 212.

Previously we noted that Professor Dov Rappel suggests a comparison of Nehama to Socrates,[107] but he ends the comparison at a certain point, for Nehama's focus was ultimately not on the student's own opinions but on the text and its interpreters. One student challenged her: "But Nehama, aren't there seventy facets to the Torah?" She replied, "Yes, but what you said is not one of them!" Nehama was also not interested in personal and emotional reactions to the text. On the contrary, she believed that they interfered with correct interpretation:

> When analyzing or interpreting a literary work… [there is a risk] that the interpreter will speak about himself… about his own elevation of spirit, about what is going on inside himself… instead of about the text.[108]

She cared greatly about general relevance, but not about the personal relevance for each individual. Precious class time was reserved for the correct answers, of which Nehama had a very clear idea; and personal issues and questions, even those of existential urgency for the student, must be saved for outside the classroom walls. Her frank nature would not allow her to coddle her students. She would not respond, "Good point!" or "That's an interesting idea" if she did not actually think so, as some contemporary lecturers might do in order to validate the student. She called this "encouragement for idiots," and preferred instead to throw back a resounding, "*Lo nachon* (wrong)!" "It was clear that there was a right answer and a wrong answer, and not a lot in between," remarks Nechama Tamler. "Nowadays, this kind of pedagogy is referred to as 'teacher answers.' The students know that the teacher is looking for a specific answer; and it is not regarded highly – but Nehama came from another time."

Ultimately this rigor achieved its goals, for Nehama brought many to an entirely new intellectual approach to the Tanach, and taught them how to read a text properly. Even those from knowledgeable backgrounds underwent a revolution. R. Daniel Tropper: "Until I met Nehama I couldn't see that a verse existed on its own, I always read it with Rashi and Ramban; but her method brought me to be able to view the verse as they did."

Outside the classroom Nehama permitted herself to be less severe, as illustrated by her encouraging response to a street-sweeper's Torah ideas even though they were based on inaccurate understandings.[109] In the absence of the need to train a student to think correctly, she could allow her more nurturing side to the fore.

---

[107] See page 199 above.
[108] N. Leibowitz, "*Al nituah*," 617.
[109] See pages 137–138 above.

Conclusion

What emerges from the above is that for Nehama, pluralism was primarily a means, not an end – a technique, not a value. Indeed, we notice that in contrast to her most cherished values and like in the case of the value of modesty, she *implements* pluralism but does not purposefully *educate* towards it.[110] In this chapter, we have explored an area in which Nehama's complex aims and beliefs come especially to the fore. Nehama was flexible, but within a set framework, and has therefore been characterized by some as teaching with "an open dogmatism." Her genuine love for independent thinking was balanced by a rigorous – some might even say doctrinaire – training in the correct methodology and answers. Both elements play an important role in her writings.

Frankel suggests that this is a balance that constitutes a challenge for educators from the traditional camp in particular.[111] Yedgar adds that this issue deserves more attention in educational forums despite its difficulties and problematics, since too many educators apply Nehama's method in no more than a partial and deficient manner.[112] In the end, we must recognize that this duality, like her other complexities, served her in her ability to teach, and in particular to reach many different kinds of people simultaneously.

---

[110] For example, the story of the Tower of Babel lends itself to a discussion of pluralism in its themes of unity and diversity. Aware of this, Yeshayahu Leibowitz dedicated a radio talk on this story to the need for the existence of differences of opinion in preventing totalitarianism (see his *Accepting the Yoke of Heaven: Commentary on the Weekly Portion*, Jerusalem: Urim Publications, 2002, 17–19). But Nehama in her study of this portion avoided the topic of pluralism or multiple voices, preferring to stick with her favored themes of civilization and technology (*NSB*, 91–108). For more on this, see Dr. Ruth Ben-Meir's lecture in *VLN* and the questions at the end of the session.

[111] Frankel, "Teacher," 370.

[112] Yedgar, "*Ha-iyunim*," 34–35. See pages 575–577 below.

CHAPTER 19

NEHAMA'S BIBLE SCHOLARSHIP:
STRADDLING WORLDS

LET US NOW take a step backwards in order to view Nehama's work in the larger context of Jewish and general trends.[1]

The burgeoning Zionist movement and her neo-Maskilic upbringing were background influences to Nehama's approach.[2] But the primary milieus and scholars that she directly engaged – through continuity, dialogue, or refutation – were:

1) Traditional Jewish Tanach scholarship throughout the centuries
2) Twentieth-century academic Bible and literary scholarship
3) Jewish scholars of the nineteenth and twentieth centuries, including Orthodox and non-Orthodox scholars, who were influenced by both of the above.

The traditional Jewish world responds to challenges

Let us begin with a recap of the changes taking place in Bible study just before Nehama's time. This survey will, of necessity, be a brief summary of a large topic, aiming simply to provide some broad outlines for understanding Nehama's scholarship.

Looking back through Jewish history, the Tanach did not always play the central role that one might have expected. This role was reserved instead for the Talmud. In Ashkenazic Jewish society, Tanach study was fragmented, with a few verses from each weekly Torah portion learned in the *heder*. But the Enlightenment saw a move away from Talmud study, considered overly-legalistic and pilpulistic, and back to the Tanach, though often specifically to the prophets for their aesthetic and moral sensibilities. The nineteenth

---

[1] See also Aryeh Newman's detailed introduction to Nehama's *Studies* series (*NSB*, xx–xxix).

[2] Amit describes how Nehama came to Palestine "bearing the weight" of two ideologies: the Haskalah and Zionism ("Hebrew Bible," 8). HaCohen sees Nehama's work as continuing the path of the more liberal Germanic *"Torah im Derech Eretz"* school ("*Shma*," 73, n. 6); though she differed with its founder, Hirsch, on important points, both in questions of biblical interpretation and in outlook (see pages 34, 39, 322 and 326 above).

century saw an intense preoccupation with the Tanach. Biblical criticism became increasingly popular, with the Torah assumed to have emerged under multiple authorship and regarded as literature and folklore, parallel to that of other peoples. This viewpoint, together with the growing Reform movement and the secular Zionist approach that advocated a Judaism devoid of God and His commandments, served to undermine the fundamentals of traditional Jewish faith, leading to crisis within the Western European and American Jewish traditional worlds.

Professor B. Barry Levy has categorized Ashkenazic Tanach interpreters of the nineteenth century as specializing in three main areas of interest: the Midrashic-Kabbalistic; the Talmudic-Midrashic; and the anti-mystical Rational-Scientific school, favoring philological accuracy and historical credibility.[3] This last was exemplified particularly by several medieval thinkers, notably Maimonides. These models also serve to delineate different traditional responses to the various challenges posed by biblical criticism and the Reform and Zionist movements. Such responses both derived from and serve to differentiate between different sociological camps. Many in the yeshivah world, belonging primarily to the Midrashic-Kabbalistic and Talmudic-Midrashic camps, reacted by clinging to traditional works as the only true route to Torah. But those of the Rational-Scientific bent, which had always by definition meant engaging with intellectual developments in the wider world, could not ignore the new challenges with the opportunities for understanding that they introduced. However, their reactions varied. Some adopted the new scientific approaches, although this was a slow process even within non-Orthodox circles,[4] while others took up defensive positions against the new theories. Still others carefully incorporated some elements from the academic world. For the first time in a long while, several monumental Orthodox Tanach commentaries were produced such as those of Luzatto, Hirsch, Mecklenburg, Malbim, Netziv and Hoffmann. The latter especially did much to confront the challenge of critical theory.

As the nineteenth century waned and the twentieth century progressed, Diaspora and Israeli Orthodoxy developed somewhat different approaches

---

[3] Levy, "Periphery," 161–163. The Midrashic-Kabbalistic school derived its impetus from Talmud, Midrash and Zohar (inclusive of Hasidic literature), while the Talmudic-Midrashic school was non-Zoharic, its focus being on the rabbinic interpretation of Torah. A few important writers cut across these lines of demarcation – for example, the Vilna Gaon.

[4] Wellhausian criticism was prohibited in the Jewish Theological Seminary, but Szold and Ehrlich were more radical. Eventually Levine and Milgrom overturned the Jewish "quasi-taboo" against higher Pentateuchal criticism in the period immediately preceding 1965 (for more, see Sperling, *Students*, 38, 45–53, 69–107, 115–147).

to scholarly study of Tanach.[5] Diaspora Orthodoxy tended to steer away from academic scholarship for the most part, though R. Joseph H. Hertz (1872–1946), Chief Rabbi of Britain and author of the popular English Torah commentary, included some academic assumptions.[6] Yeshiva University was also established as an Orthodox university integrating an academic approach with a commitment to tradition. Though the documentary hypothesis was not accepted, developments in biblical scholarship were noted, and courses emphasizing *peshat* were on the curriculum.[7] In Israel, the Rational-Scientific approach was more common among Orthodox Bible scholars, perhaps because scientific research of the land was much closer at hand.[8] Tanach became increasingly studied both in the yeshivah and in religious scholarly environments such as the Bible Department at Bar-Ilan University. In later decades, R. Mordechai Breuer undertook the ground-breaking work of admitting the documentary hypothesis in a way consonant with Orthodox sensibilities. He suggested that God, via the agency of Moses, wrote the Torah in several different styles, making the Bible critics' work valuable even if their premise is erroneous. Although the critical theories upon which Breuer has based his work are now under fire,[9] his work has been appreciated as significant, and he received the Israel Prize for it. Many other religious scholars began incorporating history and archeology into a specifically religious understanding of Tanach.[10]

Nehama and the new biblical theories

Where does Nehama fit in the above description? Though she studied for several years in German academic frameworks, both Jewish and non-Jewish,

---

[5] For a more comprehensive discussion, see Levy, "The State and Directions of Orthodox Bible Study," in *Modern Scholarship in the Study of Torah*, edited by Shalom Carmy, 53–58 (Northvale, NJ: Jason Aaronson, 1996).

[6] These appear in his notes at the end of each book of the Torah. He also comes out explicitly against the documentary hypothesis.

[7] For more details, see Levy, "Periphery," 173–178.

[8] Levy, "State," 61. He also suggests that it is because Israelis can specialize in more ways than North American scholars, and are significantly enriched by non-Orthodox academia.

[9] The classical documentary hypothesis has been modified and even rejected by many modern scholars. For more on Breuer and Bible criticism see M. Breuer, "The Study of Bible and the Primacy of the Fear of Heaven: Compatibility or Contradiction?" in *Modern Scholarship in the Study of Torah*, edited by Shalom Carmy, 159–180 (Northvale, NJ: Jason Aaronson, 1996); see also S. Carmy, "Introducing Rabbi Breuer," in *ibid.*, 147–158, and S.Z. Leiman, "Response to Rabbi Breuer," in *ibid.*, 181–187.

[10] This will be discussed in greater detail in chapter 24.

she was not part of the Diaspora scene.[11] Her emphasis was on Hebrew language, and she was a link in the chain of Jewish biblical exegesis in Hebrew. Most twentieth-century scholarship in Hebrew emerged from Israel, the Zionists continuing the trend that the maskilim had begun, and Israeli Bible scholars were Nehama's most immediate peer group. With the secular Zionists she shared a love of Tanach and a belief in the realization of the prophetic utopian vision in modern-day Israel. However, the Zionists' research, like that of many Bible scholars around the world, revolved in the main around historical and geographical factors, which did not particularly interest her. She also rejected their view of the Tanach as a humanist and historical document; for her it was a Divinely authored text, albeit written in "human language" and, as such, authoritative and binding. She had the most in common with Israeli scholars who came from strongly traditional backgrounds such as Cassuto, Segal, Buber, and Kaufmann.[12]

Nehama's teachers at the German universities did not share many of her dearest assumptions about the Tanach, drawn instead to the new theories (when mentioning the Bible critics, Nehama would add disparagingly, "And I studied with the best of them!"[13]) Over the course of her lifetime, she also saw Jewish scholarship move to an increasingly modern biblical-critical stance. Nevertheless, she consistently declined to jump onto the biblical-critical bandwagon, remaining loyal to the traditional perspective, which she considered the unassailable truth. It was important for her to be educated and involved in the academic world, but without compromising her convictions.

Nehama had her reasons for remaining unimpressed by the new theories. First, the scholars simply did not know Hebrew, as she never tired of mentioning. She told of the occasion when a famous German Bible scholar attended the Congress of Jewish Studies at the Hebrew University, and, as a German speaker, she was asked to accompany him. At one point, she informed him that a session on his subject, Ezekiel, was beginning, and no doubt Herr Professor would wish to attend? The latter objected: "But they are speaking in Hebrew, no?!" Although there is a difference between classical and modern Hebrew, for Nehama this story sufficed to explain why

---

[11] However, she was at least somewhat familiar with it, more than once quoting Jewish Bible scholars from the Diaspora, such as Ehrlich.

[12] For more on pre-State biblical scholarship see M. Haran, *Heker ha-mikra bi-leshon ha-Ivrit.* Jerusalem: Magnes, 5729 17–22; and Yael Unterman, *Background and Examples of Nechama Leibowitz's Literary Approach to Bible,* Master's thesis submitted to the graduate faculty in Jewish Studies, Touro College, Israel Branch, 2002, 21–22.

[13] Dr. Baruch Schwartz, interview. See chapter 1 n.18 for Nehama's personal testimony regarding various professors of Bible studies. See also Horwitz, "*Nehama,*" 209.

these scholars interpreted so preposterously. They possessed a basic lack of understanding of their subject, and a shocking laxity towards the Hebrew nuances, making them go "completely astray" in their understanding.[14] They demonstrate a gross insensitivity to the tone of the text:

> We shall decline to follow that non-Jewish commentator who endeavored to trace Jacob's limp, after the wrestling bout with the angel, to an attack of rheumatism, caused by sleeping in the open, all night, in the damp atmosphere of the brook. Such a mechanical approach to supernatural mystical events must be ruled out in favour of the primary demand of interpretation – response to the spirit, tone and intention of the narrative. (NSB, 366)

The biblical-critical exegetes were time and again surpassed by the traditional Jewish commentators in getting at the text's true meaning.[15] Only uneducated and prejudiced scholars could suggest that God's question to Cain (Genesis 4:9), "Where is Abel your brother?", represents a need for information on God's part (LP, 5, n. 5).

The second factor causing Nehama to be wary was her belief that many of these scholars were prejudiced. She liked to repeat Solomon Schechter's line that the theories were really "Higher Anti-Semitism," using the Torah to criticize Jews.[16] She writes:

> Modern non-Jewish biblical scholars, particularly those moved by animosity to Judaism, have cited this as a proof of the moral superiority of Christianity.[17]

She disparages the

> science that pretends to be unprejudiced and yet in actuality is full to the brim of anti-Semitism and contempt for the Old Testament, such as Gunkel and Skinner. (LP, 5 n. 5)

Their attitude is patronizing:

> This school of thought imputes to ancient peoples the lowest and coarsest of motives as a direct consequence of its oversimplistic

---

[14] See, for example, her criticism of E.A. Speiser in LP, 37, n. 1.

[15] This was particularly true of translations. For example, in NSS, 25, we hear that only the Jewish translators (and some English modern versions) got it right, or similarly in IHBV, 202, n. 2, where she calls the New Catholic translation "dreadful!" She especially liked the Buber-Rosenzweig translation, which often clung to nuances others overlooked – see chapter 20 n. 50.

[16] R. Nathaniel Helfgot, interview.

[17] NSB, 457. The Hebrew wording is even sharper – "many of whom allow their animosity to taint their scholarship" (IBB, 325). See also NSB, 307: "But another objection still remains – one often employed as a weapon against us by malicious critics"; Horwitz, "Nehama," 211; and Breuer, "Yahasah," 12.

evolutionary standpoint, which holds that the earlier a person lived, the more primitive and coarse he must of necessity be in his beliefs and practices; and the later, the more refined and spiritual. *(LP, 51, n. 1)*

They are also biased by their theology. She quotes Kaufmann's statement:

It was the Liberal Christian theology that presented Jeremiah as repudiating the sacrificial cult, by omitting and ignoring the passages at will, as is their notorious habit. *(NSV, 20)*

Having classified this scholarship as tendentious and ignorant, Nehama felt no need to meaningfully engage with it. She occasionally polemicized openly with prevailing "biblical critical" views, for example:

[The author of the Midrash] certainly did not subscribe to the critical view that the superscription of the Psalms is but a later, arbitrary addition. *(SD, 360)*

She also quoted others scholars' polemics with them.[18] But by and large, she preferred simply to ignore the theories of multiple authorship promoted by Graf and Wellhausen. Instead, she adopted an approach to the text that was literary and educational and that remained basically unchanged throughout her life.

Nehama only rarely brought findings from historical scholarship, such as comparative Near East or philological research.[19] When she did, it was generally in order to bolster the traditional viewpoint[20] or to prove the uniqueness and superiority of the Tanach.[21] She was almost never interested in manuscripts, versions, and other tools of the scholarly trade.[22] She

---

[18] For example, Cassuto's non-Documentary-Hypothesis explanation for discrepancies in the Noah story *(LP, 220)*.

[19] For example, in studying the generic names "Pharaoh" and "Agag" *(LP, 186)* or Cassuto's citation of a Phoenician inscription *(NSS, 351, n. 2)*.

[20] For example: "These words of the Sages are not *derash*, they are *peshuto shel mikra*. See the words of the scholar Speiser, who is free of any suspicion of being biased towards the Sages" *(LP, 54)*.

[21] For example, the singular Tower of Babel story *(NSB, 103)*, the comparison with the Code of Hammurabi (see *NSB*, 154, *NSS*, 361) and the unique biblical dietary laws *(NSV, 144)*. See also Frankel, *Iyun*, 150–151, 155.

[22] Grossman notes that she avoided important questions of copyists and additions even within Rashi and sometimes did not even check the Berliner version ("*Pulmus*," 204, n. 37). Nevertheless, when it came to post-biblical sources she was certainly more amenable to scientific research. She does, for example, mention Berliner in *NSS*, 333, n. 2 and *NSV*, 92; and various editions of Rashi in *TI*, 57, n. 2. She references scientific editions of Onkelos *(NSS, 333, n. 1)* and Rashbam *(IHBS, 54, n. 1)* and compares versions of Midrashim (see Gabriel Cohn, "*Ha-parshanut ha-midrashit be-mifalah ha-Torani shel Nehama*," in *PN*, 94, n. 6). She also is willing to mention emendation of the *Sifri* when Hoffmann cites it (see *SD*, 149).

avoided all mention of biblical emendation and took pains to ensure that no one could accuse the classical commentators of wanting to emend the text.[23] When Professor Martin Lockshin asked her opinion on making changes in the text in order to solve difficulties, Nehama replied that textual emendation is speculative and not good methodology.

Nehama also hardly ever made explicit distinctions between the Torah and rabbinic materials. One rare example is:

> In the Bible we do not have this dichotomy known to us from the later works on ethics. Such distinction between body and soul… is not found in the Bible. (*TI*, 80)

කා ல්

Oddly enough – or perhaps entirely understandably – it was the approach of R. Mordechai Breuer, a strictly Orthodox Jew, that elicited the most antagonism from Nehama. In an article published a few years before his death, R. Breuer reported that when he first presented his work publicly at a conference, Nehama was the harshest of his many attackers.[24] He recalled her complaining to his son: "I do not understand what your father sees in the Bible critics; those people simply knew no Hebrew!" Even his suggestion that a traditional commentator, the *Sha'agat Aryeh*, discovered the scientific approach before the gentiles did, failed to elicit her usual response of delight when traditional insights were shown to pre-empt modern ones. Instead it was met with a cold shoulder because the approach itself was anathema: "There are no contradictions in the Torah! And whoever finds them will also discover them in Shakespeare, and will thus prove there were two Shakespeares!"[25]

R. Breuer regretted Nehama's intransigency. Had she been more open to critical findings, she could have solved several perplexing biblical puzzles; but the only contradiction she was willing to discuss was the first two chapters of Genesis, because R. Soloveitchik had "solved" the tensions by developing the notion of two archetypal Adams in his seminal essay "The Lonely Man of Faith."[26] On this, R. Breuer wrote with great pathos:

---

[23] *LP*, 43. She points out a printing error in the printed *Humash* – see *IHBV*, 107, n. 3 – but never discussed the questions of versions of the Torah.

[24] "*Yahasah*," 11. Ironically, Breuer believed his method to have been anticipated by Rosenzweig, whom Nehama admired (reported by Horwitz, "*Nehama*," 217).

[25] Breuer, "*Yahasah*," 12.

[26] Breuer, "*Yahasah*," 13 – 14. In truth, even before encountering this essay she had already resolved the problem, citing comments by Cassuto and Rashi (see *NSB*, 15, n. 1, and 16, n. 4).

Should all the scholars in the world prove to her that there are contradictions in the Torah, she would not listen, for this will lead to heresy. She would, however, accept without hesitation the selfsame things from the mouth of R. Soloveitchik.[27]

Although R. Breuer believed that all "biblical critical" theories may be extrapolated from R. Soloveitchik's idea, he despaired of convincing Nehama of this.[28] He suggested, furthermore, that she was afraid to deal with the *peshat* of the text without commentaries for fear that it might lead her to biblical criticism.[29] Judy Klitsner disagrees with this premise: "I don't think Nehama was afraid of biblical criticism or felt that a serious delving into the text would of necessity lead to critical answers. She did not have enough respect for the critics to believe that. She used to say, 'Well, in that case, who said the prophet Jeremiah lived at all?' I think her approach was that you take the Bible on faith anyway, and once you take it you take it all."

– –

However, Nehama was not insensible to the actual difficulties raised by the Bible critics. She simply preferred to explain them differently.[30] In this she took her cue from her predecessors:

> Those Bible critics who exult in shredding apart God's perfect Torah, who see it as a fragments of scrolls and "sources" and various documents, find evidence for their theories in the conflicting sources here, to prove thereby that they did not all emerge from one pen. But Hoffmann [explains the issue without recourse to documentary theory].[31]

She resolved certain conflicts between the first four books of the Torah and Deuteronomy by suggesting that the last book was Moses's interpretation of the previous historical events (*SD*, 24); or that in Exodus and Numbers, Moses speaks as a historian, but in Deuteronomy as a lawgiver and moralist (*SD*, 251.) She pointed out repetitious material in the Tanach, but rather than attributing it to different documents, suggested literary and educational meanings.

---

[27] Breuer, "*Yahasah*," 12.

[28] Breuer, "*Yahasah*," 12–13. His theory was that ten generations after that R. Soloveitchik's Adam I comes Noah I, and ten generations after Adam II Noah II, who experienced flood I and flood II, and so on for the rest of the Bible.

[29] Breuer, "*Yahasah*," 11.

[30] Nehama notes historical inconsistencies in the Prophetic writings, but resolves them without positing multiple authorship (Frankel, *Iyun*, 193).

[31] Combination of *IBD*, 16 and *SD*, 18. See also *NSS*, 615, n. 2 where a problem that "confounded many modern critical scholars" has been easily solved by Arama.

In 1965, the editors of a certain pamphlet wrote to ask several educators their opinion on teaching biblical criticism in religious high schools:

> The question is, is it preferable – from a religious, educational approach, etc. – to teach specific claims of biblical criticism so as to demonstrate their wrongness and lack of scientific basis; or is it better to completely ignore this problem?[32]

Nehama was their quickest respondent. She explained to them that alongside a good deal of shoddy and absurd scholarship, they could find useful materials in biblical criticism. It covered such a broad spectrum of scholarship that their very question was faulty:

> It is as if someone were to ask whether it is worthwhile to read the works of "poets."[33]

A superficial approach to the matter was of no use whatsoever, and she rebuked them that their very question demonstrated that

> you have not probed and delved and learned. Not that I am advising you to delve into these problems – but how can someone even speak of a matter which he has not researched properly?[34]

Hence, this was not a subject to which they should devote an article in their journal. Indeed, scattered throughout Nehama's works are several references to biblical-critical ideas and scholars, though primarily in footnotes.[35] At times these are cited as support, while at other times because she wishes to refute them.

Dr. Leah Leeder, while a student at the Hebrew University, approached Nehama to discuss the strong arguments in favor of biblical criticism. Nehama admitted that sometimes even she felt unqualified to answer their claims, which – while propagandist and often spurious – constituted, when

---

[32] N. Leibowitz, "*Teshuvah*," 621. The journal was intended for graduates of the Bnei Akiva yeshivah high school in Raanana.

[33] N. Leibowitz, "*Teshuvah*," 622.

[34] N. Leibowitz, "*Teshuvah*," 622.

[35] Scholars mentioned in the *Studies* include: In *NSB*, Herder (58, n. 2) and the archeologist Pritchard (213, n. 2, spelled there "Prichard"). In *NSS*, Delitzsch and Dornseif (37, n. 2) and Pritchard (255, n. 2, where she also quotes Yadin); Daube (363 and 371, n. 4), Driver (371, n. 9), Jouon (400, n. 6), Guidman (652, n. 4), and the stylistics scholar Koenig (595, n. 21). In *NSV*, she quotes Gesenius (66); and she quotes no Bible scholars by name in *SBM* or *SD*. In her *gilyonot* she quotes Gunkel and Dilman once each, according to Sokolow's *Mafte'ah*. Nehama also cites various non-Jewish grammarians and translations. Furthermore, in *TI* she quotes Harper (45), and in *LP* she cites many biblical scholars not mentioned in her other writings including – repeatedly – Driver (1, n. 1, 46, 79, n. 6, 92, n. 4, 128, n. 3 and 146, n. 7). See Frankel, "*Ha-te'oriyah*," 434, n. 43.

presented well enough, the type of argument one could not necessarily win. Certainly, she said, someone who lacked a full grasp of Bible had no chance. Leeder valued Nehama's honesty. In lieu of a clear solution, at least knowing that even Nehama Leibowitz was unable to surmount all the difficulties made her feel better.

Being an Orthodox Bible scholar[36]

Nehama's world, as mentioned, was somehow both complex and yet relatively harmonious, and not characterized by tremendous struggle. She did not lose much sleep over the clash between the traditional versus the "biblical critical" approaches to Tanach. This stands in contrast to the tension felt by many contemporary Orthodox Bible academics, who often experience themselves as neither fish nor fowl. On one side, they are berated by academics for ignoring universal scholarship, becoming, in Carmy's words,

> intellectual Marrano[s]; compelled to feign neutrality in discussing matters in which [they hold] firm, unshakeable convictions.[37]

From the other direction, they are seen as "not kosher" in the eyes of their home communities, for Orthodox society does not wish to engage with biblical scholarship, or feels inadequate doing so, perhaps due to a lack of clarity about the Tanach's ideal role in general.[38] These religious scholars deal with these tensions in different ways: They compartmentalize the two, or specialize, or suspend judgment and hope that trends will eventually shift in more traditional directions; or they try to synthesize the critical and traditional positions in some way.[39] Some feel they cannot share their viewpoints in public, especially not in print. Their genuine opinions are heard only when they teach. Levy remarks:

---

[36] Those interested in delving further into the tensions between biblical criticism and Orthodoxy are referred to the books cited herein, by Sperling, Levy and Carmy, as well as the online journal at www.atid.org and the archives of the LookJed internet discussion group, particularly digest VI:20–23. An expanded version of this discussion appears in Unterman, *Background*, 23–29.

[37] S. Carmy, "A Room with a View but a Room of Our Own," in *Modern Scholarship in the Study of Torah*, edited by Shalom Carmy, 1-38 (Northvale, NJ: Jason Aaronson, 1996).

[38] Levy, for example, received criticism for suggesting that the Torah be given primacy as a central religious text ("State," 74–75).

[39] For more discussion see Levy, "Periphery," 180–181.

> We appear to be witnessing the creation of a new oral tradition, which, like the esoteric teachings of the Middle Ages, cannot be committed to writing – at least, not yet.[40]

In fact, there is a constantly evolving dialogue in today's world of Orthodox Tanach scholarship that raises many possibilities.[41] There may in fact be some positive outcomes from the dissonance experienced by the Orthodox Tanach scholar. Sokol, for example, argues that it may lead to the emergence of a unique hermeneutic, combining classic and modern interpretation.[42] Carmy suggests the need to create a *derech*, a path of study with positive insights, adding that this is difficult to do under the "hostile shadow of the academic establishment," with all one's energy squandered on defense. It is only an option for the rare Orthodox scholar whose attainments in this field permit bucking the consensus.[43] This brings us back to Nehama who, unattached to any Bible department, free from the constant pressure to publish, and with her primary achievements falling outside the realm of formal academia, seems to fit this description well.

In Nehama's early teaching days, Tanach study was largely a free-for-all, cropping up at random on pages of Talmud in the yeshivah world, limited to archeological and historical aspects in the secular world, and even in National Religious schools relegated to the secular curriculum. While this situation was far from ideal – and indeed, Nehama played an important part in rectifying it, restoring the Tanach to its rightful place in the center of Jewish study – in some ways it allowed her to do what she liked. She forged ahead with a *derech* of her own (to borrow Carmy's terminology), rich with academic and traditional elements, methodology and insight. Instead of experiencing struggle and dissonance, she made the most of straddling the two worlds. Her traditional background brought her several advantages. She was capable of reading the text very closely, being deeply familiar with

---

[40] Levy, "State," 69. He proposes some solutions to the problem that are less underground in nature, such as re-embracing the marginalized Rational-Scientific school of exegesis and reframing the rabbinical material discarded by the mainstream ("Periphery," 182–190). See also Yeshayahu Maori, "Rabbinic Midrash as Evidence for Textual Variants," in *Modern Scholarship in the Study of Torah*, edited by Shalom Carmy, 104 and *passim* (Northvale, NJ: Jason Aaronson, 1996), for a brief discussion of the need not to publish material which undermines tradition. Frankel also mentions this issue, referring us to Leo Strauss's "Persecution and the Art of Writing" (*Iyun*, 227, n. 53).

[41] Zvi Grumet, conversation.

[42] See Yedgar, "*Parshanut*," 109 and Moshe Z. Sokol, "How Do Modern Jewish Thinkers Interpret Religious Texts?" *Modern Judaism* 13/1 (1993): 25–48.

[43] Carmy, "Room," 37.

Hebrew and with the range of Jewish interpretative literature. She also had more leeway to accept or reject prevalent theories, and in this, at least, was intellectually freer than her non-Orthodox colleagues.

Nehama probably did experience some of the restraints affecting many Orthodox Tanach scholars. For example, there are indications that she was willing to say certain things that she would not publish and believed things that she would not say.[44] But she avoided much of the problem by skirting academic biblical scholarship altogether. She harbored a certain dislike of the academic enterprise in general – educating towards Jewish values seemed a more worthwhile way to spend one's time. But her wariness of academic Bible scholarship was most pronounced. She indignantly wrote:

> What a terrible expression to use to describe the words of the living God – "material"!!! (*TI*, 26)

She refused to go along with the predominant research directions or compromise her beliefs for the sake of career. She especially detested the prevalent assumption that traditionalists are prejudiced while others are not. Schwartz recalls her pronouncement: "Everyone has prejudices, but I at least *know* that I have them!" Academia was not a worldview, to be adopted wholesale, but rather a set of tools and findings to be implemented selectively and with caution. As Yedgar writes:

> Nehama's academic approach does not lie in disinterested openness to any and every scholarly conclusion, but rather in a methodological approach incorporating academic elements, resting on a basis of the pre-existing religious approach. She postulates that even the student of Tanach with traditional beliefs can and must submit to academic and rational standards.[45]

Nehama employed the academic way of thinking more than its conclusions – the "how" rather than the "what"; utilizing devices such as definition of terms, selection and categorization, comparing and contrasting, and more.[46] Her core methodology – evaluating commentaries for their faithfulness to the text – required probing and investigation, and hers was a systematic, objective and encompassing approach.[47] She ruthlessly rejected weak arguments and refused to bend the truth in order to reconcile

---

[44] See page 331 above.

[45] Yedgar, "*Ha-iyunim*," 19. Yedgar suggests that other modern Orthodox Bible scholars, for example Professor Uriel Simon, are located in the wider intellectual world and are part of it in a way that Nehama never was; and that Nehama's true location was in the Orthodox world – she imported and "koshered" universal material in a manner not unlike that of the Hirschian *Torah im Derech Eretz* philosophy (interview).

[46] See Yedgar, "*Bein*," 70 and "*Ha-iyunim*," 23–24 for more details.

[47] Yedgar, "*Ha-iyunim*," 19.

commentaries; on the contrary, she delighted in highlighting their differences.

This, then, was her academic *derech* in biblical scholarship, one with which she could live in peace. It focused on Jewish traditional interpretations, falling chronologically between the study of the ancient biblical text and the scholarship of recent centuries, and a far less problematic topic of study than either.[48] While the biblical scholars spent their time trying to reconstruct the text and how it came into being historically, she was studying what Greenberg calls "the received text," its present layers and meanings.[49] When Nehama did focus on the text, it was often on literary aspects of the Tanach.

∾ ∾

Nehama was known to actively discourage students from studying Bible at university. R. Chaim Weiner, who specialized in Talmud, reflects: "Nehama was probably responsible for my career choice. I guess she didn't consider what happened in the Bible Department to be a continuation of the Torah study she loved." In the case of Professor Yisrael Knohl, she had the opposite effect. Knohl knew Nehama from a young age, through his relatives, the Ben-Sassons; and even as a child, could tell that the Leibowitzes were "a very special couple." Nehama spoke to him for hours about his Tanach studies in school. These conversations "had a certain influence," and Knohl eventually switched from the field of Talmud to Tanach, making his academic career as a critical Bible scholar, a choice that displeased Nehama. Knohl recalls with discomfort standing at the entrance to the National Library while she berated him unsparingly for being involved with "all that rubbish and heresy." Yet he remarks: "While we have differences of opinion, I truly believe that she made a great contribution to Jewish society, and I don't see her method and the academic method as coming at each other's expense."

Not all his colleagues are so kind. Today, in certain non-Orthodox circles, attempts to resolve biblical puzzles while avoiding textual emendations are greeted with the dismissive rejoinder: "Oh, that's Nehama Leibowitz!" Her name has become representative there of a narrow-minded traditional approach that rejects the theories accepted by the academic world for two centuries now. In the 1950s, Boaz Evron wrote of Nehama's Tanach lessons on *Kol Israel*, Israel's national radio station:

---

[48] Carmy notes that the study of *parshanut* or rabbinic interpretation "can become an agreeable 'city of refuge' enabling the Orthodox scholar to participate in the academic field without affronting the ancestral pieties" ("Room," 11).

[49] Frankel, "*Ha-te'oriyah*," 426, n., 6; 429, n. 20 and 437.

> Dr. Leibowitz's lessons are an outstanding example of the simultaneously positive and negative aspects of Scriptural interpretations heard on *Kol Israel*, which always stay within traditional parameters, giving no foothold to scientific criticism. The speaker brought many in-depth explanations for the contradiction (that she discovered in the weekly Torah portion); but this very multiplicity testifies to the need for a scientific-critical clarification of how the contradiction came into being, independent of the attempt to solve it on a theological basis.[50]

Nevertheless, to her credit, Nehama was also accepted by many in the secular world as a respected academic, or at least a scholarly force to be reckoned with. The critic Yosef Oren praised her for

> demonstrating that traditional exegesis manages to explain textual difficulties better and more profoundly than biblical criticism does; so that the latter, even if only by inference, comes off as tendentious, aiming to undermine the sacredness of the Tanach and the value of its ideas.[51]

And Professor Yair Hoffman remarks:

> Nehama Leibowitz's admirers, it appears to me, are distributed equally between two camps: those who adopt all of her principles unquestioningly, and those who reject many of her assumptions. But even this latter camp cannot free itself of the "Nehama" within. Every essay, every theory one tries to formulate demands serious consideration of the alternative – perchance the "Nehama method" is the more correct?[52]

Nehama's primary academic career took place in Tel Aviv University, the bastion of secular Israeli academia. That she was both popular and successful there we can hear from the following letter by a reader of the *Jerusalem Post*:

> Nehama took the bus from Jerusalem to Tel Aviv once a week in order to share her unique gift as a Torah scholar and teacher with the score of students, me among them, in the newly established Tel Aviv university.... The problem which faced all of us who wanted to drink from the fountain of her legendary knowledge was that there wasn't a room quite big enough to fit us all in. I was fortunate enough to have a big and strong friend who utilized his brawn to win us both a good seat at her lectures, which were the most fascinating of all.[53]

---

[50] Sheleg, "*Kalat*," 71.
[51] Sheleg, "*Kalat*," 71.
[52] Hoffman, "*Yoter*."
[53] Rachel Kapen, "Marvelous Teacher," Letters, *Jerusalem Post*, May 9, 1997.

At the time, secular Israeli academics had little acquaintance with classical Jewish commentaries, which had been deliberately sidelined as old-fashioned with little to offer. It was Nehama who was largely responsible for salvaging from the musty attic of obscurity this precious legacy of commentaries and reintroducing their insights into the academic discourse. Hoffman recalls:

> The fifties – the early days of Tel Aviv University. The first encounter with academic Torah study, enchanting the students with its iconoclasm and captivating them in its daring evaluation and dismissal of sacred cows. For a moment, it appears that we may now leave behind the traditional approach, which no longer has the power to satisfy anyone bitten by the bug of critical analysis in academic Tanach study. But along Nehama comes, and in just one or two lessons, relights the flames of doubt, creates respect for the Sages' and medieval commentators' interpretations, turns Rashi and Ibn Ezra into contenders with Wellhausen and Gunkel who regularly "win" – and not infrequently due to the force of Nehama's personality.[54]

Abba Oren, a teacher in secular Israeli circles, writes:

> At Oranim I thought I had to make a choice between the obscurantism of the Uppsala School of Bible criticism, the latent anti-Semitism of Wellhausen, or the mean-spirited superiority of Martin Noth on the one hand and the ingenious but apologetic contributions of Cassuto. The latter was just too cerebral for me, and the first three plucked the Bible out of the bosom of Judaism, much as an instructor in medical school might plop the heart of a frog onto a dissecting table. It is very clear (a) that the instructor feels superior to the frog, (b) that the heart no longer belongs to the frog but to science, and (c) that the instructor, in the name of science, could overcome his disdain or squeamishness and is therefore to be applauded. Nehama Leibowitz was the one who put the heart of Judaism back into its rightful place for me…. The entire series really belongs in the home of every committedly curious and spiritually creative Jew.[55]

Here, Nehama succeeded in one of her main goals: to introduce the Jewishly ignorant to the richness of their tradition. As Professor Urbach wrote:

> In circles which had distanced themselves from Torah study, the *gilyonot* woman has restored the study of the Torah to its former glory.[56]

---

[54] Hoffman, "*Yoter.*"
[55] Oren, "That," 157, 159.
[56] Urbach, "*Le-mikra,*" 55.

Levy: "She restored confidence in classical rabbinic interpretation of the Bible in general, and in Rashi in particular, at a time when neither was taken seriously in the wake of the capture of the Bible by archaeology and comparative semitic studies."[57]

Nehama did not simply reintroduce the commentaries, but also injected new academic dimensions into their study. Professor Israel Rozenson:

> She played a vital role in the battle to prevent the decline of traditional commentary into an assortment of random explanations often left to the mercies of various sermonizers; and in turning it into a "science" with stringent methodological requirements.[58]

From this we learn that not all revolutions introduce the new – Nehama's revolution reintroduced the old, though in a new way. It filled a vacuum for many people. Dr. Gabriel Cohn remarks: "Why did so many educated people ignore the secular Zionists, abandon Gordon and follow Nehama? Because she was teaching the Jewish Bible. People don't want to study the Tanach as archeology – what's Jewish about that? The Bible is neutral – there is a Christian Bible and a Muslim Bible. What makes it Jewish is the Jewish commentaries." As Nehama herself writes:

> The teacher of Tanach in a Jewish school is not teaching a book of ancient Near Eastern literature, but rather the sacred text from which generations have drawn and continue to draw nourishment, and upon which all of Jewish literature through the ages – Halachah and Aggadah, prayer and liturgy, lament and *selichah*, Kabbalah and scientific research, books of Mussar and Hasidism – are nothing but expositions. They are all offshoots of the Torah, in their ideas, idioms, allusions and concepts.[59]

Academic scholar or educator?[60]

The price Nehama paid for keeping a foot in both worlds was that she never officially became a fully-fledged academic Bible scholar. Her professorship was in the Department of Education of Tel Aviv University, and not in the Bible Department, where she also taught. At the Hebrew University, despite her good relations with the faculty, she was likewise never hired to teach in the Bible Department. Ultimately, this left her freer to pursue her own agendas. So was this a deliberate choice? Was Nehama happy to be seen as a

---

[57] Levy, private communication.

[58] Rozenson, "*Ha-parshanit*," 434.

[59] N. Leibowitz, *Shiurim*, sheet 17, 3, "Note to teachers."

[60] The discussions in chapter 22 also have bearing on this question, for they explore what was more important to Nehama, the *peshat* or the relevance, with the former of more interest to the Bible scholar and the latter to the educator.

"Tanach Educator," as her professorship implied; or did she see herself as a Bible scholar, no matter how the academic world viewed her?

The answer is unclear. On the one hand, she explicitly said, "I'm not a scholar, I'm a teacher."[61] Her *Studies* were inspirational and her highest goals involved her educational agendas.[62] Her work did not follow academic norms. It chiefly comprised collating, comparing and teaching commentaries. It exhibited an almost completely synchronic-ahistorical approach. She reserved the right to select her texts using subjective criteria – picking out the more interesting and educational passages, in a neatly packaged length and format which indicated a choice more rhetorical and didactic than methodological.[63] Her approach lacked the systemization characteristic of academic work – apparently deliberately so, since she could be very clear and orderly when she wished, for example in her pedagogical work.[64] Systemization would involve taking verses out of their original context, which Nehama did not want to do, preferring to deal with the Tanach by units and by topic:

> For their beauty and impact are greater by far if each is taught in its context and the students come across them suddenly and unexpectedly.[65]

This study by units according to aesthetic or homiletic factors allowed Nehama to avoid questions arising when dealing with larger units, with the specter of biblical documents hovering over them.[66]

On the other hand, Nehama strongly objected to characterization of her approach to Tanach as "educational," a word that, in this context, smacked

---

[61] Breuer, "*Yahasah*," 14.

[62] See Frankel, *Iyun*, 220.

[63] See Amit, "Hebrew Bible," 11–12; Yedgar "*Ha-iyunim*," 27.

[64] For many, Nehama represented the height of systemization, creating order in what was previously a haphazard jumble of text and commentary (see Lieberman, *PN*, 23; Ahrend "*Mi-toch*," 32). Nonetheless, many of her principles were scattered. Her university courses on exegesis were organized topically, and she devoted lessons to "the difficult word" and other elements. There was also some laying out of principles in her work, e.g. in comparison of passages (*NSB*, 513) and use of metaphors (*NSS*, 291–293). Her most systematized work was her Open University course book on Rashi, which she only wrote very late in life.

[65] N. Leibowitz, "*He'arot metodiyot le-limmud*," 487.

[66] Nehama believed the text to be omnisignificant – namely, any part can stand on its own or be compared to any other part. She notes that the Sages viewed every verse within the setting of the Torah as a whole (*NSS*, 665). Any verse may be elucidated by comparison with verses with a similar theme or wording from other books (for example, using Psalm 78 to explain the word "*hinam*" in Numbers 11:5, in *SBM*, 95–97). Notwithstanding, Nehama was aware that, in a literary sense, different books were different units.

of tendentiousness and preaching. She insisted that she was an objective teacher of text – that she taught the *peshat*.[67] Independent thinking and intellectual effort were an integral part of her world. She derides one scholar for evaluating certain explanations as "amusing," without granting the reader the possibility to assess why.[68] Nehama was critical, if not with a capital C then certainly with a small one, promoting rational and analytical thinking, and making assessments based on logic and consistency.

Nevertheless, Dr. Marla Frankel differentiates between the type of critical thinking that Nehama espoused (*"hitbonenut bikortit"*), which is accompanied by certain assumptions about the text, and the critical thinking (*"hashivah bikortit"*), implemented in scientific scholarship where nothing is taken for granted.[69]

≫ ≪

So where does this leave us on the question of Nehama as Bible scholar? She did not fit all of the criteria for a modern Bible academic. But perhaps we should stop trying to squeeze her into the categories of "academic" or "non-academic." Another classification system might fit her better. Let us return to Levy's model of the Midrashic-Kabbalistic, Talmudic-Midrashic, and Rational-Scientific schools. A significant segment of contemporary Orthodoxy tends to favor the Midrashic-Kabbalistic and Talmudic-Midrashic approaches, often overlooking rationalistic *peshat*-orientated thinkers, including respected figures such as Rashbam and Ibn Ezra, and even deliberately expurgating them from popular anthologies.[70] Nehama, in contrast, quoted these commentators abundantly. Avoiding the Kabbalistic-Hasidic approach, she drew her material from the Talmudic-Midrashic and the Rational-Scientific schools, utilizing a wide range of views, including the philosophers, grammarians and *pashtanim* of the medieval and modern age, as well as others.

Yedgar has noted that certain academic-type aspects are present in many of the traditional commentaries.[71] It seems clear that Nehama viewed herself as following the critical thinking that she, like Yedgar, saw in them. Perhaps, then, we can state that Nehama was not trying to be a modern academic, but rather to be loyal to a traditional rational model of old, in the footsteps of great medieval Jewish *pashtanim* such as Rashbam, Ibn Ezra *et al.*, and thinkers such as Maimonides. Like them she maintained a keen sense for the

---

[67] Ahrend, "*Mi-toch*," 45.
[68] *NSS*, 371, n. 4. The scholar was Daube.
[69] Frankel, "*Ha-te'oriyah*," 432
[70] Levy, "Periphery," 165.
[71] Yedgar, "*Ha-iyunim*," 19.

peshat, searching for it both inside rabbinic interpretation and outside of it. Like them, she was willing to cite from external sources.[72] Undoubtedly a modern thinker, she was interested in new scholarship when useful, and assimilated many of its terms and ways of thinking; yet she retained a certain old-world flavor.

Nehama's position on important questions of Tanach study is in line with this kind of rational traditionalism. This can be seen when examining several axioms that Levy outlines, which in his opinion have become the normative Orthodox view of Tanach – and erroneously so, for in each case, some highly regarded rabbinic writers have not subscribed to them. These axioms are:

One: The Patriarchs lived an Orthodox lifestyle.

Two: The entire Torah was given on Sinai.

Three: There were no human contributions to the composition of the Torah.

Four: The authors of all biblical books are who the Talmud and Midrash say they are.

Five: The Torah text was transmitted with one hundred percent accuracy down the generations.

Six: All biblical narratives, including the miraculous, are literal, accurate historical events.

Seven: Rabbinic interpretation, particularly Talmud and Midrash, is unchallengeable.

Eight: Halachah represents the primary intention of the text; the Tanach receives no "independent hearing."

Nine: Non-traditional sources are inadmissible.[73]

We may suggest one further axiom, omitted by Levy but clearly part of this pantheon: That the Patriarchs, and indeed all biblical heroes, were perfect and never sinned.

Nehama had something to say about many of these axioms. Regarding the first axiom, she says:

> Our Sages… credit [Abraham] with observing the whole Torah even before it was given. Our Sages probably wished to emphasize that in Judaism belief in one God and the true faith were impossible without

---

[72] Nehama quoted even Bible critics, when useful. We might compare this to Ibn Ezra's choice, on occasion, to quote his polemical adversaries, the Karaites, when they said something valuable; but this is speculation and requires further study.

[73] See further in Levy, "Periphery," 167–172 and 196, n. 28. These axioms appear applicable mainly within North American Jewry ("as taught in the Artscroll series"), although may probably be extrapolated to conservative-minded Jews everywhere.

observance of the precepts. Whoever acknowledges one God must logically carry out His precepts. (*NSB*, 118)

A close reading of her wording, and especially "they probably wished to emphasize" implies that their words were not, perhaps, intended to be taken entirely literally.[74]

The second and third axioms were accepted by Nehama, though she was willing to admit later prophetic additions. Her work *Limmud parshanei ha-Torah u-derachim le-hora'atam: Sefer Bereshit*, intended for a broad audience of teachers, contains as an addendum,[75] a passage from the *Tzafenat Pane'ah*, a fourteenth-century work of commentary on the Ibn Ezra. In this passage, the author, R. Joseph ben Eliezer Bonfils, relates to the apparently anachronistic statement (Genesis 12:6)

...and the Canaanite was then in the land.

This verse appears to have been written at a time when the Canaanite inhabitants have disappeared, which was long after Moses's time. R. Bonfils had no problem suggesting that parts of the narrative (though not the legal material) in the Torah may have been authored by a prophet other than Moses – a radical position today.[76] Nehama confided to Levy that she reprinted this in her book to keep it in the public view because people had lost sight of this thinking.[77]

Moving to axiom six, we find that, rather than take a stance on the question of the literal historical accuracy of events in the Tanach, she declared herself uninterested in this issue.[78] Axioms seven and eight are linked – the infallibility of rabbinic understandings and the Halachah as primary interpretation. Nehama felt at liberty to challenge rabbinic understanding, albeit more so in the case of modern or medieval commentators than that of the Sages. Like many *pashtanim* before her, she was willing to argue that talmudic interpretations were not admissible as *peshat*, and to remove them from the playing field of discussion. For example:

However profound and striking the truth of the idea contained in this excerpt from the Palestinian Talmud, we must admit that no hint of it is to be found in our text. (*NSS*, 144)

---

[74] See the Hebrew wording in *IBB*, 85.

[75] *LP*, 221–222.

[76] See *Tzafenat Pane'ah*, *Lech Lecha*, 12. However, Nehama offers a different explanation when discussing this verse in her *Studies* (*NSB*, 124) and does not mention Bonfils there, due perhaps to the different audiences for the two works.

[77] Levy, private communication.

[78] See page 462 below.

Although Nehama sometimes went to great lengths to prove that the talmudic-halachic understanding was in fact *peshat*,[79] she was also able to reject it as such, knowing that they were not one and the same. While halachic practice is mandatory, when it comes to text Halachah represents *an* interpretation, not the sole one:

> Of course, Rashbam never for a moment opposed the traditional interpretation that the Torah was commanding us here to wear Tefillin, as did the Karaites. In his view, the plain sense of the text was one thing, the Halakha, the determining of Jewish precept another. There were many levels of Torah interpretation, including both the primary, literal sense and the concomitant oral tradition. (*NSS*, 223, n. 1)

Halachic readings may sidetrack the reader from the *peshat*:

> Yet the text hardly suggests a halakhic discussion, but rather a justification offered by Aaron for his intuitive decision. (*NSV*, 140)

Nehama's rejection of Levy's ninth axiom and her acceptance of non-traditional sources have been dealt with already at length; as has her approach towards our suggested tenth axiom, the assumption of perfect biblical heroes.[80]

All of the above is cited as support for the contention that, in her devout and yet simultaneously critical outlook, Nehama fits best into a certain traditional Rational-Scientific model, extant for many centuries within Jewish intellectual life. Predating biblical criticism, this model's proponents did not have to expend all their energies on defense of the sacred text. Although polemics existed, with Christians and Karaites, for the most part the medieval and pre-modern Jewish interpreters were free to engage the text directly, proceeding undisturbed with the act of interpretation. Or at the very least, that was how Nehama perceived them, and how she herself wished to be. Though unable to turn her back completely on Bible research trends, she wanted to waste as little time as possible on apologetics or justification.

Nehama saw herself as imitating these traditional predecessors, whose proto-academic approach she admired. For her, they had invented the critical approach to Tanach, through their intellectual attitudes, their debating and their justifications for their positions. Medieval did not mean primitive; she was always battling this conception. She proudly highlighted occasions when the medievals anticipated various modern theories, such as Abravanel who

> in the fifteenth century formulated this idea in words that might have been taken from a contemporary manual of psychology. (*NSB*, 427)

---

[79] See for example in "Rules for the Fruit Picker," *SD*, 229–230.
[80] See page 341 above.

or the Netziv:

> This nineteenth-century talmudist, steeped in Rabbinic law, expresses,
> in his own language, the distinctions between prose and verse that have
> been defined for us, today, in technical terminology by modern literary
> critics and students of semantics. (*SD*, 354)

Similarly, the problems "discovered" by the Protestant Bible scholars in
the late eighteenth century onwards were nothing new, having been noted
centuries before by the Jewish exegetes.[81] Once, at the Annual Conference
for Bible Research, a young scholar gave a lecture outlining his discoveries in
the Bible. At the end Nehama stood up and proclaimed that all these
"innovations" were actually to be found in the medieval Jewish
commentaries. She crusaded for the traditional commentaries, introducing
them as serious players to a "biblical critical" environment that had
neglected them. Professor Yairah Amit of the Tel Aviv University Bible
Education Department, notes:

> Paradoxically, Nehama's method has been and continues to be
> applauded by the very people who regret her relative disregard of
> general biblical scholarship. For them, the real significance of her
> method lies in its creation of a meeting point between traditional Jewish
> exegesis and the school of historical-philological research developed by
> Protestant scholars beginning in the late eighteenth century. Presenting
> both schools side by side, Nehama shows that such problems as
> duplications or even contradictions, which served as the starting points
> for historical criticism, are nothing new. Jewish exegesis had already
> taken note of these problems and dealt with them in its own fashion.
> By setting out a variety of exegetical schools, Nehama brings traditional
> commentary out into the open, transforming it into a basic factor to be
> reckoned with by scholars whenever they wish to elucidate a biblical
> text.[82]

Hoffman writes similarly:

> Nehama brought her students to an ongoing encounter between [the
> "biblical critical" school and traditional interpretation]. In her

---

[81] However, Dr. Baruch Schwartz believes that here, Nehama may have been guilty of
overtaxation of the commentators' actual words. He recalls her saying in a disparaging
way, "Why does he have to quote Gunkel here? The Alshech already said it!'" when this
was not quite true. As an example, he cites *IHBV*, 190, where Nehama notes the
unusual style of the verses. Her comment, says Schwartz, is more consistent with the
biblical critics' theory of a new literary stratum (designated "H") than with the
homogeneity assumed by the traditional commentaries. Yet Nehama immediately quotes
Alshech, implying that it is his idea, and therefore, since Alshech had discovered a "new
style," there was no need to postulate a separate source or redactor (Schwartz, lecture).
[82] Amit, "Hebrew Bible," 11.

worksheets, books and lessons she brought both of them: Driver and Rashi, Mowinckel and Radak. In this way Nehama Leibowitz bestowed legitimacy, so to speak, upon traditional interpretation, not as a separate, aloof discipline but as an approach that is integral and crucial to a scholar's intellectual integrity.[83]

Summary

Nehama persistently trod a careful line between "acceptable" rationalism and "dangerous" criticism, between academia and tradition. Her work was overall affirmative rather than defensive or polemical, and she beat out her own *derech* of insight and analysis. Although educational factors were important to her, for the most part she read the Tanach with a determinedly rational-critical stance.

I have suggested here that what Nehama did was to draw her inspiration from an earlier time, when one could be traditional and rational without becoming a Bible critic, and without retreating into the kind of rigid axioms that Orthodoxy had increasingly adopted as a result of centuries of polemics with reformist trends. Her approach seems to have grown organically from previous models, while biblical criticism produced a thorough break with them. As Levy notes, transforming into a Bible critic is not a prerequisite for every rational thinker:

> Archeology and historical perspective, not rational thinking, are the primary differences between modern writers and many of their pre-modern counterparts.[84]

From within this organic traditional-rational approach, Nehama was willing to co-opt modern academic methodologies and analytical tools wherever useful, in order to introduce rigorous discipline into Tanach study; but only insofar as such elements as were consonant with the traditional direction. Thus, although by no means a "pre-modern," she in some ways had much more in common with some of the earlier exegetes than she did with various contemporaries. Arguably, her scholarship thus remained more "Jewish," in its independence of Western scholarship, than was the case for most of her peers. As Levy notes:

> The rational-scientific position that emerged during the Enlightenment and continued to evolve throughout the past two centuries undoubtedly assumed many critical values and postures, and diverged even further

---

[83] Hoffman, "*Yoter.*" It should not be deduced from these last two citations that Nehama set out methodically to compare the biblical critics with the classic commentators, bringing them literally side by side; but rather that she introduced the critical sources from time to time (Amit and Hoffman, conversation).

[84] Levy, "Periphery," 160.

from what came to be perceived as the more traditional ones. In fact one might question if or how the work of many modern Jewish scholars differs from the work of their non-Jewish colleagues.[85]

The Modern Orthodox community as a whole accepted Nehama's scholarship despite its controversial elements. Little criticism was heard within the community's ranks, for she functioned as a beacon, a scholarly standard-bearer for the Torah. Her ability to confront modern challenges with integrity saved others from being troubled by them. As Jay Harris observes:

> People do not necessarily need to be able to articulate a response to challenge, so long as they have an authoritative source to which they can confidently refer for such a response.[86]

But at the same time that she was defending the Tanach from Bible critics, she was also reversing the negative effects of certain aspects of Orthodox Judaism upon it! She successfully rehabilitated it from its previous neglected status and, furthermore, reclaimed the *peshat* and made it popular. In other words, she restored the boundaries of accepted traditional Torah scholarship to its former broad positions, held before Orthodoxy began to hunker down in the face of perceived attack.

The status, respect and work opportunities that Nehama received outside the academic world allowed her freedom from the rules governing academic life – to "buck the consensus" and do more or less as she pleased. She never demanded to be called a Bible scholar, was not attached to a Bible Department, and did not do academic research in the accepted manner. Nonetheless, the next two chapters will be devoted to arguing that Nehama made a tremendous contribution to modern Bible scholarship, perhaps more than some who proudly go by the label "Bible scholar."

---

[85] Levy, "Periphery," 163–164. Nehama appears to have done what Uriel Simon suggests is unfeasible – he writes: "The paths blazed by the medieval commentators cannot simply be resumed, for in view of modern developments in Bible research, this exegetical method is immeasurably more critical today [than in medieval times]… so much so that it challenges not only the unity of the Written and Oral Law but even the sanctity of the Bible itself" ("The Place of the Bible in Israeli Society: From National Midrash to Existential Peshat," *Modern Judaism* 19:3 [October 1999]: 231).

[86] Jay M. Harris, *How Do We Know This? Midrash and the Fragmentation of Modern Judaism*, Albany: State University of New York Press, 1995, 233.

CHAPTER 20

NEHAMA'S LITERARY APPROACH:
PART I: BACKGROUND AND INFLUENCES[1]

IN THE COMING TWO CHAPTERS it will be argued that though Nehama was not a *critical* Bible scholar, she was a *literary* Bible scholar (in the places where she chose to use literary analysis);[2] and that she should receive due credit for the way in which her pioneering work has influenced this field.

Background

In the second quarter of the twentieth century, a wind of change blew through the world of scholarly Bible study as a new literary direction developed in reaction to the historical-critical overload in that field. While literary Bible interpretation existed already in various forms, in the 1950s it made great inroads into the academic world, eventually becoming a significant sub-field in biblical studies.

From an Orthodox Jewish perspective, this was good news. It offered an asylum for Orthodox scholars, since it bypassed niggling questions of earlier or later texts of various authorship, instead presenting works as unified wholes.[3] Rabbinic corpuses were reclaimed from their banished status, their primary assumptions now at least partially acceptable to the academic mind. At last the dialogue could shift to less defensive ground, and the gap between Orthodox and non-Orthodox was transcended to some extent.[4]

---

[1] Much of the material in this chapter and the next one is based on research for my MA thesis, written for Touro College Israel under the supervision of Dr. Baruch Schwartz (see bibliography for details). The conclusions of that paper have been refined here.

[2] In fact, most of her work does not comprise literary analyses; but even her occasional use of this tool, as an integral part of the interpretative process, made her revolutionary (Yedgar, "*Bein*," 67). Yedgar explains that Nehama adopted three main methods in her work: literary analysis, academic-methodological analysis, and a faith-based, values-oriented approach. Unlike the first two, the third cannot be similarly applied to any other text and is reserved for the Tanach as a Holy Scripture ("*Ha-iyunim*," 20).

[3] According to Carmy, most, though not all, literary readers do not presuppose the documentary hypothesis in their analysis (see "Room," 31–32).

[4] See Sperling, *Students*, 118; Carmy "Room," 31–32. See also S. Carmy, "Biblical Exegesis: Jewish Views," in *The Encyclopedia of Religion*, edited by Mircea Eliade, 2, 141 (NY:MacMillan, 1987).

However, some Bible scholars feared this new direction, calling it "neo-fundamentalism." They cautioned against a facile viewing of the new literary readings as identical to the traditional, pre-critical outlook.[5] Academic literary readings still require a solid base of reliable texts, text criticism, comparison with other Near Eastern texts and plausible historical context.[6]

In response, Orthodox scholars insist that their findings not be rejected *a priori* simply because they are traditionalists.[7] However, coming from the other perspective, Orthodox scholars do agree, for their own reasons, that the new literary readings differ from the traditional outlook. First – and most important – the Tanach is not mere literature, but the Divine word.[8] Furthermore, the Tanach contains historical information and moral instruction, two elements ignored in modern literary theory, as well as much legal material.[9] Ultimately it is a secular approach, and benefit must be derived selectively.[10]

---

[5] Segal, Cassuto, Buber, Rosenzweig and Jacob all came under fire in this way (see Sperling, *Students*, 118; Berger, "Morality," 139–140). Even Robert Alter, a secular scholar, had his work labeled "fundamentalism" by Hyam Maccoby (letter in *Commentary* 77:2 [February 1984]: 14). See also R. Knierim, "Criticism of Literary Features, Form, Tradition and Redaction," in *The Hebrew Bible and Its Modern Interpreters*, edited by D.A. Knight and G.M. Tucker, 123–165 (California: Scholars Press, 1985). See especially page 126, where he warns against "canon criticism" (focusing on the canonized version while ignoring its historical growth). Sperling emphasizes that while the idea of redaction as Israelite or Jewish creativity is more pleasing than one of "pasting together of jumbled fragments by small-minded post-exilic priests," there has nonetheless been a redaction process (*Students*, 118–119).

[6] Sperling laments the decline of these disciplines (*Students*, 119), but Amit feels, on the contrary, that textual and higher criticism are increasingly used within literary analyses, and herself advocates familiarity with their findings (Yairah Amit, *Reading Biblical Narratives: Literary Criticism and the Hebrew Bible*. Minneapolis: Fortress Press, 2001, 23–31). However, Berger warns against overuse of the documentary hypothesis in literary readings, since literary patterns must imply a certain unity. "You can allow the 'redactor' just so much freedom of action before he turns into an author using various traditions as 'raw material.' Such an approach must ultimately shake the foundations of the regnant critical theory, not merely tinker with its periphery" ("Morality," 146). This is a reaction to the work of Fokkelman, Alter and Fishbane.

[7] See Berger, "Morality," 139–140.

[8] For example, Breuer warns against importing the literary assumption that the author's intention is irrelevant (which he rejects also in general literature) into biblical interpretation ("The Study," 178–180).

[9] Carmy, "Room," 32. However, Schwartz has undertaken literary analysis of legal biblical material (see *Torat ha-kedushah: iyunim ba-huka ha-kohanit she-ba-Torah*, Jerusalem: Magnes: 1999, 12–17).

[10] See Newman's introduction to *NSB*, xxix, where he quotes T.S. Eliot on the difference between literature and a work that has had literary influence, specifically the Bible.

❧ ❧

The literary direction could not have come at a better time for Nehama as a haven from the biblical-critical methodologies. She was delighted to be able to dismiss the documentary hypothesis by explaining textual irregularities as literary devices.[11] Nehama wanted to deal with what the text said rather than who wrote it. When she first discovered a group of scholars of literature – eventually named the New Critics – who agreed with her, she was very excited. Dr. Gabriel Cohn reports Nehama's great enthusiasm when she leafed through works by two of these New Critics, Empson and Brooks. Nehama quickly understood that if this approach could also be used regarding the Tanach, it could preserve fundamental Jewish beliefs while still allowing for academic analysis. Perhaps more significantly, this new methodology might also reveal fascinating new dimensions in the Torah.

By nature, Nehama possessed a literary orientation. She studied, and later taught, literature at university. She loved the skilled use of words to create atmosphere and meaning. She was partial to *piyyutim* – liturgical poetry – and inserted them into her teachings,[12] sometimes waxing poetic in her own writings. Although we cited some examples of this in a previous chapter,[13] let us once again enjoy Nehama's poetic language as a reminder:

> A degenerate world, overflowing with violence, had been purified, rinsed and cleansed in mighty waters, sanitized and scrubbed – and is now fresh, sparkling and new, with no trace of the sin and wrongdoing, robbery, violence and degradation formerly saturating it.[14]

Nehama emphasized that the study of literature, even in high school, goes beyond just the reading of poems and stories. It constitutes the in-depth scrutiny of philosophical reflections from the world's greatest thinkers.[15] Her awe at the literature's greatness made students want to explore it in depth. Professor Dov Landau studied literature with Nehama at Bar-Ilan University and went on to become a professor of literature himself.

---

[11] For example, according to Nehama, Exodus 16:35, which appears to be an anachronistic interpolation, is actually a statement highlighting the Israelites' ingratitude (*NSS*, 269), and a geographical incongruity in Numbers 13:21–22, used as proof for the P and J authorship, is resolved by paying attention to a grammatical nuance (see Frankel, *Iyun*, 112, for discussion and references).

[12] See Shlomit Elitzur, "*Iyun be-piyuttei 'berah dodi' she-be-mahzor Pesah*," in *PN*, 609, and Nehama's essay on the poem "*Berah dodi*" in *PN*, 610–615.

[13] See page 313 above.

[14] *IBB*, 53. The English translation, in its brevity, loses the poetics and rich language (see *NSB*, 74).

[15] N. Leibowitz, "*He'arot metodiyot le-keriyat*," 144. The entire article is worth reading as a statement of Nehama's opinion on how to read literature.

He says: "Nehama's literary approach was to decode the inner meanings of the text, which are connected to the world of the emotions, and to emphasize the 'great experiences' found there. She taught the text from the inside perspective – how it understood itself." Initially, Landau felt uncomfortable with Nehama's suggestion that *Anna Karenina*, with its adulterous heroine, was a holy book. But she convinced him, arguing: "This book demonstrates that a person can never ultimately profit from sin. Karenina couldn't love the child she bore illegitimately." For Nehama, it was not the content but the attitude that defined the morality of the literature. Thus, she was partial to Gabriel Garcia Marquez's *One Hundred Years of Solitude* despite its sexual content.

Nehama stopped teaching literature relatively early, channeling her love for this genre by applying it to the Tanach. In her writings Nehama tended to apply literary analysis only upon the Tanach, though she occasionally did close reading on post-biblical sources.[16] Her close reading of the Torah derived from a fundamental theological postulate – that the Torah, being Divine, is omnisignificant, its every jot and tittle full of meaning. But she also believed that close reading worked for all literature, even without Divine basis, exactly as the New Critics did. She writes:

> Anyone who understands literature knows that the style is not merely a garb for an idea, an outer shell for its kernel; and neither is the style an embellishment or adornment for the subject. Style, sentence structure, choice of words and their arrangement, length and brevity, all form part of the body and content of the subject. This is true also of Rabbinic literature and, of course, of the Torah. Repetitions, stylistic oddities and variations are not incidental, nor do they aim merely to achieve aesthetic effect but rather to convey a message or teaching.[17]

For her students, this parallel was often an eye-opener. R. Ben Hollander says: "Before I met Nehama, I was going to teach English literature. After I met her I realized Torah *was* literature."[18] But Landau, who experienced her teaching of both, adds: "Nehama's teaching of Tanach differed somewhat from her teaching of literature. Rashi's commentary is modular; he deals with separate words, without looking for an encompassing interpretation, and Nehama too sometimes spent an entire lesson on one word. On the other

---

[16] For example, a Mishnah (see *SBM*, 182).

[17] Combination of *IHBV*, 164, and *NSV*, 207. Schwartz points out "this is almost verbatim Weiss" (interview). Nehama's lack of citation of Weiss only serves to illustrate how deeply she had internalized this approach. See also comments by Yedgar ("*Bein*," 58).

[18] Quoted in Heilman, "A Passion."

hand, the *Akedat Yitzhak* and Abravanel deal with ideas, and these commentators also appeared not infrequently in Nehama's lesson."

Nehama realized the potential for this new literary direction in Tanach long before many of her colleagues. She preempted its entry into mainstream academia by a decade or two, after which close reading and literary analysis became increasingly popular. A handful of other Jewish academics also sensed the value of this approach early on, and they had a great influence on her. This is the topic of the rest of this chapter.

Influences

The scholars Nehama most liked to quote were several Jewish contemporaries, all of whom took a close reading approach to Tanach. Their example bolstered her in adopting a minority academic position within the predominantly historical-critical field of Bible studies. Many of Nehama's influences are listed in the following passage:

> Our Sages have taught us the importance of every word in the text and to appreciate correspondences between similar phraseology and key words, recurring in different places. In our day, several scholars – primarily Buber and Rosenzweig, Benno Jacob, Cassuto and Meir Weiss – have cultivated this approach and through it unearthed meanings which were hidden between the folds of the text, unseen.[19]

The first thing to note here is her contention that close reading, a primary tool of the literary method, was already being done two millennia ago. In the Talmud and Midrash, the detailed attention that the Sages paid to the Tanach is evident.[20] Nehama presented modern close reading as a return to the midrashic close reading method[21] – except that she believed the traditional sources read *more* closely, as she writes, quoting Isaac Heinemann:

> Modern scholars have proved that the Scripture uses key words and phrases in order to underline the links between the different stories in the Bible or parts of the same story. But our Sages went much further than modern scholarship. They emphasized the identity of expressions in order to connect the incidents concerned.[22]

---

[19] Combination of *NSS*, 475 and *IHBS*, 348.

[20] See examples in *NSB*, 62, *NSS*, 87, 380, 390 and 474; *NSV*, 48; *SD*, 12; and see Cohn, "*Ha-parshanut*," 102, 105 and 107 for discussion.

[21] Cohn, "*Ha-parshanut*," 107.

[22] *NSB*, 120 (repeated on 338). She also refers us to the use of the method of identity of expressions in the Midrash (*ibid.*, 271, 336) and Rashi (*SD*, 5). When the same phrase appears in two separate passages, it may also indicate a linkage between them (e.g. *NSS*, 7, 383, and 618). This kind of linkage is one of the "commonplaces of rabbinic exegesis" (*NSB*, 271).

Moving forward in Jewish history, some of the medievals, especially Rashi, Abravanel, Ramban and the *pashtanim*, scrutinized the text particularly closely.[23] Maimonides, too, actively denounces those who would skim the Tanach as if it were just another storybook (*NSB*, 476). Radak anticipated many of the New Critics' innovative ideas, interpreting the text based on context.[24] Rashbam developed a literary approach, finding patterns in the text. This is significant because he had a narrower background than many of his contemporaries,[25] which implies that this type of literary reading may develop purely from the fertile ground of the traditional mindset.

Nevertheless, the approach of the traditional commentators was not an exact fit for modern New Critical theory.[26] They may have read very closely, but they still had the disadvantage of living many centuries ago without the benefit of subsequent research. An update was needed, and as Nehama informs us, Buber and Rosenzweig stepped forward to do precisely that:

> Jewish commentators from the very earliest of times showed keen awareness of the crucial importance of structure and style in communicating the message of a particular piece of narration... but they did not dwell on the stylistic aspects of the text in any systematic fashion. It was left to Buber to expound and explore in great detail the potentialities of this approach. (*NSS*, 19 n. 1)

> Our Midrash too knew of this principle ("It says here... and also says there...," and similarly "measure for measure," etc.). It is, however, to Buber's and even more so to Rosenzweig's credit that they elaborated

---

[23] See Weiss, *The Bible*, 37.

[24] "The whole question of context was pivotal in Radak's approach" (F. Talmage, *David Kimhi, The Man and His Commentaries*, Cambridge: Harvard University Press, 1975, 67, and see also 118). For further discussion, see Unterman, *Background*, 66, n. 315.

[25] Martin Lockshin. "Rashbam as a 'literary exegete,'" in *With Reverence for the Word*, edited by Jane Dammen McAuliffe, Barry D. Walfish and Joseph W. Goering, 83–91 (Oxford University Press: 2003). Nehama was not satisfied with Rashbam's readings, calling him an over-literalist (see pages 461, 506 below).

[26] Schwartz explains that the New Critics assume a work to be autonomous, deriving meaning solely from itself; whereas the midrashic mind derived significance from systems external to the text, including not only literary or aesthetic meanings but also halachic, moral and theological ones (Schwartz, interview). The medieval literalists were perhaps a closer fit, yet still maintained a "vigorous separation of form and content which, in the final analysis, precludes any real compatibility between their exegesis and modern close reading" (Weiss, *The Bible*, 37, n. 24). For example, Radak's rule *Kefel inyan be-milim shonot* deviates sharply from close reading by implying that repetitions do not introduce any new content. Nehama rejected this rule. See *NSS*, 380; Ahrend, *"Mi-toch,"* 37; and Zafrany, *"Darkah,"* 75.

this topic and discovered several places that I did not find in any earlier source.[27]

[Buber reveals] delicate insights, only some of which have been previously referred to in our ancient commentators. (*NSS*, 592, n. 6)

Buber and Rosenzweig, and also Jacob, Cassuto[28] and Weiss, all built upon the earlier traditional work, and also developed new methods.

Meir Weiss[29]

Professor Meir Weiss (1909–1998) was a colleague and close personal friend of Nehama's. She attended his family celebrations, and left her post at Bar-Ilan University in solidarity with him.[30] He was among the people she admired most, and two of his works appear in a list of what she calls "several truly important books written on the Tanach at an advanced level."[31] Weiss provided initial advice and guidance while she wrote her *Studies* series,[32] and was subsequently a reader for her Open University course on Rashi. Nehama esteemed Weiss's opinion to the point that she was willing to defer to it over her own, surrendering at least one cherished theory to his judgment.[33]

Weiss wished to turn the tide of the historical approach, which had transformed the Tanach text into a source for scientific information alone.[34] As a young man, he had been exposed to the wave of New Critical analysis sweeping the field of general literature studies.[35] The New Critics labored from the early to mid-twentieth century to shift attention from historical factors back to the literature itself. Uninterested in the author and his times, they focused solely on the text, reading it closely in terms of its own

---

[27] Letter to Ansbacher, *PN*, 658. Weiss too notes the debt owed by Buber and Rosenzweig to classic Jewish interpretation; they systematized the lead of the Midrash to their own more modern ends (*The Bible*, 37).

[28] Nehama believed that Cassuto owed more to traditional Jewish interpretation than he would admit, and she censured him for concealing his indebtedness to the Midrash, for example, when scientifically elaborating on the Sages' method of juxtaposing passages by verbal association (*NSV*, 65).

[29] Biographical material on Weiss may be found in Meir Weiss, *Emunot ve-de'ot be-mizmorei Tehillim*, Jerusalem: Mossad Bialik, 2001, 7–11.

[30] See page 104 above.

[31] Letter to Helfgot, *PN*, 662. The works are *Ha-mikra ki-demuto* (translated as *The Bible from Within*, see bibliography) and *Mikra'ot ke-chavanatam* (Jerusalem: Bialik, 1987).

[32] See introduction to *IBD*.

[33] See Ahrend "*Mi-toch*," 39–40; see chapter 21 n. 96.

[34] See Weiss, *The Bible*, 30.

[35] See his discussion in *The Bible*, 3, onwards. Weiss had studied in Bar-Ilan University under Moshe Schwartz, professor of Philosophy, Aesthetics and Literature, who promoted the work of Staiger and Croce. It is conceivable that Nehama also picked up some of her knowledge from Moshe Schwartz directly (Yehudah Friedlander, interview).

Meir Weis. Courtesy of Gabi Weiss.

Meir Weiss. Courtesy of Baruch Schwartz

language, structure and context. This work began with T.S. Eliot, and continuing with Richards, Empson, Wellek and others.[36] Weiss enthusiastically imported the new approach into the field of Tanach study, gradually formulating his own method which he called "Total Interpretation."[37] Through his close reading of the Bible, he was able to discover hidden treasures such as subtle psychological processes, dramatic tension and more.

Nehama and Weiss had very different personalities. Weiss worked in the methodical and perfectionist manner characteristic of the "dry" academics whom Nehama generally criticized. Indeed, R. Elhanan Samet recalls that when Weiss presented her with a copy of his monumental work on Amos, all eight hundred pages of it, she exclaimed: "Why did you do this? Had it been two hundred pages long, everyone would have read it as the definitive work – but now no one will touch it!" Notwithstanding, they both gained tremendously from the relationship. They published joint studies,[38] and Nehama quotes him in her writings.[39] According to Dr. Baruch Schwartz, his close student, Nehama learned a substantial amount of the literary theory she knew from Weiss,[40] and adopted his "Total Interpretation" approach to some extent.[41] As an observant Jew of unbending integrity with rabbinical ordination besides, Weiss may have functioned for Nehama as certification that these theories were "kosher,"[42] though in practice he actually went

---

[36] The Swiss-German school of *Werkinterpretation* had similar aims. For more details on the New Critics, see Unterman, *Background*, 54–62.

[37] See Weiss, *The Bible*, 27; B. Schwartz, "*Mishnato shel Rabbi Meir: ha-interpretatzia ha-kuli'it*," in *Le-zichro shel Professor Meir Weiss*, Jerusalem: Institute for Jewish Studies, 5759, 15–16. Besides his methodological *magnum opus*, *Ha-mikra ki-demuto*, he published research on Psalms, Amos, Job, and more (Schwartz, *ibid.*, 10–14). His quoting of the New Critics in *The Bible from Within* is sporadic, with far more citations of Bible scholars and other commentaries.

[38] *Shiurim be-firkei nehama u-ge'ula*, Jerusalem: World Zionist Organization, Department for Torah and Culture in the Diaspora, 1957.

[39] He is mentioned in *NSB*, 135; *NSS*, 302, 495 and 600; *NSV*, 612; *SBM*, 164, n. 1 (one of the few footnotes, if not the only one, in her *Studies* where she cites a colleague as bringing something to her notice); and *IBD*, 44. Additionally see worksheets for portions of *Lech Lecha* 5716 and *Noah* 5717, where a "tip" (*etzah tovah*) refers the reader to his articles, and *TI*, 48, 50 ("I particularly liked the explanation offered by Weiss").

[40] Her favorite example of the kind of question we must not ask of a text – "How many children had Lady Macbeth?" – is the title of a scholarly article also cited by Weiss (*The Bible*, 50) – see chapter 17 n. 17.

[41] Ahrend "*Mi-toch*," 38; Yedgar, "*Bein*," 67–68, n. 46.

[42] Weiss initially worked as a pulpit rabbi and educator (Meir Weiss, *Emunot ve-de'ot be-mizmorei Tehillim*, Jerusalem: Mossad Bialik, 2001, 7). This suggestion follows Breuer's idea that R. Soloveitchik "koshered" "biblical critical" ideas for Nehama: see page 419 above.

further with academic methodology than Nehama did.[43] Nehama in turn contributed to Weiss's scholarship, sensitizing him to elements analogous to modern literary theory in the commentaries. He mentions her several times in his work and clearly admired her, writing:

> She has pointed the way to be followed if the plain sense of the Bible is to be understood.[44]

Here then were two scholars, both steeped in the traditional approaches and familiar with the academic arena, yet choosing different paths. As the years progressed, Weiss chose to invest his effort in reading and contending with the Bible critics, whilst Nehama focused on the traditional commentaries. It might be argued that, starting out with more or less the same background and sensibilities, they became "mirror images" of each other. Weiss incorporated the ancients within his modern discussions, while Nehama incorporated modern scholarship into her traditionally-oriented teachings. Every time they worked together they reopened the dialogue between their respective domains, and thus enriched each other's work.

Martin Buber and Franz Rosenzweig

These two scholars developed a scientific literary approach to Tanach even before the New Criticism infiltrated Bible studies. Professor Mordechai Martin Buber (1878–1965), was termed by Weiss, who studied with him, "one of the modern pioneers of the system of close reading."[45] Buber's close colleague, Dr. Franz Rosenzweig (1886–1929), suffered, like Nehama, from his academic peers' contempt for biblical Hebrew and phraseology.[46] Buber and Rosenzweig anticipated several of the New Critics' methodological conclusions, such as the notion of form as content, the unity of the text, and the importance of every word.[47] They were especially interested in repeated

---

[43] Believing that a scientific and critical scholar cannot, once committed, let his faith interfere with his academic research, Weiss was willing in principle even to emend biblical texts – albeit in close cooperation with the method of Total Interpretation, and in practice hardly ever (Schwartz, interview; and also see B. Schwartz, *Mishnato shel Rabbi Meir: ha-interpretatzia ha-kuli'it,*" in *Le-zichro shel Professor Meir Weiss,* Jerusalem: Institute for Jewish Studies, 5759, 19; Weiss, *The Bible,* 70).

[44] Weiss, *The Bible,* 38. See also 76 and 131, n. 5.

[45] Weiss, *The Bible,* 35, n. 18. Weiss wrote the introduction to Buber's work *Darko shel mikra: iyunim bi-defusei-signon ba-Tanach,* Jerusalem: Bialik 1964.

[46] See Horwitz, "*Nehama,*" 210. See also *NSS,* 485, n. 5, and Horwitz, "*Nehama,*" 218, n. 26, concerning Rosenzweig's attack on Kautzsch, a Bible translator from the 1920s, a story recounted by Nehama.

[47] They believed in a multi-layered text, but that the Redactor R (renamed "Rabbenu" by Rosenzweig) gave the text unity such that it could no longer be pried apart (Horwitz,

words, coining the term *Leitwört* ("lead-word") to refer to a keyword that appears repeatedly within a given passage or unit. This term subsequently became familiar to many, even outside academic circles.

Nehama helped these two scholars with their monumental translation of the Tanach into German, which she greatly esteemed.[48] She studied it carefully, including the earlier drafts,[49] and frequently praised its accuracy over other Bible translations.[50] She also learned important methodologies and principles from them. More than once, Nehama declared her debt to Buber's work.[51] She writes:

> I, and many observant teachers, learned several correct things in the Bible from him, and especially the topic of the *Leitwört* and the deep significance hinted at in the Torah by its means. (*PN*, 658)

As for Rosenzweig, although she does not often quote from his works,[52] Nehama esteemed him so greatly that she appended the abbreviation *zt"l* ("of sainted memory") to his name (*PN*, 661). This title is generally reserved for the greatest Jewish people and is not used lightly.

Benno Jacob

Rabbi Benno Jacob (1862–1945) was a German-Jewish rationalist, a Reform rabbi who had studied with Graetz in the rabbinical seminary in Breslau.[53] Jacob was an early proponent of a literary approach, including sensitivity to keywords.[54] He was not interested in source analysis, emendations, Near East cultures and higher biblical criticism. Although he avoided dogmatic traditional interpretations, rejecting Mosaic authorship of the Torah, he believed in the textual thematic unity of the Torah and

---

"*Nehama*," 217). Weiss said of Buber that the main principle in his exegesis was that of the intrinsic unity of content and form (Frisch, "*Shitato*," 315, n. 8).

[48] See page 49 above.

[49] See *NSS*, introduction, 20, n. 2, and 399.

[50] Posen, "*Ha-targum*," 111–113. The translation avoided the critical theories, infused new life into German Jewry, and even generated in its readers a desire to become religious (Horwitz, "Nehama," 213). Nehama had access to notes that Rosenzweig, deprived of speech by illness, sent to Buber during the translation process, and she would describe how Rosenzweig went about trying to solve the riddles in difficult verses (Horwitz, 219; Rappel, interview). For examples of Nehama's partiality to this translation, see *IBB*, 23; *NSS*, 20, n. 2, and 687, n. 2; *NSV*, 535; *IBBM*, 355, *IBD*, 122; *SD*, 312; *LP*, 198, n. 4; and *TI*, 90 (Buber only).

[51] Nehama comments that several points in her *Studies* were inspired by Buber's article "Abraham the Seer" (from *On the Bible*, edited by N. Glatzer, New York, 1968. See *NSB*, 66, n. 1).

[52] See *TI*, 140 for a rare quote.

[53] The following information is from Horwitz, "Nehama," 208–217.

[54] See e.g. *NSB*, 482 on the keyword *sh-l-h*.

zealously defended it. He wanted to understand the Tanach from within its own framework of values, to delve into its original meaning. He believed that commentary should be written by Jews, the Tanach's intended audience, and strongly opposed Christian interpretations because of their anti-Semitic bias. When he wrote against the documentary hypothesis in the first decade of the twentieth century, his was a lone voice crying in the wilderness.

Though opposed to his religious viewpoint, Nehama was a great admirer of Jacob's commentary on Genesis and Exodus.[55]

> From Benno Jacob... I learned... more than I did from many, many books by God-fearing people. His claims against biblical criticism and his proofs of their recklessness and inaccuracies are unparalleled even by R. David Zevi Hoffmann. (*PN*, 657)

She saw Jacob's work as

> an essential aid for anyone wishing to make a close study of the biblical text and modern insights into it. (*NSB*, 409 n. 1)

She took the trouble to read his books on microfilm, the only format in which they were available for a long time.[56] Her interest brought his work to the notice of many for the first time. He has, in fact, been described as one of the most neglected Jewish religious scholars of this century.[57] Shalom Carmy observes that people were convinced that Jacob could not be a "real" Reform rabbi because of Nehama's attitude towards his commentary.[58]

Cassuto

Professor Umberto Cassuto (1883–1951), also known as Moshe David Cassuto, was an Italian-born rabbi and also a professor at the Hebrew University. He and Nehama were both on the faculty at the seminars in Bayit Vegan under Shimshon Rosenthal. Cassuto studied ancient Near Eastern culture, particularly Canaanite literature and its relationship to the Bible. He composed commentaries on Genesis and Exodus. Cassuto shared with

---

[55] Rosenzweig, who shared her admiration, hoped Jacob would be "the new Rashi of the generation" and initially invited him to collaborate on his German Bible translation (Horwitz, "*Nehama*," 210–211.) Jacob's writings have been described by some as reading like Orthodox works (see Aryeh Rubenstein "Finer Shades of Meaning," *Jerusalem Post*, June 4, 1993, 26). Hence Nehama's partiality.

[56] She received a copy of part of the manuscript on Leviticus from his son (*NSV*, 30). She also quotes from articles by Jacob (see *NSS*, 139, n. 1 and, 160, n. 5).

[57] See Aryeh Rubenstein "Finer Shades of Meaning," *Jerusalem Post*, June 4, 1993, 26.

[58] Carmy, "Re: 'Tikkun Olam' and One-year Yeshiva Students in Israel," Lookjed archives, August 1, 2004. Carmy also notes there that Jacob's relative anonymity spared him the vilification Buber received.

Benno Jacob (with whom he may have studied[59]) an assumption of the unity of the Tanach and hence a largely "post-critical" stance of literary study, though they still assumed a prehistory for particular books.[60] Despite his Orthodox ordination, Nehama appears to have approved less of Cassuto's approach than of that of Buber and the others.[61] Cassuto wanted to understand what the Torah was saying to the readers of its own time – an objective approach; whereas Nehama sought its eternally relevant messages – a "subjective" approach.[62] Nevertheless her scolding of Cassuto for ignoring

> his own careful and close reading of the biblical text which attributes significance to every nuance and variation (*NSS*, 152)

implies that his general approach, even if he did not always stick to it, was one close to her heart.

Strauss

One final influence, absent from Nehama's list in the quote above but important nonetheless, was Professor Aryeh Ludwig Strauss (1892–1953). He was Buber's father-in-law and the greatest Israeli theoretician of literature in the first half of the twentieth century. Although he came from an assimilated family, he later reclaimed his Jewish heritage, and his poetry was suffused with deeply religious themes. A literary critic and Hebrew University lecturer, Strauss had a profound influence on the literary scene in Israel. Several important figures number among his students, including author S. Yizhar and poets Dan Pagis and Leah Goldberg – the latter wrote him a poem for his sixtieth birthday.[63]

Nehama greatly admired Strauss. Although he was not a Bible scholar and she did not quote him in her *Studies* or worksheets, he taught her about aesthetic sensibilities in literature:

> Ludwig Strauss has taught us to sense the power of the poetical "not" which, instead of canceling that which is negated, makes us conscious of it. (*TI*, 81)

When Strauss was asked to teach Psalms at the Mizrachi teacher's seminary, Nehama seized the opportunity to sit in on his lessons. His teaching presented an entirely new way of viewing the biblical text using

---

[59] Horwitz, "*Nehama*," 216. She observes that they met in Italy.
[60] Sperling, *Students*, 118.
[61] She includes Cassuto in the list of "literalists" whose explanations are flawed (*NSS*, 488–489). He also relied on research that she did not find particularly convincing – see e.g. *NSS*, 648.
[62] Touitou, "*Rashbam*," 222.
[63] From "*Ma omer lecha ha-shem Aryeh Ludwig Strauss?*" *Haaretz*, August 22, 2003.

poetic tools and left a deep impression which accompanied her for the rest of her life. When Strauss taught the famous Psalm 23 ("The Lord is my shepherd"), she lamented, "How is that I say this every week and never noticed what you've just taught me?" Before his death, she urged him to write down his lessons so that others could benefit from his method of analyzing poetry. He dictated his material to Nehama from his sickbed; and the resulting discourse on three Psalms was subsequently published.[64]

Strauss's viewpoint was also in line with that of the New Critics, though he largely predated them and never explicitly mentioned them in his works.[65] In some aspects of Nehama's work she continued what he had begun, as can be seen in her article, *Keitzad likro perek ba-Tanach* ("How to Read a Chapter of Tanach"), written in his memory.[66]

Uncredited pioneers

With the exception of Strauss, who was not a Bible scholar, the scholars mentioned were not as influential in their own lifetimes as they might have been. This was probably due to academic suspicion and the prevailing trends. In time, ideas similar to theirs gained much ground within Bible scholarship – in fact, Cassuto and Jacob prefigured the holistic approach later developed by Greenberg.[67] Nevertheless, their pioneering work is not always sufficiently credited in surveys of biblical scholarship. Not coincidentally, neither is Nehama's.[68] Indeed, having familiarized ourselves with her influences, it is time to turn to Nehama's own literary contributions.

---

[64] Professor Tamar Ross, interview. The book was named *Al shelosha mizmorim mi-Sefer Tehillim*, published by the Jewish Agency, Department for Child and Youth Immigration, 1951.

[65] Weiss, *The Bible*, 38. Weiss feels that Strauss fell short of the Total Interpretation method by analyzing the text in terms of aesthetic appreciation and thus not truly understanding its meaning (*ibid.*, 374–376).

[66] For a lengthy excerpt from the article, see pages 471–472 below. The article was first published in the same series as Strauss's discourse on Psalms, and later included in his memorial volume *Nefesh ve-shir (devarim be-yom iyun le-zichro shel A.L. Strauss)*, *Iyunim*, 19–20 (Jerusalem, 1954) on pages 90–104. It was then reprinted in *Lilmod u-le-lamed Tanach*, and subsequently in translation as "Joseph and His Brothers" in *TI*, 163–176. Another English version appears in *On Teaching Tanach* (trans. Moshe Sokolow, Torah Education Network, 1986, 1–13).

[67] Sperling, *Students*, 3. While there were also a few Christian scholars who prefigured Greenberg, Sperling notes that it was predictable that Jews might claim this new subfield as their own in its earliest days, when literary reading was being viewed with disdain outside of departments of English literature.

[68] Schwartz notes that Robert Alter's survey of the literary approach in biblical studies does not give due credit to Weiss, Nehama and the others (Schwartz, private communication and *"Bikoret sefer al Robert Alter: The Art of Biblical Narrative," Shnaton le-mikra le-heker ha-mizrah ha-kadum*, 5–6 [1983]: 268).

CHAPTER 21

NEHAMA'S LITERARY APPROACH:
PART II: NEHAMA'S LITERARY WORK

Traditional and modern literary reading

ALTHOUGH FOR NEHAMA the Tanach was ultimately sacred literature, and hence unlike any other, the literary approach worked for her within certain parameters, and her use of it was significant. If the work of the pioneering Jewish scholars mentioned in the last chapter was set upon a foundation of traditional interpretation, this was even more applicable in Nehama's case. She reports deriving a number of close reading principles from the Sages' rules and sayings;[1] and remarks repeatedly upon Rashi's close reading and sensitivity to context.[2] In "How to Read a Chapter of Tanach," one of the few essays where she reflects on her own methods, she writes:

> I learned to read Tanakh from our great medieval commentators, Rashi, Ramban and Rashbam, and from their successors who to some extent followed in their footsteps, including Malbim and Rabbi Naphtali Tsevi Yehudah Berlin (author of *Ha'amek Davar*).
>
> In approach and method of explanation they may be far apart from one another and from the basic approach of Ludwig Strauss. Yet they and Strauss have something in common, something which I regard as very important to teach. This is the serious importance which they attach to the written word: to every word, not only the major words that possess deep religious, philosophical and ideological significance (such as *kedushah*, *mishpat*, *tsedakah*, *hesed ve-emet*, or *segulah*,[3] but even to the *vav ha-hibur* [the prefix meaning "and," "but," "or," etc.]). They took this

---

[1] Such as the rule of the repeated topic or word – the second instance will always hold some innovation, as will changes in style (for more, see Zafrany, "*Darkah*," 71, 75, 77, 82). Zafrany notes that Nehama also attributes rules to the Sages which did not appear in their own lists (76), and has at least one rule – sensitivity to changes in style – with no basis at all in the Sages' statements. He assumes that she deduced it from the Sages' work (*ibid.*, 77); but in light of this chapter's findings, I would suggest that perhaps she actually derived it from the New Criticism.

[2] A few examples: *NSB*, 12, 48, 286.

[3] Translated as holiness, judgment, charity, lovingkindness, truth and chosenness respectively.

serious attitude, and paid this serious attention, not only to gravity of the words but even to their sequence, to the sentence, to the sentence structure, repetition, parallelism; to everything written – and unwritten. (*TI*, 164)

Nehama continues by lyrically expressing the underlying basis for such close study of Torah:

Let me quote a modern commentator who was far from the sphere of modern poetry or belles-lettres, but whose remarks about correct reading of poetry are close to what we learned from Strauss. Commentators disagree as to whether the words "this song" in Deuteronomy 31:19 (*Va-yelekh*) ("And now, write this song for yourselves") refers to the song of *Ha'azinu* (Deuteronomy 32) or to the entire Torah, depicted as a song or poem.

The author of *Ha'amek Davar* (in *Kidmat ha-Emek*, §3) supports the latter view: "How can the whole Torah be called a poem when it is not written in the language of poetry? What is meant is that it has the nature and unique properties of poetry. The poetic idiom differs, as we all are aware, from narrative prose. In poetry, the subject is not described as fully as in a prose narrative, and marginal notes are required to explain what each verse refers to. This is not "midrash" but demanded by the nature of the poem, even a secular one. Furthermore, someone who recognizes the source of this idiom will appreciate the poem more than one who does not... and this is the nature of the Torah, in which stories are not all told in full detail, and notes, interpretations and linguistic analysis are required. All this is not "midrash" but necessary in order to understand the *"peshat"* (straightforward meaning) of the text.[4]

This view of the Bible as poetry is sensed in Nehama's visual presentation of the Torah text, with full voweling and short lines. Professor Uriel Simon notes that she learned to do this from Buber and Rosenzweig and suggests that the result is an incomparable and enduring work of art (*VLN*).

Nehama developed the literary sensitivities in the Midrash and the medieval commentaries, using modern methodical and academic tools.[5] She wove the ancient and the modern together in what appeared, at least on the surface, to be a harmonious whole.[6] She may not have invented most of the tools herself, as she writes, but she made these methods accessible and

---

[4] *TI*, 164–165. Compare with similar comments in N. Leibowitz, "*Ahavat,*" 466, and the same quote with different translation brought in *SD*, 353, in the context of the assertion: "It is no empty thing for you." In *LP* (91) she also compares reading text to poetry.

[5] Weiss, *The Bible*, 37; Yedgar, "*Ha-iyunim,*" 29.

[6] Rozenson argues that below the surface there are hermeneutical tensions, created by linking commentaries from the past to the newest literary tools ("*Diber,*" 325).

familiar, popularizing them as none before her.[7] She maintained a great interest in academic developments on the literary and biblical-literary front. As mentioned, Nehama was exposed to the New Critics, and was enthusiastic about her work, but the precise extent to which she was familiar with it is unclear. Weiss attests that she exhibited "expertise in the New Criticism."[8] Dr. Rachel Salmon agrees:

> She is very well-read in the theory and practice of Anglo-American New Criticism, and finds the methods of the New Critics congenial to her own practice.

However, Salmon then adds:

> I am quite certain that she did not learn her skills or close reading from them – the rabbis of the classical and medieval periods were masters enough – but they perhaps helped her in making applications to the contemporary educational situation.[9]

Although Nehama never quotes any of the New Critics explicitly,[10] their terminology and methodology appear throughout her work. Dr. Baruch Schwartz remarks: "Anyone wondering whether Nehama ought to be classified as a pre-modern or modern scholar need only open at the portion of *Aharei Mot* to her first two sentences on the command 'Neither shall you emulate their practices.' The words 'style', 'preamble' and 'ceremony' indicate her familiarity with modern literary study."[11] Other terminology scattered throughout her books, such as structure, poetics, chiasm and parallelism,[12] and keywords[13] as well as her noting of flashbacks,[14] and even

---

[7] Yedgar, "*Bein*," 67.

[8] Weiss, *The Bible*, 38.

[9] Salmon, "Nehama," 19.

[10] The literary scholars that she quotes are Herder (*NSB*, 58, n. 2) and the stylistics scholar Koenig (*NSS*, 595, 21), both predating New Criticism. But in at least one case Nehama is, according to Schwartz, clearly drawing on a New Critical idea, an insight of Staiger's (*IHBV*, 195, n. 7; Schwartz, interview). Yet she quotes him neither by name, nor even anonymously as "a certain scholar," as she occasionally does. See discussion later in this chapter, pages 477–483, esp. n. 144.

[11] Schwartz, interview. See *IHBV*, 190. The English version, *NSV*, 241–242, contains only some of the words cited.

[12] For more examples see Unterman, *Background*, 90 and Kagan, "Review."

[13] She learned this from Buber (*PN*, 658). Some examples of Nehama's use of the *Leitwört* include: *NSB*, 476; *NSS*, 15, 232, 244–245 and 663; *NSV*, 93; *SBM*, 205 and 408; *SD*, 92, 311–313. She quotes Buber's essays *'Leitwortstil in der Erzahlung des Pentateuchs*" (see *NSB*, 270, n. 2) and *"Ha-milah ha-manhah ve-ha-av tzurah shel ha-ne'um"* (see *NSS*, 592, n. 6). Cassuto also used keywords (see *NSB*, 34; *SD*, 312).

some methodological statements,[15] reveal the modern literary influence in her works.

Nehama as close reader

The act of close reading of text, so important to New Critics, was a thread running through Nehama's work from the early days.[16] Jewish people often take the Book of Books for granted, reading it with what Professor Moshe Greenberg has called "sacred inattention,"[17] oblivious to the mysteries and messages squirreled away inside each detail. R. Hanan Schlesinger reports that Nehama used to say, "Students read the Bible like a madly galloping war-horse." This was especially true for the narrative sections, which many traditional Jews read more superficially than the legal ones.[18] Nehama forced people to slow down and read what was actually written – every letter and word, the structures and patterns, keywords and repeated phrases.[19] The questions on her worksheets compelled the reader to actually look at the text and keep returning to it:

> And if previously he was like a person who sits in a car while the views fly past unseen, now he is like someone climbing a mountain with the view unfolding before him as he sweats and toils, increasingly with every new ascent.[20]

She wished to enhance students' appreciation of the multilayered nature of the Torah:

> The student will never love and esteem the Torah while believing the chapter to be simple and easily comprehended upon first reading, with nothing to be gained from a second reading.[21]

She succeeded, for the act of close reading with Nehama brought people into a new relationship with Torah and even restored their faith in it. R.

---

[14] For example, when Joseph's cries in the pit are mentioned for the first time, twenty-two years after the event (*NSB*, 464; see also *NSB*, 342–343). Nehama claimed that this flashback had been formulated by the Sages as a hermeneutical rule – see *NSS*, 597.

[15] As was her wont, Nehama did not systematically lay out her literary goals and techniques. We find some strongly New-Critical-sounding methodological statements in "*He'arot metodiyot le-limmud*" and "*Al nituah*"; and *NSB*, 513 is also worth noting. But the closest she comes is in "How to Read a Chapter of Tanach." Frankel argues that this article is not representative of Nehama's work due to the absence of commentaries.

[16] Evidence of this exists from as early as 1945 – see "*Sihah*," 458, and see also her comments from 1951 in "*Ahavat*," 466.

[17] Lecture at Yakar, 1998.

[18] *IBB*, 338 (not as clear in the English version, *NSB*, 476).

[19] See, for example, *TI*, 31.

[20] N. Leibowitz, "*Mi-bereshit*," 451.

[21] N. Leibowitz, "*He'arot metodiyot le-limmud*," 485.

Chaim Weiner: "Over the two years I attended Nehama's class, we studied only two chapters. I hear you ask – how is it possible to spend two years on two chapters of Bible?! I will only say this: Each hour-and-a-half lecture was rarely dedicated to more than one verse, and sometimes only one word. And the whole Bible was illuminated through the study of that word."

Nehama paid attention to every nuance in the text.[22] She had no interest in the details for their own sake – on the contrary, she condemned educators who drowned pupils in a sea of meaningless minutiae – but rather for their tremendous significance, as the medium for the Torah's message. Like the New Critics, she held that the form – the words used and their arrangement – was not random, but carried a portion of the Torah's meaning:[23]

> The order of words in the verse is not accidental. Changes in emphasis, approval and disapproval, and shades of meaning are not imparted, in the Torah, through long-winded psychological explanations or verbose analysis, but by a syntactical device or seemingly insignificant but definitely unusual turn of phrase, combination, order or choice of words. (*NSB*, 122)

One small detail might contain an entire philosophy or a crucial moral point.

> We can see from here how every word and turn of phrase in the Torah is weighted with significance, and realize the wealth of moral guidance that is to be extracted from an apparently unimportant expression. (*SD*, 7)

> Even from a single letter of a text which seems so abstruse, we can derive important moral lessons.[24]

And not only words but even the Torah's silence may be suffused with meaning (*NSS*, 85).

Due to all this, changing one word could change the entire sense of the verse.[25] Hence, Nehama argued, metaphors cannot be interchanged, however similar they might seem.[26] She illustrated this point by telling of an educational discussion that took place in the State's early years regarding whether the Tanach's language was too flowery for students to comprehend.

---

[22] Ahrend, "*Mi-toch*," 37. See also Peerless, *To Study*, 59–97 for his discussion of Nehama's approach to textual difficulties, and 173–174 for a list of some common textual difficulties.

[23] Ahrend reports: "Nehama never tired of declaring the unity of the content and the form" ("*Mi-toch*," 37).

[24] *NSV*, 216. Similarly *NSV*, 52: "Significant indeed are the lessons harbored even in the faintest minutiae of biblical stylistics!"

[25] See *LP*, 17–18 for some examples.

[26] See *NSB*, 291–293 for a discussion of metaphors.

Professor Joseph Klausner suggested that the text should be rewritten in colloquial modern Hebrew. For example, Amos 9:13,

> ... and the mountains shall drop sweet wine...

should become

> ... and the mountains shall drip grape juice...[27]

As Nehama told this story, she laughed, for the image reminded her of the old kiosks selling carbonated sweet sticky red liquid that dripped from the valves of barrels while flies buzzed around. The Tanach's language should not be altered, she concluded, but dissected and understood properly.

These assumptions also meant that no repetition was insignificant – whether of words or entire passages.

> The Torah is never guilty of repetition for the sake of rhetorical effect and there is no recapitulation that does not introduce some new idea or nuance. (SD, 90)

This was a lesson Nehama learned from her traditional predecessors:

> Our Sages have taught us that there is no repetition of any precept in the Torah unless the text wishes to add some new point, detail or aspect. (SD, 161)

> A salient feature of Ramban's explicatory method in his Torah commentary is his insistence that the lengthy recapitulation of what appears to be mere technical and other details incidental to the central core of the narrative must possess some spiritual significance. Otherwise the Torah would not have gone to the trouble of recording it.[28]

In fact, a favorite tool of Nehama's was to undertake thorough comparisons of two texts that appear to overlap, checking for their similarities and their differences.[29] This was a tool that some of her predecessors had used (TI, 11). It could be implemented on adjacent or non-adjacent texts, on verses, story units, or legal texts.[30] The nature of the repetition was irrelevant – it could be first narrative and then recounting, or first command then implementation, or any other permutation.[31] She was particularly fond of comparing the two accounts of Abraham's servant's

---

[27] See Joseph Klausner, *Sefer Amos im parshegen*, Tel Aviv, 5703, 56.

[28] *NSS*, 664. For a list of examples of Ramban's close reading see *IBBM*, 102, n. 6.

[29] See Sokolow, "*Samchut*," 298–299, Peerless, *To Study*, 45–58; and note also her essay "The Recapitulations," dealing with repetitions regarding the Mishkan (*NSS*, 644–653). At times she brings commentaries to make the comparisons, but she often makes her own (*NSB*, 418 and many others).

[30] For a legal text, see *SBM*, 151.

[31] See her quite lengthy and methodological introduction in *NSB*, 513.

encounter with Rebecca, publishing it no fewer than nine times in her worksheets;[32] and comparing the words of Moses with that of the Reubenites and Gadites in order to illustrate the difference in their outlooks.[33] The activity of comparing repeated materials was particularly important to Nehama because these texts were used as primary evidence for biblical-critical theories. It was claimed that the two versions of a story or a law had originated in different authors or schools, and hence the discrepancies between them. Nehama countered these claims by citing the traditional hermeneutical rule that details missing from one story are frequently provided in another[34] and by teaching that psychological and ethical messages are learned from the differences. She writes:

> Very often, Scripture contains similar accounts in which a person or group of people experiences similar happenings on different occasions. They are there in order to teach a specific lesson regarding their reactions. The person's character is revealed in his success or failure, showing us the way in which the person or group meets a series of challenges.[35]

Nehama contended that the "biblical critical" scholars were ignorant of important principles and that the close reading that was the key to true comprehension was beyond their reach:

> Since the modern non-Jewish interpreters of the Bible were not aware of this principle of biblical narration [that when there are two appeals or requests, the second is always more modest or convincing] – or deliberately ignored it, these duplications were explained in terms of two variant sources or documents.[36]

Thus, in discussing the similar events in I Samuel 24 and 26, she declares combatively:

> No one will suggest that we have here two accounts of the same incident.[37]

---

[32] Sokolow, "*Samchut*," 298. This comparison also appears as Addendum 6 in *LP* (227–228).

[33] See N. Leibowitz, "*Ahavat*," 467; *SBM*, 382–383.

[34] See *SBM*, 114.

[35] *SBM*, 114 and see also Sokolow "*Samchut*," 299.

[36] *NSS*, 101–102, n. 3. See also *NSB*, 457; *SD*, 18; and also Nehama's article outlining the significance of the repetition of "And he said," "*Vayomer... vayomer*," in *PN*, 495–502, especially 502, where Nehama informs us that the biblical critics mistook one word, containing worlds of emotion, for a "corruption or dittography."

[37] See *SBM*, 117 and *IBBM*, 121, and note also *NSS*, 48, n. 3.

Context was held by the New Critics to be extremely important – in fact, "close reading" later came to be called "contextualism." Nehama, for her part, writes:

> The rule is: every word is interpreted according to the context in which it appears. (*IHBV*, 228)

> You must beware of two dangers when trying to explain a chapter systematically: (a) teaching each verse isolated from its context, and in too much detail, so that you lose sight of the message as a whole and fail to see it as an entity; (b) paraphrasing the verse into "easy" Hebrew, thus depriving it of the structure given to it by the author.[38]

Sound, rhythm and tone were also to be carefully scrutinized. For example:

> The 4–4–4–3 word rhythm of the verse is also significant.[39]

Judy Klitsner recalls how Nehama taught the importance of tone by asking the students to imagine someone who says, "Look, I have proof that the article I wrote is wonderful!", triumphantly producing a publisher's letter which reads, "Dear sir, we are very sorry, but we will not be able to publish your article." "See that!" cries the would-be author. "They're very sorry!"

Tone becomes significant when Joseph's brothers throw him into a pit and then say (Genesis 37:20):

> And we will see what will become of his dreams.

Ramban hears cynicism in these words, but Rashi takes it literally – they would indeed wait and see. Nehama explained that Rashi could not believe them capable of such cruelty. It was one thing to plot to kill their brother, but it was quite another to do it so hard-heartedly. Only professional killers, such as those in Shakespeare's Macbeth, could so make light of the act of killing (*LP*, 170 n. 9).

Professor Martin Lockshin learned a lot from Nehama about the literary layers of the text: "For instance, she taught me to differentiate between *referential meaning* (where something new may be learned) and *rhetorical meaning*." An example of this is found in the verse (Exodus 22:23):

> And my anger shall burn hot, and I will kill you with the sword; and your wives shall be widows, and your children orphans.

The second half seems simply to be aiming for effect, since killing a man *ipso facto* leaves his wife a widow and his children orphans. Rashbam indeed

---

[38] *TI*, 68. See also *NSB*, 288, 557 and *NSS*, 69, 582.
[39] *NSV*, 322. See *NSS*, 629 for another example.

believes these words to be rhetorical, but Rashi understands it as an extra curse, binding the widows to extra restrictions.

Literary and psychological reading

Nehama's ability to detect the text's emotional tone owed much to the fact that she was a genuine student of human nature. Just as she writes of the Midrash, she too understood that

> reality is often stranger than any fiction, that history is full of mysteries and that the human heart is very complex. (*NSS*, 251)

In this she was following midrashic and other leads:

> R. Yose the Galilean's explanation is true to human experience. (*SD*, 128)

But she was also expressing her own personality and inclinations. Professor Israel Rozenson comments:

> Nehama was unrivalled in her ability to unearth the hidden depths of the human heart in various external circumstances.[40]

Menahem Ben-Yashar, who documented several psychological aspects within Nehama's teachings, adds that every good educator is of necessity a good psychologist by nature.[41]

On the one hand, Nehama was against over-psychologizing the Tanach characters:

> The Torah is not a psychological novel and is not concerned with satisfying biographical curiosity. (*NSS*, 39)

> The Torah does not describe the character of its figures by direct psychological analysis, but only indirectly, through their utterances, actions and even lack of action. (*NSB*, 131)

She insisted that a person's psychology can only be understood when observed standing on line at the grocery store, while the Tanach presents only selective views of biblical characters.[42] They are literary figures, and we have no other details about them as individuals:

> The man Moses is hardly known to us. (*NSS*, 50)

> The Torah similarly gives not the slightest hint of Abraham's sufferings and soul-searchings as he went to sacrifice Isaac. (*NSS*, 48 n. 1)

---

[40] Rozenson, "*Ha-parshanit*," 434, n. 1, paragraph 5.
[41] Menahem Ben-Yashar, "*Panim psichologiyot ve-hinuchiyot be-parshanutah shel Nehama Leibowitz*," in *PN*, 341 and *passim*. See also Kagan, "Review," in which he cites several interesting examples of Nehama's psychological and emotional sensitivity to the text.
[42] Judy Klitsner, interview.

In line with this, Nehama often preferred to view the biblical figures as transcending their particular time and place, as archetypes whose actions represent historical movements.[43] And yet she also saw them as individuals, with human psychological make-up;[44] and she loved to explore interpretations in this vein, provided that they made textual sense.[45] She used psychological intuition in order to solve ambiguities of tone and intent in the text:

> Did Abimelech really wish to provoke [Abraham]? He is after all described as a righteous gentile, and Abraham will pray for him. If he speaks here ironically, that is tactless on his part.[46]

Nehama had a good idea of human weakness, its excuses and rationalizations in avoiding responsibility.[47] Regarding the seventy elders who slipped away one by one, she cries:

> How typical! How true to life! (*NSS*, 87)

Her discussions of the process behind the gradual enslavement in Egypt,[48] the outsider as leader (*NSS*, 40), and the interpretation of dreams (*NSB*, 426), are just a few examples of Nehama's many psychological insights. She even revealed aspects of this type in legal parts of the Torah. In discussing the verses (Exodus 22:25–26):

> If you take your neighbor's garment as a pledge, you shall deliver it to him by sundown. For that is his only covering, it is the garment for his skin. In what shall he sleep? And it shall come to pass that when he cries to me I will hear, for I am compassionate,

she says:

> This is not the only context where the text inserts a direct emotional plea into what is a dry, terse legal ruling; the Torah does not simply decree, but rather instills its demands into the heart.[49]

---

[43] See for example her treatment of Potiphar's wife, who comes to represent manipulative and utilitarian behavior down the ages (*NSB*, 419–420; see page 275 above).

[44] She insists that Esau be viewed not only as an archetype but also as an individual, with positive and negative traits (*NSB*, 283–284; see also page 320 above.

[45] In *NSS*, 315 she observes: "Psychologically true as is the commentator's observation, it hardly qualifies for a true reading of the text itself."

[46] *PN*, 677. See also her rejection of Ramban's explanation of Joseph's motives in advising Pharaoh to appoint a wise man – she did not believe that this fit Joseph's psychological-spiritual profile (*NSB*, 447).

[47] See pages 356–363 above.

[48] See page 39 above.

[49] Combination of *NSS*, 420 and *IHBS*, 308.

She encouraged readers to likewise analyze characters' actions and motivations, to plunge into their inner worlds and make connections to their own lives.[50]

Her predilection for psychological explanations led Nehama to side fairly often with Ramban over Rashi.[51] While Rashi's explanations contained some psychological elements,[52] she felt that in general Ramban possessed deeper and more complex insights. She noted that when he could not decide based on linguistic factors, he used his intuitive understanding of human nature (*LP*, 38, n. 2). Nehama became impatient with the "over-literalists," such as Kaspi, Ibn Ezra, Rashbam and Radak, whose lack of close reading led them to misread the emotional atmosphere of the text. She believed that their ignorance of the Tanach's nuances led in general to inferior interpretations[53] and that at times they completely trampled the psychological tone of the text:

> Perhaps all the explanations of the philosophers and rationalists referred to missed the point in our text, because they failed to detect the sigh of disappointment behind Moses's words and regarded them as a statement of fact. (*SD*, 293)

She dismisses an explanation of Rashbam's:

> In the presence of the burning bush that was not consumed would [Moses] have expressed doubts of a political, diplomatic nature?[54]

In fact, she felt that the seemingly far-fetched Midrashic explanations were sometimes more on target in their insight into human nature:

> Hitherto we have cited all those who try to explain the text literally…. But it seems to us that our rabbis evinced a profounder understanding of the Israelites' character.[55]

Nehama's explanation of the differences between two commentators also sometimes rested upon their differing psychological conceptions.[56]

Ahistorical approach

Nehama's approach was deliberately ahistorical.[57] Like the New Critics, her commitment was to the text alone. The historical interpretation was too

---

[50] Deitcher, "Between," 9. See also *ibid.*,11 for his discussion of direct and indirect means of penetrating each biblical character, such as feelings or internal dialogues.

[51] Ben-Meir, "*Le-darkei*," 134–136.

[52] See for example *IBBM*, 55, n. 2.

[53] See her comments in *NSS*, 85, 87, 102, n. 4, 251, 382, 488 and 495 n. 4.

[54] *NSS*, 70. See page 506 below.

[55] *SBM*, 100–101. For more on Nehama and Midrash, see chapter 22.

[56] For example *SBM*, 176, question 2b.

narrow and localized; it did not explain the Torah, only its external structure.[58] She was interested in questions of meaning, not of fact. Though she paid more attention to the prophet's historical context, ultimately she recommended ignoring it in favor of his message.[59] In this, she was following midrashic methodology, as this quote she cites from Isaac Heinemann indicates:

> The question historical science asks is: what were the factors (political, economic, religious) which motivated Egypt's persecution and enslavement of Israel? But the question the Midrash asks is: why was Israel persecuted and enslaved more than the other nations of the world?[60]

Schwartz recalls Nehama saying many times: "I have no idea what actually happened and it does not interest me in the least!" But in practice, there was a little more to it than that. She certainly held this approach towards post-biblical texts, such as the Midrash and Aggadah, which, with their often-fantastic descriptions and elaborations, were meant to be symbolic and not literal.[61] She did not care whether or not Abraham really smashed idols, as described in the Midrash. But Nehama's approach was less decisive when it came to Tanach. Here, as a traditionalist, she believed that the events took place, even though her primary focus was on the ideas they conveyed.[62] Therefore, a differentiation must be made between the two types of text. She said that if students are expected to accept as fact the midrashic suggestion that the Israelite women bore sextuplets in Egypt, they are liable to reject both this and also the splitting of the Red Sea, "which we do believe."[63]

In any event, her focus was not the facts but on the message; any scientific information was purely incidental:

---

[57] See further on this subject, Rozenson "*Ha-parshanit*," *passim*.

[58] Yedgar, "*Ha-iyunim*," 20.

[59] Frankel, *Iyun*, 193. Rozenson believes that this attitude caused Nehama's extensive work on Prophets and Writings to fall short of the success of her other work. He explains: "Her book on Jeremiah was not up to standard, and my intuition says this is because you cannot teach Prophets in the same way as Torah. They must be based on the events of the time, and Nehama did this, but not nearly enough. The book did not achieve popular success, and neither did her book with Weiss, *Shiurim be-firkei nehama u-ge'ula*" (interview).

[60] *NSS*, 1. Also see Frankel, *Iyun*, 97, 120.

[61] See also N. Leibowitz, *Darkei*, 4.

[62] Frankel, *Iyun*, 96, 127.

[63] Schwartz, interview.

Our Torah is not meant to be a saga of past glories but a tale of truth and moral edification.[64]

[We must] unstintingly explain and emphasize that the book of *Bereshit* is not a history book, and its aim is not to survey the annals of ancient peoples. Rather it has its own goals: It is Torah [instruction], [aiming] to teach a message and a way of life, and the entire range of events, and its choices of when to be cryptic and when to elaborate, all are undertaken with this aim in mind.[65]

Likewise, she cites Cassuto's warning to the modern

history-ridden student who approaches the Holy Writ with nothing but archeological curiosity. (*NSB*, 91)

Nehama was not interested in biblical realia – the physical and cultural environment of the Tanach. She chose not to follow in the footsteps of certain traditional commentators who looked at historical explanations, such as Gersonides,[66] or who dealt with biblical realia such as Ibn Ezra[67] or Mendelssohn. She criticized commentators for over-realism.[68] Near Eastern customs or laws were always brought as a footnote to the issue at hand, never as the focus, for

no chapter in the Torah was written in order to teach us the trading laws of the Near East and ancient Canaan.[69]

---

[64] *NSS*, 127. See also *LP*, 83.

[65] *LP*, 155. See also *LP*, 83, and *NSB*, 91: "It should never be thought that the Torah is concerned merely with relating the past of peoples and countries, the annals of the ancient east for their own sake."

[66] She takes pride in the inventiveness displayed in one such historical interpretation by Gersonides, yet simultaneously dislikes the historical perspective implied (*IHBS*, 457; see Unterman, *Background*, 106 for discussion).

[67] See Ibn Ezra's commentary on Genesis 24:2, for example.

[68] Ibn Ezra attacks Saadya Gaon's explanation that Abraham's righteousness was revealed publicly by the binding of Isaac, and argues that "at the time no one was there, not even his servants." Nehama calls this argument "petty naive realism," adding incredulously, "And with this claim he wants to rebut the idea that the purpose of the binding was to teach a lesson and example to all the world!"(*IBB*, 134, compare *NSB*, 189). Elsewhere, Saadya too comes in for her reproach: "Saadya Gaon also tried to solve our difficulty by offering a rather unconvincing geographical explanation" (*SD*, 377).

[69] *Teacher's Guide* for *Hayyei Sarah* 5722. Abraham's negotiation with Ephron the Hittite "is not a source of information on customs and manners in the ancient east, particularly in the realm of buying and selling… it would be indeed strange if the Torah had dwelt on these details, just for the purpose of the realistic coloring" (*NSB*, 207). Nonetheless, in her questions at the end (*ibid.*, 213), she cites the scholar Lehman's findings and asks, "Which passages in our chapter are illuminated by the Hittite laws?"

The teacher of Tanach in a Jewish school is not teaching a book of ancient (Near) Eastern literature, but rather the sacred text from which generations have drawn and continue to draw nourishment.[70]

On one of the rare occasions when Nehama admits realia, we see that she did so reluctantly and only after Rashi did so.[71] Moreover, Rozenson notes that even in those few instances when Nehama did refer to the historical setting of the Torah, it was not to make a historical point but a psychological one.[72] She follows Rashi in turning geographical directions into theological concepts.[73] Maps, geography and zoology were of limited use in understanding the Tanach. Anyone suggesting that a discussion of the botanics of wheat and barley adequately explains the meaning of the verse (Deuteronomy 8:8)

A land of wheat, and barley, and vines, and fig trees, and pomegranates; a land of olive oil, and honey

is sorely mistaken:

The Torah does not insert realistic coloring for its own sake, or to provide background and atmosphere as in a modern novel.[74]

These realistic explanations cannot satisfy the mind that searches for ethical and intellectual inspiration (NSS, 492). Nehama was once teaching Psalm 23 ("The Lord is my shepherd...") when someone stood up and declared "Anyone who is not a shepherd cannot understand this Psalm!" A former shepherd himself, he proceeded to explain the Psalm based on his craft. But Nehama felt that his explanation lacked any meaningful insight, in contrast (she added, when retelling this incident) to the non-Jewish English

---

[70] N. Leibowitz, *Shiurim*, sheet 17, 3, "Note to teachers."

[71] She notes that creating a "Covenant between the Pieces" was a custom of the time (*NSB*, 145), basing herself on Rashi's quoting of the prophet Jeremiah (Rozenson, "*Diber*," 335).

[72] Rozenson, "*Ha-parshanit*," 448–449. He points out that regarding Pharaoh's act of "readying his chariot" (Exodus 14:6) Nehama mentions that Thotmes (Thutmose) III of Egypt personally went to the forefront of his battalion (see *NSS*, 252). But this seeming interest in history is misleading, for she was in fact bolstering Rashi's psychological interpretation, that Pharaoh was eager and did the act himself. As evidence, Rozenson points out that Nehama goes on to quote a second "proof" – King Abdullah's personally firing the first shot during Israel's War of Independence, an incident from an entirely different historical-cultural context, and comparable to the first only in a psychological sense.

[73] See *TI*, 116. In this, Nehama was following the path of non-Zionist Diaspora interpretations, whereby all terrains become internal ones. This reaches its most extreme form in Hasidic interpretation, which often transforms the entire Torah into psychological and spiritual symbols.

[74] *NSB*, 314, and see also *NSB*, 196–198, 396. See also Ahrend, "*Mi-toch*," 47–48.

physicist who asked to be read this Psalm on his deathbed. The latter truly understood King David's words.[75] Similarly she writes:

> Surely it is the Psalmist's definition of the qualities of the Torah and not considerations of archeological, historical, geographical and scientific importance that has been accepted by its students in every generation. (*SBM*, 388)

To teach history via the physical artifacts of the period, attempting to bring it to life by asking students to reproduce its clothing, architecture and furniture from clay and carton, was, Nehama said, a misinterpretation of the concept of active learning:

> [This] is clearly not a method of teaching history… but for teaching the history of objects and their manufacture.[76]

Any benefit gained is overshadowed by the harm caused by placing the wrong things at the center of attention.[77] Once, hearing of a reputedly superb teacher in Haifa, Nehama asked to sit in on his lesson. He asked the students to chart the probable site of the *Akedah*, based on which mountain would require a three days' walk for Abraham, as mentioned in Genesis 22:4. The students spent the lesson poring over maps and guessing at mountains with great interest, but Nehama walked out dissatisfied. The question was a fair one – she even discusses it herself in her writings[78] – but not a single word had been expended on the meaning of the story. She afterwards agreed with a colleague who pronounced: "*Akdu et ha-Akedah!*"[79] Nehama pointed out repeatedly that while modern literature would have described the mountains and the walk to the *Akedah*, the Torah omits such details as unimportant. She took her cue from the Torah itself.

Not that she was advocating ignorance of history and geography – familiarity with the language, history and land of Israel was important; but it

---

[75] R. Elhanan Samet, interview. See her analysis of this Psalm in her *Leader's Guide to the Book of Psalms* (NY: Hadassah Education Dept., 1971), especially 41, where she asks "Do you think that a knowledge of Eretz Yisrael and its nature is helpful to an understanding of the Psalm?" and "The National Geographic of 1926 carried an article on the life of shepherds in Israel with a photograph for each verse of Psalm 23…. Do the photographs contribute to our understanding of our chapter?" (Here it is not clear that the answer is an unequivocal no!)

[76] N. Leibowitz, "Active Learning," 5, n. 2.

[77] Ahrend, "*Mi-toch*," 47.

[78] *LP*, 66, where she speculates that it might be Mount Zion, citing a Catholic scholar who suggests that Abraham saw the mount from a distance at the eastern edge of today's Abu Tor.

[79] Lit: "They bound the binding!" i.e. they crippled the story's meaning for the sake of the details.

could never replace the act of finding meaning in the Torah. R. Raphael Posen recalls her asking her students how much water Rebecca must have drawn in order to slake the camels' thirst. She told them that she once requested this information from an Arab, who told her "Ten oil-storage canisters." Nehama then asked her class who still had such canisters in their homes, and a lively discussion commenced of how long it would take to fill one up. This brought the scene alive for them, but it was not enough for Nehama, for she immediately went on to teach the message of showing kindness to lost strangers, and this was the main point of the lesson.[80]

Nehama's rejection of this approach resulted in many hours of debate with students who felt that the Tanach might be experienced as more relevant when connected to geography and history. Aryeh Rotenberg recalls that when students asked her questions on biblical geography, she sent them to Professor Elitzur. "The literary perspective and the geographical seemed like two different worlds," says Rotenberg. Nonetheless, he found a way to integrate his passion for realia with his love of Nehama's work, leading hikes for American day school teachers who had studied with Nehama and quoting her teachings while out in the field. For instance, standing in the Elah valley, the site of David's battle with Goliath, Rotenberg mentioned Nehama's insight that David's conclusion of his pre-battle speech (Samuel I:17:36),

> Your servant slew both the lion and the bear; and this uncircumcised Philistine shall be as one of them, seeing he has defied the armies of the living God,

elicits no reply from Saul – for we see that in the next verse David speaks again:

> And David said, The Lord who saved me from the paw of the lion, and from the paw of the bear, he will save me from the hand of this Philistine…

and this time succeeds in convincing the king:

> … and Saul said to David, Go, and the Lord be with you."

When this explanation was quoted at the actual scene, it took on a power and vividness greater than in the classroom.

Nehama was extreme in her ahistoricism. She went even further than two of her favorite scholars, Heinemann and Weiss.[81] She applied it not only to the

---

[80] Posen, "*Mehanechet.*"

[81] See Rozenson, "*Ha-parshanit,*" 437, regarding Heinemann. Nehama's radicalness almost equaled that of the scholar Benedetto Croce, for whom art was never an

Bible but also frequently to its interpreters. Weiss was willing to admit the possibility of historical influence on a commentator, while Nehama absolutely disagreed in the case of Rashi and others:

> It was not his worldview, his beliefs or his personal experiences which guided Rashi in his exegetical work, but the Bible itself, the language of the text, the context.[82]

While Nehama was writing her comprehensive book on Rashi, it was proposed that a chapter be included detailing his background and influences. Nehama was adamant that this would be not only superfluous but also detrimental. Information about Rashi's personality and lifestyle – "what pants he wore," as she put it – would divert the students from what he said and why he said it from a textual standpoint.[83] What Nehama was doing, in essence, was reading not only the Tanach but also Rashi's commentary in New Critical fashion. She assumed that in his intellectual honesty, he was capable of freeing himself of any outside influences. Her educational agenda required her to take up this stance, since allowing for external influences would diminish the eternal nature of the commentators' words. The commentator was writing in reaction to the Divine text, not to particular events of his day. It was this standpoint that allowed her to seat commentators of different epochs "around the table together," to juxtapose them in a dialogue transcendent of time and circumstances.[84]

What is interesting, though, is her selectivity. She included later commentators in this timeless category and even non-Orthodox writers such as Benno Jacob;[85] but unhesitatingly excluded others, such as the Israeli poet Nathan Alterman:

> [Alterman's] words were written as all of Egypt's plagues descended upon Europe and filled them with blood, fire and pillars of smoke. Rashi too saw with his own eyes the horrors of the massacres of 1096,

---

expression of anything external (Croce is mentioned in Weiss, *The Bible*, 50). The other New Critics only opposed the historical angle as the sole prism of interpretation; the Swiss-German school was, moreover, actually interested in it, for its contribution to understanding the text's language (Weiss, *The Bible*, 8–9, 11).

[82] *Perush Rashi la-Torah*, 2, 460. She admits that scholars dissent from her view, but also asserts: "Everyone concedes that the influence of historical events in Rashi's commentary... is negligible" (n. 6).

[83] Ahrend, lecture. Although this historical chapter, written by Avraham Grossman, was ultimately included in the book – Nehama was even reportedly quite pleased with it – it was placed at the end rather than at the beginning, as is more common (see Mondschein, "*Akedat*," 118; Rozenson, "*Ha-parshanit*," 443).

[84] See Rozenson, "*Ha-parshanit*," 448, and Cohn, "*Ha-parshanut*," 97.

[85] Ahrend "*Mi-toch*," 42.

and grieved over them; but when he approached the text, all that was important was the verses and context.[86]

∾ ∾

Nehama was criticized for this highly ahistorical approach to Bible and commentary. Regarding the Bible, Rozenson feels that in viewing it through a timeless lens, Nehama lost the opportunity to highlight the advances made between earlier and later Judaism, as well as the contribution of biblical ethics to the moral evolution of the world.[87] Regarding the commentaries, many felt her view to be shortsighted.[88] Touitou, for example, argues that had she been interested in Rashbam's polemic with the Christians, she could more effectively have explained some of his unusual deviations from the *peshat*.[89] She rejects Rashbam's suggestion for why Moses broke the two tablets of stone, writing:

> Rashbam, a literalist par excellence, veers far from the plain sense here. There is no clue in the text for his interpretation that Moses's physical strength had ebbed away. (*NSS*, 606)

Yet, notes Touitou, she does not stop to ask why he veers thus. He proposes that Rashbam was avoiding supporting the Christian belief that a new covenant would replace the old one (*VLN*).

Nehama was aware of the scholarly arguments against her; and these only increased as time went on.[90] In fact, there is some evidence that towards the end of her life she became more amenable to the historical viewpoint.[91] Professor Moshe Ahrend argues that all along Nehama was not entirely

---

[86] *IHBS*, 126, n. 1. For more of Nehama's thoughts on Alterman's poem "*Shirei Makkot Mitzrayim*," see Nili Ben-Ari, "*Makkot Mitzrayim*," *Amudim, Nissan/Iyyar* 5767, 4–7.

[87] Rozenson, "*Ha-parshanit*," 450. He claims that Nehama does this only once, in comparing Sarah's behavior with the laws of Hammurabi (*ibid.*, n. 32).

[88] Yairah Amit, for example, rejects Nehama's separation between the historical approach and the values-educational approach. Values, she argues, are formed by time and place, and ignoring the historical viewpoint denies the entire picture (*VLN*).

[89] Touitou, "*Bein peshuto*," 229. Nehama was sensitive to the topic of Jewish-Christian polemics in general (*LP*, 213, n. 7; *SD*, 132). However, in the context of textual study she believed that this polemic might hold "no more than historical value" for the students (*LP*, 215). She was aware of Rashbam's agendas (see *NSV*, 391, n. 4) but would not concede that these shaped his exegesis: "Whether Rashbam's explanation is largely motivated by apologetic considerations in his theological disputations with the hostile critics of Judaism is a moot point" (*NSV*, 149 and see also n.1; see also discussion Touitou, "*Bein peshuto*," 232). She discusses the effect of the polemic with the Karaites on Ibn Ezra and Rashbam in *NSS*, 217–218 and 223, n. 1.

[90] Ahrend, "*Mi-toch*," 42–43. See also Grossman "*Pulmus*," 188.

[91] Grossman "*Pulmus*," 187, n. 3, and Yedgar report on pages 120 above and 558 below..

opposed; she simply felt that the historical approach was taken too far.[92] Indeed, we find in her writings an occasional sudden interest in historical and linguistic questions, included seamlessly in the discussion.[93] This is especially true of Prophets.[94] She also sometimes mentioned a commentator's background,[95] especially if this could serve an educational agenda.[96] Abravanel came in for special attention, with Nehama frequently attaching historical motivations to him – but this was cited negatively, as evidence that outside influence can distort a commentator's outlook, with the implication that the other commentators were not similarly susceptible.[97]

Postmodern elements in Nehama's approach

The above examination of Nehama's New Critical methodologies was achieved through an artificial putting asunder of what she deliberately joined[98] – namely, isolating certain elements from her general approach, and spotlighting them as a consistent system. But Nehama's approach actually

[92] He notes ("*Mi-toch*," 43) that Nehama praised the article by Sarah Kamin, "*Perush Rashi al Shir ha-Shirim ve-ha-vikuah ha-Yehudi-Notzri*" (from S. Kamin, *Bein Yehudim le-Notzrim be-farshanut ha-mikra*, Jerusalem: Magnes, 1992, 31–61).

[93] See, for example, *SD*, 366; *TI*, 56; or *NSV*, 168, n. 6, where she notes that the dialogues between R. Akiva and Turnus Rufus are "claimed to be historically authentic." She used historical research to serve her educational message (see chapter 19 n. 20, 21).

[94] Frankel, *Iyun*, 192.

[95] For example, Arama, Hirsch, Ibn Ezra, Ibn Kaspi, Netziv, Ramban, Rashbam. See Unterman, *Background*, 108–109, for more details and examples.

[96] For example on the verse "and he believed in God; and he counted it to him for righteousness" (Genesis 15:6), with its ambiguous "he" "he" and "him." Ramban insists that it was Abraham who recognized God's righteousness in giving him descendants. Nehama believed that Ramban's view derived from an anti-Christian stance – for if the second "he" was said to refer to God, this would imply, in line with Christian dogma, that God may be pleased with belief alone, without deed. (Nehama was very attached to this idea, but Weiss, as a reader for her book on Rashi, deemed it "superfluous." Nehama protested: "But I wanted to show the superiority of Judaism over Christianity!" However, such was her respect for Weiss that she removed it [Ahrend, "*Mi-toch*," 39–40]).

[97] While Nehama defends Abravanel's right to "detect in the Torah a message of comfort for his sorely tried coreligionists" (*SD*, 54) she contrasts this with the Midrash's "timeless application bearing a message of courage in every generation" (*ibid.* 156; and see other mentions of Abravanel's subjectivity in *NSB*, 93; *NSS*, 501–504). Nonetheless she also writes: "Abravanel thus drew from the sacred text a message for his generation. May we not learn from him to find in the words of the Torah a similar message for our own time and our own generation?"(*SD*, 302; and see also *IBBM*, 182, n. 3, cited on page 491 below, and *SD*, 295). See Rozenson "*Ha-parshanit*," 439–441 for more discussion of Nehama and Abravanel.

[98] Yedgar notes that Nehama's literary interpretations were often woven tightly with her discussions of classic commentaries ("*Ha-iyunim*," 23).

embraced a multiplicity of interpretations, based on both the *peshat* and on other layers of meaning hidden within the text.[99] As Frankel notes:

> The narrow context of the text, which is everything for the New Critical scholars, is only one of the factors in Nehama's work when she comes to determine "the area of context" for the study and teaching of Tanach.[100]

For this reason, Frankel suggests that a more accurate description of Nehama's approach would be not "close reading" but "close study" (*iyun tzamud*), applying to all of the layers of meanings, not only the surface one.[101]

Nehama, for her part, certainly did not see herself as bound to any particular literary theory.[102] She was happy to adopt elements from the New Critical/Total Interpretation approach, when useful, as part of the larger process of interpretation.[103] But sometimes she also broke all the New Critical rules, and aspects of her work resemble very different literary approaches, such as the postmodern one.

In the last few decades of Nehama's life, postmodern theory was on the ascent in both literature and Bible studies. Ever open to learning something new, Nehama took an interest in these developments.[104] When Simi Peters mentioned that she was reading Daniel Boyarin's *Intertextuality and the Reading of Midrash*,[105] Nehama asked her to explain the deconstructionism theory, for until then she had failed to find anyone who could get beyond a faltering start. Dr. Ruth Ben-Meir reports seeing another postmodernist work next to Nehama's bed; Nehama, she recalls, was fascinated by it.[106]

Nehama demonstrated an affinity for the deconstructionist position that meanings are to be found within the reader.[107] This is illustrated in four

---

[99] See Yedgar, "*Bein*," 67–68, especially footnotes 45–46.

[100] Frankel, *Iyun*, 4. See also *ibid.* 130, n. 15.

[101] Frankel, *Iyun*, 4–5 and footnotes.

[102] Frankel, "*Ha-te'oriyah*," 437.

[103] Ahrend informs us that Nehama "categorically stated that there is no purpose in making a grocery list of 'literary and stylistic elements' such as the *Leitwört*, the parable, the metaphor, the alliteration, the metonym, the anaphora etc. etc.; rather, they should be mentioned only when it may be demonstrated what they are expressing within the work and how they impact its meaning" ("*Mi-toch*," 37).

[104] Eliezer (Ed) Greenstein, "*Parshanutah rabat ha-panim shel Nehama Leibowitz ve-ha-parshanut ha-postmodernit*," *Limmudim* 1 (2001): 21. See also Ahrend, "*Mi-toch*," 46.

[105] Bloomington: Indiana University Press, 1990.

[106] The book was Stanley Fish, *Is There a Text in This Class?: The Authority of Interpretive Communities*, Cambridge, MA: Harvard University Press, 1980.

[107] See Ahrend, "*Mi-toch*," 45–47; Yedgar, "*Bein*," 54, 61.

separate passages from her writings.[108] The first sets up a religious foundation for the need for individual readings:

> This reading of the Torah as addressed directly to us, our time and generation – is this not the authentic way to approach the Torah's words? And what is true for every generation may also be said of each individual, who must study Torah as a personal listening to God's word.[109]

In the second, she elaborates on the individual's experience while reading the Tanach:

> My purpose is not to have you read these Psalms as documents from an ancient time, as records of Israel in olden days, but rather as poetry which transcends time. The "I" who speaks in these chapters is not the "I" of King David, or of Asaph, or of Ben-Korah. That "I" who speaks, weeps, expresses joy, offers thanks to God, cries for help, is the "I" of the reader at that very moment of reading. For indeed, all great literature is contemporaneous with the reader of any time.... Each generation brought to the words of the Psalms its own experiences, its joys and tribulations, its problems and tensions, its faith and its trust, its hopes and its disappointments.[110]

The individual reader experiences unique emotion, and possibly unique interpretation alongside it, though this it is not made explicit.

The third passage goes further to make this clear:

> It is doubtful, in general, whether an individual can establish a reading process for the many. Should not each individual attempt to establish his own reading, a reading suitable to his spirit and soul? Just as his spirit and soul comprise a unique and one-time phenomenon in this world, so his reading of Tanakh, his understanding of the text, should be a one-time phenomenon – uniquely his – and not an imitation of something else which once was.

> Ludwig Strauss taught us, according to the formulation of Nathan Rotenstreich, that true reading is: "The completion of the work (of literature), as though it were taken from the potential to the actual." Reading a poem is: "A reproduction which the reader accomplishes by means of his voice and soul." It is true that the reader is bound to the

---

[108] See also *SD*, 295 where, ironically, she says of Abravanel, whom she castigates elsewhere (see n. 97 above) that it is exactly his subjective approach, "colored by the religious persecutions of his times" which is more suited to the wording of the text than Rashi's in this particular instance.

[109] *IBD*, 61; compare *SD*, 55: "Each generation must view the Torah as personally addressed to it and directly applicable to the contemporary situation."

[110] N. Leibowitz, *Leader's Guide*, 1.

printed word. He does not, however, merely absorb it into his soul; he gives it expression from within his soul in order to bring the letters to life. "The relationship of words to a living work is like that of an architect to a constructed house. The reader is true in his reading to the blueprint, but it is he who builds the house of literary creativity from the material of his voice and soul.

After these words it is even more understandable how difficult it is for one person to teach another to read, since the responsibility for rebuilding the book anew belongs to the builders themselves, according to the instructions of the book, and by means of the material of their voices and souls, in which they differ one from the other just as their appearances differ. (*TI*, 163-164)

Here there is no hint of the Nehama who dismissed her students' ideas. Instead, she appears to assume an infinite number of unique interpretations. These plainly cannot all be derived using rigorous New Critical type methodologies alone, but are rather to emerge from the uniqueness of the reader, echoing the postmodern reader-response theory of Stanley Fish *et al.* in which the reader is said to complete the work's meaning through interpretation.[111] Perhaps precisely because she had strayed so far from New Critical territory, Nehama hastens to qualify the above:

If, in spite of this, we are still trying to teach reading, our justification is that the instructions given to the builder (namely, the architect's blueprint with all its verses, words and letters) are the precise data, the objective facts, the authority. It is towards the understanding of these (letters, words and verses) and to the acceptance of their authority, that we wish to lead the reader; and this is what our teacher Ludwig Strauss taught us in his lectures. (*TI*, 164)

A fourth passage unambiguously promotes subjective interpretation, albeit for educational reasons:

Each student feels that one particular interpretation (depending on his personality and character) is compatible with his sentiments. He is drawn to that interpretation and makes a great effort to convince his friends that only "his" interpretation is correct.... A personal connection is formed between the chapter and the student. (*TI*, 155)

Thus Nehama's assumption of the Torah's direct relevance to every generation and every individual, and the unique emotion and interpretation that creates a personal connection to the text, combine to create a relatively postmodern dimension in her approach.[112]

---

[111] See also Yedgar's comments in "*Bein*," 55, n. 26.
[112] Yedgar, "*Bein*," 61.

ও ও

Nehama's work with Midrashim also took her far from the New Critics and closer to postmodernism. Although she chiefly focused on Midrashim that furthered the text's primary meaning, and avoided interpretations that broke up the verse or uprooted it from its context,[113] at times she would introduce midrashic explanations that were in no way *peshat*, as she herself testified.[114] This was because she had other goals in mind, beyond text and context – namely, getting the reader to identify with the text, and teaching moral meanings relevant to the reader. These were types of readings to which most New Critics were completely opposed, as spoiling the autonomy of the work.[115]

Nehama's extreme anti-historicizing approach and her lack of interest in the externals of the commentators' lives also anticipated postmodernism before its advent. Even her classic question "What's bothering Rashi?" rather than "What is the difficulty in the text?" is, claims Professor Ed Greenstein, a wink in the direction of postmodernism and the commentator's phenomenological world.[116] Greenstein argues for a deconstructionist tendency within the body of Nehama's *Studies*. He cites as an example her essay on the midwives (*NSS*, 31–38). Here, he argues, Nehama approached postmodernism. Firstly, she gave preference to the marginal minority over practically all of the important commentators' views. Secondly, she provided, instead of her usual text-based interpretations, moral-psychological reasons reflecting her own personal views and values, as evinced by her closing comments, a clear reference to events in Nazi Germany.[117] Also, her accompanying statement, "if this is the correct interpretation," leaves room for doubt, and legitimates the alternatives, another postmodern element.[118]

Nehama moved away from the monolithic approach of much of the traditional world, as Dr. David Bernstein notes: "Within the parameters she set up there was room to see the advantages of each commentator's

---

[113] *TI*, 82; and see Cohn, "*Ha-parshanut*," 95–97.

[114] Cohn, "*Ha-parshanut*," 97 and examples on 105. See also pages 509–510 below.

[115] Some American New Critics did believe in reading texts for their moral statement (see *The Johns Hopkins Guide to Literary Theory and Criticism*, edited by M. Groden and M. Kreisworth, 530 [Baltimore/London: Johns Hopkins University Press, 1994]).

[116] Greenstein, "*Parshanutah*," 32.

[117] Greenstein "*Parshanutah*," 30–31, 33. Nehama speaks there of those who hid behind "superior orders" (*NSS*, 36).

[118] She writes "if we accept" (*NSS*, 36) and "it seems to me" (*IHBS*, 20, n. 5 – the English translation – "all the evidence points" – fails to illustrate the subjective dimension).

approach. Mostly, you were not to think in unequivocal categories of right and wrong, but rather that from one point of view, Rashi makes more sense, whereas from another Ramban does. This contrasts with the educational approach which teaches 'Rashi says this and Rashi is always right.'" Professor Dov Rappel recalls that the students at Mizrachi could not grasp this idea, of many legitimate meanings. Since the Scripture was written with a certain intention, they argued, then only the interpreter who hits upon the *peshat*, the meaning closest to that intention, may be right. In order to disabuse them of this notion, Rappel, Nehama and Elyakim ben Menahem each taught a lesson on the same Psalm, and each with a different understanding of the *peshat*. Then the students were at last convinced that *peshat* could be many things simultaneously.[119]

This was so obvious to Nehama that, as Greenstein reports, after making an effort to understand deconstructionism, especially its notions of the "hermeneutics of suspicion" and "textual indeterminacy," she eventually decided that it had little new to add. She questioned the difference between textual indeterminacy and the approach taken in Torah study whereby several legitimate interpretations may exist simultaneously, as per the adage, "Both these and those are the words of the living God" (Eruvin 13b).[120]

In truth these two are not quite the same.[121] But even her question indicates that in her devotion to multiple meanings, she came closer to postmodern than to modern theory, in contrast to Weiss, who aimed to derive one interpretation from the Scripture.[122] She even occasionally refrained from deciding at all between commentaries, leaving an essay open-ended so that the reader could choose:

> We do not wish to force any particular interpretation on the student but merely to indicate how susceptible are the words of the Torah to many and even contradictory explanations.[123]

Though Nehama rarely did this in the Torah, Frankel discovered that in Prophets, she was consistently open to contradictory findings and did not resolve them.[124] Frankel believes that this more accurately represents Nehama's true standpoint than the careful moral wrap-up at the end of her essays.[125] This is arguable, and will be discussed in the next chapter.

---

[119] Rappel, *"Tehillim mizmor kaf-bet,"* in *PN*, 441.

[120] Eruvin 13b; Greenstein, *"Parshanutah,"* 22.

[121] See Greenstein, *"Parshanutah,"* 23, for his explanation.

[122] Yedgar, *"Bein,"* 68, n. 46. See also Yedgar, *"Ha-iyunim,"* 18, n. 14.

[123] *NSB*, 150. See chapter 18 n. 99.

[124] Frankel, *Iyun*, 191.

[125] Frankel, *VLN*. She argues that the wrap-up was a result of educational demands from Nehama's publishers. She also notes that the extent to which this is used varies

๛ ๖

All this notwithstanding, the fact remains that in closing most of her essays with a message and in rejecting interpretations when she wished, Nehama was clearly not a full postmodernist. Frankel suggests that Nehama's approach brings her to the border of the postmodern approach but not into it. Even if she accepted many interpretations of a text, they were still distinct and disagreeing rather than leaving the ambiguity of the text intact; legitimate contenders for *peshat* had to be anchored in the text, maintaining the original objective of the verse and complying with it.[126]

Professor Moshe Sokolow does not even believe that Nehama maintained multiple interpretations in tandem. He claims that she was always consciously pushing for evaluation and selection of the commentary closest to the *peshat*.[127] Salmon similarly notes:

> Nehama... is wary of the approaches to textuality developed after, and to some extent against, New Criticism because she fears that they will relativize the text and weaken its moral imperative.[128]

Professor Warren Zev Harvey suggests that in fact Nehama was closer to Plato than to Derrida, in that each position she brought was sharply delineated and distinct from the others, with none of the ambiguity of the postmodernists (*VLN*).

The bottom line seems to be that for Nehama, despite the above four quotes, interpretation abides not in the reader alone, but in the finite, bounded realm of the text.[129] Dr. Mordechai Cohen observes: "Just the title of *How to Read a Chapter of Tanach* does not correspond well with reader-response theory" (*VLN*). In fact, Nehama at times warned of the dangers of subjectivity.[130] She praised Ramban for avoiding the pitfall of inappropriate preaching on a verse:

> [He] does not take advantage of this opportunity to exploit the verse to "recount the virtues of Eretz Yisrael" but on the contrary takes Ibn Ezra to task for doing so, since his is not an interpretation that fits the

---

with the particular text. In the *Studies*, texts that deal with revelation and Divine mystery are more often left open-ended. See further in Frankel, *Toratah*, chapters 3 and 4.

[126] Frankel, *VLN* and *Iyun*, 191.

[127] As mentioned on page 385 above, Nehama declared, "*These and those means no learning!*" and, "When Ramban says of Rashi's explanation 'This is incorrect!' his intention is not 'You are also right!' See Sokolow, *Samchut*, 297 and *passim*.

[128] Salmon "Nehama," 19.

[129] Greenstein's replies to Nehama's query regarding the difference between textual indeterminacy and the Torah approach fall along similar lines to her own view ("Parshanutah," 22).

[130] See "*Al nituah*," 617–619 and her critiques of Abravanel's subjectivity, n. 97.

verse. This teaches us that opinions and beliefs, likes and dislikes are not to dictate the interpretation, but only the text – its language, style, grammar and context.[131]

Perhaps then it is most accurate to state that Nehama read in both modern and postmodern ways, as Erella Yedgar remarks:

> Nehama unites two seemingly contradictory elements, both of which appear to her imperative in studying the text, which in other hermeneutical approaches are liable to exist independently: A literary approach limiting study to the text's rules and details, and a dialogical approach, opening the (text's) significance to personal interpretation deriving from the reader's unique perspective and from the supposition that the text speaks personally to the reader.[132]

Yedgar suggests, therefore, that even Nehama's literary work should be more accurately termed "literary-dialogical."[133]

Nehama's postmodernist leanings stand in her defense against accusations that she was not a true scholar, that she functioned with external educational agendas and by a method that was unscientific and biased in comprehending the text. Such allegations hold water only from the modern perspective. From the postmodern perspective, Nehama's focus on the views and values of the commentators, of herself and of her students, is admissible and even admirable.[134]

Nehama as original commentator

Much of the above information brings us to another important revelation: That, in addition to her important work with biblical commentators, Nehama Leibowitz is also worthy of the title "commentator" in her own right. This is an oft-overlooked fact, for reasons that will be discussed below.

While Nehama's primary goal was to teach text with commentaries, there were textual patterns and difficulties that she noticed on her own. It should not be too surprising to find her applying her keen literary sensibility, shaped by many years of exposure to the midrashic, medieval and modern approaches to text. On the contrary, it would have been remarkable had a person of such creativity and skill failed to come up, from time to time, with insights of her own. Since she developed theories for literary analysis, for example regarding how to read dialogues in the text,[135] it is logical that she

---

[131] *LP*, 83–84 (see page 267 above for longer quote). See also *NSB*, 207 for a similar point.
[132] Yedgar, "*Ha-iyunim*," 18–19.
[133] Yedgar, "*Ha-iyunim*," 18, n. 14.
[134] Today's scholars are increasingly coming round to her way of thinking. See page 511 above.
[135] See N. Leibowitz, "*Va-yomer*," *passim*.

would apply these theories herself. Hence, original literary analyses, as well as original psychological and ethical insights, are to be found scattered at irregular intervals throughout Nehama's *Studies*.

ॐ ॐ

The material in the *Studies* may be separated out into three categories. First, text and commentary. Second, Nehama's explanations before and after her quotes of text and commentary. These explanations sometimes contain interpretations that are not given in the name of any commentator. Such explanations are most likely Nehama's own, but they are easily missed, obscured and embedded in the other material or appear as bridges between citations of others.[136] Hence, the superficial reader might easily mistake them for mere rewordings, and only a closer examination reveals their innovation.[137]

The third category is less easy to miss: analyses and insights that appear with no commentators cited in the vicinity at all, for part or all of an essay. Several essays in the *Studies* are almost entirely comprised of such – presumably original – interpretation, particularly those on the Joseph story.[138] One example is her essay "Anatomy of a Blessing," which illustrates her sensitivity to tone and richness of language.[139]

Yedgar speculates that having learned the literary technique primarily from modern thinkers, including Buber *et al.*, Nehama allowed herself to be at her most original in the literary area.[140] In fact, she anticipated work by

---

[136] Red flags alerting us to such sections might include her use of words such as "perhaps" and "it appears" (Kagan, "Review") or "we may note" (see e.g. *NSB*, 81). For example, in *NSS*, 449, the absence of comment from Rashi's supercommentaries forces her to make her own, with the preface "it seems to me"; or *NSV*, 273 ("The commentators have not solved this problem. Perhaps…" etc).

[137] For example, in *NSS*, 433, her comments on the difference between the word "meet" and the word "see" – introduced by the words, "There is a further point to consider." Or see her profile of Lot, based on an analysis of the word order in the verse (*NSB*, 122–123); or *NSS*, 561 – "But a more careful look…." (the Hebrew is even more forceful, see *IHBS*, 404). For more examples of independent analyses, see Unterman, *Background*, 86–88, and also those cited in the earlier part of this chapter in the context of her close reading techniques.

[138] See *NSB*, 430–438, 470–482. Her essay, "Joseph and His Brothers," (*TI*, 163–176) is a mix of insights from commentators and her own literary analyses. See further in Frankel, *Iyun*, 42–64.

[139] *SBM*, 290–296. See also her pyramidal structured breakdown of Pharaoh's dreams, set out beautifully in *IBB*, 311 (the English translation, in *NSB*, 441, is not equivalent). Her careful comparison between Samuel I, 24 and 26 is also well worth noting (*SBM*, 114–118 and see page 457 above).

[140] Yedgar, "*Ha-iyunim*," 22.

later literary Bible scholars.[141] In this she was a pioneer of the literary-biblical method, as Professor Yair Hoffman tells us:

> Before the principles [of the Close Reading method, as established by Weiss] were even formulated systematically, Nehama Leibowitz paved the way for them. She cleared away the stumbling blocks of prejudice, uprooted weeds from the field of study, which all too quickly piled up "critical" solutions without first scrutinizing the text....

> There are times when one reads a nice article about biblical prose and wonders, "Where did I read this already?" And then remembers that it was in one of the *gilyonot*.[142]

It seems very likely that these analyses, not brought in the name of anyone else, are Nehama's own. There is, however, the possibility that she imported an occasional idea from someone else without attribution – not due to plagiarism, which she loathed,[143] but rather to her deep internalization of the insight, to the point where it appeared obvious.[144] We see a clear example of this, involving not New Critics but traditional interpreters, in her discussion of Exodus 1:13–14 (*NSS*, 6–8). The Egyptians are described there as enslaving the Israelites ruthlessly (*"be-farech"*). Nehama points out that the only other mention of this word in the Torah appears in the description of the proper ethical treatment of a slave/manservant (Leviticus 25:43):

> You shall not rule him ruthlessly.

This insight, sensitively connecting two distant places by use of a common word, is likely her own. But then, using this literary observation as a springboard, she weaves a powerful argument: that the collective memory of the traumas in Egypt (the context of the first verse) must be preserved and channeled into sympathy for the downtrodden and the stranger (the

---

[141] For example, a footnote by Frisch ("*Shitato*," 317, n. 14) suggests that Nehama's analysis of the David and Bathsheba story reaches similar conclusions to those reached later on by Fokkelman, Alter and himself.

[142] Hoffman "*Yoter.*"

[143] Nehama declared: "Shall I hide the source [of my teachings]? I cannot. Whose are the waters that we drink yet whose names we fail to mention?" (letter to Ansbacher, *PN*, 658). But we do find that she on occasion does not attribute fully. For example, she informs the reader that "an Egyptian nobleman always prepared in his lifetime his own grave," without providing a source for this statement (*NSB*, 532).

[144] In n. 10 above, we mentioned that she quoted an insight that Staiger discovered without citing him by name. She may have heard it herself once and forgotten its source, or she may have reached the same conclusion independently. But she may also not have felt it necessary to distinguish so sharply between her own and others' analysis – as in the example below.

context of the second verse). She cites the Torah itself as her support, in its repeating refrain:

For you were slaves/strangers in the land of Egypt.[145]

In other words, she works with both the nuances of the verses, and the broader context of the Torah, exactly as a New Critic would.

Notable for our discussion here is the fact that she makes her point in this essay without recourse to any commentators. It seems to be her own. Yet in another discussion, later in *New Studies in Shemot*, she cites this same reason for the enslavement – the creation of sympathy – in the name of Rashi and Ramban.[146] Why, then, does she not cite it in their name here? After all, she had no interest in passing their views off as her own – if anything, the opposite is true, as Leah Abramowitz reports:

> Nehama rarely said, "This is my idea"; instead she would say, "I saw this somewhere.... Professor Shmuel Adler gave a shiur in her memory in which she used some famous explanation she assigned to Rashi. "I searched through all the Rashi commentaries again and again but couldn't find where he said that. It's obviously one of her ideas, which she developed and claimed it was Rashi's."[147]

Furthermore, in the second essay Nehama goes on to actually *reject* this position regarding the creation of sympathy, with no qualms whatsoever, as "naïve"; and ultimately prefers a different conclusion.[148] This is something one generally does not do so facilely with one's original readings. This example suggests that Nehama's view of herself was overwhelmingly not as a commentator but as a teacher of commentaries,[149] as she indeed declared: "I teach only what the commentators have written – I do not innovate!"[150] and: "My book [is] no more than a compilation of commentaries on the weekly Torah portion, of which there are many today."[151] She did not make a clear distinction as to where others' readings stopped and hers began; hers was done in the context of theirs and needed no neon letters pronouncing it

---

[145] This theme appears in Exodus 22:20, 23:9, Leviticus 19:34, and in Deuteronomy 5:15, 10:19, 15:15, 24:22.

[146] See *NSS*, 382–384 and especially the second Rashi on 383. She also cites her first essay, from the beginning of *NSS*, in a footnote there (389 n. 5), which only serves to strengthen the question.

[147] Abramowitz, *Tales*, 60.

[148] *NSS*, 384, and 389, n. 6. See also page 94 n. 33 above, where a suggestion is made to resolve this contradiction in terms of her personality.

[149] Yedgar, "*Bein*," 75.

[150] Bonchek, "*Darko*," 143.

[151] Letter to Tal, *PN*, 666; see Yedgar, "*Ha-iyunim*," 30.

"original." This explains why an idea might appear once from her own pen, seemingly, and a second time attributed to someone else.

Nehama's belief was that all close reading ought to be done in conjunction with the commentaries, and with the ultimate goal in mind:

> Reflection and depth of thought, and... sensitivity to the most delicate nuances and associations of the words of scripture... can only be achieved by reading the text with the aid of the great scholars, that is, by examining the commentaries, comparing them with each other and weighing their words against the text itself, while bearing in mind its wording and style, its context, and its structure. The ultimate aim is to make students fully aware of the great light which shines out of the Torah – Torah both written and oral, Torah in its legends and interpretations, and Torah in its most literal form, down to the last letter – so that they will cherish it and its Giver.[152]

જી ન્ઉ

Had she put her mind to it, Nehama might well have written an outstanding work of Torah interpretation. In fact, before the *Studies* came out, Professor E.E. Urbach made a call for Nehama to go beyond others' works and write a complete and systematized commentary of her own:

> The *gilyonot*, for all their good qualities, cannot take the place of the commentary we lack.... Dr. Nehama Leibowitz can and should provide us with the commentary we lack.[153]

Urbach wanted Nehama to create a new commentary that would be suitable for a traditional audience yet updated for the times. We might suppose this to be a project Nehama would support; yet her belief in the eternal relevance and greatness of her predecessors' ideas was evidently the stronger impulse, for she never acceded to the request. Dr. Gabriel Cohn explains: "What Professor Urbach failed to understand is that the idea of writing a commentary went against everything Nehama was trying to achieve. The idea behind her method was not to write a commentary, but to enable the student to arrive at his or her own interpretation – the most accurate and personal interpretation possible."

There may have been other reasons too.[154] Her humility may also have played a role, for example.[155] Taking on the mantle of the first female

---

[152] N. Leibowitz, "*Shiur be-Torah*," *Ma'ayanot* 4 (1954): 34, translated by Amit ("Hebrew Bible," 9).

[153] Urbach, "*Le-mikra*," 56, 58. This was written just as the first *Studies* were coming out in 1954.

[154] R. Mordechai Breuer suggests that Nehama avoided writing her own commentary for fear that it would bring her into an undesirable full-blown confrontation with biblical criticism ("*Yahasah*," 11). Others disagree strongly with this assumption.

Tanach commentator would have been a tremendous responsibility. Although she had the confidence to contradict the commentators in a localized way, it was quite another thing to write an entire commentary. "Me write a commentary?" she exclaimed. "I don't know anything! I don't know Semitic languages like Moshe Greenberg. I don't know archeology."[156] Nehama argued that "only a tremendous scholar" could write about Tanach. She would not allow herself to imagine placing herself in the same league as the illustrious people whose work she studied.

Such a role would also have brought more unwanted attention to Nehama as a "revolutionary," undermining her most important goals. In her work, Nehama wanted the attention to go to the Torah and her predecessors, not to her own genius. When precedents for her methods were discovered in earlier writings, this gratified her rather than otherwise.[157] On one occasion, after writing "The reason is clear to me," she quickly works to deflate any self-importance by soon adding, "Now I come to my 'discovery'" (PN, 496–497), with the quotation marks around "discovery" defusing any appearance of pride.

R. Nathaniel Helfgot observes: "Her whole approach militated against innovation, against creativity *qua* creativity. She was not into the notion of new-fangled readings of Tanach. She focused instead on uncovering the assumptions of the commentators, not differentiating between their work and her own." In fact, Nehama believed that true innovation was beyond the reach of most. She lamented that most students did not have anything original to say; hence, she preferred exams to written papers which, far from encouraging independent thinking, seemed to produce nothing of value. She rejected the cult of originality, astonished that

> even yeshivahs, which are aware of what knowledge, comprehension and erudition are, encourage the students – far from Torah giants – to write "novellae." (PN, 685)

The Jewish academic world was no better, granting as it did a platform to countless second-rate articles written by people suffering from what she called "graphomania." Full of uninformed and clichéd ideas, these articles appeared in all sorts of pamphlets and minor publications. This was not the way to deal with contemporary challenges, Nehama admonished:

---

[155] Kagan "Review"; Bonchek, "*Darko*," 147.

[156] R. Nathaniel Helfgot, interview.

[157] Such as the work of R. Isaac Campanton (see page 373 above) or Judge Zvi Tal's discovery of support for her method in the Tosafot (see page 511 below).

You want "to raise the level of your religious and general education." Very good. But is this the way to do it? To have Hayyim read Yossi's musings, and Uzi read Gideon's contemplations?[158]

Upon hearing of a new journal of articles by women, she responded: "That money could have gone to supporting another scholar!" She felt that such journals emerged from a widespread ignorance, stemming from insufficient perusal of quality books.[159] Any spare time ought to be spent on works that were truly great, by the likes of R. David Zevi Hoffmann and others. These were difficult books that should be read not once, but many times.[160] Nehama was pained that fewer and fewer books were being read, and she deplored the widespread academic reliance on bibliographies containing only segments of books, grumbling, "No one reads complete books these days." In 1988, when R. Helfgot asked her to contribute an article to a Yeshiva University publication aimed at promoting creative, serious Tanach study within the walls of the *bet midrash*, he received the following sharply-worded reply:[161]

> I received your letter, and thank you for remembering me positively and for honoring me with an invitation to participate in this collection. I cannot accede to your invitation, both due to my inability to contribute anything of genuine importance to Tanach study, and also from lack of time. But let me take this opportunity to tell you what I really think: I believe that there is absolutely no need to bring out a book such as this, because few people will read it. After all, there are several truly important and high-level books written on the Tanach, such as Meir Weiss's two books *Ha-mikra ki-demuto* and his recent work *Mikra'ot ke-chavanatam* (the first was translated with additions into English as *The Bible from Within*) and there is also an exceptional work by Leah Frankel *z"l* called *Pirkei mikra*, and the excellent book by H. Tz. Enoch[162] and so on and so on – and who of all your yeshivah students has read even one line of these books?? I don't know who the Tanach teachers are over there. If they include anyone who is truly great (like the truly great Talmud/Halachah scholars you have over there) then let him write his book. But for a collection of mediocre articles to be put together (you

---

[158] N. Leibowitz, "*Teshuvah*," 623.

[159] N. Leibowitz, "*Teshuvah*," 623.

[160] N. Leibowitz, "*Teshuvah*," 622; letter to Ahituv.

[161] See *PN*, 662–663 for full letter(s).

[162] In her second letter to Helfgot (*PN*, 663) she cites additional valuable and overlooked works by Enoch, Leah Frankel, Weiss and Rappel, and also her own *Limmud parshanim ve-hora'atam* (sic) from which "a teacher could learn something" and her brother's book "*He'arot le-parashat ha-shavua*" (see chapter 23 n.67) and laments that students do not read R. Soloveitchik's works. See also her letter to Reinitz, *PN*, 684–685, where she lists further works of merit.

write that student authors will be included) – what for? And for whom? Kohelet already protested, "And more than these, my son, be wary of creating infinite books....[163]

The urge to publish also steals time from good teaching, she informed R. Yaakov Koppel Reinitz:

> Far better that a teacher prepare lessons well than waste time writing underdeveloped articles.... Far better that the teacher sit with students in an optional extra-curricular afternoon class (students come to such a class gladly, since there are no exams or grades, just study for its own sake), and even simply to converse on current affairs, than to squat upon the birthstones to produce a stillborn. (PN, 685)

She adds that money is much better spent on study days and sample lessons than on paper and ink for articles which in any event will not – and, in most cases, should not – be read.

Nehama also innovated in other realms, besides the literary analysis of the text. For example, the Midrashim she cited frequently lacked commentaries, forcing her to invent her own and become a *de facto* commentator on Midrash.[164] Also, her moral message statements that appeared chiefly, though not solely, at the end of each *Studies* were not quite the simple summaries they appeared to be. A closer look reveals careful selection and rewording of others' ideas, which also constitutes an act of original interpretation.[165] It might also be argued that in connecting seemingly unrelated passages of the Bible, Nehama created her own Midrash.[166]

Lastly, Nehama developed certain philosophical concepts in unique directions. For example, her somewhat radical association between the concepts of *tzelem elohim* (Image of God) and *kedoshim tihyu* ("You shall be holy") are not found in any of her predecessors' ideas,[167] and her

---

[163] Ecclesiastes 12:12. Although R. Helfgot was somewhat disheartened by her response, the volume was eventually published under the name *Rinat Yitzhak.* "I felt that she was mistaken and that people should be encouraged to think creatively in Tanach," he says (interview).

[164] Cohn, "*Ha-parshanut,*" 95.

[165] Yedgar, for instance, points out how Nehama slightly changes Ramban's understanding of God's commandment in Genesis to subdue or conquer the earth ("*Ahrayut,*" 386–387).

[166] See for example *NSB*, 178 where she suggests that a seemingly unrelated passage from Isaiah may "possibly" be connected to a passage from Genesis.

[167] Yedgar, "*Ahrayut,*" 389, n. 28.

interpretation of the "idolatrous sinner" as someone who shirks responsibility is strikingly original.[168]

"Nehama as Bible scholar" revisited

We have already touched upon the question of whether Nehama is seen, or ought to be seen, as a Bible scholar rather than an educator. We examined this question using the criteria of attitude towards biblical criticism and academia, and capability for critical thinking. But subsequent to our discussion in the past two chapters, we may now return to the question from a different angle – in terms of her biblical-literary work, and her original contributions to biblical scholarship.

There is argument concerning what place Nehama ought to be accorded in the annals of modern Bible scholarship. Moshe Ahrend believes she should take up a place of honor, but Professor Uriel Simon suggests that her original work is minimal, and that, though no less talented than Meir Weiss, the absence of systematic interpretation on her part meant that her impact was much more limited than it might have been (*VLN*). He writes:

> Nehama Leibowitz's *Studies* indeed accustom students to identifying fine nuances in the language and style of the Hebrew text.... One cannot deny, however, that Nehama Leibowitz, venerated teacher though she was, saw herself above all as an educator, and not as a scholar. Hence the five volumes of her *Studies* are more in the nature of excellent textbooks but not systematic commentaries.[169]

Professor Robert Alter, in his seminal work *The Art of Biblical Narrative*, does not mention Nehama at all, not even in chapters devoted to topics on which she wrote extensively, such as repetition.[170] Presumably, had she

---

[168] *SD*, 309. See discussion on page 357 above.

[169] Simon, "The Place," 232.

[170] Alter writes: "Until the mid-1970s the only book-length study in English by a professional Bible scholar that made a sustained effort to use a literary perspective was Edwin M. Good's *Irony in the Old Testament*" (Alter, *The Art of Biblical Narrative*, New York: Basic Books, 1981, 15). However, Weiss's book was published in 1962; and Schwartz in fact criticizes Alter's omission of Nehama and Weiss from his survey of biblical scholarship ("*Bikoret sefer al Robert Alter*, The Art of Biblical Narrative," *Shnaton le-mikra le-heker ha-mizrah ha-kadum* 5–6 [5743]: 268). When asked about his choice, Alter responded in a private communication: "It has never been my intention in any of my writings to provide an exhaustive representation of secondary literature. I mention only what is absolutely relevant to what I'm doing. I read Meir Weiss a long time ago, and found his work intelligent but not focused in a way that was especially helpful for what I wanted to do. I think that Nehama Leibowitz is an acute commentator on details of the text, but does not frame a poetics of biblical narrative, which is what I attempted; and in any case, I prefer to draw directly from Ibn Ezra, Rashi, Radak, etc., whom she uses abundantly."

gathered and systematized her work on repetition in its own volume, it would have achieved much greater recognition.

However, the popular perception is very different, as reflected in the *Jerusalem Post*'s description:

> Nehama Leibowitz was hailed by many as the most brilliant Torah commentator of our generation.[171]

R. Ben Hollander hastened to respond to this:

> Leibowitz would insist that she was not a commentator but... a teacher.[172]

Yet the battle is already lost, for a glance at the way in which Nehama is described in many different forums reveals that they often include the word "commentator" or "interpreter."[173]

Scholars too give Nehama credit as an interpreter – for example, Professor Israel Rozenson, who resists Simon's definition of "interpretation."[174] He writes:

> Certainly a "summary" like Nehama Leibowitz's, resolving substantial questions such as the closeness of a particular commentary to *peshat* or the influence of his time period, ought to be considered an independent commentary of its own.[175]

He also laments the neglect of Nehama's groundbreaking literary work on Tanach by many, including her own students: "Every great person's followers end up taking on the easier parts. I had thought that in the footsteps of Nehama Leibowitz we would see someone from the world of teacher-training in Tanach become a leading scholar of literary analysis in Tanach; but this did not happen – we find them only within academia." Dr. Baruch Schwartz believes that Nehama deserves to be credited more for her

---

[171] Calev Ben-David, "No More Yentls," *Jerusalem Post*, April 2, 1999, B3.

[172] Ben Hollander, "Nehama Leibowitz, Teacher," Letters, *Jerusalem Post*, May 19, 1999, 8.

[173] For example, Grace B. McMillan speaks of "Nehama Leibowitz's commentaries" ("Fifty Feminist Rabbis on Torah," *Jerusalem Post*, Jan 5, 2001, 12B, reviewing *The Women's Torah Commentary: New Insights from Women Rabbis on the 54 Weekly Torah Portions*, edited by Elyse Goldstein). For the full quote see page 273 above. In another example, Harvey J. Fields, in *A Torah Commentary for Our Times* (New York, UAHC, c. 1990–1993) calls Nehama a "modern commentator" (*Exodus and Leviticus*, 40) and a "modern interpreter" (*ibid.*, 100) and utilizes her work widely.

[174] Rozenson, "*Diber*," 326, n. 3.

[175] Rozenson, "*Predah mi-devarim*," *Ha-Tzofeh*, 21 Tishrei 5755, 4, and see Rozenson, "*Ha-parshanit*," 434 n. 1, paragraph 5.

contribution to biblical-literary scholarship, as does Weiss.[176] The committee who awarded Nehama the Bialik Prize referred to her analyses of the Tanach's literary narrative (a "deeply aesthetic experience" for her audience) and to her original philosophical insights.[177] And in *Hogim ba-parashah*, a Hebrew volume published in 2005 devoted to various philosophers and commentators, from Maimonides and R. Kook to Spinoza and Freud, Nehama is centrally featured in three of the essays.[178] Their authors clearly see her as not just a collector of others' comments but as an interpreter and thinker in her own right. So does Michael Bahat, who has published a book in which articles by thinkers such as R. Soloveitchik, Buber and Rosenberg are juxtaposed with Nehama's moral teachings, from her *Studies* on Genesis.[179]

In Conclusion

Nehama Leibowitz has been pigeonholed by some as a teacher rather than a Bible scholar. It seems that this was also her own self-definition. However, the last three chapters have served to demonstrate the erroneous nature of this assumption. While not a biblical-critical scholar, Nehama was a probing, rationalistic analyst of the Tanach, of a type perhaps more familiar from pre-biblical-criticism days. Furthermore, rebelling against the historical approaches and influenced by a mix of traditional literary approaches, modern Jewish thinkers and the New Critical literary movement, she built up literary methodologies and applied them in new analyses which, because they are scattered and unemphasized by their author, remain largely overlooked to this day.

In creating her method and greatly influencing the direction of Tanach interpretation for her students, Nehama may even be said to have founded a school of thought. Traditional Tanach teachers have drawn on the many literary techniques she utilized, including intertextuality, the *Leitwört* and other tools used widely today. Nehama popularized these methods before they were in fashion, prefiguring later work. Although Robert Alter expresses astonishment in his book, published in 1981, that "at this late date literary analysis of the Bible of the sort I have tried to illustrate here… is

---

[176] Schwartz, interview. Others who remark Nehama's original insights on both Scripture and Rashi include Dr. Avigdor Bonchek ("*Darko*," 143) and Professor Yaakov Kagan ("Review").

[177] Their comments are reproduced in Nissenbaum, Booklet, 4.

[178] The essays are by Ohana, Yedgar and Rosenak – see bibliography for details.

[179] The book is called *Iyunim le-parashat ha-shavua mi-yesodam shel Nehama Leibowitz* (Haifa, 5750). According to the author's introduction, it was written with Nehama's approval and aid.

only in its infancy,"[180] Nehama was in fact already doing this kind of work, albeit on a minor scale, decades earlier. Professor Yairah Amit writes that Nehama's work elicits "the approval of enlightened, critical scholars," explaining:[181]

> Her faithfulness to the principle of close reading has made Nehama Leibowitz a pioneer in the literary-aesthetic approach to biblical interpretation. With this approach, she has shown the extent to which the literature of the Bible represents artistic creativity of unique distinction, well able to stand up to modern textual-aesthetic analysis.[182]

What Nehama lacked in systematization, she made up for in the sheer scope of her impact, going well beyond academic circles. With literary study today widespread in both the academic world and that of the modern sector of Orthodox Torah study, her contribution merits more recognition. It should take its rightful place in surveys of twentieth-century Bible scholarship.

---

[180] Alter, *The Art of Biblical Narrative*, New York: Basic Books, 1981, 14.
[181] Amit, "Hebrew Bible," 11.
[182] Amit, "Hebrew Bible," 11.

CHAPTER 22

THE MEDIUM AND THE MESSAGE:
PESHAT, DERASH AND WHAT LIES BETWEEN

HAVING DISCUSSED two foundations of Nehama's approach – her use of commentaries and her close literary reading – we now come to the third foundation: the practical or moral lesson.

Nehama held two dimensions to be fundamental when studying text: the *peshat*, the intended meaning of the verse; and the moral message, embedded within the text, which remained with the student after studying the Torah and commentaries. Once again, we find a delicate balance between these two disparate elements, leading to a unique flavor in Nehama's work.

Introduction: *Peshat* and *derash*

Today, the words *peshat* and *derash* are seen as a pair of opposites, referring respectively to the plain/objective/simple/intended meaning, and the homiletical/allegorical/imaginative meaning. But in talmudic times, neither term meant what it does today; in fact, the two may even have been synonyms, at least on occasion.[1] It was Rashi who in medieval times began to use the words "*peshat*" and "*derash*" to differentiate between simple and non-simple explanations, and subsequently, many others began to think in these terms. Ibn Ezra, for example, noted that *peshat* was tied to grammar and reason.[2] Though there is still debate today about the exact meaning of these terms, a consensus has been reached amongst many scholars. Segal's definitions are widely accepted today:[3]

> The *peshat*... aims to comprehend and explain the words of the text according to the revealed, direct ("simple") intention emerging from the words' meaning as well as the context... [and] to explain the text in an objective fashion.... The *derash*, however... searches within the text for

---

[1] See Cohn, "*Ha-midrash ke-parshan ha-midrash ke-pashtan*," *Mahanayim* 7 (1994): 92, and Louis Rabinowitz, "The Talmudic Meaning of *Peshat*," *Tradition* 6/1 (1963): 67–72. Rabinowitz suggests that both *peshat* and *derash* meant "the usual, accepted traditional meaning as it was generally taught." See the entry "*Peshat*" in the *Encyclopaedia Judaica*, which Rabinowitz authored.

[2] Cohn, "*Ha-midrash*," 90–91.

[3] See Cohn, "*Ha-midrash*," 91.

matters of interest to the interpreter, non-existent in the revealed, simple intention. The *derash* reads the text's words carefully, and expands and fills them out, removing them from the regular meaning and context.... In other words, the *derash* constitutes subjective interpretation of the text.[4]

Nehama certainly worked within these categories of thought and trained her students to differentiate between the two.[5] But she was also aware of the shifting nature of these two terms, joking: "*Peshat* is what I say – *derash* is what you say!" (or, in its other version, "My *peshat* is your *derash!*") She rejected most of the popular definitions of *peshat*, such as "the plain meaning," "the literal meaning," or "what we have before us," declaring, "What we have before us is a bunch of letters and vowels!"[6] For Nehama the true *peshat* was the *intended* meaning, one consistent with the text's overall thrust, and not necessarily the literal meaning. True, the actual words used are never pushed aside (*SD*, 241); but this represents only one of many true meanings, and do not always constitute the *peshat*.

Defining the *peshat* as the intended meaning allowed Nehama to multiply the interpretations admissible as *peshat*, since she was not limited by the actual words used.[7] In this way she was able to blur the lines between *peshat* and *derash*, as will be discussed in this chapter.

Nehama and *peshat*

There is no doubt that Nehama saw herself as ever questing for the *peshat*. Even R. Mordechai Breuer, who felt that Nehama hesitated to fully confront the text as it was, admits that all her efforts were bent towards revealing the *peshat*.[8] She wanted to know the text's primary meaning. It was like an inexhaustible riddle, with Nehama in the role of Sherlock Holmes. She made clear distinctions and categorizations and cut to the core of the issue in the text. The answer was obvious – once she had pointed it out.

As we explained in the last chapter, for Nehama, the text alone, with its nuances and structures, was the central subject matter. The *peshat* was not "what was happening at the time." While an explanation might be very nice from an aesthetic, psychological or logical perspective, it was not *peshat*

---

[4] M. Segal, *Parshanut ha-mikra*, Jerusalem: 5712, 2–3.
[5] See examples in Cohn, "*Ha-parshanut*," 105.
[6] Ahrend, "*Mi-toch*," 43.
[7] Thus for example, Nehama worked to show the *peshat* dimensions in some commentaries whom her contemporaries had rejected as *darshanim* (see N. Leibowitz, "*Ahavat*," 468).
[8] Breuer, "*Yahasah*," 11.

unless it was anchored in the text.[9] No commentator, however beloved, was spared critique when deviating from this rule:

> How appropriately do Ramban's words fit the picture psychologically!... But do his words similarly fit in with the wording of the text? Where is the warrant in the text itself?[10]

> But there is one unfortunate drawback to this type of explanation. It runs counter to the wording of the text. (*NSS*, 639)

> With all its pointedness, the foregoing answer does not carry conviction. (*NSS*, 125)

Even the Sages were required to adhere to the maxim, "Scripture never departs from its plain meaning,"[11] and when this was not the case, even their views could not be considered *peshat*, for example:

> Some of our Sages expressed a more positive attitude to vows. In our study we have confined ourselves to the more general view which finds support in the emphasis given by the text itself. (*SD*, 226)

Relevance and actualization

However, ascertaining the *peshat* was only half the job done, since it did not guarantee that students would not retort: "So what?" This response was one that Nehama considered debilitating and which she combated all her life long. In her view, this malady afflicted much of academia.[12] Analytical research without memorable conclusions was a waste of time. Nehama told of a friend's lengthy doctoral dissertation on whether or not people in Shakespeare's time believed in ghosts. The conclusion, after all that effort? Some did, while others did not! The Torah must never be experienced like this. It is not a source for scientific information or intellectual pleasure, but for eternally relevant values and ethics. It requires existential commitment from the student, motivated by personal search, and not just by Divine command or community requirements.[13] She explains:

> We must... show that comprehending the verse is not solely a philological undertaking involving clarifying words and grammatical forms, but rather that our understanding of a particular verse is one

---

[9] See Rozenson "*Diber*," 332.

[10] *NSS*, 79. Similarly *NSS*, 315.

[11] Shabbat, 63a. Nehama quotes this well-known phrase in *SD*, 241 and in her essay "*He'arot metodiyot le-limmud*," 488.

[12] Susan Handelman has written on this subject, in "We Cleverly Avoided Talking about God: Personal and Pedagogical Reflections on Academia and Spirituality," *Courtyard: A Journal of Research in Jewish Thought and Education* 1 (1999): 101–120.

[13] Cohn, "*Ma ahavti*," 28; Frankel, *Iyun*, 215. The intensive occupation with the sources will hopefully bring the student to become devoted to them (Frankel, *Iyun*, 225, n. 25).

brick in the edifice of what (is commonly referred to as) the Jewish worldview. To this end, selections have been brought from scholarly and ethical works that bear a connection to the verses.[14]

The lack of thought content, the dearth of a religious message must be traced to the incapacity of the student in failing to detect the eternal inner significance underlying the apparent, dry technical, historical details. "If it seems a vain thing, it is your fault." (*SBM*, 393)

In this, Nehama was a link in a long chain of Jewish philosophers and exegetes who aimed at the edifying message.

Our commentators in every age were deeply conscious of the timeless quality of Holy Writ, ever able to convey comfort, a warning or a summons particularly appropriate to their own generation. (*SD*, 51)

Just one example is the Malbim, who asks:

What contribution does such a story make to the spiritual message and mission of the Torah? (*NSB*, 207)

This emphasis went all the way back to the prophets:

Your duty, as a teacher, is to teach these words as if they were being said *to-day*, not merely because the claims of education demand it but because we are told to do so by Jeremiah himself!... The Talmud [Megillah 14a] makes this plain: "Messages that were needed for subsequent generations were written down, those that were of no use later were not written down." (*TI*, 62)

Nehama writes of Abravanel:

There was no commentator like him who read the words of the prophets as being wholly directed at himself and his generation and time, and who heard in their words the answers to the questions of his period – and this is the only authentic way in which to read the Torah and Prophets.[15]

Buber, too, looked for the relevance in the text, and Nehama's affinity for him stemmed from this, not only from his literary approach to text.[16]

ಶ್ರ ೀ

Nehama was always looking out for the pedagogical payoff. When she had concluded examining the text and commentaries, she almost always suggested a specific point to take away from the discussion. She carefully chose which of all the ideas mentioned in a class or essay should be the last

---

[14] From "*Mi-bereshit*," 452–453.

[15] *IBBM*, 182, n. 3. However, she also criticized him for subjective reading, see: paes 356 n. 29, 469 n. 97 above.

[16] Frankel, *Iyun*, 107.

taste in the students' mouths. These could be even minority opinions or marginal topics, if she felt them to be the most educational.[17] Her personal preference came strongly into play, and for the same reason, certain subjects are repeated many times in her work – though generally with some innovation[18] – whilst others never appear. Erella Yedgar notes that this educational approach was another expression of Nehama's feelings of responsibility – this time, to her readers, who eagerly anticipated what she would draw out of the text for them.[19]

The secret to Nehama's success was her unerring sense for what interested people. She knew how to sift through a vast sea of material, pinpointing what caught her attention – the most compelling subject matter, the strong moral message – under the assumption that it would do so for others too.[20] She intuited what would prove popular, focusing more on narrative sections than halachic ones, and saving more difficult material for select forums such as the worksheets. But she did not limit herself to the most colorful parts of the Torah – she was also a champion at taking seemingly dull material and making it come alive, finding philosophical issues behind banal details:

> Accordingly, what appeared to be purely technical instructions intended to enhance the aesthetic aspect of the offering, proves to constitute a reminder of the most fundamental principle of our faith. (*NSV*, 385)

In this she was following her predecessors:

> Our Sages and commentators have drawn moral lessons even from such apparently purely ritual instructions [as the signs for a kosher animal]. (*NSV*, 157)

Even minute details could contain an interesting idea:

> And these commentaries taught us an ethical lesson from an extra *vav!* (*IBBM*, 98)

For this reason, many of Nehama's students found themselves unable to take her grammatical questions at face value, and always looked for the subtle moral point they felt sure was lurking under the surface.

Those texts which could not be brought to life in this way she largely avoided. Much as she liked grammatical insights, she was adamant that they must not take over:

---

[17] See Yedgar, "*Bein*," 71; "*Ha-iyunim*," 32. One example of this was her study on the midwives. See pages 356–357, 473 above.

[18] See Yedgar, "*Ha-iyunim*," 32. For a list of some of the lessons that she favored and those she avoided, see pages 169–170 and 331–332 above, respectively.

[19] Yedgar, "*Bein*," 79.

[20] Judy Klitsner, interview; Amit, "Hebrew Bible," 11–12.

But it seems to me that in a chapter so full of fundamental ideas of the Torah… we should not detour and get involved in grammatical matters that are not crucial to comprehension of the issues. (*LP*, 7, n. 9)

Such [grammatical] matters are best dealt with at the end… and not in the middle of a discussion on the verses themselves. Robbing the poor to build luxurious palaces at their expense (and similar wickedness) is of infinitely greater importance than the exchange of two letters of the alphabet. (*TI*, 43)

For the same reason, she avoided realia:

What significance does the Torah which, on the evidence of the Psalmist in Psalms nineteen "enlightens the eyes," "rejoices the heart" and "restoreth the soul," find in this dry list of names that are undoubtedly an important object of study for archeologists and geographers interested in identifying them? (*SBM*, 388)

Academic scholars are often interested in the Torah's meaning for its earliest readers, but Nehama wished to know what the Torah says to the reader of today:[21]

We want the prophet's words to penetrate the heart and affect the deeds; for the verse be a creative force in the student's life and a resource at times of crisis. That at times of decision and trial the verse will materialize, light up dark places and speak to the person as if said solely for him and for this hour. (*KA*, 482)

Erella Yedgar remarks that for Nehama there was no gap between the biblical values and our own, something not applicable to all religious academics.[22] She campaigned for the contemporary significance of seemingly archaic issues, for example the prophets' denunciations of the misuse of sacrifices:

The prophets' battle has not become obsolete with the cessation of the sacrifices; and its relevance has not expired with the destruction of the Temple. This is not a battle against misconceptions surrounding the sacrifices, but rather a perpetual struggle against the human desire to shirk the fulfillment of God's demands in all areas of life, every day and every hour, restricting them instead to limited places and times. A battle against the desire to be satisfied with the symbol, while avoiding the demands symbolized by it.[23]

---

[21] See Yedgar, "*Bein*," 78. Rozenson critiques this approach (see page 468 n. 37 above).
[22] Yedgar, interview.
[23] *IHBV*, 23–24, compare *NSV*, 20–21.

> At school, with all the attention paid to the historical background to the messages of the *neviim* [prophets], we must never forget that the essential is the lesson for future generations. (TI, 51)

When Joy Rochwarger asked Nehama what topic to teach on Tisha be-Av, Nehama interpreted her question to refer to what lessons could be learned from the destruction of the Temple, and how they could be best conveyed to the students. Rochwarger:

> Her first association was with everlastingness.… She taught me how to find inspiration in a story that for most people would have spoken only of evil and corruption, and she succeeded in engaging my undivided attention by taking the present back to the past and by making history as relevant as present-day reality.[24]

To make the ancient text less alien and more accessible to contemporary ears, she enlisted modern language and concepts. Joseph's policies in Egypt were described by her as "the first example of land nationalization" (*NSB*, 525). Yehudit Ilan still remembers the first of Nehama's questions that she ever managed to answer. She had skipped an outing to the cinema in favor of Nehama's class, given to counselors of the *Ha-no'ar ha-oved ve-ha-lomed* movement, and it proved worthwhile, for when Nehama asked: "What would we today call Moshe's killing of the Egyptian?" to Ilan's pleasure, her own reply, "A political murder," was exactly the answer Nehama sought.

While teaching, Nehama would from time to time reference current events, for example noting that Sarah, in her treatment of Hagar, was perhaps responsible for the birth of

> that individual whose descendants have proved a source of trouble to Israel to this very day. Who knows? (*NSB*, 157)

Another example concerns the verse in Deuteronomy 24:15:

> On his day you shall give him his hire, nor shall the sun go down upon it; for he is poor, and sets his heart upon it; lest he cry against you to the Lord, and it shall be a sin to you.

Nehama compared this with the Delay of Wage-Payment Bill, which had its first reading in the Knesset in 1955 and which indeed cited this verse.[25] She also drew up parallels between the slavery in Egypt and the Holocaust.[26]

Nehama trained her students to similarly make their own connections to the text, encouraging them to bring examples from their communities and lives (*TI*, 33, 51). R. Mordechai Spiegelman recounts how Nehama as a

---

[24] Rochwarger, "Words," 75.
[25] *NSV*, 294–295, and see further Frankel *Iyun*, 161.
[26] See pages 38–40 above.

young teacher was assigned to teach Hebrew composition to some elementary school students. She asked them to write an essay on the topic, "What person would you want to be if you could become somebody else?" Most chose Jewish biblical and historical figures – King David, R. Akiva, etc. But one student wrote that he would become an owner of a kiosk in the Sinai desert at the time that the Israelites were encamped there – "because imagine how many cups of soda I could sell!" Nehama was effusive in her praise of the teacher in that school for making the Torah so real to this student.[27]

Nehama's books, full of ready-made captivating messages, proved a sterling resource for those who needed to make the Torah interesting and accessible, such as teachers and rabbis. Jacobus Schoneveld writes:

> The greatest doubt arising with regard to [the orthodox Jewish educational ideal] is whether it is capable of keeping in touch with life as contemporary man actually feels and experience it.[28]

Nehama was able to bridge that gap, and she was recognized for this talent. She was employed by Gesher to prepare their counselors to facilitate secular-religious dialogue, for they were yeshivah graduates and untrained in the art of deriving contemporary values from the Torah. Professor Michael Rosenak found himself, as a young man, impressed with Nehama's ability to demonstrate how texts that had not agitated or attracted Jews for a long time could be electrifying. He cites Moshe Sokol, who writes that the modern person not only finds redemption in the text, but may also redeem the text in turn, by taking it seriously.[29] Rosenak explains: "All of the people who taught me at the Jewish Agency seminar in 1954 took the text seriously. I had had a good Jewish education, but my questions had always been met with an evasion before."

Nehama believed that not only Torah but other subjects too must be taught skillfully so as not to push away the student – history, for instance. She warned against using long lists of names, or intellectual phrases that raise no associations in the student's mind, such as "regimes" and "social strata." Far more useful are stories of real people with whom the student can identify – the ordinary person of the time, struggling with real-life difficulties.[30]

---

[27] Spiegelman, review of Peerless, *To Study*.
[28] Schoneveld, *The Bible*, 83.
[29] See Moshe Z. Sokol, "How Do Modern Jewish Thinkers Interpret Religious Texts?" *Modern Judaism* 13/1 (1993): 25–48, especially 42.
[30] N. Leibowitz, "Active Learning," ix.

Both *Peshat* and Moral Messages

However, important as both *peshat* and relevance were to Nehama, they have not always gone hand in hand. On the contrary, many see them as opposites, for in the history of Jewish interpretation, moral messages have frequently been derived from texts by methods far from *peshat*. The *darshan*, or homiletical preacher (the forerunner of today's synagogue sermonizer) was often an inventive weaver of disparate texts and proposer of imaginative interpretations, leading to inspiring messages. His primary aim was not elucidation but education.[31] Therefore, we must ask the following question: in Nehama's work, did *peshat* and inspiration/education indeed clash? Was it a case of two impulses struggling for ascendancy?

Nehama's innovation was to argue that on the contrary, the two are inseparable. For the Torah text intends *a priori* to teach edifying lessons. Its primary meaning is geared toward that end. Hence, far from imposing a moral agenda on the text, Nehama believed that she was simply letting it speak in its naturally instructive tones:

> The Bible imparts its teachings not by direct indoctrination, by a moral tagged on the story, but through the medium of the narrative, its structure and style and the organization of the plot. (*NSS*, 12)

She wished only to bring out those messages that were built into the text. She warned many times against superimposing pre-conceived ideologies or value systems onto the Tanach. Rather, we must search, as the commentators do, for nuanced philological and contextual clues implanted in the text that suggest its meaning, and the educational messages must spring from them.[32] When the interpreters deviated from the *peshat* (whether consciously or unconsciously), Nehama made sure to draw the student's attention to it.[33] She disapproved of wild interpretations. Concerning *"vorts"* (Torah interpretation based on fanciful association and wordplay, far from the primary meaning), she said that they could be bandied around between courses at a meal but were not to be passed off as serious Torah learning or published as such.[34] She was certainly aware of the difference between exegesis and eisegesis (subjective/biased interpretation):

---

[31] Cohn argues, though, that since there is still much sensitivity to grammar and to rules of language in such *derashot*, many of them cannot be clearly classified as exclusively *peshat* or *derash* (Cohn, "*Ha-midrash*," 93–94).

[32] See also her comments in "*Al nituah*," 618.

[33] Yedgar, "*Bein*," 63.

[34] See her exchange with Reinitz in *PN*, pp. 698–702, particularly her pungent words in 698 and 702.

We must demonstrate how the verse (or story or biblical character) lives on long after it was first presented. How the generations perceive and reflect it back; how they utilize a story or a single verse, deepen their comprehension and fill it with new content and even distort it (consciously or unconsciously).... It is preferable that the student learn to discern this later use of the verses, and become adept at differentiating between legitimate usage, that maintains the original import of the verse, and an illegitimate usage that conscripts the verse to contemporary needs.[35]

Here, Nehama refers to over-simplistic parallels frequently made between current events and the Tanach, which she termed "cheap political analogies."[36] She warns:

We should also oppose all sorts of unfounded and invalid analogies (as appear in current actualizations).[37]

These involve preaching, and partial and shallow understandings of the text. The very opposite of eternal, they are time-bound, and, once the events are over, become passé. For this reason, Nehama's references to current events were limited, and she did not base her entire essay on them.[38] Politicization of a text would inescapably have alienated some readers, and by being apolitical, Nehama allowed everyone to connect to her Torah. She therefore took care to phrase her moral messages in general language, that would not sound too preachy or biased.[39] While she advocated using modern terminology, she warned that any such terminology must loyally represent the text and its concepts without compromising the Torah's meaning or honor.[40] Using *Akedah* terminology when referring to fallen Israeli soldiers constituted cheap actualization of the text.[41] Facile translations of Tanach concepts into secular language could lead to distortions; to speak of "chosenness" without the existence of a Divine Chooser can become very problematic.[42] Similarly, she writes:

---

[35] N. Leibowitz, *Shiurim*, Sheet 15, 3.

[36] Sylvetsky, "*Zichron*."

[37] *Teacher's Guide* to *Va-yikra* 5722.

[38] See R. Yohanan Fried's comments in Sheleg, "*Kalat*," 71, where he contrasts her with charismatic contemporary teachers who connect their teachings extensively to current events; and Yedgar, "*Ha-iyunim*," 31, especially, n. 55.

[39] Frankel, "*Ha-te'oriyah*," 437.

[40] Frankel, *Iyun*, 33.

[41] Mondschein, "*Akedat*," 117.

[42] *Teacher's Guide* for *Yitro*, 5715, quoted in Reiner and Peerless, *Haggadat*, 61. Nehama warns against nationalistic chauvinism, against a sense of chosenness as entitlement rather than as commandedness and responsibility. See pages 319, 363–364 above.

It goes without saying that that the equation of our enemies with God's enemies can only be done when we are truly bearing His standard and carrying out His will, and authentic representatives of our Torah. (*IBBM*, 113)

The balance between cheap actualization and genuine relevance-making is, in truth, a difficult and delicate one:

We must consider whether it is preferable to keep the number of [contemporary] examples to a minimum for fear that the Torah lesson will turn into some cheap newspaper article; or whether, on the contrary, it is a positive thing [to include numerous examples] so that the lesson will be lively and speak to the student's heart – or, as our students and friends in the USA say, "To prove that the Torah's words are relevant." Essentially, this – like many pedagogic questions – is not one that can be answered yes or no, but is one of quantity, of time and place. (*LP*, 138, n. 11)

As great as Nehama's dislike of dry teaching was, her fear of its opposite – using the text to preach – was even more pronounced. In the first case, the teacher is passive, but in the second, the student is passive. The teacher must first and foremost create comprehension of the text itself, and only after that assume the role of educator.

☙ ❧

Nehama was thus a careful teacher, aware of possible pitfalls, and she genuinely believed herself to be always presenting the *peshat*, except in cases where she explicitly noted otherwise.

Many concurred with her own assessment of her method, believing her fully worthy of the name *peshat* scholar of Tanach. Dr. David Bernstein: "She was definitely a *peshat* person. She loved to introduce *derash* for the ethical and moral teaching, as long as you didn't pretend that it was *peshat*. She was always making that distinction clear. *Derash* was not her main emphasis, but when she did bring it, it was with a smile on her face." R. Nachum Amsel adds: "Whoever says she had a superagenda does not understand Nehama." Frankel insists that *peshat* was her chief goal and that Nehama remained true to the text's voice, her educational understandings stemming directly from her close literary reading.[43] Others suggest that if her interpretation appears to us not to be *peshat*, perhaps we ought first to ascertain how she arrived at it before jumping to conclusions. Perchance our own insensitivity to nuances is to blame? Furthermore, it has been argued, the proportion of her teaching she granted to the moral message was minimal – the last ten minutes of a

---

[43] See Frankel, *Iyun*, 21, 214, and 225, n. 17, defending Nehama from accusations of implementing the type of interpretation that Zakovitch calls "homiletical acrobatics."

lesson, or the final paragraph of an essay, after a lengthy examination of the text and commentaries.

Not all agree, however. Professor Elazar Touitou recommends calling Nehama's approach "conscripted *peshat*," since, while she did not impose herself on the text, she nevertheless drew spiritual and moral conclusions from it that fit in with her worldview.[44] Others claim even more strongly that at times, Nehama's powerful educational impulse brought her to loosen her grip on the *peshat*; that she allowed both the halachic and her own moral code to color her understandings.[45] They believe that she projected onto the text instead of allowing it to speak for itself, compromising the most accurate reading of the text or citation of sources.[46] She made sure to include often and prominently those commentaries who expressed her own opinion, so that her messages were received loud and clear – for example, the *Meshech Hochmah*'s comments on the breaking of the two tablets, warning against the misuses of symbols.[47] The very title of her series, "*Studies in Bereshit*" etc. indicates that in her books the text constituted a jumping-off point for further studies, rather than being thoroughly investigated for itself. Dr. Howard Deitcher remarks: "Although she always claimed that she was looking for the *peshat*, when you asked her what the *peshat* was she found it difficult to answer. Her driving force was the educational one. She said, 'How can I educate people to a certain lifestyle and set of values? That is how I define the *peshat*.'" Professor Uriel Simon says: "Nehama simply found the *peshat* too simple, too plain" (*VLN*). He believes that in blurring the lines between *peshat* and *derash*, she does both a disservice, because they need not, and should not, overlap. Each has its own domain, and it is precisely its separation from the *derash* that allows the *peshat* its own existence.

Undoubtedly, certain amounts of non-*peshat* material did creep into Nehama's lessons. There are essays which are clearly less *peshat*-focused,[48]

---

[44] Touitou, "*Rashbam*," 222, and see S. Garfinkel, "Applied Peshat," *JANES* 22 (1993) 19–28.

[45] Yedgar, "*Bein*," 72–75, and see also the discussion on page 327 above of Nehama's humanism that caused her to read selectively.

[46] See discussion and examples in Yedgar, "*Bein*," 72–75.

[47] *NSS*, 612–614. See pages 317–318 above.

[48] Her essay "The Eternal God a Dwelling Place," for example, is devoted primarily to a midrash that is not anchored in the text, and concludes with an interpretation from the Netziv which "though apparently far from the immediate sense of the passage is worth our attention" (*SD*, 402–403). Only a few lines of the essay are devoted to more *peshat*-type explanations.

including those exploring the halachic ramifications of the verse.[49] In her discussion of kosher and non-kosher animals, after a short survey of some possible moral reasons, she brings a midrashic explanation suggesting that these animals symbolize the four kingdoms that persecuted the Jews. She is cognizant that this explanation travels quite a distance from the immediate world of the Tanach, but chooses nonetheless not only to bring it, but to end with it.[50]

Due to all of the above, Nehama was sometimes described as teaching not Bible but Torah – i.e. the Jewish worldview (under the assumption that there is such a thing!), an educational endeavor. This was not necessarily a negative statement. Professor Chana Safrai says: "Nehama did not teach Bible, Nehama taught Judaism; and that was exactly what I wanted from her in the Lieberman Institute. I liked the fact that the verse was for her a value, a truth. This was her special quality." Abba Oren writes:

> There is all the difference in the world between the scholarly detachment of such modern literary criticism and her deep Jewish religious moral commitment.[51]

This is why, for him, Nehama "put the heart of Judaism back into its rightful place."[52]

Yedgar suggests a different resolution to this conflict within Nehama between *peshat* and education: That while she said one thing (*peshat*) she actually did the other (education). Ultimately, her obligation to the text was overruled by her obligation to the student and to theological positions.[53] Yedgar also notes that Nehama's purpose in bringing morals varies in

---

[49] Yedgar demonstrates that Nehama even expands halachic parameters, equating a passive failure to "mark graves" with the active transgression of "You shall not place a stumbling block before the blind," when this is clearly not the Talmud's halachic intention ("*Bein*," 74, relating to *NSV*, 307–313). See also *NSV*, 333–340, 358–365 and 554–568, and *SBM*, 171–175 on ritual fringes.

[50] See *NSV*, 159–161. For another example where Nehama explicitly chooses to end with something that, although it does not accord with the rules of grammar, is too much in tune with universal and Jewish life for her to resist, see *IHBS*, 108. See also her quote of Hirsch, ("A 'far-fetched' explanation – but interesting!" *IBBM*, 67); or of Abravanel ("Does this do violence to the text? It is certainly not its plain meaning, but such interpretation is legitimate and even obligatory," *SD*, 55); or of Alshech's comment which, although it "can hardly be said to reflect the primary meaning," is her choice for ending the essay (*NSS*, 338).

[51] Oren, "That," 157.

[52] Oren, "That," 157. For the full quote, see page 427 above.

[53] This is the topic of Yedgar's article "*Bein*," and see also her article "*Ha-iyunim*."

different works. Sometimes they serve an interpretative purpose, and are a means, and other times they are ends in themselves.[54]

– –

The above debate functions, interestingly enough, as a modern counterpart to a similar scholarly discussion on Rashi.[55] He also announced (in his commentary to Genesis 3:8),

> I have come to deal only with the plain meaning of the verse.[56]

Nevertheless, his use of Midrash has led many to question this claim. Although Nehama sometimes rejected interpretations by Rashi as being non-*peshat* and educationally driven,[57] she often accepted them. It might be argued that she was more or less continuing in his footsteps and in those of the traditional commentators who supposed that they were explaining the text, yet in reality also used it to expound their philosophies (though Lockshin, for one, believes that Nehama was far less tendentious than many of the commentators she quotes).

Whichever way one looks at it, Nehama's approach was an eclectic one – embraced both a strong sense for *peshat* together with moral, emotional, psychological, literary or philological conclusions. Yedgar writes:

> On the one hand, in combination, these [different approaches] create an insoluble tension, inevitably leading to compromise between their conflicting educational aims. On the other, they also point the way to a more complex educational approach in an increasingly complex world, an educational approach that mediates between continuity and renewal, consistency and flexibility, commitment and openness, responsibility and creativity.[58]

Her approach differed from the often monolithic approaches found in academia, reflecting more accurately the multifaceted nature of reality and of her students' needs.[59] The precise balance between one pole and another shifted with the audience. The *Studies* students, considered intelligent beginners, were provided with closing messages at the end of almost every essay, a necessarily guiding voice. The worksheet correspondents, who were

---

[54] Yedgar, "*Bein*," 48.
[55] For more on these scholarly discussions see Ahrend, "*Mi-toch*," 42–43; Grossman "*Pulmus*," 188, 204–205; and Shmuel P. Gelbard, "Rashi's Objectives in His Commentary to the Torah" (*Hebrew*), *Megadim* 33 (2001): 59–74 (cited in Angel, "Paradox," 127).
[56] Nehama quoted this several times in her *Studies* (*NSB*, 283, 313, 337 and *NSS*, 174).
[57] See pages 345 and 377 n. 40 above.
[58] *Limmudim* 1 (2001) xiv–xv (abstract of article).
[59] Yedgar, "*Bein*," 80.

considered to be more advanced, were not given messages, but had to work them out for themselves.[60] Nehama once remarked to Deitcher that the *gilyonot* "are for Sunday to Thursday," while the books "should be read on Shabbat after the *cholent*." Study on Shabbat, she observed elsewhere, should be *oneg*, pleasure, focusing on aesthetic aspects and ideas. Perhaps, then, for Nehama, the "medium," with its rigor, was for the weekday, while the "message" was for that taste of the World to Come, for Shabbat.[61]

Nehama and Midrash[62]

The above discussion remains incomplete without exploring Nehama's approach to Midrash. Nehama loved the Midrash. Her fondness for Thomas Mann's work *Joseph and His Brothers* was due to its being based in a large part on Midrashim. Dr. Gabriel Cohn suggests that she felt the Midrash to be the basis for all Jewish exegesis. This was a novel idea at the time, though it is now propounded by important scholars such as Greenberg.[63] Since the same rabbis who wrote the Midrash also determined the definitive Jewish reading of the Tanach from among all possible readings of their day, Nehama's extensive use of Midrash is more evidence of her desire to teach the "Jewish Bible" and no other, says Cohn.

In her works, Nehama incorporated many hundreds of midrashic extracts taken from collections of Midrash and from the Talmud. These texts, which she carefully studied in Jerusalem's National Library, were old, error-ridden, and difficult to read.[64] She had to add punctuation and vowels and sometimes translate them, with the help of Professor Isaac Heinemann, a Midrash expert whose work she respected tremendously. She thus made many segments much more available to the wider public.

Moreover, her explanations of Midrash went beyond punctuation and translation, since she had no choice but to interpret and elucidate. The study of Midrash had been relatively neglected for centuries, even in traditional

---

[60] *IBD*, introduction, where we hear that the *gilyonot* "require great effort from the student, invested in accurate reading of the Torah and its commentators and the problems with which they deal," while the *Studies* are intended for "those who wish to become a little familiar with our Torah, by unimpeded reading of Midrash and commentaries throughout the generations."

[61] See Nehama's comments in *Darkei*, 8. Her recommendations are to study text and Aggadah and avoid in-depth study of commentaries, with the emphasis on the ideas, to achieve a wider and more elevating sweep, not as detail-oriented as the regular study.

[62] See also the discussion of Nehama and Midrash in the context of postmodernism, page 473 above.

[63] Interview. See also Cohn, "*Ma ahavti*," 28–29 and "Nehama Leibowitz," 11–12.

[64] Cohn, "*Ha-parshanut*," 95; Cohn, "Nehama Leibowitz," 13.

circles, in favor of medieval or modern commentaries.[65] This neglect meant that the idea of writing a commentary on the Midrash was unpopular, which in turn left the Midrashim quite unintelligible and even less likely to be studied, instead gathering dust on the uppermost shelves of the Jewish bookcase. Some work had been done previously, for example by Ramban, who translated Midrash into everyday concepts (*NSB*, 160). But Nehama went further: With the help of a few existing commentaries such as those of Maharal, Maharsha, and her contemporary Heinemann, as well as a great deal of inventiveness and insight, she opened up the cryptic world of the Midrash to the average reader.[66] Cohn: "I believe there was no one who advanced the understanding of the use of Midrash on Tanach as Nehama did."

The academic world in Nehama's day dismissed Midrashim as a bunch of far-fetched fables, an ahistorical, largely non-literal body of exegesis that often crossed the line into eisegesis.[67] But she took it seriously, and developed a methodology for studying it.[68] As with other commentaries, she would juxtapose two or more Midrashim with each other or with another commentary, teaching that each represented a different philosophical approach.[69] She would also assume that the Midrash's impenetrable thicket of strange details might intend to represent concepts:

> Professor Heinemann… notes that our Sages, in contradistinction to the scientific approach, do not generalize the concrete, but on the contrary, express abstractions in concrete terms.[70]

Nehama taught that the Midrash, like the Torah, prefers the tangible over the theoretical. One example concerns the Midrash on Cain and Abel:[71]

> "And Cain spoke with Abel his brother." What were they arguing about? They said: Come, let us divide the world. One said: The land on which you are standing is mine; and the other replied: The clothes you are wearing are mine. One said: Take them off! The other: Get off! In the course of this, "Cain rose up against Abel his brother and slew him."

---

[65] Cohn, "*Ha-parshanut*," 94.

[66] Cohn, "Nehama Leibowitz," 12.

[67] Simon writes: "In the early 1950s, when I was pursuing my studies in the Hebrew University's Bible Department, one could not study midrashic exegesis there, as it ran counter to *peshat*" ("The Place," 224).

[68] See *TI*, 82–83.

[69] Cohn, "*Ha-parshanut*," 104.

[70] *NSB*, 39, and also in similar words in *NSB*, 138–139. See also *NSV*, 39.

[71] *NSB*, 38–39. The Midrash is from *Bereshit Rabbah* 22:6, on Genesis 4:8.

R. Joshua of Sachnin said in the name of R. Levi said… what were they disputing about? One said: In my domain shall the Temple be built. The other said: In my domain shall the Temple be built…. In the course of this, "Cain rose up against Abel his brother and slew him."

Yehudah bar Ami said: They were disputing over Eve.

At first glance, these suggestions appear anachronistic and alien; the reader does not know what to make of them. But Nehama explained the broader picture:

> It is quite evident… that the Midrash gives the story of Cain and Abel a universal application. It is concerned not merely with the individual case of Cain and Abel, but with the motives underlying man's desire to quarrel, make war, kill and murder his fellow. (*NSB*, 39)

In other words, these concrete examples combine to make up a philosophical premise, that at the root of all murder lie three broad arenas of conflict: material possessions, religion, and sexual passion (and here Nehama would add with a twinkle: "Is it an issue that concerns Marx, the Pope or Freud?")[72] The Midrash has been transformed from bizarre and inexplicable to profoundly insightful.

If Nehama's work contributed greatly to the Midrash, the Midrash also contributed greatly to Nehama's work. Though we have suggested that Nehama was influenced by Rashi, the truth is that both were influenced by the Midrash, with its sensitivity to texts and its moral instruction.[73] Indeed, the Midrash may be said to be the royal road for the Jewish educator. Dr. Marla Frankel's notion of the "pedagogue," the strict educator who plays an important role in Nehama's instructional theory, is

> based on the function of the *darshan*, described by the talmudic Sages, namely a wise man who rests his teachings on the written Midrash or at least refers to it and whose duty is to sway the hearts of his listeners and to teach them moral principles and religious laws…. [The pedagogue] does not look for the original meaning and the original contexts of the text, but seeks a way to express new contents that arise out of the text (and are significant to him).[74]

Since the Midrash is often viewed as interpretation with an educational agenda, Nehama's extensive use of Midrash convinced some that she was not a true *pashtanit*. But Nehama disagreed strongly, turning the argument

---

[72] Abramowitz, *Tales*, 49–50, quoting Cohn. For more discussion of Nehama's work on this Midrash see Cohn, "*Ha-parshanut*," 99, and Peerless, *To Study*, 27–28.

[73] See Cohn, "*Ha-parshanut*," 108.

[74] Frankel, "The Teacher," 371, n. 8.

around with a radical contention: That Midrash and *derash* are not synonymous; and that in fact the Midrash often expresses a form of *peshat* – not always readily apparent, yet *peshat* nonetheless.

This assertion represented a new way of looking at Midrash. The assumption that the Midrash contains only *derash* (i.e. non-*peshat*) material, and that midrashic interpretation is synonymous with *derash* interpretation as we know it today, is a common one; but it is based on a historical inaccuracy. The Hebrew root *d-r-sh* underwent a change in meaning. Originally the root meant to "study" in the Tanach, while in talmudic times it meant "interpretation." As mentioned above, only in Rashi's day did the word *derash* clearly come to mean the opposite of *peshat*, non-simple interpretation. The Midrash, which constitutes all of the Sages' interpretations of the Bible, then became tarred with the same brush, even though its name really refers to the act of study and interpretation. To be sure, it appears to be replete with inventive, non-*peshat*-based material, owing less to the text than to a vivid imagination. Nonetheless, the truth is that the midrashic corpus actually contains a vast mixture of materials, from straightforward interpretation to improbable tales.[75] As Nehama explained, the percentage of the Midrash derived by non-*peshat* means is significant, but not as much as one might think.

Nehama's work helped to reduce such misconceptions. Though in the minority for most of her life, she resolutely continued to declare that the Midrash is a commentary like any other. Her readers became used to seeing midrashic opinion take its place in the discussion alongside Rashi and Ibn Ezra, with a demonstrably clear and rational point to make. In fact, the Midrash was sometimes shown to be the more careful reader of the text:

> Luzzatto's interpretation… has not the slightest basis in the wording of the text. Accordingly the words of the Midrash… are to be preferred. (*SD*, 79)

Indeed, Nehama claimed that, contrary to the popular understandings of *peshat* and *derash*, some Midrash was closer to the intended *peshat* than more literalist readings:

> The literal explanation is limited to the surface meaning, whereas the homiletic exposition uncovers a deeper level of meaning… the plain sense looks at the outward appearance, but the homiletic sees into the heart. (*SBM*, 103)

---

[75] Cohn, "*Ha-midrash*," 90 and 91 n. 17.

Here we have a *derash* that when probed deeply is found to grasp the depth of the verse better than all the explanations of the *pashtanim.*[76]

Such statements were simultaneously a praise of the Midrash and an indictment of over-literalists. The text must be read in its emotional-psychological context;[77] and Nehama had some biting things to say about "pursuers of *peshat*" who failed to do so, with their "slavish adherence to the literal wording" which could "blind one to the real inner meaning."[78] This was "not *peshuto shel mikra* (the intended meaning of the text) but rather *ivvut shel mikra* (a distortion of the text), she said.[79] One of the primary culprits was the Rashbam, whom she lambasts in several places:

> Here we have a convincing example of how the so called rationalist, the adherer to the strict literalness of the text, the eschewer of all homiletic exegesis may be forced into deviating from the plain sense and the underlying meaning.... [Rashbam is] unaware that he has transplanted us from the burning bush to the practical, matter-of-fact atmosphere of the council chamber of a military headquarters... while the text cries out against him (*NSS*, 68-69).

Nehama liked to illustrate the literalists' mistake by telling of the man who comes home from work and says to his wife, "I'm dead!" Of course, his wife does not call a mortician, but replies, "Lie down for a few minutes until dinner is ready."[80] She noted the "erroneous perception of *derash* as the opposite of *peshat* instead as a deeper level of the *peshat*."[81] She taught that some interpretations that are rejected as *derash* are in fact "*omek peshuto shel mikra*" – the genuine, in-depth *peshat*, going beyond the cursory reading of the words:

> Must we not admit that the Midrash has plumbed the depths of the text's plainest and literal sense? (*NSB*, 489)

> It is quite mistaken to regard this homiletic interpretation of our Sages as in any way doing violence to the plain meaning of the text.... Their homiletic explanation is, in actual fact, simply another and a deeper level of the real meaning of the text.[82]

---

[76] *IBBM*, 135. Regarding the ignoring of nuances, see page 461 above and discussion in Frankel, *Iyun*, 115–116. It was actually Nehama's sensitivity to context that led her to search for the best interpretation in the *derash*.

[77] For further discussion see Peters, *Learning*, 14–15.

[78] *NSS*, 488 and see *SBM*, 209.

[79] Bruriah Eisner, interview.

[80] Abramowitz, *Tales*, 46.

[81] *IBB*, 290, missing from the English version (*NSB*, 413).

[82] *NSB*, 412. See also *NSB*, 247; N. Leibowitz, "*Sikkum*," 468; and discussion in Cohn, "*Ha-parshanut*," 105–107.

Nehama likewise felt that many of the Midrashim that Rashi cited were indeed *peshat* or at least "close to *peshat*,"[83] clarifying the primary meaning of the text (*NSS*, 254).

Midrash transcended logic and order to adequately explain the Torah text (*NSV*, 65). It was to be understood not historically but symbolically.[84] Judy Klitsner: "I once asked her what type of truth was expressed in the Midrash quoted by Rashi claiming that Rebecca was three years old when she married Isaac.[85] She said it should not be understood literally, but is rather a statement concerning her precociousness, maturity and suitability to be a matriarch."

Nehama could not countenance the dismissal of Midrash as fantastic ramblings:

> It must be noted carefully that where contradictions, illogicality and the absurd are patently apparent even to the student – it is impossible that the Sages were not sensitive to them.[86]

They did not invent the midrashic material out of thin air:

> Whence did our Sages elicit their data regarding Abraham's internal struggle...? We may answer that their description was prompted by the one conversation that is reported to have taken place between father and son. (*NSB*, 199)

For this reason, Midrash was not to be read as a separate body of work from the Torah but in tandem with it, so that its creative ideas would then be seen as interpretation, not fabrication, for example:

> As in many cases of this nature, both the homiletical and the literal sense complement each other. The waters were indeed bitter, but were it not for the fact that the people themselves were embittered, they would not have been disturbed or demoralised by the unpleasant taste of the water. (*NSS*, 283, n. 3)

The following is an example of Nehama's belief that the Midrash is capable of extraordinary textual insight, superior to more literal explanations.[87] In Numbers 11:5 the Israelites gripe:

> We remember the fish, which we ate in Egypt for free; the cucumbers, and the melons, and the leeks, and the onions, and the garlic.

---

[83] *Perush Rashi la-Torah*, 363–364; but see also *ibid.*, 405–406 for a slightly softer formulation. See also *NSV*, 325–326, and Mondschein, "*Akedat*," 118, n. 27.
[84] See page 462 above.
[85] Rashi on Genesis 25:20.
[86] N. Leibowitz, "*He'arot metodiyot le-limmud*," 489.
[87] For another example and discussion, see Frankel, *Iyun*, 112, third example.

The Midrash has an unexpected take on this verse:

> We remember the fish: Does it say that the Egyptians actually gave them fish for free? Surely it is stated: "Now go and work; for no straw shall be given you" (Exodus 5:18). If they did not give them straw for free, why would they give them fish for free? How then do I explain the term "For free"? [It means] free from Divine commandments.[88]

The average reader, who has understood "for free" as meaning "without payment" is taken aback by this interpretation, "free from the commandments." Aware of this, Nehama remarks that it indeed sounds "far removed from the world of their murmurings" (*SBM*, 97). But after examining other possible solutions, she concludes:

> Hitherto we have cited all those who try to explain the text literally.... But it seems to us that our rabbis evinced a profounder understanding of the Israelites' character.... Perhaps this was merely the outward form their inner dissatisfaction took... when discontent lurks in the heart of the public or individual, grumblings and murmurings, criticism and defamation will flare up at the slightest pretext.... Our Sages detected this. (*SBM*, 100–101)

A similar explanation applies to a later verse in the same chapter, where the people of Israel complain about the lack of food (Numbers 11:10):

> Then Moses heard the people weep throughout their families, each in the door of his tent; and the anger of the Lord was kindled greatly; and Moses also was displeased.

The Sages, and in their footsteps Rashi, explain that the phrase "throughout their families" indicates that their true underlying concern was family matters. Their sexual practice was now limited by the newly-imposed Torah law (*SBM*, 102-103). Once again, the phrase is removed from its most obvious meaning to reflect an inner discontent, concealed behind their words. A student once asked in puzzlement why Rashi turned to sexual matters when the text was clearly talking about food. Without batting an eyelash, Nehama replied, "If you take a look at Freud's book *Civilization and Its Discontents*, you will see that when people want to protest about something but can't, they will grumble about something else. This is what Rashi is trying to point out here."

However, Nehama emphasized that all of the above was only true within certain limits. Not all Midrash is *peshat*, only select Midrashim. She cautions:

---

[88] *Sifrei, Beha'alotcha.*

> We must note especially those places where the Sages, deliberately and not due to any lack of understanding, disregarded the *peshat* and historical accuracy, in order that the Torah speak to their contemporaries in their own language and about their own interests and troubles.[89]

Midrashim vary greatly:

> Some of them take the syntactical structure of the verse and crush it to small pieces from which they build up an entirely new and wonderful world…. Others on the contrary adhere to the structure, language and word-order of the text, but lift the whole verse out of context.[90]

The former type are not to be confused with the *peshat*. Nehama was certainly willing to define a Midrash as forced or problematic:

> However profound and striking the truth of the idea contained in this excerpt from the Palestinian Talmud, we must admit that no hint of it is to be found in our text.[91]

> Of course the Midrash was not concerned with the syntactical problem. This was simply the starting point for the discussion of a philosophic problem…. But our commentators have not found any such philosophical allusions in the text… (*SD*, 402)

And at times she even set up, as is the more common perception, Midrash as differing from *peshat*. For example, she wrote:

> Note: If the students are not drawn to Midrash, and particularly if they evince an inner resistance, then it should be minimized and not forced upon them; instead, *peshat* should be taught – the historical side, the lifestyle of the ancients, etc. But from my own experience – albeit, only with girls – both native Israelis and immigrants from Germany take great pleasure in any Midrash that contains an artistic portrayal or deep life wisdom or an emotional expression of love of the land, nation, or Creator. But the teacher needs to emphasize the difference between *peshat* and *derash*.[92]

The fact remains, however, that Nehama still taught and included the Midrash frequently, which brings us back to the question of whether she was a *pashtanit* or a non-*peshat*-orientated educator. The truth is that she sometimes preferred the Midrash to the *peshat*, even when it subverted the

---

[89] N. Leibowitz, *Darkei*, 4.

[90] *TI*, 82. See also *NSS*, 254: "Did Abraham know that he had to counteract the effect of Balaam's machinations against his descendants?… This is not the intention of our Sages." See also Cohn, "*Ha-parshanut*," 94–95.

[91] *NSS*, 144, and see also *NSB*, 404 (the Midrash's explanation "is forced"); *IBBM*, 27.

[92] N. Leibowitz, "*He'arot metodiyot le-limmud*," 490.

plain meaning entirely. One extreme example is her citation of a Midrash equating Esau's escort of four hundred armed men with four hundred Amalekite men who lived many centuries later. The Midrash, basing itself on these men's sudden mysterious disappearance from the Esau story, posits that they were rewarded for their abandoning of Esau hundreds of years later when, as Amalekites, they escaped from King David's sword. Nehama's reaction to this suggestion is:

> True, the text states explicitly that it was the camels that [the Amalekites] rode on which saved them, but that is the superficial explanation. (*TI*, 96)

Nehama knew that midrashic stories had tremendous educational power. She once asked a group of high-ranking Israeli army officers to open their Tanachs at the story of Abraham breaking his father's idols. One officer, after flipping back and forth in frustration, at last exclaimed, "Where is the Tanach I learned from when I was a child?" Her point was that many people recall well-known midrashic stories, especially those learned in childhood, as part of the biblical text.[93] As an educator, this did not trouble her as much as it might some others. She mentioned that she overheard a woman informing her children that hospitality is an important mitzvah as learned in the Torah, which "tells us how Abraham's tent was open on all four sides, so that visitors would pass through it on their way." She added, "I wouldn't go up to that woman and say: 'Excuse me, madam, but that's not written in the Torah – that's a Midrash!'" The ideas had been assimilated and something had been learned. Fine distinctions could be made at a later stage.[94]

Nehama believed that Midrashim were particularly successful in getting students to identify with the text. For this reason, despite her extensive methodology, she was not always desirous of dissecting them:

> Reading such Midrashim should come as a conclusion at the end of the lesson, so that the impression they create should not be spoilt by explanations. Imaginative Midrashim such as these can easily be killed by analysis. (*TI*, 83)

Some types of analysis, however, were useful. Nehama brought psychological insight to her understanding of Midrash and took it to a new level. She suggested that certain dramatic conversations appearing in Midrashim, seemingly between two or more persons, are in fact symbolic representations of conflicting voices inside one person. When Satan appears to Abraham in the guise of an old man, dissuading him from offering up his son, Nehama writes:

---

[93] Peters, *Learning*, 99.
[94] See Peerless, *To Study*, 23.

> As in many places... the conversation is not one that takes place between two actual people, but rather an external projection of an internal process.[95]

Who is Satan? Abraham's thoughts and doubts. (*TI*, 33)

"The mighty men of Saul" are similarly a personification of Saul's thoughts and doubts.[96] In this approach, Nehama anticipated contemporary scholarship on Midrash; though she notes that she takes her cue from some of her predecessors:

> Resh Lakish's observation (Bava Batra 16a) that the Satan is the evil inclination provides the clue to the above passage.[97]

High Court Judge Zvi Tal, an avid fan of Nehama's work, wrote to inform her that he had discovered support for her approach in the Tosafot; she responded that she herself had noted a precursor in the Ritva (*PN*, 664–665). However, she unquestionably developed this methodology further, and in doing so, both clarified the Midrash and cleared the way for further psychologistic interpretations after her.

Over the years, Nehama's attitude to Midrash met with great resistance amongst her colleagues, including Professor Yonah Frankel, a prominent Midrash scholar. Some scholars, such as Professor Israel Rozenson, objected primarily to her divesting of the Midrash from its historical context.[98] Others objected to her defining Midrash as commentary. Yet as today's scholars, influenced by postmodern trends, increasingly come round to her line of thinking, Nehama, who was in the minority for so long, has been vindicated.[99] Simi Peters notes: "Nehama's work on Midrash is likely to find a more appreciative audience amongst today's generation of scholars who, unlike their predecessors, are able to recognize even in forms that are not linear prose arguments, such as the midrashic parable, a type of

---

[95] *IBB*, 138; compare *NSB*, 196. See also *NSB*, 494, n. 1 and worksheets for *Va-era* 5708, *Va-yigash* 5712 (referenced in *IBBM*, 122, n. 3).

[96] *SBM*, 117. See also *NSB*, 493 for her comments on Judah's conscience. See further in Cohn, "*Ha-parshanut*," 101; Menahem Ben-Yashar, "*Panim psichologiyot ve-hinuchiyot be-parshanutah shel Nehama Leibowitz*," in *PN*, 347.

[97] *NSB*, 201. Erich Auerbach's essay *Mimesis*, from which she quotes extensively (*NSB*, 196–198; referenced also in *TI*, 32) takes a similar direction.

[98] Rozenson accepts her psychological approach, but feels it overshadows other ways of understanding Midrash ("*Ha-parshanit*," 447). Breuer argues that Nehama's lack of knowledge of "biblical critical" theory made her overlook exegetical dimensions within Midrash ("*Yahasah*," 19–20).

[99] Examples are Boyarin (see Cohn "*Ha-parshanut*," 96, n. 11) and Kugel. See also Cohn, "*Ha-midrash*," 96, n. 34, where he lists several authors who compare the midrashic and literary approaches.

interpretation." Yet even such contemporary scholars who are more amenable to the midrashic mindset have on the whole overlooked the Midrash's pedagogic dimensions.[100]

Several of Nehama's students developed her approach. Peters, through an exacting close reading of the Midrash, took the idea of the Midrash as exegesis even further than Nehama did. While Nehama generally stayed with accessible Midrashim – rationalistic, close to the *peshat* and with a clear moral point – Peters demonstrates that many of the others are a form of commentary too. She suggests that, although remarkably prescient in her more holistic approach to Midrash, Nehama was "tone-deaf" to certain types of Midrashim. Due to Nehama's rationalist intellectual training, she sometimes dismissed these texts as sermons conveying ideas. Peters feels that in this, Nehama represents a transitional figure between the New Critical and postmodern approaches.[101]

Conclusion

We close this chapter having seen the complexity of Nehama's attitude towards textual elucidation and educational messages – *peshat* and *derash* – in her dual identity as scholar and educator; and how these dualities played out in her approach to Midrash in particular, a body of work that she loved. With this we also close the methodological section of the book.

---

[100] Professor Susan Handelman writes: "Deconstruction, semiotics, cultural poetics, anthropology, and hermeneutic theory have all recently been applied to the rabbinic genre of Midrash with interesting results, but the intense pedagogical self-consciousness of midrashic texts has been little discussed" ("The 'Torah' of Criticism and the Criticism of Torah: Recuperating the Pedagogical Moment," *Journal of Religion* 74 [1994]: 356–371, reprinted in *Interpreting Judaism in a Postmodern Age*, edited by Steven Kepnes, 363–364, New York: 1996.)

[101] Peters, interview. See Peters, *Learning*, for a full account of her methodology.

PART IV

YESHAYAHU LEIBOWITZ

Yeshayahu Leibowitz and his wife, Grete. Courtesy of Mira Ofran.

Yeshayahu Leibowitz in his lab, circa mid 1930's, Mt. Scopus, Jerusalem. Courtesy of Mira Ofran.

CHAPTER 23

YESHAYAHU LEIBOWITZ:
"SAY TO WISDOM: YOU ARE MY SISTER"

Preface

BEFORE BEGINNING this chapter, a caveat is in order. We should apply the same lesson that Nehama learned from her brother after she published an article on R. Kook's introduction to Song of Songs.[1] Yeshayahu urged her, "Nehama, you stick to *parshanut!* You don't understand the first thing about Rav Kook!" From this reprimand she understood the importance of working within one's limits, and she would tell the story with a smile, recommending: "Before talking of unfamiliar matters, first go study them!" This lesson applies here, too. An in-depth study upon which a proper comparison of Yeshayahu and Nehama Leibowitz might be based has yet to be published.[2] Yeshayahu Leibowitz's thought alone is difficult to encompass, and even those who consider themselves experts on it disagree on some major issues. Therefore, the following is only a start in this direction, initial and partial, and should be taken as such.

By now the reader is familiar with Nehama's life, but a brief survey of Yeshayahu's biography is necessary before any comparison may be undertaken.

Yeshayahu's life and work

Yeshayahu Leibowitz (1903–1994) was known during his lifetime as a radical Jewish philosopher and outspoken activist.[3] Having studied chemistry in

---

[1] See page 121 above.

[2] The only occasion that I know of on which this topic has been examined is Professor Uriel Simon's lecture on the subject at the Van Leer Institute (*VLN*). I have quoted some of his findings here.

[3] Some of the following information is from the *Encyclopaedia Judaica*, 10:1587–1588, and from the Jewish Virtual Library (http://www.jewishvirtuallibrary.org/jsource/biography /yleib.html), a project of the Pedagogic Center of the Jewish Agency. Popular biographical material about Yeshayahu should be treated with caution, as many myths and errors have crept into it. I thank Avi Katzman for reading over this chapter and helping to maintain its accuracy.

Berlin[4] and attaining his doctorate by age twenty-one, he went on to study medicine in Cologne and Basel, receiving a second doctorate. In 1935 he moved to Palestine. He joined the staff of the Hebrew University, where he taught biochemistry and neurophysiology and, later on, the history and philosophy of science and other subjects. He received his professorship in 1961. He wrote many books and articles, lectured extensively, and edited several volumes of the *Encyclopedia Hebraica*. For many, he represented the foremost Israeli intellectual of his time. He was an extraordinary personality: an independent thinker with a razor-sharp mind, he adopted an uncompromisingly militant debating style, believing that

> when speaking about crucial and complicated matters... one must speak in a firm tone – soft, pleasant words are meaningless in these contexts.[5]

Sir Isaiah Berlin termed Yeshayahu "the conscience of Israel."[6] He was not some detached intellectual, but was involved with and indignant about all the issues he took up.[7] He was critical of reality – all reality – and always strove for the ideal.[8] After failing to be elected to the first Knesset,[9] he never ran for a political position again; not for lack of ambition, but because he did not feel comfortable joining any of the existing parties ("Whom could I run with?" he would ask rhetorically[10]). Instead, he was active in several political and social organizations and championed various causes, including protests against the introduction of nuclear weapons.[11] His establishment of a new religious educational stream and his protest against the forced secularization of religious immigrants contributed to the breakup of the first Knesset.[12]

According to one of his grandsons, Yeshayahu's greatest gift was delivering complicated ideas in a clear, coherent way.[13] Yeshayahu himself

---

[4] In his biography of Yeshayahu Leibowitz, Asa Kasher notes that Yeshayahu also studied philosophy in Berlin.

[5] Y. Leibowitz, *Ratziti*, 209. Yeshayahu put this into more colloquial form when he told Michael Shashar: "We live in a world in which the flow of information that lands on us from the radio, television and the press is so great that if one speaks neither dairy nor meat but *parve*, no one will hear" (quoted in Aviv Lavie, "*Yeshayahu Leibowitz hai*," *Haaretz* weekend supplement, February 21, 2003. 20).

[6] Eliezer Goldman, introduction to Y. Leibowitz, *Judaism*, viii.

[7] Goldman, introduction to Y. Leibowitz, *Judaism*, xxxiii–xxxiv.

[8] David Ohana, "*Tzionuto shel Yeshayahu Leibowitz*," *Kivvunim* 45 (1995): 171.

[9] Avi Katzman, interview.

[10] Y. Leibowitz, *Al olam*, 168.

[11] For more details see Y. Leibowitz, *Ratziti*, 11, and Goldman, introduction to Y. Leibowitz, *Judaism*, xi and xxviii.

[12] Avi Katzman, interview.

[13] Shula Kopf, "Analyzing the Analyst," *Jerusalem Post* Magazine, January 10, 2003.

believed that he expressed himself clearly, but he also liked to quote the philosopher Karl Popper: "It is impossible to speak in such a way that you cannot be misunderstood."[14] Understood or not, during his lifetime he gained many admirers, as well as many critics, in both religious and secular circles. Some found his views extremely convincing or at least thought-provoking. Young intellectuals discovered in Yeshayahu a way of thinking that they could respect, and while few followed him in all his radical ideas, many found themselves challenged to rethink their opinions. "His dogmatism caused others to awaken from their own dogmatism," writes Professor Avi Sagi.[15] Father Marcel Dubois, who participated in an eight-hour debate on Judaism and Christianity with him, remarked: "Yeshayahu Leibowitz, who agreed with me rarely, is sorely missed by me now... a man whose freedom of thought and deed instructed him to behave according to his views and not his needs."[16]

It was difficult to take a neutral stance towards Yeshayahu's views. He managed to upset people to the point of apoplexy, with both the iconoclastic content of his arguments and their prickly form. Such was his galvanizing effect on his opponents that an entire volume of articles disputing his thought was published.[17] He was described by one of his fellow professors at the Hebrew University as "the most logical but also the most unreasonable person I ever met."[18] His philosophical conception of Judaism was so out of the ordinary that he was accused of being a heretic or a "religious atheist," observing the commandments without believing in God. One person said to him: "You're very religious, but your religion isn't Judaism!"[19]

Because of this, and particularly because of his political opinions, he became largely *persona non grata* within the national-religious camp, though at the same time some of them admired him for daring to confront the flaws in religious society. This rejection was painful to him.[20] He was passionately

---

[14] Or "to avoid someone interpreting your words to mean the exact opposite of what you intended" (Y. Leibowitz, *Al olam*, 188).

[15] *Yeshayahu Leibowitz: olamo ve-haguto*, edited by Avi Sagi, Jerusalem: Keter, 1995, 12.

[16] Read by Professor Naftali Rothenberg, *VLY*, beginning of fourth session.

[17] *Shelilah li-shmah klapei Yeshayahu Leibowitz*, edited by H. Ben-Yeruham and H.E. Kulitz, Jerusalem, 1983.

[18] Michael Shashar, introduction to Y. Leibowitz, *Al olam*, 13.

[19] Jeffrey Saks, "Letters on Religion without Theology" (review essay of Y. Leibowitz, *Ratziti lishol otcha, Professor Leibowitz*). *Tradition* 34 (3): 2000, 94, n. 12.

[20] Avi Sagi reports: "I once asked him: 'Explain to me how it is that with respect to the people who are closest to you – the religious public – you are the most lethal of critics, whereas for the left-wing public, with whom you can't even drink a glass of water, you are a hero.' Suddenly, Yeshayahu fell silent. He looked at me and said nothing for a few

devoted to his Judaism and always counted himself among the community of the Torah-observant. Not once did he think of freeing himself from religion's demands.[21] He was involved in the founding of the religious kibbutz movement, and was respected and loved by its leaders in his early years.[22]

இ ௸

Though Yeshayahu's views on human knowledge were strongly shaped by Maimonides and Kant, his overall philosophy was all his own. For him, being a Jew meant accepting the yoke of heaven as embodied within the Torah and mitzvot, without reasons and rationalizations, regardless of needs and desires.[23] Although this might appear very restrictive to some, for him true freedom lay specifically therein.[24]

Religion, Yeshayahu said, is not a means to any greater personal or social good, but rather an end in itself. In contrast to Christianity, Jewish faith is not a benefit, an awareness that grants redemption. It is an obligation to the service of God through mitzvot.[25] The ultimate act in Judaism and the true expression of dutiful service of God – or at least the best attempt at such a thing, for ultimately the Divine cannot be served or known – is the strict practice of Halachah. In doing so, no reward or meaning is to be sought, whether spiritual, psychological or moral:

> Performing a mitzva of the Torah is not an ethical act but an act of religious faith.[26]

---

minutes. I saw a sad person. Being cut off from his public was a great tragedy for him" (quoted in Lavie, "*Yeshayahu*," 22).

[21] See Y. Leibowitz, *Al olam*, 68; and *Ratziti*, 500.

[22] He had tremendous impact on the religious kibbutz movement's ideological positions. His religious thinking, neither primitive nor mystical as it was, was embraced by the kibbutz leaders, as was his position that observant Jews should be involved in all walks of life, rather than delegating halachically challenging jobs to the non-observant (Eliezer Goldman, "*Ma hayav lo ha-kibbutz ha-dati?*" *Amudim* 580 [5755]: 11). See also Avi Sagi, *Olamo*, 13.

[23] This is a prevalent theme. For just one example see in his book of Bible commentary, *Accepting the Yoke of Heaven* where he states this decisively in his opening paragraph to Genesis (11).

[24] Professor Avital Wohlman, *VLY* (this lecture has been transcribed at tpeople.co.il/Leibowitz).

[25] Y. Leibowitz, *Ratziti*, 108. Goldman notes that Yeshayahu viewed Christianity as a form of paganism, and also that "follow[ing] from his conception of the halakhic life as the essence of Judaism," Yeshayahu saw Christianity as "the great historic adversary of Judaism, not merely its competitor," due to its rejection of the law (see Eliezer Goldman, introduction to Y. Leibowitz, *Judaism*, xxxi).

[26] Y. Leibowitz, *Accepting*, 140.

Yeshayahu Leibowitz. Photo: Bracha Ettinger.

Yeshayahu Leibowitz. Photo: Bracha Ettinger.

In fact, searching for any meaning beyond the practice of Halachah constitutes idolatry. Even prayer derives from the obligation to pray, and not from emotions or beliefs. There is no unique Jewish culture beyond Halachah, for no other facet of Jewish religion has been as continuous.[27] Since Jewish philosophers disagree upon almost every Jewish article of faith, the definition of Judaism cannot lie within philosophy, but only within practice. Yeshayahu claimed that there is no specifically Jewish philosophy, theology, mysticism or science. He critiqued various religious thinkers and trends of his time that, in his view, deviated from this emphasis on the practice of Halachah.[28] Gershom Scholem, the great scholar of Jewish mysticism, once said to Yeshayahu: "You believe in the Torah, but not in God." He retorted: "You neither believe in the Torah nor in God but in something bizarre, hidden in the Jewish people – and I do not share this belief."[29]

However, his conception of Halachah was far from static. He advocated fresh halachic deliberations to confront modern challenges, and new legislation for the new State – for example, a substitute solution to the Diasporic reliance on gentiles, the *Shabbos goy*. He did not expect that such legislation would emerge from the rabbis. It must therefore be given over into the hands of the halachically observant community – thus democratizing the Halachic system.[30]

---

[27] Goldman, introduction to Y. Leibowitz, *Judaism*, xvii.

[28] For example, R. Abraham Joshua Heschel, who he felt had been corrupted in America by the "sappy-sentimental-anthropocentric" religion of Jews who wanted Judaism without commandments (Y. Leibowitz, *Ratziti*, 165, explaining his refusal to join a committee for the publication of Heschel's works in Hebrew. For more on Yeshayahu's attitude towards Heschel see [Warren] Zev Harvey, "*Mekorotav ha-Yehudi'im shel Leibowitz*," in Sagi, *Olamo*, 45). Similarly, he reviled the growing trend, exemplified by the interest in "that clown, R. Shlomo Carlebach" and in the Lubavitcher Rebbe, of the exploitation of religion for satisfaction of one's own desires, writing: "I am not against entertainment as long as it is seen as such and not raised to the level of a religious act" (Y. Leibowitz, *Ratziti*, 209).

[29] See Y. Leibowitz, *Ratziti*, 483. A slightly different version of the conversation is reported by Yeshayahu in *Al olam* (47) where he retorts, "You don't believe in Torah and you don't believe in God, yet for some reason you believe in the uniqueness of the Jewish people!" Yeshayahu also claimed: "The Kabbalah is an intrusion of paganism into the world of Torah" (*Ratziti*, 259) and that it owed its popularity to its expression of subterranean pagan desires that classical Judaism had failed to stamp out (*Ratziti*, 255–257). Avi Katzman notes, that more than once, Yeshayahu would quote from Kabbalistic sources, announcing "You will never believe where this is from!" (interview). For an interview with Yeshayahu on the subject of Kabbalah, see www.radicaltorahthought.com/IndexArticles.htm.

[30] Hellinger, *VLY*.

Yeshayahu was a Zionist in the sense that he preferred living under Jewish political sovereignty to the Gentile rule of the Diaspora. His given definition of Zionism was "We are fed up with being ruled by the *goyim!*"[31] He felt that Torah could only be fully realized within an autonomous Jewish collective, and not when – as in the Diaspora – confined to a bubble of personal commandments, divorced from the surrounding economic, political and societal frameworks.[32] Therefore, he noted, Zionism functions as "escape from escapism,"[33] from the escapism that religious life in the Diaspora represents and the taking on of full responsibility.

But Zionism could also be idol worship. When secular Zionism assumes that the chief purpose of Halachah is Jewish survival, this is worship of the Jewish nation rather than God.[34] Religious Zionism was also problematic, since religion and state ought to be separated in order for religious society and government to function with integrity and independent of the other, avoiding a parasitic relationship. He criticized the dominant religious camp for following R. Zvi Yehudah Kook, who merged religion and state entirely. Of the political arm of this movement, *Gush Emunim*, he wrote:

> *Gush Emunim* are not interested in Jews or Judaism, only in the State.[35]

For Yeshayahu, the State was not a religious ideal but an instrument, and a flawed one at that. He habitually made sharp comments concerning the political system, government corruption, the excessive influence of parties on individuals, and the proliferation of nuclear weapons. He quoted his namesake's lament (Isaiah 1:21):

> How has the faithful city become a whore! It was endowed with justice; righteousness lodged in it, but now murderers!

He added ominously:

> These words sound as if they are addressed to us today; and 150 years after Isaiah came the destruction.[36]

The stormiest arguments came after the 1967 war, when Israel took control of the West Bank and Gaza. Yeshayahu was extremely apprehensive of the repercussions of this move. He predicted that within a short time, the area's workers and farmers would be Arabs while the Jews would become administrators, inspectors, and officials;[37] and worse, that a totalitarian state

[31] Y. Leibowitz, *Al olam*, 28.
[32] Goldman, "*Ma hayav*," *Amudim* 580 (5755): 10.
[33] Ohana, "*Tzionuto*," 163.
[34] Goldman, introduction to Y. Leibowitz, *Judaism*, xxi.
[35] Y. Leibowitz, *Ratziti*, 375.
[36] Y. Leibowitz, *Accepting*, 164.
[37] Goldman, introduction to Y. Leibowitz, *Judaism*, xxix.

would ensue, with all its citizens in the pay of the Secret Service.[38] Fearing that this occupation portended the State's moral destruction, with the land turning into an object of idol worship, he became a lone voice calling for the then unimaginable – absolute withdrawal. Professor David Ohana writes:

> Till the day of his death, Leibowitz strove to uphold the seventh day of the Six Day War: To struggle against an increasingly dangerous mythologizing tendency in modern Israeli history, emphasizing always that a free people cannot be a conquering people.[39]

Such views led some to erroneously suppose Yeshayahu to be a spiritual father to the humanistic left-wing peace camp.[40] But in truth, his views were couched in terms of political and religious considerations, not humanistic ones, and his moral philosophy was driven by his religious outlook.[41] Although his social, political and intellectual endeavors were undertaken primarily within a community of secular humanists, he would not admit this fact into his self-definition,[42] insisting loudly that he was not a humanist:[43]

> As far as I understand, humanism, in the spirit of Kant, envisages the human person as the supreme value and end within any reality which man is capable of knowing.... From the stand-point of Judaism... [human] existence can be meaningfully evaluated only in terms of his position before God as expressed in his mode of life. Judaism recognizes no expression of such a position other than "The acceptance of the yoke of the Kingdom of Heaven and the yoke of Torah and its mitzvot."[44]

---

[38] Avi Katzman, interview.

[39] Ohana, "*Tzionuto*," 165.

[40] Naftali Rothenberg, *VLY*. He notes that Yeshayahu differed from the left-wing camp in general, for he was willing to act against democracy and the rule of law under certain circumstances, while they held these two ideals sacrosanct.

[41] Moshe Halbertal demonstrates that although Yeshayahu argued for a complete separation between religion and ethics, in practice his strong moral principles emerged directly from his views on religious categories such as holiness and idolatry. See Halbertal, *Yeshayahu Leibowitz: bein hagut datit le-bikoret hevratit*, in Sagi, *Olamo*, 221–227.

[42] He claimed there could be no connection between the religious and secular, announcing to his secular peers: "I can't even eat in your house!"

[43] Y. Leibowitz, *Al olam*, 147, and see further comments there.

[44] Letter published in *Haaretz*, April 15, 1983, cited in Goldman, introduction to Y. Leibowitz, *Judaism*, viii. However, Eliezer Schweid believes that Yeshayahu took up an ambivalent attitude towards humanism (*VLY*), while Avi Katzman notes that for Yeshayahu, the human was, while not the supreme value, the starting point and the yardstick for everything else (interview).

He regularly pointed out that Leviticus 19:18 does not say "You shall love your neighbor as yourself," but rather, "You shall love your neighbor as yourself; I am God."[45] Without this ending, there is no meaning to the verse.

Furthermore, Yeshayahu claimed that being a humanist included being four things: A cosmopolite, an atheist, a pacifist and an anarchist;[46] and that he was none of these.[47] When it came to pacifism, for example, Yeshayahu was not of that opinion, believing that peace was still a long way off. Not only was the War of Independence entirely justified in attaining sovereignty for the Jewish people, but fighting to defend Israel was essential. Nonetheless, he found himself fighting alongside the Israeli peace camp and the humanists, due to his belief that Zionism's unique mission to demonstrate humane government was betrayed the moment that it began to dominate another people.[48] He supported soldiers' refusal to serve in the territories and in Lebanon. Indeed, his most provoking statement of all came in 1982 when he used the terms "Judeo-Nazi" to characterize the policies of the government and the army, in Lebanon and the disputed territories of Judea and Samaria.[49] This elicited an eruption of outrage in large sectors of Israeli society, and was not quickly forgotten. He continued to make controversial observations in public, and the decision to award him the Israel Prize in 1993 caused an uproar, with Prime Minister Yitzhak Rabin insisting that he would not attend the ceremony. Yeshayahu declared his own refusal to accept the prize, and the matter was closed.

---

[45] Y. Leibowitz, *Judaism*, 19.

[46] See Y. Leibowitz, *Al olam*, 147, and Aviezer Ravtizky, *Vikuchim al emunah u-philosophiah*, Tel Aviv, 2006, 35. Avi Katzman emphasizes that while these four conditions are included in humanism, they do not encompass its whole (interview).

[47] Avi Katzman suggests that although Yeshayahu was not any of these four types in their absolute state, nevertheless he approached these types in his anti-nationalism and anti-militarism, his opposition to governmental abuse of power and to the belief in an interventionist God, and is thus "the most humanist of the non-humanists" (interview).

[48] Ohana, "*Tzionuto*," 161.

[49] Avi Katzman states that contrary to the widespread belief, Yeshayahu never called the actual soldiers or settlers themselves "Judeo-Nazis," only certain policies and actions (interview). But this fact seems to make little difference in the way the comment is remembered. When Michael Shashar asked him, "Wasn't it an exaggeration to use the expression 'Judeo-Nazis'? Do you really believe that we could degenerate to the level of the Nazis?" Yeshayahu replied, "When the nation (or, in Nazi terminology, 'the race') and its sovereign power become supreme values, no restraint remains to human behavior. This mentality has become widespread in us too. Our conduct in the occupied territories, the Gaza Strip and Lebanon, already resembles the Nazis' behavior in their occupied territories of Czechoslovakia and the West. We haven't set up concentration camps as they did in the East, but how dreadful for this fact to be presented as the one differentiating us from the Nazis!" (Y. Leibowitz, *Al olam*, 78).

ॐ ॐ

Michael Shashar, who interviewed Yeshayahu at length about his life, is at pains to emphasize that Yeshayahu did not hate people, only ideas that he considered immoral or wrong.[50] Yeshayahu himself explained that his rationale in saying such harsh things was for the sake of the minority who might be capable of hearing him and changing their minds. "Many people say to me, 'You express what we cannot articulate for ourselves,'" he observed.[51]

Another Yeshayahu existed alongside the sharp-tongued ideologue. Some might be surprised to hear him portrayed as an affable, soft person, a "sweet granddad," yet thus he was known by those who were close to him.[52] A family member remarks:

> He rattled everyone when he talked about the "Judeo-Nazis," but at the same time, he was the man with the fedora and the old satchel who hurried every morning for sixty years to pray at the Yeshurun Synagogue.[53]

At home, he suddenly became pleasant and open to conversation.[54] His fatherly side also expressed itself in his letters, which contained his home address and telephone number so that troubling issues might receive proper attention in a long personal conversation.

The above-cited family member says:

> Everyone has his own Leibowitz. Since he was such a diversified person, everyone can connect with the area of his personality and activity that appeals to him.[55]

Yet this very diversity that allowed him to connect with so many different people and fields may have come at a price. Dr. Yehudah Meltzer, a publisher, observes:

> No one else was able to be dominant in all his fields… [but] when we celebrated his seventy-fifth birthday I asked him whether, if he could go back to age twenty in Berlin, he would concentrate on biochemistry. "If you had done that, you probably would have received the Nobel Prize," I told him. He was very moved by the question. He thought a bit and then said, "God gave me many shortcomings, and modesty is not one of them. As for the Nobel, of course I would have received it. But on

---

[50] Michael Shashar, introduction to Y. Leibowitz, *Al olam*, 11.
[51] Y, Leibowitz, *Al olam*, 185.
[52] Lavie, "*Yeshayahu*," 20.
[53] Lavie, "*Yeshayahu*," 20.
[54] Sagi, *Olamo*, 12.
[55] Lavie, "*Yeshayahu*," 20.

the substance of the question, I don't know what to tell you." In other words, he knew that the decision to touch on so many fields, the desire to connect so many worlds, and above all, the need to be politically active, to address painful questions of daily life and to travel the country disseminating his philosophy came at the expense of something. It is a reasonable conjecture that if he had devoted his life to the study of one subject he would have achieved breakthroughs that would have advanced science.[56]

In any event, the fact that Yeshayahu's thought still reverberates powerfully within Israeli intellectual discourse and the media is certainly a great achievement. It says a great deal that the published volume of his letters, *I Wanted to Ask You, Professor Leibowitz*, remained at the top of the *Haaretz* bestseller list for six months.[57]

Having become somewhat acquainted with Yeshayahu, we can now turn to the relationship, similarities and differences between him and his sister.

Extraordinary siblings

Professor Uriel Simon likens Nehama and Yeshayahu Leibowitz, in their scope and influence, to two of Rashi's illustrious grandchildren, Rabbenu Tam and Rashbam. Like them, the Leibowitz siblings between them conquered the Jewish world, their combined impact on Israeli and Jewish society too immense to measure.

It is a tribute to both Yeshayahu's and Nehama's stature that they were both well-known in their own right and not as the "brother of" or the "sister of." For different segments of society, though, one of them is more likely to be better-known than the other. For much of the Diaspora, and especially for American Jews, the primary association with the name Leibowitz is Nehama, whereas for many Israelis it is Yeshayahu.[58] But for many, both names ring a bell. Both represent a watershed in their respective fields: Jewish philosophy has been known to be divided into "before and after

---

[56] Quoted in Lavie, *"Yeshayahu,"* 20. See also Y. Leibowitz, *Al olam*, 177.

[57] Saks, "Letters," 91. The volume was entitled *Ratziti lishol otcha, Professor Leibowitz.* See bibliography for details.

[58] A Google search in English brings up more hits for Nehama's name, while in Hebrew Yeshayahu's is more popular. In the original *Encyclopaedia Judaica*, Nehama's entry, which was appended to that of Yeshayahu, was about one-third the length of his, but this was probably more reflective of the *Encyclopaedia*'s neglect of women in general (Moshe Shalvi calls the Yeshayahu/Nehama entry "one egregious example of the [*Encyclopaedia*'s] obtuseness," and claims that "of the fifteen million words in the *Encyclopaedia Judaica*, only approximately 400,000 – 0.27 percent – were devoted to women and women-related topics...." (M. Shalvi, "Publishing as Empowerment," *Bet Debora* 3 [2003]). The updated *Encyclopaedia Judaica* granted Nehama her own entry.

Yeshayahu Leibowitz"[59] and Tanach study into "before and after Nehama Leibowitz."[60]

The two had great mutual respect and affection. Yeshayahu praised Nehama with a verse from Proverbs (7:4):

> Say to wisdom: You are my sister.[61]

He considered Nehama a leading expert in Tanach, turning to her with questions in her field,[62] and remarking, "She brought people to open the Tanach," and "My sister is the only person in Israel who knows what Tanach is."[63] Yeshayahu in turn was a very significant figure in Nehama's life, and she praised him to others as a "wonderful man."

Nehama was the younger by two years, and growing up as Yeshayahu Leibowitz's little sister may not have been a simple matter. She mentioned to Dr. Shmuel Adler that at home her brother was considered a genius while she was considered average.[64] Nehama also claimed that "Shaya" always beat her in their father's Tanach quizzes, though this may have been her modesty talking, since others claim that she actually won.[65] While she never gave the appearance of being intimidated by him in later life, she may have, consciously or unconsciously, experienced herself as inferior to Yeshayahu, who had a breadth of expertise that she did not. On the other hand, the companionship of such a brilliant brother probably also accelerated her development and influenced its direction.

Even after they left home, the two continued to correspond. Among Yeshayahu's published letters, the earliest dated are to Nehama, sent at age twenty-five from Cologne, where he was studying medicine.[66] In one of these, he explains to her the basics of epistemology and recommends articles for her to read.

Yeshayahu settled in Israel not long after Nehama, and their connection, resting on affection and on a shared capacity for intellectual exchange, continued throughout their lives. They periodically spent time together, sitting on a Shabbat afternoon arguing volubly on Nehama's balcony, or traveling back together from Tel Aviv University, where Yeshayahu also

---

[59] See for example Sagi, *Olamo*, 15.

[60] Nigal, "*Morah.*"

[61] HaCohen, "*Shma*," 75, n. 11.

[62] For example: "… and I asked experts on Rashi, I asked my sister Nehama who is more of an expert in this field than I" (quoted in Aviezer Ravitzky, *Vikuchim al emunah u-philosophiah*, Tel Aviv, 2006, 15).

[63] Sheleg, "Kalat," 73, Strikovsky, "Nehama on Women," 187, and *Daf*, 5.

[64] Shmuel Adler, interview.

[65] See Sheleg, "*Kalat*," 70.

[66] Y. Leibowitz, *Ratziti*, 515–516.

lectured from time to time. Her brother's family was the closest thing to Nehama's own, and after her husband's death she spent every Passover Seder with them.

Their fields of interest were generally different enough not to bring the siblings into competition with each other. When this did happen, as in a period during the years 1985 and 1986 when Yeshayahu gave a twelve minute radio talk about the Torah portion every Friday afternoon, he waited before putting these talks in print because Nehama was still publishing her books.[67] In general, essays on the weekly portion, though commonplace today, were unusual for the time, and between them, Yeshayahu and Nehama netted a large audience, filling a genuine need for the weekly portion to be made relevant and accessible. Their books proved so popular that they were often in their second print run within a year of publication.[68]

Commonalities

Yeshayahu and Nehama resembled each other in important ways. Both demonstrated precision of thought, and their intellectual output was courageous, genuine and original. Their sharp minds, outstanding memories and long lives brought people to marvel at the "Leibowitz genes."[69] They possessed eclectic interests, a provocative teaching style and the ability to simplify complex concepts.[70] They both dedicated their lives to higher ideals, teaching *li-shmah* (literally "for the sake of heaven" though also "for its own sake"). They were firmly convinced of their opinions, categorically rejecting entire systems of thought, such as psychoanalysis (in Yeshayahu's case) or feminism (in Nehama's). Both had little patience for what they perceived as nonsense. To one person who wrote inquiring as to the difference between "anger, fury and rage" Yeshayahu responded that the difference was like that between "fool, idiot and blockhead."[71] When someone phoned to invite him to lecture on the topic of "The Resurrection of the Dead," Yeshayahu barked, "There's no such thing!" and hung up. Nehama was also perfectly capable of hanging up, especially on people who wanted to interview her.

---

[67] But since her last two books were a long time in coming, he did end up publishing *"He'arot le-parashat ha-shavua"* (Academon, Jerusalem) before them in 1988. Nehama termed it a "fine book... worthwhile reading for every teacher" (Letter to Helfgot, *PN*, 663). It was subsequently published in English in 1990 as *Notes and Remarks on the Weekly Portion* and recently reissued in a corrected edition as *Accepting the Yoke of Heaven* (Jerusalem: Urim Publications, 2006). Another, longer book came out in the year 2000, *Sheva shanim shel sichot al parashat ha-shavua* (1976–1982).

[68] Simon, *VLN* (this lecture has been transcribed at tpeople.co.il/Leibowitz).

[69] Sheleg, *"Kalat,"* 70.

[70] Sheleg, *"Kalat,"* 70.

[71] Y. Leibowitz, *Ratziti*, 514–515.

Yeshayahu Leibowitz. Courtesy of the artist, Charles Szlakmann.

Yeshayahu Leibowitz. Courtesy of the artist, Charles Szlakmann.

Simon recalls: "They were both scary people, with a commanding presence and tremendous concentration. You could see them hunched over in the audience – they were physically similar – and you could feel the wheels of their minds turning; and you would wait for the outburst or the criticism or the flame that would flare up at your words" (*VLN*). Yet both possessed a soft heart beneath their sharp tongues. They were private about their personal lives and did not talk much about their families.[72]

Nehama and Yeshayahu shared a belief in autonomy as a crucial value, and a fierce independence of spirit in their own lives; and yet both maintained at the same time an unquestioning loyalty to Judaism and to the will of God as defined by the observance of mitzvot. They were uninterested in biblical criticism or in readings of the Tanach outside the Jewish context. For them, the Tanach was autonomous and independent of its historical origins.[73] Both took on, in different ways, the question of Judaism in a Jewish State – Yeshayahu involved in the political and practical ramifications, and Nehama working to boost the cultural stamina of the State by teaching the Tanach as a specifically Jewish work. They shared a focus on the future, on the State and Jewish empowerment, not on the Holocaust. Yeshayahu would say, "The Holocaust is not our problem. We did not do it; it was done to us."[74] He wished to see an end to the perception of the Jews as history's victim.

Both were engaged and active in society. They were driven by feelings of responsibility and an unwillingness to turn a blind eye to injustice or hypocrisy. Extremely sensitive to moral issues, they were like "prophets of doom," speaking out frankly and dramatically against wrongs. This was more pronounced in Yeshayahu, who consciously took his cue from the forthright and plain-speaking prophets of old.[75] He noted that he had correctly

---

[72] Shula Kopf, "Analyzing the Analyst," *Jerusalem Post* Magazine, January 10, 2003.

[73] For a discussion of Yeshayahu's approach see Avi Sagi, "*Kitvei ha-kodesh u-mashma'utam be-hagutam shel Leibowitz ve-Soloveitchik,*" *Be-khol derakhekha daehu* 1 (5755): 49–62. We can infer from Sagi's conclusions that Nehama was closer to R. Soloveitchik than to Yeshayahu in her thinking.

[74] Quoted by Hanoch Ben-Pazi in a lecture given on January 29, 1996 for the Open University (transcribed at tpeople.co.il/Leibowitz). (Avi Katzman notes that generally Yeshayahu made this statement regarding all anti-Semitism, not the Holocaust in particular.) However, Ben-Pazi goes on to argue that the Holocaust actually had a profound influence on Yeshayahu's thought, for example in shaping his fear of nationalism and its corruptions. Yeshayahu's quote regarding "the deaths by choking and burning of 1.5 million Jewish children" (page 545 below) takes on new significance in light of this view.

[75] Sagi, *Olamo*, 12.

predicted certain events, just like a true prophet;[76] though at his ninetieth birthday gathering he declared a prophet to be a person who prophesies not what will be but what ought to be.[77]

Rejecting the ivory tower, Yeshayahu and Nehama also taught outside their respective universities, in teachers' enrichment courses, adult education programs, youth groups, army bases and many other places. They also appeared on the radio, though only Yeshayahu appeared on television. The siblings, who spent numerous hours in correspondence with all sorts of people, had no set office hours, receiving strangers and students alike for conversations in their homes. They also enjoyed teaching smaller study groups at home. Impromptu teaching would occur outside the reading rooms of the National Library, where Nehama conversed with questioners and Yeshayahu "held court" on a wide variety of topics, surrounded by eager students.[78]

Lacking all snobbery, the Leibowitzes were happy to talk to anyone, from scholar to street cleaner. They traveled long distances in order to lecture, and continued to teach and to accept speaking engagements even in their advanced years. At the age of eighty-six, Yeshayahu thought nothing of flying to Germany to participate in a television panel and returning the following day to Israel to keep several appointments.[79] Nehama took advantage of this trait of her brother's, wriggling out of speaking invitations by saying, "Ask my brother – he loves to do that sort of thing!"

Though Nehama was not a formal scientist as Yeshayahu was, she too was rigorous and analytic, and her work constituted both an art and a science in its own fashion. When, in 1982, Nehama was nominated to receive the Bialik Prize for the Jewish Sciences, two members of the committee, former students of hers, pushed strongly for her candidacy. Professor Dov Landau was one of them, and he explains: "She was the one who taught us scientific thinking in university, in writing articles and in Bible study." However, the third member contended that Nehama was "not a scientist but a teacher." The stalemate was broken when Professor E.E. Urbach became a co-nominee for the prize.

For some students of a scientific bent, Nehama's approach made the Tanach intelligible to them for the first time. One of these students was

---

[76] Y. Leibowitz, *Ratziti*, 484.

[77] Ohana, "*Tzionuto*," 163. Ohana claims that Yeshayahu did not like being called a prophet. See also Asa Kasher's words regarding how a prophet or social critic should be treated in "*Bein Yahadut le-bikoret hevratit*" (*Yediot Ahronot*, February 9, 1990). There were also those who termed Yeshayahu a "false prophet."

[78] Ruth Fogelman, private communication.

[79] Goldman, introduction to Y. Leibowitz, *Judaism*, vii.

Yonatan Ahituv, who recalls his first experience of Nehama when she gave a radio talk on Numbers 27:18–20. She asked, in the footsteps of the Midrash, in what manner Moses was to pass his "spirit" on to his successor Joshua. Would it be like the pouring of liquid from one vessel to another or like the lighting of one candle from another?[80] She then discussed the difference between these two images and suggested that the second is the more apt, for just as fire is not diminished by lighting another candle, thus too, Moses's spirit was not reduced in the act of transmission.[81] Such precision of thinking impressed Ahituv, who until then had believed the Tanach to consist of great artistry but little content.

Nehama respected the advance of science. She omitted certain passages from her quote of Ramban on Numbers 21:9, though they were essential to his argument, because they did not correspond with up-to-date scientific theory and might appear foolish to modern minds.[82]

❧ ☙

Turning now to the works of Nehama and Yeshayahu Leibowitz, even a superficial investigation brings to light some significant common elements. Some of these derived from their father, who imbued them with a love of universal wisdom sources and provided them with a rationalistic upbringing which led them both to reject the supernatural and superstitious. Yeshayahu writes:

> Anyone who views the *mezuzah* as protecting the house and its inhabitants debases religion and is guilty of pagan belief.[83]

Their upbringing also brought them to emphasize halachic practice and be wary of Hasidism and of ecstatic religious life,[84] which they viewed as compromising halachic observance. These two elements often went together, as Nehama writes of R. Naphtali Zvi Yehudah Berlin (*Netziv*), the nineteenth-century Lithuanian Rosh Yeshivah:

---

[80] See *Bamidbar Rabbah* 21:15.

[81] See *IBBM*, 152–153; *SBM*, 345; and a brief mention in *NSS*, 517.

[82] See Frankel, *Iyun*, 140, n. 138. For Yeshayahu, in contrast, science and religion were totally separate and irrelevant to each other.

[83] Y. Leibowitz, *Ratziti*, 120, and see *ibid.*, 496.

[84] Yeshayahu himself, before quoting R. Zadok ha-Cohen of Lublin, notes how unusual it is for him to be doing so, for Hasidic thought is very alien to his mindset (*Ratziti*, 179). This opposition may also have been due to his rejection of holiness created by humans – see Aviezer Ravitzky's personal anecdote in "*Arachim u-reshamim*," in Sagi, *Olamo*, 16. Yeshayahu shares Nehama's opinion that even moments of Divine revelation are not enough to sustain an ongoing religious habit; see pages 314–317 above. See also, for example his essay "*Nissim ve-emunah*" in *Emunah, historiah ve-arachim*, Jerusalem: 5742, 65–66.

As an ardent follower of the Gaon of Vilna, [Berlin's] reference to those "who seek with zeal the love of God, but not within the limits set by the Torah" might well have alluded to the Hasidic movement of his time, whose ecstasy and focus on *devekut*, the great opponents of Hasidism feared, might breach the walls of the Halachah.[85]

The emphasis on Halachah was paramount in Yeshayahu's case, for he attributed ultimate value to Halachah to the exclusion of all other religious expression. Professor Moshe Halbertal, who has described him as the "Lithuanian's theologian," points out that in the volume of Yeshayahu's letters, many of the correspondents are yeshivah students of the non-Hasidic (often termed "Lithuanian") persuasion (*VLY*). Yeshayahu's devotion to Halachah is illustrated in his response upon hearing of the premature death of his son. He immediately said to Nehama, "Ah, that means I won't lay *tefillin* tomorrow" (a mourner is exempt from positive commandments until the time of burial.) Nehama was much moved that her brother's first impulse in such circumstances was the halachic one.[86]

But while both were devoted to Halachah, neither advocated taking on strict injunctions such as separation between men and women (specifically in social or academic circumstances, not in prayer or ritual). Yeshayahu even writes that where it is already in place, mixed dancing should not be forbidden, for these kinds of prohibitions are sociologically determined and may change with the new Israeli reality.[87]

Another trait that Yeshayahu had in common with the Lithuanian yeshivah world was the talmudic-style love of debate. Arguing and disputing constituted the *sine qua non* of his intellectual and political life. Nehama, who also valued passionate debate, possessed a desire for harmony that her brother did not. Moreover, although she sometimes adopted unequivocal or even extreme viewpoints, she also frequently recognized a complex middle ground of disparate truths. In contrast, Yeshayahu tended to view the world

---

[85] *NSV*, 107. However, in another essay, Nehama quotes a different position of the Netziv's in which he distinguishes between the performance of a *mitzvah* and the state of holiness and communion with God, for practical mitzvot link one with mundane matters (*SD*, 286–287). Here he sounds less "Leibowitzian."

[86] Nehama told this story to Avi Katzman in an interview. Ravitzky recounts an incident with similar sentiments. Several months after his son's death, Yeshayahu gave a lecture and said, "When a person gets up in the morning and says, 'Blessed is He who spoke and the world came into being' – if it is his wedding day, this is not an act for the sake of heaven; but if he says this following the death of his son, this is *Torah li-shmah* (*VLY* – this lecture has been transcribed at tpeople.co.il/leibowitz).

[87] Y. Leibowitz, *Ratziti*, 151.

in unqualified dichotomies of right and wrong, though the contradictions in his writings ultimately hint at a recognition that reality is not that simple.[88]

Other commonalities may be due to the direct influence of the strong-minded Yeshayahu on his sister. Indeed, R. Elhanan Samet suggests that Nehama's approach resembles Yeshayahu's in his less radical youth. Nehama suggested that her brother's most unbending principles may have developed only gradually, as he battled against the Reform movement as a young man.[89]

ᔆ ᔆ

We can see one example of the similarity of their ideas in Nehama's discussion of the sin of eating the forbidden fruit in Eden:

> The evil is not the evil of punishment but the evil in the sin itself, in the deviation of man from the will of God that it involves. (*NSB*, 24)

Here, as in Yeshayahu's philosophy, the significance lies in God's command and obedience to it, not in any external rewards or punishments. Nehama also held unquestioning obedience to be of the highest importance, as can be seen in an essay about the sanctification of God's name.[90] Here, she discusses the topic of the importance of decent behavior on the part of Torah students – an issue very close to her heart. Yet instead of choosing to emphasize it, she highlights the theme of service of God:

> Man was created for the sole purpose of serving his Creator. Whoever is not willing to lay down his life for his master is not a good servant. It is a fact that men lay down their lives for their masters, how much more so in obedience to the command of the King of kings, the Holy One, blessed be He. Throughout history this precept has been faithfully carried out by Jews. (*NSV*, 405)

Though more philosophical than Nehama, Yeshayahu was also interested in moral applications rather than theoretical questions:

> It's not what comes after life that should concern a person... rather what is in his life and what he does with this gift.[91]

Like Nehama, he was relatively uninterested in discussing metaphysical concepts such as revelation or prophecy, about which he believed we can know nothing and say nothing. He maintained, for example, that the first

---

[88] Moshe Hellinger, *VLY*.

[89] Professor Menahem Ben-Sasson, interview. Eliezer Goldman suggests that "the thesis that Jewish faith is basically the commitment to observance of the Halakhah as worshipful service of God has a polemical thrust. Among others, it is directed against Reform Judaism, which regards the Halakhah as a husk hiding the essential core of religion" (introduction to Y. Leibowitz, *Judaism*, xvii).

[90] "You Shall Not Profane My Holy Name," *NSV*, 398–410.

[91] Y. Leibowitz, *Ratziti*, 16.

verse of the Torah is entirely opaque; not one word is comprehensible to us. The only thing we can learn from it is

> the great principle of faith, that the world is not God – [this is] the negation of atheism and pantheism.[92]

Yeshayahu and Nehama shared a lack of faith in "isms," the various ideologies that have pervaded Western culture at one time or another. They termed such ideologies "idol worship," as we see when Nehama enlists Rosenzweig's help in defining idolatry as:

> Culture, civilization, people, state, nations, race, art, science, economy and class – here you have what is certainly an abbreviated and incomplete list of the pantheon of our contemporary gods.[93]

The siblings used the word "idolatry" liberally, expanding its definition from its archaic connotations of sacrifices to Moloch and the like to

> the transformation of means, even perfectly legitimate ones, into ends in themselves. (NSS, 320)

> Turning any means, however kosher and decent, into an end, into our life's goal, is transgressing "You shall have no other gods besides Me".... [E]ven non material goals [such as] homeland, nation and state, when they cease to be means and implements to the service of the creator, and become the goal... become idol worship – the most dangerous of its kind (IHBS, 235).

In such views, Nehama was probably strongly influenced by both her father and her brother, as comes across in one of the earliest published letters of Yeshayahu, written to Nehama from Cologne:

> I was going to write to you a week ago on the topic of idol worship which interests you, but after I read what Father wrote, I hesitated; why should I repeat the same things? I don't know if he read my mind or I read his, because I was also going to quote the verse from Va-ethanan with the Midrashim and commentaries on it.[94]

Yeshayahu insisted repeatedly that turning something of human origin – a value, person, institution, place etc. – into something holy, into a supreme value holding sway to the exclusion of other values, constituted idolatry:

> The conversion of the term kedushah – as a task and a duty which the Jewish people is obligated to accomplish – to a quality which is innate in the Jewish people – means the conversion of faith to idolatry.[95]

---

92 Y. Leibowitz, *Judaism*, 140.
93 *NSS*, 321; see also *ibid.* 331, quoted on page 163 above.
94 Y. Leibowitz, *Ratziti*, 516.
95 Y. Leibowitz, *Accepting*, 114.

He was not willing to call the Jews a "holy people." He continues:

> I opened my morning newspaper and found it full of accounts of the murders that have taken place in our midst, and incest and prostitution and lust and rape and theft and armed robbery, and – superfluous to say – idolatry. And yet, there are people who say: "We are by nature a holy people."[96]

We recognize a similar conviction in the following statement by Nehama:

> What strange commandment is this that enjoins us, who are not holy, to sanctify God's name? (*NSV*, 401)

Like Nehama, Yeshayahu instead defines the holiness of the Jewish people in terms of actions and responsibility:

> Holiness is expressed as the most lofty state that can be attained through man's decisions on religious faith…. On the other hand, we have holiness according to Korah and his adherents, which is something base and disreputable: in essence, the person absolves himself of responsibility, of the mission imposed upon him and of the obligation to exert himself; he is smugly sure that he is already holy.[97]

Yeshayahu indeed opposed the investment of any object or value with intrinsic holiness:

> There is no holiness in anything in the world – not in a land, or a people, or a building, or an object, or a person: Only God is holy.[98]

Nehama's statement is very similar:

> There is only one source of holiness. No intrinsic holiness resides in places, houses or vessels, not even in the greatest of men. (*NSS*, 612)

For this reason, both Nehama and her brother disapproved of practices such as praying at gravesites. A buried saint must not be turned into an object of worship. The land as idol was also a common theme for Yeshayahu, for example:

> There is nothing more dangerous than cloaking defilement in the garb of holiness. The land itself does not have any inherent quality which sanctifies everything done in it…. The Mishna asks: "What is [the

---

[96] Y. Leibowitz, *Accepting*, 116.

[97] Y. Leibowitz, *Accepting*, 142. The need for responsibility and accountability were important to Yeshayahu too, and he demanded: "The leader shares in every error, in every sin by negligence…. We have reached the stage of being led by people without any self-respect, leaders who attempt to save themselves at the expense of the sins, omissions and errors made by those under them…." (*Accepting*, 147).

[98] Y. Leibowitz, *Ratziti*, 248, and see his discourses there, 247–254.

land's] holiness? That from it one brings the *omer* and the *bikkurim* (the first fruits) and the showbread." In other words: it is the observance of the mitzvot relating to the land that imparts holiness to the land; it is not holy in itself.[99]

Nehama also believed that God "is not bound to a particular holy place, land or sanctuary,"[100] and writes:

> [That the land may become defiled] is a moral rather than a mystical notion. (*NSV*, 579)

> The return to the homeland, the transformation from dependence to sovereignty, slavery to freedom are but instruments, the means for achieving the ultimate goal – specified in our text: the service of God. (*NSS*, 71)

But there was an important difference in how Nehama applied her opinion. Firstly, what was for Nehama one of many important values was for Yeshayahu a supreme and overarching principle. His preoccupation with the theme of idolatry may be seen by its frequent appearance in his comments on the weekly Torah portion, as well as his other writings.[101] In his fight for purity of worship, he was truly a modern iconoclast. Secondly, Nehama did not politicize her views, while Yeshayahu's philosophical insights directly informed his political opinions. For example, she warned against worshipping objects in her oft-taught lesson, featuring the *Meshech Hochmah*'s idea that Moses broke the tablets of stone to prove that they were not holy.[102] This was a lesson dear to Yeshayahu as well,[103] but, unlike Nehama, he gave it a real-life application when, after the Six Day War, a new influx of pilgrims started arriving at the Kotel (Western Wall). At that time, he renamed it the *"discotel"* as an expression of his concern that it was becoming an object of worship in and of itself.[104] Another example was his

---

[99] Y. Leibowitz, *Accepting*, 158.

[100] *NSB*, 509, quoting Buber.

[101] See, for example, in *Accepting the Yoke of Heaven*, regarding the priests, "This holiness is only a special obligation imposed upon them" (117–118); and "the spiritual plague, the plague against faith, religion and morals, that has infected and still infects certain circles of that part of the Jewish people which accepts the obligation to observe the Torah and the mitzvot: to regard certain people as holy in themselves, and not in terms of the function they fill in teaching Torah…. [This] is nothing but a form of idolatry that has penetrated into Judaism, and is a sign of the withering of faith in God" (119–120). See also *ibid.* 124, 143, 163.

[102] See pages 317–318 above.

[103] See, for example, Y. Leibowitz, *Ratziti*, 240; *Sheva shanim*, 400. Harvey mentions Yeshayahu's fondness for the *Meshech Hochmah*'s interpretations in "*Mekorotav*," 45.

[104] One distressed individual wrote to him to ask if the destruction of the Temple was then, by extension, also a good thing, as it released the idea of the Divine from any

opposition to the Gush Emunim movement, with its ultimate emphasis on land.

क क

In their study of the weekly Torah portion, Nehama and Yeshayahu are at times drawn to the same sections and issues. For example, Nehama writes of some verses in the Torah portion of *Aharei Mot* (Leviticus 18:1–5):

> We have written at great length on these verses… and while it is neither proper from the Torah's perspective nor educationally sound to speak of "important verses" and less important ones… nonetheless there are certain verses in which it appears all the Torah's rays of light converge, and in which, from our standpoint, the Divine flame is evident in a way that is not true of all parts of the Torah.[105]

Yeshayahu broadly echoes these sentiments with a broader sweep in writing of "the two great *sidrot*," *Aharei Mot* and *Kedoshim*:

> Of course, we are neither authorized nor permitted to give grades to the different *sidrot* of the Torah, yet at the same time we cannot refrain from having a special emotional feeling for these two *sidrot*.[106]

Even where Nehama's work deviates from Yeshayahu's, it still exhibits at times traces of his influence. Take the issue of *ta'amei ha-mitzvot* – offering rationales for the commandments. Although this has been done by many Jewish thinkers throughout history, Yeshayahu rejected its validity – a Jew fulfills the commandments because God said so (through the agency of the Oral law) and for no other reason.

Nehama adopted a twofold approach to this issue. On the one hand, she believed it natural to look for meaningful ideas behind the commandments. Indeed, several of her teachings were devoted to the reasons behind particular mitzvot, such as circumcision, the dietary laws or the prohibition of eating blood,[107] and especially ritualistic precepts unfathomable to the modern reader, such as the sacrifices.[108] She also found symbolism and allegory in the details of certain mitzvot[109] and encouraged her students in

---

appearance of material limitation. Yeshayahu insisted that it was not (see *Ratziti*, 243–244).

[105] *IHBV*, 199 (omitted in the English version).

[106] Y. Leibowitz, *Accepting*, 113.

[107] *NSV*, 162, *NSV*, 144 and *NSV*, 84 respectively. See Frankel *Iyun*, 151–153 for other examples and discussion.

[108] Frankel, *Iyun*, 164.

[109] See for example her discussion of the menorah in *NSS*, 497–507; or the dietary laws, *NSV*, 159–161.

this activity, citing Heinemann's position that it is not only permitted but constitutes religious imperative.[110]

Still, she taught that any reasons given must be supported by the text (*NSV*, 152), and that ultimately we can never know the reason intended by the Giver (*NSS*, 494). She moreover supported *Sefer ha-Hinuch*'s contention that "actions shape character" – that it is deeds that educate, not thoughts or feelings:[111] While Yeshayahu also believed that deeds serve to shape one's inner world,[112] this was not his main philosophical emphasis; for here the commandments are still a means to an end – that of education. Rather, he believed in observance for its own sake. At the conclusion to one of Nehama's essays, she too distances herself from the view of the *Sefer ha-Hinuch*, and the similarity to Yeshayahu's view on this matter becomes apparent. After asking:

> Are the observances of Judaism an end in themselves, with the organization of society and our own education and that of our children merely the means of attaining that end? Or perhaps the Divine precepts themselves constitute the means of improving the quality of our lives…? (*NSS*, 213–214)

she ends definitively:

> In Rashi's and Ibn Ezra's views, in contrast to that of Ibn Janah and Sefer ha-Hinukh, the Divine precepts are not just a means of education, influencing man's character through action, but they constitute an end in themselves as an example of service to God. Human and national life in all their aspects, political, cultural and economic, constitute the vehicles through which we may perform the will of the Creator: "The Lord brought us out of Egypt for one purpose only, to serve Him."[113]

Likewise, in Nehama's preface to her discussion of the commandment to send away the mother bird and take the eggs (Deuteronomy 22:7), she writes:

> We have on more than one occasion referred to the reasons for religious precepts advanced by our Sages. Research into these reasons does not necessarily promote observance. The loyal Jew obeys the behests of the Torah, irrespective of whether he understands the reasons behind them. (*SD*, 217)

She ends the essay with the same point, writing that irrespective of any reasons given for commandments, they must be accepted first and foremost

---

[110] See *NSS*, 496 n. 5; *SD*, 217–218; see also Frankel, *Iyun*, 156 and n. 105.
[111] See *NSS*, 180 and chapter 1 n. 39.
[112] See Rosenak, "*Parashat Mi-ketz*," 135.
[113] *NSS*, 214. The quote is from Ibn Ezra.

as an expression of God's will and observed in obedience to that will (*SD*, 221). Moreover, Nehama at times rejects the search for symbolic meaning:

> We are not to look for and ferret out its symbolism in the form of the bow, its color or physical characteristics to determine the connection between them and what it represents for us. It is the same as in the case of the *zizit*. We are not to look for its meaning in the number of its knots or threads. The text simply says: "Ye shall behold it and ye shall remember." (*NSB*, 87)

And in one place, she notes that *ta'amei ha-mitzvot* come and go, but the law remains unchanging.[114]

Thus it seems that Nehama was in two minds about this topic, positioned between an emphasis on practice and obedience that she shared with her brother, and her own strong affinity for connection and meaning, which she also tried to impart to others.

In light of his influence on her, it is surprising how little Nehama quotes Yeshayahu in her work, mentioning him only once in her *Studies* and never in her *gilyonot*.[115] Yeshayahu mentioned his sister often in conversation, but he too quotes her very little, if at all. Simon suggests that Yeshayahu did not read Nehama's studies, some of which were already published by the time he gave his radio talks, or at the very least bypassed them, not wanting to engage them directly. "I wonder if Nehama was upset at the fact that she never managed to impose upon her older, admired brother a measure of discipline in his interpretations," Simon remarks: "He does everything she fought against, with his superficial, hasty reading of the text. I also wonder if Yeshayahu was disappointed that he never influenced Nehama to fight zealously for her beliefs as he did" (*VLN*). This brings us directly to the next section.

Differences

Nehama and Yeshayahu differed in various ways. For example, Yeshayahu was more of an unmitigated rationalist, dismissing experiential aspects of religion, while Nehama was sensitive to emotional dimensions and disliked inflexible rationalism. Nehama's work was accessible and tailored for mass consumption by an intelligent lay population, while Yeshayahu, alongside his more popular work, also dealt with more demanding fields of study such as biochemistry and philosophy.[116] Nehama focused at an early point in her

---

[114] N. Leibowitz, *Darkei*, 8.
[115] See *NSV*, 350, n. 6 and Sokolow's *Mafte'ah* respectively.
[116] Sheleg, "*Kalat*," 70.

career on the area of Tanach at the expense of other interests such as the teaching of Hebrew language, history and essay writing. Yeshayahu, in contrast, maintained broad interests for many years. Nehama also believed that the Torah must pervade and encompass all aspects of life, while Yeshayahu, at least in theory, held religion to be completely separate from other areas of life such as science or morality.[117]

To those who knew them, the most outstanding personality distinction between them was the manner in which they went about making their impact on society. Simon marvels at the prescience of the Leibowitz parents who named their son after the great rebuker of the Jewish people, the prophet Isaiah, and then, as if to offer a measure of consolation, named their daughter Nehama.[118] Nehama was an optimistic, warm personality, drawn to the inspiring and adept at smoothing over clashing elements, while Yeshayahu, true to his namesake, was an uncompromising and unharmonious character. Like the thinker Albert Camus, he refused to surrender to the desire for the comforting or redemptive, remaining without illusions in his struggle.[119] Yeshayahu was a radical whose statements called for civil disobedience, if not outright sedition.[120] His sister, in contrast, believed in good citizenship as a Torah value. Yeshayahu delighted in iconoclastic and provocative statements made in high-profile settings, while Nehama fled the spotlight and avoided being seen as revolutionary, preferring to innovate quietly.[121] Yeshayahu's willingness to be interviewed anytime and in any media was matched only by Nehama's feelings of revulsion for the same. Although both were convinced of the rightness of their viewpoints, Yeshayahu was far more eager to engage in public debate over his ideas, and, unlike Nehama, was willing to permit a volume to be published in his honor within his lifetime.

Note, however, that it would not be correct to say that Nehama was more of a compromiser than Yeshayahu. They simply had different ideals. For example, for decades Nehama never relinquished her principle of staying within Israel's borders, zealously reprimanding others on this subject to the point of absurdity, while Yeshayahu did not feel strongly about this particular issue.

---

[117] See above, n. 41.

[118] Quoted in Sokolow, "Nehama Leibowitz: She taught Torah out of Love," *The Jerusalem Report*, May 15, 1997, 48. However, Simon adds that even the book of Isaiah itself has two parts: the chapters of rebuke and the chapters of consolation.

[119] Sagi, *Olamo*, 15.

[120] Naftali Rothenberg, *VLY* (4th session).

[121] Sheleg, "*Kalat*," 71.

The two siblings had real differences of opinion, which they aired articulately and at high decibels. Students recollect Yeshayahu's visit to Nehama during a lesson. They went into the kitchen, from whence could be heard a lot of loud talking. At one point, Nehama exclaimed emphatically: "That's not what we learned from our holy father!"[122] The disagreements began early. Nehama recounted that as very small children, Yeshayahu told her the story of the Maccabees. After the first battles, he informed her, Judah the Maccabee was left with three hundred people. He then asked: "Nehama, is that a lot or a little?" "It's a lot!" said Nehama. "No, it's a little!" shouted Yeshayahu, giving her a smack.[123] For the rest of her life, Nehama remembered that blow as her brother continued to "smack" everyone around him. Her great love and respect for him did not cancel out her deep-seated reservations about his standpoints. She once gave a lecture at a seminar for education officers in the IDF. Stepping off the dais, she noticed her brother in the audience awaiting his turn to speak, and said to him, "Shaya, don't undo everything I just did!"[124] But all her attempts to change his mind were to no avail.[125]

In public, Nehama mostly refused, even when goaded, to say anything negative about him, dismissing people's complaints in a lighthearted fashion. When Robert Bogen informed her that Yeshayahu had ejected him from his class for not understanding something, Nehama replied indulgently, "My brother's a mischievous child." To someone else she suggested: "Don't take his words seriously. This is only one side of him." And to some shocked acquaintances she said, "Look, we both received a Lithuanian education, so you have to expect contrary and headstrong opinions! This does not mean, though, that I agree with all his views." However, those close to her were privy to her genuine discontent. She recommended avoiding Yeshayahu's more injurious attitudes, advising Rahel Kossowsky: "If he's talking politics I wouldn't bother, but if it's on the Rambam then I highly recommend attending his lecture." However, she also cautioned Chana Rabinowitz: "Make sure you learn to differentiate between the Rambam and Shaya!"

A comparison between the siblings' published essays on the weekly Torah portion reveals that while the structure is similar – namely, quotes from the text and Jewish sources accompanied by discussion – the content differs. While Nehama stayed close by the text and its many interpreters, expressing

---

[122] Abramowitz, *Tales*, 65.
[123] Shalom Rosenberg, interview.
[124] Sheleg, "*Kalat*," 73.
[125] Michael Shashar, introduction to Y. Leibowitz, *Al olam*, 12.

her own ideas quite delicately, Yeshayahu was essentially a *darshan*, roaming far and wide and using the text as a platform for his own ideas, couched in hyperbolic language. At the end of seven years of radio talks, he clarified: "Make no mistake, I did not teach Torah. I did not intend to teach Torah. All these talks were simply my reflections on the weekly portion, to which I attached my own thoughts."[126] It is interesting that Yeshayahu the scientist was less rigorous when it came to the text. That was Nehama's science. In light of this, it is ironic that he felt that Nehama's work, though praiseworthy, was not true to the primary intention of the text, saying: "What Nehama does is first-rate, but irrelevant as far as the essence of the Tanach is concerned."[127] He also criticized her for not engaging directly with the text, observing: "She wants to know everything: What Rashi says, and what all the rest of the commentators say. Only one thing does not interest her: what the Tanach itself says."[128]

In their writings on the Tanach the Leibowitzes employed many sources, both Jewish and universal. But Yeshayahu ranges farther afield, even mentioning Jesus as part of his discussion.[129] Neither Yeshayahu nor Nehama granted importance to the historical background of the Tanach, but Yeshayahu was also uninterested in literary analysis of the text,[130] calling the Tanach

> at least in parts of it, second-rate literature, unable to compete with Sophocles, Shakespeare, Goethe or Pushkin.[131]

In their essays on the weekly Torah portion, Yeshayahu and Nehama are sometimes interested in entirely different topics. For example, in the portion of *Naso*, Yeshayahu ponders the nature of God's voice "speaking" to Moses while Nehama deals with robbery, the Nazirite and the priestly blessings.[132] This may be connected to the fact that Yeshayahu was more obviously a philosopher than Nehama – who, although she touched upon many profound issues, never studied philosophy to any great depth and claimed not to be conversant with such topics. Yeshayahu, on the other hand, was familiar with the classic philosophical sources. Names such as Plato, Socrates and Spinoza appear regularly in his studies of the Torah, and his thinking

---

[126] Y. Leibowitz, *Sheva shanim*, 955.
[127] Sheleg, *"Kalat,"* 73.
[128] Breuer, *"Yahasah,"* 11.
[129] Y. Leibowitz, *Accepting the Yoke of Heaven*, 150. True, Nehama alludes to Jesus in *LP*, 213 n. 7, but does not call him by name; and furthermore the context is one of discussion of Jewish-Christian polemic, not any interest in Jesus for his own sake.
[130] Hamiel, *"Moral"*; Saks, "Letters," 89.
[131] Y. Leibowitz, *Ratziti*, 116–117.
[132] Compare Y. Leibowitz, *Accepting*, 130–133 with *SBM*, 38–87; there is no overlap.

was greatly informed by Kant, whom he admired tremendously. Moreover, although he was known to claim that he had no overarching philosophy ("No one can pretend to possess a worldview, only a view on certain things in the world," he would state[133]), and never wrote a comprehensive outline, the recurrence of certain major themes makes it possible to draw up a philosophical outline of Yeshayahu's thought, even if its precise nuances are disputed to this day.[134] Nehama's philosophy, however, comes through less obviously, and needs to be carefully culled.[135] It proves to be almost entirely of a moral-ethical nature, as Professor Rivka Horwitz notes: "Philosophically, Nehama belonged to a generation that saw an ideal in building the land, in austerity, in good-heartedness, charity, and creating a new society in Israel. The philosophers she liked most concentrated on man and the notion of goodness. She did not want to delve into questions of who or what God is in His essence, but rather questions of this world and what God is in this world."

While Yeshayahu shared some of these values, his training and focus were different. His comments to the first verse of Genesis are instructive:

> The world is not God, and God is not in the world – God is beyond the world, beyond any reality to which man's concepts are bound, and beyond the needs and the interests which stem from man's existence in the world. Neither the world nor man is prime; God is not for the world, as with the Platonic Demiurge; and He is not for man. Rather, God is prime and the world (including man in it) is subordinate.[136]

Nehama never employed this kind of terminology or referred to such concepts. Contrast this with Nehama's opening essay to *Studies in Genesis*, which deals not with God or the world but with mankind, with the humanistic and moral themes in the verse "Let us make man"(Genesis 1:26):

> Every individual is equally significant before God, since every man was created in His image. (*NSB*, 3)

It is notable that Yeshayahu taught the exact opposite message – that "the image of God" reflects humankind's insignificance compared with the Divine.[137]

---

[133] Aviezer Ravitzky, "*Arachim u-reshamim*," in Sagi, *Olamo*, 17. Yeshayahu was justifying himself against Ravitzky's claim that his writings contained many contradictions.

[134] Professor Asa Kasher states that there has not been, and it seems will never be, a successful attempt at encompassing Yeshayahu's philosophy, or even the majority of it, for there are too many ambiguities and paradoxes (*VLY*).

[135] See introduction to chapter 16.

[136] Y. Leibowitz, *Accepting*, 14–15.

[137] See Harvey, "*Mekorotav*," 39–40.

When Nehama did discuss the nature of God, as she did infrequently, we see a different conception from that of her brother. Yeshayahu believed that the encounter with God takes place only through deeds, through Halachah.[138] God, being transcendent, cannot be discussed using any ordinary categories – is indeed not an object of religious thought at all, only an object of worship:[139]

> A God who can be known through history or nature is a very inferior God indeed – in truth, he is not a real God at all, but rather an accessory to one's thought or feelings.[140]

Though Nehama too did not believe God to be knowable, she would not concede the God-as-object of her brother, instead teaching God-as-subject, an immanent God of relationship. She did not reject the idea of God's transcendence, but rather felt it to be an incomplete portrait:

> God's transcendence does not contradict His immanence. He is both far (not a part of the world in contradistinction to heathen conceptions) and near, not indifferent to human welfare but involved in giving the world He created for His glory, direction. (NSS, 575)

Nehama's preference for the interventionist, relational view of God, in the footsteps of Halevi, Rashi, Ramban and others, comes through clearly.[141] She writes:

> Halevi, unlike Ibn Ezra, teaches us that metaphysical conceptions of God are a poor substitute for the real thing and are designed for those who are incapable of rising to the level of faith. (NSS, 309–310)

The mysterious *Ehyeh* name of God represents the involved, caring God:

> Ramban also rejected the sophisticated "philosophic" explanation that might elude the grasp of his readers of God's "continuous being," choosing the intimate homely exposition of His passionate concern for His creatures, of His sharing their suffering and "being with them." (NSS, 131, n. 6)

---

[138] Shalom Rosenberg, "*Paradoxim ve-emunah be-mishnato shel Yeshayahu Leibowitz*," *Limmudim*, 102.

[139] Avi Sagi, "Yeshayahu Leibowitz – a Breakthrough in Jewish Philosophy: Religion without Metaphysics," *Religious Studies* (33): 1997, 204. See also *Ratziti*, 17 and 53.

[140] Y. Leibowitz, *Ratziti*, 103.

[141] NSS, 309–310. Frankel even suggests that Nehama adopted Halevi's approach positing that God's revelation through history, and specifically to the Jewish people, is the fundamental premise of Judaism (*Iyun*, 92). Yeshayahu was not partial to Halevi's philosophy. See, for example, in his books *The Faith of Maimonides* (Tel Aviv, 1989), 48, and *Judaism*, 120 (thanks to Paul Widen for these references).

She continues this thought by informing us that Moses Mendelssohn renders God's name in a philosophical, transcendent way, too remote from his readers' experience, while

> Rashi, Ramban and others… understand *ehyeh asher ehyeh* in terms of God's providence rather than His existence. (*NSS*, 131, n. 6)

In discussing the topic of revelation, she begins with a philosophical postulate that seems somewhat distancing, though not as much as Yeshayahu's:

> We cannot perceive the actual essence of the Godhead… only through His manifestations in the world, through His deeds as they impinge on us. (*NSS*, 133)

However, she then segues into God's relationship with the Patriarchs and the topic of Divine Providence. She was a proponent of recognizing God's hand in history, including modern Israeli history,[142] whereas Yeshayahu attributed no religious significance to historical events, but only to the meaning created by the religious consciousness of the participants.[143] He writes:

> And if you perceive our victory in the Six Day War as the action of "Divine providence" then you must perceive it also in the deaths by choking and burning of 1.5 million Jewish children. There is nothing more mindless or presumptuous than to lug out the "Divine Providence" card from one's pocket when it's convenient, yet not to when it isn't.[144]

In her childhood, Nehama's father had rejected her theory that she was struck by a tram as punishment for skipping her prayers.[145] This paternal outlook expressed at such an impressionable age might have been expected to influence Nehama greatly. Yet we find it more prevalent in Yeshayahu's thought, for instance:

---

[142] See Frankel's comments in *Iyun*, 119.

[143] Avi Sagi, "Yeshayahu Leibowitz – a Breakthrough in Jewish Philosophy: Religion without Metaphysics," *Religious Studies* (33) 1997: 207.

[144] Y. Leibowitz, *Ratziti*, 224 and see Y. Leibowitz, *Al olam*, 97. For another example, see Y. Leibowitz, *"Nissim."* Yeshayahu followed Maimonides's definition of Divine Providence: that it refers not to God's knowledge of humans but rather to human knowledge of God. Nevertheless, he admitted, "I know that millions of Jews understand this differently" (Y. Leibowitz, *Al olam*, 97).

[145] See page 26 above.

Belief in God is not belief in Divine intervention in the world's workings and in humanity's destiny.[146]

Nehama disagreed entirely, believing the relational God to be the one emerging from a close reading of the Torah:

> Moses did not speak of the nature of God, of His being the immanent or transcendent cause of the world... but of God's relationship to Israel. (*SD*, 402)

Nehama taught that this conception had been distorted by later philosophers:

> Followers of the Rambam, in their attempts to eradicate all traces of anthropomorphism from the biblical text, tended to dull the sense of Divine immanence and transform the Jewish religion into a remote mechanical monotheism. (*NSS*, 357)

We can only speculate if by "followers of the Rambam" Nehama was also referring to her brother, critiquing his religious life. It is intriguing to imagine her polemicizing with him in the pages of her *Studies*. At the very least, these words serve to encapsulate the gulf between them.

The bottom line is that Nehama's more traditional religious outlook entailed belief in a compassionate, involved God, and she herself may have yearned to sense the Divine presence in her life.[147] For Yeshayahu, on the other hand, the Divine presence was expressed solely through the commandments, when carried out as an act of worship of God. Hence, his own religious emphasis was on praxis. This dichotomy fits in with the final words of R. Haym Soloveitchik's essay, "Rupture and Reconstruction: The Transformation of Contemporary Orthodoxy," regarding religious-experiential shifts in Jews of modern times. He writes:

> Having lost the touch of His presence, they seek now solace in the pressure of His yoke.[148]

Importing these words into our context, it appears that Nehama would be unhappy about such developments, while her brother would be gratified at the shift towards what he had proposed all along.[149]

---

[146] Y. Leibowitz, *Ratziti*, 221. For more discussion see Daniel Statman, "Negative Theology and the Meaning of the Commandments in Modern Orthodoxy," *Tradition* 39/1 (2005): 63.

[147] See page 380 above.

[148] *Tradition* 28 (1994): 103. Interestingly, both Nehama and Yeshayahu are credited in Soloveitchik's acknowledgments.

[149] Soloveitchik writes there: "Zealous to continue traditional Judaism unimpaired, religious Jews seek to ground their new emerging spirituality less on a now unattainable intimacy with Him than on an intimacy with His Will" (103). Daniel Statman suggests

≥∂ ≈∂

Nehama also diverged greatly from Yeshayahu in her affinity for Rabbi A.I. Kook. In one essay, she brings a recommendation typical of Yeshayahu's thinking, concerning

> our duty to accept the yoke of His commandments... based on the belief that He made us and we are His. (*NSV*, 515)

However, she moves on from this message, preferring to conclude the essay with a thought of R. Kook's, who

> sees a means of purifying the soul and of uncovering and activating the Divine treasure which dwells in the soul of the nation. (*NSV*, 522)

Her atypical final remark,

> Nothing more need be added to his words,

indicates her esteem for R. Kook.[150] She was drawn to his poetic brand of spiritual-mystical religion, though she felt incapable of entirely plumbing its depths:

> It is difficult indeed to catch the full flavor of Rabbi Kook's highly figurative style, charged with a deep mystical content, elusive and allusive. (*SD*, 313)

When it came to certain fundamental matters, Yeshayahu was the antithesis of R. Kook. They met in 1929, when Yeshayahu sat in the rabbi's *sukkah*, talking with him for many hours. "I immediately perceived that I was in the presence of a great man," Yeshayahu recalled, "but one whose world was exceedingly foreign to me, and even invalid from a faith perspective."[151] Yeshayahu's philosophy may even have developed partly as a reaction to what R. Kook and his son, R. Zvi Yehudah Kook, taught.[152] He did not subscribe, as his sister did, to R. Kook's evolutionary model of human

---

that in fact modern Jewry, uncomfortable with definitive statements about God and meaning, is essentially Leibowitzian. This would imply that Yeshayahu is not radical but, on the contrary, an accurate reflection of his time, expressing – at least in philosophical terms – the *zeitgeist* of contemporary Orthodoxy. Under other circumstances, Statman argues, he might even have become its spokesperson (*VLY* and "Negative Theology etc." [full ref. n. 146 above], 71).

[150] She ends again with R. Kook in *NSV*, 543, as well as quoting him several times elsewhere in her work (describing his comments as "profound" – see *NSV*, 43); and particularly regarding the issue of vegetarianism (see page 129 above).

[151] Y. Leibowitz, *Al olam*, 93.

[152] Ravitzky, *VLY*. He emphasizes that this is only speculation, but notes that Yeshayahu became more extreme in his later years, when R. Zvi Yehudah Kook became dominant in shaping the political opinion of many. Ravitzky's lecture is entitled, "Yeshayahu Leibowitz: Antithesis of Rabbi A.I. Kook?"

progress or to his beliefs in Divine sparks existing within heresy and idol worship. Yeshayahu believed that R. Kook's viewpoint had lamentable political consequences, for he "sought and found holiness in the very existence of the Jewish people and thereby led his disciples astray."[153] Here, the two were opposites – Yeshayahu reduced the holy to God alone, while R. Kook expanded the notion of the holy to include all of existence. As an illustration, Professor Aviezer Ravitzky tells of the time he remarked to Yeshayahu, "I wonder how R. Kook made *havdalah*, how he could say the sentence, 'He who makes a distinction between the holy and the mundane.'" Yeshayahu smiled, but prematurely, for Ravitzky then continued, "In your case, of course, it is difficult to understand how you can make Kiddush and say, 'He who makes Israel and the seasons holy'!" (*VLN*)

At least partially due to his rejection of this philosophy, Yeshayahu's brand of religious Zionism differed from that of many of his contemporaries, including his sister. He felt that the connection of religion and state would ultimately lead to the corruption of Judaism. For him, the institution of the Chief Rabbinate was an enfeebled one, the result of the effects of prolonged Diaspora Judaism upon the halachic process.[154] It was "one of the most contemptible institutions in the history of the Jewish people," entwined with bureaucracy and politics and "a prostitution of religion, destruction of the Torah and desecration of God."[155] He refused to lend his name to a letter inviting R. Soloveitchik to become the Chief Rabbi of Israel, claiming that it constituted a violation of the injunction: "Do not place a stumbling block before the blind."[156] He decried the religious establishment's attitude towards women, writing to one of Nehama's students:

> Your problem (like most of your friends in the National Religious camp) is that you do not understand – or try not to understand – the deep crisis among religious Jews today. You don't feel at all the contradiction between your involvement with Nehama's "enterprise" and your obsequious prostrations to the rabbis who distance women from Torah and Torah study and even negate the value of learning from a woman.[157]

In general, Yeshayahu rejected any value in women voluntarily fulfilling those mitzvot that are traditionally performed by men, for the entire significance of mitzvot derives from their being commanded. He compared

---

[153] Y. Leibowitz, *Accepting*, 144.
[154] Goldman, "*Ma hayav*," 11.
[155] Leviticus 19:14. See Y. Leibowitz, *Ratziti*, 364.
[156] Y. Leibowitz, *Ratziti*, 364; see Saks, "Letters," 90.
[157] Y. Leibowitz, *Ratziti*, 483, translated by Saks, "Letters," 92–93, n. 2.

this to a layman desiring to accept upon himself a priest's restrictions regarding contact with the dead. But the act of learning Torah fell into a different category altogether, as a basic Jewish right.[158] Barring women from this most important spiritual activity was unjust. Even if it was socially dictated, Halachah did not require it. While Nehama also considered Torah learning a basic right for women, Yeshayahu went further, calling for religious legislation to change women's status in the public and political spheres so that they could participate more fully in religious culture. He felt that the failure to deal with this issue properly could endanger the entire future of Judaism.[159]

Nehama argued with her brother on questions of religion and state. She chided: "It's easy for you to talk because we had a father who could afford to hire private tutors for us. But if religion and state are separated, who will pay for the religious education of children from disadvantaged homes?" Yeshayahu replied: "If the sizable affluent sector of religious Jewry can't provide religious education for all, then it has no right to exist."[160]

Nehama also did not share Yeshayahu's views regarding the occupation of Judea, Samaria and Gaza. Though opposed to conquest,[161] she did not feel that Zionism fell into that category. It was not a form of colonialism or chauvinism, for the land of Israel was a Divine gift and therefore belonged to the Jews, as any land belonged to the people whom God had settled there.[162] The phrase "Judeo-Nazis" caused her great pain and she begged

---

[158] Y. Leibowitz, "The Status of Women," in Y. Leibowitz, *Judaism*, 128–129.

[159] Y. Leibowitz, "The Status of Women," in Y. Leibowitz, *Judaism*, 128. For the contradictions inherent in his approach towards women's Torah learning, see lecture by Avinoam Rosenak, *VLY*.

[160] Y. Leibowitz, *Al olam*, 86–87.

[161] See *Teacher's Guide* to *Matot-Masei* 5716: "How important is the Ramban's emphasis here against imperialistic ambitions to conquer lands that are not ours."

[162] See *Teacher's Guide* to *Matot-Masei* 5716. "That God did not only give this people its land, but being the Lord of the World, He led every nation from its previous dwelling-place to its land of inhabitance." When we read her essay on "Abraham and Lot" (*NSB*, 121–128) it is evident that Nehama was more concerned with the issue of robbery than of occupation. Lot's wicked shepherds assume that the land is theirs by right. Abraham's shepherds, in contrast, know that while this would constitute stealing at this moment, after it would fall into the Israelites' possession (as the Midrash says, "when I drive out the Canaanite and the Perizzite from its midst") settling the territory would not, by implication, be morally wrong. However, Schoneveld feels that Nehama is reticent about discussing the motif of the promised land in the *Akedah*, "as if she fears a nationalistic and chauvinistic misuse of the promise of the land" (*The Bible*, 166). See also chapter 6 n. 17; and for more on her attitude toward Zionism see chapter 13.

him not to put it into print, but to no avail.[163] For months afterwards, this phrase was practically her only topic of conversation. Professor Chana Safrai recalls it as the only time she had ever seen Nehama in a bad mood and lacking her usual buoyancy – though she never let her teaching suffer from it.

Nehama did not lack sensitivity to the moral problematics of killing other peoples.[164] In fact, although Yeshayahu is usually seen as the great moralist of the two, Professor Warren Zev Harvey disagrees (*VLN*): "Yeshayahu had a political relativistic ethics, whereas Nehama had a deontic [pertaining to duty and obligation], almost Kantian, ethic." He cites an article written by Yeshayahu in 1953 after a series of terrorist incidents led to Israeli retaliations against the Arab village of Kibiya, with many civilian casualties. Entitled "After Kibiya," the critical tone in the article foreshadowed his reaction to events after the Six Day War. He called the Israeli actions "justified but cursed," saying, "we *could* justify it, but let us not justify it!"[165] As support for his position, he cited the biblical story of Simeon and Levi's massacre of the residents of Shechem, an act that though it had valid reasons[166] led their father to curse them (Genesis 49:7):

> Cursed be their anger, for it was fierce; and their wrath, for it was cruel;
> I will divide them in Jacob, and scatter them in Israel.

But whereas Yeshayahu was theoretically willing to justify the brothers' act, Nehama was adamantly opposed to any such thing, notes Harvey. No matter how successful Simeon and Levi's tactic proved, it was still not morally justified or Divinely approved, she asserted, taking a stand against some major commentators.[167] Nehama maintained her opinion despite the

---

[163] Sheleg, "*Kalat*," 73, quoting Shashar, referring to its being printed in Y. Leibowitz, *Al olam u-melo'o: sichot im Michael Shashar.*

[164] See her column in *Yediot Ahronot* on the weekly portion of *Va-yishlach*, November 29, 1990, reprinted in *PN*, 526–527, on "And Jacob was afraid." However in her *Studies* on this portion, this issue is relegated to a question at the end of the essay (356); why she does not choose to feature it more prominently is unclear.

[165] Harvey, *VLN*, and see also his lecture at *VLY*. "After Kibiya" was published in *Be-terem*, 1953/1954, and republished in *Torah u-mitzvot ba-zeman ha-zeh* (Tel Aviv: Masada, 5714) and a third time in *Yahadut, Am Yehudi u-Medinat Yisrael* (Schocken, 1975). It may be read in translation in Y. Leibowitz, *Judaism*, 185–190. Yeshayahu blamed the Kibiya incident on the erroneous attribution of holiness to the State, granting legitimacy to immoral actions. The disputations about the incident spread to the pages of Britain's *Jewish Chronicle* (December 1953).

[166] See Genesis 34:31: "Should he treat our sister like a harlot?"

[167] See pages 347–349 above for more discussion. Note however a different tack in *NSB*, 545, where she suggests that these zealous qualities would prove vital in the future

existence in the story of real grounds for complaint. After all, Jacob and his family are manipulated by the Shechemites, which Nehama found very upsetting, echoing as it did the repeated experience of the Jews in foreign lands:

> This was how it always ended. The stranger came, toiled and accumulated wealth which ultimately reverted to his hosts.[168]

Nonetheless, she refused to condone in any way the murder of the Shechemites, even as a deterrent or in self-defense. Erella Yedgar feels that Nehama's essay on this incident is particularly revealing. She suggests: "Nehama had a subtle political agenda here, as hinted by her use of the word 'retaliation' and by her addition of the phrase 'women and children' where the text does not mention them, to indicate her opposition to such retaliatory actions as Kibiya."[169]

Nehama also insisted powerfully – possibly even more than Yeshayahu in certain cases – on individual responsibility. She writes:

> A person is no speck of dust or cog in a machine, but is created in the image of God, responsible for his every action,[170]

while Yeshayahu felt that Eichmann's trial had been mishandled because

> he was a small, worthless cog in a larger system... a product of 2000 years of Christian history, whose entire *raison d'être* was the destruction of the Jews.[171]

Thus, though some might believe Yeshayahu to be the greater moralist, we have seen instances where Nehama took the more uncompromising view. More research is needed on this subject.

Comparisons, juxtapositions and continuations

The fields of Yeshayahu and Nehama's intellectual activity only partly overlapped. Had they not been related, they would probably have not invited much comparison, except inasmuch as they both wrote on the weekly Torah portion at roughly the same time. However, the fact of their being siblings explains why they have been repeatedly (though not systematically) compared, contrasted and brought together in diverse contexts. At times this comparison has been used somewhat ignobly, for the purpose of

---

exile – though she also ends her essay with two equally presented views, implying that she was undecided on this point.

[168] *NSB*, 384. See Yedgar, "*Parashat va-yishlach*," 109.

[169] Yedgar, interview, relating to what Nehama writes in *NSB*, 380. See also Yedgar, "*Parashat va-yishlach*," 104.

[170] Combination of *IBB*, 125 and *NSB*, 175.

[171] Y. Leibowitz, *Al olam*, 79.

highlighting shortcomings in the other – primarily by sectors of religious society who would juxtapose Yeshayahu unfavorably with his sister in order to accentuate his more controversial traits.[172] On the positive end of the spectrum, however, their ideas have been brought into fruitful dialogue with each other. Some have examined their thoughts on the same topic – for instance, Professor Michael Rosenak, who compares their words side by side on the weekly Torah portion of *Mi-ketz*.[173]

Joint conferences have been organized around the Leibowitz siblings, and a volume by the name of *Limmudim* containing articles about their respective work has been published. They were also memorialized by the inauguration of the Nehama and Yeshayahu Leibowitz prize, awarded first to Adam Baruch, and then to Ari and R. Mordechai Elon at the Kfar Blum Judaism festival.[174]

Today, Yeshayahu's work is still making waves. A generation of Israeli intellectuals, including prominent professors, continues to develop and discuss his thought. Many of his followers are politically left-wing, although Yeshayahu was often critical of the left's leaders and it is questionable how many in this camp truly understand his ideological outlook and its religious roots. Certain segments of the younger religious population in Israel have also re-embraced his thought in reaction to strong right-wing messianic currents in their communities. The adjective "Leibowitzian" has entered the lexicon of Jewish philosophical discourse, and today we can speak of "neo-Leibowitzians" who have developed Yeshayahu's thought in new directions.[175] But can the same be said of Nehama? This will be discussed in our final chapter.

---

[172] Reportedly, someone said, "There's only one good thing about Leibowitz: Nehama!" A newspaper columnist urged: "If this year indeed has to be 'Leibowitz Year,' as some have proclaimed, then it should be the year of Nehama, rather than of Yeshayahu" (Moshe Kohn, "An Oscar for Leibowitz," *Jerusalem Post*, January 29, 1993, 8.)

[173] Rosenak, *"Parashat Mi-ketz."*

[174] The prize was awarded by the Shorashim Institute. Adam Baruch, author of the *Shishi* column in *Maariv*, received it on December 17, 1998. His mother had studied with Nehama in her youth. His acceptance speech appears in *Limmudim* 1, 113–118. The second prize was awarded on July 4, 2000.

[175] Shalom Rosenberg cites Asa Kasher as an example, but suggests that Kasher has undertaken a significant deviation from Yeshayahu's approach (*"Paradoxim ve-emunah be-mishnato shel Yeshayahu Leibowitz,"* Limmudim, 93–94).

PART V

LOOKING TO THE FUTURE

Nehama Leibowitz. Courtesy of the artist, Dvir Derovan.

CHAPTER 24

TODAY'S WORLD AND TOMORROW'S:
NEHAMA'S TORAH INTO THE
TWENTY-FIRST CENTURY

> One must not regale oneself in pomp for that which belongs to
> the past; it is superseded by the present mitzvah that each day
> bids us observe. (Nehama Leibowitz, *New Studies in Vayikra*, 69)

THE FINAL REMAINING CHALLENGE is to understand where Nehama's work
fits in with current trends and, without undervaluing her achievements, to
provide a platform for a discussion of her work's future.

Today more than ever, with countless competing stimuli from the media
and the Internet, the educational challenge is how to prevent all the bar- and
bat-mitzvah gifts of Torah books from gathering dust in the bookcase. New
generations of young Jews must be shown how these books speak their
language so that they will come to open them on their own, with genuine
excitement; otherwise, the future of Jewish education is bleak.

So where does Nehama's Torah fit in? Fashioned as it was in the
cauldron of the twentieth century, does it have what it takes to speak to the
twenty-first? Or is Nehama, to borrow the words of Batya Gur, "one of the
last giants of the old world"?[1] The following remarks will attempt to answer
this question, focusing primarily on the Israeli scene, though the conclusions
may well be equally valid elsewhere. It will include observations by many
experts, as well this author's own suggestions.[2] But the facts will be at the
disposal of the readers so that they may make their own judgment. We begin
with a survey of recent changes within Tanach study and education.

---

[1] For full quote see pages 209–210 above.

[2] Several of the interviewees mentioned in this chapter also read it over and commented,
which contributed greatly to its accuracy. However, since there was disagreement as to
the true nature of the developments described here, particularly the extent of R. Bin-
Nun's influence, I have chosen to present the facts in as balanced a way as possible and
hope that any disagreements will serve to spark fruitful dialogue amongst educators and
scholars. The reader is also referred to the Hebrew Wikipedia entry *Mahapechat ha-
Tanakh*, and to Hayyim J. Angel, "*Torat Hashem Temima*: The Contributions of Rav Yoel
Bin Nun to Religious Tanakh Study," *Tradition* 40/3 (Fall 2007): 5–18.

New Orthodox approaches to Tanach

Without a doubt, Nehama advanced the study of Tanach tremendously, especially within the Orthodox community. No one before her had made a science of analyzing the commentaries or had invited the student to join in a discussion spanning two millennia – and as an equal to boot. Her work had enormous repercussions for women, both in the role model she provided of a woman scholar and (arguably) the first Jewish woman commentator; and also in providing a non-talmudic corpus for study and inspiration upon which Jewish women could establish their spiritual lives. She also legitimized the Tanach as an alternative central Jewish text for men. This represented a major shift in a male world that revolved almost entirely around the Talmud, and it might have been expected to cause more discomfort than it ultimately did. Perhaps the resemblance of Nehama's method to talmudic debate, as well as her respectful citations from Talmud and Halachah, made yeshivah students feel more comfortable and unaware of the shift taking place. The problematics of Talmud study as the sole focus of male Jewish learning remains controversial to this day, and is discussed passionately in certain educational circles;[3] and yet Nehama's contribution to this shift is not often mentioned.[4]

In brief, Nehama set the ball rolling for high-level Judaism-based study of Tanach by both men and women. What followed in traditional Jewish Tanach study – for example, its substantial expansion within the more modern yeshivah world – owed much to her work, with rabbis specializing in Tanach and developing new approaches. However, these new directions have also moved away from Nehama's work, influenced by the secular academic world and other factors.

In this context, the revolutionary method of R. Yoel Bin-Nun is particularly notable. Catalyzed by insights of R. Zvi Yehudah Kook, R. Bin-Nun's method diverged from Nehama's on several fronts: Firstly, it demanded a hearing for Tanach at face value and without commentaries (at least initially), as part of a strong return to the *peshat*. In addition, where Nehama was concerned with the micro, Bin-Nun focused on the macro, examining broad strokes, structures and processes throughout Tanach, not just small units as Nehama did for the most part. Finally, it also emphasized realia – the historical, archeological, anthropological, geographical, zoological

---

[3] See articles at www.atid.org/journal/Talmud.asp.

[4] Ya'akov Beasley tries to rectify this wrong, writing: "Many people would crown Nechama Leibowitz, not Yehoshua Bachrach, as the founder of the new methodology of Bible studies," in "Of Fainting Maidens and Wells: Bible Study in the Yeshiva Curriculum: A Halachic, Historical, and Ideological Overview" (www.atid.org/journal/journal98/beasley.doc).

and botanical dimensions of Tanach, synthesizing this kind of study into traditional Tanach learning.

This new approach, and others influenced by it, have been characterized as "The Torah of the Land of Israel," in contrast with "The Torah of the Diaspora." During the long period of Jewish exile and dispersion, stories of kings and wars seemed far removed from Jewish life and were little studied. The secular Zionists were the first to re-embrace such narratives, causing the religious world to be wary of reclaiming its own sacred stories, until the emergence of a new religious Israeli identity, whose focused shifted to "The Torah of the Land of Israel."

Nehama, though undeniably Zionist, reached her prime too early for this rejuvenation (although she was very likely one of the people who made it possible). It was only in the late 1970s that religious Israelis felt comfortable enough to move beyond the traditional and familiar, and beyond even Nehama's innovations, to entirely new ways of looking at the Tanach. These new approaches made their earliest inroads within post high school religious education. Building on the work of others,[5] R. Bin-Nun led the way to a wider movement in his then-hometown of Ofra and at Herzog College, whose association with the highly esteemed Har Etzion yeshivah provided a solid platform for the launch of these revolutionary endeavors. From R. Bin-Nun and his student/colleague, R. Yaakov Meidan, hundreds of students learned the new approaches, in turn importing them to other institutions and forums. Concurrently, other Orthodox scholars and teachers, even those not directly influenced by R. Bin-Nun, were moving in the same direction – the general direction of the broader academic world. The return to direct engagement with Tanach text, the historical approach, and the use of realia gained greatly in popularity in these circles. Tanach-based hiking increased as part of the new awareness, and many articles on related subjects appeared, especially in the Herzog College's journal *Megadim*.

Nehama knew of R. Bin-Nun's work and praised portions of it.[6] However, he also recalls disputing a number of times with her (he notes wryly, "She would say 'I don't understand' which meant 'I don't approve'!"). In true Nehama style, these debates took place not in auditoriums or on the pages of a journal, but in taxis on the way to Gush Etzion. They argued over specific verses and about pedagogy in general, she asserting that students forget everything except skills, while he countered that no one forgets

---

[5] Such as Rabbis Mordechai Breuer, Hanan Porat, Yeshayahu Hadari and Yehudah Shaviv, and Professor Yehudah Elitzur in the field of realia (Cherlow, 10).

[6] For example, his work on the particular meaning of the Tetragrammaton, about which Nehama said, "All teachers have to teach this one" (Bin-Nun, interview). See "*Havaya pe'ila ve-kiyumit ba-mikra*" in *Megadim* 5 [5748]. See also Cherlow, 20.

beloved songs, so if the Torah is learned melodically, through cantillation (following its own reference to itself as a "song" in Deuteronomy 31:19), it will be remembered. "At any rate, that was how I learned it!" he informed her.

R. Bin-Nun reports gaining insights from these conversations. Perhaps they also affected Nehama, for about six months before her death, she astonished Erella Yedgar by saying: "I hear that Rabbi Bin-Nun and Professor Elitzur go out into the field and that it really boosts the understanding of the text. You know, I was always opposed to these methods, but I think now that the real reason was because I didn't know how to do them properly! People create all these elaborate pedagogical theories simply due to their own ignorance." Notwithstanding, for most of her life she represented the polar opposite to these new methods; and, some suggest, was responsible for significantly impeding the development of unmediated Tanach study in Israel.[7]

∾ ∿

Today, while R. Bin-Nun's method still arouses controversy from time to time,[8] it is relatively well-established. Every summer, Herzog College hosts a popular three-day Tanach seminar in which ideas may be showcased, many of them in the new directions. This program inspired a similar one in the USA, which was established by R. Nathaniel Helfgot. R. Menahem Leibtag has also exposed thousands of English-speakers to the new approaches through his weekly essays on the Internet. Rabbi Dr. Yonatan Grossman, a young scholar from Bar-Ilan University's Bible department, who has taught for the past decade at the Herzog College, reports that R. Bin-Nun's approach has been highly influential on the new generation of scholars and students in national-religious circles. It has affected, at least indirectly, even those who view themselves as entirely independent, or who self-identify with a different school of thought, such as Nehama's.

Those who subscribe to these new developments view Nehama's work as old-school. Despite what she wrote in her methodological articles or what her students might claim to the contrary, they believe that her method insufficiently engages the Tanach text and gives too much credit to the commentators, thus interfering with the search for the best *peshat*. It is therefore not considered as valuable as it once was. Grossman: "I still send my students to Nehama's books, for there is much to be gained from them in terms of method. But her work can only give partial answers to today's students, and so its popularity has lessened over time." For many

---

[7] Cherlow, 8, 12.
[8] Cherlow, 27.

contemporary scholars, especially in more academic frameworks, Nehama does not confront biblical criticism enough to be useful for them. She was daring for her time, citing such non-Orthodox figures as Benno Jacob and Buber. However, the work of R. Mordechai Breuer, which R. Bin-Nun adopted, though with some major differences, has changed the way the Tanach is viewed, going much further than Nehama did.[9]

Professor Israel Rozenson, head of Efrata College (formerly the Mizrachi seminary), a religious teacher-training college for women that had close ties to Nehama, believes that her method can be detrimental to the study of Tanach when it is used exclusively. Rather, it should appear in conjunction with approaches that are its polar opposite. He personally is drawn to such approaches precisely for their contrast to Nehama's method: "I have been built dialectically through Nehama by disagreeing with her. There were many times when I asked myself what Nehama Leibowitz would have said and then set out to say the opposite." Rozenson is aware that Nehama had serious reservations regarding his work, but he is convinced that other approaches should be given their due, and particularly that of R. Bin-Nun.

ə» «ə

Thus, a crucial complement and serious alternative arose to the predominant Nehama-based approach within religious Tanach education. R. Bin-Nun's approach succeeded in capturing much of the post–high-school religious system; while the matriculation examination – and hence the majority of the curriculum in the religious high schools – firmly remains Nehama territory, consisting primarily of analyzing commentaries, with some searching for key words, themes and motifs. The only exception is the *bekiut* unit, testing the command of large amounts of material.

From the outset, Nehama's method was deemed useful for the matriculation examinations, for with its clear questions and answers it, lent itself to easy grading. But in the process of adaptation for the matriculation examination's format, it became reduced to a repetitive formula of "What does this commentator say and what does that commentator say?" This was against Nehama's most basic educational principles. Professor Moshe Ahrend insists: "The matriculation exam is based on a substandard imitation of Nehama's method. Students have to repeat mechanically what each commentator said. The goal has become to impart information through memorization, when Nehama's aim was the exact opposite." The tedious, one-dimensional experience of Tanach study that resulted has continued unchanged more or less until this day, to the great frustration of some.

---

[9] See Cherlow, 23–24.

Rozenson, for example, attempted to introduce written papers as part of the grade, creating a more direct and personal encounter with the text, but met with only limited approval. In the meantime, the non-religious educational stream, though far from perfect, had gone on to encompass in its curriculum the study of archeology, history, and literature, as well as topics such as leadership in the Bible and women in the Bible, and also findings from research articles.

At one point, R. Bin-Nun was offered the position of supervisor of the religious high-school Tanach study unit. His dream was to expand the curriculum, broadening the students' horizons and heightening interest in Tanach. He planned to preserve Nehama's methodology, with focus on skills and traditional interpretations, for half of the material. The other half would be taught according to topics, not the textual units Nehama favored, and would be multi-disciplinary, including history, geography and interconnections with Jewish philosophy. He also proposed to set up a National Center for Tanach Instruction.

The Minister of Education, Zevulun Hammer, was willing to provide the budget, but the plan met with strong opposition from Nehama and others, many of them her students.[10] The emergence of these two factions surrounding himself and Nehama pained R. Bin-Nun greatly. He felt that the Religious Education Authority was using Nehama's reputation to appear open-minded and forward-looking, while in practice resisting innovations. To his great disappointment, the plan was eventually shelved and he never took up the position, instead channeling his ideas into the new pedagogical Tanach center at the Herzog College. Rozenson, working alongside R. Bin-Nun in the 1980s to promote more integrative teaching, saw it as a wasted opportunity. "This entire topic is a painful one. We did it in all innocence. We weren't trying to come out against the Nehama method but, on the contrary, to broaden its impact, to take certain marginalized elements of her approach and bring them to the fore, such as her literary analysis."

Rozenson himself had pulled away from the mainstream educational system, which seemed to imbue Nehama's work with unassailable authority and suppress any dissenting voices. He recounts: "In my early career, I was one of two supervisors present at a teacher-assessment test. The other supervisor, my senior, was a student of Nehama's. We watched the young teacher-in-training presenting a lesson on the Joseph story. He pointed out where the story's events took place on the map, and the locations of Joseph, Jacob and the brothers. To me his work seemed very good, but my partner

---

[10] Fierce opposition to the new approaches in general was expressed by other conservative elements, unaffiliated with Nehama – notably R. Zvi Thau of Yeshivat Har ha-Mor. See Angel's article *Torat Hashem* etc. (full ref. in n. 2 above).

reprimanded him: 'In a lesson of only fifty minutes, a lengthy introduction on the map of events is a complete waste of time!'" Rozenson found this incident disturbing; and he later published an article arguing that maps are important even in literary analysis and can lead to interesting philosophical conclusions.[11]

However, although he spent his life resisting Nehama's approach, Rozenson mentions her twice in his book on *Bamidbar* and was delighted to write an article in the memorial volume, *Pirkei Nehama*, for he recognized her vast contribution to Jewish intellectual life. "The feeling of immense admiration we all had for her makes this happen," he says. This fact reflects positively on the atmosphere of open debate surrounding Nehama's work. R. Bin-Nun, too, always venerated Nehama's moral integrity and humility. He is convinced that Nehama's intention was "*le-shem shamayim*," untainted by political considerations of any kind. She genuinely believed that her methods were the best ones. At Nehama's funeral, when someone asked him if he forgave her, he replied unhesitatingly in the affirmative.

The result of all these developments is that teachers today have a wider range of approaches from which to choose. Rami Yannai, a teacher at Herzog College who studied with both Nehama and R. Bin-Nun, finds it beneficial to have both Nehama's methods and several others at his disposal. He says that the key for contemporary Tanach teachers is to employ a discerning mix in the classroom so that students are stimulated and receive the broadest picture. The teachers at the Efrata College also profess eclectic approaches. They strongly emphasize close reading and some reader autonomy as Nehama did, but differ from her in locating each commentator firmly within his historical period. Rozenson stresses the importance of this difference.

> My fear, after speaking to scores of teachers and students, is that the combination of Nehama Leibowitz's incredible authority and the manner in which she presented Rashi and the Midrashim, will create in the students' minds an image of a superior commentator who rises above the historical contingencies of his time and who... to all appearances successfully reads the text's intention.[12]

---

[11] "*Va-yishlachehu me-emek Hevron*," in *Mayim mi-dalyav* (Lifshitz Teacher's College), 1993, 111–122. He argues there that Joseph's brothers moved northwards due to lack of rainfall. This represented a Divine manipulation of the climate and allowed them enough distance from their father to choose their attitude towards Joseph freely.

[12] Rozenson, "*Ha-parshanit*," 436.

He further elaborates: "I need the student to understand that Rashi's hostile attitude towards Esau was shaped by the Crusades. If you present Rashi as a *pashtan* as Nehama did, you run the risk of developing an inbuilt enmity towards the Christian world because of Rashi." Rozenson believes that because each commentator is affected by his circumstances, it makes no sense to create a dialogue between commentators of various periods and social backgrounds as Nehama did. But some feel this criticism to be too extreme, for after all Nehama showed a certain sensitivity to the historical background of commentary and text, especially Prophets. It may be argued that Rashi comes across in her work in a less one-dimensional fashion than Rozenson implies.[13]

New global trends

The above is only a partial picture of the new developments. The effect of deconstructionism has also been felt in the world of Orthodox Tanach study.[14] Nehama's method, as discussed, came close to these postmodern approaches, closer ironically than some of the newer approaches described above, whose focus on realia is more modern than postmodern.

Other recent trends pertinent to this discussion include the rise to prominence of individual spirituality and creativity in Western culture. Every age comes with its *zeitgeist*, its own particular emphases and challenges.[15] While any adequate description of our own *zeitgeist* is impossible here, it seems reasonable to suggest in a general way that one of the great influences on Western society for the past few decades has been a growing tendency toward individualism. This has gradually pushed to the margins all the ideologies and "isms" that consistently failed to bring redemption in the twentieth century. Today, the personal appears to have moved to center stage, spawning a plethora of psychological-spiritual theories and self-awareness techniques. The increased value placed on personal freedom has affected the way that organized religions function, with many of them

---

[13] He does not, for example, come across as a Christian-hater in his commentary on Genesis 27:41, where Esau announces, "Just wait for the days of mourning for my father and I will kill Jacob." Rashi remarks there: "[This sentence should be read] in its plain sense – so as not to grieve Father," omitting the Midrash that enforces the picture of Esau as the archetypical Jew-hater. See "Just Wait for Father's Death," *NSB* 280–285.

[14] Yedgar, "*Parshanut*," 108.

[15] This idea is found in Jewish sources as well. The Vilna Gaon writes: "In every generation a different attribute rules [from the attributes by which God runs the world] and it is because of this that natures change, and all the doings of that generation, their behavior and their leaders, are all according to the nature of that attribute, and it is dependent on their free choice... and all this is included in the Torah" (*Even shelemah* 11:9, cited in Devorah Heshelis, *The Moon's Lost Light*. Targum Press: 2006, 62).

compelled to exchange the stick for the carrot, at least to some extent. Sweeping transformations have come about as sacred cows are slaughtered one after the other – with absolute morality nibbled away by relativism, personal narrative replacing nationalism, and the toppling of science's claim to objectivity. The demands made of tradition today are often no longer for scientific empirical evidence or internal coherence but for personal relevance, with buzzwords including "authenticity," "meaning" and "emotional connection." Being methodical and rigorous is no longer in fashion. Attention spans have shortened, contributing to the rise of shallow and fuzzy thinking.

Some lament these changes, employing derogatory labels such as the "me generation" and the "MTV generation" to describe what they see as the narcissism and vapidity of today's youth. But viewed through a different lens, the focus on the individual can also be a challenge and lead to positive developments: independent thinking, a level of self-awareness and an unprecedented desire for the truth, or at least the subjectively authentic.

These, then, are some of the burdens and opportunities of our times.[16] In this realm, as throughout this book, Nehama's position appears to fall in the middle place, within the clash between old and new.

On the one hand, Nehama's work appears ahead of its time. Her books still repeatedly surprise with their freshness and contemporary tone. In her Bible scholarship, she anticipated emerging modern and postmodern literary theories. In her educational outlook, she heralded current trends. "Nehama understood the rupture of the modern world," remarks Chana Rabinowitz. She feels that Nehama truly understood the internal struggles of the younger generation, and that her desire to help secular youth fill a certain vacuum in their lives through Torah stemmed from a real understanding of their world. Rabinowitz also reports that Nehama, unusually, accepted from her a gift of a collection of modern poetry – a genre that Nehama greatly desired to understand. She grasped poetry by the likes of Nathan Zach and Yehudah Amichai with impressive ease, despite their departure in both form and content from Bialik and her beloved old-timers. This also indicates that her finger was on the pulse of the new generation, says Rabinowitz.

Nehama was certainly interested in the individual. She encouraged a unique response to every text:

---

[16] For more on such challenges as opportunities, see Yael Unterman, "If You Seek Him with All Your Heart: Nurturing Total Individual Growth in Yeshivah," in *Wisdom from All My Teachers: Challenges and Initiatives in Contemporary Torah Education*, edited by Jeffrey Saks and Susan Handelman, Jerusalem: Urim Publications, 2003, 176–178.

Reading a poem is: "A reproduction which the reader accomplishes by means of his voice and soul."[17]

That "I" who speaks, weeps, expresses joy, offers thanks to God, cries for help, is the "I" of the reader at that very moment of reading.[18]

She wanted to use the students' individuality, not repress it. Professor Moshe Ahrend cites a talmudic quote regarding the evil inclination (Kiddushin 30b):

If this scoundrel assaults you, lure him to the study hall.

He suggests that Nehama channeled the students' "evil inclination" – in this case, the individual ego with all its argumentativeness and self-absorption – into Torah by harnessing its positive aspects, such as the desire for debate and relevance, into generating class discussion.[19] Her educational methods were designed to elicit more individuality, in line with today's thinking. Writing in the introduction to Nehama's article "Active Learning in the Teaching of History," Jon Bloomberg remarks that

[although the article] is predicated upon an educational scene which is rather different from the prevailing reality in our schools in the United States in the latter part of the twentieth century, it is remarkable that so much of what Professor Leibowitz wrote some fifty years ago remains relevant to today's Jewish history classroom.[20]

He notes that skilled history teachers now use role-playing and discussion. They deal with issues in addition to texts and, as in Nehama's class, the range of views that the students and the teacher express are presented for evaluation.[21]

In all this, therefore, Nehama comes across as a teacher who would be eminently capable of engaging today's teenagers, just as she did the group of Yeshivah high school students who gave up their Saturday nights to study with her.[22]

ಇ⊸ ⊸ಲ

On the other hand, Nehama's Torah appears to fall short of what many young people seek today. She was a beacon for her day, with her harmonization of elements from traditional and modern life a breath of

---

[17] *TI*, 163 – see pages 471–472 above for rest of quote.
[18] N. Leibowitz, *Leader's Guide*, 1 – see page 471 above for rest of quote.
[19] Ahrend *"Mi-toch,"* 49.
[20] N. Leibowitz, "Active Learning," iv.
[21] N. Leibowitz, "Active Learning," iv.
[22] See page 471 above.

fresh air for many.[23] But the postmodern period has brought other struggles: The search for meaning in a highly fragmented world, and the pursuit of self-awareness, wholeness and belonging; and Nehama's work only partly addressed these issues. She created meaning, raised awareness of the complexity of certain issues, and provided her readers with a sense of belonging to a community of intelligent Torah learners – indeed, to a larger Jewish society responsible to each other and to the world. But ultimately, the individual's needs were not Nehama's focus. Her search for relevance in the Torah did not touch greatly on personal relevance. Rozenson: "Nehama spoke in general terms. For the most part, she related to the reasons for the mitzvot rather than to their significance on a personal level. She did not deal with the issue of 'What did a sacrifice do for the ancients, what does it do for us, and what is the difference?'"

The psychologically complex language that constitutes the *lingua franca* of the educated younger generations exists only partly in Nehama's work, and often appears only fleetingly between other materials. Behavior interested her more than intention did because "actions shape character."[24] She taught that psychological factors are secondary to behavior and cannot be used to excuse it,[25] the opposite message to many psychological theories. Although she liked to quote Ramban's psychological explanations, sometimes preferring them above all others,[26] she did not approve of exaggerated self-analysis. In the words of Buber, which she cited in an essay at the end of her book *Limmud parshanei ha-Torah*:

> Effective introspection is the beginning of a person's life path; and occasionally of humanity's path too. But it is not effective unless it indeed leads to the path; for there exists a certain sterile introspection that leads only to self-torture, despair and ever-increasing overcomplication. (*LP*, 219)

Nehama said this plainly in a letter to R. Raphael Posen. He had advised a young woman desiring to become a youth counselor in Bnei Akiva (a coeducational religious youth movement) that her actions should be dictated by her motives, and she must ask herself whether her true intention was to save souls or to meet young men. Nehama remonstrated:

> My dear friend, is this really the way? If I were to begin probing my own motives, what percentage of my drive to teach, to travel to all

---

[23] R. Zvi Grumet suggests that in a similar way, R. Soloveitchik's work was revolutionary for its time in its encompassing of modern and traditional worlds, but today is far less so (private communication).

[24] See chapter 1 n.39.

[25] See page 361 above.

[26] See examples in Ben-Meir, "*Le-darkei*," 134–135.

corners of the country and check thousands of worksheets was motivated by a genuine desire to disseminate Torah, and what percentage by a need to earn money, or by self-love or love of praise – which one does hear, from friends and students alike – after a successful lesson; or (perhaps?) by the need to flee loneliness, from the empty house, since my husband died?... Far better not to examine such things. And can this ever really be ascertained anyway? Better leave such inspections to the One who knows inner thoughts. He will judge.

So how could a young girl introspect in this fashion? Furthermore, it's completely unconstructive! Better she should believe she's doing something worthy, saving children from the street and lawlessness, bringing them closer to their Father in Heaven – even if a psychoanalyst or an ordinary psychologist might discover that her strongest motivation is the desire to meet boys. Far better that she not know this and not think about it... [and remain passionate about the movement's activities].

By the way, this is how I interpret the sentence "If this scoundrel assaults you, lure him to the study hall," i.e., keep him busy with spiritual matters – what the psychologists call sublimation. This is the only way, certainly in our times! (*PN*, 670)

Nehama's Torah was primarily located on the axes of relationship of self to God and self to other. It dealt far less with the relationship of self to self, and interest in the self was not seen as a positive thing. This was an issue on which Nehama was in agreement with her brother rather than with her esteemed R. Kook. Professor Aviezer Ravitzky notes that Yeshayahu Leibowitz and R. Kook were on opposite sides when it came to the question of the self (*VLY*). The latter, in keeping with his view that all of existence is holy, believed that the self, its desires and needs, is a repository for the Divine; while Yeshayahu held that the self is separate from the Divine and must be subjugated to it. Nehama too was suspicious of the self, so often coupled with words like "-absorbed" or "-centered." As Simi Peters notes: "Nehama was self-aware, but her generation's definition of this term was different from ours. A lot of what we might call self-awareness she would see as self-indulgence."

Nehama minimized the place of self in her own life. She never pampered herself materially, and in her teaching role in the classroom and in conversation she took a step back to make room for others. She largely put her work before her private life, and she likewise expected others to push their individual desires or problems to the margins as far as possible and get on with right living. As she wrote comically in her column in the *Yediot* newspaper:

> Don't say "First of all me, then after that comes me, and next comes me again, and then after that perhaps my wife." And what about your fellow human being?[27]

And a few weeks later, in the same newspaper:

> The true rebellion is that of the sensual self against the manacles of the Torah's morals.[28]

Her *Studies* contain similar sentiments:

> The assertion of individual selfish ambitions outweighs their group feeling as a "kingdom of priests and a holy nation." (*SBM*, 183)

She wrote that deifying the inner world constituted the "original fount of sin," (*SD*, 368) and similarly that

> it is possible to repudiate the entire Torah [by] idol worship, by deifying our own ambitions and aspirations, by saying (in the words of the prophet Hosea, 14:4) "to the work of our hands, you are our gods" (where "the work of our hands" signifies also the aspirations of our soul and anything we have fabricated from our hearts and turned into a god).[29]

For Nehama, each age has its own idolatry and suffering (*SD*, 53–54); and the emphasis on the self is the idolatry of ours. Her Torah was aimed towards society, not the individual. Her student was to follow a path laid down long before by the Jewish people as a whole, and updated by Zionism, also strongly oriented towards the Jewish collective. She was aware of the tension between individual and collective needs, writing of the

> highly topical issue… [the] dilemma between the choice of a career – personal advancement – or the fulfillment of a mission. It is a choice which has faced and continues to face Jewish youth, especially those intent on discharging the cardinal precept of settlement in the Land of Israel. (*SBM*, 379)

But her focus was strongly on the mission nonetheless.

৵ ৵

However, Nehama could not stop the inevitable course of history and, to her distress, the collectivist Israel that she knew gradually dwindled. In the Western world, psychology, self-help books and the New Age movement became increasingly popular, and in the Jewish world, interest grew in Hasidism and Kabbalah, in mystical and psychospiritual dimensions, in ecstatic worship – precisely the topics Nehama disliked or avoided.

---

[27] *Parashat Be-har*, May 17, 1990; reprinted in *PN*, 509.

[28] *Parashat Be-ha'alotcha*, June 7, 1990; reprinted in *PN*, 512.

[29] *IBBM*, 183; she quotes this also in *NSS*, 321, in a discussion of wealth as idolatry.

No one can blame Nehama for not keeping up with this flood of new approaches. She never lost interest in new developments, but her main duty remained to transmit the Torah that she had created and knew so well, and this she did not shirk. She continued with the same methods – and much of the same material – at ninety as she had at forty. Her perseverance itself is a sign that she was not of today's *zeitgeist*, all about change and movement as it is. But the fact remains that her Torah, which was revolutionary at its outset, had become mainstream by the time of her death. It was left to others to take the next steps in the evolving process of Torah teaching.

One of these was Dr. Avivah Zornberg, and it is instructive to contrast Nehama's work with hers. An internationally acclaimed lecturer and scholar, Zornberg is recognized by many as a leading creative teacher and interpreter of Torah for the English-speaking world. Her approach is, like that of Nehama, intellectually broad and critically probing, yet at the same time fully conversant with the traditional commentaries. Like Nehama, Zornberg is Jerusalem-based and much in demand, attracting large crowds of both men and women. Her books also incorporate diverse materials and open new vistas for the study of the weekly Torah portion. But the resemblance ends at a certain point. Though Zornberg found Nehama's work and methods valuable, she traveled a different path. "I found her a very inspiring figure, but our styles are very different," she says.[30] R. Ben and Judy Hollander wrote in a letter to the *Jerusalem Post*:

> Both are multi-disciplined thinkers of keen psychological insight, but one bores down into the many-sided pshat of Torah, while the other flies out on the wings of Midrash.

> Leibowitz is rigorously rational, tightening thought; Zornberg is richly associative, loosening imagination. Leibowitz is the ultimate pedagogue, the master facilitator deftly enabling Torah and commentators to speak with their startling immediacy. Zornberg speaks for herself, the poet and philosopher, inviting us to "eavesdrop" on her exquisitely personal response to the dialogue of life and text.

Zornberg employs a greater range of sources than Nehama did, drawing heavily on contemporary psychology, literary theory and philosophy, and Hasidic sources. She makes deeper forays into the realm of the imaginative and emotive, working, in Professor Susan Handelman's words, "at the edge of the vulnerable, the unknown, dealing with the angst and the shadow." Zornberg delicately excavates subterranean psychic layers, probing religious and spiritual mysteries with a poetry all her own. In articulating their

---

[30] Calev Ben-David, "One Woman's Exodus," *Jerusalem Post*, March 23, 2001, B12. See also page 235 above.

personal struggles and yearnings, she creates existential meaning for her audience, who at times are even moved to tears by her words. We could suggest that Nehama's Torah might be characterized as archetypically masculine in its analytical, rigorous and linear form, while Zornberg's may be more archetypically feminine in its non-linear form and its emotional content.[31] Yedgar puts it differently: Where the feminine within Nehama's approach was unconscious, in Zornberg and others it is more conscious.[32]

The Hollanders, however, warn against too-facile comparisons, continuing their letter:

> Since, in addition to their different agendas, neither woman intends a feminist statement by her work, comparing their contributions by the lowest common denominator of gender does a disservice to both.

> That being said, however, it is certainly noteworthy that the person who has done the most to broaden the study of Torah and commentary in the twentieth century is a woman, and that it is now another woman who is charting new directions for Torah thought in the coming century.[33]

The last sentence summarizes for us the key benefit in the comparison. Nehama was ultimately a transitional figure between the modern and the postmodern era. What she intuited only in patches, Zornberg teaches in full force. But as the Hollanders suggest, it may indeed not be coincidental that two women pioneered new directions in Torah learning in both the previous century and this one. Whether this is due to sociological reasons – that women, who lack a traditional yeshivah education and rabbinical position, are much freer of constraints; or more metaphysical ones – that the Jewish world thirsts for the feminine aspects of the Torah, the emergence of which marks a national rebalancing and even redemption – is a matter of perspective.[34]

All these shifts in emphasis have affected the world of education, giving rise to new techniques that promote experiential and emotional components in learning. The full range of creative and imaginative tools, such as music,

---

[31] Tamar Rotem writes: "Zornberg's way of thinking… is associative. In that sense her way of thinking is considered to be very feminine" ("From George Eliot to the Garden of Eden," *Haaretz* magazine [English edition], September 10, 2004, 14).

[32] Yedgar, "*Parshanut*," 116.

[33] "Multi-disciplined thinkers," *Jerusalem Post* magazine, July 21, 1995, 2.

[34] Devorah Heshelis, in *The Moon's Lost Light* (Targum Press, 2006), outlines how the strong emergence of women's talent in Torah learning is one of the changes that Kabbalistic and other works predicted for the immediate pre-messianic era.

dance, art, drama and writing are being integrated, together with regular frontal learning and discussions.[35] Here Nehama was again ahead of her time, with buds of these creative techniques appearing in her teaching. She integrated drama into her classroom, and evinced a talent for dramatically envisioning a biblical scene. We sense this in her essay on Rashi's comment to Exodus 5:1:

> "The elders slipped away one by one." How typical a picture! How true to life! All greet the dramatic tidings with expressions of joy and gratitude. Enthusiasm is boundless.... Early next day, they march en masse towards Pharaoh's palace. But soon, sobriety begins to set in. Doubts sprout up like mushrooms. Will Pharaoh heed? What are the chances? Will our appearance really make a difference? Is it all *worth* it? And so one by one they begin to drop out. Not according to a prearranged plan, not by a "unanimous" vote, but quietly, stealthily. The further the delegation advances, the closer the palace, the greater the number of palace guards who come into view, and the nearer the moment of meeting Pharaoh face to face – the more rapidly does the number of delegates diminish. And upon arrival, Moses and Aaron are alone, two individuals facing the king of the great Egyptian empire, a powerful and ruthless monarch. They were but two old men, without an army, without military force... alone, yet not alone. (*NSS*, 88)

When teaching this Rashi to some children, Nehama asked them to get into a line and pretend to be Moses with the elders behind him. The children playing the elders gradually all stole away, until, when the child playing Moses finally looked round, there was no one left.

Nehama was talented at filling in the gaps, of descriptions that the Tanach omits, replete with vivid details:

> Pharaoh, as it were, rose from his throne and drew himself up to his full stature, adjusted his crown and brought to bear on them the full impact of his regal authority. (*NSS*, 97)

> Note that in three days' travel there is only one conversation between father and son. You can hear the echo, the sound of slow steps, heavy, monotonous, from the heavy silence. (*TI*, 30)

At times she would also ask the students to do the imaginative filling in of gaps, and in this she anticipated a technique called Bibliodrama, a

---

[35] See www.atid.org for their work on the role of the arts in Jewish education. Another pioneering organization is "Bet Av," founded by R. Dov Berkowitz and providing platforms for the likes of Yonadav Kaploun (see their publications, and Kaploun's book *Ra'iti ve-hinei* [Jerusalem 2004], containing examples of his psychological creative writing technique on the weekly portion).

psychodramatic role-playing method developed by Dr. Peter Pitzele.[36] This technique, very much a fruit of our age, will be used as a case in point to show how Nehama goes halfway towards anticipating the spirit of the early twenty-first century.

Bibliodrama engages students in ways beyond the traditional. It is not identical to acting, for the entire group, rather than just one person, builds the inner life of the biblical character. The participants are asked questions as if they were the people in the story. For example: "Moses, what did you feel standing in front of the burning bush?" Participants are required to answer in character, and, since the answer is not explicit in the text, imaginative responses tumble out: "I felt overawed," "I felt puzzled," "I knew that this was a symbol of something." This first-person language deepens the emotional identification with the text, following, in fact, the Torah's own guidelines, when it instructs the person bringing the first fruits to the Temple is to declare in first-person language (Deuteronomy 26:3):

> I have come to the Land which the Lord swore to our fathers to give to them.

As Nehama points out, this person

> does not say: My fathers came to the land; [rather] he himself has come unto the land, in the same way as our Pesah Haggadah states, "That in every generation every Jew is obliged to see himself as if he had gone out of Egypt." (*SD*, 260)

Bibliodrama, with its direct approach, similarly throws the student right back into Egypt. If, as Nehama explains, the Midrash converts the abstract into the emotional and the general to the specific, thereby helping the students to identify personally with the text (*TI*, 87), this technique has the same effect. It also creates space for interpretative intuitions based on the subtlest nuances of the text, and these often coincide marvelously with the Midrashic view. Indeed, Pitzele calls Bibliodrama "modern Midrash."[37]

I would suggest that Nehama's dramatic flair and desire to create identification with the biblical characters brought her in an intuitive, spontaneous way to approach Bibliodrama at times. She asked her young students to tell her at whom Jacob was looking during a key moment or

---

[36] See Peter Pitzele, *Scripture Windows: Towards a Practice of Bibliodrama* (Torah Aura Productions: 1998) and *Our Fathers' Wells: A Personal Encounter with the Myths of Genesis* (Harper Collins: 1996).

[37] In Bibliodrama, participants extrapolate from small clues in the text, reminding us of Nehama's statement (*NSB*, 199): "Whence did our Sages elicit their data regarding Abraham's internal struggle…? We may answer that their description was prompted by the one conversation that is reported."

what Joseph might have said as he was pleading for his life from the pit.[38] In this she anticipated the two Bibliodramatic questions: "Jacob, whom are you looking at right now?" and "Joseph, what do you call out from the pit?" (though this direct address, rather than asking "If you were Joseph/Jacob," as Nehama did, constitutes a significant difference).

Bibliodrama also allows access to Tanach even for students not very familiar with the Bible. This was of great importance to Nehama, who notes that the advantage of discussion in the classroom is that such students

> in respect of understanding the passage as such... are not inferior.... In a debate over two interpretations, they are well able to penetrate the minds of the personalities and motivations of the characters in the chapter and to grasp the substance and spirit of the story. (*TI*, 148)

It seems therefore as if Bibliodrama, despite its untraditional form, might well have intrigued and pleased Nehama had she known of it;[39] though Yedgar believes that she would have found it imprecise.[40]

Nevertheless, even traditional Jewish educators today are much more aware of the need for experience and creative expression in the lesson than Nehama was. In the end, many of the creative aspects in Nehama's work – her drama, anecdotes, imagination and humor – depended largely on her personality and appeared very little in her writings. With Nehama gone, the amount of creativity infusing her teachings is up to the individual teacher.

The relevance of Nehama's work today

As the old adage has it, the proof of the pudding is in the eating. Therefore, leaving the theoretical question of how Nehama's work is or is not in tune with new developments, we turn to the concrete question: Have today's young Israeli and Diaspora Jews in fact heard of Nehama Leibowitz and her work? Do they open her books? And if so, do they understand what they discover in there, and want to read more?

---

[38] See pae 188 above.

[39] Suitable for both child and adult education, the technique works very well alongside more traditional learning methods, including Nehama's in-depth study of commentaries. Many of the commentators' questions may be formulated as Bibliodramatic questions. After role-playing them out with the full power of their imaginations, the students' understanding of the commentaries' questions is immensely improved. From my own experience, Bibliodrama serves as a powerful complement to regular Jewish education, and I strongly recommend that educators familiarize themselves with it.

[40] She feels that all art forms introduced into Nehama's lesson, such as poetry or dramatic readings, served mostly to further the students' grasp of the *peshat* as Nehama saw it, rather than to allow subjective understandings and personal expression (Yedgar, private communication). It is true that Bibliodramatic interpretation can move far from the text – hence its resemblance to Midrash.

Without doing an exhaustive scientific survey, the answer to these questions would appear to be "yes and no." Nehama's name is still widely known and respected, even amongst those who had not reached adulthood when she passed away. Nehama functions as an inspiration and role model for religious high school girls, some of whom make her the subject of their projects. Rabbanit Chana Henkin, the dean of Nishmat, a Jerusalem-based advanced Torah learning institute for women, testifies that despite real changes in students' needs, Nehama's books remain popular in the *bet midrash*. Other young adults also value Nehama's books, as this author has become aware simply through casual observation: A young woman who received the *Studies* as a bat-mitzvah gift, and, inspired by their critical approach, chose to study Bible at university; a religious professional couple in their thirties, whose dining room table is heaped with open *Studies*, clearly very much in use; an Israeli in his early forties, involved in the world of music, who keeps Nehama's books by his bed to read at the end of his day; or a middle-aged graduate of a secular Israeli school, who lights up at the name Nehama Leibowitz, and says, "When we studied the book of Job, I was so disappointed by the ending, because God offers no real answer to Job's questions. But then my Tanach teacher brought Nehama's explanation, that God was telling him: 'You have human wisdom, not Divine wisdom. Your understanding is limited.' Today as a science teacher I often quote this, informing my students that human wisdom can be examined empirically, but there are many things beyond the reach of science and those are Divine wisdom."[41]

A simple search on the Internet reveals many thousands of appearances for Nehama's name. Her work is quoted in books, articles, newspapers and sheets on the weekly Torah portion. Torah teachers, rabbis and youth movement counselors continue to use Nehama's writings to prepare classes and sermons (and many still do not credit her!)[42]

However, there are also many today who have never heard of Nehama Leibowitz. Her books are rarely opened within the secular school system, and the general Israeli public does not know of her. Studying one of Nehama's books on the subway, Eidel Rudman noticed a young Israeli reading over her shoulder. Catching her eye, he exclaimed: "What is this book?! I didn't know such a thing existed! Where can I buy it?" And those

---

[41] Rita Gilad, interview.
[42] This author witnessed her teenage Israeli relative returning from school with a sheet on the weekly portion prepared by her teacher. The sources, which seemed familiar, had indeed been lifted directly from one of Nehama's *Studies* without attribution.

who have heard of her, sometimes know only that she is Yeshayahu's sister (when they are not busy mistaking her for his wife)! Tzvi Mauer, the founder of Urim Publications, was unprepared for the response when he approached a large publishing house in Israel with an invitation to co-publish a Hebrew edition of the Nehama Leibowitz Haggadah, which had been released the previous year in English to strong acclaim. To his surprise, the secular Israeli publisher had never heard of Nehama, while the head editor knew little more of her than her connection to Yeshayahu.

Even Israeli youth within national-religious circles do not always know very much about her, venturing: "She wrote commentaries on the Torah" or "In her learning she reached the level of a rabbi." She seems like a distant figure to them. As young people tend to do, they have bundled her indiscriminately with illustrious figures from centuries past, never dreaming that she passed away just a few years previously and that their teachers met her personally. There has been a falling-off of interest in Nehama's work. Academics writing on the subject do not tend to fall into the younger brackets; conferences in her honor tend to draw middle-aged audiences, with the younger crowds preferring psychological, Hasidic and Kabbalistic subjects or political issues. When there are popular Tanach forums for younger people, such as a monthly lecture in the Givat Shmuel neighborhood that draws four hundred people, they often follow newer approaches rather than Nehama's.

Unfortunately, Nehama's method is no longer associated with innovation and excitement. Quite the reverse. Because the religious matriculation examinations for Tanach are largely based upon it, comparing commentaries has for many Israeli students become a tiresome activity done only in order to get good grades. The sad truth is that instead of bringing students to love Torah, as Nehama desired, her method as implemented in the high schools today frequently has the opposite effect. Based on many conversations, Yedgar reports that students' recollections of their Tanach classes contain real dislike, along the lines of: "I don't remember a thing except that the whole time was spent on commentaries."[43]

Chaviva Speter, an Israeli Tanach teacher, enjoyed attending Nehama's lessons, but never found herself drawn to her books. They seemed heavy and old-fashioned, part of her parents' generation. Only when she needed to ransack the *Studies* series for texts in English did Speter finally discover, to her surprise, the gems inside, sounding as if they had just been written yesterday. Part of what had put her off for so long was her experience in school: "Nehama's method was initially an innovation, but by the time I was

---

[43] Yedgar, "*Ha-iyunim*," 14–15, and interview.

in high school, my teachers were overusing it," she says. "We did end up knowing what Rashi and Ibn Ezra said, but it became exhausting and burdensome. We saw the trees but not the forest. I would still use it in teaching, but our generation want a more global picture, one that systematically puts more emphasis on the commentator's broader context and historical background."

Addressing this phenomenon, Dr. Marla Frankel suggests that if the students leave alienated from Tanach, they are not being taught through the prism of Nehama's teachings. Nehama would doubtless have been distraught to hear that one could spend years studying with her method and still know nothing about the Tanach. Certainly school, with its intense pressure and competition, is not the ideal context for learning to love a subject. While Nehama herself was able to overcome this using her agile mind, her sense for relevant and thought-provoking material and her lively, mischievous presence bringing high-schoolers to love Torah, the dry matriculation examination format has sucked all the fun out of her methods. Rozenson: "The matriculation examination has transformed the study of Tanach into an experience like learning a page of Talmud – analytical and methodological."

The students are also not the same population they once were, as Yedgar notes: "Spoken Hebrew has developed at an incredible rate, and is much further today from the language of the commentators than was Nehama's generation's Hebrew. Today, the effort required to understand the commentary can end up preventing access to the verse and the broader context." Students become bogged down in details in the commentaries or verse, lacking the larger picture or even the sense of why it is important. As Yedgar pithily puts it, instead of the act of reading the Tanach being slowed down, as Nehama wished, it is brought to a near standstill.[44]

Nehama knew of this risk. She always warned against attending to isolated nuances while overlooking central ideas.[45] But she also erred in assuming that the relevant ideas and values would emerge naturally from the text and commentaries, while in fact, a capable guide and teacher is needed, for otherwise all but the most astute students will fail to grasp the relevance.[46] And if even under Nehama's own tutelage only the more mature, self-motivated students could keep up with the demands of her method,[47] what happens when the teacher is palpably not Nehama? There are many unimaginative teachers who focus on the *gilyonot*-type process of

---

[44] Yedgar, "*Ha-iyunim*," 34.
[45] N. Leibowitz, "*Gilyonot le-iyun*," 19, 48.
[46] Yedgar, "*Ha-iyunim*," 34.
[47] Yedgar, "*Ha-iyunim*," 34.

questioning and comparing commentaries, without ever arriving at *Studies*-like lessons to be learned.[48] The study remains an intellectual endeavor rather than a personal-emotional one. Technique comes at the expense of content, such as the social or theological issues behind the interpretations. In this, they miss out on important goals of Nehama's.[49] Her goals are even more undermined in the case of those teachers who abandon the technique entirely," to teach and compare text and commentaries frontally, without allowing discussion and involvement by the students.[50]

It is a sad truth that those teachers who sense the problematics of all this largely have their hands tied by the current matriculation examination framework. Young teachers trained in newer approaches find themselves unable to introduce them into the high schools because of the pressure to get through the material, which leads to great frustration on their part. Even devoted followers of Nehama's method believe that change is urgently necessary. Some suggest that other commentators, not the ones that she chose, can explain the text better for today's generation. Others, such as R. Elhanan Samet, believe that the exclusive focus on commentaries should be replaced with more direct dealing with the text.

Perhaps such pressures will have their effect on the matriculation examination soon. It is extremely regrettable that Nehama should be the inspiration for an unbalanced curriculum and her method implemented in such a constricted, formulaic manner. Yet those teaching outside the matriculation examination cannot rest on their laurels, for the problematic implementation is not limited to it or even to Israel alone. R. Francis Nataf remarks:

> While, thanks to the efforts of Nechama Leibowitz, her students and others like them, more and more classrooms are asking the question, "What's bothering Rashi?", once we figure that out, we are content to get Rashi's (or Ramban's or Seforno's) answer to what was bothering him and to move on to the next problem. In other words, that which was once an exercise in literary analysis has become more akin to work on math problems.[51]

---

[48] Yedgar, "*Ha-iyunim*," 15.

[49] See Yedgar, "*Ha-iyunim*," 15–16 for a list of the goals. Those focusing on personalization and relevance have especially been neglected.

[50] Yedgar, "*Ha-iyunim*," 35.

[51] Francis Nataf, "Learning Torah with Our Own Eyes: Initial Feedback to *Redeeming Relevance*," Cardozo Academy email list, Ideas number 86, Tuesday, November 23, 2006 (see www.cardozoschool.org – the essay appears under Essays>Contemporary Issues>Education).

How much of this is due to erroneous implementation of her method, and how much to its intrinsic limits, is arguable. Yedgar defends Nehama, arguing that her critical method of interpretation and comparison invites students to suggest their own interpretative analysis.[52] But in the long run, in her emphasis on commentaries and in limiting the role of originality, Nehama may have unwittingly encouraged a tradition of stagnation and mediocrity, thus failing to nurture the next generation's best minds. Creativity needs to be not just permitted but cultivated if it is to thrive.[53]

Solutions and developments

The good news is that ways are being found to bring Nehama's methods up to date while preserving a healthy sense of what works and what does not. The key here is for teachers not to try to imitate Nehama exactly, but rather to make the material their own. We can cite here the words of the Baal Shem Tov, founder of the Hasidic movement:

> One must live and conduct himself according to one's own spiritual level. When one tries to conduct one's life by the standards of someone else's spiritual level, one will fail by both standards. This is the meaning of the Sages' teaching (Berachot 35b): "Many tried to emulate R. Shimon bar Yohai, but they were unsuccessful."[54]

And Parker Palmer, a leading philosopher of education, writes:

> Good teaching cannot be reduced to technique; good teaching comes from the identity and integrity of the teacher.[55]

Admittedly, there are obstacles to this. Nehama's method is a difficult one, which is why she felt the need to publish leaflets to guide teachers in using her worksheets. It is conceivable that only teachers with Nehama's range of talents are capable of carrying her techniques off successfully; the rest will skip stages.[56] The relevance stage especially falls by the wayside, for the exhaustive analysis of commentaries leaves most teachers (and students) with little energy or time for meaning-making.[57]

Also, the conservative nature of religious society and Nehama's own opposition to innovation together conspire to inhibit teachers in several ways. Many teachers, awed by her stature, are afraid to make necessary

---

[52] Yedgar, "*Ahrayut*," 406.

[53] See discussion "The waning of Parshanut," Lookjed archives, July 26, 2004 and onwards, regarding why (Orthodox) Jews have ceased to write systematic Tanach commentary.

[54] *Keter shem tov* 1:4.

[55] Parker Palmer, *The Courage to Teach*, Jossey-Bass: 1998, 10.

[56] See Yedgar, "*Ha-iyunim*," 35.

[57] Yedgar, "*Ha-iyunim*," 34, 35.

updates to the methods. The teachers' own original interpretations are not nurtured, for if Nehama – a person of such charisma and intellect – fled from all appearances of originality in her interpretations, how dare ordinary teachers allow themselves to do so? It goes without saying, then, that students' original interpretations are not encouraged. Although some might insist that Nehama wished above all to empower students' interpretations, in practice, as her technique is used today, it often prevents direct access to the verse. Yedgar: "The teachers teach only the commentaries, giving short shrift to looking at the verse. The result is that for the pupils, instead of being the gateway to the verse, the commentaries become a wall blocking it from them."[58]

Teachers must overcome all of these impediments and, understanding Nehama's method in its broadest sense, figure out how to extrapolate from it in a manner that will be successful for today. Frankel argues that Nehama's work has been done a disservice in being interpreted so narrowly, and that certain groups have embraced her methodology while consistently ignoring aspects of her educational philosophy. Frankel: "To teach in Nehama's footsteps today you would have to be willing to quote Shalom Rosenberg, Admiel Kosman, Meir Shalev, or a great non-Jewish writer or scholar. It's not just about the kind of questions she asks – you have to find the contemporary thinkers. It is clear to me that she added a shelf to the Oral Law, and anyone who thinks they can teach Nehama Leibowitz without doing that is missing something very significant. Just as she used Buber's translation, we need to use Fox's translation. If she could not teach Genesis without Benno Jacob, we can't teach Exodus without Childs."

She notes that certain religious circles are willing to teach Buber and Jacob – or at least, the selected segments that Nehama "koshered" – yet not their modern counterparts. She is confident that today Nehama would have read Mary Douglas on purity and ritual: "It follows from everything she's done. Douglas seeks meanings in the text, and would therefore be useful to Nehama." Because Nehama was interested in whatever enlightened the text and made learning a positive and challenging experience, Frankel feels that in utilizing media – movies, theater, etc. – in her teaching she is following Nehama's lead. "We shouldn't focus her methods alone, we should apply her instructional principles," she insists.

Other former students of Nehama's have expanded her teaching, developing it in new directions. Some spend much more time with the text, such as Dr. Gabriel Cohn and R. Elhanan Samet, two original and insightful Israeli Tanach teachers who use the literary approach. Cohn does not

---

[58] Interview. Yedgar has written about this in *"Ha-iyunim,"* 34.

experience this as a violation of Nehama's aims: "Her ultimate goal was the text. However, she spent too much time getting to it and placed the commentaries too much in the center, so over the years I emphasized them less. I believe that even she felt, towards the end of her life, that it needed modification. Today's students are less educated, so it is more difficult for them to approach the text via the commentaries." R. Samet has continued the literary direction that Nehama began, but in a more methodical fashion, with his own literary principles and on broader units than she generally dealt with; and also without her strong aversion to realia. He feels confident in suggesting his own interpretations even when they contradict the commentaries. "My goal is the understanding of Tanach, not of the commentaries *per se*," he explains. He adds: "I possess more talmudic and halachic knowledge than Nehama did. But she had a broad universal education that I lack – languages, general literature, etc. Today such people are rare."

There are those who place more emphasis on the historical background of the commentator than Nehama did, such as Dr. Ruth Ben-Meir. There are those who develop their own original interpretations, influenced by the directions Nehama laid out.[59] There are also those who have gone on to allow students more creative license to interpret on their own. "Nehama's starting point is the commentaries; mine is the Tanach," explains Yedgar. "My students engage in a lot of open discussion, more than in Nehama's class. I spend more time asking for the students' impressions of what they have read, inviting creative interpretation based on a close reading of the text." But she hastens to add: "Though I am two generations after her, and use more modern techniques, it is she who gave me the confidence to be so open."

She outlined an alternative structure for lessons based on Nehama's method, whereby

> the student comes up with the questions, the commentaries and the methods. Especially in the age of the computer, with its databases, we can look forward to greater autonomy on the part of pupils in accessing study materials and topics.[60]

She actually debated this topic with Nehama, discussing how controlling the teacher ought to be, and learned from her to impose limits – students' interpretations should not be a free-for-all, but rather supported by the text. Another development Yedgar instigated was to teach by topic. Nehama did

---

[59] Two examples of recent books are R. Shmuel Klitsner's *Wrestling Jacob* and Professor Moshe Sokolow's *Hatzi Nehama*, both published by Urim Publications.
[60] Yedgar, "*Ha-iyunim*," 36.

not like this method, but Yedgar feels that there are topics worth teaching, such as the image of Jerusalem in the Psalms, or laws of damages in the Torah. "I utilize her tools even when teaching things Nehama never did," she says.

Judy Klitsner also empowers student interpretation. She considers this to be a logical extension of everything Nehama taught her: "She was saying, 'You student, you novice who just came into this room, you can read a text carefully too!' It did not matter whether the student had been studying for years or for one day. The approach was the same – understand the words, look closely at the context, and use your interpretive skills to find the best reading of the text." Coming from an educational background that created no room for her own intuition, Klitsner found Nehama's class enormously liberating. "She enabled me to take that great initial step of letting the text speak to me, and helped me take part in the interpretive process. Instead of immutable authorities, the commentators became living, creative people in animated dialogue with one another. To me it was obvious that the next step was to start without the commentaries and just assess what the verse said." Klitsner reports that to her surprise, students consistently discover almost all the questions the commentators ask. "By the time we actually look at the commentators, we already have in hand the difficulties that bothered them."

What all of these teachers share is the belief in Nehama's system together with an understanding that it needs to be interpreted liberally, in terms of spirit and not only letter. Change is unavoidable. "The fact that so many major teachers of Tanach today who consider themselves Nehama's followers have translated her teaching into new channels proves that her system was fundamentally a dynamic one," argues Cohn. Yedgar puts it in stronger terms: "To continue Nehama is in some way to rebel against her."

Such teachers do not fear that their modifications will damage Nehama's system. On the contrary, they will only enhance its usefulness while remaining true to its intention. Cohn feels that Nehama would have approved of such approaches, for her chief goal was to lead the student to independent interpretations and existential meaning: "She always managed to elevate her studies beyond the level of the details to something much more significant. Not just a lesson about the past but about the present."

Some of these teachers are in part influenced by other systems – for example, in returning to focus on the text and not the commentaries, they may have been influenced by new literary movements. Consequently, many of Nehama's successors are not in fact teaching "pure Nehama," so to speak. The lines between Nehama's school of thought and others are becoming more and more blurred and the feeling of separate "camps" is dissipating. Today's students are simultaneously exposed to a variety of approaches without knowing exactly whose is whose. Indeed, future generations may be entirely unaware that the founders of these approaches once thoroughly disagreed. They also may well be ignorant of the debt that their teachers owe to Nehama Leibowitz, who pioneered so many elements that are now commonplace.

The future

There is no one obvious successor to Nehama. Besides the tremendous number of people influenced by her work, she left behind a small band of scholars and teachers who are intimately involved with it, who research it for articles, books and doctorates, work to disseminate it, and view their teaching as a direct continuation of hers.

In the course of writing this book it became clear to this author that these people function largely as individuals. The *Amitei Tzion* class is the closest that Nehama came to a group of disciples, but with Nehama gone, the sense of a group largely dissolved. Unlike in the case of many other great minds, no coherent school or group dedicated to her work exists. Interesting work has been done by individual scholars, and some fruitful debate takes place in conferences and public forums. Those who have succeeded in transferring the worksheets to the internet appear to have the clearest vision for taking Nehama's work into the twenty-first century. Overall, the impression remains that those most involved in analyzing and disseminating Nehama's approach have yet to sit down together to create any kind of cohesive program for the future of her work. Each is busily engaged in his or her own Nehama.[61] In the meantime, what used to be the Nehama "camp" is shrinking, wedged between the new methods for Tanach study on the one hand and the right-wing nationalist camp on the other.

Yedgar suggests that this lack of cohesion occurred because Nehama, who kept her philosophy and method largely unsystematized, never invited public debate of her method or discussion by colleagues in academic conferences or other media. In contrast, her brother actively solicited debate on his ideas, and his intellectual legacy is discussed today and categorized in ways that Nehama's is not. This volume has been at attempt to create categories and bring various "Nehama scholars" into dialogue with each other over significant issues.

In the critical debate as to the future of Nehama's work, scholars are not all of one mind. Some question to what extent to which her work will survive long-term. Erella Yedgar notes that the appeal of Nehama's work

---

[61] There has been some collaboration by various former students of Nehama's, such as Yitshak Reiner and Shmuel Peerless or the editors of the memorial volume, *Pirkei Nehama*. The journal *Limmudim* has potential as a forum too.

has decreased, and offers three reasons. Firstly, she was not sufficiently attuned to the gap between contemporary moral sensibilities and the Tanach concerning issues such as the attitude towards slavery, killing, homosexuality, racial superiority, and the status of women.[62] In particular, religious women, a minority within a minority, often cannot turn to their own holy book for their redemption due to various problematic elements.[63] Secondly, and on the other side of the spectrum, many people today are too religiously conservative to be comfortable with Nehama's work. Lastly, young people do not want to work too hard, but want to be instantly gratified and exposed to exciting new ideas. "Today's generation wants instant," says Yedgar. "Nehama was not about instant. She was about process."

Rabbi Dr. Yonatan Grossman testifies from his own experience: "The respect in which Nehama is universally held is a remarkable thing, and her work is still at the basis of what we do, but today's students open her books less and less." Professor Eliezer Schweid wonders whether a system exists today that is capable of assimilating what Nehama can give.[64] In her day, Nehama functioned as a bridge between two worlds, connecting religious and secular Israeli populations to one another's values – to Zionism and to tradition, respectively. She was one of the few proponents of the religious educational system who went beyond defensiveness and apologetics, to actually influence broader society.[65] The question remains whether she can still do so. The Tanach would have to be appreciated in both sectors, says Schweid, and expresses concern for the fact that the secular system no longer views the Tanach as a source of values. In order for Nehama's work to be appreciated there, it would have to seen once more as educational rather than as fossilized historical information.[66]

Due to all these factors, Nehama's audience appears to have narrowed. However, Dr. Gabriel Cohn is not concerned about the future: "Her method is strong enough that its momentum will continue even without a formal movement. Her principles will guarantee the continuity. Since we have Nehama's method, we do not need Nehama herself. I do not know if this can be said of others as well." He senses Nehama's imprint everywhere he turns. "I hear lectures on the weekly portion all over Israel, and think of Nehama. I see women studying Tanach as Talmud is studied, and I think of her. I go to Alon Shvut, a vibrant center for Tanach learning, and witness

---

[62] Yedgar, "*Parshanut*," 109, and interview.
[63] Yedgar, "*Parshanut*," 110, 112.
[64] Schweid, *VLN*, public session.
[65] Schoneveld, *The Bible*, 258.
[66] In this context, see Simon's suggestions for the future of Tanach in his article "The Place," 235 and *passim*.

creative students of Tanach who want to go further than the classic Jewish commentaries to experience the biblical text in fresh ways, and again I see her influence. And in the Diaspora, I think of the Limmud conferences, thousands of people learning Torah for the love of it, and I feel Nehama's presence in this *Torah li-shmah*."

Professor Michael Rosenak also believes that Nehama's work will endure. In his view, every culture has its "language" – its timeless essence, which is not up for discussion – and its "literatures," which are creative developments on the basis of the "language." Nehama guaranteed her continuity by approaching the "language" of Judaism (the Torah text) by way of many "literatures" (the commentaries). Yedgar asserts: "I think her method is important, even if people don't like it – her precision, her adherence to the text, the connection to previous generations. Her words carry authority and many worthwhile principles of study. Her *Studies* benefit high schoolers, provided there is guidance and explanations." R. Elhanan Samet believes that the brevity of Nehama's *Studies* will keep them popular as some of the newer studies, including his own, are less accessible to young people simply because of their length. He also notes that the newer studies lack educational messages, another point in Nehama's favor. Rozenson agrees that people will continue to open her books in the future: "Not only because of their quality and methodical nature, but because they are conveniently arranged by weekly portion. Moreover, based on current trends rightward within the religious world, she will continue to be popular due to her avoidance of biblical criticism and her personal piety." Rozenson favors developing aspects of her work that have not been emphasized thus far as an important part of its continuation. What is needed, therefore, are upgrades of Nehama's work to meet today's needs.

Might Nehama have changed her mind and broadened her views on Tanach study had she lived today? Were she to read this chapter, would she conclude that her method indeed needs an update? We can only speculate. Some believe that she wanted her method to be used exactly as she had done, and hence left her work to be continued by those students who would most honor this wish. Others argue that Nehama, who recanted on some important issues even in the last years of her life, would certainly make changes if she were developing her method today. People must not be afraid to outline the limitations in Nehama's approach so that the method may be improved for its future survival. She herself cautioned sensitivity and flexibility in teaching:

> If the students are not drawn to Midrash, and particularly if they evince an inner resistance, then it should be minimized and not forced upon them….[67]

Ben-Meir raises the question of whether Nehama had a method at all, for she was known to deny that she had one. Although her system had some clear lines, her personality had a great impact on the teaching. Nehama argued that what she taught was entirely bound up with her unique combination of traits and therefore only she could teach the "Nehama Leibowitz method." According to this view, she would have encouraged flexibility in her followers and approved of updates and changes.

In any event, serious thought should be devoted to maximizing Nehama's contribution to the present and future, including careful evaluation and critique of her work. Such critique sometimes meets with resistance in certain circles, where Nehama has been virtually canonized and made immune to any criticism, however constructive. One rabbi and scholar who dissected Nehama's work in a well-thought-out article received letters lambasting him for daring to criticize her. This is clearly against Nehama's wishes; she never wanted to be turned into a saint. As Yedgar notes, Nehama's critical method invites us to critique Nehama herself.[68] Defensiveness is counterproductive. Nehama was a complex figure, and a worthy subject for analytical study, in order to clarify and magnify her contribution to the world; hence, more critical study is required, not less! Yedgar proposes: "We need more research on her pedagogical method. We still need to identify the measure of the student's expected knowledge at the outset, the parameters of the student's autonomy, the role of the teacher and the ratio of pedagogical versus theoretical knowledge. We need to understand Nehama's didactic methods and their application – how they apply to certain populations and not others, to certain areas and not others."

❧ ❦

Based on all of the above, it seems to me that if Nehama's method is taken up, intelligently adapted in line with twenty-first century developments, and integrated alongside other Tanach-teaching methods, it can continue to play a vital role in Jewish education.

Updates are certainly needed. Some of Nehama's teachings are difficult for young people to understand. Her worksheets are not easy to navigate without guidance. But her *Studies* are still accessible to those with a reasonable understanding of the field, and can be made so to others by a knowledgeable teacher. Her critical approach to the texts and commentaries,

---

[67] N. Leibowitz, "*He'arot metodiyot le-limmud*," 490. See page 509 above for full quote.
[68] Yedgar, "*Ahrayut*," 406.

together with her moral sensitivities, remains inspiring. Interest in her work is still strong, at least amongst some of the more educated sectors of the Israeli public, and as some evidence we return to the story of the Nehama Haggadah. Notwithstanding the aforementioned Israeli publisher's uncertainty as to the Haggadah's viability in the Israeli market, Urim Publications proceeded to publish *Haggadat Nehama*, which ended up generating much interest and continues to do so every Passover, especially in Israeli stores classified as "secular."

We need clearly-written books and insightful teachers to serve as a bridge to the new generations and to entice young people to open Nehama's *Studies* and venture into her territory. Her work, which is still very useful, is in some ways more needed than ever. It serves to remind students of the necessity for patience, hard work and proper understanding of Hebrew and grammar, without which *peshat* interpretation is like groping in the dark. It provides a rationalistic, methodical balance to the highly personal approach, outlasting highs that quickly fade. Her grounded, ethical spirituality complements today's esoteric and emotional currents. While both of these qualities are necessary to create a Torah that nourishes the human spirit in all its diversity, Nehama's Torah is particularly needed to stir students towards personal growth, humility, and responsibility towards their community rather than just themselves, in this age of the individual.

Nehama's capability for "complex thinking," for navigating and balancing contradictory ideas, emphasized throughout this book, is one that the high-school system should address overtly. Jewish teenagers in the Western world suffer from an onslaught of contradictory messages, and they yearn to know the one "truth." Some educational systems are dedicated to providing that single, monolithic truth. They may succeed for a while, but the young people may also discard their teachings wholesale when they become adults and can think for themselves. Nehama, with her ability to see several sides, maintaining paradoxes while still remaining a pious believer, is a figure worth discussing with such teens in order to prepare them for the complexities of adult life. Moreover, her recommendation to get on with life without paying attention to distracting nonsense or to feelings of self-pity, together with her gratitude for every new day, is also a valuable lesson, not just for our disaffected youth but for us all.

Finally, Nehama's work will also serve as a reminder to teachers to introduce varied techniques while maintaining rigor and integrity; to activate the class and ask questions rather than lecture; to bring in elements from their own lives and take a personal approach. Teachers should recall how much students enjoy solving the riddles in the Tanach. Here we may note that some of the teachers of the new Tanach methods today have forgotten what Nehama taught about active learning and, eager to transmit the new ideas, have unfortunately reverted to frontal teaching. The loss may outweigh the gain.

For Chaviva Speter, Nehama provides a model of someone who does not live in constant fear of heresy. Today, Speter complains, religious people tremble when faced with intellectual challenges and developments. She says: "With all my criticism, I feel that she is *the* teacher. She caused us to think and to take pleasure in our studies, and that is the sign of an excellent teacher." Teachers would do well to remember this too.

Conclusion

Every revolution eventually becomes standard practice and may stagnate if subsequent generations do not bring it up to date. If Nehama's work is taught well, with an eye to today's generation and its needs, it can continue to be relevant, profound and refreshing to students who are mature enough to absorb its contribution, and it can provide an excellent set of principles and tools for approaching text. On the other hand, narrow and partial interpretations, especially by uninspired or overworked teachers, may well turn students off. As the Talmud (Yoma 72b) warns of the Torah itself:

> If you merit it, it is a life-giving medicine; if you do not merit, it is a deadly poison.

Let us, with God's help, work together wisely and with humility so that Professor Nehama Leibowitz's work will be cherished for many years to come.

EPILOGUE

WHAT'S IN A STREET NAME?

> I should really have finished here, but my regard for all who
> teach Torah to Jewish children everywhere, and my wish to help
> as far as I can, prompt me to add here a few observations, simply
> because… I find it difficult to part from you. (Nehama
> Leibowitz, *Torah Insights*, 34)

THURSDAY, APRIL 11, 2002, 4:30 PM

Picture the scene: a hazy heat blazes upon a lazy hilltop in southeast
Jerusalem, where a future suburb sprawls in its clutter of half-built houses,
piled rubble and swinging cranes. Warm winds gust across the dusty streets.
Signs announce: "This site will become the Har Homa (Homat Shmuel)
neighborhood." It is an optimistic pronouncement. Bethlehem is a stone's
throw from here, with Zur Baher lying on an adjacent hilltop to the east, and
the past few weeks have brought nothing but bloodshed. Yet construction
goes on.

Several rows of plastic chairs are lined up near a microphone on a
makeshift dais. Policemen and security personnel stand at the sides, watching
as a small crowd of people mingle and talk – the family and devotees of the
late Professor Nehama Leibowitz. Today a distinctive tribute is being made
to Nehama, for the city of Jerusalem is honoring her with a street named in
her memory.

It was just a matter of time, for a broader consensus for a street name
would probably be hard to find. Indeed, the only person likely to frown at
this occasion would be Nehama herself. Knowing this, people in the crowd
nudge and whisper: "If Nehama were here, she'd say, "What's all this for?
For me?!" And when the speakers finally ascend the dais, each begins with
an apology to Nehama for praising her now that she cannot protest.

The first speaker, R. Raphael Posen, says: "How Nehama would have
hated a street named for her! But let me reassure her by saying: Nehama, the
population of this particular neighborhood will not be diplomats and
professors. It will be the ordinary people who loved your Torah so much."
Next, Nurit Fried takes the microphone: "Nehama nurtured everyone with

whom she came into contact. While teaching one day, I became aware that I was doing a 'Nehama imitation' – of her movements, her voice, her method. When I told her, she denied it. 'No, no, it's all from you!'"

Finally, Ehud Olmert, mayor of Jerusalem, gets up to speak. Behind him are the flags of Israel and the Jerusalem municipality and a bodyguard with sunglasses, staring at the crowd. "I first got to know Nehama at the Hebrew University in the 1960s. Having heard her 'Chapters of Commentary' on the radio, I wanted to hear her lecture. I still remember it as an amazing experience. She had a definite presence on the campus, this small woman with her beret always tilted at a careful angle." Suddenly, he is interrupted by a request from the audience: "Mr. Olmert, would it not be fitting for the adjacent street to be named for Yeshayahu Leibowitz, uniting brother and sister?"

Ever the deft politician, Olmert parries with a smile: "I don't believe Yeshayahu's followers would be happy to have a street named for him in this particular area." No one can contradict him. Even in death, the siblings' divergent views express themselves in the most concrete way.

The mayor invites Nehama's niece, Dr. Mira Ofran, to unveil the street sign. The municipality have respected Nehama's wishes – the standard blurb is absent, and instead next to her name there is one word only: *morah* (teacher).

The brief ceremony ends.

"I've been to many street-naming ceremonies," comments Dr. Gabriel Cohn, "but this was exceptional, truly a spiritual experience." There are smiles as a shiny paperback volume is passed from hand to hand. Hot off the presses, it is *New Studies in Shemot*, translated into Russian. Another volume is handed round – a journal entitled *Limmudim*, dedicated to Yeshayahu and Nehama Leibowitz.

As the little band disperses until the next tribute or conference or memorial day, they have the pleasure of knowing that Nehama lives on not only in her books and her worksheets, in her students' learning and teaching, in the history and hearts of the Jewish people, but now immortalized on a street in the Holy City, in the old-new land that she loved so much. May her memory be a blessing.

ראש העיר ירושלים
אהוד אולמרט
וחברי מועצת העירייה

מתכבדים להזמינך
לטקס קריאת רחוב

"נחמה"

ע"ש

פרופ' נחמה ליבוביץ
מורה
(תרס"ה-תשנ"ז)
(1997-1905)

ביום חמישי, כ"ט בניסן תשס"ב, 11.4.2002
בשעה 16:30 בשכונת חומת שמואל (הר חומה), ירושלים.

הטקס יתקיים בכל מזג-אוויר.

להגעה ראה מפה הרצ"ב.

Invitation to the ceremony for the naming of Nechama Street
in Har Homa, Jerusalem, April 2004.

Sign for Nechama Street in Har Homa, Jerusalem.
Reads: "Named for Professor Nehama Leibowitz, Teacher. 5665–5757."

BIBLIOGRAPHY[1]

1. Cited works by Nehama Leibowitz:

"Active Learning in the Teaching of History." Trans: Moshe Sokolow, introduction Jon Bloomberg. New York: 1989.[2]

"*Ahavat Torah ve-limmudah.*" In *PN*, 464–468.

"*Al nituah safruti ve-al parshanut.*" Unpublished book review. In *PN*, 617–623.

"*Daf la-lomdim.*" In *PN*, 456–457.

Darkei ha-hora'ah shel Humash im mefarshim la-aliyat ha-no'ar ha-dati. Jerusalem: Organization Committee for Youth Aliyah Counselors, 5701.

"*El kol lomdei parashat ha-shavua mi-toch iyun ba-gilyonot ba-asher hem sham.*" In *PN*, 469–470.

Gilyonot le-iyun be-Sefer Yirmiyahu. Department for Torah and Culture in the Diaspora, 5737.

"*Ha-amlanut be-hora'at ha-historiah be-veit ha-sefer ha-amami ve-ha-tichoni.*" In *PN*, 631–650.

"*Hadracha be-ketivat hiburim.*" Originally printed in *Hed ha-hinuch* 10 (Folio 11–13), 318–321 (5696), reprinted in *PN*, 625–630.

"*He'arot metodiyot le-limmud Humash im mefarshim be-veit sefer tichoni.*" First printed in *Hed ha-hinuch* 15 (1–3): 13–16 and (4–5): 58–60 (5741); reprinted in *PN*, 485–494.

"*He'arot metodiyot le-keriyat ma'amar shel ha-Rav Kook (Le-metodika shel keriyat sifrut mahshavah be-kitot gevohot).*" *Ma'ayanot* 3 (5713): 144–146.

"*Iyun be-mizmorei Tehillim.*" In PN, 577–590.

---

[1] For abbreviation key, see front page. Note that cited works of only minor or tangential importance have been omitted from the bibliography, and appear only in the relevant footnotes.

[2] This article may be read online at http://www.lookstein.org/articles/active_learning. pdf

Iyunim be-Sefer Ba-midbar. Jerusalem: WZO, Department for Torah and Culture in the Diaspora, 5756.

Iyunim be-Sefer Bereshit. Jerusalem: WZO, Department for Torah and Culture in the Diaspora, 5726.

Iyunim be-Sefer Devarim. Jerusalem: WZO, Department for Torah and Culture in the Diaspora, 5754.

Iyunim hadashim be-Sefer Shemot. Jerusalem: WZO, Department for Torah and Culture in the Diaspora, 5730.

Iyunim hadashim be-Sefer Va-yikra. Jerusalem: WZO, Department for Torah and Culture in the Diaspora, 5743.

"Keitzad anu lomdim Tanach?" In *PN*, 475–484.

"Keitzad lamadnu Torah im mefarshim." In *PN*, 471–473.

Leader's Guide to the Book of Psalms. NY: Hadassah Education Dept., 1971.

Lilmod u-le-lamed Tanach. Eliner Library, WZO, Department for Torah and Culture in the Diaspora, 1995; published in English as *Torah Insights* (see below).

Limmud parshanei ha-Torah u-derachim le-hora'atam: Sefer Bereshit. Jerusalem: Joint Authority for Jewish Zionist Education, Department for Torah and Culture in the Diaspora, 1975, 1978.

"Mi-bereshit ad le-einei kol Yisrael: bi-melot shana la-gilyonot." In *PN*, 451–455.

New Studies in Shemot (Exodus): Jerusalem: WZO, Department for Torah and Culture in the Diaspora, 1976.

New Studies in Vayikra (Leviticus). Jerusalem: WZO, Department for Torah and Culture in the Diaspora, 1980.

"Parashat ha-Akedah." *Derachim ba-mikra u-ve-hora'ato* (5757), 11–34.

Perush Rashi la-Torah: iyunim be-shitato (with Moshe Ahrend), 2 volumes. Open University: 1990.

"Shiur be-Torah." *Ma'ayanot* 4 (1954): 34–40.

Shiurim be-firkei nehama u-ge'ula (with Meir Weiss). Jerusalem: WZO, Department for Torah and Culture in the Diaspora, 1957.

"Sihah al limmud parashat ha-shavua be-michtavim." In *PN*, 458–461.

"*Sikkum benayim al mifal ha-gilyonot.*" In *PN*, 462–464.

Studies in Bamidbar (Numbers). Jerusalem: WZO, Department for Torah and Culture in the Diaspora, 1980.

Studies in Devarim (Deuteronomy). Jerusalem: WZO, Department for Torah and Culture in the Diaspora, 1980.

"*Teshuvah le-mishal shel talmidim.*" In *PN*, 621–623.

Torah Insights. Jerusalem: Joint Authority for Jewish Zionist Education, Department for Torah and Culture in the Diaspora, 1995 (translation of *Lilmod u-le-lamed Tanach*).

"*Va-yomer… va-yomer.*" In *PN*, 495–502.

2. Cited works by others

Abramowitz, Leah. *Tales of Nehama.* Gefen, 2003.

Ahrend, Moshe. "*Ha-katuv tzarich iyun.*" *Bi-sdei hemed* 11 (1968): 30–37.

Ahrend, Moshe. "*Mitoch avodati im Nehama a"h.*" In *PN*, 31–49.

Ahrend, Moshe, Ruth Ben-Meir, and Gabriel H. Cohn, eds. *Pirkei Nehama.* Jerusalem: Jewish Agency, 2001.

Amit, Yairah. "Hebrew Bible – Some Thoughts on the Work of Nehama Leibowitz." *Immanuel* 20 (Spring 1986) 7–13.

Angel, Hayyim J. "The Paradox of *Parshanut*: Are Our Eyes on the Text, or on the Commentators? Review of *Pirkei Nehama.*" *Tradition* 38/4 (Winter 2004): 112–128.

Bedein, David. "Goodbye, Nechama." http://israelbehindthenews.com/ Apr–14.htm#Nechama.

Ben-Meir, Ruth. "*Le-darkei parshanuto shel Ramban.*" In *PN*, 125–142.

Ben-Sasson, Menahem. "*Ha-teshuvah be-iyunehah shel Nehama Leibowitz – iyun be-megamatam ha-hinuchit shel ha-iyunim.*" In *PN*, 357–368.

Berger, David. "On the Morality of the Patriarchs in Jewish Polemic and Exegesis." In *Modern Scholarship*, edited by S. Carmy (see below), 131–146.

Bonchek, Avigdor. "*Darko shel Rashi be-ferush milim mukarot ba-Torah le-fi gishatah shel Nehama.*" In *PN*, 43–147.

Bonchek, Avigdor. "Professor Nechama, Teacher of Israel." *Jewish Action* 54 (Fall 1993): 16, 18–20, 27.

Breuer, (Professor) Mordechai. *"Professor Nehama Leibowitz a"h."* In *PN*, 17–19.

Breuer, (Rabbi) Mordechai. *"Yahasah shel Nehama Leibowitz el mada ha-mikra."* *Limmudim* 1 (2001) 11–20.

Carmy, Shalom. "A Room with a View but a Room of Our Own." In *Modern Scholarship*, edited by S. Carmy (see below), 1–38.

Carmy, Shalom, ed. *Modern Scholarship in the Study of Torah*. Northvale, NJ: Jason Aaronson, 1996.

Cherlow, Yuval. Introduction to *Pirkei ha-avot* by Yoel Bin-Nun, 7–28.

Cohn, Gabriel H. *"Ha-midrash ke-parshan ha-midrash ke-pashtan."* *Mahanayim* 7 (1994): 88–97.

Cohn, Gabriel H. *"Ha-parshanut ha-midrashit be-mifalah ha-Torani shel Nehama."* In *PN*, 93–108.

Cohn, Gabriel H. *"Ma ahavti Toratecha."* In *PN*, 25–30.

Cohn, Gabriel H. "Nehama Leibowitz – Teacher of Torah." *Be-khol derakhekha daehu*: Journal of Torah and Scholarship at Bar-Ilan University 6 (Winter 1998): 1–16.

Cohn, Gabriel H. *"Shiput musari li-demuyot mikra'iyot?: le-ha'arachat demutah shel Sara Imenu."* In *Derachim ba-mikra u-ve-hora'ato,"* edited by Moshe Ahrend and Shmuel Feuerstein, 199–213. Bar Ilan University Press, 1997.

Deitcher, Howard. "Between Angels and Mere Mortals: Nechama Leibowitz's Approach to the Study of Biblical Characters." *Journal of Jewish Education* 66: 1 (Spring/Summer 2000): 8–22.

Frankel, Marla. *"Ha-te'oriyah ha-hora'atit shel Nehama."* In *PN*, 425–439.

Frankel, Marla. *Iyun ve-hora'ah: hanharat shitatah shel Nehama Leibowitz* [A Clarification of Nechama Leibowitz's Approach to the Study and Teaching of Bible]. Jerusalem: Hebrew University, 1997.

Frankel, Marla. "The Teacher in the Writings of Nechama Leibowitz." In *Abiding Challenges: Research Perspectives on Jewish Education*. London and Tel Aviv: Freund, 1999, 359–374.

Frankel, Marla. *Toratah shel Nehama Leibowitz: darkah be-limmud ha-Tanach u-ve-hora'ato*. Yediot Aharanot: Sifrei Hemed, 2007.

Frisch, Amos. *"Shitato shel RSh"R Hirsch be-sugiyat hetei ha-avot."* In *Derachim ba-mikra u-ve-hora'ato*, edited by Moshe Ahrend and Shmuel Feuerstein, 181–198. Bar Ilan University Press, 1997.

Goldman, Eliezer. *"Ma hayav lo ha-kibbutz ha-dati?"* *Amudim* 580 (5755): 10–11.

Greenstein, Eliezer (Ed). *"Parshanutah rabat ha-panim shel Nehama Leibowitz ve-ha-parshanut ha-postmodernit."* *Limmudim* 1 (2001): 21–33.

Grossman, Avraham. *"Pulmus dati u-megamah hinuchit be-ferush Rashi la-Torah."* In PN, 187–205.

HaCohen, Aviad. *"Ha-im Esav soneh le-Yaakov?"* *Meimad* 12 (5758): 16–19.

HaCohen, Aviad. *"Shema ha-emet mi-mi she-omra: zeh kelal gadol be-torat Nehama Leibowitz."* *Alon Shvut* 13 (5759): 71–92.

Hamiel, Haim. *"Leibowitz, Nehama."* *Ha-encyclopedia shel ha-tzionut ha-datit.* Vol. 6, 572–582.

Hamiel, Haim. *"Morat ha-dor."* *Ha-Tzofeh*, April 18, 1997, 6.

Harvey, (Warren) Zev. *"Mekorotav ha-Yehudi'im shel Leibowitz."* In *Yeshayahu Leibowitz: olamo ve-haguto*, edited by Avi Sagi, 39–46. Jerusalem: Keter, 1995.

Harvey, (Warren) Zev. "Professor Nehama Leibowitz, Israel's Teacher of Teachers." *Canadian Zionist*, vol. 50/4 (April/May 1981): 10–11, 18.

Heilman, Uriel. "A Passion for Teaching." *Jerusalem Post*, April 18, 1997, 13.

Heilman, Uriel. "Teacher of the People of Israel Mourned." *Jerusalem Post*, April 14, 1997, 12.

Helfgot, Nathaniel. "Recalling a Master Teacher." *New York Jewish Week*, April 1997.

Hoffman, Yair. *"Yoter me-hokeret, yoter mi-martzah."* *Yediot Ahronot* culture supplement, December 24, 1982, 1–2.

Horwitz, Rivka. *"Nehama Leibowitz ve-ha-parshanim ha-Yehudi'im be-Germania ba-me'ah ha-20 – Martin Buber, Franz Rosenzweig, u-Benno Jacob."* In *PN*, 207-220.

Kagan, Yaakov. "A Review of Nechama Leibowitz's *Eyunim – Studies on Torah*." www.lookstein.org/articles/nechama.htm.

Lavie, Aviv. "*Yeshayahu Leibowitz hai*." *Haaretz* weekend supplement, February 21, 2003, 18–22.[3]

Leibowitz, Yeshayahu. *Accepting the Yoke of Heaven: Commentary on the Weekly Portion*. Jerusalem: Urim Publications, 2002.

Leibowitz, Yeshayahu. *Al olam u-melo'o: sichot im Michael Shashar*. Jerusalem: Keter, 1987.

Leibowitz, Yeshayahu. *Judaism, Human Values and the Jewish State*. Translated and edited by Eliezer Goldman. Cambridge, MA: Harvard University Press, 1992.

Leibowitz, Yeshayahu. "*Nissim ve-emunah*." In *Emunah, historiah ve-arachim*. Jerusalem: Academon, 5742, 65–66.

Leibowitz, Yeshayahu. *Ratziti li-shol otcha, Professor Leibowitz*, edited by Mira Ofran, Avi Katzman *et al*. Jerusalem: Keter, 1999.

Leibowitz, Yeshayahu. *Sheva shanim shel sihot al parashat ha-shavua*. Jerusalem: 2000.

Levy, B. Barry. "On the Periphery: North American Orthodox Judaism and Contemporary Biblical Scholarship." In *Students of the Covenant*, edited by S. David Sperling (see below), 159–204.

Levy, B. Barry. "The State and Directions of Orthodox Bible Study." In *Modern Scholarship*, edited by S. Carmy (see above), 39–80.

Lookjed archive (www.lookstein.org/lookjed/search.php?f=1).

Mondschein, Aaron. "*Akedat Yitzhak – bein emunah le-tehiyah*." *Bet Mikra* 44/2 (5759): 107–118.

Moskowitz, Yehiel Zvi. "*Al ha-gilyonot ve-al ha-iyunim*." *Daf le-tarbut Yehudit* 228: *Nehama Leibowitz z"l*, edited by Aryeh Strikovsky, 11–14. Torah Education Department of Education Ministry, Iyar 5757/1997.

"Nehama herself" (author unknown). *Kol emunah*, Spring 1987, 18.

Nigal, Gedalyah. "*Morah degulah*." *Ha-Tzofeh*, May 9, 1997, 6.

---

[3] All translation taken from the article in the English edition, entitled "Prophet in His Own Country."

Nissenbaum, Avraham, ed. Booklet for study day about Nehama Leibowitz. Open University, Department for History, Philosophy and Judaism, 1999.

Ochs, Vanessa L. *Words on Fire: One Woman's Journey into the Sacred*. San Diego: Harcourt, Brace, Jovanovich, 1990.

Ofran, Mira. "*Le-ha'ahiv et ha-limmud: 'shitat Nehama' – be-chol ha-miktzo'ot.*" In *PN*, 407–424.

Ohana, David. "*Parashat Noah: Nimrod bein Nehama Leibowitz le-Yitzhak Danziger.*" In *Hogim ba-parashah*, edited by Naftali Rothenberg (see below), 31–42.

Ohana, David. "*Tzionuto shel Yeshayahu Leibowitz.*" Kivvunim 45 (1995): 161–171.[4]

Oren, Abba. "That Thy Word Hath Quickened Me: Review of *Studies in Bamidbar.*" *Forum*, Jerusalem: WZO, 38 (Summer 1980): 155–159.

Peerless, Shmuel. *To Study and to Teach: The Methodology of Nechama Leibowitz*. Jerusalem: Urim Publications, 2003.

Peters, Simi. *Learning to Read Midrash*. Jerusalem: Urim Publications, 2004.

Posen, Raphael. "*Ha-targum bi-chtavehah shel Nehama.*" In *PN*, 109–123.

Posen, Raphael. "*Mehanechet idialit.*" *Ha-Tzofeh*, May 9, 1997, 6.

Posen, Raphael. "*Te'uv ha-golah.*" *Ha-Tzofeh*, March 27, 1998.

Rappel, Dov. "*Tehillim mizmor kaf-bet.*" In *PN*, 441–450.

Reiner, Yitshak. *Mo'adei Nehama*. Eliner Library, WZO, Department for Torah and Culture in the Diaspora, 2005.

Reiner, Yitshak, and Shmuel Peerless, eds. *Haggadat Nehama*. Urim Publications, 2003.

Reiner, Yitshak, and Shmuel Peerless, eds. *Studies on the Haggadah from the Teachings of Nehama Leibowitz*. Urim Publications, 2002.

---

[4] This article, translated as "Sane and Democratic Zionism," may be read at http://www.hagshama.org.il/en/resources/view.asp?id=207. The translations in this book have largely stayed with that translation.

Rochwarger, Joy. "Words on Fire: Then and Now – In Memory of Nechama Leibowitz." In *Torah of the Mothers: Contemporary Jewish Women Read Classical Jewish Texts*, edited by Susan Handelman and Ora Wiskind Elper, 57–81. Urim Publications, 2000/2006.

Rosenak, Michael. "*Parashat Mi-ketz: ha-omnam tzaddik? Ha-Rambam, Yeshayahu Leibowitz u-Nehama Leibowitz mesohahim al Yosef.*" In *Hogim ba-parashah*, edited by Naftali Rothenberg (see below), 129–140.

Rosenak, Michael. *Roads to the Palace: Jewish Texts and Teaching.* Providence: Berghahn Books, 1995.

Rothenberg, Naftali, ed. *Hogim ba-parashah* ("Meditations on the Parasha: The Weekly Torah Portion as an Inspiration for Jewish Thought and Creativity"). Tel Aviv: Van Leer Institute, Maskel, 2005.

Rozenson, Israel. "*Diber Hashem be-mahazeh: hashkafatah shel Nehama Leibowitz al ha-parshanut ha-alegorit.*" In PN, 325–339.

Rozenson, Israel. "*Ha-parshanit, ha-perush ve-ha-historiah: he'arot al tefisat ha-parshanut shel Nehama Leibowitz.*" In *Al derech ha-avot* 2001, 433–453.

Sagi, Avi, ed. *Yeshayahu Leibowitz: olamo ve-haguto.* Jerusalem: Keter, 1995.

Saks, Jeffrey. "Letters on Religion without Theology" (review essay of Y. Leibowitz, *Ratziti* – see above). *Tradition* 34/3 (2000): 88–94.

Salmon, Rachel. "Nehama Leibowitz, Scholar and Teacher." *Kol emunah*, Spring 1987, 16, 19.

Schoneveld, Jacobus. *The Bible in Israeli Education: A Study of Approaches to the Hebrew Bible and its Teaching in Israeli Education.* Amsterdam: Van Gorcum, 1976.

Seeman, Don. "The Silence of Rayna Batya." *The Torah U-Madda Journal* 6 (1996): 91–128.

Shapiro, Marc B. *Between the Yeshiva World and Modern Orthodoxy: The Life and Works of Rabbi Jehiel Jacob Weinberg, 1884–1966.* Littman, 1999.

Sheleg, Yair. "*Kalat ha-Tanach.*" *Kol ha-ir*, October 27, 1995, 70–73.

Sheleg, Yair. "*Keter shel Torah.*" *Otiot* (Iyar 5757): 8–9.

Simon, Uriel. "*Ha-parshan nikkar lo rak be-shitato ela gam bi-she'elotav.*" In PN, 241-262.

Simon, Uriel. "The Place of the Bible in Israeli Society: From National Midrash to Existential Peshat." *Modern Judaism* 19:3 (October 1999): 217–239.

Sokolow, Moshe. *Hatzi Nehama: Studies in the Weekly Parashah Based on the Lessons of Nehama Leibowitz.* Jerusalem: Urim Publications, 2007.

Sokolow, Moshe. *Mafte'ah ha-gilyonot* (Index to the worksheets). Department for Torah Education and Culture in the Diaspora, 1993.

Sokolow, Moshe. "*Samchut ve-atzma'ut: ha-hashva'a ve-ha-mahloket be-mishnatah shel Nehama.*" In *PN*, 297–306.

Sperling, S. David, ed. *Students of the Covenant: History of Jewish Biblical Scholarship in North America.* Atlanta: Scholars Press, 1992.

Spiegelman, Mordechai. Review of Shmuel Peerless, *To Study and to Teach* (see above). Lookstein Center Internet Archive, November 2003.

Strikovsky, Aryeh, ed. *Daf le-tarbut Yehudit* 228: *Nehama Leibowitz z"l.* Torah Education Department of Education Ministry, Iyar 5757/1997.

Strikovsky, Aryeh. "*Nehama Leibowitz al nashim ve-nashiyut.*" In *Bat Mitzvah,* edited by Sara Friedland ben Arza, 302–316. Jerusalem, 2002.

Strikovsky, Aryeh. "Nehama on Women and Womanhood." In *Traditions and Celebrations for the Bat Mitzvah,* edited by Ora Wiskind Elper, 186–195. Jerusalem: MaTaN and Urim Publications, 2003.

Sylvetsky, Rahel. "*Zichron la-holchim.*" *Ha-Tzofeh,* May 14, 1997, 7.

Touitou, Elazar. "*Bein 'peshuto shel mikra' le-'ruah ha-Torah': yahasah shel Nehama Leibowitz le-perush ha-Rashbam la-Torah.*" In *PN*, 221–240.

Unterman, Yael. *Background and Examples of Nechama Leibowitz's Literary Approach to Bible.* Master's thesis submitted to the graduate faculty in Jewish Studies, Touro College, Israel Branch, 2002.

Urbach, Ephraim Elimelech. "*Le-mikra ha-gilyonot le-parashat ha-shavua.*" *Ma'ayanot* 4 (1954): 55–58.

Weinberg, David. "Remembering Nehama." *Jerusalem Post,* April 5, 1998, 8.

Weiss, Meir. *The Bible from Within: The Method of Total Interpretation.* Jerusalem: Magnes, 1984.

Wiskind Elper, Ora, ed. *Traditions and Celebrations for the Bat Mitzvah.* Jerusalem: Urim Publications/MaTaN, 2003.

Yedgar, Erella. *"Ahrayut ishit u-beinishit bi-chtaveha shel Nehama Leibowitz – iyun be-megamatah ha-erkit-hinuchit."* In *PN*, 377–406.

Yedgar, Erella. *"Bein megamah parshanit-didaktit le-megamah erkit-hinuchit."* *Limmudim* 1 (2001): 45–80.

Yedgar, Erella. *"Ha-iyunim shel Nehama Leibowitz ke-degem le-shiur Tanach."* *Derech Efrata* 9–10 (2001): 13–37.

Yedgar, Erella. *"Parashat va-yishlach: ha-shiput ha-musari be-iyuneha shel Nehama Leibowitz: ma'aseh ha-ahim bi-Shechem ke-mikreh mivhan."* In *Hogim ba-parashah*, edited by Naftali Rothenberg (see above), 102–116.

Yedgar, Erella. *"Parshanut nashim datiyot o parshanut nashit-datit la-mikra?"* *Lihyot isha Yehudiya* 1 (2001): 106–121.

Zafrany, David. *"Darkah shel Nehama Leibowitz z"l be-hava'at ma'amarei Hazal."* In *PN*, 71–92.

INDEX

ABOUT THE AUTHOR

YAEL UNTERMAN grew up in the UK and resides in Jerusalem. She holds degrees in Psychology and Talmud, Jewish History and Creative Writing. She has lectured worldwide, and has published in various genres, including articles in the critically acclaimed books *Torah of the Mothers* and *Wisdom From All My Teachers*. She facilitates bibliodramas and performs in educational theater productions, including original pieces, and she is also a life coach.

Website: www.yaelunterman.com.